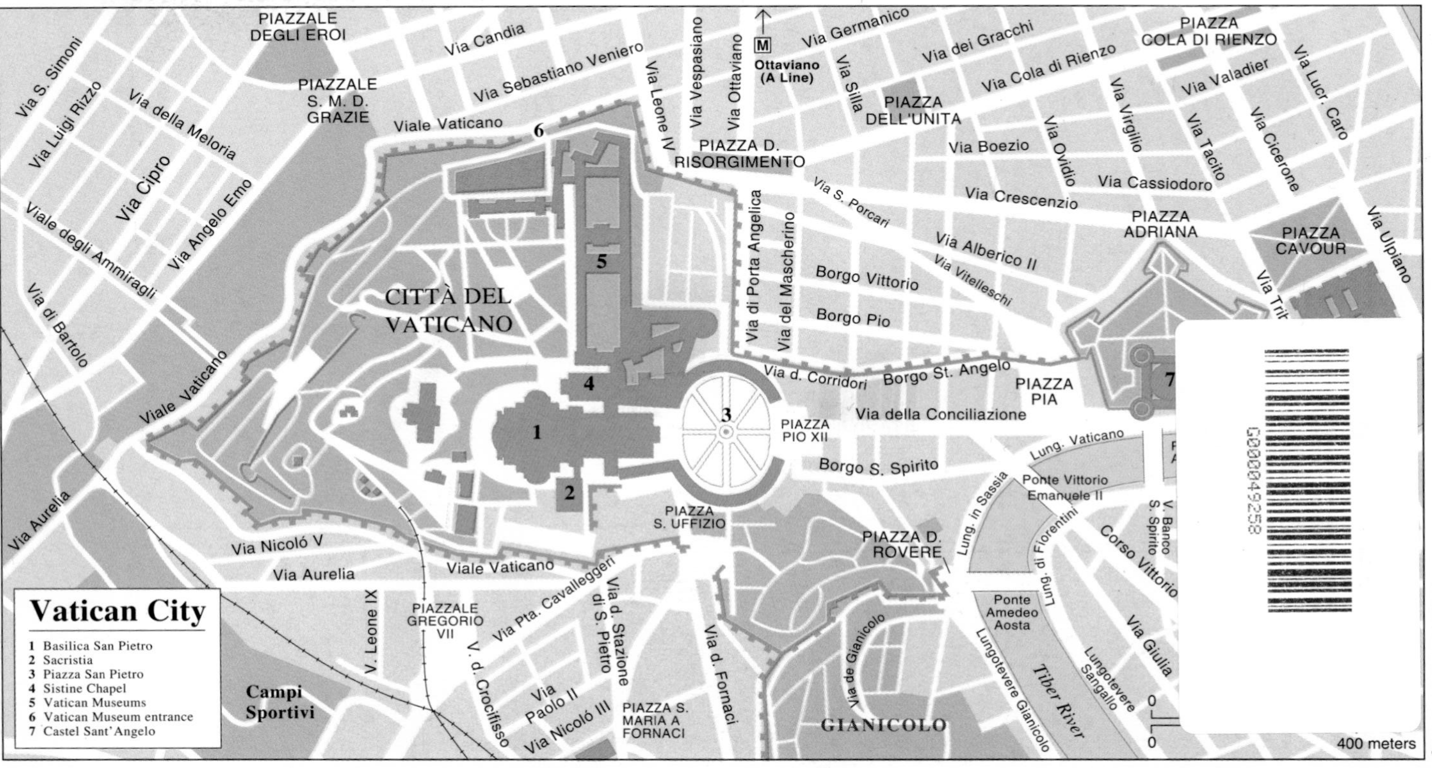

Vatican City
1 Basilica San Pietro
2 Sacristia
3 Piazza San Pietro
4 Sistine Chapel
5 Vatican Museums
6 Vatican Museum entrance
7 Castel Sant'Angelo
CITTÀ DEL VATICANO
GIANICOLO
Campi Sportivi
Tiber River
0
0
400 meters
Ottaviano (A Line)
PIAZZALE DEGLI EROI
PIAZZALE S. M. D. GRAZIE
PIAZZA COLA DI RIENZO
PIAZZA DELL'UNITA
PIAZZA D. RISORGIMENTO
PIAZZA ADRIANA
PIAZZA CAVOUR
PIAZZA PIA
PIAZZA PIO XII
PIAZZA S. UFFIZIO
PIAZZA D. ROVERE
PIAZZALE GREGORIO VII
PIAZZA S. MARIA A FORNACI
Via S. Simoni
Via Luigi Rizzo
Via della Meloria
Via Cipro
Via Angelo Emo
Viale degli Ammiragli
Via di Bartolo
Viale Vaticano
Via Aurelia
Via Candia
Via Sebastiano Veniero
Via Leone IV
Via Vespasiano
Via Ottaviano
Via Germanico
Via Silla
Via dei Gracchi
Via Cola di Rienzo
Via Valadier
Via Lucr. Caro
Via Boezio
Via Ovidio
Via Virgilio
Via Tacito
Via Cicerone
Via Cassiodoro
Via Crescenzio
Via Ulpiano
Via S. Porcari
Via Alberico II
Via Vitelleschi
Via di Porta Angelica
Via del Mascherino
Borgo Vittorio
Borgo Pio
Via d. Corridori
Borgo St. Angelo
Via della Conciliazione
Borgo S. Spirito
Lung. Vaticano
Lung. in Sassia
Ponte Vittorio Emanuele II
Lung. di Fiorentini
V. Banco S. Spirito
Corso Vittorio
Ponte Amedeo Aosta
Lungotevere Gianicolo
Lungotevere Sangallo
Via Giulia
Via Nicoló V
Via Aurelia
Viale Vaticano
V. Leone IX
Via Pta. Cavalleggeri
Via d. Stazione di S. Pietro
V. d. Crocifisso
Via Paolo II
Via Nicoló III
Via d. Fornaci
Via de Gianicolo

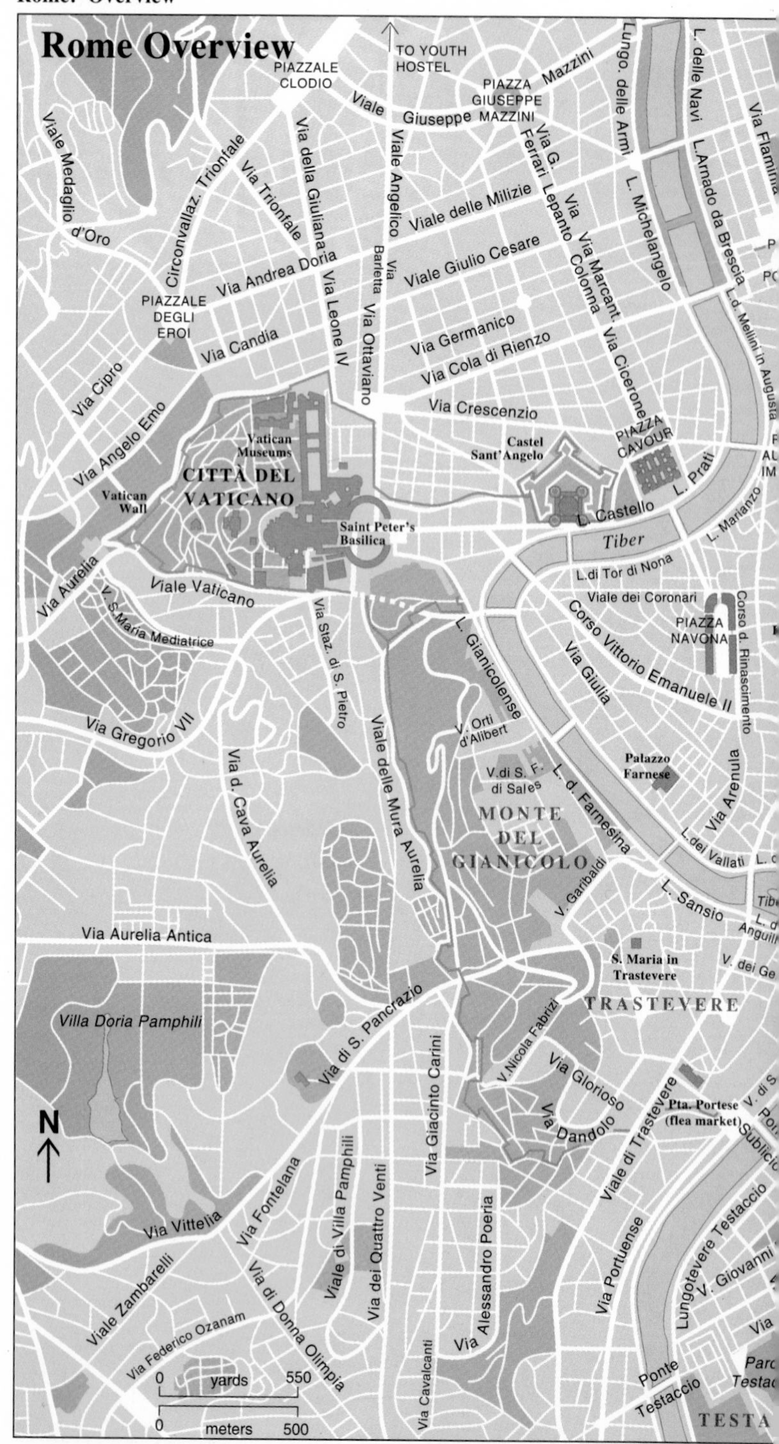
Rome Overview
PIAZZALE CLODIO
TO YOUTH HOSTEL
PIAZZA GIUSEPPE MAZZINI
Viale Giuseppe Mazzini
Viale Medaglio d'Oro
Circonvallaz. Trionfale
Via Trionfale
Via della Giuliana
Viale Angelico
Via G. Ferrari
Lepanto
Via Marcant. Colonna
Lungo. delle Armi
L. Michelangelo
L. delle Navi
L. Arnado da Brescia
Via Flaminia
Viale delle Milizie
Via Barletta
Viale Giulio Cesare
Via Andrea Doria
Via Leone IV
Via Ottaviano
PIAZZALE DEGLI EROI
Via Candia
Via Germanico
Via Cola di Rienzo
Via Cicerone
L. d. Mellini
Via Cipro
Via Crescenzio
Via Angelo Emo
Vatican Museums
CITTÀ DEL VATICANO
Vatican Wall
Castel Sant'Angelo
PIAZZA CAVOUR
L. Prati
Saint Peter's Basilica
L. Castello
Tiber
L. Marianzo
L.di Tor di Nona
Via Aurelia
Viale Vaticano
V. S.Maria Mediatrice
Via Staz. di S. Pietro
Viale dei Coronari
Corso Vittorio Emanuele II
PIAZZA NAVONA
Corso d. Rinascimento
L. Gianicolense
Via Giulia
Via Gregorio VII
Via d. Cava Aurelia
Viale delle Mura Aurelia
V. Orti d'Alibert
V.di S. F. di Sales
L. d. Farnesina
Palazzo Farnese
Via Arenula
MONTE DEL GIANICOLO
L.dei Vallati
V. Garibaldi
L. Sansio
L. Anguill
Via Aurelia Antica
S. Maria in Trastevere
V. dei Ge
TRASTEVERE
Villa Doria Pamphili
Via di S. Pancrazio
V.Nicola Fabrizi
Via Glorioso
Via Dandolo
Via Giacinto Carini
Viale di Trastevere
Pta. Portese (flea market)
N
Via Vittelia
Via Fontelana
Viale di Villa Pamphili
Via dei Quattro Venti
Via Alessandro Poeria
Via Portuense
Lungotevere Testaccio
V. Giovanni
Viale Zambarelli
Via di Donna Olimpia
Via Federico Ozanam
Via Cavalcanti
Ponte Testaccio
TESTA
0 yards 550
0 meters 500

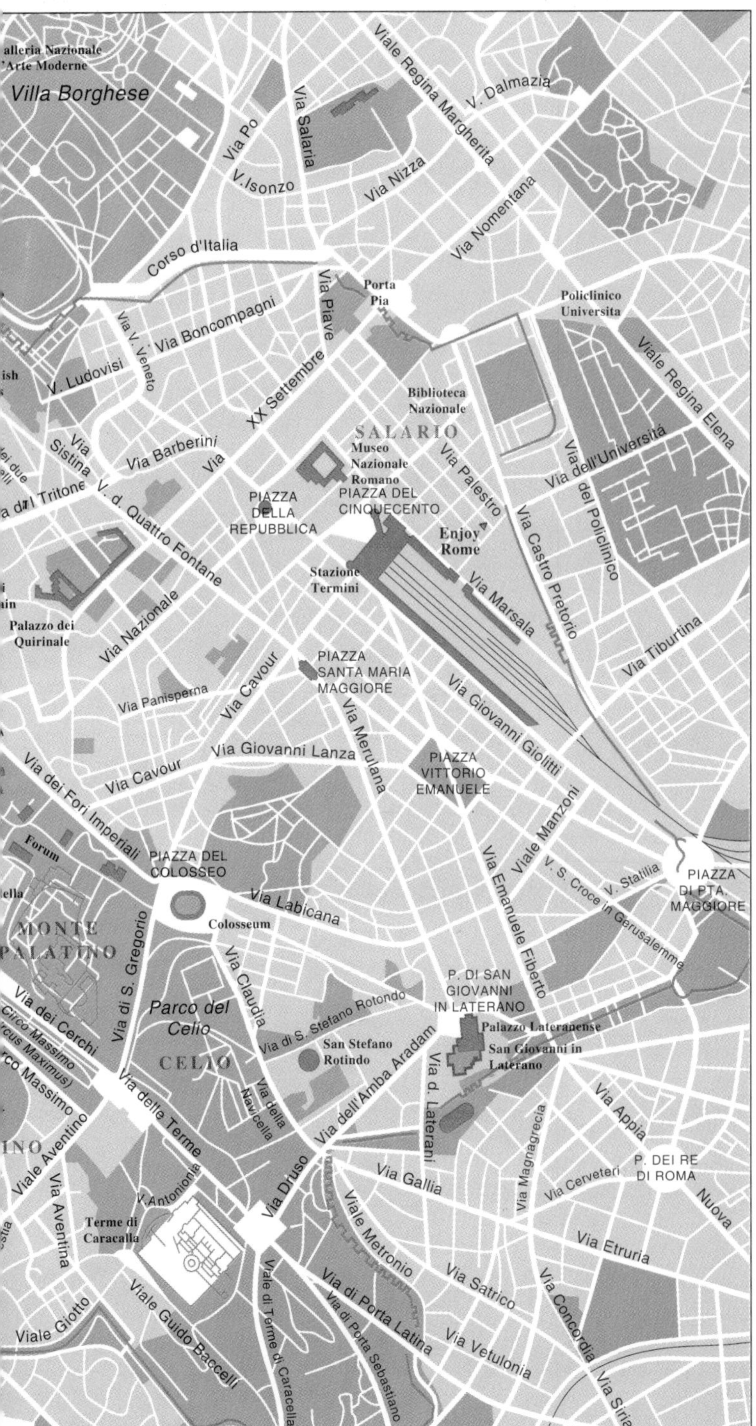
Villa Borghese
Viale Regina Margherita
V. Dalmazia
Via Salaria
Via Po
V. Isonzo
Via Nizza
Via Nomentana
Corso d'Italia
Porta Pia
Via Piave
Policlinico Universita
Via Boncompagni
Via V. Veneto
V. Ludovisi
Viale Regina Elena
XX Settembre
Biblioteca Nazionale
SALARIO
Via Sistina
Via Barberini
Museo Nazionale Romano
Via Palestro
Via dell'Università
Via del Policlinico
PIAZZA DELLA REPUBBLICA
PIAZZA DEL CINQUECENTO
Enjoy Rome
Via Castro Pretorio
V. d. Quattro Fontane
Stazione Termini
Via Marsala
Palazzo dei Quirinale
Via Nazionale
Via Tiburtina
PIAZZA SANTA MARIA MAGGIORE
Via Panisperna
Via Cavour
Via Giovanni Giolitti
Via Merulana
Via Giovanni Lanza
PIAZZA VITTORIO EMANUELE
Via dei Fori Imperiali
Viale Manzoni
Forum
PIAZZA DEL COLOSSEO
Via Emanuele Filiberto
V. S. Croce in Gerusalemme
V. Statilia
PIAZZA DI PTA. MAGGIORE
Via Labicana
Colosseum
MONTE PALATINO
Via di S. Gregorio
Via Claudia
P. DI SAN GIOVANNI IN LATERANO
Parco del Celio
Via di S. Stefano Rotondo
Palazzo Lateranense
Via dei Cerchi
San Stefano Rotindo
San Giovanni in Laterano
CELIO
Via d. Laterani
Via della Navicella
Via dell'Amba Aradam
Via delle Terme
Via Appia
Viale Aventino
Via Magnagrecia
P. DEI RE DI ROMA
Via Gallia
Via Cerveteri
V. Antonioniana
Via Druso
Viale Metronio
Nuova
Terme di Caracalla
Via Aventina
Via Etruria
Via Satrico
Via Concordia
Viale Giotto
Viale Guido Baccelli
Viale di Terme di Caracalla
Via di Porta Latina
Via di Porta Sebastiano
Via Vetulonia
Via Siria

Rome Transport

TO YOUTH HOSTEL
Viale Giuseppe Mazzini
PIAZZA GIUSEPPE MAZZINI
Via G. Ferrari
•19•70•490•913•
Viale Angelico
•32•
Viale delle Milizie
Viale Giulio Cesare
LEPANTO
Via Lepanto
Via Marcant. Colonna
•280•
OTTAVIANO
A-LINE
•990•
V. Ottaviano
Via Leone IV
•49•
Via Cola di Rienzo
•81•
Via Crescenzio
•23•49•492•
•23•34•
•34•49•492•990•
Via Cicerone
PIAZZA CAVOUR
•87•
Castel Sant' Angelo
•23•
•41•
•64•
Vatican
St. Peter's Basilica
•34•46•46b• 62•65•98•
•62•
Urban Train Service (F.S.)
S. PIETRO
Tiber
Viale dei Coronari
Corso Vittorio Emanuele II
•26•44•46•56•60•61•62•64•70•81•492•
Via Giulia
•23•
PIAZZA NAVONA
C. d. Rinascimento
•492•913•
•26•81•
PIAZZA DEL POPOLO
Via Flaminia
FLAMINIO
A-LINE
Via di Ripetta
•90•90b•
Via del Babuino
Via del Corso
Via del Corso •56•60•62•81•85•90•90b•
•119•
•119•
Pantheon
PIAZZA COLONNA
PIAZZA VENEZIA
95•116•492•
Via Condotti
V. dei due Macelli
•52•52b•53•56•
•58•61•62•80•
Via del Tritone
•95•119•492•
Trevi Fountain
Palazzo dei Quirinale
SPAGNA
Viale del Muro Torta
•95•490•495•
VILLA BORGHESE
Via Sistina
V. d. Quattro Fontane
•71•81•
BARBERINI
Via Barberini
•61•62•492•
•95•
Via V. Veneto
Corso d'Italia
Via Po
Via Salaria
Via Piave
•490•495•
Via Nizza
Viale Regina Margherita
V. Dalmazia
Via Nomentana
•61•65•
SALARIO
CASA PRETORIO
•65•
Via XX Settembre
•60•61•62•
P. D. CINQUECENTO
P. D. INDIPENDENZA
•64•65•75•492•
REPUBBLICA
P. D. REPUBBLICA
A-LINE
Via Nazionale
•57•64•65•
•70•75•170•
•71•
•70•
•71•
Via Cavour
Stazione Termini
•93•93b•
•93•
•93b•613•
TERMINI
B-LINE
B-LINE
Via Marsala
Via Castro Pretorio
Via Merula
•70•
•16
•70•

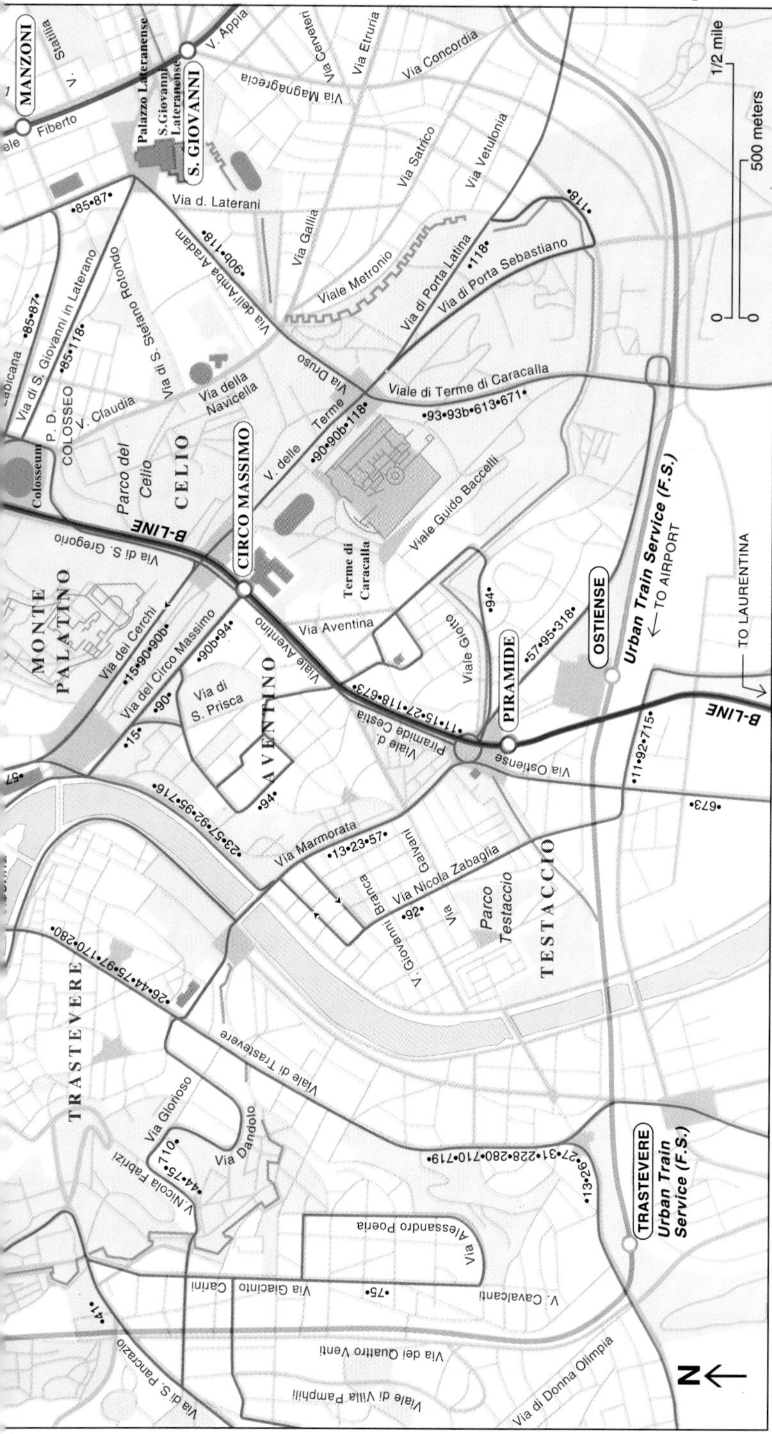

MANZONI
S. GIOVANNI
CIRCO MASSIMO
PIRAMIDE
OSTIENSE
TRASTEVERE
Urban Train Service (F.S.)
Urban Train Service (F.S.) ← TO AIRPORT
TO LAURENTINA
B-LINE
MONTE PALATINO
CELIO
AVENTINO
TESTACCIO
TRASTEVERE
Colosseum
P. D. COLOSSEO
Parco del Celio
Palazzo Lateranense
S.Giovanni Laterano
Terme di Caracalla
Parco Testaccio
Via di S. Giovanni in Laterano
Via di S. Stefano Rotondo
V. Claudia
Via della Navicella
Via dell'Amba Aradam
Via d. Laterani
Via di S. Gregorio
Via dei Cerchi
Via del Circo Massimo
Via di S. Prisca
Viale Aventino
Via Aventina
V. delle Terme
Via Druso
Viale di Terme di Caracalla
Viale Guido Baccelli
Viale Giotto
Viale d. Piramide Cestia
Via Ostiense
Via Marmorata
Via Nicola Zabaglia
V. Giovanni Branca
Via Galvani
Viale di Trastevere
Via Glorioso
Via Dandolo
V. Nicola Fabrizi
Via Alessandro Poerio
Via Giacinto Carini
V. Cavalcanti
Via dei Quattro Venti
Viale di Villa Pamphili
Via di Donna Olimpia
Via di S. Pancrazio
Via Appia
Via Magnagrecia
Via Cerveteri
Via Etruria
Via Concordia
Via Satrico
Via Vetulonia
Via Gallia
Viale Metronio
Via di Porta Latina
Via di Porta Sebastiano
V. Statilia
Fiberto
•85•87•
•85•118•
•90b•118•
•90•90b•118•
•93•93b•613•671•
•118•
•15•90•90b•
•90b•94•
•90•
•15•
•94•
•57•95•318•
•11•15•27•118•673•
•11•92•715•
•673•
•23•57•92•95•716•
•13•23•57•
•92•
•26•44•75•97•170•280•
•27•31•228•280•710•719•
•13•26•
•44•75•
•710•
•75•
•41•
•57
0 — 1/2 mile
0 — 500 meters
N ←

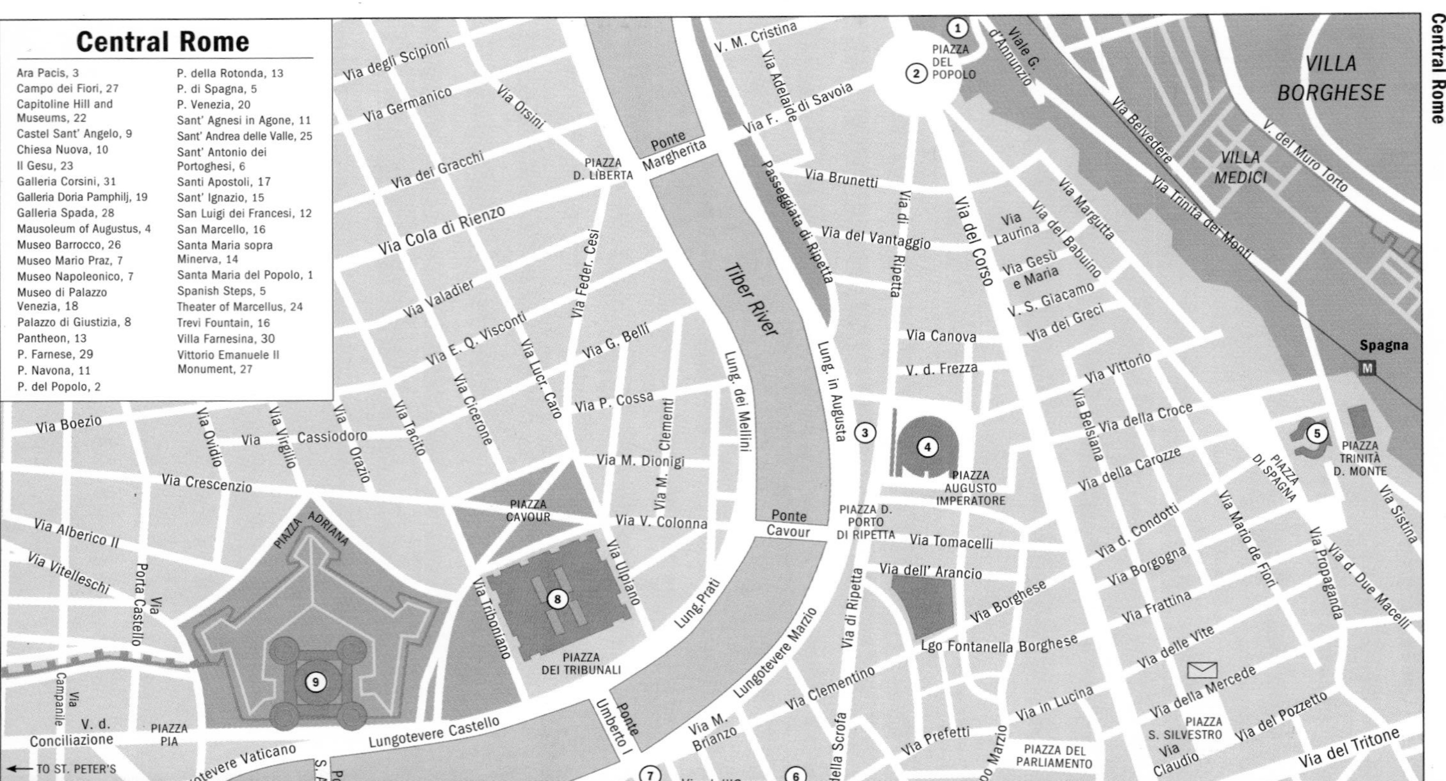

Central Rome
Ara Pacis, 3
Campo dei Fiori, 27
Capitoline Hill and Museums, 22
Castel Sant' Angelo, 9
Chiesa Nuova, 10
Il Gesu, 23
Galleria Corsini, 31
Galleria Doria Pamphilj, 19
Galleria Spada, 28
Mausoleum of Augustus, 4
Museo Barrocco, 26
Museo Mario Praz, 7
Museo Napoleonico, 7
Museo di Palazzo Venezia, 18
Palazzo di Giustizia, 8
Pantheon, 13
P. Farnese, 29
P. Navona, 11
P. del Popolo, 2
P. della Rotonda, 13
P. di Spagna, 5
P. Venezia, 20
Sant' Agnesi in Agone, 11
Sant' Andrea delle Valle, 25
Sant' Antonio dei Portoghesi, 6
Santi Apostoli, 17
Sant' Ignazio, 15
San Luigi dei Francesi, 12
San Marcello, 16
Santa Maria sopra Minerva, 14
Santa Maria del Popolo, 1
Spanish Steps, 5
Theater of Marcellus, 24
Trevi Fountain, 16
Villa Farnesina, 30
Vittorio Emanuele II Monument, 27
VILLA BORGHESE
VILLA MEDICI
V. del Muro Torto
Via Belvedere
Via Trinità dei Monti
Viale G. d'Annunzio
PIAZZA DEL POPOLO
Spagna
PIAZZA TRINITÀ D. MONTE
PIAZZA DI SPAGNA
PIAZZA AUGUSTO IMPERATORE
PIAZZA D. PORTO DI RIPETTA
PIAZZA D. LIBERTA
PIAZZA CAVOUR
PIAZZA DEI TRIBUNALI
PIAZZA ADRIANA
PIAZZA PIA
PIAZZA S. SILVESTRO
PIAZZA DEL PARLIAMENTO
Tiber River
Ponte Margherita
Ponte Cavour
Ponte Umberto I
Via del Corso
Via di Ripetta
Via del Babuino
Via Margutta
Via Laurina
Via Gesù e Maria
V. S. Giacamo
Via dei Greci
Via Canova
V. d. Frezza
Via Brunetti
Via del Vantaggio
Passeggiata di Ripetta
Lung. in Augusta
Lung. dei Mellini
Lung. Prati
Lungotevere Marzio
Lungotevere Castello
Via Vittorio
Via Belsiana
Via della Croce
Via della Carozze
Via d. Condotti
Via Borgogna
Via Frattina
Via delle Vite
Via della Mercede
Via del Pozzetto
Via del Tritone
Via Claudio
Via Mario de Fiori
Via Propaganda
Via d. Due Macelli
Via Sistina
Via Tomacelli
Via dell' Arancio
Via Borghese
Lgo Fontanella Borghese
Via Clementino
Via in Lucina
Via Prefetti
Via della Scrofa
Via M. Brianzo
V. M. Cristina
Via Adelaide
Via F. di Savoia
Via degli Scipioni
Via Germanico
Via Orsini
Via dei Gracchi
Via Cola di Rienzo
Via Valadier
Via E. Q. Visconti
Via Feder. Cesi
Via G. Belli
Via P. Cossa
Via M. Dionigi
Via M. Clementi
Via V. Colonna
Via Ulpiano
Via Lucr. Caro
Via Cicerone
Via Tacito
Via Orazio
Via Cassiodoro
Via Virgilio
Via Ovidio
Via Boezio
Via Crescenzio
Via Triboniano
Via Alberico II
Via Vitelleschi
Via Porta Castello
Via Campanile
V. d. Conciliazione
Lungotevere Vaticano
TO ST. PETER'S

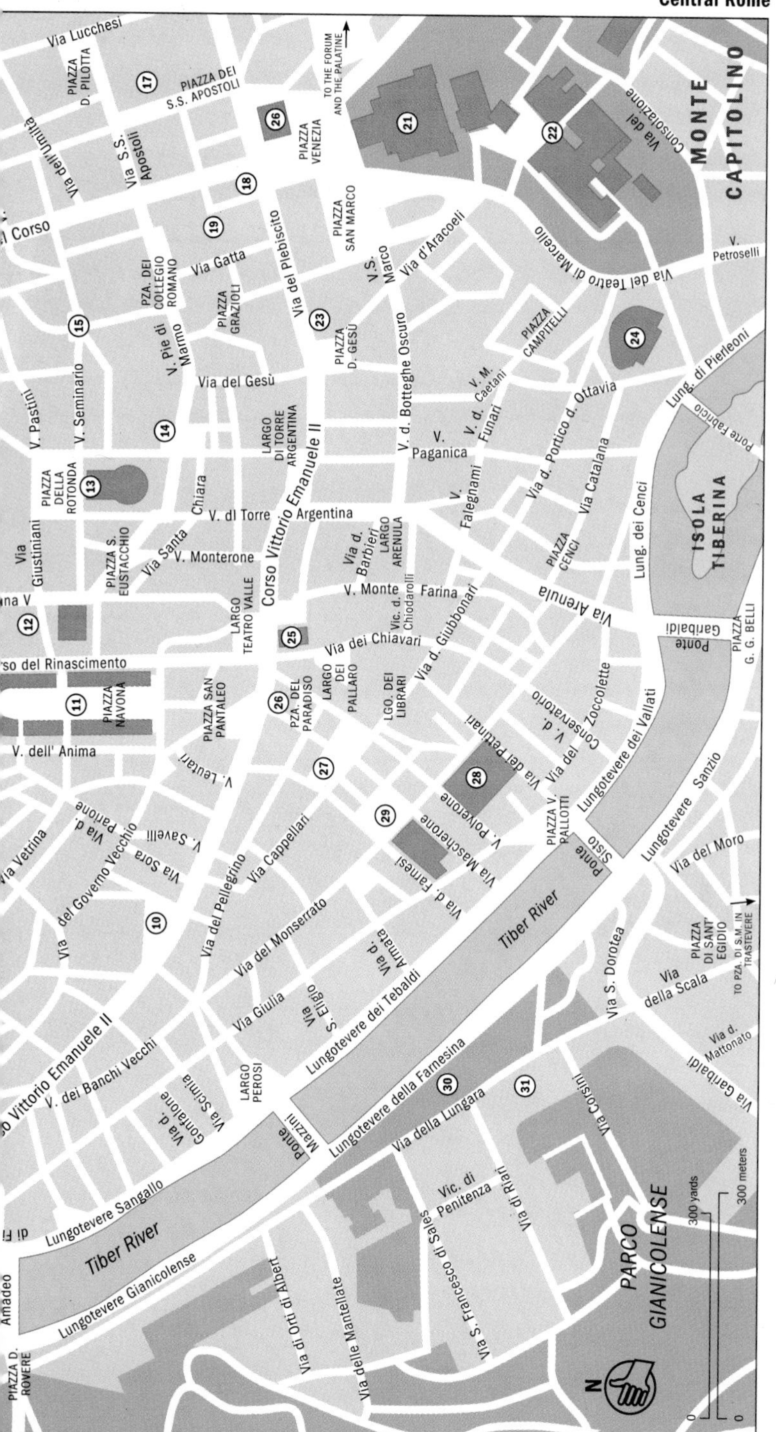
Via Lucchesi
PIAZZA D. PILOTTA
PIAZZA DEI S.S. APOSTOLI
TO THE FORUM AND THE PALATINE
MONTE CAPITOLINO
Via dell'Umiltà
Via S.S. Apostoli
PIAZZA VENEZIA
PIAZZA SAN MARCO
Corso
Via del Consolazione
V. Petroselli
Via del Teatro di Marcello
PZA. DEI COLLEGIO ROMANO
Via Gatta
PIAZZA GRAZIOLI
Via del Plebiscito
V.S. Marco
Via d'Aracoeli
V. Pie di Marmo
V. Seminario
V. Pastini
PIAZZA D. GESÙ
V. d. Botteghe Oscure
PIAZZA CAMPITELLI
V. M. Caetani
Via del Gesù
LARGO DI TORRE ARGENTINA
V. Paganica
V. d. Funari
Via d. Portico d. Ottavia
Lung. di Pierleoni
Ponte Fabricio
PIAZZA DELLA ROTONDA
Corso Vittorio Emanuele II
V. Falegnami
Via Catalana
ISOLA TIBERINA
Via Giustiniani
V. dl Torre Argentina
Via Santa Chiara
Lung. dei Cenci
PIAZZA S. EUSTACCHIO
V. Monterone
Via d. Barbieri
LARGO ARENULA
PIAZZA CENCI
LARGO TEATRO VALLE
V. Monte Farina
Vic. d. Chiodaroli
Via Arenula
Via dei Chiavari
Via d. Giubbonari
Ponte Garibaldi
PIAZZA G. G. BELLI
rso del Rinascimento
PIAZZA NAVONA
PIAZZA SAN PANTALEO
PZA. DEL PARADISO
LARGO DEI PALLARO
LGO. DEI LIBRARI
V. d. Conservatorio
Via del Zoccolette
Lungotevere dei Vallati
V. dell' Anima
V. Leutari
Via dei Pettinari
PIAZZA V. PALLOTTI
Lungotevere Sanzio
Via d. Parione
Via Sora
V. Savelli
Via del Governo Vecchio
Via Vetrina
V. Polverone
Via Mascherone
Ponte Sisto
Via del Moro
Via del Pellegrino
Via Cappellari
Via d. Farnesi
Tiber River
Via del Monserrato
Via d. Armata
PIAZZA DI SANT' EGIDIO
TO PZA. DI S.M. IN TRASTEVERE
Via S. Dorotea
Via della Scala
Via Giulia
Via S. Eligio
Lungotevere dei Tebaldi
Via d. Mattonato
Via Garibaldi
V. dei Banchi Vecchi
LARGO PEROSI
Lungotevere della Farnesina
Via d. Gonfalone
Via Scimia
Ponte Mazzini
Via della Lungara
Via Corsini
Vic. di Penitenza
Via di Riari
PARCO GIANICOLENSE
o Vittorio Emanuele II
Lungotevere Sangallo
Tiber River
Lungotevere Gianicolense
Amadeo
PIAZZA D. ROVERE
Via di Orti di Albert
Via delle Mantellate
Via S. Francesco di Sales
N
0
300 yards
300 meters
10 11 12 13 14 15 17 18 19 21 22 23 24 25 26 27 28 29 30 31

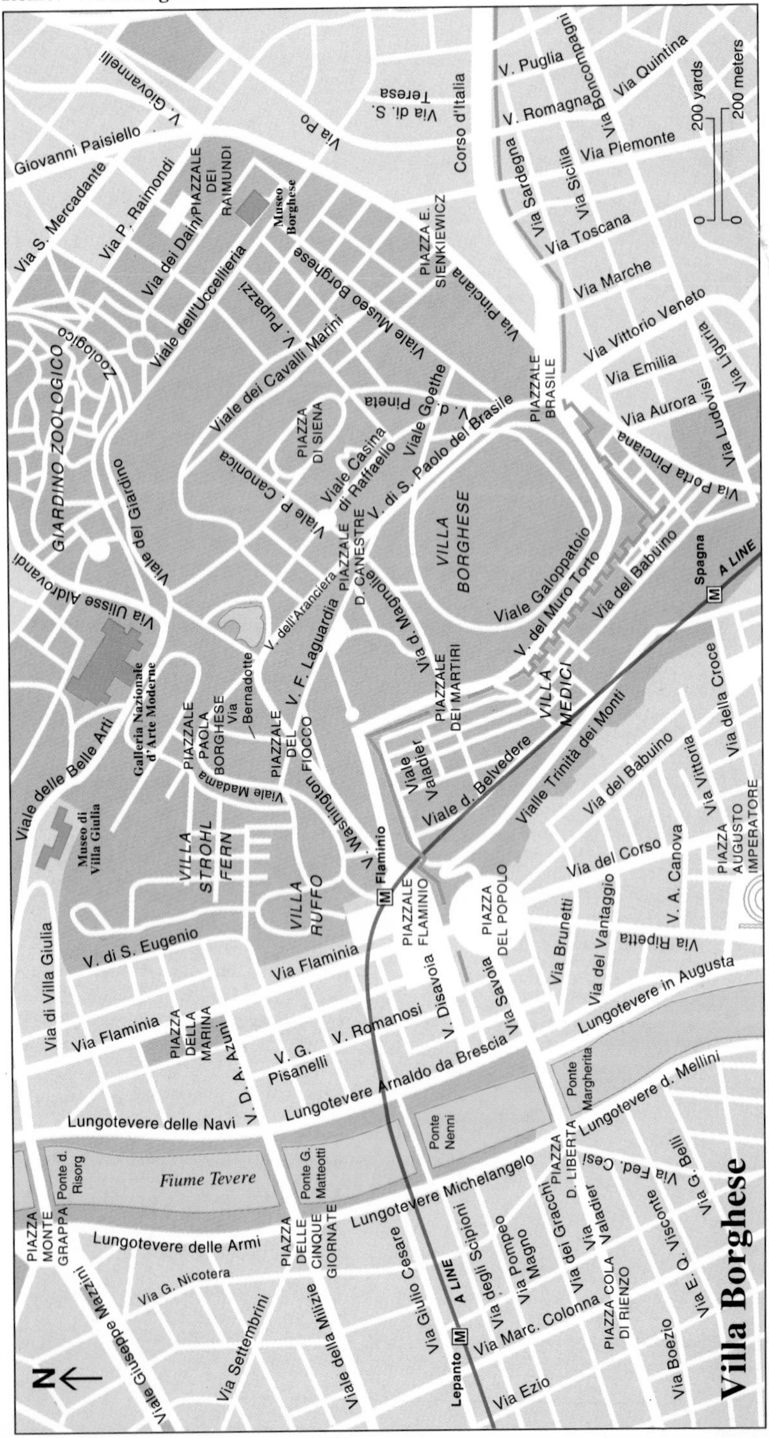

Rome: Villa Borghese

Villa Borghese

N

200 yards
200 meters
0
0

A LINE
Spagna
Flaminio
Lepanto

Fiume Tevere

VILLA BORGHESE
VILLA MEDICI
VILLA STROHL FERN
VILLA RUFFO
GIARDINO ZOOLOGICO
Museo Borghese
Galleria Nazionale d'Arte Moderne
Museo di Villa Giulia

PIAZZALE DEI RAIMUNDI
PIAZZA E. SIENKIEWICZ
PIAZZALE BRASILE
PIAZZA DI SIENA
PIAZZALE D. CANESTRE
PIAZZALE PAOLA BORGHESE
PIAZZALE DEL FIOCCO
PIAZZALE DEI MARTIRI
PIAZZALE FLAMINIO
PIAZZA DEL POPOLO
PIAZZA AUGUSTO IMPERATORE
PIAZZA DELLA MARINA
PIAZZA MONTE GRAPPA
PIAZZA DELLE CINQUE GIORNATE
PIAZZA D. LIBERTA
PIAZZA COLA DI RIENZO

Ponte d. Risorg
Ponte G. Matteotti
Ponte Nenni
Ponte Margherita

Giovanni Paisiello
V. Giovannelli
Via Po
Via di S. Teresa
Corso d'Italia
V. Puglia
Via Boncompagni
Via Quintina
V. Romagna
Via Piemonte
Via Sardegna
Via Sicilia
Via Toscana
Via Marche
Via Vittorio Veneto
Via Liguria
Via Emilia
Via Aurora
Via Ludovisi
Via Porta Pinciana
Via Pinciana
Via S. Mercadante
Via P. Raimondi
Via dei Daini
Viale dell'Uccelliera
V. Pupazzi
Viale Museo Borghese
Viale dei Cavalli Marini
Zoologico
Viale del Giardino
Viale P. Canonica
Viale Casina di Raffaello
Viale Goethe
V. d. Pineta
V. di S. Paolo del Brasile
Via Ulisse Aldrovandi
V. dell'Aranciera
V. F. Laguardia
Via d. Magnolie
Viale Galoppatoio
V. del Muro Torto
Via del Babuino
Via Bernadotte
Viale Madama
V. Washington
Viale Valadier
Viale d. Belvedere
Vialle Trinità dei Monti
Via della Croce
Via Vittoria
Via del Corso
V. A. Canova
Via Ripetta
Via del Vantaggio
Via Brunetti
Viale delle Belle Arti
Via di Villa Giulia
V. di S. Eugenio
Via Flaminia
V. Disavoia
Via Savoia
V. Romanosi
V. G. Pisanelli
V. D. A. Azuni
Lungotevere in Augusta
Lungotevere Arnaldo da Brescia
Lungotevere delle Navi
Lungotevere d. Mellini
Lungotevere Michelangelo
Lungotevere delle Armi
Via Fed. Cesi
Via G. Belli
Via Visconte
Via E. Q. Visconte
Via Boezio
Via Valadier
Via dei Gracchi
Via Pompeo Magno
Via degli Scipioni
Via Marc. Colonna
Via Ezio
Via Giulio Cesare
Viale della Milizie
Via Settembrini
Via G. Nicotera
Viale Giuseppe Mazzini

Let's Go writers travel on your budget.

"Guides that penetrate the veneer of the holiday brochures and mine the grit of real life."

—*The Economist*

"The writers seem to have experienced every rooster-packed bus and lunar-surfaced mattress about which they write."

—*The New York Times*

"All the dirt, dirt cheap."

—*People*

Great for independent travelers.

"The guides are aimed not only at young budget travelers but at the independent traveler; a sort of streetwise cookbook for traveling alone."

—*The New York Times*

"A guide should tell you what to expect from a destination. Here *Let's Go* shines."

—*The Chicago Tribune*

"An indispensible resource, *Let's Go*'s practical information can be used by every traveler."

—*The Chattanooga Free Press*

Let's Go is completely revised each year.

"A publishing phenomenon...the only major guidebook series updated annually. *Let's Go* is the big kahuna."

—*The Boston Globe*

"Unbeatable: good sight-seeing advice; up-to-date info on restaurants, hotels, and inns; a commitment to money-saving travel; and a wry style that brightens nearly every page."

—*The Washington Post*

All the important information you need.

"*Let's Go* authors provide a comedic element while still providing concise information and thorough coverage of the country. Anything you need to know about budget traveling is detailed in this book."

—*The Chicago Sun-Times*

"*Let's Go* guidebooks take night life seriously."

—*The Chicago Tribune*

Let's Go Publications

Let's Go: Alaska & the Pacific Northwest 2002
Let's Go: Amsterdam 2002 **New Title!**
Let's Go: Australia 2002
Let's Go: Austria & Switzerland 2002
Let's Go: Barcelona 2002 **New Title!**
Let's Go: Boston 2002
Let's Go: Britain & Ireland 2002
Let's Go: California 2002
Let's Go: Central America 2002
Let's Go: China 2002
Let's Go: Eastern Europe 2002
Let's Go: Egypt 2002 **New Title!**
Let's Go: Europe 2002
Let's Go: France 2002
Let's Go: Germany 2002
Let's Go: Greece 2002
Let's Go: India & Nepal 2002
Let's Go: Ireland 2002
Let's Go: Israel 2002
Let's Go: Italy 2002
Let's Go: London 2002
Let's Go: Mexico 2002
Let's Go: Middle East 2002
Let's Go: New York City 2002
Let's Go: New Zealand 2002
Let's Go: Paris 2002
Let's Go: Peru, Ecuador & Bolivia 2002
Let's Go: Rome 2002
Let's Go: San Francisco 2002
Let's Go: South Africa with Southern Africa 2002
Let's Go: Southeast Asia 2002
Let's Go: Southwest USA 2002 **New Title!**
Let's Go: Spain & Portugal 2002
Let's Go: Turkey 2002
Let's Go: USA 2002
Let's Go: Washington, D.C. 2002
Let's Go: Western Europe 2002

Let's Go *Map Guides*

Amsterdam
Berlin
Boston
Chicago
Dublin
Florence
Hong Kong
London
Los Angeles
Madrid
New Orleans
New York City
Paris
Prague
Rome
San Francisco
Seattle
Sydney
Venice
Washington, D.C.

Rome 2002

Carla Mastraccio editor

researcher-writers
Charles DeSimone
Amber Lavicka
Christina Rosenberger

Jenna Robins map editor
Naz F. Firoz managing editor
Luke Marion photographer

Macmillan

HELPING LET'S GO If you want to share your discoveries, suggestions, or corrections, please drop us a line. We read every piece of correspondence, whether a postcard, a 10-page email, or a coconut. Please note that mail received after May 2002 may be too late for the 2003 book, but will be kept for future editions. **Address mail to:**

Let's Go: Rome
67 Mount Auburn Street
Cambridge, MA 02138
USA

Visit Let's Go at **http://www.letsgo.com,** or send email to:

feedback@letsgo.com
Subject: "Let's Go: Rome"

In addition to the invaluable travel advice our readers share with us, many are kind enough to offer their services as researchers or editors. Unfortunately, our charter enables us to employ only currently enrolled Harvard students.

Published in Great Britain 2002 by Macmillan, an imprint of Pan Macmillan Ltd.
20 New Wharf Road, London N1 9RR
Basingstoke and Oxford
Associated companies throughout the world
www.panmacmillan.com

Published in the United States of America by St. Martin's Press.

ISBN: 0-333-90610-1
First edition
10 9 8 7 6 5 4 3 2 1

Let's Go: Rome is written by Let's Go Publications, 67 Mount Auburn Street, Cambridge, MA 02138, USA.

Printed in the USA on recycled paper with biodegradable soy ink.

Contents

nightlife 183

entertainment 195

shopping 203

daytripping 213

planning your trip 241

accommodations 265

living in rome 277

service directory 289

index 298

maps 307

RESEARCHER-WRITERS

Charles DeSimone *Southern Rome, Termini and San Lorenzo, Centro Storico*

After a summer in Cairo for *Let's Go: Middle East 2000* and one in Southern Italy for *Let's Go: Italy 2002*, our roguish researcher brought extensive knowledge of the Classics and croquet with him on his return trip to the Land of the Latins. He untangled the mysteries of ancient ruins, Baroque architecture, and, even more amazingly, the Roman subway system. He added daytrips, bargained with street vendors, and joined the throngs of crazy soccer fans, sending back clear, incisive prose. You know what we mean.

Amber Lavicka *Ancient City, Trastevere, Testaccio, Lazio, Pontine Islands*

Amber turned skills honed researching the beach towns of Sardinia for *Let's Go: Italy 2001* to the bustling streets of Rome's Testaccio district, savoring Roman nightlife and evoking the true flavor of Italian life with her rich, poetic writing style. After hot days wandering in the ruins of the Ancient City, Amber kept her cool and made it to the rocky shores of the Pontine Islands.

Christina Rosenberger *Borgo, Prati, and Vatican City, Principal Collections, Piazza di Spagna*

Christina's background in visual arts and her lucid, clever prose made her both a joy to work with and the ideal candidate to reorganize coverage of Rome's most famous museums. Given assigments like shoe shopping on the V. Condotti and researching *gelaterie*, Christina perservered, sending back copy that made us doubly swoon, first with envy, and then with pleasure.

Celeste Fine *Pompeii, Herculaneum, Paestum*

Shannon F. Ringvelski *Editor, Italy*

David James Bright *Associate Editor, Italy*

Sarah Yasmin Resnick *Associate Editor, Italy*

HOW TO USE THIS BOOK

BEFORE YOU GO. Start planning your jaunt to the big city with **Discover Rome,** which lists the city's top 15 sights along with suggested itineraries, themed tours, Let's Go Picks (the best—and quirkiest—of Rome, and three fantabulous **walking tours** (complete with maps) if you need help strategizing your sightseeing. Thumb through **Life and Times** for a quick and easy-to-swallow survey of Rome's history and culture, from Puccini to Europop. For the nuts and bolts details of planning your urban sojourn, flip to the end of this guide, where you'll find **Planning Your Trip** (with advice about passports, plane tickets, insurance, and more), the **Accommodations** section for booking a room from home, and even a chapter on **Living in Rome,** which details everything from obtaining a visa to finding housing for those planning to spend months (or years) in Rome .

ONCE THERE. When you touch down in Rome, **When in Rome** will be your best friend, dishing the dirt on the city's neighborhoods and offering tips on how to act like a true Roman. For easy navigating, the neighborhood breakdown here mirrors the breakdown found in the other chapters of the book. You'll spend most of your time in the city flipping through the chapters that follow: **Sights, Museums, Food & Drink, Nightlife, Entertainment,** and **Shopping.** Listings in these sections are oganized in the order of our preference within each neighborhood; if you want to know which restaurant we think is the best, just look at the top of the list. The Let's Go thumbs-up (☒) next to a listing lets you know it's one of our favorites—those places that are either super cheap, super hip, or just plain super.

MAPS AND MORE. All neighborhoods—complete with their hotels, museums, monuments, restaurants, bars, and Metro stops—are plotted in the **map appendix** at the back of this book, marked off with a black strip running down the side. Right before the maps comes the **Index** and a useful **Service Directory,** listing all the different services you might require during your trip, from taxis to pharmacies. Should you want you leave the city, **Daytripping** will help you strike out on your own into surrounding Lazio, with trips to the ruins at Pompeii, the beaches of Anzio and Nettuno, and excursions to the nearby cities of Florence and Naples.

THE INSIDE SCOOP. Tips on how best to explore Rome are found in the nifty **black sidebars** found on various pages scattered throughout the guide. Aside from the unnamed sidebars that give the low-down on all that is quirky, interesting, and fab about the city, there are On the Cheap and Big Splurges which outline establishments that are particularly good deals or special treats worth an extra expense, respectively. The absolute essentials are highlighted in white **Essential Information** boxes.

Just a final note: remember that this guide is great, but it's just that—a *guide*, not the be-all-end-all of travel in Rome. Just like Dante ditched that pesky pagan Virgil once he got out of the bowels of hell, put this book down once in a while and strike out on your own; you'll be glad you did.

A NOTE TO OUR READERS The information for this book was gathered by *Let's Go* researchers from May through August of 2001. Each listing is based on one researcher's opinion, formed during his or her visit at a particular time. Those traveling at other times may have different experiences since prices, dates, hours, and conditions are always subject to change. You are urged to check the facts presented in this book beforehand to avoid inconvenience and surprises.

ACKNOWLEDGMENTS

The Let's Go 2002 series is dedicated to the memory of Haley Surti

ROMA THANKS: The existential wonder that is the basement—plagues and all—and Anne Chisholm for delivering us from them. Naz for being the line-editing uber-ME that you are! Jen and Caleb for that sweet sweet production magic. Team Italy for the crunch.

CARLA THANKS: Everyone—Eric, Nikki, Anne, Monica, Sarah, Jean, Joseph, Chris, and Angela—in the basement! Karen for always being ready to medicate me with caffeine, and for being my absolute favorite marmot. Anne for helping me beat the machine from hell into submission and keeping me company through deadline... Kate D. for being a fabulous mommy and/or roommate, and constantly offering me the fruits of the mediteranean (even on public streets). Matt G. for surviving another summer of my excessive capitalist mentality without going mad. Sarah for lending me her shirt and looking deep into my eyes. Angie for aiding in my mission to eat. and eat. Jean and Angela for posing against the window. Joseph, Eric, and Chris for nobly handling all the female madness.... Cody for speaking *beautiful* Italian to me. Sarah R. for being an index-proofing angel of mercy. Naz for helping me create header schemes so sexy they should be kept from minors. Yuan for rescuing my cardigan, from the ghosts of neuroses past, tea downtown, and for being my sister in prissiness, and in just about everything else—mwah! jiejie. Mishy for sharing her chicken fingers and her apartment with me, may we have many and longer roadtrips in our future (provided you drive!).... Jen for saving me from the rain at Park St. and being so utterly loverly. Suzanne for introducing me to big brother and test-tasting the jell-o with me. Bec and Ves The Wei-How for what else? the sunlight... Mom, Dad, and Joe for all the love, support, shopping and nutella. yumm.... And Jason. Oh, Jason.

Editor
Carla Mastraccio
Managing Editor
Naz F. Firoz
Map Editor
Jenna Robbins

ABOUT LET'S GO

FORTY-TWO YEARS OF WISDOM

For over four decades, travelers crisscrossing the continents have relied on *Let's Go* for inside information on the hippest backstreet cafes, the most pristine secluded beaches, and the best routes from border to border. *Let's Go: Europe,* now in its 42nd edition and translated into seven languages, reigns as the world's bestselling international travel guide. In the last 20 years, our rugged researchers have stretched the frontiers of backpacking and expanded our coverage into the Americas, Australia, Asia, and Africa (including the new *Let's Go: Egypt* and the more comprehensive, multi-country jaunt through *Let's Go: South Africa & Southern Africa*). Our new-and-improved City Guide series continues to grow with new guides to perennial European favorites Amsterdam and Barcelona. This year we are also unveiling *Let's Go: Southwest USA,* the flagship of our new outdoor Adventure Guide series, which is complete with special roadtripping tips and itineraries, more coverage of adventure activities like hiking and mountain biking, and first-person accounts of life on the road.

It all started in 1960 when a handful of well-traveled students at Harvard University handed out a 20-page mimeographed pamphlet offering a collection of their tips on budget travel to passengers on student charter flights to Europe. The following year, in response to the instant popularity of the first volume, students traveling to Europe researched the first full-fledged edition of *Let's Go: Europe.* Throughout the 60s and 70s, our guides reflected the times—in 1969, for example, we taught you how to get from Paris to Prague on "no dollars a day" by singing in the street. In the 90s we focused in on the world's most exciting urban areas to produce in-depth, fold-out map guides, now with 20 titles (from Hong Kong to Chicago) and counting. Our new guides bring the total number of titles to 57, each infused with the spirit of adventure and voice of opinion that travelers around the world have come to count on. But some things never change: our guides are still researched, written, and produced entirely by students who know first-hand how to see the world on the cheap.

HOW WE DO IT

Each guide is completely revised and thoroughly updated every year by a well-traveled set of nearly 300 students. Every spring, we recruit over 200 researchers and 90 editors to overhaul every book. After several months of training, researcher-writers hit the road for seven weeks of exploration, from Anchorage to Adelaide, Estonia to El Salvador, Iceland to Indonesia. Hired for their rare combination of budget travel sense, writing ability, stamina, and courage, these adventurous travelers know that train strikes, stolen luggage, food poisoning, and marriage proposals are all part of a day's work. Back at our offices, editors work from spring to fall, massaging copy written on Himalayan bus rides into witty, informative prose. A student staff of typesetters, cartographers, publicists, and managers keeps our lively team together. In September, the collected efforts of the summer are delivered to our printer, who turns them into books in record time, so that you have the most up-to-date information available for your vacation. Even as you read this, work on next year's editions is well underway.

WHY WE DO IT

We don't think of budget travel as the last recourse of the destitute; we believe that it's the only way to travel. Our books will ease your anxieties and answer your questions about the basics—so you can get off the beaten track and explore. Once you learn the ropes, we encourage you to put *Let's Go* down and strike out on your own. You know as well as we that the best discoveries are often those you make yourself. When you find something worth sharing, please drop us a line. We're Let's Go Publications, 67 Mount Auburn St., Cambridge, MA 02138, USA (feedback@letsgo.com). For more info, visit our website, www.letsgo.com.

BYRON

INSIDE

Discover Rome

Italy will return to the splendors of Rome, said the major. I don't like Rome, I said. It is hot and full of fleas. You don't like Rome? Yes, I love Rome. Rome is the mother of nations. I will never forget Romulus suckling the Tiber. What? Nothing. Let's all go to Rome to-night and never come back. Rome is a beautiful city, said the major.

—Ernest Hemingway, *A Farewell to Arms*

So you think you're a player. Been there, done it all, and almost fell asleep? No one, nowhere has ever been able to shake your unflappable cool, to wipe that bland smile off your stunning, self-satisfied face. You smile patronizingly when others speak of the nadirs and zeniths, of the heights of ecstasy and the sloughs of despair, to which they have been carried, and subsequently dropped. You have never mouthed enthralled cliches or had your heart broken. You have never been to Rome.

Rome will shake the cynicism from your world-weary soul, and dump you breathless at the Trevi fountain. It will have you tossing pennies in the fountain, like the giddiest of Gidgets in Rome. You will discover a heretofore unknown cache of butterflies in your stomach, as you stare open-mouthed at the best the world has to offer in art, architecture, and plain, simple style. Knock-kneed as any cheerleader invited to the big dance by the handsomest of starting quarterbacks, you will stumble out of the Pantheon, filled with dreams of pagan gods. You will lose yourself and find yourself again in the narrow streets of Trastevere. And you will know what it is to fall in love. So please, relax and embrace a madness so divine that it is called eternal. Afterwards, curled on your couch, 3 pints into an ice-cream binge, as you gaze at your photoalbum, and remember what you knew, all too briefly, there will be time to repine. For now, there is only Rome.

ROME BY THE NUMBERS

Area: 577 mi^2. In that space are crammed 981 churches and 280 fountains.

Distance from the Mediterranean: 17 mi.

Official Age of the City: 2754 years. In That Time, there have been 168 popes, 73 emperors, and 9.3 million pairs of tight leather pants.

Population: 2.8 million (Metro Rome is home to over 4.5 million). Of those, 94% have their children baptized Catholic; 12% go to mass and confession weekly; and 37% believe they've been afflicted with the "evil eye."

Tourists: 15 million per year. (That's more than five tourists per Roman per year—but who's counting?)

Cars on Rome's Streets: 2 million daily.

Cats on Rome's Streets: do you *really* want to know?

Passengers on Rome's Metro: 3 million daily.

Ticket Inspectors: 120.

Gallons of Water Delivered by Ancient Aqueducts: 312,000 hourly.

"Egyptian" Obelisks: 13.

Egyptian Obelisks: 7.

Egyptian Obelisks in Egypt: Fewer than that.

Pyramids in Rome: 1.

Pyramids in Egypt: 4.

WHEN TO GO

Few would dare call a Roman **spring** anything less than heaven. The weather is pleasantly balmy (hovering around 50 to 70°F), but the tourists haven't yet caught on. Rome's gardens and green spaces catch fire, and Lazio's freshest produce fills the streets. By June, the rains have ceased and hotels are booming. A Roman **summer** is sweltering (65-85°F) and congested, but you can catch major exhibitions, exciting festivals, and concerts under the stars. When the city gets too thick, cool off in the Mediterranean or in cold volcanic lakes. In August, the Romans leave town; you may not find as many hole-in-the-wall *trattorie* open, but the crowds will subside a bit. The trend continues into the **fall,** when the temperatures drop (45-60°F) and the prices do, too. **Winter** brings cold (expect temperatures between 40°F and 55°F), rain, and some of the lowest prices of the year, but it also brings the holidays, which are a major to-do in the city of St. Peter.

ROME ON FILM

So you're going to Rome. Learn from the mistakes of those who came before you—Gregory Peck (don't fall in love with a stranger), Spartacus (crucifixion sucks), Matt Damon (despite the face, Jude Law is not divine), etc.

Gladiator. So what if Rome's hills aren't that big and Marcus Aurelius was no altruistic Republican— all gladiators should be as hot as Russel Crowe. Mmmm....

The Talented Mr. Ripley. Learn all about how to dispose of bodies in the Eternal City. Once you get past the inordinate amount of time the film spends in those boring *northern* Italian towns, it's a pretty good psychological thriller.

Rome, Open City is the Rossellini classic about Rome during WWII, covertly filmed while the city was still occupied by the Nazis.

La Dolce Vita, by Fellini, is just plain good. That's all there is to it. Actually, what makes it really good is the sea monster at the end.

Roma, another Fellini flick, this basically plotless portrait of Rome combines autobiography with both insane and insanely beautiful visual images.

Spartacus. It's Kubrick and it's flawed, but it's got a young Charlton Heston. 'Nuff said.

Roman Holiday features Audrey Hepburn and Gregory Peck, and is so sweet you may need to visit a dentist after watching. Watch out for that pesky Bocca della Verità!

Caligula is Penthouse publisher, Bob Guccione's infamous sex-fest.

TOP 15 SIGHTS...

1. Musei Vaticano (p. 140). Rome's largest collection, the Vatican holds an ungodly percentage of the world's art, showcasing the personal tastes of Popes since 1506.

2. Galleria Borghese (p. 150). A lovely 17th-century villa in a lovely wooded park houses this lovely museum. Highlights: lovely Caravaggios and a very lovely nude of Napoleon's sister.

3. Basilica San Pietro (p. 110). Dwarfing cathedrals the world over, the house that Bernini built offers the delicate beauty of Michelangelo's *Pietà,* and the breathtaking, best birds' eye view of Rome.

4. Colosseum (p. 76). Too many tourists? Yes. Still mind-blowing? Definitely.

5. The Spanish Steps (p. 101). With attractions ranging from fashion shows to flower stalls, these famous stairs have drawn poets and tourists for centuries.

6. Capuchin Crypt (p. 102). 4000 dead friars. The Capuchin Crypt will satisfy anyone's desire to see molding made out of femur and tibia. The Counter-Reformation facade is spiffy, too.

7. Piazza Campidoglio (p. 83). Climb Michelangelo's stairway to this blindingly white square for a stunning view of the Forum.

8. Trevi Fountain (p. 104). This new (1762) addition to the Roman tourist will tempt you to re-enact a classic Fellini moment—but please refrain; it will cost you heavily in fines.

9. Palatine Hill (p. 78). So sayeth the Imperial real-estate agents: Location, location, location... The suckling site of Remus and Romulus, the hill has some of Rome's best ruins.

10. Church of San Clemente (p. 127). Two churches older than Methuselah, a mithraeum older than that, walkways through ancient sewers—is there anything this church doesn't have? Well, yes, but you can buy booze at St. Paul's Outside the Walls (see p. 127).

11. The Pantheon (p. 90). The huge dome of this pagan temple-turned-church still puzzles architects, who can't figure out how it was erected using 2nd-century building techniques.

12. Basilica Santa Maria Maggiore (p. 124). After its grand Baroque facade, Maggiore's striking classical interior is a surprise. Don't miss the apse's 13th-century mosaics of Mary dressed as a Byzantine Empress.

13. Museo Nazionale Etrusco di Villa Giulia (p. 153). You can go to Etruria (p. 234) and see the ruins of this ancient people's civilization, or you can come here and see all the artifacts plundered from them. Or you can do both.

14. Il Gesù (p. 88). Worldy and gold-encrusted, this 16th-century church was headquarters of the Jesuit order, the hardcore priests who brought us the Counter-Reformation and the Hoyas.

15. Church of San Giovanni in Laterano (p. 129). Former home of the Pope, resting place of the noggins of Peter and Paul, and a bad-ass *baldacchino.*

Roman Fourum

Vittorio Emanuele II

Chiesa Nuova

...AND OTHER PICKS

WHERE TO GO FIRST, LAST, AND WHENEVER CONFUSED. Pierluigi and Fulvia, proprietors of **Enjoy Rome** (p. 23), dish all the dirt on Rome, tell you what to do with it, and make all the necessary arrangements. Small miracles performed on request.

BEST CHURCH IN WHICH TO BUY LIQUOR. **Basilica San Paulo Fuori la Mura** (p. 135), where monks sell homemade benedictine to thirsty believers and passersby.

BEST BATHROOM. **Jonathan's Angels,** without a doubt (p. 187). Though **Termini**'s (p. 251) aren't too shabby, either.

HANDS DOWN BEST ITALIAN BEER. **Peroni.** Peroni, Peroni, Peroni.... Was there ever really a doubt?

SUGGESTED ITINERARIES

ONE DAY

Trying to cram the Eternal City into a day is going to be difficult, but you can try. In the morning, take our half-day **walking tour** through the medieval Centro Storico (p. 6), which begins and ends at P. Navona. After lunch nearby at one of the fantastic restaurants along V.d. Governo Vecchio, hop a bus to P. Venezia, and take our other half-day **walking tour** of the best of the rest of Rome, ending at St. Peter's Basilica in Vatican City. Head south and finish up with dinner at a *pizzeria* in Trastevere (p. 173), then head back across the Tiber for some nighttime fun (p. 186).

THREE DAYS

DAY ONE: GETTING ORIENTED. Begin with our **Best of Rome** walking tour (p. 5). Take your time touring the sights, stopping off in the **Roman Forum** (see p. 67) and the **Church of Santa Maria in Cosmedin** (see p. 85). When you're through, walk down the Tiber to Trastevere, and head for an outdoor *pizzeria* (see p. 173). Finish up by heading back up to the Borgo to catch some jazz at **Alexanderplatz Jazz Club** (p. 199).

DAY TWO: VATICAN CITY. Wake up early, go to the **Vatican Museums,** get in line, and race through the galleries to get to the Sistine Chapel before the crowds (p. 140). After you've caught your breath and had your fill of Michelangelo, spend a few hours in the rest of the museum. Be sure to spend some time at **St. Peter's** (p. 110), and make the climb to the top of the dome. Before heading off to dinner, explore Hadrian's mausoleum, better known as **Castel Sant'Angelo** (p. 115).

DAY THREE: BORGHESE AND THE SPANISH STEPS. Your first stop is the **Galleria Borghese** for the most concentrated two hours of art you've ever experienced in your life (p. 150). Relax afterward by wandering through the gardens of the Villa Borghese until you find yourself at the top of the **Spanish Steps** (p. 101). Catch lunch and do some **shopping** (p. 203), then take in the big sights in the area—don't miss the ancient Roman monuments (p. 108) or the **Trevi Fountain** (p. 104). Grab dinner near P. del Popolo (p. 171), and head back to the Spanish Steps to take the relaxing **after-dinner walking tour** (p. 183).

FIVE DAYS

In addition to the previous three-day tour, try the following:

DAY FOUR: SOUTHERN ROME. Spend some time examining the Colosseum up close, then head toward the grand **Church of San Giovanni in Laterano** (p. 129), stopping by the odd little **Church of San Clemente** (p. 127) along the way. From San Giovanni, take bus #218 to south to explore the **catacombs** and other sights along the **Appian Way** (p. 131).

SEVEN DAYS

So you wanted a tropical vacation, but got the hustle and bustle of Rome instead? Not to worry. After five days in Rome, take a two-day sojourn in the **Pontine Islands** (p. 230), just three hours from Rome by public transit. The islands offer pristine shoreline, fantastic seafood, and a little relaxation. You deserve it; this vacation has been hard work.

WALKING TOURS

For an after-dinner walk, see p. 183—after dinner, of course.

BEST OF ROME—VITTORIO TO THE VATICAN

P. Venezia to St. Peter's Basilica. This walk explores the Capitoline Hill, the Forum, the Jewish Ghetto, Campo di Fiori, Piazza Navona and St. Peter's Basilica. The walk will take approximately 3-3.5 hours, longer if you visit any of the museums along the way. The walk is also enjoyable at night, when many of the sites are lit up and the bars in Campo dei Fiori and P. Navona are open.

We begin in Piazza Venezia, where the mammoth **Vittorio Emanuelle II monument** simply refuses to be ignored. The monument—alternately know as the Vittoriano, Altar of the Nation, the giant wedding cake and Mussolini's typewriter -- was built between 1885-1911 to celebrate Italy's unification. The tomb of an unknown Italian soldier from WWI is guarded by two honor guards just above the staircase, and a giant equestrian statue of Vittorio rises above that. The monument is 200m high and 500m long—a dinner party for 24 was held in the horses's belly before the head was welded on.

When you reach the crest of the hill, take the stairs down to the intersection of Vico Jvgano and V.d. Teatro di Marcello. To your left you'll see more ruins—the fenced-off *Area Sacra di Sant'Omobono* holds the remains of the Temples of Fortuna and Mater Matua—well as the **Temple of Vest**a (round) and the **Temple of Fortuna Virilis** rectangular) further down the street. Duck under the arches and cross V.d. Teatro di Marcello; the **Teatro di Marcello** will be on your left a few paces. This theater, a designed in homage to the Colosseum, was dreamed up by Julius Caesar and dedicated by Augustus to the memory of his nephew Marcellus, who died at the tender age of 19.

Foro Borario

View from Aventine Hill

Church of Sant'Agnese in Agone

At the end of the Teatro di Marcello, take a right onto V. Montanara (which turns into V. Campitelli, featuring the Baroque **S. Maria in Portico**), your first left onto V. Trib., your first right onto V.d. Portico d'Occtavia, and then turn yourself about. You're in the heart of the **Jewish Ghetto**, the four blocks that pleasant Pope Paul V relegated to the city's Jewish population in the 1550s. While you're here, stop at **Forno del Ghetto**, the unlabeled bakery at 1 V.d. Portico d'Occtavia, for some of the city's best pastries—we recommend you buy by the kilo.

CENTRO STORICO—THE MEDIEVAL CITY

This is a loop through the medieval city, beginning and ending at P. Navona. 2½-5½hr.

The walk begins in **Piazza Navona** (p. 93), an elliptical *piazza* built on the site of a stadium constructed by Emperor Domitian in the first century AD. Take a moment to shoo off pushy vendors and take in the *piazza*'s fountains, which include Bernini's **Fountain of the Four Rivers.** The **Church of Sant'Agnese in Agone** is also worth a look—the dead saint's skull is prominently displayed.

From the southeast corner of P. Navona—with the three fountains to your left and the church looming behind you—walk down V. di Canestrari (V. Sediari) to P.S. Eustachio. Take V. Santa Chiara to P. della Minerva, where you can take in Michelangelo's *Risen Christ* at the **Church of Santa Maria Sopra Minerva** (p. 92). Take V. Minerva to P. della Rotonda and pay a visit to the hulking **Pantheon** (p. 90).

From there, take V.d. Seminario east, then turn right onto V. Sant'Ignazio into **Piazza Collegio Romano** (p. 89). Take in the **Galleria Doria Pamphilj** (p. 159) or continue on, turning left, crossing the Corso, and following V. d. S.S. Apostoli to V. di San Marcello. Turn left, then right at the dead end onto V. d. Ulmita'. Take the next left onto V. d. Vergini. A right on V.d. Murate will lead you directly to the **Trevi Fountain** (p. 104).

Continuing east from the P. di Trevi, take V.d. Lavoratore, stopping briefly at **San Crispino** for the world's best *gelato* (p. 105). Take V.d. Scuderie, cross V.d. Traforo, and walk up V. Rassella. At V.d. Quattro Fontane, go left into **Piazza Barberini** (p. 105). Go up V. Veneto 50m to see the **Capuchin Crypt** in Chiesa Santa Maria della Concezione, then double back and take V. Sistina up the hill to the busy **Spanish Steps** (p. 101).

From the top of the Steps, take V. Trinita' dei Monti (V. G. D'Annunzio) to the left-hand turn-off onto P. del Popolo. Admire the Raphael chapel and the Caravaggios in the **Church of Santa Maria del Popolo** at the north end of the *piazza* (p. 106), then take V. di Ripetta from the southern side. Grab a bite at **Pizza Re'**, a block down on the left (p. 172).

V. d. Ripetta runs into the **Ara Pacis** and **Mausoleum of Augustus** (p. 108). Continue down and take a left onto V. Borghese. Follow it and V. Divino Amore to P. Firenze. Continue down V.d. Maddalena, pull back into P. d. Rotonda, and rejuvenate at **Tazza d'Oro** (p. 177). From P.d. Rotonda, take V. Giustiniani and go right through P.S. Luigi d. Francesi onto V.d. Scrofa, stopping by **Chiesa San Luigi dei Francesi** (p. 92) for a glimpse at three more Caravaggios. From V.d. Scrofa, go left onto V.S. Agostino, stopping into **Chiesa Sant'Agostino** to see Caravaggio's *Madonna* and Raphael's *Isaiah.* From there, P. Cinque Lune spills into V. Angolare on the west, which runs back into the top end of P. Navona.

ROME BY SEASON

SPRING. As soon as the azaleas bloom at the end of March, piles of them are brought to the Spanish Steps to celebrate **La Festa di Primavera,** the coming of spring. The exhibition lasts until the flowers die, usually a week or two. **Good Friday** brings the Pope's **Procession of the Cross** from the Colosseum to the Palatine and a week of services in basilicas across the city, culminating in the Pope's Easter **Urbi et Orbi** blessing in 50 languages. Don't miss **Rome's birthday;** April 21 sees the Capitoline Hill alive with partyers, Latin poetry, a concert, and fireworks set off from the Circus Maximus. The **Rose Show** arrives in early May at Valle Murcia, on the Aventine above the Circus Maximus, and lasts through June. Also, the **Italian International Tennis Tour-**

nament brings excitement to the Foro Italico during the first two weeks of May.

SUMMER. Festivals and concerts abound, so be sure to check *Roma C'è*. On June 23, the **Church of San Giovanni in Laterano** sponsors a gluttonous banquet of snails and roast pork. **Festa dei Santi Pietro e Paolo,** June 29, is an awe-inspiring religious ceremony for Rome's patron saints, taking place in the Basilica dei Santi Pietro e Paolo. The 3rd Sunday in July brings **Noantri,** a 10-day celebration of the planet called Trastevere, complete with midway rides and grand religious processions. Finally, on August 5, the **Festa della Madonna della Neve** is a blizzard of white flower petals representing the legendary out-of-season snow at the **Church of Santa Maria Maggiore.**

FALL. In September, watch out for the **art festival** featuring the works of over 100 painters along V. Margutta. Vats of wine make for hazy evenings at the **Sagra delle Uva** in the Forum's Basilica of Maxentius, and a torch-lit **medieval crafts fair** (late September to early October) on V.dell'Orso complements the V.d. Coronari **antique fair** (last two weeks of October).

WINTER. Christmas sees P. Navona full of crêche figures for sale and children begging for toys and candy and reciting poems and speeches. It's hopelessly cute. On December 8, the Pope and other worshipers leave elaborate floral tributes to the statue of the virgin in P.d. Spagna for the **Festa dell'Immacolata Connezione. Capodanno** (New Year's) merrymaking includes sparklers, throwing old dishes (or clothes, or old bathtubs) from windows, eating *cotecchino* (pig's feet), and washing it all down with *spumante* and an amazing fireworks display. On the first, the faithful light candles and make their way through the catacombs of Santa Priscilla, while the pope gives a solemn High Mass at St. Peter's. On January 17, during the **Festa di Sant'Antonio,** pet cats, dogs, and canaries are blessed after mass on the steps of the Church of Sant'Eusebio all'Esquilino. The **Carnevale** parade (the day before Ash Wednesday) down the Corso is a sight to be seen. Throw on a fancy costume and bring some silly string.

Living in Rome

Pompeii

Castel Sant'Angelo

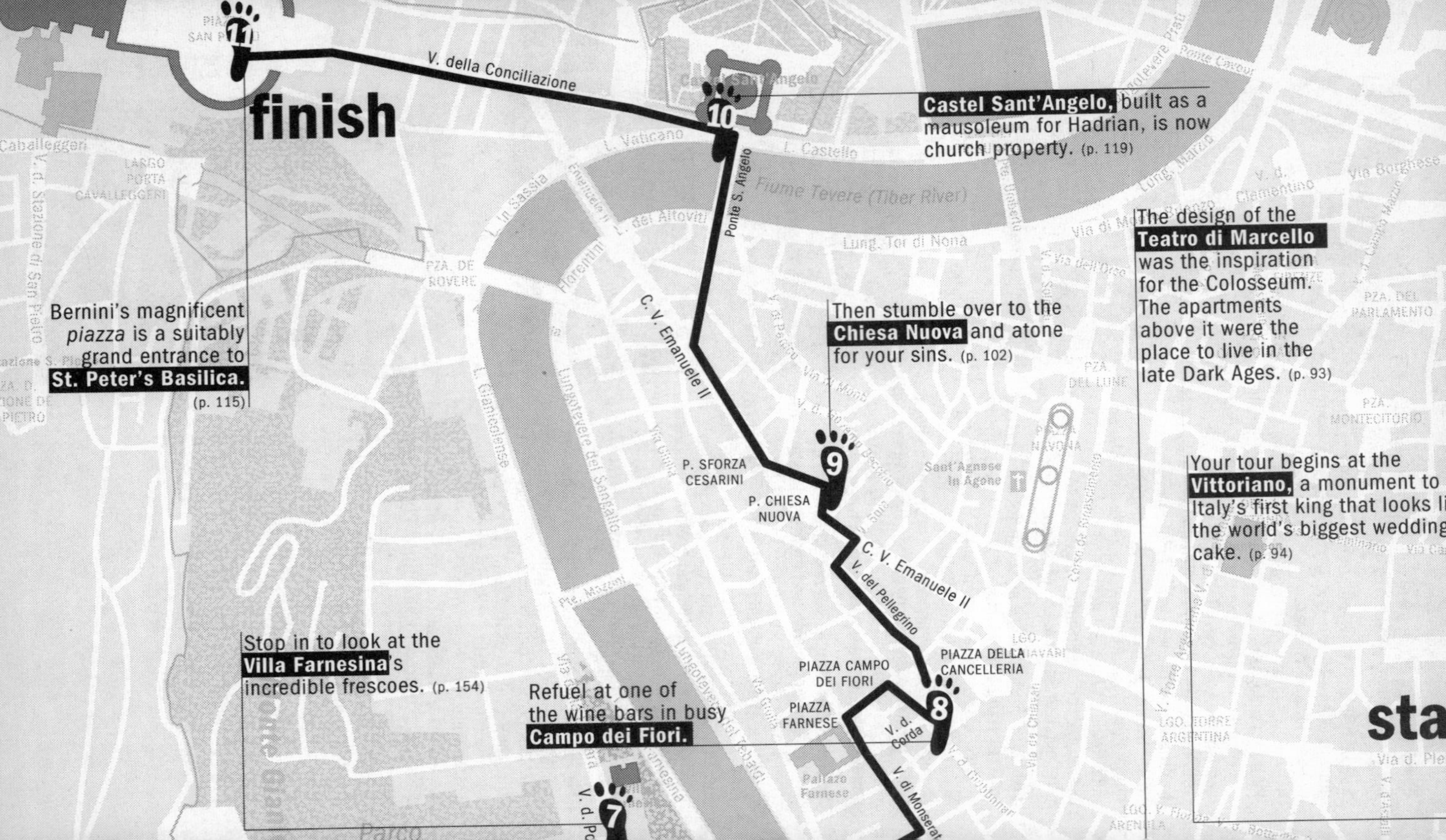

finish
star
Castel Sant'Angelo, built as a mausoleum for Hadrian, is now church property. (p. 119)
The design of the Teatro di Marcello was the inspiration for the Colosseum. The apartments above it were the place to live in the late Dark Ages. (p. 93)
Then stumble over to the Chiesa Nuova and atone for your sins. (p. 102)
Your tour begins at the Vittoriano, a monument to Italy's first king that looks like the world's biggest wedding cake. (p. 94)
Bernini's magnificent piazza is a suitably grand entrance to St. Peter's Basilica. (p. 115)
Stop in to look at the Villa Farnesina's incredible frescoes. (p. 154)
Refuel at one of the wine bars in busy Campo dei Fiori.
V. della Conciliazione
Ponte S. Angelo
Fiume Tevere (Tiber River)
C. V. Emanuele II
P. SFORZA CESARINI
P. CHIESA NUOVA
C. V. Emanuele II
V. del Pellegrino
PIAZZA DELLA CANCELLERIA
PIAZZA CAMPO DEI FIORI
PIAZZA FARNESE
V. d. Corda
V. di Monserat
V. d. Po
PZA. DE ROVERE
LARGO PORTA CAVALLEGGERI
L. Vaticano
L. Castello
Lung. Tor di Nona
Lungotevere dei Sangallo
L. Gianicolense
Sant'Agnese in Agone
Palazzo Farnese
PZA. DEL PARLAMENTO
PZA. MONTECITORIO
LGO. TORRE ARGENTINA
Via d. Plebisc
V. d. Stazione di San Pietro
PZA. D. STAZIONE DE S. PIETRO
Porta Cavalleggeri
Via Borghese
Ponte Cavour

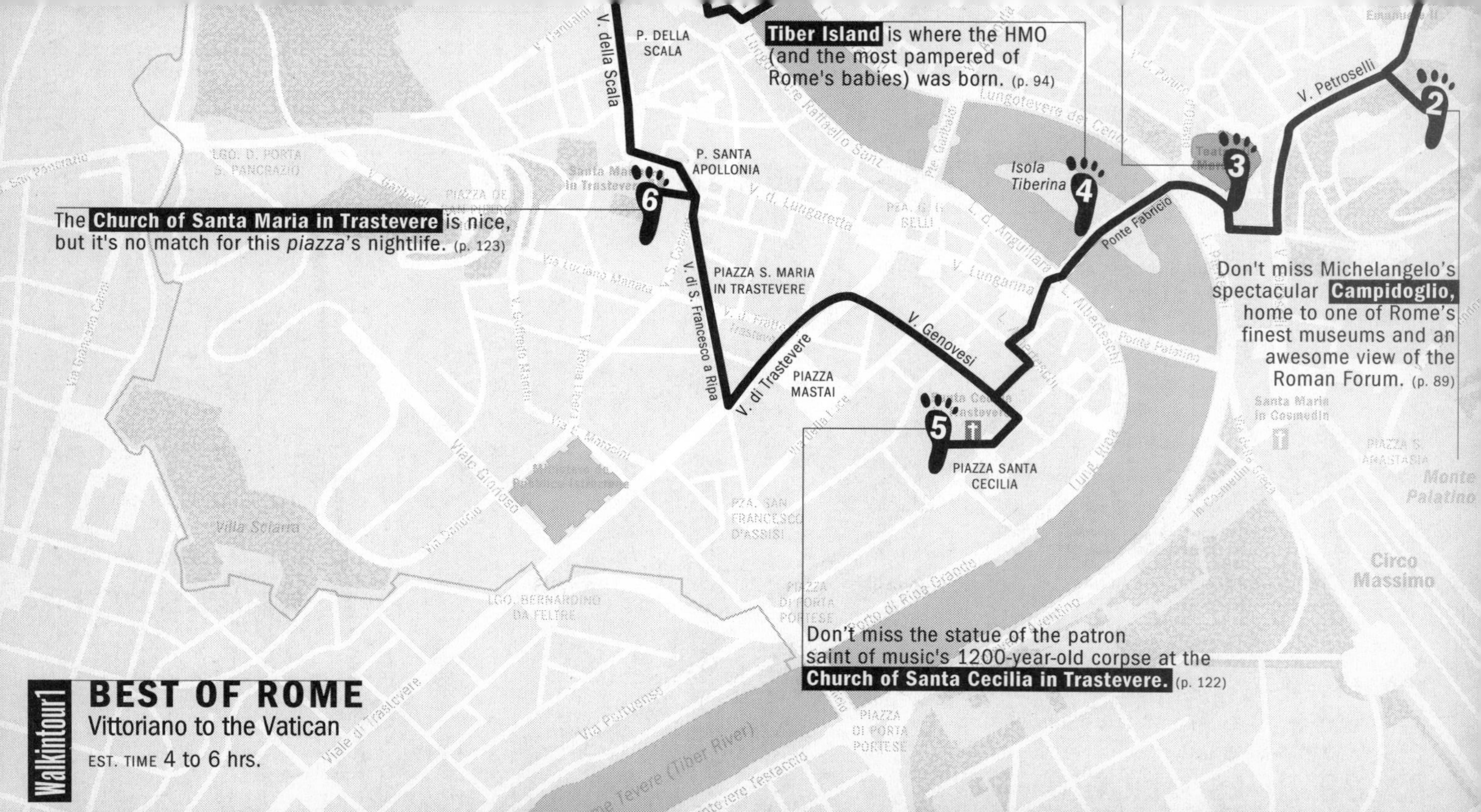
Walkintour1
BEST OF ROME
Vittoriano to the Vatican
EST. TIME 4 to 6 hrs.
Tiber Island is where the HMO (and the most pampered of Rome's babies) was born. (p. 94)
The Church of Santa Maria in Trastevere is nice, but it's no match for this piazza's nightlife. (p. 123)
Don't miss Michelangelo's spectacular Campidoglio, home to one of Rome's finest museums and an awesome view of the Roman Forum. (p. 89)
Don't miss the statue of the patron saint of music's 1200-year-old corpse at the Church of Santa Cecilia in Trastevere. (p. 122)
V. della Scala
P. DELLA SCALA
P. SANTA APOLLONIA
PIAZZA S. MARIA IN TRASTEVERE
V. di S. Francesco a Ripa
V. di Trastevere
PIAZZA MASTAI
V. Genovesi
PIAZZA SANTA CECILIA
Ponte Fabricio
Isola Tiberina
V. Petroselli
Santa Maria in Cosmedin
Circo Massimo
Monte Palatino
Viale Glorioso
Villa Sciarra
Flume Tevere (Tiber River)

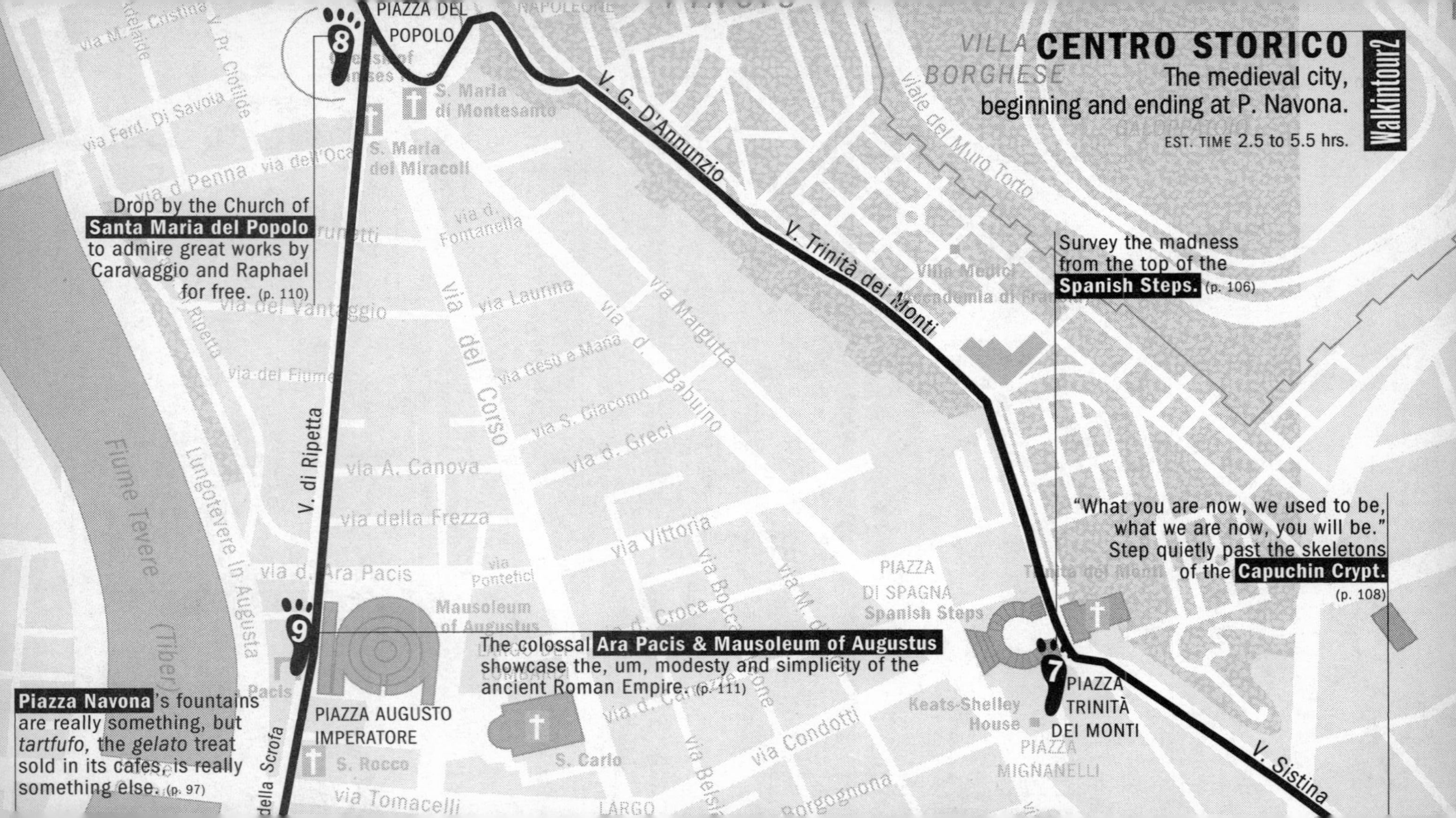
Walkintour2
CENTRO STORICO
The medieval city, beginning and ending at P. Navona.
EST. TIME 2.5 to 5.5 hrs.
VILLA BORGHESE
viale del Muro Torto
PIAZZA DEL POPOLO
8
S. Maria di Montesanto
S. Maria dei Miracoli
Drop by the Church of Santa Maria del Popolo to admire great works by Caravaggio and Raphael for free. (p. 110)
V. G. D'Annunzio
V. Trinità dei Monti
Villa Medici
Survey the madness from the top of the Spanish Steps. (p. 106)
"What you are now, we used to be, what we are now, you will be." Step quietly past the skeletons of the Capuchin Crypt. (p. 108)
7
PIAZZA TRINITÀ DEI MONTI
V. Sistina
PIAZZA DI SPAGNA
Spanish Steps
Keats-Shelley House
PIAZZA MIGNANELLI
via Condotti
Borgognona
via Vittoria
via Margutta
via d. Babuino
via d. Greci
via S. Giacomo
via Gesù e Maria
via Laurina
via d. Fontanella
Via del Corso
via A. Canova
via della Frezza
via d. Ara Pacis
via del Vantaggio
via del Fiume
via d. Penna
via dell'Oca
via Ferd. Di Savoia
V. Pr. Clotilde
V. di Ripetta
Lungotevere in Augusta
Fiume Tevere (Tiber)
9
Mausoleum of Augustus
The colossal Ara Pacis & Mausoleum of Augustus showcase the, um, modesty and simplicity of the ancient Roman Empire. (p. 111)
PIAZZA AUGUSTO IMPERATORE
S. Rocco
S. Carlo
via Tomacelli
LARGO
della Scrofa
Piazza Navona's fountains are really something, but *tartfufo*, the *gelato* treat sold in its cafes, is really something else. (p. 97)

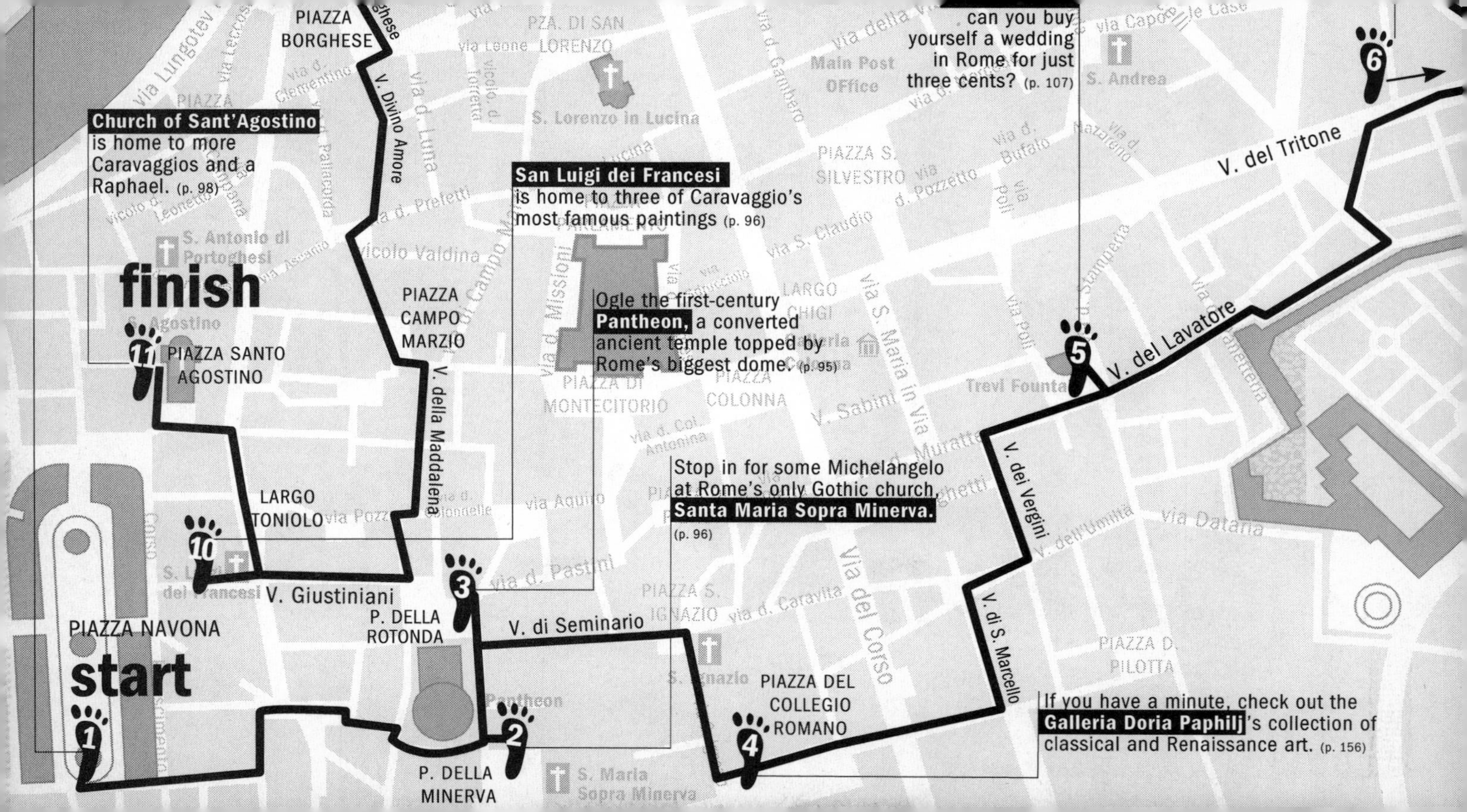

Church of Sant'Agostino is home to more Caravaggios and a Raphael. (p. 98)
San Luigi dei Francesi is home to three of Caravaggio's most famous paintings (p. 96)
Ogle the first-century Pantheon, a converted ancient temple topped by Rome's biggest dome. (p. 95)
Stop in for some Michelangelo at Rome's only Gothic church, Santa Maria Sopra Minerva. (p. 96)
If you have a minute, check out the Galleria Doria Paphilj's collection of classical and Renaissance art. (p. 156)
. can you buy yourself a wedding in Rome for just three cents? (p. 107)
start
finish
PIAZZA NAVONA
PIAZZA BORGHESE
V. Divino Amore
PIAZZA CAMPO MARZIO
V. della Maddalena
PIAZZA SANTO AGOSTINO
LARGO TONIOLO
V. Giustiniani
P. DELLA ROTONDA
P. DELLA MINERVA
V. di Seminario
PIAZZA DEL COLLEGIO ROMANO
V. di S. Marcello
V. dei Vergini
V. del Lavatore
V. del Tritone
Trevi Fountain
Via del Corso
via S. Maria in Via
PIAZZA COLONNA
PIAZZA DI MONTECITORIO
PIAZZA S. IGNAZIO
PIAZZA D. PILOTTA
Via Dataria
S. Maria Sopra Minerva
S. Lorenzo in Lucina
PZA. DI SAN LORENZO
Main Post Office
S. Andrea
PIAZZA S. SILVESTRO
S. Antonio di Portoghesi
Pantheon

STAR
OLITA
OLIO DI
SEMI VARI

INSIDE

When in Rome

The best way to inspect the streets of Rome, if you wish to study as well as see them, is to break your pocket-compass and burn your maps and guidebooks...take Chance for a mentor and lose yourself.
—George Sala, 1866

In his *History of Rome*, Livy concluded that "the layout of Rome is more like a squatter's settlement than a properly planned city." Two thousand years of city planning later, Rome still seems like an unnavigable sea of one-way streets, dead ends, clandestine *piazze*, and incurable traffic. The following pages will help you get your footing the minute your plane touches down in the Eternal City. Chances are you're still going to get lost—even Roman residents lose their way in Rome's sprawling streets. And when in Rome....

UPON ARRIVAL

Most international flights touch down at Leonardo da Vinci International Airport (☎06 65951), referred to as **Fiumicino** for the coastal village in which it is located. Up-to-the-minute information on both of Rome's airports is online at www.adr.it.

FIUMICINO

EPT (Rome Tourist Authority) (☎06 65956074), directly in front of the customs exit of Terminal C. Hotel reservations and brochures. English spoken. Open daily 8:15am-7pm.

Banca di Roma, a small branch sits immediately to the right of customs; go right from customs to the end of the hallway to find the large office. Decent exchange rates. Open M-F 8:25am-1:25pm and 2:30-3:40pm, Sa. 8:25-11:55am. **ATM** at both locations accepts AmEx, Cirrus, MC, and V. Its **currency exchange** office is to the right of customs. Open daily 6am-midnight.

Luggage Storage, on the right at the end of the hall as you exit customs. Open 24hr. L4100/€2.11 per bag per day ending at midnight.

Post Office, next to luggage storage and the large Banca di Roma office. Services include fax and telegrams. Open M-F 8:30am-3:15pm, Sa 8:30pm-1:45pm.

Rent-A-Car/Autonoleggi, two conveyer belts away from the train depot.

CIAMPINO

Most charter and a few domestic flights arrive at Ciampino airport (☎06 794941). To get to Ciampino from Rome, take the COTRAL bus (every 30min., 6:10am-11pm, L2000/€1.03) to Anagnina station on Metro Linea A (see p. 19). To get to Ciampino, reverse these directions. Another option is taking a train from Termini to Ciampino station and a bus to the airport; check with FS (☎1478 88088; www.fs-on-line.com) for details. After 11pm, to take a cab to and from Ciampino. Although Ciampino is inside the Rome city limits, there is a supplemental charge of L10,000/€5.16.

TO AND FROM THE AIRPORT BY TRAIN

Upon seeing the dozens of people crowded outside customs waiting for loved ones, you may feel compelled to pretend to be related to one of these people and convince them to take you to their Italian home, where you'll enjoy home-cooked meals and a warm bed. Resist this urge. Instead, follow the signs to your left for **Stazione FS/Railway Station.** Go up 2 floors to the pedestrian bridge to the airport train station. From here you can take one of the two trains to the center of Rome.

TERMINI STATION

The Termini line runs nonstop to Rome's main train, Termini (30min.; 2 per hr. 12 and 37min. past the hour 7:37am-10:37pm, extra trains 7:37am, 6:37, 8:37pm; L16,000/€8.23, L40,000/€20.30 on board). Buy a ticket *"Per Termini"* at the FS ticket counter, the *tabacchi* on the right, or from one of the machines in the station. A train leaves Termini for Fiumicino from track #22 or #23, which is at the end of #22 and a bit of a walk (40 min.; houly at 20min. past the hour 7:20am-9:20pm; extra trains 6:50am, 3:50, 5:50, 7:50pm; L16,000/€8.26). Buy tickets at the Alitalia office at track #22 at the window marked *"Biglietti Per Fiumicino"* or from other designated areas and machines in the station. Validate your ticket before boarding.

TIBURTINA STATION

The Tiburtina/Orte/Fara Sabina train stops at many of the minor train stations (but NOT Termini) on the outskirts of the city center, all of which are, in turn, connected to the city center by bus or Metro. Service is erratic on Sundays and in August, and trains may arrive at Tiburtina after the Metro closes (40min.; every 15min. 6:27am-9:27pm; extra trains 5:37am, 9:57, 10:27, 10:57, 11:27pm; L8000/€4.13). Buy tickets *"Per Tiburtina"* on the right, or from the machines in the station, or on the train after hours. Note that the final destination of this train may be indicated on the signs by "Orte (6th stop)," "Tiburtina (8th stop)," or "Fara Sabina (15th stop)." Validate and retain your ticket for the entire trip.

The most convenient way to reach the city center when using this line is to get off at the Tiburtina station, which is connected to the Metro stop "Tiburtina" (Linea B). When you get off the train (track #1), go down the stairs, following the signs for the *Metropolitana.* Buy a ticket (L1500/€0.77), validate it, and take Metro Linea B (dir: "Laurentina"). A train leaves Tiburtina for Fiumicino from track #4 or #5 (40min., every 15 to 60min. 5:04am-10:33pm, L8000/€4.13). Buy tickets at the ticket booths.

EARLY AND LATE FLIGHTS

If your flight arrives at Fiumicino after 10pm or leaves before 8am, you may have transportation difficulties. The most reliable, if expensive, option is to take a **cab,** which costs L65-85,000/€37.00-44.30. (Request one at the kiosk in the airport or call ☎06 3570, 06 4994, or 06 6645.) In the wee hours, the cheapest option is to take the blue **COTRAL bus** to Tiburtina from the ground floor outside the main exit doors after customs (1:15, 2:15, 3:30, 5am; L8000/€4.13, pay on board).

From Tiburtina, take bus #40N to Termini. Reserve a room in the area ahead of time to avoid setting up camp in Termini. To get to Fiumicino from Rome late at night or early in the morning, take bus #40N from Termini to Tiburtina (every 20-30min.), then catch the blue COTRAL bus to Fiumicino from the plaza outside (12:30, 1:15, 2:30, 3:45am; L8000/€4.13).

LET'S GET ORIENTED

Most sights and establishments listed in *Let's Go: Rome 2002* are grouped by location and then ranked by interest and quality. Each neighborhood corresponds to a map at the back of this book (on which sights and establishments are plotted). Street names change frequently in Rome; in directions to establishments, this is denoted by placing another street name in parentheses after the initial name. For instance, Via del Quirinale turning into Via XX Settembre would be denoted as "V.d. Quirinale (V. XX Settembre)." **Abbreviations** used include: V. for Via, P. for Piazza, and C. for Corso. First names (as in C. V. Emanuele II) and San/Santa are abbreviated in addresses.

ROME BY NEIGHBORHOOD

No longer defined by the Seven Hills, modern Rome is huge, sprawling over a large area between the hills of the Castelli Romani to the north, the beach at Ostia to the west, and Lake Albano to the south, counting within its boundaries such memorable eyesores as Anagnina, Spinaceto, and Infernetto ("little Hell"). Encircling it is the Grande Raccordo Anulare (GRA), whose name loosely translates as "traffic jams of Biblical proportions." Luckily for you, though, most major sights lie within a comparatively small radius, which can be neatly divided into eight areas.

ANCIENT CITY

Accessible by Metro (Linea B) and buses serving P. Venezia. For sights, see p. 67.

The Ancient City begins directly south of **Piazza Venezia** (the center of the city and home to the huge Vittorio Emanuele II monument; see p. 88). Directly behind the monument, the **Capitoline Hill,** capped by Michelangelo's P.d. Campidoglio, is accessible by **Via di Teatro di Marcello,** which runs southwest toward the Velabrum and the Tiber. On the other side of the monument, **Via dei For Imperiali** runs all the way to the **Colosseum.** Off V.d. Fori Imperiali are the **Imperial Fora** and the **Roman Forum** itself. Behind the Forum looms the **Palatine Hill** and, beyond that, the **Circus Maximus.**

CENTRO STORICO

Accessible by buses #60 and #117 on the Corso, as well as a number of buses along C. Vittorio Emanuel II. For sights, see p. 87.

The medieval neighborhood of Rome spreads north and West from **Piazza Venezia,** bordered by Via del Corso on the East and the Tiber to the west. **Corso Vittorio Emanule II** runs northwest from Piazza Venezia toward the Vatican; much of the third of the Centro south of this thoroughfare is taken up by the **Jewish Ghetto.**

PIAZZA DI SPAGNA AND THE CORSO

Accessible via Metro Linea A and many buses, including #60 and #492 to P. Barberini and #117 to the P.d. Spagna. For sights, see p. 101.

East of the Corso, stretching from Piazza Venezia up toward Villa Borghese, is the area around the **Spanish Steps.** The famous steps themselves, which climb from **Piazza di Spagna** up to **Piazza Trinità dei Monti,** are four blocks from the Corso along Rome's most exclusive shopping area, **Via Condotti.** On the western side of the Corso lie the famous Mausoleum of Augustus and the Ara Pacis. South of the Spanish Steps is the über-crowded **Trevi Fountain.** East of the fountain is the **Quirinale,** headquarters of Italian government. **Via del Tritone** runs east from the Corso to **Piazza Barberini,** and continues on toward Termini as **V. Barberini.**

VILLA BORGHESE

M: A-Flaminio or M: A-Spagna. Bus #490 runs through the park. For sights, see p. 109.

Northeast of Piazza del Popolo and the Spanish Steps is the **Villa Borghese,** a vast park that is home to the **zoo** and several museums. Since it is a park, there are kilometers of verdant paths. The neighborhood of the Villa Borghese stretches around Piazza del Popolo east to cover the environs north of Termini and **Via XX Settembre.**

BORGO, PRATI, AND THE VATICAN CITY

Accessible via Metro (Linea A) and many buses, including #64, #492, and #490, which serves northern Prati. For sights, see p. 110.

Across the Tiber, northwest from the Centro Storico is the **Vatican City.** Crossing the Ponte Vittorio Emanuele II from C. Vittorio Emanuele II takes you directly to **Via della Conciliazione,** the avenue that leads west to P.S. Pietro and **Saint Peter's Basilica.** The **Vatican Museums** are just next door. At the eastern end of V.d. Conciliazione, **Castel Sant'Angelo,** the Pope's historic residence, overlooks the Tiber. Between Castel Sant'Angelo and the Vatican is the quiet **Borgo** neighborhood. To the north is less quiet **Prati,** home to scattered hotels, restaurants, and pubs. **Via Cola di Rienzo** runs through Prati from **Piazza del Risorgimento,** next to the Vatican, across Ponte Regina Margherita to **Piazza del Popolo.**

TRASTEVERE

Tram #13 runs the length of Viale di Trastevere from Largo Argentina in the Centro Storico south past Stazione Trastevere. Among others, buses #23 and 170 provide service to southern Trastevere and bus #870 serves the Gianicolo. For sights, see p. 117.

Trastevere, easily Rome's most picturesque neighborhood, and certainly its most entertaining to navigate, is south of the Vatican and west, across the Tiber, from the Centro Storico. Viale Trastevere runs across Ponte Garibaldi all the way to Largo Argentina and C. Vittorio Emanuele II and is the main drag of the neighborhood. Most of Trastevere's points of interest lie near this street, and not far from the river. Between Trastevere and the Vatican is the exclusive and park-like Janiculum Hill, or the Gianicolo.

TERMINI AND SAN LORENZO

Termini is the transfer point between the 2 Metro lines and is served by countless buses. San Lorenzo is served by bus #492, Esquilino is accessible by buses #70 and #714, and bus #60 runs out of the city along V. XX Settembre (V. Nomentana). For sights, see p. 121.

Located east of the center of town, this is the area most people see first when arriving in Rome. Get used to it, because it's also where most budget travelers stay. The neighborhood immediately northeast of **Stazione Termini** is jam-packed with hotels, hostels, restaurants, and Internet cafes. East of the station is the **Città Universitaria,** home to Rome's La Sapienza university. South of that is **San Lorenzo,** the student neighborhood, which is home to many cheap and delicious restaurants, as well a healthy dose of left-wing student spirit. South of Termini, along V. Giovanni Giolitti and V. Merulana, is the **Esquilino** neighborhood. San Lorenzo is connected to Esquilino by **Via Tiburtina. Via XX Settembre (Via Nomentana)** cuts through the quieter area northwest of the station. In front of the station, **Via Nazionale** runs from **Piazza della Repubblica** west toward the older center of town. **Via Cavour** runs southeast from the station to the Colosseum.

SOUTHERN ROME

Testaccio, the Aventine, and EUR are served by Metro Linea B and buses including #23 and 673. Metro Linea A and buses #673 and 714 run to the Caelian and southeast Rome. For sights, see p. 127.

Across the river from Trastevere and south of the Jewish Ghetto and the Ancient City are the posh **Aventine Hill** and the working-class **Testaccio** district. The former home to Rome's slaughterhouses is named after a hill of ancient amphora shards and has many of Rome's most popular nightclubs (not to mention its only pyramid).

Farther south are **Ostiense** and **EUR,** Mussolini's prototype neighborhood of wide boulevards, nationalistic slogans, and museums. East of the Tiber are the **Caelian Hill,** southeast of the Colosseum and home to the San Giovanni neighborhood, and farther south, the **Appian Way.**

MAPS

It's impossible to navigate the streets of Rome without a map, and using the free and omnipresent **McDonald's** map will probably get you lost (though you're likely to find at least one of the 35 McDonald's locations in the Eternal City). Instead, pick up the concise and detailed **Charta Roma** map (at EPT or PIT kiosks) or the one published by Enjoy Rome. *Let's Go* publishes a **map guide** to Rome, a pocket-sized map of transportation, sights, etc., with 32 pages of advice on where to sleep, eat, and dance in Rome. The compact Bus/Tram/Metro map available at Termini (free) is relatively ueless, so buy a **Roma Metro-Bus** map at a newsstand (L8000/€4.13). **Rome A to Z** (sold with **Lazio A to Z**) includes a pocket guide of 20 bike routes (available at newsstands; L12,000/€6.20). **Tuttocittà,** distributed yearly with Roman phone books, is the best atlas, but isn't sold in stores; ask Roman friends or store owners if you can look at it.

View from Piazza Garibaldi

LET'S USE PUBLIC TRANSPORTATION

Bus and subway tickets (L1500/€0.77) are one and the same and can be bought at *tabacchi*, newsstands, some bars, and vending machines (in stations, on occasional street corners, and at major bus stops). Look for the ATAC label. Each ticket is valid for either one ride on the Metro or for unlimited bus travel within 75 minutes of validation. A BIG **daily ticket** costs L8000/€4.13 and allows for unlimited bus or train travel everywhere in the *Comune di Roma,* including Ostia but not Fiumicino; a CIS **weekly ticket** costs L32,000/€16.32. If you'll be in Rome for more than a few weeks, consider purchasing the *abbonamento mensile,* which allows 1 month (beginning the first of the month) of unlimited transport for L50,000/€25.55. Ask for the pass anywhere tickets are sold. Student passes are cheaper, but are only for Italian students or students at Italian universities.

Subway

BUSES

Though the network of routes may seem daunting at first, Rome's bus system is very efficient and inexpensive. Buses also cover far more area than the rather scanty metro system. The **ATAC** (*Aziende Tramvie Autobus Communali;* ☎800 555666, 8am-8pm) intracity bus company

On the Street

has a myriad of **information booths,** including one in Termini. The invaluable **Roma Metro-Bus map,** published by Lozzi, is available at newsstands for L8000/€4.13. Ask at the tourist office (see p. 24) for a useful Bus/Tram/Metro map of central Rome. Each bus stop *(fermata)* is marked by yellow signs listing routes that stop there and key streets and stops on those routes. The name of the stop at which you are standing is boxed; the bus will take you to any of the places listed below the boxed stop. **To go to a stop listed above the box,** cross the street to catch the same bus in the opposite direction.

Temporary bus signs are simple yellow poles with the route marked in cursive; you'll need to check a map to know all the stops. Some buses run only on weekdays *(feriali)* or weekends *(festivi)*, while others may have different routes, depending on the day of the week. Hours vary, but most buses begin around 6am and stop around midnight. Board buses from the front or back doors, not from the middle, then stamp your ticket in the orange machine at the back; exit only through the middle, helpfully marked *uscita*. The ticket is then good for any number of transfers over the next 75min. Stamp the other end of the ticket after your first transfer. If you exceed 1¼hr., you must stamp a new ticket. There is a **L100,000/€51.67 fine** for not carrying a validated ticket or bus pass, and inspections are becoming more common. Playing the dumb tourist won't help. Buy several tickets and keep them on you: at night and on weekends they can be hard to find.

Night routes are indicated on signs by black shields, owls, and the letter N following the route number. Below the bus itinerary should be listed the approximate time that the bus will pass. Signal a night bus to stop by standing right under its sign and flailing wildly. They run infrequently, and you may have to transfer several times to get where you want to go. Don't depend too heavily on *notturno* buses, as they are often unreliable. **ATAC** offers *Giro Turistico*, a no-frills, 3-hour circuit of the city. (Bus #110; leaves Termini 10:30am, 2, 3, 5, and 6pm; L15,000/€7.75.) They provide a map and some explanation in Italian and quasi-English, whirling you around the city for a comprehensive peek at the city's more visible monuments.

A word on **bus etiquette:** If you are young , you really should give your seat to elderly people. Inexplicably, Romans on the bus like to prepare for their grand descent several stops in advance by crowding around the exit doors. If you are standing in their way near the exit, you will be asked repeatedly, *"Scende (la prossima)?"* which means, "Are you getting off at the next stop?" Answer appropriately.

POPULAR ATAC BUS ROUTES

Rome is always revamping its transportation system. Be sure to check a map for the most up-to-date route information.

DAY BUSES

46: Vatican, C. V. Emanuele II, Largo Argentina, P. Venezia.

60: V. Nomentana, V. XX Settembre, Teatro Marcello. P.d. Republica P. Venezia, Coleosseo, P.le Ostiense.

64: Termini, V. Nazionale, P. Venezia, Largo Argentina, C. V. Emanuele II, Vatican (known as the "wallet-eater." AVOID THIS BUS!)

81: P. Malatesta, San Giovanni, Colosseo, Bocca della Verita, P. Venezia, Largo Argentina, P. Cavour, V. Cola di Rienzo, Vatican.

117: S. Giovanni, Colosseum, Largo Tritone, P.d. Spagna, P. del Popolo, V.d. Corso, P. Venezia, Colosseum. Weekdays only, from 8am-9pm.

170: Termini, V. Nazionale, P. Venezia, Largo Argentina, V. Marmorata, southern Trastevere, S. Paolo Basilica, P. Agricoltura (EUR).

492: Tiburtina, Termini, P. Barberini, P. Venezia, C. Rinascimento, P. Cavour, P. Risorgimento.

TRAMS

8: Largo Argentino, Porta Portese, Trastevere, Gianicolum.

19: S. Lorenzo, Villa Borghese, V. Ottaviano, P. Risorgimento (Vatican).

30B: Porta San Paolo, Colosseo, S. Giovanni, S. Lorenzo, Villa Borghese. Stops 10pm.

NIGHT (NOTTURNO) BUSES

You must signal a night bus to stop for you. Buses are supposed to come at 30min.-1hr. intervals, but can be unreliable; try to avoid waiting alone.

29N: Testaccio, Lungotevere de' Cenci, V. Crescenzio (Vatican), V. Belle Arti, V. Regina Marherita, S. Lorenzo, Colosseum.

40N: Approximately the same route as Metro B, from Termini to Tiburtina. Runs every 30min.

45N: P. Capecelatro, P. della Rovere (Vatican), C. Vittorio Emanuele, Largo Argentina, P. Venezia, V.d. Corso, P.S. Silvestro. Leaves Capecelatro 12:51, 1:50, and 4:50am; leaves Silvestro 12:23, 1:22, 2:21, and 4:22am.

55N: Approximately the same route as Metro A, from Termini to Cinecittà. Runs every 30min.

60N: P. Vimercati, V. Nomentana, V. Veneto, P. Venezia. Leaves Vimercati 12:08, 12:38, 1:38, 2:08, 3:08, 3:38, and 4:38am.

78N: P. Clodio, Vatican, V. Flaminia, P. Cavour, C. Rinascimento, P. Venezia, Termini. Leaves Clodio 12:30, 1:30, 3, 4, 5, and 5:30am. Leaves Termini 1, 3:30, 4:30, and 5:30am.

BUSES TO RURAL LAZIO

COTRAL buses between Rome and the province of Lazio (☎06 5915551) leave from outside the city center; take the subway to an outlying area and catch a bus from there: M: A-Anagnina for Frascati and the Colli Albani; M: B-Rebibbia for Tivoli and Subiaco; M: A-Lepanto for Cerveteri, Tarquinia, Bracciano, Lago Vico, and Civitavecchia. *Let's Go* lists information in the Daytrips chapter (see p. 213). For more information, contact COTRAL (☎06 5915551) or a tourist agency (see p. 294).

METRO

Every time they tried to dig more tracks for their subway system, the Romans discovered more ancient ruins. As a result, Rome's subway system is sparse. Many of Rome's sights are a trek from the nearest stop, but for covering large distances quickly, the subway beats the bus—it's comparatively fast and reliable. The two lines (A and B) of the *Metropolitana* intersect at Termini and can be reached by several entrances, including the stairway between the station and P. del Cinquecento. Entrances to Metro stations elsewhere are marked by poles with a white "M" on a red square. **The subway runs daily from 5:30am to 11:30pm.**

You don't actually have to validate your ticket to pass through the turnstiles on the subway; however, ATAC's ticket inspectors prowl trains and stations, and, as on the buses, checks are becoming much more common.

TAXIS AND RADIO TAXIS

Taxis in Rome are convenient but expensive (though less so than in other major cities). You can flag them down in the street, but they are easily found at stands near Termini and in major *piazze*. Ride only in yellow or white taxis, and make sure your taxi has a meter (if not, settle on a price before you get in the car). The meter starts at L4500/€2.47. Surcharges are levied at night (L5000/€2.55), on Sunday (L2000/€1.03), and when heading to or from Fiumicino (L14,000/€7.23) and Ciampino (L10,000/€5.16), with a charge per suitcase of L2000/€1.03. Standard tip is 15%. Expect to pay about L15,000/€7.75 for a ride from Termini to the Vatican. Taxis between the city center and Fiumicino cost around L70,000/€36.20. **Radio taxis** will pick you up at a given location within a few minutes of your call. Beware: radio taxis start the meter the moment your call is answered! See the **Service Directory,** p. 294, for a listing of taxi and radio taxis.

Rome Transport

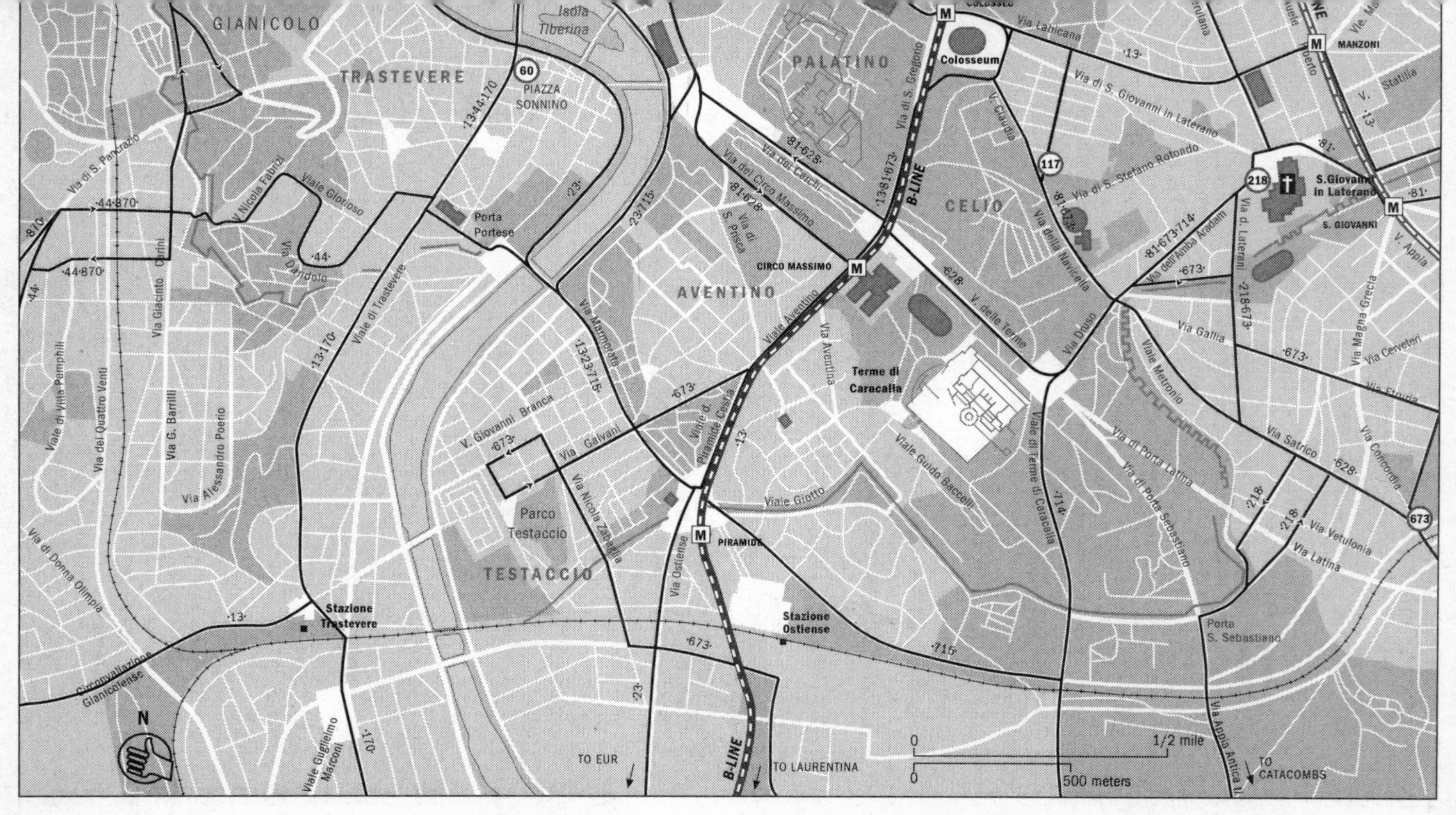
GIANICOLO
Isola Tiberina
TRASTEVERE
PIAZZA SONNINO
PALATINO
Colosseum
MANZONI
Via Labicana
Via di S. Giovanni in Laterano
Via di S. Gregorio
V. Claudia
CELIO
Via di S. Stefano Rotondo
S.Giovanni in Laterano
S. GIOVANNI
V. Appia
Via d. Laterani
Via dell'Amba Aradam
Via della Navicella
Via di S. Pancrazio
V. Nicola Fabrizi
Viale Glorioso
Via Dandolo
Porta Portese
Via dei Cerchi
Via del Circo Massimo
Via di S. Prisca
CIRCO MASSIMO
AVENTINO
B-LINE
V. delle Terme
Via Druso
Via Gallia
Via Magna Grecia
Via Cerveteri
Via Etruria
Viale Metronio
Via Giacinto Carini
Viale di Trastevere
Via Marmorata
Viale Aventino
Via Aventina
Terme di Caracalla
Viale di Villa Pamphili
Via del Quattro Venti
Via G. Barrili
Via Alessandro Poerio
V. Giovanni Branca
Via Galvani
Viale d. Piramide Cestia
Viale Guido Baccelli
Viale di Terme di Caracalla
Via di Porta Latina
Via di Porta Sebastiano
Via Satrico
Via Concordia
Viale Giotto
Parco Testaccio
Via Nicola Zabaglia
PIRAMIDE
Via Vetulonia
Via Latina
Via di Donna Olimpia
TESTACCIO
Via Ostiense
Stazione Trastevere
Stazione Ostiense
Porta S. Sebastiano
Circonvallazione Gianicolense
N
Viale Guglielmo Marconi
TO EUR
TO LAURENTINA
0
1/2 mile
500 meters
Via Appia Antica
TO CATACOMBS

LET'S DRIVE

CARS

Driving in Rome is a bad idea. Roman drivers are aggressive, and those who drive mopeds appear not to care whether they live or die. Parking is expensive and very difficult to find, and if you don't keep your eyes peeled, you may drive into a car-free zone (certain streets are reserved for public transportation and the police) and incur a fine. Car theft and robberies on cars are rampant, even during the day in busy areas. As if that weren't enough, gas (**benzina** in Italian) is exorbitantly priced (approximately L2000/€1.03 per liter). Luckily, most gas stations accept credit cards.

Rome is linked to the north and south of Italy by a great north-south highway called the **A1,** which feeds into the **Grande Raccordo Anulare (GRA),** the beltway that encircles Rome. Tolls on these roads are high; a trip to Florence can cost around L20,000/€10.30. Besides the highway, there are several good *strade statale* that lead into Rome. From the north, enter on V. Flaminia, V. Salaria, or V. Nomentana. Avoid V. Cassia, V. Tiburtina, and V.d. Mare at all costs; the ancient two-chariot lanes can't cope with modern-day traffic.

When leaving the city, don't try to follow the green *Autostrada per Firenze* signs—get on the GRA instead and follow it around; it's longer but faster. To get to the Adriatic coast, take highway A24. To reach beaches and port towns, try V. Pontina, which sticks close to the sea and connects you to most coastal spots.

INTERNATIONAL DRIVING PERMITS (IDP)

If you plan to drive a car while in Italy, you should obtain an **International Driving Permit (IDP).** Although most car rental agencies don't require the permit, it is required for legal reasons if you drive for more than a month. Your IDP, valid for one year, must be issued in your own country before you depart and must be accompanied by a valid driver's license. You must be 18 years old to receive the IDP. Applications usually need to include one or two photos, a current local license, an additional form of identification, and a fee. Those driving in Italy for more than one year must obtain an Italian license (L70,000/€36.20).

Australia: Contact local **Royal Automobile Club (RAC)** or **National Royal Motorist Association (NRMA)** in NSW or ACT (☎ (08) 9421 4444; www.rac.com.au/travel). AUS$15.

Canada: Contact any **Canadian Automobile Association (CAA)** branch office or write to CAA, 1145 Hunt Club Rd., #200, K1V 0Y3 (☎(613) 247-0117; www.caa.ca/CAAInternet/travelservices/internationaldocumentation/idptravel.htm.) Permits CDN$10.

Ireland: Contact the nearest **Automobile Association (AA)** office or write to the UK address below. Permits IR£4. The Irish Automobile Association, 23 Suffolk St., Rockhill, Blackrock, Co. Dublin (☎(01) 677 9481), honors most foreign automobile memberships (24hr. breakdown and road service ☎ (800) 667 788.)

New Zealand: Contact your local **Automobile Association (AA)** or their main office at Auckland Central, 99 Albert St. (☎(9) 377 4660; www.nzaa.co.nz). Permits NZ$8.

South Africa: Contact the Travel Services Department of the Automobile Association of South Africa at P.O. Box 596, 2000 Johannesburg (☎(11) 799 1400; fax 799 1410; http://aasa.co.za). Permits SAR28.50.

UK: Contact your local AA or the **AA Headquarters** (☎(0990) 44 88 66), or write: The Automobile Association, International Documents, Fanum House, Erskine, Renfrewshire PA8 6BW. To find the nearest location that issues the IDP, call ☎(0990) 50 06 00 or (0990) 44 88 66. For more info, see www.theaa.co.uk/motoringandtravel/idp/index.asp. Permits UK£4.

US: Visit any **American Automobile Association (AAA)** office or write to AAA Florida, Travel Related Services, 1000 AAA Drive (mail stop 100), Heathrow, FL 32746 (☎(407) 444-7000; fax 444-7380). You don't have to be a member to buy an IDP (US$10). AAA Travel Related Services (☎(800) 222-4357) provides road maps, travel guides, emergency road services, travel services, and auto insurance.

CAR RENTALS

Economy cars are around L500,000/€258.00 per week (L90,000-180,000/€45.00-90.00 per day), though you may be able to find deals (without radio or A/C) as low as L300,000. By reserving in advance, non-residents of Italy are eligible for discounts of up to 60%. Insurance is required, augmenting the rates by as much as L100,000/€51.60 a week. Paying by credit card may give you free insurance on rentals; check with your credit card company. All agencies require either a credit card or a cash deposit of at least L300,000/€155.00, and most take only plastic. You must be 21 and have a valid driver's license, and preferably an International Driver's Permit (see above); the IDP is required for those who drive for more than one month.

You can make arrangements to pick up cars at Termini, the airports, or in the city offices. You may return your car at any rental location in Italy (with an additional charge of roughly L50,000/€25.80 north of Rome and a monumental L300,000/€155.50 or more to the south). Before making a reservation, ask your airline or travel agent about special deals. For car rental agencies in Rome, see the **Service Directory,** p. 290.

HITCHHIKING

Let's Go does not recommend getting around by thumb as a safe means of transportation, and none of the following is intended to imply otherwise. Never get in the back of a two-door car. Never let go of your bag, and don't put anything in the trunk. If you feel threatened, experienced hitchers recommend you insist on being let out immediately, regardless of where you are. If the driver refuses, many people act as though they're going to open the door or vomit on the upholstery.

BIKES AND MOPEDS

Rome's hilly cobblestone streets, dense traffic, and *pazzo* drivers make the city a challenge for bikes and mopeds. Bikes cost around L5000/€2.55 per hour or L15,000/€7.75 per day, but the length of that "day" varies according to the shop's closing time. In summer, try the stands on V.d. Corso at P.d. San Lorenzo and V. di Pontifici. (Open daily 10am-7pm.) You need to be 16 years old to rent. Helmets are required by a strictly enforced law, and should be included with your rental. Prices do not include 20% sales tax. For those just interested in an afternoon on a bike, Enjoy Rome (p. 23) offers an informative, albeit harrowing, tour of the city's best sights. For bike and moped rental agencies in the city, see the **Service Directory,** p. 290.

LET'S GET INFORMED

TOURIST OFFICES

Enjoy Rome, V. Marghera, 8a (☎06 4451843 or 06 4456890; fax 06 4450734; www.enjoyrome.com; info@enjoyrome.com). From the middle concourse of Termini (between the trains and the ticket booths), exit right, with the trains behind you. Cross V. Marsala. The office is on the 3rd block down V. Marghera. Owners Fulvia and Pierluigi answer questions and offer useful tidbits about the city free of charge and in perfect English. Enjoy Rome arranges hotel accommodations (as well as short-term apartments), walking and bicycle tours (see p. 294), and bus service to Pompeii (see p. 236). Additionally, Enjoy Rome offers a full-service travel agency, booking transportation worldwide and lodgings throughout Italy. Branch office at V. Varese, 39 (walk down V. Marghera another block and turn right). Open M-F 8:30am-7pm, Sa 8:30am-2pm.

PIT (Tourist Information Point) (☎06 48906300), at track #4 in Termini. Run by the city, this English-speaking office provides limited information on events, hotels, restaurants, and transportation, as well as countless brochures and a serviceable map of Rome with sights listed on the back. Open daily 8am-8pm. **PIT kiosks** offer the same services at various spots around Rome. **Castel Sant'Angelo** (P. Pia; ☎06 68809707), **Fori Imperiali** (V.d. Tempio della Pace; ☎06 69924307), **P.d. Spagna** (Largo Goldoni; ☎06 68136061), **P. Navona** (P. delle Cinque Lune; ☎06 68809240), **Trastevere** (P. Sonnino; ☎06 58333457), **San Giovanni** (P.S. Giovanni in Laterano; ☎06 77203535), **Santa Maria Maggiore** (V.d. Olmata; ☎06 47880294), **V.d.**

Corso (V. Minghetti; ☎06 6782988), **V. Nazionale** (Palazzo delle Espozioni; ☎06 47824525), **Termini** (P. dei Cinquecento; ☎06 47825194), and **Fiumicino** (international arrivals area; ☎06 65956074). All kiosks except Fiumicino open daily 9am-6pm. Fiumicino open daily 8:15am-7:15pm. You can get the same info from the **Call Center Comune di Roma** (☎06 36004399), which operates daily 9am-7pm.

EPT, V. Parigi, 5 (☎06 48899255 or 06 48899253; fax 06 48899228) generally has the same information as PIT. Walk from the station diagonally to the left across P. del Cinquecento (filled with buses) and go straight across P. della Repubblica. Turn right onto V. Parigi, which starts on the other side of the church, at the Grand Hotel. English spoken, but not very well. *Alberghi di Roma e Provincia* lists all hotels and *pensioni* around Rome registered with the EPT. Open M-F 8:15am-7:15pm, Sa 8:15am-1:45pm.

USEFUL PUBLICATIONS

BROCHURES AND PAMPHLETS

The PIT offices and Enjoy Rome have free brochures and maps of downtown Rome. Enjoy Rome's aptly titled booklet, **Enjoy Rome,** is packed with information geared toward the English-speaking budget traveler. The EPT (via Parigi, 5) publishes **Un Ospite a Roma** (A Guest in Rome), a free pamphlet updated bi-weekly, listing events, exhibits, and concerts, as well as vital phone numbers for museums, galleries, and emergency services. It is also available at "finer hotels."

MAGAZINES

Roma C'è (L2000/€1.03) is the comprehensive, tried-and-true guide to everything from restaurants to church services to discos. It is written in (easily decipherable) Italian with a small English language section at the end. **Time Out: Rome** (L2000/€1.03), a flashy up-and-comer in the market of entertainment and culture mags, has plenty of useful information (entirely in Italian), including special info for women and gays. Both magazines are available on Thursdays. Also on Thursdays, **La Reppublica** publishes **Trovaroma** (L1500/€0.77), which lists events and recreational possibilities. The daily **Il Messaggero** has some of the best entertainment listings, but is written in hard-to-decipher Italian.

LET'S KEEP IN TOUCH

BY TELEPHONE

CALLING ROME FROM ABROAD

Phone numbers range from five to eight digits in length. Rome is changing all numbers to seven or eight digits. In Italy it is necessary to dial the city code for all numbers, even if you are calling from within the same city. Calls to Italy must begin with your country's **international access code** (011 in the US), then Italy's counry code (39), and the **city code** without the initial zero (06 becomes 6). **Toll-Free numbers:** *numero verde* numbers begin with 800 or 167.

CALLING ABROAD FROM ROME

To dial direct internationally, dial **two zeros** and the **country code** (Australia 61, Ireland 353, New Zealand 64, South Africa 27, United Kingdom 44, US and Canada 1), then the area/city code and number. If you normally dial a zero before the area/city code when calling within your country, do not when calling to your home country from Italy. Miraculously, **rates** have dropped lately for international calls from Italy. At their most expensive, rates to the US are L2127/€1.05 for the first minute and L1675/€0.80 for each additional minute. Rates are highest on weekdays from 8am to 8pm. Lowest rates are from 11pm to 8am, on holidays, and between 2:30pm on Saturday and 8am on Mondays.

The easiest way to call home is with a pay phone and pre-paid phone card (see **Pay Phones,** below), but a call of any length may require several cards. The English-speaking operator in Italy can put through **collect calls** (☎170), though it's cheaper to find a pay phone and deposit just enough money to be able to say "Call me" and give your number (though some pay phones can't receive calls). Some companies have created callback phone services: you call a specified number, let it ring once, and hang up. The company's computer calls back and gives you a dial tone. You can then make as many calls as you want, at rates 20-60% lower than many phone cards. This option is most economical for loquacious travelers, as there may be a monthly minimum of US$10-25. For info, call **Telegroup** in the US (☎800 338 0225).

Depending on your calling plan, a **calling card** may be your best and cheapest bet; your long distance provider has an international access number (billed as a toll-free or local call) you can dial from Italy to make collect or calling card calls: **AT&T** (☎1721011), **MCI** (☎1721022), **Sprint** (☎1721877), **Bell Canada Direct** (☎1721001), **British Telecom Direct** (☎1720044), **Telecom Éireann Ireland Direct** (☎1720353), **Telstra Australia Direct** (☎1721161), **Telecom New Zealand** (☎1721064), and **Telkom South Africa** (☎1721027). Call your long distance provider before your trip and do some research.

Italy is in the Western European **time zone,** six hours ahead of Eastern time in North America, one hour ahead of Britain and Ireland, one hour behind South Africa, nine hours behind Australia, and 11 hours behind New Zealand. Italy participates Daylight Savings but doesn't necessarily change on the same weekend as your home country.

PAY PHONES

Orange pay phones are all over the city, although ubiquitous cell phones *(telefonini)* are gradually driving them out. Some still take change (L100, L200, and L500 coins), but it is far more convenient to use pre-paid phone cards *(schede telefoniche)*. They come in denominations of L5000, L10,000, and L15,000, and are available at bars, *tabacchi*, and vending machines. As these cards will only pay for a 3min. call to the US during peak hours, some *tabacchi* now carry cards in denominations up to L50,000. Once you have purchased the card, break off the perforated corner and insert it into the machine with the magnetic strip facing up. The amount left on the card will be displayed on the screen. Dial away. An initial L100 will be taken when your call goes through. It costs L200 to connect to mobile phones, which all have the area codes 0337, 0338, or 0339. A clicking noise warns you that you're about to run out of money; you can insert another card (or some coinage). Once you have hung up, wait around and savor *la dolce vita* until the phone spits your card back.

ESSENTIAL INFORMATION

HELP!

Carabinieri: ☎112.

Police/Fire/Ambulance: ☎113.

Police Foreigner's Office: ☎06 46862876.

Police Headquarters: ☎06 46861.

Medical Emergencies: ☎118.

Fire Service: ☎115.

TELEPHONIC FACTS

To call abroad when in Rome, dial:

1. **00 + the country code** (Australia 61, Ireland 353, NZ 64, S. Africa 27, UK 44, US/Canada 1)
2. **area/city code**
3. **phone number**

Telephone codes

Italy's country code: 39

Rome's city code: 06

Directory Assistance

Italy: ☎12 (L2000 /€1.03 to connect, but you'll get it back when you hang up).

Europe and Mediterranean: ☎176 (L1200/€0.62).

Intercontinental: ☎17 90 (L1200/€0.62).

English-speaking operator: ☎170.

BY MAIL

Although the Italian postal system has drawn snickers from the rest of Western Europe, things are better, partly thanks to new EU standards. Airmail from Italy takes anywhere from one to three weeks to arrive in the US, while surface mail takes a month or longer. Letters and small parcels rarely get lost if they are *raccomandata* (registered), *espresso* (express), or *via aerea* (air mail). Stamps are available at face value in *tabacchi* (they're everywhere; look for the big, white T), but mail letters from a post office to be sure they are stamped correctly.

Rome's main post offce is at P.S. Silvestro, 19, south of P.d. Spagna (take bus #62, 80, 116, or 492). Stamps are at booths #23-25. Currency exchange is available at booth #19. Fax and telegram service is also available; see p. 27. (☎06 6798495; fax 06 6786618. Open M-F 9am-6pm, Sa 9am-2pm.) Come to S. Silvestro with especially large packages, or if you need to insure your mail. Another large post office is at V.d. Terme di Diocleziano, 30, near Termini. (☎06 4745602; fax 06 4743536. Same hours as San Silvestro branch.)

RECEIVING MAIL IN ROME

Those sending you mail in Rome from North America should plan on it taking up to two weeks. Mail can usually be sent to your hotel, though you should let the proprietor know something is coming. The **American Express** office (see **Service Directory,** p. 291) will hold mail for up to 30 days for AmEx cardmembers or travelers' check holders. Have the sender write "client mail" on the envelope, as well as your name, with surname capitalized and underlined. Letters addressed to the main downtown post office should be labeled **Fermo Posta** (held mail) and look like this: FIELDING, Carla; *Fermo Posta;* Piazza San Silvestro, 19; 00187 Roma. You must claim your mail in person at booth #72 at the P.S. Silvestro post office (see below) with your passport as ID. The fee is L3000 per piece of mail.

SENDING MAIL FROM ROME

EXPRESS MAIL, OVERNIGHT MAIL, AND PARCELS. Priority mail through the Italian Postal Service is called *Posta Prioriaria.* It's faster and more reliable than regular mail. Packages of up to 2kg are accepted starting at L1200. (Info ☎800 222666.) *Posta Celere* guarantees 24hr. delivery to most locations within Italy for packages up to 30kg. Rates start at L12,000/€6.20. (Info ☎800 009966.) Parcels, and unsealed packages under 1kg (500g for Australia) may be mailed from the San Silvestro post office. Sealed packages of up to 20kg and 200cm total outside dimensions (length plus width and height) may be shipped, provided they are wrapped in brown paper, available at any *tabacchi.*

COURIERS

The quickest, most reliable service is available through private couriers. Service and rates are the same between companies. It costs L60,000/€36.20 to send documents abroad (up to 500g) with guaranteed 48hr. delivery. Mailboxes, Etc. (see p. 27) will accept courier packages, or you can visit the following offices. See the **Service Directory** (p. 292) for a list of courier services available in Rome.

PAPAL MAIL

The Vatican administers its own postal service, which is supposedly faster and more reliable than Italy's yet costs the same. Visit the locations in P.S. Pietro: one on the left, near the tourist office and another on the right, near the center of the colonnade. There is a branch office on the 2nd floor of the Vatican Museum (open during museum hours, but with no *Fermo Posta*). Packages up to 2kg and 90 cm^3 are accepted. (☎06 69883406. Open M-F 8:30am-7pm, Sa 8:30am-6pm.)

BY EMAIL

Internet points, Internet cafes, and even Internet laundromats (p. 292), are breeding like rats. *Let's Go* lists a few with good rates or other attractions. Contact your Internet service provider for information before arriving in Rome. To set up a new account, check the Yellow Pages under "Internet." Be sure to turn off your modem's "Detect Dial Tone" setting in order to be able to connect.

Trevi Tourist Service: Trevi Internet, V. dei Lucchesi, 31-32 (☎/fax 06 6920 0799), 1 block from the Trevi Fountain (toward P. Venezia on the road that becomes V.d. Pilotta). Central location, fast connection, and great rates (L5000/€2.58 per 30min., L10,000/€5.16 per

1½hr.; if you don't use all your time, come back again at a later date to do so). You want more? How about printing (L200/€0.13 per page b/w, L2000/€1.03 per page color), scanning (L2000/€1.03 per page), video conferencing, photocopying, fax service (see below), Western Union money transfers, money exchange, newfangled cheap international calls on a newfangled phone system, and scooter rentals, all in A/C comfort. Open daily 9am-10pm.

Splashnet, V. Varese, 33 (☎06 49382073), 3 blocks north of Termini. Offers a match made in heaven: a laundromat with internet access. While weeks' worth of mud disappears from your socks (wash and dry L6000/€3.20 each) you get 15 min. of internet time free. Internet access L5000 per hr., ask about the *Let's Go* discount. Open daily 8:30am-10:30pm.

Internet Café, V. dei Marrucini, 12 (☎/fax 06 4454953; www.Internetcafe.it; info@Internetcafe.it.), in S. Lorenzo. Bus #492 bus from Termini or take a 15min. walk. Swank Internet cafe with stocked bar, fast connections, and A/C. L5000/€2.58 per 30min., L8000/€4.13 per hr.; after 9pm L6000/€3.62 per 30min., L10,000/€5.16 per hr. Special lunch deal 11am-3pm gets you a sandwich, a drink, and an hour of Internet access for L10,000/€5.16. 7-9pm, the same deal's L12,000/€6.20. Open M-F 9am-2am, Sa-Su 5pm-2am.

Mail Boxes Etc., V. dei Mille 38-40, off V. Marghera near Termini. (☎06 4461945; fax 06 4461338). Trusty MBE offers fax, photocopying, UPS and FedEx shipping, as well as cheap Internet access. Computers are limited, but prices (L3000/€1.55 per hr.) can't be beat.

Internet Café, V. Cavour, 213 (☎06 4782 3051). Just south of the Cavour (B) Metro stop on the right. While there's nothing particularly exciting about this place, it gets the job done nicely. Also offers game machines should you not feel particularly communicative. L10,000/ €5.16 per hr., 10hr. pass L60,000/€30.62. Open daily 9am-1am.

The Netgate Internet Point, P. Firenze, 25 (☎06 6893445). Down P.d. Parlamento from V.d. Corso. Large (40 computers) and A/C with webcams and microphones. L7500/€3.85 per hr.; students L6500/€3.40. Open M-Sa 10:30am-9pm, Su 4-8pm. AmEx/MC/V.

Internet Café, V. Cavour, 213 (☎06 4782 3051). M: B-Cavour, on the right. While there's nothing particularly exciting about this place, it gets the job done nicely. Also offers game machines should you not feel particularly communicative. L8000/€4.13 per hr., L50,000/ €25.80 for 10hr. pass. Free internet Su 9am-noon. Fax, Western Union, and photocopying. Open daily 9am-1am. AmEx/MC/V.

Freedom Traveller, V. Gaeta, 25 (☎06 4782 3682; www.freedom-traveller.it). North of P. del Cinquecento. Run by a youth hostel, Freedom's just another word for Internet café with full bar and couchful common room featuring movies in English. L5000/€2.58 per hr. with card; otherwise L8000/€4.13. Internet train franchise. Open daily 9am-midnight.

BY FAX

Fax service is common at *tabacchi* and photocopy shops. Public fax service is available at the main post office in P.S. Silvestro (9am-6pm) at booths #73-76. (Faxes can be received 24hr. a day; they can only be picked up during business hours; see p. 25.)

XeroMania, V. S. Francesco a Ripa, 109 (☎06 5814433; fax 06 5817507). Off V. di Trastevere. Sending: L3000/€1.55 first page, L1000/€0.52 each additional page plus cost of phone call. Receiving: L2000/€1.03 1st page; L1800/€0.98 each additional page (24hr. receiving services). Open M-F 9am-1pm and 3:30-7:30pm, Sa 9am-1pm. Cash only.

Trevi Tourist Service, V. dei Lucchesi, 31-32 (☎/fax 06 69200799). One block from the Trevi Fountain (toward P. Venezia on the road that becomes V.d. Pilotta). Sending 1st page abroad L5000/€2.58 (L3000/€1.55 per additional page), L3500/€1.55 in Italy and L1500/€0.77 in Rome. Receiving L1000/€0.52 per page. Also Internet access (see above), printing, scanning, photocopying, Western Union money transfer, money exchange, phone service, and scooter rental. Open daily 9am-10pm.

Mailboxes, Etc., V. dei Mille, 38-40 (☎06 4461945; fax 06 4461338). South of P. Indipendenza near Termini. Sending: to US 1st page L7000/€3.62; L2000/€1.03 per additional page (varies according to destination). Receiving: L2000/€1.03 per page. Open M-Sa 9am-2pm and 3-7pm. AmEx/MC/V.

LET'S SPEAK ITALIAN

VOWELS

There are seven vowel sounds in standard Italian. **A, I,** and **U** are always pronounced the same way; **E** and **O** have are either tense or lax, depending on where the vowel appears in the word, whether it's stressed or not, and regional accent. It's difficult for non-native speakers to predict the quality of vowels. We illustrate the *approximate* pronunciation of the vowels below; don't worry too much about **E** and **O.**

a	*a* as in f*a*ther *(casa)*	**o** (tense)	*o* as in b*o*ne *(sono)*
e (tense) **e** (lax)	*ay* as in b*ay* *(sete)* *eh* as in s*e*t *(bella)*	**o** (lax)	between *o* of b*o*ne and *au* of c*au*ght *(zona)*
i	*ee* as in ch*ee*se *(vino)*	**u**	*oo* as in dr*oo*p *(gusto)*

CONSONANTS

Consonants shouldn't be too bad, just remember **H** is always silent and **R** is trilled.

C and G: before **a, o,** or **u, c** and **g** are hard, as in *cat* and *goose* or as in the Italian word *colore* (koh-LOHR-eh), "color," or *gatto* (GAHT-toh), "cat." They soften into "ch" and "j" sounds, respectively, when followed by i or e, as in the English *cheese* and *jeep* or the Italian *ciao* (CHOW), "good-bye," and *gelato* (jeh-LAH-toh), "ice cream."

CH and GH: **h** returns **c** and **g** to their "hard" sounds in front of **i** or **e** (see above); making words like *chiave* (key-AH-vay), "keys," and *tartarughe* (tahr-tah-RU-geh), "tortoises."

GN and GLI: pronounce **gn** like the **ni** in *o*ni*on*, thus *bagno* ("bath") is "BAHN-yo." **Gli** is like the **lli** in *million*, so *sbagliato* ("wrong") is said "zbal-YAH-toh."

S and Z: An **s** between two vowels or followed by the letters **b, d, g, l, m, n r,** and **v** is pronounced as a **z;** thus *casa* ("house") sounds like "KAH-zah" and *smarrito* ("lost") like "zmahr-REE-toh." A double **s** or an **s** followed by any other letter has the same sound as English initial **s,** so *sacco* ("bag") is SAHK-koh. **Z** has a **ts** or **dz** sound; thus *stazione* ("station") is "staht-see-YOH-nay," while *zoo* ("zoo") is pronounced "dzoh" and *mezzo* ("half") is "MEH-dzoh."

SC and SCH: when followed by **a, o,** or **u, sc** is pronounced as **sk,** so *scusi* ("excuse me") yields "SKOO-zee." When followed by an **e** or **i,** the combination is pronounced "**sh**" as in *sciopero* (SHOH-pair-oh), "strike." **H** returns **c** to its hard sound **(sk)** in front of **i** or **e,** as in *pesche* (PEH-skeh), "peaches," not to be confused with *pesce* (PEH-sheh), "fish."

Double consonants: The difference between double and single consonants in Italian is likely to cause problems for English speakers. When you see double consonants, think about pronouncing it twice or holding it for a long time. English phrases like "bad dog" approximate the sound of double consonants. Failing to make the distinction can lead to confusion; for example, *pe**nn**e all'arrabbiata* is "short pasta in a spicy red sauce," whereas *pe**n**e all'arrabbiata* means "penis in a spicy red sauce." How long you hold the consonant is a matter of taste.

STRESS & PLURALITY

In many Italian words, stress falls on the next-to-last syllable. When stress falls on the last syllable, an accent indicates where stress should fall: *cit***tà** (cheet-TAH) or *per***ché** (pair-KAY). Stress can fall on the third-to-last syllable as well. It's not easy to predict stress, so you'll have to pick this up by listening to Italian speech.

Italians words form their plurals by changing the last vowel. Words that end in an **a** in the singular (usually feminine), end with an **e** in the plural; thus *mela* (MAY-lah), "apple," becomes *mele* (MAY-lay). Words that end with **o** or **e** in the singular take an **i** in the plural: *conto* (COHN-toh), "bill," is *conti* (COHN-tee) and *cane* (KAH-neh), "dog," becomes *cani* (KAH-nee). There are several exceptions to these rules; for example, *braccio* becomes *braccia* in the plural. Words with final accent, like *città* and *caffè*, and foreign words like *bar* and *sport* do not change in the plural.

PHRASEBOOK

DAYS OF THE WEEK

ENGLISH	ITALIAN	PRONOUNCIATION
Monday	*lunedì*	loo-nay-DEE
Tuesday	*martedì*	mahr-tay-DEE
Wednesday	*mercoledì*	mair-coh-leh-DEE
Thursday	*giovedì*	joh-veh-DEE
Friday	*venerdì*	veh-nair-DEE
Saturday	*sabato*	SAH-bah-toh
Sunday	*domenica*	doh-MEH-nee-kah

MONTHS

ENGLISH	ITALIAN	PRONOUNCIATION
January	gennaio	jehn-NAH-yoh
February	febbraio	Fehb-BRAH-yoh
March	marzo	MAHRT-soh
April	aprile	ah-PREE-lay
May	maggio	MAHJ-joh
June	giugno	JOON-yoh
July	luglio	LOOL-yoh
August	agosto	ah-GOH-stoh
September	settembre	seht-TEHM-bray
October	ottobre	oht-TOH-bray
November	novembre	noh-VEHM-bray
December	dicembre	dee-CHEM-bray

TIME

ENGLISH	ITALIAN	PRONOUNCIATION
At what time...?	*A che ora...?*	ah kay OHR-ah
What time is it?	*Che ore sono?*	kay OHR-ay SOH-noh
It's 3:30.	*Sono le tre e mezzo.*	SOH-noh lay tray ay MEHD-zoh
It's noon.	*È mezzogiorno.*	eh MEHD-zoh-JOHR-noh
now	*adesso/ora*	ah-DEHS-so/OH-rah
tomorrow	*domani*	doh-MAH-nee
today	*oggi*	OHJ-jee
yesterday	*ieri*	YAIR-ee
right away	*subito*	SU-bee-toh
soon	*fra poco*	frah POH-koh
already	*già*	jah
after(wards)	*dopo*	DOH-poh
before	*prima*	PREE-mah
early/earlier	*presto/più presto*	PREHS-toh/pyoo PREHS-toh
late/later	*tardi/più tardi*	TAHR-dee/pyoo TAHRdee
early (before scheduled arrival time)	*in anticipo*	een ahn-TEE-chee-poh
late (after scheduled arrival time)	*in ritardo*	een ree-TAHR-doh
daily	*quotidiano*	kwoh-tee-dee-AH-no
weekly	*settimanale*	seht-tee-mah-NAH-leh
monthly	*mensile*	mehn-SEE-leh
vacation	*le ferie*	lay FEH-ree-eh
weekdays	*i giorni feriali*	ee JOHR-nee feh-ree-AH-lee
Sundays and holidays	*i giorni festivi*	ee JOHR-nee fehs-TEE-vee
day off (at store, restaurant, etc.)	*riposo*	ree-POH-zo

TIME

ENGLISH	ITALIAN	PRONOUNCIATION
a strike	*uno sciopero*	SHOH-peh-roh
a protest	*una manifestazione*	mah-nee-fehs-taht-see-OH-neh

PHRASES

ENGLISH	ITALIAN	PRONOUNCIATION
Hi!/So long! (informal)	*Ciao!*	chaow
Good day./Hello.	*Buongiorno.*	bwohn JOHR-noh
Good evening.	*Buona sera.*	BWOH-nah SEH-rah
My name is...	*Mi chiamo...*	mee Key-YAH-moh
What is your name...?	*Come ti chiami? (informal)/Come si chiama Lei? (formal)*	KOH-may tee key-YAH-mee/KOH-may see key-YAH-mah lay
I'm/We're from . . .	*Vengo/Veniamo dal/dalla. . .*	VAIN-goh/VAIN-ee-Am-oh doll
How are you?	*Come sta/state?*	KOH-may STAH/STAH-tay
Good night.	*Buona notte.*	BWOH-nah NOHT-tay
Goodbye.	*Arrivederci./ArrivederLa.*	ah-ree-veh-DAIR-chee/ ah-ree-veh-DAIR-lah
please	*per favore/per cortesia/ per piacere*	pair fah-VOH-ray/ pair kohr-teh-ZEE-ah/ pair pyah-CHEH-reh
Thank you.	*Grazie.*	GRAHT-see-yeh
You're welcome. May I help you? Go right ahead.	*Prego.*	PRAY-goh
Pardon me.	*Scusi.*	SKOO-zee
I'm sorry.	*Mi dispiace.*	mee dees-PYAH-cheh
Yes./No./Maybe.	*Sì./No./Forse.*	see/no/FOHR-say
I don't know.	*Non lo so.*	nohn loh soh
I have no idea.	*Boh...*	boh
Let's Go! (our favorite)	*Andiamo*	ahnd-ee-AH-moh
Could you repeat that?	*Potrebbe ripetere?*	poh-TREHB-beh ree-PEH-teh-reh
What does this mean?	*Che vuol dire questo?*	kay vwohl DEE-reh KWEH-stoh
Okay./I understand.	*Ho capito.*	Oh kah-PEE-toh
I don't understand.	*Non capisco.*	nohn kah-PEES-koh
I don't speak Italian.	*Non parlo italiano.*	nohn PAR-loh ee-tahl-YAH-noh
I'm an artist	*Sono artista*	SOH-noh ahrt-EE-stah
Is there someone who speaks English?	*C'è qualcuno che parla inglese?*	cheh kwahl-KO-noh kay PAR-lah een-GLAY-zay
Could you help me?	*Potrebbe aiutarmi?*	poh-TREHB-beh ah-yoo-TAHR-mee
How do you say...?	*Come si dice...?*	KOH-may see DEE-chay
What do you call this in Italian?	*Come si chiama questo in italiano?*	KOH-may see key-YAH-mah KWEH-stoh een ee-tahl-YAH-no
this/that	*questo/quello*	KWEH-sto/KWEHL-loh
who	*chi*	kee
where	*dove*	DOH-vay
which	*quale*	KWAH-lay
when	*quando*	KWAN-doh
what	*che/cosa/che cosa*	kay/KOH-za/kay KOH-za
why/because	*perchè*	pair-KEH
more/less	*più/meno*	pyoo/MEH-noh

DIRECTIONS AND TRANSPORTATION

ENGLISH	ITALIAN	PRONOUNCIATION
Where is...?	*Dov'è...?*	doh-VEH
How do you get to...?	*Come si arriva a...*	KOH-meh see ahr-REE-vah

ENGLISH	ITALIAN	PRONOUNCIATION
Do you stop at...?	*Ferma a...?*	FAIR-mah ah
...the beach	*la spiaggia*	lah spee-AH-jah
...the building	*il palazzo/l'edificio*	eel pah-LAHT-so/leh-dee-FEE-choh
...the bus stop	*la fermata d'autobus*	lah fair-MAH-tah DAOW-toh-boos
...the center of town	*il centro*	eel CHEN-troh
...the church	*la chiesa*	lah kee-AY-zah
...the consulate	*il consolato*	eel kohn-so-LAH-toh
...the grocery store	*l'alimentari*	lah-lee-men-TAH-ree
...the hospital	*l'ospedale*	los-peh-DAH-lay
...the market	*il mercato*	eel mair-KAH-toh
...the office	*l'ufficio*	loo-FEE-choh
...the post office	*l'ufficio postale*	loo-FEE-choh poh-STAH-lay
...the station	*la stazione*	lah staht-see-YOH-nay
near/far	*vicino/lontano*	vee-CHEE-noh/lohn-TAH-noh
Turn left/right	*Gira a sinistra/destra*	JEE-rah ah see-NEE-strah/ DEH-strah
straight ahead	*sempre diritto*	SEHM-pray DREET-toh
here	*qui/qua*	kwee/kwah
there	*lì/là*	lee/lah
the street address	*l'indirizzo*	leen-dee-REET-soh
the telephone	*il telefono*	eel teh-LAY-foh-noh
street	*strada, via, viale, vico, vicolo, corso*	STRAH-dah, VEE-ah, vee-AH-lay, VEE-koh, VEE-koh-loh, KOHR-soh
Take the bus from... to...	*Prenda l'autobus da... a...*	PREN-dah LAOW-toh-boos dah... ah...
Do you believe in UFOs?	*Credi negli UFO?*	CRAY-dee nay-lyee ooh-eff-oh
What time does the... leave?	*A che ora parte...?*	ah kay OHR-ah PAHR-tay
...the (city) bus	*l'autobus*	LAOW-toh-boos
...the (intercity) bus	*il pullman*	eel POOL-mahn
...the ferry	*il traghetto*	eel tra-GHEHT-toh
...the plane	*l'aereo*	lah-EHR-reh-oh
...the train	*il treno*	eel TRAY-no
I would like a ticket for...	*Vorrei un biglietto per...*	vohr-RAY oon beel-YET-toh pair
How much does it cost?	*Quanto costa?*	KWAN-toh CO-stah
How much does... cost?	*Quanto costa...?*	KWAN-toh CO-stah
I would like...	*Vorrei...*	voh-RAY
...a ticket	*un biglietto*	oon beel-YEHT-toh
...a pass (bus, etc.)	*una tessera*	OO-nah TEHS-seh-rah
one way	*solo andata*	SO-lo ahn-DAH-tah
round-trip	*andata e ritorno*	ahn-DAH-tah ey ree-TOHR-noh
reduced price	*ridotto*	ree-DOHT-toh
student discount	*sconto studentesco*	SKOHN-toh stoo-dehn-TEHS-koh
What time does the train for... leave?	*A che ora parte il treno per...?*	ah kay OH-rah PAHR-tay eel TRAY-noh pair
What platform for...?	*Che binario per...?*	kay bee-NAH-ree-oh pair
Where does the bus leave from...?	*Da dove parte l'autobus per...?*	dah DOH-vay PAHR-tay LAU-toh-boos pair
Is the train late?	*È in ritardo il treno?*	eh een ree-TAHR-doh eel TRAY-no
When will the strike be over?	Quando finisce il sciopero?	KWAN-doh fee-NEE-shay eel SHOH-peh-roh
the arrival	*l'arrivo*	la-REE-voh

DIRECTIONS AND TRANSPORTATION

ENGLISH	ITALIAN	PRONOUNCIATION
the departure	*la partenza*	la par-TENT-sah
the track	*il binario*	eel bee-NAH-ree-oh
the terminus (of a bus)	*il capolinea*	eel kah-poh-LEE-neh-ah
the flight	*il volo*	eel VOH-loh
the reservation	*la prenotazione*	la pray-no-taht-see-YOH-neh
the entrance/the exit	*l'ingresso/l'uscita*	leen-GREH-so/loo-SHEE-tah

HOTEL RESERVATIONS

ENGLISH	ITALIAN	PRONOUNCIATION
Hello? (used when answering the phone)	*Pronto!*	PROHN-toh
Do you speak English?	*Parla inglese?*	PAHR-lah een-GLAY-zay
Could I reserve a single/double room for the second of August?	*Potrei prenotare una camera singola/doppia per il due agosto?*	POH-tray pray-noh-TAH-ray OO-nah CAH-meh-rah SEEN-goh-lah/DOH-pee-yah pair eel DOO-ay ah-GOH-stoh?
with bath/shower	*con bagno/doccia*	kohn BAHN-yo/DOH-cha
with bathroom	*con un gabinetto/un bagno/una toletta*	eel gah-bee-NEHT-toh/eel BAHN-yoh/ lah toh-LEHT-toh
open/closed	*aperto/chiuso*	ah-PAIR-toh/KYOO-zoh
a towel	*un asciugamano*	oon ah-shoo-gah-MAH-noh
sheets	*le lenzuola*	lay lehn-SUO-lah
a blanket	*una coperta*	OO-nah koh-PAIR-tah
heating	*il riscaldamento*	eel ree-skahl-dah-MEHN-toh
How much is the room?	*Quanto costa la camera?*	KWAHN-toh KOHS-ta lah KAM-eh-rah
My name is...	*Mi chiamo...*	mee key-YAH-moh..
I will arrive at 2:30pm.	*Arriverò alle quattordici e mezzo.*	ah-ree-vair-OH ah-lay kwah-TOHR-dee-chee eh MED-zoh
Certainly!	*Certo!*	CHAIR-toh
I'm sorry but...	*Mi dispiace, ma...*	mee dis-pee-YAH-chay, mah...
We're closed during August.	*Chiudiamo ad agosto.*	kyu-dee-AH-moh ahd ah-GOH-stoh
No, we're full.	*No, siamo al completo.*	no, see-YAH-moh ahl cohm-PLAY-toh
We don't take telephone reservations.	*Non si fanno le prenotazioni per telefono.*	nohn see FAHN-noh lay pray-noh-tat-see-YOH-nee pair tay-LAY-foh-noh
You'll have to send a deposit/check.	*Bisogna mandare un acconto/un anticipo/un assegno.*	bee-ZOHN-yah mahn-DAH-reh oon ahk-KOHN-toh/oon ahn-TEE-chee-poh/oon ahs-SAY-nyoh
You must arrive before 2pm.	*Deve arrivare primo delle quattordici.*	DAY-vay ah-ree-VAH-ray PREE-moh day-lay kwah-TOHR-dee-chee
Okay, I'll take it.	*Va bene. La prendo.*	vah BEHN-eh. lah PREHN-doh

RESTAURANTS

ENGLISH	ITALIAN	PRONOUNCIATION
the breakfast	*la (prima) colazione*	lah (PREE-mah) coh-laht-see-YO-nay
the lunch	*il pranzo*	eel PRAHND-zoh
the dinner	*la cena*	lah CHEH-nah
the appetizer	*l'antipasto*	lahn-tee-PAH-stoh
the first course	*il primo (piatto)*	eel PREE-moh pee-YAH-toh
the second course	*il secondo (piatto)*	eel seh-COHN-doh pee-YAH-toh
the side dish	*il contorno*	eel cohn-TOHR-noh

RESTAURANTS

ENGLISH	ITALIAN	PRONOUNCIATION
the dessert	*il dolce*	eel DOHL-chay
the fork	*la forchetta*	lah fohr-KEH-tah
the knife	*il coltello*	eel cohl-TEHL-loh
the spoon	*il cucchiaio*	eel koo-kee-EYE-yoh
the bottle	*la bottiglia*	lah boh-TEEL-yah
the glass	*il bicchiere*	eel bee-kee-YAIR-eh
the napkin	*il tovagliolo*	eel toh-vahl-YOH-loh
the plate	*il piatto*	eel pee-YAH-toh
the waiter/waitress	*il/la cameriere/a*	eel/lah kah-meh-ree-AIR-ray/rah
the bill	*il conto*	eel COHN-toh
the cover charge	*il coperto*	eel koh-PAIR-toh
the service charge/tip	*il servizio*	eel sair-VEET-see-oh
included	*compreso/a*	KOHM-pray-zoh/ah

MEDICAL

ENGLISH	ITALIAN	PRONOUNCIATION
I have...	*Ho...*	OH
...allergies	*delle allergie*	lay ahl-lair-JEE-eh
...a blister	*una bolla*	lah BOH-lah
...a cold	*un raffreddore*	oon rahf-freh-DOH-reh
...a cough	*una tosse*	OO-nah TOHS-seh
...the flu	*l'influenza*	lenn-floo-ENT-sah
...a fever	*una febbre*	OO-nah FEHB-breh
...a headache	*un mal di testa*	oon mahl dee TEHS-tah
...a lump (on the head)	*un bernoccolo*	eel bear-NOH-koh-loh
...a rash	*un'esantema /un sfogo/ un'eruzione*	leh-zahn-TAY-mah/ eel SFOH-goh/ leh-root-see-OHN-eh
...a stomach ache	*un mal di stomaco*	oon mahl dee STOH-mah-koh
...a swelling/growth	*un gonfiore*	eel gohn-fee-OR-ay
...a venereal disease	*una malattia venerea*	lah mah-lah-TEE-ah veh-NAIR-ee-ah
...a vaginal infection	*un'infezione vaginale*	leen-feht-see-OH-nay vah-jee-NAH-lay
My foot hurts.	*Mi fa male il piede.*	mee fah MAH-le eel PYEHD-deh
I'm on the pill.	*Prendo la pillola.*	PREHN-doh lah PEE-loh-lah
I haven't had my period for (2) months.	*Non ho le mestruazioni da (due) mesi.*	nohn oh lay meh-stroo-aht-see-OH-nee dah (DOO-ay) may-zee
I'm (3 months) pregnant.	*Sono incinta (da tre mesi).*	SOH-noh een-CHEEN-tah (dah tray MAY-zee)
You're (a month) pregnant.	*Lei è incinta (da un mese).*	lay ay een-CHEEN-tah (dah oon MAY-zay)
blood	*il sangue*	eel SAHN-gweh
a gynecologist	*un ginecologo*	jee-neh-KOH-loh-goh
the skin	*la pelle*	lah PEHL-lay

EMERGENCIES

ENGLISH	ITALIAN	PRONOUNCIATION
I lost my passport.	*Ho perso il passaporto.*	oh PAIR-soh eel pahs-sah-POHR-toh
I've been robbed.	*Sono stato derubato.*	SOH-noh STAH-toh deh-roo-BAH-toh
The ATM has eaten my credit card.	*Il Bancomat ha trattenuto la mia carta.*	eel BAHN-koh-maht ah trah-tehn-OO-toh lah MEE-ah CAHR-tah
Wait!	*Aspetta!*	ahs-PEHT-tah

EMERGENCIES

ENGLISH	ITALIAN	PRONOUNCIATION
Stop!	*Ferma!*	FAIR-mah
Help!	*Aiuto!*	ah-YOO-toh
Leave me alone!	*Lasciami in pace!*	LAH-shah-mee een PAH-cheh
Don't touch me!	*Non mi toccare!*	NOHN mee tohk-KAH-reh
I'm calling the police!	*Telefono alla polizia!*	tehl-LAY-foh-noh ah-lah poh-leet-SEE-ah
Go away!	Vai via!	VY VEE-ah
Go away, cretin!	*Vattene, cretino!*	VAH-teh-neh creh-TEE-noh

LOVE

ENGLISH	ITALIAN	PRONOUNCIATION
May I buy you a drink?	*Posso offrirle qualcosa da bere?*	POHS-soh ohf-FREER-lay kwahl-COH-zah dah BAY-ray
Would you buy me a drink?	*Può offrirmi qualcosa da bere?*	pwoh ohf-FREER-mi kwahl-COH-zah dah BAY-ray
I'm drunk.	*Sono ubriaco.*	SOH-noh oo-BRYAH-coh
Are you drunk?	*È lei ubriaco?*	ay LAY-ee oo-BRYAH-coh
You're cute.	*Lei è bello.*	LAY-ee ay BEHL-loh
I'm an anarchist.	*Sono un'anarchica.*	Soh-noh uhn ann-AHR-key-cuh
Your friend is cute.	*Il suo amico è bello.*	eel SOO-oh ah-MEE-cah ay BEHL-loh
I have a boyfriend/ girlfriend.	*Ho un ragazzo/una ragazza*	oh oon rah-GAHT-soh/ oo-nah rah-GAHT-sah
I love you, I swear.	*Ti amo, te lo giuro.*	tee AH-moh, tee loh JOO-roh

GLOSSARY

abbazia	also badia, an abbey
anfiteatro	ampitheater
arco	arch
apse	a semicircular, domed niche projecting from the altar end of a church
atrium	an open central court, usually to an ancient Roman house
baldacchino	stone or bronze canopy supported by columns over the altar of a church
basilica	a rectangular building with aisle and apse; no transepts. Used by ancient Romans for public adminstration. The Christians later adopted the style for their churches
battistero	a baptistry, usually a separate building near the town's duomo, where the town's baptisms were performed
borgo	ancient town or village
campanile	a bell tower, usually freestanding
cappella	chapel
cartoon	full-sized drawing used to transfer a preparatory design to the final work, especially to a wall for a fresco
castrum	the ancient Roman military camp. Many Italian cities were originally built on this plan: a rectilinear city with straight streets, the chief of which was called the decumanus maximus
cenacolo	"Last Supper"; A depiction of Christ at dinner on the evening before his crucifixion, often found in the refectory of an abbey or convent
chancel	the space around the altar reserved for clergy and choir
chiaroscuro	the balance between light and dark in a painting, and the painter's ability to show the contrast between them
chiesa	church
cloister/chiostro	a courtyard; generally a quadrangle with covered walkways along its edges, often with a central garden, forming part of a church or monastery

comune	the government of a free city of the Middle Ages
corso	a principal street or avenue
cosmati work	mosaic on marble, found in early Christian churches around Rome
cupola	a dome
diptych	a painting in two parts or panels
duomo	cathedral; the official seat of a diocesan bishop, and usually the central church of an Italian town
facade	the front of a building, or any wall given special architectural treatment
fiume	a river
forum	in an ancient Roman town, a square containing municipal buildings and/or market space. Smaller towns usually have only one central forum, while large cities, such as Rome, can have several
fresco	affresco, a painting made on wet plaster. When it dries, the painting becomes part of the wall
frieze	a band of decoration in any medium. Architecturally, can also refer to the middle part of an entablature (everything above the columns of a building) between the architrave and the cornice
giardino	garden
gabinetto	Toilet, WC
Greek Cross	a cross whose arms are of equal length
grotesque	painted, carved, or stucco decorations of fantastic, distorted human or animal figures, named for the grotto work found in Nero's buried Golden House
in restuaro	under restoration; a key concept in Rome
Intarsia	inlay work, usually of marble, metal, or wood
Latin Cross	a cross whose vertical arm is longer than its horizontal arm
loggia	a covered gallery or balcony
lungo, lung	literally "along," so that a lungomare is a boardwalk or promenade alongside the mare (ocean)
lunette	a semi-circular frame in the ceiling or vault of a building that holds a painting or sculpture
mausoleum	a large tomb or building with places to entomb the dead above ground
nave	the central body of a church
necropolis	ancient burial site; definitely spooky
palazzo	an important building of any type, not just a palace. Many were built as townhouses for wealthy families
Pietà	a scene of the Virgin mourning the dead Christ
polyptych	altarpiece with more than three panels
ponte	bridge
presepio	nativity scene
putto	(pl. putti) the little nude babies that flit around Renaissance art occasionally, and Baroque art incessantly
reliquary	holding place for a saint's relics, which usually consist of bones, but are often much much stranger
sinopia drawing	a red pigment sketch made on a wall as a preliminary study for a fresco.
scalinata	stairway
spiaggia	beach
stigmata	miraculous body pains or bleeding that resemble the wounds of the crucified Christ
thermae	(terme in Italian) ancient Roman baths and, consequently, social centers
telamoni	large, often sensual, statues of men used as columns in temples
transept	in a cruciform church, the arm of the church that intersects the nave or central aisle (i.e. the cross-bar of the T)
travertine	a light colored marble or limestone used in many of the buildings in Rome
triptych	a painting in three panels or parts
trompe l'oeil	literally, "to fool the eye," a painting or other piece or art whose purpose is to trick the viewer, as in a flat ceiling painted to appear domed
tufa	a soft stone composed of volcanic ash (tufo in Italian)
villa	a country house, usually a large estate with a formal garden. In Rome, villa refers to the area surrounding the estates that have become public parks.

INSIDE

Life & Times

HISTORY

VARIOUS BEGINNINGS

Arms, and the man I sing, who, forc'd by fate,
And haughty Juno's unrelenting hate,
Expell'd and exil'd, left the Trojan shore.
Long labors, both by sea and land, he bore,
And in the doubtful war, before he won
The Latian realm, and built the destin'd town
Virgil, The Aeneid

Once upon a pagan time, **Aeneas** (a fine fellow remembered as either the progeny of the goddess of love or a distant relative of that famous boatbuilder, Noah) perturbed by the recent wave of certain undesirable elements (i.e. Greeks) into his native Troy, grabbed his aging father, hopped in the Volvo, and commuted to the sunny suburbs of the land of the Latins. Pleased with the climate, friendly peoples, and generous income tax policies, he stuck around and married their princess, Lavinia. He then crowned himself king, and creatively christened the kingdom Lavinium. At this point, Virgil's *Aeneid* leaves off, but that's scarcely all there is to say on the matter.

Shortly after all this happened, according to the ancient Roman historian, Livy, a Vestal "Virgin" named Rhea Silvia went bad and gave birth to a bouncing pair of baby boys; fathered by Mars, the god of war. Well, as the title implies, this lifestyle choice wasn't really an option for someone in her profession, and her twins were set adrift in the Tiber.

Luckily, the boys were found by a motherly she-wolf who had just lost her cubs, and thought the tiny refugees a suitable substitute, until a shepherd came along and "rescued" the twins, who were called **Romulus** and **Remus.** Despite a somewhat troubled childhood, the twins managed to stay off the smack and even founded a city on the Palatine Hill, which they called **Rome,** on April 21, 753 BC, after much debate. Remus's brief insistence on naming the new town after himself ended in the metropolis's first murder. We won't give away which twin won the day, but we'll give you a hint—you're not currently enjoying the witty, irreverent prose of *Let's Go: Reme...*

Pretty as this tale of gods and wolf-boys is, its veracity is somewhat suspect. Pottery dating from as far back as 1200 BC has been found, suggesting older origins. Remains of villages in the area date from about 800 BC; the people who first ruled Rome were the **Sabines.** Three Sabine kings ruled Rome: Numa Pompilius, who took charge in 715 BC, Tullus Hostilius, and Ancus Martius.

The Sabines were soon supplanted, by the **Etruscans,** a tribe from the North. (See **Cerveteri,** p. 234, and **Tarquinia,** p. 234, for more information on Etruscan villages.) Responsible for the adaptation of the Latin language and the Latinization of the Greek gods, Etruscan kings controlled Rome starting in 616 BC. Some remains of their civilization can still be seen: most notably, the Etruscans built the Cloaca Maxima, the pride and joy of the Roman sewer system. Their rule came to an end in 509 BC, when the son of King **Tarquinius Superbus** raped the famously chaste Roman matron **Lucretia.** She committed suicide, and her outraged family led the Roman populace to overthrow the Tarquin dynasty in 509 BC. The next day, the first Roman republic was founded.

Free from Etruscan rule, the Romans began to breastfeed their bouncing baby republic. Originally, the government was an oligarchy in which land-owning patricians (and after 450 BC, wealthy plebeians) gathered in the Senate to make laws, hear trials, and declare war. A complex bureaucracy made up of *praetores* (judicial officer), *quaestores* (tax collectors), *aediles* (magistrate), and *tribunes* oversaw the city's burgeoning infrastructure, and Rome strutted its stuff with loads of new temples, roads, bridges, and aqueducts. From its power base in the Tiber valley, the city expanded, conquering neighbors with astounding efficiency and generally rabble-rousing in the surrounding countryside. In 395 BC, the Etruscans were put down for good when the Romans captured Veia, their capital. Southern Italy was made safe for Romans in 275 BC, when **Pyrrhus,** the Greek ruler of Tarentum, was defeated at the Battle of Beneventum.

THE REPUBLIC GROWS...

> What did Caesar really whisper to his protégé as he fell? *Et tu*, Brute, the official lie, is about what you'd expect to get from them—it says exactly nothing.... When one speaks to the other then it is not to pass the time of day with et-tu-Brutes. What passes is a truth so terrible that history—at best a conspiracy...to defraud—will never admit it. The truth will be repressed or in ages of particular elegance be disguised as something else.
>
> —Thomas Pynchon, *Gravity's Rainbow*

After the conquest of Italy, the republic waged a series of three, count 'em, three, **Punic Wars** (264-146 BC), against Carthage (modern-day Tunisia) for control of key Mediterranean trade routes and territory in Spain and Sicily. During the second of these wars, the Carthaginian general **Hannibal** famously marched his army—elephants and all—up through Spain and across the Alps. He swooped down the peninsula, surprising a series of Roman generals, and made it all the way to the walls of Rome, but once there failed to breach them (his long-suffering wife comforted him with assurances that this happens to all generals occasionally, especially since he was under a lot of pressure and had drunk a lot the night before). His campaign devolved into a cat-and-mouse game with **Fabius Maximus,** who eluded the overeager Hannibal for several years until the starving Carthaginians refused to play anymore and took their tired elephants home. Carthage was decisively defeated at Zama, in Africa, in 202 BC by another great Roman general, **Scipio Africanus.** Pressing the advantage, **Cato the Censor** encouraged Romans to raze the powerless Carthage in the Third Punic War of 146 BC. Rumor has it that Roman soldiers sowed Carthaginian fields with salt to keep the city from causing trouble again.

Traditionally Roman society had been austere and pious, but, drunk with a heady mix of bloodlust and riches, it became a veritable swamp of greed and corruption. Yeoman farmers were pushed off their land by avaricious landowners and driven into slavery or starvation. Less than grateful, the yeomen protested; by 131 BC, popular demands for land redistribution led to riots against the corrupt patricians, culminating in the **Social War** (91-87 BC). Tribes throughout the peninsula fought successfully for the extension of Roman citizenship.

Fed up, **Sulla,** the general who had led Roman troops during the conflict, marched on Rome (traditionally a demilitarized zone), seizing control of the city in a bloody military coup. Over 1600 nobles and senators were executed without trial. Sulla's strong-arm tactics set a dangerous precedent for the Republic as generals began to amass private armies funded by huge personal fortunes. In 73 BC, **Spartacus,** rebellious gladiatorial slave, and generally fine piece of manflesh, led a 70,000-man army of slaves and farmers in a two-year rampage down the peninsula. When the dust cleared, 6000 slaves had been crucified, and **Pompey the Great,** an associate of Sulla, took de facto control of Rome.

Disallowed by the Senate from ruling alone, Pompey ran the city with **Julius Caesar** and **Crassus,** forming the **First Triumvirate.** The threesome went sour, and Caesar, the charismatic conqueror of the Gauls, emerged victorious, having poor Pompey assassinated in 48 BC. Caesar's reign was brief but memorable: a small senatorial faction, fearful of his growing power, assassinated him on the Ides (15th) of March in 44 BC. In the ensuing power vacuum, a **Second Triumvirate** was formed. This time the ruling all stars were made up of Caesar's grand-nephew and adopted son, Octavian, Marc Antony (soon to be tangled up with that royal hussy Cleopatra and sent off to Africa), and Lepidus, a no-account rascal (who is now a regular contestant on the fine program Hollywood Squares. Octavian soon declared war on Marc Antony and Cleopatra, and spanked them soundly—so soundly, in fact, that they killed themselves in 30 BC. And Lepidus? Well, lets just say X takes the square...

...AND BECOMES AN EMPIRE

Under his new name **Augustus,** Octavian consolidated power and began assembling an imperial government in 27 BC. His reign (27 BC-AD 14) is considered the golden age of Rome, a flourishing of culture ushering in the 200 years of the **Pax Romana**. Augustus's power was not only political: he declared himself a god, paving the way for all sorts of mischief among future emperors. Nonetheless, Rome benefited from a huge building boom including a new forum and the first Pantheon. However, the peace was not extended to those who wouldn't sensibly shut up and consent to be ruled. As a result, the emperor's generals busied themselves hacking up Germans.

SONS & LOVERS: JULIO-CLAUDIANS

The descendants of Augustus proved unequal to the task of world government, as drunk with megalomania, they slipped into fevers of debauchery and insanity. **Tiberius** (AD 14-37), who allegedly conducted sexual experiments on goldfish, ushered in an era of decadence. Deranged **Caligula** (who once made his horse *consul*), drooling **Claudius** (41-54), and sadistically wacky **Nero** drained the treasury to support their lifestyles. Much of Rome was burned in the great fire of 64. Nero may or may not have been responsible for the blaze, but took advantage of the situation, building himself a new house, the **Domus Aurea** (see p. 80). Nero found a fine set of scapegoats for the fire in the early Christians. Common Romans were entertained and appeased watching Christians dressed in the hides of animals torn to shreds by savage beasts. The Christians who died came to be known as "martyrs," from the Greek "witnesses."

FLAVIANS & ANTONINES

Tired of his "quirks," the Senate forced Nero to commit suicide in AD 68. **Vespatian** (69-79) cleaned up Nero's mess, tearing down the Domus Aurea and erecting the Colosseum. His sons **Titus** (79-81) and **Domitian** (81-96) continued in Vespatian's footsteps. The **Antonine** emperors, starting with **Nerva** (96-98), marked the apex of the Empire. Spanish emperor **Trajan** (98-117) expanded the Empire to its greatest size, conquering Dacia (modern Romania) and the Danube region with feats of engineering and tactical brilliance. Trajan died while conquering Persia, and the general **Hadrian** (118-138)managed to carpe diem his way right into the throne. Hadrian preferred philosophy to war and decied to focus his energies on redecorating Rome with his own architectural designs, including another **Pantheon** (see p. 90) and his colossal mausoleum, now **Castel Sant'Angelo** (see p. 115).

Unfortunately, it was all downhill after Hadrian. The city clung to its status as *Caput Mundi* (head of the world) until the death of the philosopher- emperor **Marcus Aurelius** in 180, but by then, the Empire had grown too large to defend. Emperors, forced to relegate power and money to generals in the field, lay vulnerable to military coups. The tumultuous 3rd century saw no fewer than 30 emperors—only one of them lucky enough to die of natural causes. Despite some enlightened administrations, the brutality and depravity of despots like the unfortunately named **Commodus,** Caracalla (see **Baths of Caracalla,** p. 84), and the confused Elagabalus (who believed he was the sun), did much to undermine the stability of the Empire.

RISE OF CHRISTIANITY AND FALL OF ROME

By the 3rd century, Rome was in poor shape. **Aurelian** (270-275) thought that the surest way to solve the city's military and economic crises was to build a wall around it. **Diocletian** (284-305) secured control of the fragmented Empire in 284, established order, and subdivided the Empire into four spiffy and manageable parts. He also intensified the persecution of Christians. Nonetheless, by the end of Diocletian's reign, approximately 30,000 Christians lived in Rome.

After Diocletian, the fortunes of Christianity took a turn for the better. Gallerius, ruling the western part of the Empire, granted freedom of worship to Christians in 311. In 312, while battling it out with Maxentius for the imperial throne at the Milvian Bridge (which now lies near Rome's Olympic Stadium), **Constantine** (312-337) saw a huge cross in the sky along with the phrase, *In hoc signo vinces* (By this sign you shall conquer). Constantine being a quick study, sure enough, victory followed, and the next year Constantine's **Edict of Milan** made Christianity the official religion of the Empire. Despite the attempts of **Julian the Apostate** (361-363) to revive old Roman rituals, Christianity became the dominant religion. In 391, **Theodosius** (379-395) issued an edict against paganism.

Constantine hastened the end of Rome's supremacy by moving the capital east to Byzantium (which he humbly renamed **Constantinople**) in 330. Right on cue, armies of northern barbarians knocked politely on Rome's crumbling fortifications, asking if they could please be let in to steal anything not nailed down. First came the pre-Attila **Huns,** who showed up in 375. In 410, **Alaric,** king of the Visigoths, sacked the city. Sacker-extraordinaire **Attila the Hun** arrived on tour in 452, but fast-talking Pope Leo I convinced him to pillage elsewhere. Unfortunately three years later, Genseric the Vandal batted clean-up. In 476, the Western Roman Empire was finally done in when **Odoacer the Goth** ousted Romulus Augustulus. The Roman Empire was through. Gothic rule wasn't such a bad thing: under Odoacer and his son Theodoric, Roman life proceeded peacefully, perhaps due to the novelty of outside rule.

MIDDLE AGES

The Byzantine emperor **Justinian** brutally conquered much of the western division between 535 and 554, and imposed the *corpus juris,* or codified law of the Empire, which served as Europe's legal model for 500 years. By the 6th century, the Eternal City, once home to nearly a million people, supported only several thousand. When King Totila of the Goths pillaged the aqueducts in 546, the city's fate was sealed. The hills of Rome, once *the* place for Roman domiciles, gave way to the suddenly more appealing neighborhoods on the Tiber. In these days some of the most famous neighborhoods of Rome—Trastevere, Campo de' Fiori, and the area around Piazza Navona—were settled. Starvation and plague ran rampant in ramshackle alleyways near the river, while periodic invasions by barbarians lowered property values.

Rome owed its salvation from the turbulence of the Dark Ages in large part to wealthy popes who attracted cash-laden pilgrims and invoked the wrath of God to intimidate would-be invaders. Pope **Gregory the Great** (590-604) devised efficient strategies for distributing food and spreading the word of God across Europe. His actions laid the framework for the temporal power subsequent popes would wield.

MEDIEVAL CHAOS, PART I

Faced again with the threat of invasion from the German Lombards in 752, Pope Stephen II was forced to ask for help from the Frankish warlord Pepin the Short. Pepin's forces prevailed and he gave the city to the "Republic of the Holy Church of God" instead of the Byzantine emperor. Pepin's **Gift of Quiersy-Sur-Oise** effectively set up the papal states. Pepin pushed the fledgling republic along for a bit until God took over. Under the short one's benevolent protection, **Pope Adrian I** repaired the city's aqueducts and restored its churches. Adrian's successor, **Pope Leo III,** slipped a crown on the head of Pepin's son **Charlemagne** on Christmas Day, 800, declaring him "Emperor of the Romans." The relationship between the popes and the Holy Roman Emperors was difficult to maintain. Charlemagne's death in 814 set off another 200 years of near-anarchy as his descendants killed each other to rule Europe.

In 846, Muslim **Saracens** rowed up the Tiber and plundered several basilicas. Many felt this was God's retribution for clerical misbehavior; indeed, all manner of licentiousness was going on. The most bizarre tale from these years is the posthumous trial of **Pope Formosus**. Formosus's successor **Pope Stephen VI** dug up Formosus and dressed him in ecclesiastical robes to attend a "cadaver synod." After a poor defense, the corpse was convicted on all counts, including coveting the papacy, and, confusingly, perjury. Its three blessing fingers were severed (one can never be too careful), and the corpse formerly known as Formosus was chucked into the Tiber. Pope Stephen himself was later murdered, the next pope was overthrown, and the pope after that was murdered as well.

Around the turn of the 10th century, eight popes took the throne in eight years; nine popes were murdered during the 1100s. It was not a good time to be pope.

With the papacy in arrears, power was seized in 880 by a woman named **Theodora** who set up a secular dominion over Rome. Starting with Anastasius III in 911, the family managed to choose eleven popes, many of them lovers and children of Theodora's daughter Marozia. Unfortunately, they never lasted very long. A slightly better fate was that of Marozia's son **Alberic the Younger,** who came to power in 932. Alberic attempted to wrest temporal control of Rome away from the Church. Alberic had no idea how mammoth this task was; the Vatican wouldn't officially excise itself from Roman politics for nearly a millennium.

In 954, Alberic appointed his degenerate teenage son **John XII** as pope. Getting his priorities straight, John installed a harem at the Vatican shortly after his father's death. Before he stroked out while in bed with a married woman in 964, John crowned German monarch **Otto I** Holy Roman Emperor, for protection against the Northern Italian **Berengar.** Panicked by thoughts that he had allied himself with the wrong leader, John asked Berengar for protection. Otto was victorious and took the city and the papacy. For the next century, the pope was picked by the Emperor.

The next century of Roman history was dominated by a gruesome tit-for-tat as Romans revolted against imperialist papal appointments and popes imposed punishments on the rebels (e.g. grounding them in their *palazzi*). At the turn of the 11th century, **Otto III** developed a penchant for ripping out the eyes of members of the **Crescenzi** family, the persistent and powerful nobility who periodically stormed the papal fortress, Castel Sant'Angelo, to declare themselves "Consuls."

In 1075, Pope **Hildebrand** demanded an end to the Holy Roman Emperor's interference with the Church, forcing Emperor Henry VI, whom he had excommunicated, to beg in the snow for forgiveness. It turned out to be a trick; the next time the emperor was excommunicated he laid siege to Rome, and Hildebrand's followers jumped ship. In 1084, Norman conqueror **Robert Guiscard** remembered—ahead of schedule—that Rome was due for its tercentennial sacking and made convincing work of it.

MEDIEVAL CHAOS, PART II

Around the same time that King John was buying time with the Magna Carta in England, Romans received a measure of self-rule. The 1122 **Concordat of Worms** transferred the balance of power from the Emperor to the Church. Tipsy on its gains, the Church soon predictably arrived in an advanced state of corruption. A secular senate was formed in 1143, but a few hangings later, in 1155, power over the city returned to the pope, Adrian IV, the only English pope.

Unhappy with the popes, Romans kicked them out of the city in 1181. In 1188, during the papacy of **Clement III** (a Roman by birth) the rebels and the Church struck a bargain. The papacy's (super)powers were accepted, and members of the senate swore their loyalty to the pope. In exchange, the Church agreed to recognize the city of Rome as a *comune*, with the power to declare war or peace. This agreement paved the way for the unprecedented power of **Pope Innocent III.** Innocent excommunicated England's King John, declared the Magna Carta null and void, and fought heresy with a vengeance. Innocent declared the Pope to be Vicar of Christ on Earth, "set midway between God and Man," in charge of "the whole world." Innocent's power over the city itself, however, was weak: the citizens maintained earlier reforms, leading to a period of widespread prosperity, if not peace.

Boniface VIII, elected in 1294, antagonized nearly every ruler in Europe with a string of excommunications and the papal edict **Unam Sanctam,** which decreed that it was necessary for salvation that every living thing be subject to the Pope. Fed up, the French assaulted Boniface in his home and accused him of such crimes as sodomy and keeping a pet demon. Poor Boniface died of shock. His successor, the Frenchman Clement V, moved the papacy to Avignon, France, beginning the **Babylonian Captivity** in 1309. For most of the 14th century, popes would conduct their business from Avignon under the watchful eyes of the French kings. Freed from the Church, the city struggled to find peace, but feuding between the Orsini and Colonna families and the outbreak of the **Black Death** in 1348 kept Rome exciting.

At the behest of St. Catherine of Siena, **Pope Gregory XI** agreed to return the papacy to Rome in 1377, restoring the city's greatest source of income. The **Great Western Schism** (1378-1417), the period during which there were two (and occasionally three) popes, however, jeopardized the power of the papacy, and war was widespread. The **Council of Pisa** (1409-1417) resolved the situation to Rome's satisfaction.

RENAISSANCE AND BAROQUE

UP COME THE PROTESTANTS

Taking charge in 1417, **Pope Martin V** initiated a period of Renaissance urbanity and absolute rule in Rome that lasted until 1870. No-nonsense Martin widened and paved roads, and buildings in new Renaissance styles went up. **Julius II** (1503-13) began an ambitious building program, setting out plans for Rome in general and for St. Peter's dome in particular (p. 110). He hired Bramante (p. 56), who demolished medieval Rome with such enthusiasm and intent that Raphael nicknamed him *Ruinante*.

When Protestant upstart **Martin Luther** returned to Rome in 1510, he was sorely disappointed by the city's aesthetic indulgence and spiritual dissolution. He was revolted by the sight of Raphael's ornate *Stanze* in the Vatican, in which Christian and pagan symbols mingled—in the buff, no less. While the pope went "triumphing about with fair-decked stallions, the priests gabbled Mass," Luther went about writing the *95 Theses* that kicked off the **Protestant Reformation.**

After excommunicating Luther, **Pope Leo X** (1513-1521) asserted his interest in the humanities, drawing up plans for a new St. Peter's dome and commissioning artists Michelangelo and Raphael. To support their caviar taste, Renaissance popes taxed Romans and their country cousins. Lazio and Umbria soon filed for bankruptcy, and much of the distressed agricultural population up and left. The popes curried favor with and extracted money from whichever foreign nations suited them best at the time. Fragmented alliances left Rome vulnerable to invasion, and soon proved fatal.

SACK OF ROME

The **Sack of Rome,** an intense eight-day pillage by German warriors, Spanish marauders, and 15,000 angry Lutherans, came in May 1527. The city fell to bloodthirsty imperialist troops, who stormed through the Borgo, destroying everyone and everything in sight. Little respect was shown for religious artifacts. One priest was murdered because he refused to kneel and give the Holy Communion to a donkey. The pope, Clement VII, escaped by holing himself up for six months in Castel Sant'Angelo, besieged by the troops of the French King Charles V.

Pope Paul III, disappointed by the sack, set up the **Inquisition** in 1542. It took hold remarkably well (with even more voracity than in Spain), and the burning of books, infidels, and freethinkers carried on until 1610 when all of Rome was clearly in line and behaving. Powerful families and the papacy were still hopelessly corrupt, but they didn't seem to be hurting anyone. Having created such havoc, the popes lost much of their political credibility and relevance in the play among European powers during the Thirty Years's War. Most of the 17th and 18th centuries were relatively quiet for Rome.

19TH CENTURY

Pius VI amiably mishandled conflicts between the church and the Revolutionary French government, inducing anti-clerical sentiment to explode in Paris. Effigies of Pius were set on fire and a severed head landed in the lap of the Papal Nuncio as he was traveling in his coach. Romans, roused from their usual complacency, attacked a French delegation on the Corso in 1793. Homes of French sympathizers were vandalized and the French Academy was set on fire with shouts of "Long live the Catholic religion."

Napoleon Bonaparte arrived on the scene in 1796 to deal with the problem and to refill French coffers with the treasures of Italy. Napoleon refused to depose the pope for strategic reasons, but he brought the Church to its knees, extorting millions in tribute and carrying off precious works of art. Romans watched 500 wagons leave the city loaded with booty; some of the most important pieces of Italian and Roman art are still found in Parisian museums. In 1798, French **General Berthier** stormed the Vatican, kidnapped the pope, and established yet another **Roman Republic.** When Napoleon's empire crumbled, however, the 1815 Congress of Vienna returned the papacy to temporal power in Rome.

In 1849, with the liberal **Risorgimento** raging, Rome voted to abolish the papal state and establish, you guessed it, another **Roman Republic. Pope Pius IX** appealed to Catholic heads of state with success; Rome was once again besieged by a Bonaparte, Napoleon III. The resistance was led by **Giuseppe Mazzini** and **Giuseppe Garibaldi.** The former preached with revolutionary fervor, and the latter led Rome against the French, who still triumphed and reinstated Pope Pius IX.

Nonetheless, regional Italian rulers united the country (except Rome and Venice), declared Rome the capital, and crowned the first Italian king, **Vittorio Emanuele II.** In 1870, when the French left for war with Prussia, there was no one to stop the Italian forces from crashing through the Vatican. The pope, who had just declared the doctrine of Papal Infallibility,

Piazza Farnese

Flower Seller

Horse Carriage

"imprisoned" himself, refused to give up, and urged all Italians to support him; he died alone in 1878.

20TH CENTURY

Rome's recent history may sound vaguely familiar. In a century marked by immense political unrest, public debate between the classes, and a resurgence in new forms of art and culture, citizens are taking part in Caesar's grand Roman tradition. Political fights have moved from the *rostra* to the capitol, although the arguments remain just as heated. Even the *fascisti* of the 1920s took their name from the symbol of authority in ancient Rome, the *fasces*, a bundle of sticks tightly wound around an axe-blade. Today, the Italians (divided principally into northern and southern alliances) are seriously rethinking the formation of a single state.

IL DUCE

The life of **Benito Mussolini** is a tribute to the bigness of which the littlest man is capable. After stints as a schoolteacher, a journalist, and, even a pacifist, Mussolini (or *Il Duce*, "the Leader") started his political career with the militant left, but soon abandoned Marx and socialism in favor of Nationalism. At the tender age of 25, Mussolini called for the appointment of a "ruthless and energetic" dictator to clean up Italy. Three months later, he conceded that he might be the man needed for the job.

In 1919, Mussolini assembled paramilitary combat groups (the *fasci di combattimenti*), known as the **Blackshirts,** who waged a fierce, anti-leftist campaign for power. They broke labor strikes for industrialists, raided newspapers soft on Bolshevism, and established mini-dictatorships in small cities. Mussolini had grown so powerful in Italy that the 1922 **March on Rome** was just for show, as were the reports that 3000 Fascist martyrs had died in the attempt. When Vittorio Emanuele III named him Prime Minister, Mussolini forged a totalitarian state, suppressing opposition parties, regulating the press, and demolishing labor unions. His few pieces of constructive legislation include revamping the train system to increase efficiency and the **Lateran Pact of 1929,** regulating Vatican-Italian relations.

In 1929, Mussolini moved his office to **Palazzo Venezia,** where he delivered his imperial orations. Mussolini fancied himself an emperor in the grandest tradition and was determined to mark his territory by a series of unfinished, gargantuan architectural schemes. Under his aegis, the government spent more than 33 billion lire on public works; he plowed down medieval, Renaissance, and Baroque works, as well as over three-quarters of the ruins he claimed to be preserving, to create a wide processional street, **Via dei Fori Imperiali.** Ironically, the pollution-belching traffic along this street is now the major cause of the rapid deterioration of the Colosseum. To symbolize Fascist achievement, Mussolini envisioned a huge forum that would make St. Peter's and the Colosseum look like Legoland. For the centerpiece of his Foro Mussoliano, he commissioned a 263ft. statue of himself as Hercules. One hundred tons of metal later, with only an enormous foot and head to show for it, the project lost its balance and collapsed.

Impressed by German efficiency, Mussolini entered World War II with Hitler in 1939. Used to relying on propaganda rather than strength, Mussolini squandered his army in France, Russia, and Greece until a coup and the Allied forces deposed *Il Duce*, who was rather ingloriously hanged.

Rome's sizable resistance movement made up for Italy's dreadful military performance, protecting Jews and anti-Fascists from the occupying Germans. Serious damage to the city was averted; Hitler had the sense to declare Rome an "open city" as liberating Allies approached in June 1944.

The dreary **EUR** area (see p. 135) is a reminder of Mussolini's unsettling vision and his ultimate failure. His legacy lives on in his granddaughter, **Alessandra Mussolini,** who is trying to revive Italian Fascism. Elected to Parliament, she made an unsuccessful bid for mayor of Naples in 1993.

A BABY NATION GETS THE COLIC

The end of World War II led to sweeping changes in Italian government. The **Italian Constitution** of 1948 established a **Republic** with a president, a parliament with a 315-

member Senate and 630-member Chamber of Deputies, and an independent judiciary. Within this framework, the **Christian Democratic Party,** bolstered by American aid (and rumored Mafia collusion), bested the Socialists. Domination by a single party did not stabilize the country; political turmoil has reigned, along with over 50 different governments since World War II.

Postwar instability and industrialization led to violence in the 1970s. The *autunno caldo* (hot autumn) of 1969, a season of strikes, demonstrations, and riots, opened a decade of unrest. The most disturbing event was the 1978 murder of ex-Prime Minister Aldo Moro, who is remembered by a plaque in the Jewish Ghetto where his body was dumped by the leftist Brigade Rosse.

Because the nation is still young, city and regional bonds often prove stronger than nationalist sentiment. The most pronounced split exists between the north's wealthy industrial areas and the south's agrarian territories.

RECENT EVENTS

The daily minutiae of Italian politics read like a soap opera that, when taken *cum grano salis*, seems more amusing than disturbing. In 1992, **Oscar Luigi Scalfaro** was elected president on a platform of governmental reform, including streamlining of the cabinet. Since then, politics have been characterized by the slow process of electoral law reform, resulting in **"Tangentopoli"** ("Kickback City"); over 2600 politicians have been implicated in corruption scandals. Reaction to the crackdown on corruption and the Mafia in politics has included such acts of violence as the 1993 bombings of the Uffizi, Florence's premier art museum, as well as several sites in Rome, including the Church of San Giorgio in Velabro (see p. 86), the "suicides" of 10 indicted officials over the past four years, and open Mafia retaliation against judges.

Current and former Prime Minister **Silvio Berlusconi** (who moonlights as a billionaire publishing tycoon) presided over a "Freedom Alliance" of three right-wing parties: his conservative **Forza Italia,** the reactionary **Lega Nord,** and the formerly neofascist **Alleanza Nazionale.** When the Lega Nord pulled out, Berlusconi lost his majority and was forced to resign as Prime Minister.

The elections of 1996 brought the center left-coalition, the **Olive Tree** (L'Ulivo), to power, and **Romano Prodi** was elected Prime Minister. Prodi's major designs were balancing the budget and the stabilization of Italian politics. He now serves as president of the European Union Commission. Despite his removal to Brussels, however, Prodi's voice still carries weight: he's in the unique position of having left the presidency without first horribly disgracing himself.

In 1998, **Massimo D'Alema** came to power also representing a variation of the center-left. His policy is largely similar to Prodi's. In June 1999, a government bureaucrat was found assassinated in the streets of Rome; the same night, a 19-page manifesto was found in trash cans across the city. It was feared that this might mark a resurgence of the anarchic Italy of the 1970s, and carabinieri in the city were on full alert. Though the incident seems to have been an isolated one, D'Alema saw his support crumble at the end of the year as he failed to push through welfare reforms and alienated unions in trying to do so.

Despite D'Alema's fleeting success, he stepped down in mid-May of 2000 and was replaced by his former Treasury Minister, **Giuliano Amato.** Known as "Dr. Subtle" for his ability to perceive the fine points of argument and his deft trimming of government spending, Amato (alongside Ciampi and D'Alema) is largely credited with the institution of the successful 1999 budgetary reforms, though his anti-graffiti campaign failed entirely. Master writers have been catching "why me?" all over *bella Italia* since Amato's first day in office. Perhaps the nickname derives from Amato's ability to avoid scandal; he was one of few to emerge unscathed from corruption crack-downs in the early 90s, one of which led to late Socialist Party leader Bettino Craxi's exile in Tunisia. Ironically, Amato benefited from Craxi's death. As the top untainted Socialist, he now heads a shaky 12-party coalition, Italy's 58th government since World War II. To expect stability would be to ignore Italian history. Perhaps the real escape artist is Silvio Berlusconi, who managed, despite a corruption conviction, to secure election in 2001 as prime minister, to the great consternation of liberal Italians everywhere. Several organizations for foreign travelers in Italy immediately issued warnings about the conservative prime minister's agenda and tendency to support insular nationalism. In reality, the fractured nature of Italian politics will probably not allow Berlusconi total(itarian) freedom when it comes to parliament. Many believe that electoral reform is the answer to Italian factionalism, but with the long tradition of Italian inter-city warring and Berlusconi's known preference for the system that brought him to his current imperial overlord status, change is nowhere in sight.

Currently, the city of Rome is being run by center-leftist Mayor Francesco Rutelli, now in his last term. Having endured criticism over his handling of preparations for the **Jubilee,** Rutelli is now faced with resentment for prioritizing his future in the European parliament over city issues. Every 25 years since 1675, the Pope has declared a Holy Year of Jubilee. Though it did not attract the crowds that were hoped for, the 2000 Jubilee saw not only a Pope apologizing for centuries of Church wrongdoings, but a city cleaner, more put-together and more welcoming to visitors than at any time in recent memory. Over 700 projects included Metro expansions, restoration of the Colosseum, and better roads to the airport.

RELIGION

Religion has been a major force in the shaping of Roman history, politically as much as socially. From the Pantheon to St. Peter's, the majority of sights in Rome are or were connected with religion. This section aims to be a history of belief: for information on religion and politics, see **History** above.

GODS OF THE ROMANS

Early Roman religion is difficult to piece together, mostly because the ancient Romans themselves were involved in forgetting it by the first century BC. All that can be certain is that the Romans had the typical Indo-European *paterfamilias* structure of a male head of household who bore sacral life-and-death power over the rest of the family. The **lares** were attached to a particular household, worshiped by the family and its slaves. The **penates** were also household gods, but they were associated more with the storage cupboards of the household and the care of the hearth. Along with war rituals, the hearth was an area of strong religious importance, and the cult of **Vesta** (with her league of Vestal Virgins; see **House of the Vestal Virgins,** p. 75) was one of the most fundamental elements of early Roman religious practice.

Like the vast majority of inhabitants of the ancient world, the Romans practiced animal sacrifice, believing it important to achieve a state of *pax deorum* (peace of the gods) instead of *ira deorum* (the wrath of heaven.) War rites of the Romans were even known to include human sacrifice in cases of dire crisis, though this was outlawed by the more refined citizenry of later centuries. Romans were introduced to the entire package of Greek gods and goddesses by the Etruscans. The awed Romans soon adopted most of the Greek religious cast, simply transposing Hellenic names into Latinate versions for use at home. As the god of war, **Mars** was declared patron of belligerent Rome.

Roman polytheism was of a tolerant sort; religion was seen as a local practice, and foreign gods were frequently "interpreted" as versions of the Greco-Roman gods under other names. The Romans didn't impose their religion on anyone, and even the notorious "cult of the emperor"—which began with Julius Caesar and Augustus, who were deified posthumously—actually began by popular demand in one of the eastern provinces, where local inhabitants had a custom of deifying their rulers. Many of the more educated Romans were non-religious, having absorbed the Stoic, Epicurean, and Platonic elements of Greek philosophy.

Toward the end of the Empire, Roman territory sheltered a variety of assorted cults and sects: the Egyptian gods Isis and Osiris were integrated into the Roman pantheon, while Mithraism (see p. 47) spread through the army. Temples were erected to Cybele, a fertility goddess of Eastern origin. Christians were persecuted anomalously in the Roman Empire because they were regarded as a renegade sect, people who had withdrawn from the local community. It didn't help that they refused to worship Julius or Augustus Caesar on demand, either.

MITHRAISM

Mithras?...It didn't fail because it was bad. Mithraism almost triumphed over Christianity. It failed because it was so nearly good.

-William Gaddis, *The Recognitions*

Mithraism, a religion with strong similarities to Christianity that flourished in the first few centuries AD, was the first successful monotheistic religion in the Empire. Imported from Persia, it centered around the god **Mitras,** who created the world by killing a sacred bull. Mithraism remains shrouded in mystery, mainly because it was a secretive cult based on the celebration of **mysteries** known only to initiates. The vast majority of our knowledge about the religion comes from archaeological remains. Their place of worship, the **mithraeum,** was usually built underground, and several Christian churches, notably the **Basilicas of San Clemente** (see p. 127) and **Santa Prisca,** were constructed on top of them. Although only eight mithraea have been excavated in Rome, there may have been over 700 at the height of the movement. Several mithrae have also been excavated in Ostia Antica (see **Daytrips,** p. 217).

The mithraeum was usually an artificial cave with stone benches facing a depiction of Mithras killing the sacred bull. Several other minor figures were present in the scene, including a scorpion, a dog, a snake, the sun, the moon, and a male figure named Cautopates holding a torch. The best-preserved artifact of the scene is the bull sculpture in the Room of the Animals at the Vatican Museums (see p. 140).

Mithras, the central figure in the religion, originated as a minor Zoroastrian and Hindu deity. An Apollo-like figure, he was the god of the sky, the sun's light, contracts, and mediation. The cult's Roman popularity began around AD 100. Historians speculate that Mithraism was a social religion for bourgeois Roman military veterans. With nothing but artificial ties to its Zoroastrian roots, it was a sort of Roman New Age religion. Mithraism's potential was seriously hindered by its exclusion of women. With the ban on paganism in 391, the death knell was sounded for Mithraism, though some isolated believers may have kept the faith in the outskirts of the Empire. In fact, some claim that the Masons represent, in concept and descent, a late outcropping of Mithraism. Other remnants of Mithraism linger on: December 25, now celebrated as Christmas, was once celebrated as the birthday of Mithras.

CHRISTIANITY & CATHOLICISM

Suppressed for the moment, the deadly superstition broke out again, not only in Judea, the land which originated this evil, but also in the city of Rome, where all sorts of horrendous and shameful practices from every part of the world converge and are fervently cultivated.

-Tacitus, *Annals* 15:44

Since Peter and Paul arrived shortly after Christ's death, Christianity has been big in Rome. Christ said to give unto Caesar what is Caesar's and unto God what is God's; in reality, separating politics and religion hasn't been quite so simple. As early as AD 35, the Senate declared Christianity to be "strange and unlawful." Nonetheless, in 42, **Saint Peter,** the first Bishop of Rome, set up shop in the city. **Saint Paul,** the codifier of Christian thought, dropped by often, until he was beheaded in 62, near EUR. Peter, met his end in upside-down crucifixion near the site of the Vatican in 67. The duo are recognized as Rome's patron saints.

Persecution of Christians began in earnest after the Great Fire of Rome in 64, and it continued sporadically for the next 240 years. From 200 to 500, Christians used the **catacombs** outside of the center of Rome as cemeteries by Christians (see p. 131). Although the Christians did not live there, as commonly assumed, much has been learned about the early church from the decorations inside.

Christian persecution in Rome ended just before Christianity was made the state religion in 315. The church struggled to find its feet. The **Nicaean Creed** of 325 was the first cohesive statement of belief by the Pistic (Orthodox) church, nailing down the basics of Christianity. Soon, with the banning of paganism, Christianity found itself with a monopoly on the soul trade. A flurry of theological ensued: The Latin translation of the Bible by **St. Jerome** standardized the work, while Rome's own **St. Augustine**

FINDING GOD

THE PANTHEON SUPER-POWER CHECKLIST

More than you ever wanted to know about the ancient Roman gods. Impress your friends!

Jupiter: King of the gods; sexual gymnast; law-maker;all around sexy beast.

Juno: Queen of heaven; goddess of women and marriage; Jupiter's wife...and sister.

Mars: God of war and the spirit of battle; represented the gruesome aspects of fighting.

Vulcan: God of fire; divine smith and patron of all craftsman; Venus's hubby; ugly.

Ceres: Goddess of the Earth and fertility. Talk about responsibility!

Venus: Goddess of love and lust; patron of prostitutes; wife of Vulcan; noted philanderer (especially with Mars).

Vesta: Goddess of the family hearth (and the city hearth on a larger scale); forever a virgin.

Minerva: Goddess of war, handicraft, and reason; born fully grown from Jupiter's head.

Neptune: God of the sea and water; Jupiter's brother; always on the prowl for dry real estate.

Apollo: God of the sun, music, and song; Diana's twin; the most revered and feared god.

Diana: Goddess of the moon, wild animals, hunting, vegetation, chastity, and childbirth.

Mercury: God of animals, wealth, commerce, shrewdness, persuasion, and travelers (yeah!).

wrote the *City of God* and *Confessions*, the framework of most Christian theology.

During this period, most of the major basilicas of Rome were begun, though in forms vastly different from their current states. The **crucifix,** today the ubiquitous symbol of Christianity, only became widely used around 550. In 490, the Council of Chalcedon declared that Jesus was of both human and divine nature, answering a question that had spawned innumerable heretic sects. In 787, the Second Council of Nicaea declared that the Holy Spirit proceeds from the Father and the Son. The first major break in the church began to form, and in 1054, the Eastern and Western halves of the church separated in an event known as the **Great Schism.** Rome and Constantinople were too far apart for effective government, and Roman religious rule grated on the Byzantines. In addition, there was theological dissent: the Eastern church believed in the special religious significance of icons, while the Western church did not.

The (Western) Church's history during the Middle Ages was tumultuous. Papal succession was political, and greed and corruption were rampant. Pope Urban II kicked off the **First Crusade** in 1047 in order to unify the Church and squelch partisanship. While this crusade, like those that followed, failed to retake the Holy Land and created all manner of havoc in the Middle East, it succeeded in bringing a rebirth to a religion in danger of becoming stagnant. For similar reasons, Pope Gregory II initiated the first incarnation of the **Inquisition** in 1232.

The 14th century, during which the papacy jumped borders, duplicating and even triplicating itself (see **History,** p. 41), was only dress rehearsal for the confusion that would come with the **Protestant Reformation** of the 1500s. In 1517, Martin Luther's accusatory *95 Theses* significantly threatened Rome's religious power. Ignatius of Loyola founded the Jesuits in 1534 to combat the Protestant menace; from 1534-1563, the Council of Trent met to plan the **Counter Reformation** and further define what had become known as Roman Catholicism.

The Catholic Church's influence on the world, while not inconsequential, has declined tremendously since the Reformation. Pius IX's **First Vatican Council** of 1869 resulted in the somewhat archaic doctrine of papal infallibility.

Since World War II, however, the Church has spread its message globally with renewed strength and vigor, particularly in Eastern Europe and the developing world. Meanwhile back in Rome, the Church has lost much of its following: less than 10% of Romans attend mass regularly. The Church's responses to public affairs during this century have been contradictory. While Pope Pius XII insisted that the Church would stay out of politics, a 1950s papal decree forbade Catholics from associating with the Communist party.

Ironically, in many other Western European countries, the Church was directly affiliated with Socialist parties.

During the 1960s, in an effort to transform the church into a 20th-century institution, the much-loved Pope John XXII agreed to open dialogue with the Communist Party, showing a new commitment to compromising with non-believers. Before his death, he convened the **Second Vatican Council** in 1962. The aim of the council was to improve relations with other religions and to make the Church more accessible to the layperson. The most visible results of the Council, which concluded under Paul VI in 1965, included the replacement of Latin with the vernacular in the mass, the increased role of local clergy and bishops in administration, and the re-evaluation of the place of scripture with regard to belief.

Since 1981, Pope John Paul II's international approach to papacy—including his overt use of the media and constant traveling—has reflected the Church's intention to establish a more direct relationship with believers without the interference of politics. The fact that the current pope is Polish (Italian newspapers don't call him Giovanni Paolo II but Wojtyla, his last name) has removed the Pope from Italian politics, and the papacy has concerned itself primarily with global issues. While it is suggested that the pope played a part in the fall of Communism, he has also denounced the excesses of capitalism.

Piazza Farnese

LITERATURE

SUM, ES, EST, SUMUS, ESTIS, SUNT

Fools laugh at Latin words.
-Ovid

Piazza Navona

Anyone who has experienced the joy of memorizing Latin verb conjugations will recall the heavy hitters of Latin literature, most of them from Augustus's golden age (see **History,** p. 39). **Plautus** (220-184 BC) wrote farces that entertained the masses. (His comedy *Pseudolus* was the basis for the Broadway musical *A Funny Thing Happened on the Way to the Forum.*)

The poetry of **Catullus** (84-54 BC) set a high standard for passion and provided a great source of Latin obscenities for future generations of Latin students. **Livy** (c.59 BC-AD 17) wrote Rome's official history, while **Julius Caesar** (100-44 BC) gave a first-hand account of the shredding of the Republic in *De Bello Civili.* Caesar's contemporary, the philosopher **Cicero** (106-43 BC), penned works notable for their carefully crafted Latin, including the political speech *In Catilinam ("O tempora, O mores!").*

Filetti di Baccala

Virgil (70-19 BC) wrote the **Aeneid,** linking the founding of Rome to the fall of Troy via the wanderings of Aeneas. **Horace**'s (65-8 BC) verse (*Odes*, *Epodes*, *Satires*, and *Epistles*) was more autobiographical. Fed up with the squalor and chaos of first-century BC Rome, both Virgil and Horace praised the simple life of the country dweller. City-lover **Ovid** (43 BC-AD 17), though originally employed by Augustus, was later banished to the Black Sea for his involvement in the escapades of Augustus's rebellious and promiscuous daughter and grand-daughter, both named Julia. His poems—among them the *Amores*, the *Metamorphoses*, and the *Ars Amatoria* (a tongue-in-cheek guide to love)—are much more light-hearted than those of his contemporaries.

Post-Augustan literature included **Petronius**'s first-century AD *Satyricon*, a blunt look at the Nero's decadence, while **Tacitus**'s *Histories* summarizes the war, politics, and scandals in the years after Nero's death. **Suetonius** (AD 69-c. 130), the Robin Leach of the era, dished the dirt on the first 12 Roman emperors in *The Lives of the Caesars*. **Marcus Aurelius**'s (121-180) *Meditations* are the philosopher king's musings during the twilight of Rome's glorious imperial era.

EARLY CHRISTIAN LITERATURE

The Christian church wasted no time in building itself up a body of work. Much of the New Testament, as well as other theological books, were written in Rome. Among the latter are the *Epistles of St. Clement of Rome*, which were actually forged well after the death of **St. Clement,** the fourth Bishop of Rome. The work is an argument for headquartering the Church in Rome, instead of Alexandria. Another forgery attributed to Clement is the so-called Clementine *Recognitions*. Called the first Christian novel, it tells the tale of a wanderer who finds meaning in life when he happens to run into St. Peter and his merry band of Christians. Naturally. Other major works by the early Christians include St. Jerome's Latin translation of the Bible, the **Vulgate,** in 405, and **Tertullian**'s defenses of orthodox Christianity from Gnostic thought. Tertullian's work went a long way toward defining Christian thought. His style also set the tone for many future works, including *The Confessions* of **Saint Augustine,** a 4th-century Roman native.

TALES OF HEAVEN, HELL, & NAUGHTY NUNS

After the fall of the Roman Empire, the focus of Italian literature moved (permanently, it would seem) away from Rome. The influence of Rome was still felt, however: during the Middle Ages,

A FIELD GUIDE TO HERETICS

In the early days of Christianity, there were plenty of heretics. A brief guide to major credences:

Arianism: Following Arius (250-336), Arianism argued that Christ was not eternal, having been created by God the Father. While Arianism was supported by Emperors Constantius II and Valens, the First Council of Nicaea in 325 denounced it.

Docetism: The Docetists (2nd century) argued that Christ's divine nature was incompatible with human suffering and that Christ was not human.

Donatism: The Donatists, a North African sect, split from the church in 312 and survived until the 7th century, when Islam arrived. They believed that the Church should not be tainted with the political and valued personal holiness.

Eunomianism: The Eunomians believed that the only proper name for God the Father, an incomprehensible concept, was "Ungenerated;" everything else, including Christ, had been generated. They were denounced as being too philosophical.

Gnosticism: Gnosticism denotes a wide variety of beliefs. In most Gnostic cosmogonies, a creator god was the supreme being; from the creator came a demiurge, a flawed figure who created a flawed world. The world was thus an evil place; salvation could be attained through knowledge, called *gnosis*, of the divine spark of god.

the literary language of choice remained Latin, in spite of the fact that the Latin of Caesar and Cicero hadn't been spoken by the people since the days of the early Empire. This gap between the written language and the vernacular, or *volgare*, eventually led to writers and poets throughout the Romance language-speaking parts of Europe rejecting Latin. Tuscan **Dante Alighieri** (1265-1321), considered as much the father of the modern Italian language as of its literature, was one of the first European poets to eschew Latin. After the death of his young love Beatrice in 1290, Dante began his masterpiece, *La Divina Commedia*, detailing his allegorical journey through the afterlife is guided by his ancient Roman counterpart, Virgil.

Although he preferred to write in Latin, **Petrarch** (1304-1374) was perhaps more influential than Dante in establishing a model for future Tuscan poets. **Giovanni Boccaccio**'s (1313-1375) *Decameron*, a collection of 100 stories told by 10 young Florentines fleeing their plague-ridden city, ranges in tone from cheeky to downright bawdy; in one story, a hard-working gardener fertilizes an entire convent.

RENAISSANCE LITERATURE

Florence continued to dominate Italian culture and literature through the Renaissance, leaving Rome in its shadow. Most of the best known Renaissance thinkers and artists, including Nicolò Macchiavelli, Michelango, and Leonardo da Vinci, lived and worked in Florence. While arguments about the Italian language, the nature of love, and the place of women erupted throughout Northern Italy, Rome remained largely silent. Commissions by the Church lured many artists to Rome, but most authors chose to write about the city rather than live there.

Among those who wrote about Rome was **Benevenuto Cellini** (1500-1571), a Florentine sculptor and goldsmith, remembered for his autobiographical *Vita*. The somewhat paranoid Cellini presents himself as a model of bravery and determination. Among other exploits, he recounts in livid detail his successful defense of Castel Sant'Angelo (see p. 115) against Imperial forces and his daring escape from imprisonment in the same in 1538. Also chronicled in *Vita* are Cellini's memories of a number of famous Romans, including Pope Clement VII.

A number of Renaissance writers, including Leon Battista Alberti, Baldassare Castiglione, and Giorgio Vasari, passed through and worked in Rome. The philosopher **Giordano Bruno** (1548-1600) never managed to leave, as he was burned at the stake for his humanist thought, which contradicted the ideas of the Church.

A FIELD GUIDE TO HERETICS *(CONT.)*

Marcionism: Marcion (84-160) denounced the Jewish scriptures as being written in honor of the evil demiurge (see Gnosticism, above) in favor of the Gospel of Luke and the Pauline Epistles. The movement lasted until the 5th century.

Monarchianism: Monarchianism, beginning in the 2nd century, denied the trinity in favor of one godhead. This marked the beginning of tensions between the Eastern and Western churches.

Monophysitism: The Monophysites of the 5th century believed that Christ was of divine and not human nature.

Nestorianism: Nestor (c.381-c.451) argued that Christ was of two persons—one human and one divine. As Mary had given birth only to the human Christ, she could not be called the Mother of God. Nestorianism survives today in Iran, Iraq, and Syria.

Pelagianism: Pelagianism, a heresy which arose in the 5th century, denied the concepts of original sin and Christian grace.

POPE JOAN

Canonical history holds that Nicholas Breakspear, Pope Adrian IV, was the only English Pope. Popular tradition, however, has it that John VIII (853-855), elected for his saintliness and Greek learning, was not only of English descent but also, to add insult to injury, a woman. "Joan" was found out when she gave birth during a procession; the enraged citizens of Rome promptly stoned her and the baby to death. The truth of the story of Pope Joan is unclear: historical records are hazy, and the tale has been used polemically to support anti-Catholic, feminist, anti-feminist, and Catholic-reformist agendas. Joan's story gave birth to a tradition in which the elected heir of St. Peter's apostolic seat was required to sit in a special chair with a carved slot for the purpose of having his testicles touched by a young cardinal to verify his gender. In popular culture, Pope Joan inspired the Popess card in the Tarot deck. Bernini may have memorialized her end in some half-hidden sculpting on the famous *baldacchino* in St. Peter's cathedral (see p. 110).

ROMAN ROMANTICISM

After the brightness of the Renaissance, Italian literature stagnated in the 17th century. But although few notable *literati* emerged, a number of new literary forms appeared, including the novel, the opera, and *commedia dell'arte*.

Italian theater came into its own in the 18th century. Roman dramatist **Metastasio** wrote melodramas while **Carlo Goldoni** transformed *commedia dell'arte* by replacing stock figures with unpredictable characters in works like *Il Ventaglio*. By the late-19th century, the written and spoken language had again drifted apart, causing another vernacular movement in literature. **Alessandro Manzoni** promoted the use of the "living and true" tongue with his hugely popular novel *I Promessi Sposi*.

Rome's unique contribution to 19th- and 20th-century writing came in the form its **dialect poetry.** One of the greatest dialect poets was **G.G. Belli** (1791-1863). An imaginary explanation by Belli of the advantages of dialects over national languages appeared in Anthony Burgess's *ABBA ABBA*: "A language waves a flag and is blown up by politicians. A dialect keeps to things, things, things, street smells and street noises, life."

Meanwhile, Rome was the "paradise of exiles," according to Percy Bysshe Shelley. **Goethe,** arriving in Rome in 1787, gushed, "Only now do I begin to live." **Frederick Jackson Turner** would later use excerpts from *Childe Harold* as inspiration for a series of Roman paintings.

No discussion of expats in Rome would be complete without mentioning **John Keats,** who came to Rome in 1820 to improve his health. Despite a posh *pensione* with a to-die-for view of the Spanish Steps (now the Keats-Shelley Memorial House, p. 161), Rome didn't do much for Keats's tuberculosis; he died three months later, at age 25. Sigmund Freud, on whom it wasn't lost that "Roma" is "Amor" spelled backwards, writes of being aroused by the city in *The Interpretation of Dreams*. Perhaps Rome's greatest fan in the 19th century was American expat **Henry James,** who made 14 visits to Italy, beginning in 1869 and ending in 1907.

20TH-CENTURY LITERATURE

As Communism, Socialism, and Fascism gave rise to anti-traditional literary movements, Italy became a center of Modernist poetry. The most flamboyant and controversial of Modernism's poets was **Gabriele d'Annunzio,** whose cavalier heroics and sexual escapades earned him as much fame as his eccentric, over-the-top, and often nationalistic verse (exemplified by his novel, *Il Piacere*, set in Rome).

The 1930s saw the rise of young Italian writers influenced by the experimental narratives and themes of social alienation found in the works of American writers such as Ernest Hemingway and John Steinbeck. These included Cesare Pavese, Ignazio Silone, and Elio Vittorini. The most prolific of these writers, Roman-born **Alberto Moravia,** wrote the ground-breaking—and promptly banned—*The Time of Indifference*, attacking the Fascist regime. To evade government censors, Moravia employed experimental surreal forms in his subsequent works. *La Romana* is the story of a Roman who slowly finds herself becoming a prostitute. Oops, how'd that happen! Two of Moravia's works became important films: *Il Disprezzo* formed the basis for Jean-Luc Godard's superb *Le Mépris*, and Bernardo Bertolucci's *The Conformist* was based on Moravia's novel of the same name.

The concept of the Modernist Italian novel was largely formed by Rome-born **Carlo Emilio Gadda**'s *That Awful Mess on Via Merulana*, a novel described as the Italian analogue to James Joyce's *Ulysses*. Gadda makes extensive use of Roman dialect, expanding what starts out as a simple detective story into a broad portrait of life under Fascism. Among Gadda's followers were **Elsa Morante,** who wrote about the Jewish experience in Rome in such novels as *Menzogna e Sortilegio*.

The other major contemporary Italian author writing in and about Rome is **Natalia Ginzburg,** author of several psychological novels centered on the interiors of the self and the family. Many, such as *Famiglia* and *Borghesia*, are set in Rome and betray a deep understanding of its streets and its mores. While most of the best known Italian writers of the 20th century hail from outside Rome, the city continues to contribute to Italian literature. **Pier Paolo Pasolini,** better known as a director (see p. 59), also wrote a significant amount of poetry. In 1997, the unlikely candidate **Dario Fo,** a *commedia dell'arte*-inspired Italian playwright and actor denounced by the Catholic church, won the Nobel Prize for literature, in honor of his comic plays and his dramatic satires of post-war Italian texts. Fo's most popular works are *The Accidental Death of an Anarchist* (1970) and *We Won't Pay! We Won't Pay!* (1974).

ART AND ARCHITECTURE

Before Rome was Rome, Etruscans lived, worked, and made art that influenced the Roman conquerors who would later take over their territory. They are most famous for their subtle, reddish pottery, which took heavy inspiration both from the Greeks and from Oriental, Phoenician, and Hittite sources. Their earliest pottery (9th century BC) took the form of funerary urns, mostly decorated with stippled or incised patterns. In the 7th century, the **bucchero** style—shiny black or grey funeral pottery that looks an awful lot like metal—came into style, a must-have for every Etruscan lady who lunched. Just as typical, however, are the earthy **terra-cotta** bas reliefs that the Etruscans introduced and the Romans went on to claim. Nationalistic Roman orator Cato even had the nerve to announce, several hundred years later: "I hear too many people praising the knick-knacks of Corinth and Athens, and laughing at the terra-cotta antefixes of our Roman gods." Etruscans liked bright colors and fluid lines, even in their still plentiful *necropoloi*, tomb paintings, and funerary statues, a taste which prompted D.H. Lawrence to wax ecstatic about the sensuality of Etruscan art: "so alive…flexible." (Mr. Lawrence, there are children present!) Etruscans ruled Rome until the last of their dynasty, Tarquinius Superbus, was kicked out by the Latins (see **History,** p. 38). Ruins of Etruscan buildings coexist with and lie just beneath the classical Roman ruins, showing traces of their former gaudy terra-cotta decorations and the **gargoyles of Greek deities** that once adorned their gables and gutters. Etruscan influence persisted beyond their political fade-out, most notably in Roman religious and domestic art.

CLASSICAL ROME

The emerging Roman styles in art fall mainly into two large categories—art in service of the state and private household art, which finds its origins in the votive statues of household gods (the *lares* and *penates*) created by ancient Roman tribes. Household art was a democratic form, splashed across the interiors of houses, courtyards, and shops, and taking everything from scenes of the gods and goddesses at play to illusionary woodland landscapes as its subject.

Most private Roman art took the form of **frescoes,** Greek-influenced paintings that were daubed onto wet plaster so that both plaster and paint would dry together, forming a lasting and time-resistant patina. (Da Vinci's *The Last Supper* is probably the most famous fresco.) Proud household owners often embellished their abodes with sneaky **trompe l'oeil** doors or columns to make the place look bigger. **Mosaic** (painting with tiles) was another popular genre from the Hellenistic period onward; a favorite subject was the watchdog, often executed on the vestibule floor, with the helpful inscription *cave canem* ("beware of dog"). Craftsmen-artists fashioned these mosaics by painting scenes into the floor (or occasionally wall) of a building, pressing finely shaded **tesserae** (bits of colored stone and glass) onto the painting's surface, and squeezing a soft bed of mortar in between the cracks to cement everything in place. An even more personalized art form of sorts—graffiti—was also widely practiced by citizens of the ancient Roman Empire. Look out for walls in Pompeii or excavated buried buildings to see the full range of uninhibited ancient self-expression—everything from love declarations to denunciations of Christianity as a cannibal religion, as well as such judiciously weighed sentiments as "Marcus Lucius is a very large ass."

Public art in Rome was commissioned by the Roman government and usually reflected the tastes and victories of whoever was in power at the time. At first the Romans simply exploited Greek design features for their buildings, but soon they developed the revolutionary technology of the **arch** from earlier Etruscan vaults. This, along with the happy invention of **concrete,** revolutionized their conceptions of architecture and made possible such monuments as the Colosseum (p. 76), triumphal arches celebrating military victories, aqueducts, amphitheaters, basilicas, and much more. The Romans then finessed the arch, lengthening it into a **barrel vault,** crossing two arches to make a **groin vault,** or rotating it in a tight circle to build **domes.** Monumental public buildings either reminded the spectator of a particular emperor's exploits in battle (like the artistically sublimated propaganda of Trajan's Column) or functioned as frenzied arenas of mass entertainment intended to pacify an unruly populace. Some of the most famous building occurred around AD 80, when the normally affable ex-plebe emperor Vespatian built the blood-soaked arches and columns of the **Colosseum** (see **Pacifying the Populace,** p. 76), and when Titus had his triumphal **Arch of Titus** constructed to provide a suitable backdrop for him to parade his booty and slaves.

Religion, Marx noticed, keeps the people busy and out of trouble. The Roman government scooped him on this, making sure to spend money on the construction of religious temples and on festivals and rites to calm and patriotically inspire the populace by offering it a spectacle of spiritual unity and power. Temples were usually constructed along the Greek model, with a triangular portico supported by the classical row of columns and decorated with strips of friezes on strategic flat surfaces. In capitals (the decorative upper portion of a column), Romans used the Greek orders of Doric, Ionic, and Corinthian, making the latter more elaborate than ever by supplementing its crown of acanthus leaves with all manner of ornate curlicues. Later on, the Romans would begin to transfer column style and the full panoply of Greek architecture to almost any building.

The earliest and most sacred man-made monument in Rome was probably the Temple to Vesta, although its white simplicity was soon overshadowed by more pragmatic temples (such as those devoted to the deified Augustus and Julius Caesar). Rome's most important architect was **Vitruvius,** who originated the idea that harmonious buildings would base their measurements and proportions on the human body—a.k.a. the "measure of man." (Cement modernist Le Corbusier, among others, picked up on Vitruvius's graceful building philosophies.) Later on, Romans became more interested in theaters and basilicas for distraction and contemplation. At this point, basilicas were still used in as courthouses and shopping arcades, although the cool and climate-adapted design of a long rectangle with arch-and-column supports would be recycled by later Christian and Byzantine emperors as the first floorplan for early churches.

BYZANTINE DECADENCE

When Constantine transferred the capital of the Roman Empire in AD 330 from Rome to **Constantinople** (then known as Byzantium, and now reincarnated as modern-day Istanbul), artistic influences in Rome took a decidedly Asiatic twist. Born from the aesthetic traditions of the Christian catacombs and the Greek and Oriental styles, Byzantine art favored immobile, mystical, slender-fingered figures against flat gold or midnight blue backgrounds, shadowy domes, and an atmosphere of enigmatic and flooding holiness. Spread the world over by the Emperor Justinian and his powerful wife Theodora, the Byzantine style reveled in gorgeously ornate mosaics, some of which can still be seen in the churches of Santa Cecilia in Trastevere, Santa Prassede, and Santa Maria in Domenica, although the best examples of this style in Italy are all in Ravenna. Despite the fact that the religious Byzantine emperors erected countless costly palaces, only their religious buildings have survived subsequent sackings, medieval recycling, and modernization. These buildings were built on the model of Roman **basilicas** (law courts); instead of having a cathedral shape, they are rectangular and domed, with stony cold sarcophagi and the dim gold glare of far-off mosaics and anemic saints.

Piazza Navona

A TOUCH OF ROMANESQUE

Given the chaos of the 3rd and 4th centuries, emperors' minds tended to focus on making war, not art. The gaze of the Christian art that eventually emerged in the Middle Ages was fixed firmly on heaven. From roughly AD 500 to 1200, Romanesque-style churches dominated Europe. In Rome, these Romanesque fashions slowly and incrementally overtook the older Byzantine style, retaining the basilica floorplan but updating it with rows of pillared round arches, low ceilings, oriel windows, peeling wooden statues of saints, and an elaborate and arcane bestiary of symbolic men and beasts cavorting in the caps of pillars and the reliefs above doorways. Wall frescoes and mosaics from this period abound in Rome, in **San Paolo fuori le Mura** (which also hoards mosaics imported *in toto* from Byzantium), **Santa Maria Maggiore,** and **Santa Prassede.**

Piazza della Rotonda

GOTHIC: NO THANKS

The Romans never approved of the Teutonic barbarian hordes living to their north, and when somebody in the Renaissance wanted to find a disparaging name for the bad old Dark Ages style that Europe was recovering from back then, "Gothic" seemed made to order. Gothic never really caught on in the Holy Roman Empire; not only is there just one Gothic church in all of Rome—Santa Maria sopra Minerva—it's more famous for an ancient altar to the owl-loving Roman goddess of Wisdom (razed by Christians) than for its current dedication to the Blessed Virgin.

Trevi Fountain

RENAISSANCE IN ROME

...if cleanliness is next to godliness, it is a very distant neighbor to chiaroscuro.

—Henry James

The succession of wealthy Renaissance popes eager to leave their mark on the city in the form of new buildings, paintings, and sculpture gave a sagging Rome its most striking stylistic tummy-tuck since its ancient days. This age heralded the split between science and faith, and the Church condemned both Galileo and Giordano Bruno for their astronomical assertions that the earth was not the center of the universe. Painters, sculptors, and architects relied heavily on subjective experience while at the same time employing the technical discoveries of the Age of Science, such as the newly reinvented trick of creating **perspective.** Although Rome was certainly not the center of the Italian Renaissance, it did manage to lure many of the most famous Florentine artists to come refurbish the imperial city's image, including Michelangelo, Brunelleschi, and Rafael. It is also home to one of the period's trendiest churches, the Mannerist Jesuit headquarters, **Il Gesù.**

The supreme artist with the supremely tortured soul, **Michelangelo Buonarroti** (1475-1564), grew up among the stonemasons of Tuscany; as the man later said: "with my wet-nurse's milk, I sucked in the hammer and chisels I use for my statues." During this period, Michelangelo honed his knowledge of the human body after he swapped his crucifix for the privilege of dissecting corpses in the Cloisters of Santo Spirito. At the age of 21, he headed to the already ancient capital city to seek his fortune. Originally commissioned by the pope for some minor works, Michelangelo was deluged with requests for work once he became well known in Rome. It is for one of these commissions that he created the profoundly sorrowful and career-making **Pietà** in St. Peter's (p. 112).

In 1502, Pope Julius II sent for Michelangelo, now almost 30 and at the height of his career, to return once more to Rome to build the pope's **tomb** (in San Pietro in Vincoli). The relationship that was to last 10 years between the overbearing, irascible, and demanding Julius II and the introverted and temperamental Michelangelo was hardly a meeting of like minds. The colossal tomb was left unfinished when Julius got carried away instead with plans for St. Peter's. Irritated, Michelangelo abandoned Rome in 1504, but Julius managed to sweet-talk the moody artist into returning to Rome to paint the **Sistine Chapel** ceiling. Mikey spent the next four years slaving over—or rather under—the problem-ridden project, beginning by learning how to paint frescoes. In the following years, he threw away the his original pictorial design, redesigned his plans, fired his assistants, and ended up doing the whole job himself. The ceiling was finished in 1512, four months before Julius's death, and Michelangelo escaped to Florence. Thirty years later, Michelangelo returned to Rome, greeted by the new Pope Paul II, who called the aged Michelangelo back to the Sistine Chapel for arguably his most important work, **The Last Judgment** (p. 148). Michelangelo would continue his architectural designs, but he would never paint again. Before his death at the age of 89, he expressed his wish to be buried in Florence. To circumvent the Romans, who would certainly want to claim Michelangelo's body, his casket was smuggled to Florence and interred.

Michelangelo's Florentine contemporary **Raphael** (Raffaello Sanzio) also made the obligatory pilgrimage to Rome for prestige and generous papal commissions. Julius had him fresco his private rooms, now world-famous as the **Raphael Stanze.** Raphael profited from his stay in the Vatican to covertly learn some of Michelangelo's techniques for creating realistic and dynamic art, much to Michelangelo's annoyance.

BERNINI + BORROMINI = BAROQUE

The Baroque in Rome can be summed up in the work of two heavily lionized artists: **Gian Lorenzo Bernini** and **Francesco Castelli Borromini.** The personality differences between effervescent, cavalier boy-genius Bernini and dark, temperamental Borromini are abundantly clear in their works. Known as the "greatest European" in his day, the architect, sculptor, painter, and dandy Bernini more than set the standard for the Baroque during his prolific career. Bernini's father, a Florentine sculptor, brought his son to Rome to start work; he was immediately signed on for training and didn't stop working until the age of 80. He died having worked for every pope that was in power during his lifetime.

Along with his charged **St. Teresa in Ecstasy** (in Santa Maria della Vittoria), Bernini's Hellenistic **David** (in the Galleria Borghese, p. 150) stands in great contrast to Michelangelo's classical version. Although sculpture was only one facet of Bernini's career, he made great contributions to Rome in the architecture department. The oval of the *piazza* of St. Peter's was the culmination of a life's work; he personally supervised the construction of each and every one of the 284 Doric columns of travertine marble. Bernini's churches and monuments (including the grand **baldacchino** at St. Peter's and his own favorite, the **church of Sant'Andrea al Quirinale**) exemplify the exuberantly showy, theatrical, illusory style that came to define the Baroque.

The non-conformist Swiss **Borromini** spent much of his career fitfully working against the gaudy showiness of the Baroque. Borromini was commissioned to design some of the details on Bernini's *baldacchino*, but it became increasingly apparent that Bernini and Borromini's styles were wholly incompatible. In works like the **church of San Carlo alle Quattro Fontane,** Borromini created an entirely new architectural vocabulary that fused sculpture and architecture. Eventually the complexity of Borromini's work caught up with him; he became obsessed with his calculations and machinations and withdrew completely from society. A few days after burning a final series of architectural plans, he impaled himself on a sword.

NEOCLASSICAL RE-REVIVAL

In the late 1700s, southern Italy would provide the long-awaited reaction to the Baroque in the form of **Neoclassicism.** Morbidly infected by the excitement surrounding the excavations in Pompeii, Herculaneum, and Paestum, Neoclassical artists reasserted the values of Greco-Roman art that the Renaissance already had taken a shot at imitating. The greatest artists of this period weren't Roman but they soon immigrated to Rome. Foremost among the Neoclassicists was **Jacques-Louis David** (1748-1825), who studied in Rome at the French Academy. In sculpture, the coldly pure lines of **Antonio Canova** also found fans, leading the Borghese to install some of his marble statues in their gardens.

Pope Benedict XIV preferred restoring Rome for tourists over conducting church business; street signs and historical markers appeared for the first time. He commissioned paintings for St. Peter's and mosaics for Santa Maria Maggiore (redesigned by prominent architect **Fernando Fuga**). Baroque artists managed to resist the tide of Neoclassicism, as **Nicola Salvi**'s Baroque Trevi Fountain (p. 104)—completed in 1762—testifies. The tumultuous Risorgimento put a damper on construction in the mid-1800s; once the country was unified, large-scale building began, to accommodate the new government. The undeveloped area east, southeast, and northeast of Termini was soon crowded with apartment buildings. A number of buildings were lost in expansion, including Henry James's favorite, the Villa Ludovisi.

FASCIST ART

Mussolini was one of the biggest builders of public works since the cadre of popes who built St. Peter's and the rest of the Vatican complex. Most of the monuments he erected, like his philosophy, are pompous, rigid, geometrical, and based on an artistic model that subjugates the individual to the public masses. Much of the Fascist legacy in Roman architecture can be found in the **EUR** neighborhood on the outskirts of Rome (p. 135), including one building (the Palace of Labor) that architect **Marcello Piancentini** described proudly as a "square Colosseum." The **Foro Italico,** meant to be the monumental symbolic center for a heroic nation, is also a prime example of the Fascist notion of artistic expression—not too different from their notion of political expression. Note the excessive use of "DUCE A NOI" in the tilework, as well as the nude figures wrestling, swimming, laboring, and piloting biplanes.

POST-FASCIST ART

Things got a little more complicated and a lot less megalomaniacal after Mussolini was out of the picture. Although Italy and Rome are perhaps best known in modern times for their celluloid art (see p. 58 for more info on Italian cinema), Italian visual artists had some degree of fame. Several turned to more traditional forms for less than traditional purposes: neo-*neo*-Classicist Felice Casarotti kicked it with the old *old* school, while **Giorgio di Chirico** painted surrealist landscapes that combined ancient Roman architecture with signs of Italian modernity like trains and cars—Vespa meets Vespatian, so to speak. Textures and artistic materials also became more important, with Lucio Fontana exploring the aesthetics of the disgusting in sculpture and painting, and multimedia sculptor **Alberto Burri** melding masterpieces out of scraps of plastic, fabric, and cellophane. No tour of Roman museums is complete without ogling **Amedeo Modigliani**'s paintings of voluptuously sexy nude women—they're always lurking around the corner in Roman museums.

MASS MEDIA: AN INTRODUCTION

Rome became my home as soon as I saw it. I was born that moment.
That was my *real* birthday.
-Federico Fellini

THE BIG SCREEN

To see Rome's most significant gift to 20th-century art, stroll past the myriad museums, and head into a movie theater. Years before Hollywood began to pump teeny-bopper flicks and creative manifestos, the **Cines** studios were alive and kicking (in addition to making the occasional movie) in the Eternal City. Constructed in 1905-6, Cines created the Italian "super-spectacle"—extravagant, larger than life productions, recreating major historical events. **Enrico Guzzani**'s incredible *Quo Vadis* enjoyed international success as the first "blockbuster" in cinematic history.

Recognizing the power of popular cinema, Mussolini created the *Centro Sperimentale della Cinematografia*, a national film school, and the mammoth **Cinecitta studios.** The famous director and secret Marxist, **Luigi Chiarini**, attracted many students—including **Roberto Rossellini** and **Michelangelo Antonini,** both of whom rose to well-deserved directorial fame after the war. Mussolini generally steered clear of the aesthetic aspects of film, but did institute a few "imperial edicts," among them one that forbid laughing at the Marx Brothers' *Duck Soup.* After the fall of Fascism, filmmakers embraced their newfound freedom, producing an explosion of **Neorealist cinema. Luchino Visconti**'s 1942 work *Ossessione* and Rossellini's *Roma, Citta Aperta.*

FELLINI

Federico Fellini rejected the Neorealists' use of such archaic elements as "plot" and "characters" to portray a world of moments and witnesses. The city of Rome is a central image in his work. In *Nights of Cabiria* (1957), his wife Giulietta Masina gives a heartrending performance as a Roman prostitute. *8½* (1963) the quintessential exploration of writer's block is one of the most critically acclaimed films of all time. In his autobiographical *Roma* (1972), a stand-in for the director encounters yet another bizarre parade of characters, focusing on the city itself, probing how imagined Rome (and the director's nostalgia) are often in direct conflict with reality. *La Dolce Vita* (1960), banned by the pope, but widely regarded as *the* representative Italian film, scrutinizes the unscrupulously stylish Rome of the 1950s. In the movie, a buxom, blonde Anita Ekberg leaps into the Trevi Fountain, starting such a widespread trend that the Italian government had to pass laws prohibiting wading.

ANTONIONI

Fellini's colleague, Michelangelo Antonioni, was even more extreme in his refusal to conform to the artificial constraints of form, in terms of plot line, conflict, and resolution. He frustrated his audiences expectations by following internal rhythms, deconstructing traditional cause and effect plot sequencing, creating a highly stylized brand of cinematic purity. His first major works form a sort of conceptual trilogy

L'Avventura (1960) examines the lack of meaning in upper-class life by focusing on the effects of a woman's disappearance on her friends. *La Notte* (1960) is a masterful study of the failure of communication. *L'Eclisse* (1962), continues his study of the moral vacuum by portraying a succession of relationships damned by materialism. *Blow-Up* (1967), filmed in English, is ostensibly the story of a photographer in London who inadvertently films a murder, and manages to utterly reconceive the uses of sound and visual imagery in film.

PASOLINI

Pier Paolo Pasolini—who spent as much time on trial for his politics as he did making movies—remains Italy's most controversial director. For Pasolini, Rome was more than his birthplace or the setting for his films—it was his inspiration. An ardent Marxist, he set his first films in the Roman underworld of poverty and prostitution. One of his early works, *Mamma Roma* (1962), chronicles the allegorical downfall of a passionate and maternal whore who repeatedly tries to prevent her son from joining a band of criminals. He moved from his Neorealist roots to an emphasis on myth and ideology, making film adaptations of *Oedipus Rex* (1967), the *Decameron* (1970), and the *Thousand and One Nights* (1974). His austere *Gospel of St. Matthew* (1964), made without professional actors, has been called the greatest film about the life of Christ. Pasolini's final film, *Salo* (1975), is an extremely controversial adaptation of the Marquis de Sade's *The 120 Days of Sodom.* He set the Marquis's novel in World War II Italy, and the nihilistic violence has been interpreted as an indictment of Italian compliance with fascism and capitalism. Often regarded as the most obscene film ever, *Salo* is still banned in Australia. Pasolini's radical politics, homosexuality, and alleged pedophilia made him rather unpopular with right-wing groups. He was murdered by a hustler in Ostia in 1975.

BERTOLUCCI

Much less controversial, although still decidedly leftist, are the films of Bernardo Bertolucci. His 1970 masterpiece, *The Conformist,* studies the effects of fascism on a weak-willed man. *Last Tango in Paris* (1972) features what some have termed Marlon Brando's greatest performance ever, playing an expatriate immersed in a doomed love affair. Once controversial for its portrayal of anonymous sexual encounters, it now seems relatively tame. The Italian film industry boycotted Bertolucci for what they saw as the pornography and excessive internationalism of his style. The boycott forced him abroad, leaving him free to direct such Hollywood epics as *The Last Emperor* (1987), a version of Paul Bowles's *The Sheltering Sky* (1990), and the rather muddled *Little Buddha* (1993). After a 20-year exile Bertolucci returned to Italy to shoot *Stealing Beauty* (1996) and *L'Assedio* (1998).

ROSSELLINI

One of the pioneers of Neorealism, Roberto Rossellini is best known for his early work—inexpensively shot, edgy films focusing on life in a war-torn nation. The most famous is the superb *Roma Citta Aperta* (1945) which boasts a performance by Anna Magnani, and was shot almost exclusively on location in real houses and apartments in a Rome ripped apart by conflict. His later films are more glossy, polished, and Romantically styled. Rossellini is also known for his publicized affair with Ingrid Bergman, who after writing him a fan letter, became his lover, subsequently leaving her husband (and the middle-class morality of Hollywood) to marry him.

COMMEDIA DELLA CINEMA

Unlike Bertolucci, Italian comic filmmakers have found a great deal of support and success at home in the mother country. Directors such as **Nanno Moretti,** creator of the *Caro Diario* (*Dear Diary;* 1994), and **Lina Wertmuller,** maker of such complex and explosively funny films as *Seven Beauties* (1976) and 1993's popular *Ciao, Professore!* have managed to provide a viable alternative to Hollywood's ubiquitous romantic comedies. Perhaps the best known of the group is the charmingly eccentric actor and director, **Roberto Benigni** (who also starred in *Ciao, Professore!*) romped victoriously through the 1999 Academy Awards for his controversial Holocaust-set comedy *La Vita e Bella* (*Life is Beautiful*).

THE SMALL SCREEN

If you thought American TV was a bit sexist, you've never checked out the male-dominated playland that is Italian television. Game shows, news, even children's programs are populated by voluptuous (frequently topless), long-legged bombshells in flashy clothes. Italian programming comes in two main varieties—the three vaguely educational, state-owned **RAI** channels, and the often shamelessly vapid networks owned by prime minister Silvio Berlusconi. Italia Uno, Rete 4, and Canale 5 broadcast all your favorite Aaron Spelling reruns (from 'Saved by the Bell" to "Beverly Hills, 90210"). The Italian music television channel is **Magic,** which brings you music videos from an idiot cousin of pop music. Late-night TV brings a barrage of dubbed movies and graphic half-hour advertisements for phone sex.

Elementary school-aged children dash home every day after school to watch **Non E la RAI,** a variety show featuring scantily clad young women dancing and lip-syncing to all their favorite tunes. You can even spy the hostess Ambra, singer of the song "Aspettavo Te," outside the studios near San Giovanni in Laterano. Those brushing up on Italian pop culture can watch and learn from countless game shows like **La Ruota della Fortuna** and **OK: Il Prezzo E Giusto,** on which Italians humiliate themselves for cash. One game show polls the audience with multiple choice questions and then publicly mocks and humiliates the people who answer incorrectly.

MUSIC

The Italians have long been slaves to a pretty tune. Italians, with help from the French, invented the system for musical notation still in use today. Before Julie Andrews came along as a singing nun in curtain couture, there was Guido D'Arezzo, who invented *solfege*, the "do, re, mi" syllable system of expressing the musical scale. A 16th-century Venetian printed the first musical scores with moveable type. Cremona offered violins by Stradivarius and Guarneri; the piano (actually *piano-forte*, which means "soft-loud") is an Italian invention. For Italians, vocal music has always occupied the position of highest glory. **Madrigals,** free-flowing secular songs for three to six voices, grew in popularity. One of the greatest contributors to Italian madrigals and sacred music was **Giovanni Pierluigi Palestrina.** Born and bred in Lazio, he served as a choirboy at the Church of Santa Maria Maggiore and went on to direct choirs at Santa Maria Maggiore, San Giovanni in Laterno.

OPERA

Born in 16th-century Florence, nurtured in Venice, and revered in Milan, the opera is the greatest musical innovation in Italian history. Invented by the **Camerata,** an artsy clique of Florentine poets, noblemen, authors, and musicians, opera began as an attempt to recreate the dramas of ancient Greece by setting lengthy poems to music. As opera spread from Florence to Venice, Milan, and Rome, the styles and forms of the genre grew increasingly distinct. Contemporaneous with the birth of opera was the emergence of the **oratorio.** Introduced by the Roman priest **St. Philip Neri,** the oratorio set biblical text to dramatic choral and instrumental accompaniment.

In opera, Baroque ostentation yielded to classical demands of moderation. To today's opera buffs, The words "Italian opera" generally connote Rossini, Bellini, Donzietti, Verdi, and Puccini—all composers of the 19th and early 20th centuries. **Giuseppe Verdi** had become a national icon by mid-life, writing such masterpieces as as the tragic, triumphal *Aïda*, and *La Traviata.* Another great composer of the period, **Gioacchino Rossini,** boasted that he could produce music faster than copyists could reproduce it, but he proved such an infamous procrastinator that his agents resorted to locking him in a room with a single plate of spaghetti until he finished composing. Aparently that was some pretty amazing spaghetti, as his *Barber of Seville* remains a favorite of modern audiences. Finally, **Giacomo Puccini,** composer of *Madama Butterly*, deserves a nod for his kick-ass female characters (despite their various predispositions toward ending in tuberculosis or violent suicide).

INSTRUMENTAL MUSIC

Instrumental music began to establish itself as a legitimate enterprise in 17th-century Rome. During the Baroque period, **Corelli** developed the *concerto* form, distinguished by its contrasting moods and tempos, which added drama to technical expertise. **Antoni Vivaldi** wrote over 400 *concerti* while teaching at an orphanage in Venice. His *Four Seasons* remains one of the best-known Baroque orchestral works. In the mid-17th century, operatic overtures began to be performed separately, resulting in the creation of a new genre. The *sinfonia* (symphony) was modeled after the melody of operatic overtures, but simply detached from its setting. At the same time, composer **Domenico Scarlatti** wrote over 500 harpsichord sonatas.

Italy's choke-hold on the music world continued into the 19th century. Relying on pyrotechnical virtuosity and a personal style of mystery and scandal, violinist **Nicolo Paganini** brought Europe to its knees. One of the first musicians to make publicized concert tours, he inspired **Franz Liszt** to become a virtuoso pianist; the pair became the 19th-century equivalent of rock stars, complete with their very own groupies.

TWENTIETH CENTURY

Italian classical music continued to grow into the 20th century. **Otto Respighi,** composer of the popular *Pines of Rome* and *Foundations of Rome*, experimented with orchestral textures. Known for his work with meta-languages, **Luciano Berio** defied traditional instrumentation with his *Sequenza V* for solo trombone and mime, and other works for solo wind instruments and voice. Among performers, **Luciano Pavarotti** retains followers, despite the loss of his voice; his 1990 concert with the two "other" tenors, Placido Domingo and Jose Carreras, drew a full-capacity crowd to the Baths of Caracalla. A 1997 repeat filled the stadium at Modena, and the 1998 reunion during the World Cup in Paris reportedly drew one million people.

POP, ROCK, AND...RAP(?)

Once upon a time, Italian pop had its own unique and indigenous character, which blended Italian folk songs and Mediterranean rhythms with pop beats. Pino Daniele, Lucio Battisti, **Vasco Rossi,** and others used to perform folk-inspired ballads for captive audiences composed largely of university students. Since the 1980s, however, traditional Italian pop has been assimilated into the global hegemony of the American/British pop scene. Some of these earlier stars have faded from the pop sky, while others, like Rossi have adapted to suit the trends, and remain very popular. There are still a good number of native pop talents, among them Renato Zero, Gianna Nannini, **Laura Pausini,** and 883. The aging Renato keeps churning out hits, and the Romans love him for it: In the summer of '99 he was able to fill the Foro Italico for six nights in a row. Nini's "Lupi Solitari" was the anthem of all angsty 15-year-olds, while 883's ballad "Come Mai" has been suggested as the new Italian national anthem. Since Laura Pausini conquered the Italian pop scene, she has begun to try to swim in more international waters, albeit with somewhat uneven success.

Italian rock acts are generally better than their pop counterparts. **Zucchero,** who has played stadiums with the likes of Pavarotti and Sting, is the tried and true warhorse of Italian rock, with a solid international fan base as well. The above mentioned Vasco Rossi has turned from folk to rock; his "Rewind" was an anthemic hit in 1999. **Liftba,** with their U2-esque stylings and a lead-singer with highly impressive cheekbones, is perennially popular, though some fans complain that they have sold out, leaving their socially conscious roots in the wake of popular success.

Though many would be hard-pressed to believe it, Italian rap exists, and its not bad. Well, its not that bad. Well, its not *terrible...* The ultra-left wing and super-socially conscious **99 Posse**'s reggae and rap hybrid stylings were featured in the controversial film *Sud*, while curly-haired **Jovanotti** has turned from TV-variety-show pop star to rapper. **Articolo 31,** though its more pop/rock than rap, also puts in a good showing—it takes its name from the Italian law banning pot smoking, in case you were wondering. Rome's contributions to Italian-language rap include **Er Piotta,** whose "SuperCafone '99" ignited dance floors and *coatti* everywhere, the pseudo-gangster rapper **Flamino Maphia,** and **Colle de Fomento,** whose "Il Cielo su Roma" explains all you'll ever need to know about why living in Rome is so damn cool.

INSIDE

Sights

Turn all the pages of history, but Fortune never produced a greater example of her own fickleness than the city of Rome, once the most beautiful and magnificent of all that ever was or will be...not a city in truth, but a certain part of heaven.

—Poggio Bracciolini

Rome wasn't built in a day, and you won't see any substantial portion of it in 24 hours, (although you can try, using our one-day tour of Rome, p. 4). Ancient temples and forums, medieval churches, Renaissance basilicas, Baroque fountains, 19th-century museums, and Fascist architecture all cluster together in a city bursting with masterpieces from every era of Western civilization.

Whichever of the thousands of sights you choose to see, there are a few pieces of advice that pertain to almost all of them. First and foremost, most sights are best visited in the morning—the earlier, the better. Not only do you avoid the crowds (the Trevi fountain is sheer madness in the afternoon), but in the summer you miss the crushing heat that descends upon the city. Second, remember that most churches are only open from 8:30am to 12:30pm and from 4 to 7pm, so plan accordingly. Rome is possibly the greatest exposition of human endeavor on the planet. Let it overwhelm you.

Rome Major Museums and Monuments

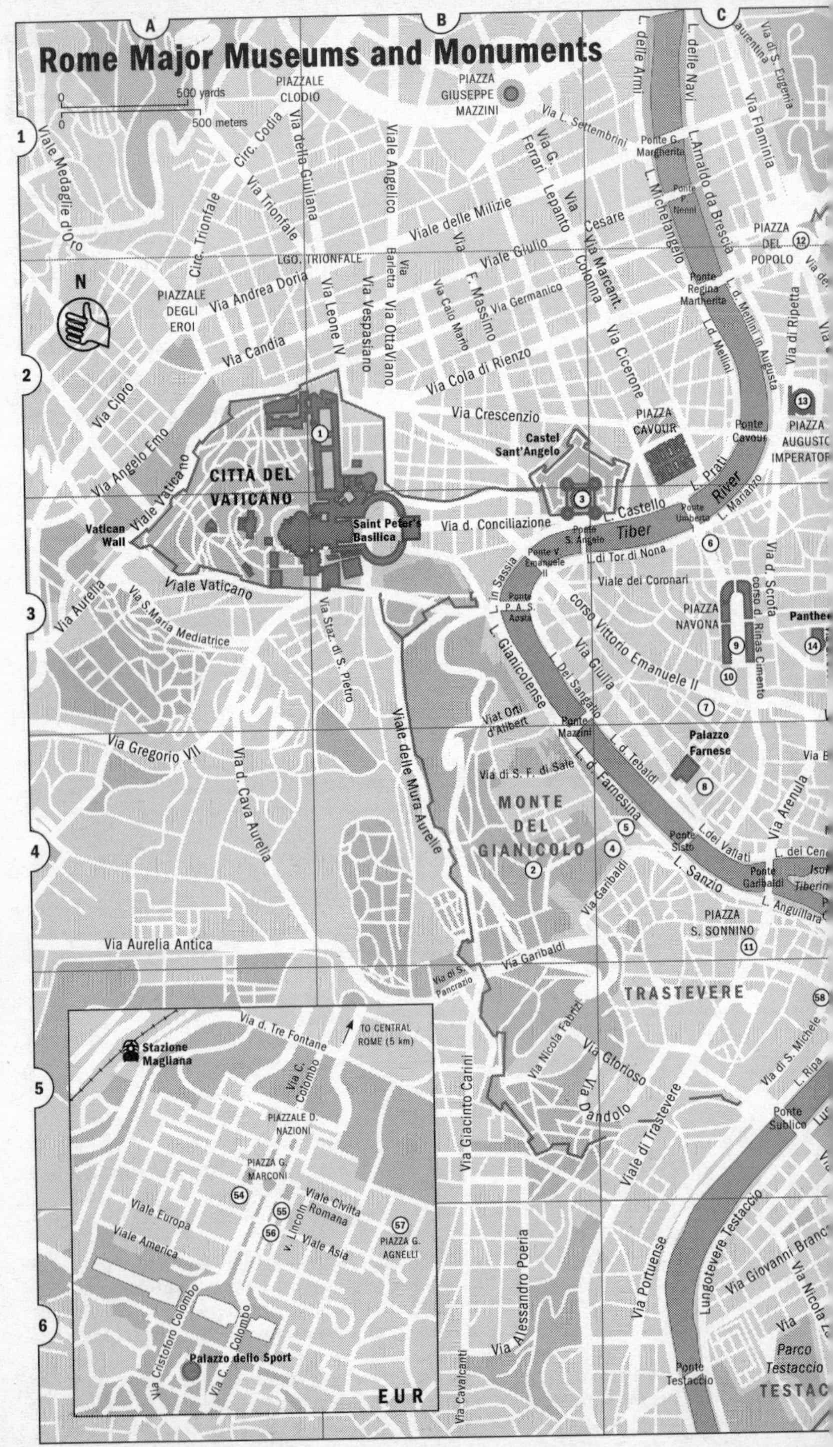

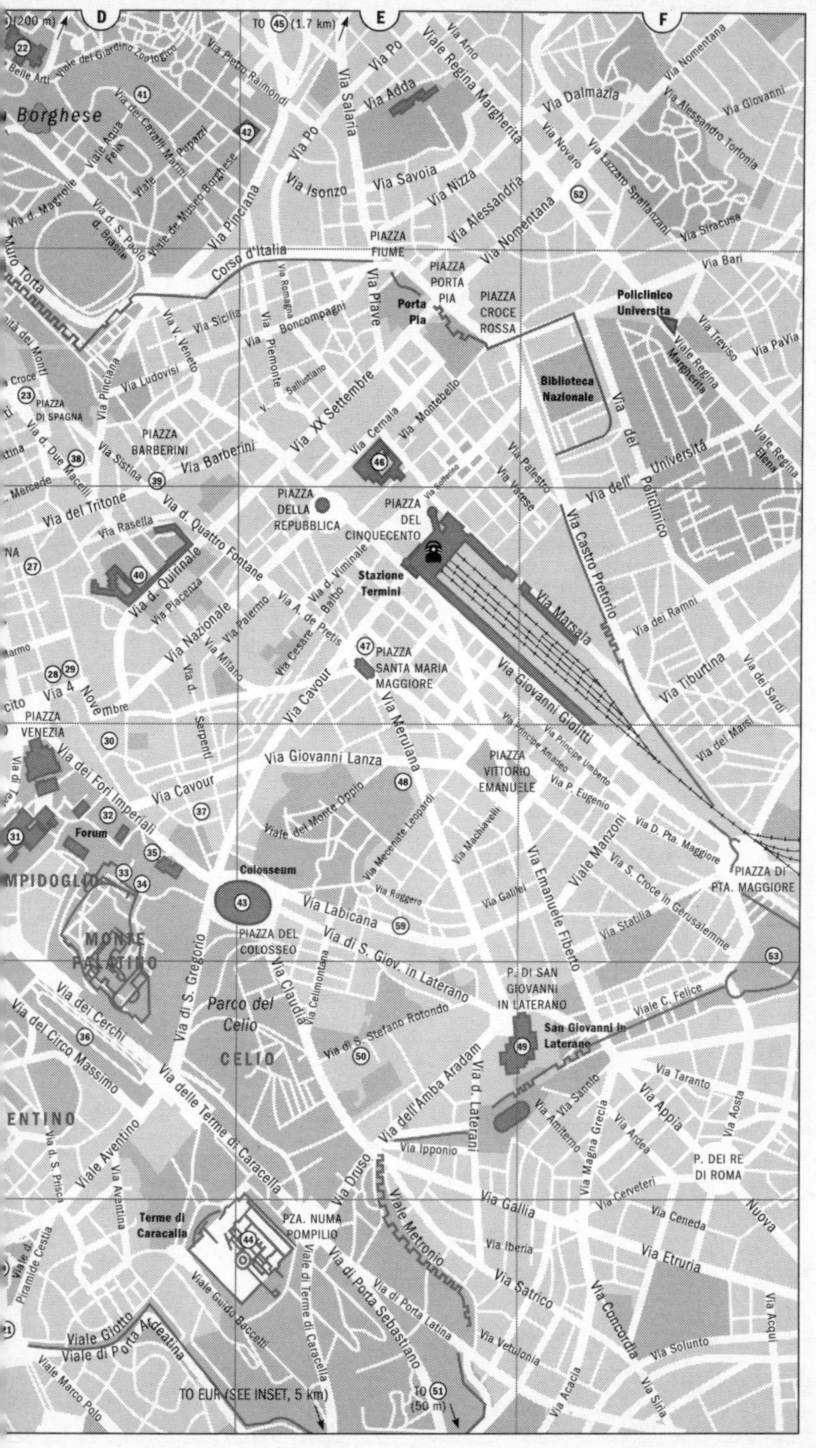
D
E
F
TO 45 (1.7 km)
Borghese
Viale del Giardino Zoologico
Via Pietro Raimondi
Via Po
Viale Regina Margherita
Via Salaria
Via Adda
Via Dalmazia
Via Nomentana
Via Alessandro Torlonia
Via Giovanni
Via Isonzo
Via Savoia
Via Nizza
Via Alessandria
Via Novaro
Via Lazzaro Spallanzani
Via Siracusa
Via Pinciana
PIAZZA FIUME
Corso d'Italia
Via Bari
PIAZZA PORTA PIA
Porta Pia
PIAZZA CROCE ROSSA
Policlinico Universita
Muro Torto
Via Piave
Via Sicilia
Via Boncompagni
Via Romagna
Via Piemonte
Via Treviso
Viale Regina Margherita
Via V. Veneto
Via Ludovisi
Biblioteca Nazionale
PIAZZA DI SPAGNA
Via Sallustiano
Via XX Settembre
Via Cernaia
Via Montebello
Via del Policlinico
PIAZZA BARBERINI
Via Barberini
Via Sistina
Via d. Due Macelli
Via Palestro
Via Varese
Via dell' Università
Viale Regina Elena
PIAZZA DELLA REPUBBLICA
PIAZZA DEL CINQUECENTO
Via Solferino
Via del Tritone
Via Rasella
Via d. Quattro Fontane
Via Castro Pretorio
Via d. Quirinale
Via Piacenza
Via d. Viminale
Via A. de Pretis
Stazione Termini
Via Marsala
Via dei Ramni
Via Nazionale
Via Palermo
Via Milano
Via Cesare Balbo
PIAZZA SANTA MARIA MAGGIORE
Via Tiburtina
Via dei Sardi
Via 4 Novembre
Via Cavour
Via Merulana
Via Giovanni Giolitti
PIAZZA VENEZIA
Via d. Serpenti
Via Principe Amadeo
Via Principe Umberto
Via dei Marsi
Via Giovanni Lanza
PIAZZA VITTORIO EMANUELE
Via dei Fori Imperiali
Via Cavour
Viale del Monte Oppio
Via P. Eugenio
Forum
Via Mecenate Leopardi
Via Machiavelli
Via D. Pta. Maggiore
Viale Manzoni
Via Emanuele Filiberto
PIAZZA DI PTA. MAGGIORE
Colosseum
Via Ruggero
Via Galilei
Via S. Croce in Gerusalemme
MONTE PALATINO
Via Labicana
Via Statilia
PIAZZA DEL COLOSSEO
Via di S. Giov. in Laterano
Via di S. Gregorio
Via Claudia
Via Celimontana
P. DI SAN GIOVANNI IN LATERANO
Viale C. Felice
Via dei Cerchi
Parco del Celio
Via di S. Stefano Rotondo
San Giovanni in Laterano
Via del Circo Massimo
CELIO
Via Taranto
Via delle Terme di Caracella
Via dell'Amba Aradam
Via d. Laterani
Via Sannio
Via Appia
Via Aosta
Via Amiterno
Via Magna Grecia
Via Ardea
Viale Aventino
Via Ipponio
P. DEI RE DI ROMA
Via d. S. Prisca
Via Aventina
Via Druso
Viale Metronio
Via Cerveteri
Via Gallia
Nuova
Terme di Caracalla
PZA. NUMA POMPILIO
Via Ceneda
Viale d. Piramide Cestia
Via Iberia
Via Etruria
Viale Guido Baccelli
Viale di Terme di Caracella
Via di Porta Latina
Via Satrico
Via Concordia
Via Acqui
Via di Porta Sebastiano
Viale Giotto
Viale di Porta Ardeatina
Via Vetulonia
Via Solunto
Viale Marco Polo
TO EUR (SEE INSET, 5 km)
TO 51 (50 m)
Via Acacia
Via Siria

MUSEUMS	
dell'Alto Medioevo, 56	A6
Antiquarium Palantino, 34	D4
d'Arte Ebraica, 17	C4
d'Arte Moderna, 22	D1
d'Arte Orientale, 48	E4
d'Arte e Tradizioni Populari, 54	A5
Barracco, 7	C3
Borghese, 42	E1
Campidoglio (Capitoline), 31	D4
Canonica, 41	D1
delle Cere (Waxworks), 28	D3
delle Civilatà Romana, 57	B6
Colonna, 29	D3
Communale d'Arte Moderna, 38	D2
Corsini, 4	C4
Doria Pamphilj, 24	D3
Keats-Shelley Memorial House, 23	D2
delle Mura, 51	E6
Mario Praz, 6	C3
Napoleonico, 6	C3
di Nazionale Etrusco, 15	C1
di Palazzo Venezia, 25	D4
Preistorico Etnografico, 55	A6
di Roma, 10	C3
Romano delle Terme, 46	E2
Spada, 8	E2
Degli Stumenti Musicali, 53	F4
Vatican Museums, 1	B2
Villa Farnesina, 5	C4

CHURCHES	
Domine Quo Vadis, 51	E6
Il Gesù, 16	C4
Pantheon, 14	C3
S. Cecilia in Trastevere, 59	E4
S. Clemente, 58	C5
S. Giovanni in Laterano, 49	F5
S. Maria in Cosmedin, 19	D4
S. Maria Maggiore, 47	E3
S. Maria del Popolo, 12	C1
S. Maria in Trastevere, 11	C4
S. Pietro in Vincoli, 37	D4
S. Stefano Rotondo, 50	E5
S. Trinità dei Monti, 23	D2
Sinagoga Ashkenazita, 17	C4

ROMAN MONUMENTS	
Ara Pacis, 13	C2
Basilica of Mazentius, 35	D4
Bocca della Verità, 19	D4
Campidoglio (Capitoline), 31	D4
Castel S. Angelo, 3	B3
Catacombs:	
S. Agnese, 52	F1
S. Callisto, 51	E6
S. Domitilla, 51	E6
S. Priscilla, 45	E1
S. Sebastiano, 51	E6
Colosseo (Colosseum), 43	E4
Circus Maximus, 36	D5
Fori Imperiali, 30	D4
The Forum, 32	D4
Mausolueum of Augustus, 13	C2
Pyramid (of Gaius Cestius), 21	D6
Teatro Marcello, 18	C4
Baths of Caracalla, 44	E6
Baths of Diocletian, 46	E2
Via Appia Antica (The Appian Way), 51	E6

PARKS AND FOUNTAINS	
Fontana dei Quattro Fiumi (Fountain of the Four Rivers), 9	C3
Fontana di Trevi, 27	D3
Fontana del Tritone, 39	D2
Giardino Zoologio, 26	D1
Orto Botanico, 2	B4
Protestant Cemetery, 20	D6

PIAZZE	
Campo dei Fiori, 8	C4
Piazza di Spagna (Spanish Steps), 23	D2
Piazza Augusto Imperiali, 13	C2
Piazza Barberini, 39	D2
Piazza del Cinquecento, 46	E2
Piazza del Colosseo, 43	E4
Piazza Navona, 9	C3
Piazza del Popolo, 12	C1
Piazza della Rotonda, 14	C3
Piazza Venezia, 25	D4

ANCIENT CITY

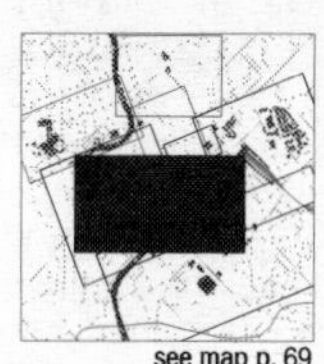
see map p. 69

In the midst of the countless, scattered stones of the **Roman Forum** and the **Palatine** stands a small, truncated column. This spot was the **Umbilicus Urbis,** the "navel of the city," marking the geographical center of the ancient city. More than any other monument in Rome, it symbolizes the Roman Forum and the larger city of Rome's past status as a veritable *ombelico del mondo*—the navel of the world, the center of all the ancient West's political, economic, social, and religious life. Despite the ravages of time, the glory of Rome's early history is still palpable. In a relatively small area, one can see the venues of Roman government, religion, entertainment, privilege, and even sanitation, although the volume of camera-and-bottled-water-toting tourists confounds attempts to recreate ancient Rome in your mind. Exploring the ancient city is time-consuming and involves a great deal of walking; **give yourself a full day to visit the Forum, Palatine, and Colosseum thoroughly.**

ESSENTIAL INFORMATION

CHURCH ETIQUETTE

It's not nice to walk into a church in the middle of mass unless you intend to participate. At all times, refrain from speaking loudly, parading directly in front of the altar, and taking flash photographs.

While some churches strictly adhere to established dress codes (no shorts, short skirts, bare midriffs, or tank tops), others may not be so adamant. Even in the latter case, however, grubbiness and bare skin will generally attract disapproving stares from pious Italians; wear modest clothing if you plan on going church-hopping. Another option is to keep a large scarf or sarong stashed in your backpack and to drape it over your immodestly bare flesh before entering houses of worship. Men may just have to suck it up and wear light cotton pants.

ROMAN FORUM

Main entrance: *V.d. Fori Imperiali (at Largo C. Ricci, between P. Venezia and the Colosseum).* ***Other entrances*** *are opposite the Colosseum (from here, you can reach the Palatine Hill, too) and at the Clivus Capitolinus, near P. del Campidoglio. M: B-Colosseo, or bus to P. Venezia.* ***Open*** *M-Sa 9am-6:30pm, Su 9am-1pm; in winter M-Sa 9am-1hr. before sunset, Su 9am-1hr. before sunset; sometimes closes M-F 3pm, Su and holidays noon. Free.* ***Guided tour*** *with archaeologist L6000/€3.20; audioguide tour for Forum L7000/€3.62 in English, French, German, Italian, Japanese, or Spanish; both available at main entrance.*

The Forum, once a marshland prone to flooding and eschewed by Rome's Iron Age (1000-900 BC) inhabitants, spreads from the Colosseum west toward the Capitoline Hill. Today, many of the Forum's structures are reduced to piles of jagged rocks, and the locations of many sites are just hypotheses. Access is unpredictable, as you never know which areas will be fenced off because of excavation or restoration.

In the 7th and 8th centuries BC, Etruscans and Greeks used the Tiber Island as a crossing point for trade and the Forum as a market. Rome was founded as a market town for sober farmers who came to trade and perform religious rites; the Romans were peacefully dominated by the more advanced Etruscans until 510 BC, when the Republic was established. The **Curia,** the meeting place of the Senate; the **Comitium Well,** or assembly place; the **three sacred trees** of Rome; and the **Rostra,** the speaker's platform, were built here to serve the young government. The earliest **temples** (to Saturn and to Castor and Pollux) were dedicated in honor of the revolution. The already extant **Via Sacra,** Rome's oldest street, became the main thoroughfare of the young city. The conquest of Greece in the 2nd century BC brought new architectural forms to the city, including the lofty **Basilica Aemilia,** used as a center for business and judicial work before Christians co-opted the form for their churches.

The Forum was never reserved for a single activity. Senators debated the fates of far-flung nations over the din of haggling traders. The **Vestal Virgins** kept the city's eternal flame burning in their house on a street full of prostitutes, who kept flames of a different sort burning. Elsewhere, priests offered sacrifices in the temples, generals led triumphal

BENITO MUSSOLINI: SAGE AND SEER

On one of the walls of the Ancient Forum, facing V.d. Foro Imperiale, four large marble maps of Europe—from Northern Africa to Scandinavia, the Atlantic Ocean to the Caspian Sea—delineate Rome's dominance over the years. Roman territories are in white, the rest of the map is in black. The first one (on the left) is of Rome in its beginnings, 8th century BC, when only the city itself is white. The next three show Rome's expanded empire, from 146 BC (the end of the Punic Wars) to AD 14 (death of Augustus) to AD 117 (end of Trajan's reign). By the fourth map, two-thirds of Europe, North Africa, Mesopotamia, and Britannia are white. Very nice. Look at the wall directly to the right of the last map. Behind a tree, there's a large discolored space on the bricks. Apparently Mussolini had constructed a fifth map to hang there in 1937, celebrating Rome's imminent renewed dominion over Europe. After Mussolini died, the map disappeared, only to be uncovered in pieces in the attic of an American soldier three decades later. Now it's to be found in the Capitoline Museums (see p. 152).

processions up to the Capitoline, and pickpockets pickpocketed tourists without the aid of bus #64.

The Forum witnessed political turbulence in the Republic in the first century BC. **Cicero**'s orations against the antics of corrupt young aristocrats echoed off the temple walls and **Julius Caesar**'s dead body was cremated, amid rioting crowds, in the small temple that bears his name. Augustus, Caesar's great-nephew and adopted son, exploited the Forum to support his new government, closing off the old town square with a temple to the newly deified Caesar and building a triumphal arch honoring himself. His successors followed suit, clotting the old markets with successively grander tokens of their majesty (often looted from the monuments of their predecessors). The construction of the imperial palace on the Palatine in the first century AD, and of new *fora* on higher ground to the north, cleared out the old neighborhoods around the square. By the 2nd century, the Forum, though packed with gleaming white monuments, had become a deserted ceremonial space. Barbarian invaders of the 5th century burned and looted the Forum, and Constantine's Christian city government had the pagan temples closed.

In the Middle Ages, many buildings were converted to churches and alms houses; marble was stolen and the Forum gradually became Campo Vaccino, a cow pasture, with only the tallest columns peeking through the tall grass. The last bits of the Forum's accesible marble were quarried by Renaissance popes for their own monumental constructions. Excavations since 1803 have uncovered a vast array of remnants, but also rendered the site extremely confusing—the ruins of structures built over and on top of each other for more than a thousand years are now exposed to a single view. For more on the Forum's past, see **History,** p. 39.

CIVIC CENTER

The Forum's main entrance ramp leads directly to V. Sacra. To the right, the Capitoline Hill and the Arch of Septimius Severus stand in the distance. V. Sacra cuts through the old market square and civic center; the ***Basilica Aemilia*** *is to your immediate right, and the brick* ***Curia*** *building is just beyond.*

BASILICA AEMILIA

Completed in 179 BC, the Basilica Aemilia was the judicial center of ancient Rome. It also housed the guild of the *argentarii* (moneychangers), who operated the city's first *cambiomat* and provided Roman *denarii* for traders and tourists (doubtless at the same great rates found today at Termini). The basilica was damaged several times by fire and rebuilt; in the pavement you can see bronze marks from the melted coins lost in these blazes. Money might have been able to buy love in some of the seedier parts of the Forum,but it couldn't stop the basilica's destruction by Alaric and the Goths in AD 410.

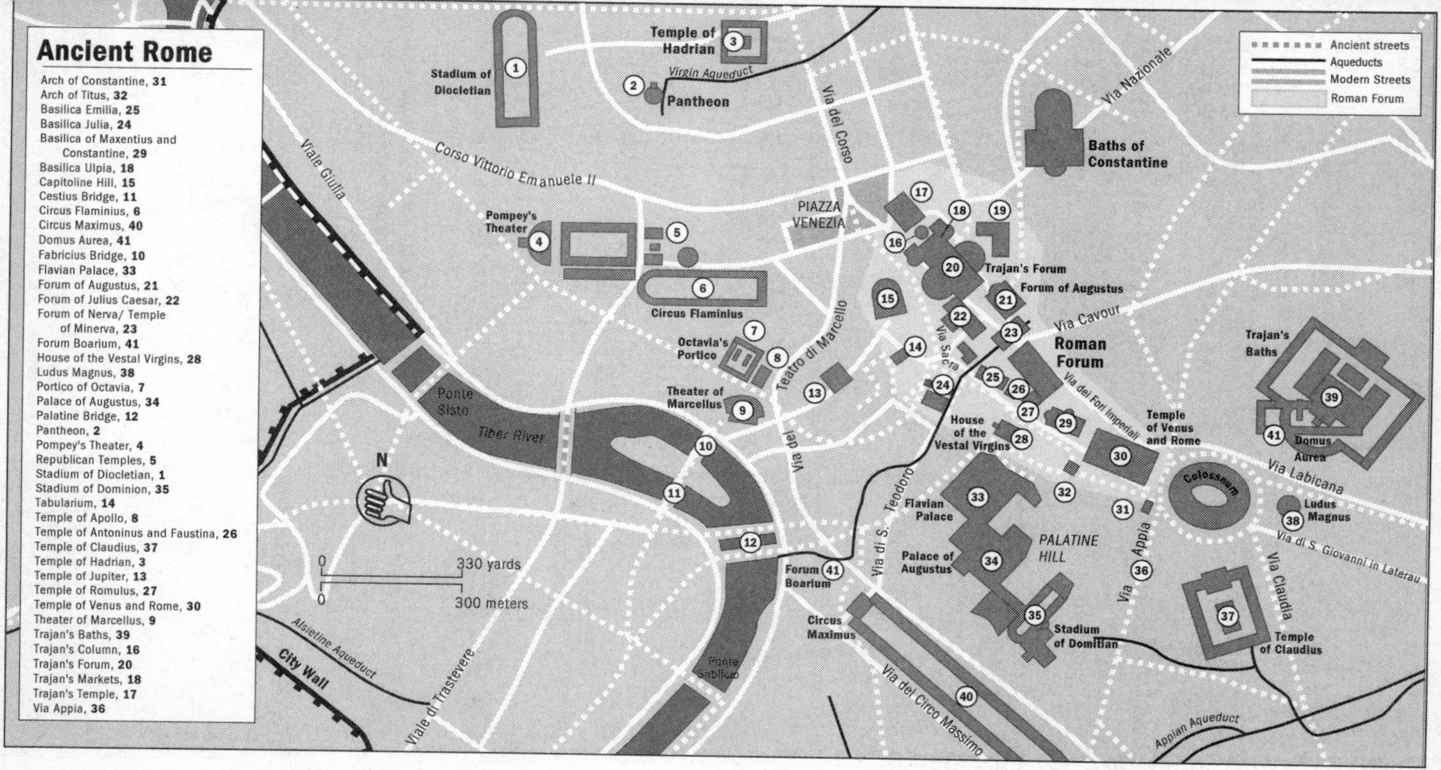

Ancient Rome

Arch of Constantine, **31**
Arch of Titus, **32**
Basilica Emilia, **25**
Basilica Julia, **24**
Basilica of Maxentius and Constantine, **29**
Basilica Ulpia, **18**
Capitoline Hill, **15**
Cestius Bridge, **11**
Circus Flaminius, **6**
Circus Maximus, **40**
Domus Aurea, **41**
Fabricius Bridge, **10**
Flavian Palace, **33**
Forum of Augustus, **21**
Forum of Julius Caesar, **22**
Forum of Nerva/ Temple of Minerva, **23**
Forum Boarium, **41**
House of the Vestal Virgins, **28**
Ludus Magnus, **38**
Portico of Octavia, **7**
Palace of Augustus, **34**
Palatine Bridge, **12**
Pantheon, **2**
Pompey's Theater, **4**
Republican Temples, **5**
Stadium of Diocletian, **1**
Stadium of Dominion, **35**
Tabularium, **14**
Temple of Apollo, **8**
Temple of Antoninus and Faustina, **26**
Temple of Claudius, **37**
Temple of Hadrian, **3**
Temple of Jupiter, **13**
Temple of Romulus, **27**
Temple of Venus and Rome, **30**
Theater of Marcellus, **9**
Trajan's Baths, **39**
Trajan's Column, **16**
Trajan's Forum, **20**
Trajan's Markets, **18**
Trajan's Temple, **17**
Via Appia, **36**

Ancient streets
Aqueducts
Modern Streets
Roman Forum

Stadium of Diocletian
Temple of Hadrian
Virgin Aqueduct
Pantheon
Via del Corso
Via Nazionale
Baths of Constantine
Viale Giulia
Corso Vittorio Emanuele II
Pompey's Theater
PIAZZA VENEZIA
Trajan's Forum
Forum of Augustus
Circus Flaminius
Via Cavour
Octavia's Portico
Teatro di Marcello
Via Sacra
Roman Forum
Trajan's Baths
Theater of Marcellus
Via dei Fori Imperiali
Ponte Sisto
Tiber River
House of the Vestal Virgins
Temple of Venus and Rome
Domus Aurea
Via del
Colosseum
Via Labicana
N
Via di S. Teodoro
Flavian Palace
Ludus Magnus
PALATINE HILL
Via Appia
Palace of Augustus
Via di S. Giovanni in Laterau
Forum Boarium
330 yards
300 meters
Via Claudia
Circus Maximus
Stadium of Domitian
Temple of Claudius
Alsietine Aqueduct
City Wall
Viale di Trastevere
Ponte Sublicio
Via del Circo Massimo
Appian Aqueduct

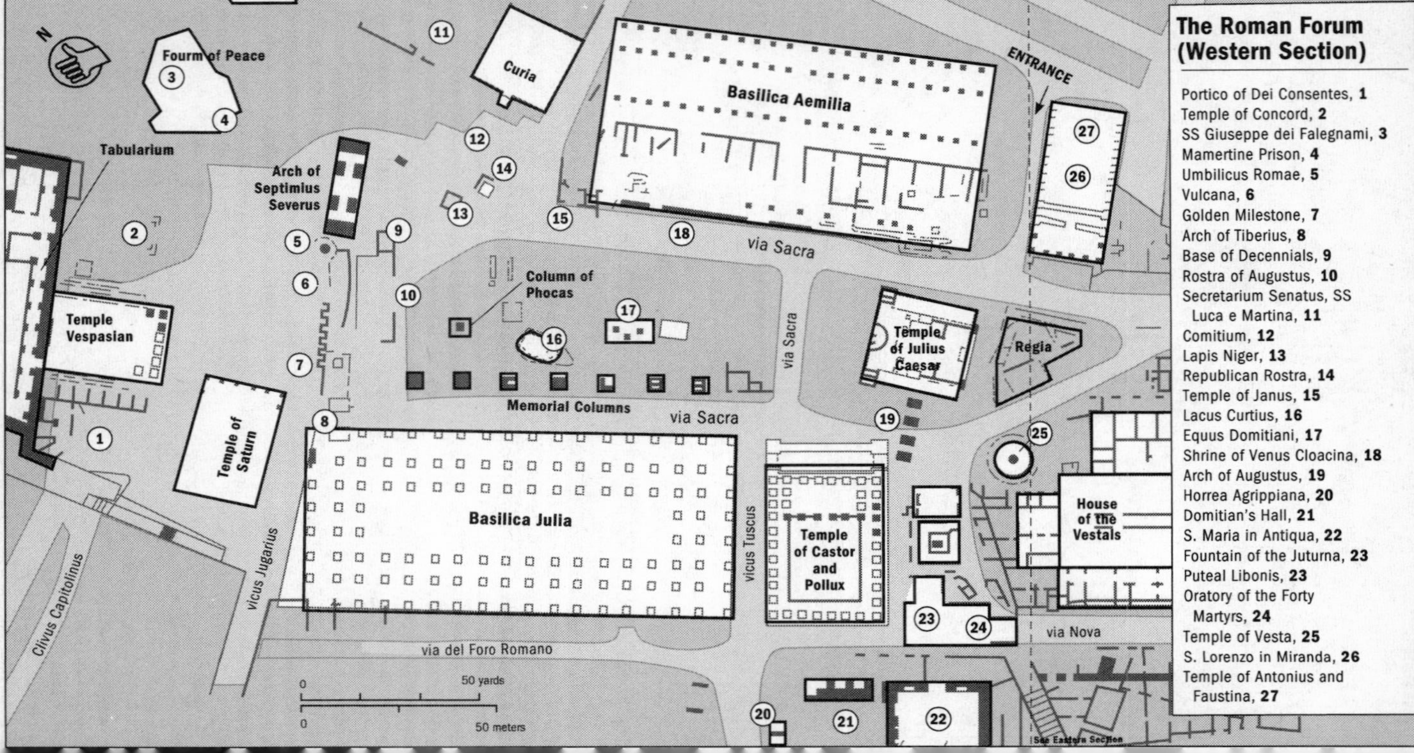

The Roman Forum (Western Section)
Portico of Dei Consentes, 1
Temple of Concord, 2
SS Giuseppe dei Falegnami, 3
Mamertine Prison, 4
Umbilicus Romae, 5
Vulcana, 6
Golden Milestone, 7
Arch of Tiberius, 8
Base of Decennials, 9
Rostra of Augustus, 10
Secretarium Senatus, SS Luca e Martina, 11
Comitium, 12
Lapis Niger, 13
Republican Rostra, 14
Temple of Janus, 15
Lacus Curtius, 16
Equus Domitiani, 17
Shrine of Venus Cloacina, 18
Arch of Augustus, 19
Horrea Agrippiana, 20
Domitian's Hall, 21
S. Maria in Antiqua, 22
Fountain of the Juturna, 23
Puteal Libonis, 23
Oratory of the Forty Martyrs, 24
Temple of Vesta, 25
S. Lorenzo in Miranda, 26
Temple of Antonius and Faustina, 27
N
Fourm of Peace
Tabularium
Curia
Basilica Aemilia
ENTRANCE
Arch of Septimius Severus
Temple Vespasian
Temple of Saturn
Column of Phocas
Memorial Columns
via Sacra
Temple of Julius Caesar
Regia
Basilica Julia
vicus Tuscus
vicus Jugarius
Clivus Capitolinus
Temple of Castor and Pollux
House of the Vestals
via Nova
via del Foro Romano
0
50 yards
50 meters
See Eastern Section

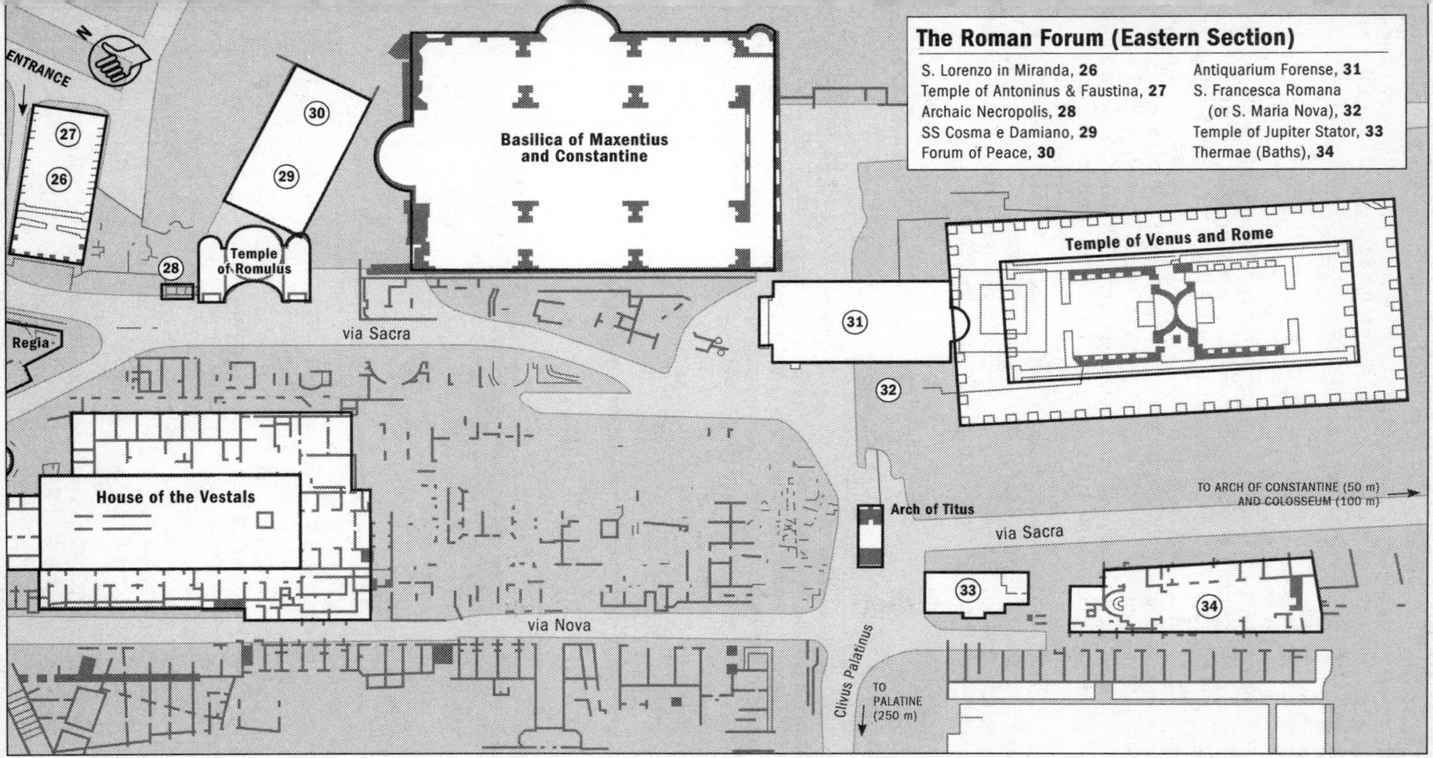

The Roman Forum (Eastern Section)

S. Lorenzo in Miranda, **26**
Temple of Antoninus & Faustina, **27**
Archaic Necropolis, **28**
SS Cosma e Damiano, **29**
Forum of Peace, **30**
Antiquarium Forense, **31**
S. Francesca Romana (or S. Maria Nova), **32**
Temple of Jupiter Stator, **33**
Thermae (Baths), **34**

ENTRANCE
N
Regia
Temple of Romulus
Basilica of Maxentius and Constantine
Temple of Venus and Rome
House of the Vestals
via Sacra
via Nova
Arch of Titus
Clivus Palatinus
TO PALATINE (250 m)
TO ARCH OF CONSTANTINE (50 m) AND COLOSSEUM (100 m)

The broken bases of columns are all that remain of the interior. The foundations of the row of *tabernae* (shops) that once faced the Forum are still visible along the path. In the back right corner of the basilica are reliefs of the *Rape of the Sabine Women* and the *Death of Tarpeia.*

CURIA

To the left of Basilica Aemilia (as you face it) stands the Curia, or Senate House, one of the oldest buildings in the Forum. Its origins go back to Tullus Hostilius, the 3rd king of Rome, though the structure of the building dates only from the time of Diocletian (AD 283). It was converted to a church in 630 and only recently restored by Mussolini to reveal inlaid Egyptian marble pavement and the long steps where the senators placed their own chairs for meetings. The stone base shows where Augustus's legendary golden statue of Victory rested until the end of the 4th century, when Christian senators irked by paganism chose to get rid of it. The Curia also houses the **Plutei of Trajan,** two sculpted parapets that decorated the Rostrum, depicting the burning of the tax registers and the distribution of food to poor children. To the left of the Curia is the **Church of Santi Luca e Martina,** once the **Secretarium Senatus.** Farther up the hill, below the **Church of San Giuseppe dei Falegnami,** is the 2nd-century BC **Mamertine Prison** (p. 84), where St. Peter is said to have been imprisoned and miraculously made water appear to use in the baptism of his cellmates.

COMITIUM

The broad space in front of the Curia was the Comitium, where male citizens came to vote and representatives of the people gathered for public discussion. This space was also home to the famed **Twelve Tables,** bronze tablets upon which the first codified laws of the Republic were inscribed. To the left of the Arch of Septimius Severus is the large brick **Rostrum,** or speaker's platform, erected by Julius Caesar in 44 BC (just before his death). The term *rostra* refers to the metal ramrods on the bows of warships. *Rostra* from warships captured at Antium in 342 BC decorated the platform. The literal *rostrum* is gone, but regularly spaced holes in its platform remain. Senators and consuls orated to the Roman plebes from here, and any citizen could mount to voice his opinion. After his assassination, Cicero's head and hands were displayed here. Augustus's rebellious daughter Julia is said to have voiced her disdain for her father's legislation promoting family values by engaging in amorous activities with Augustus's enemies on the spot where the laws had been announced.

ARCH OF SEPTIMIUS SEVERUS

The hefty Arch of Septimius Severus at the end of V. Sacra is an anachronism in this Republican square. Dedicated in AD 203 to celebrate that emperor's victories in the Middle East, the arch's reliefs depict the imperial family. Severus's classy son and successor, Caracalla, grabbed the throne, killing his brother Geta and scraping his name and portrait off the arch. Behind the arch stand the grey tufa walls of the **Tabularium,** once the repository of Senate archives, now the basement of the Renaissance **Palazzo dei Senatori.**

MARKET SQUARE

The original market square (in front of the Curia) was graced by a number of shrines and sacred precincts. Immediately down the stairs from the Curia lies the **Lapis Niger** (Black Stone), surrounded by a circle of bricks. Republican Romans believed this is where the legendary founder of the city, Romulus, was murdered. Modern scholars now think the Lapis Niger was actually an early shrine to Vulcan. The shrine was considered passé even during the Republic, when its statuary and columns were covered by gray pavement. Below the Lapis Niger rest the underground ruins of a 6th-century BC altar, along with a pyramidal pillar where the oldest known Latin inscription in Rome warns the public against defiling the shrine. Across from the far side of the **Basilica Julia,** the **Three Sacred Trees** of Rome—olive, fig, and grape—have been replanted by the Italian state (never mind that grapes grow on vines). On the other side, across from the Basilica Julia, lies a circular tufa basin (sometimes covered by a low tin roof, the purpose of which could only be to block your view of it), the **Lacus Curtius,** commemorating the swamp that had been there before. It received its name from the story of either Marcus Curtius, who sacrificed himself on the spot to save the city, or the less exciting Gaius Curtius (no relation), who once saw a lightning bolt hit it.

The "newest" part of the Forum is the **Column of Phocas,** erected in 608 to celebrate the visiting Byzantine emperor, Phocas—a sacrilege that would have probably made early Republican Romans roll in their graves. The marketplace may also have been home to three important markers: the **Umbilicus Urbis,** the **Golden Milestone,** and the **Vulcanal.** The locations of these, which marked the center not only of the city, but of the Roman world, are only hypotheses.

Circus Maximus

LOWER FORUM

To the left, behind the Arch of Septimius Severus are Basilica Julia and the 3 extant temples of the lower Forum.

TEMPLE OF SATURN

Eight columns mark the Temple of Saturn, one of the first buildings constructed in Rome. The Romans believed that Saturn had taught them the art of agriculture, and filled his statue inside the temple with fresh olive oil. Though actually built in the early 5th century BC, the temple has its mythological origins in an earlier Rome, one with no property, war, or slavery. The temple was the site of Saturnalia, the Roman winter bash that signified the end of the year. During this raucous party, class and social distinctions became void, as masters served slaves.

Behind the temple are (left to right): the **Portico of the Dei Consentes,** the last pagan monument built in Rome; the three Corinthian columns of the **Temple of Vespatian,** completed by his son Domitian in AD 81; and the foundations of the **Temple of Concord,** which was built to celebrate the peace between patrician and plebeian Romans in 367 BC.

Piazza di Campdoglio

BASILICA JULIA

Around the corner to the left of the Temple of Saturn, rows of deserted column bases are the sole remains of the Basilica Julia. Begun by Julius Caesar in 54 BC, completed by Augustus, and restored by Diocletian, it followed the same plan as the Basilica Aemilia (see above) on a larger scale. The central hall, flanked by three rows of columns on each side, was used by tribunals of judges to lay down the law. Look for grids and circles in the steps where anxious Romans, waiting to go before the judge, played an ancient version of snakes and ladders. If you've had your fill of culture, at the end of the basilica opposite the Temple of Castor and Pollux is part of the **Cloaca Maxima,** the huge sewer which drained from the Forum directly into the Tiber. Do not try to avail yourself of this resource.

Bocca della Verita

TEMPLE OF CASTOR AND POLLUX

At the end of the Basilica Julia, three white marble columns mark the massive podium of the **Temple of Castor and Pollux,** dedicated in 484 BC to celebrate the Roman rebellion against their Etruscan king, Tarquinius Superbus. The Romans attributed their victory over the Latins at Lake Regillus in 499 BC to the help of the twin gods Castor and Pollux (not the nefarious brothers of the movie *Face/Off*), who outflanked the mortal Etruscans.

Legend says that immediately after the battle the twins appeared in the Forum to water their horses at the nearby **Lacus Juturnae** (Basin of Juturna). Now marked by a reconstructed marble *aedicula* to the left of the gods' temple, the site was once the location of the ancient city's water company. Behind the temple, the **Church of Santa Maria Antiqua** is the oldest in the forum, dating to the 6th century.

TEMPLE OF THE DEIFIED JULIUS

Across from the Temple of Castor and Pollux is the rectangular base of the **Temple of the Deified Julius,** which Augustus built in 29 BC to honor his murdered adoptive father and to proclaim himself the son of a god. The circular pile of rocks inside housed an altar and likely marks the spot where Caesar's body was cremated in 44 BC after his assassination near Largo Argentina. Wistful monarchists leave flowers here on the Ides of March. In his own modest glory, Augustus built the **Arch of Augustus,** a triple arch (only the bases are visible now) that straddled V. Sacra.

UPPER FORUM

TEMPLE OF VESTA

The circular building behind the Temple of the Deified Julius is the Temple of Vesta, originally built by the Etruscans but rebuilt by Septimius Severus at the end of the 2nd century AD. Designed after a Latin hut, the temple is where the Vestal Virgins tended the sacred fire of the city, keeping it continuously lit for more than 1000 years (until the 4th century). Within one of the temple's secret rooms, visited only by the Vestal Virgins, stood the **Palladium,** the small statue of Minerva that Aeneas was said to have brought from Troy to Italy. Behind the temple, between the House of Vestal Virgins and the Temple of Antoninus and Faustina, lies the triangular **Regia,** office of the Pontifex Maximus, Rome's high priest and titular ancestor of the Pope. Long before the first Pontifex (Numa Pompilius) took it over, as early as the 6th century BC, the Regia was the site of sacrifices to the gods of agriculture (as well as Mars, Jupiter, Juno, and Janus). One of the rites performed was the October harvest ritual, in which the tail and genitalia of a slain horse were brought to the Regia in an offering to the god of vegetation. Sadly, this ceremony has been discontinued.

AMUSING THE PLEBES

When Juvenal wrote that "bread and circuses" were all that were necessary to keep the Roman populace happy, he was referring in part to the free snacks and wild spectacles staged in the 50,000-person Colosseo. In order to keep the large numbers of unemployed Romans occupied, emperors depended upon the distracting powers of ceremonial pageantry and calculated violence of gladiatorial combats. Fallen, injured gladiators could make a sign begging for mercy. While the emperor mulled over his decision, the bloodthirsty crowd howled for a thumbs-down, the death sentence. Most Romans, including the elite, saw nothing wrong with these savage spectacles. Another popular event at the Colosseum was the killing of wild animals. Lions and tigers and bears, crocodiles, giraffes, and camels (oh my!) were all released from an underground network of tunnels into a simulated forest. Professionals *(venatores)* would work the frightened animals into a feverish state and draw out their deaths.

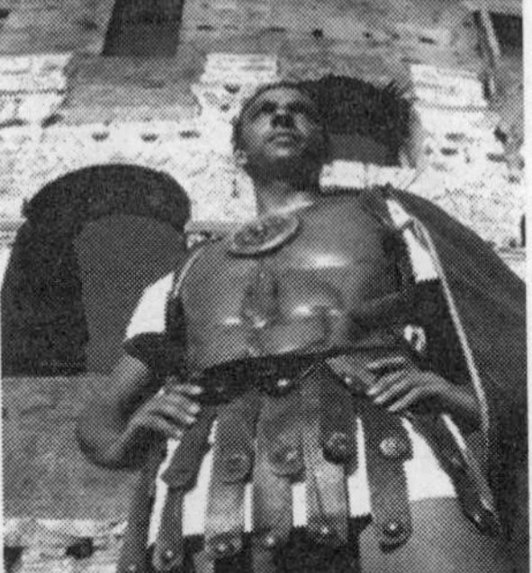

HOUSE OF THE VESTAL VIRGINS

The sprawling complex of rooms and courtyards behind the Temple of Vesta was the House of Vestal Virgins. Here, in spacious seclusion in the shade of the Palatine, lived the six virgins who officiated over Vesta's rites, chosen for their purity and physical perfection and ordained at the age of seven. As long as they kept their vows of chastity, the Vestal Virgins were among the most respected people in ancient Rome; they were the only women allowed to walk unaccompanied in the Forum and could protect or pardon anyone. This easy life had its price; if a virgin strayed from celibacy, she was buried alive with a loaf of bread and a candle, on the assumption that the sustenance that it provided would give her time to contemplate her sins during her prolonged death. Only a handful of women met this fate.

Off-and-on restoration often means that visitors can only peer through the iron gates surrounding the House of the Vestal Virgins. Still, there is a view (head up to the Palatine to get a really good view) of the central courtyard where statues of the priestesses who served between AD 291 and 364 reside, including one whose name was scraped away (8th on the left as you enter the courtyard). The erased priestess is thought to have been Claudia, the Vestal Virgin who, at the end of the 4th century, converted to that new-fangled religion from the south, Christianity.

TEMPLE OF ANTONINUS AND FAUSTINA

Back on V. Sacra is the Temple of Antoninus and Faustina (opposite the Temple of Vesta, to the immediate right as you face the entrance ramp), whose strong foundation, columns, and rigid lattice ceiling have preserved it unusually well over the ages. In the 7th and 8th centuries, the **Church of San Lorenzo in Miranda** was built in the interior of the abandoned temple. The temple's columns and frieze were incorporated into the Christian structure. This is not to say that the Christian rulers didn't try to destroy the pagan temple: the deep grooves at the top of the columns show where cables were tied in attempts to demolish this steadfast symbol of pagan worship. The original building was constructed by Emperor Antoninus and dedicated to his wife Faustina (his name was added after his death in AD 161). In the shadow of the temple (to the right as you face it) is an archaic **necropolis,** with Iron Age graves dating to between the 10th and 8th centuries BC, which lend credence to Rome's legendary founding date of 753 BC. The bodies from the ancient graveyard were found in hollow tree trunks. The remains are visible in the Antiquarium (see **Velia,** below).

TEMPLE OF ROMULUS

Farther up V. Sacra stands the round Temple of Romulus, which retains its original bronze doors, with a working lock, from the 4th century AD. The name of the structure, however, is misleading for two reasons. First, the "Romulus" in question here was probably the son of the 4th-century emperor, Maxentius, not the legendary founder of Rome. Second, the temple probably wasn't a temple at all but an office of the urban *praetor* during the Empire. The temple now houses the **Church of Santi Cosma e Damiano.** Across V. Sacra from the structure, remains of fortifications from between 730 and 540 BC have been discovered. Behind the temple, recently excavated ruins of Vespatian's **Forum Pacis** (Forum of Peace) are visible along V.d. Fori Imperiali, beginning just past the main entrance.

VELIA

Take V. Sacra out of the Forum proper, toward the Arch of Titus.

BASILICA OF MAXENTIUS AND CONSTANTINE

Antiquarium open daily 9am-1pm. Free.

The gargantuan Basilica of Maxentius and Constantine is on the left as you walk down V. Sacra. The three gaping arches that remain are only the side chapels for an enormous central hall, whose coffered ceiling covered the entire gravel court and three chapels on the other side. Emperor Maxentius began construction of the basilica in 308 but was forcefully deposed by Constantine at the Battle of the Milvian Bridge in 312. Constantine converted to Christianity during the battle, and although he oversaw completion of the basilica, some pagan reverence for the Forum kept him from ever dedicating it as a church. He built the basilica of San Giovanni in Laterano instead,

POLLUTION AMONG THE RUINS

When Mussolini created wide roads to circle the city's monuments, he also paved the way for their destruction. Today, the Colosseum faces serious damage due to the constant rush of polluting traffic around it. Thousands of cars, scooters, and buses race past the arena daily; when the subway rumbles by, the ground beneath it shakes. Restoration is a Sisyphian task: as workers slowly make their way around the Colosseum, pollution begins to tarnish the already cleaned exterior. For the past 25 years, the government has been considering designating the area from Piazza Venezia to beyond the Colosseum as an "archaeological park," closed to traffic. This would seriously aggravate the already horrible traffic that plagues the city, but it may be the only way to prevent complete collapse of the ancient monument.

with a similar plan (see p. 129). Constantine didn't let his piety get in the way of his ego, though. The middle apse of the basilica once contained a gigantic statue of him; the body was bronze, and the head, legs, and arms were marble. The remains that were found (on exhibit at the **Museo Capitolino;** see p. 152) include a 6½ ft. long foot. In the end, though, Christianity won out; all the bronze in the basilica was melted down in the 7th century to cover the first basilica of St. Peter's.

The Baroque facade of the **Church of Santa Francesca Romana** is built over Hadrian's Temple to Venus and Rome *(Amor* and *Roma)*. It hides the entrance to the **Antiquarium Forense,** a small museum that houses artifacts from the Forum. Among the items on display are skeletons from the *necropolis*.

ARCH OF TITUS

On the summit of the Velian hill, where V. Sacra intersects with the road down from the Palatine, is the Arch of Titus, built in AD 81 by Domitian to celebrate his brother Titus's destruction of Jerusalem 10 years earlier. Though the paranoid Frangipane family turned it into a fortified tower in the Middle Ages, Pope Pius VII ordered it restored to its original state in 1821. On the interior of the arch is a famous frieze depicting Titus's victory and the treasure he took from the Great Temple (which appears to have been spent by Titus on the construction of the Colosseum).

THE COLOSSEUM

M: B-Colosseo. ***Open*** *daily 9am-6:30pm; winter daily 9am-1hr. before sunset. L10,000/€5.16, EU citizens under 18 and over 60 free, EU citizens 18-24 L5000/€2.58.* ***5-day ticket book*** *good for the three Musei Nazionali Romani (see p. 154), the Colosseum, and the Palatine Hill (L30,000/€15.50).* ***Tours*** *with archaeologist L6000/€3.20; audioguide in English, French, German, Italian, Japanese, or Spanish L7000/€3.62.*

The Colosseum is the enduring symbol of the Eternal City—a hollowed-out ghost of travertine marble dwarfing every other ruin in Rome. Recently completed renovations have cleaned the exterior and reconstructed several missing sections (in brick instead of marble, unfortunately) to give a better sense of what the ancient amphitheater looked like, but it is still pretty barren and empty inside. Use your imagination (or scenes from *Gladiator*) or pick up an audioguide (*telefonini* on steroids) to make the visit more interesting. The city of Rome does its part to make the Colosseum come alive by hiring poor souls to dress up as gladiators and centurions outside, as well the occasional historically inaccurate but provocatively dressed gladiatoress. They're amusing enough to look at, but what they want is to have their picture taken with you for a cool L10,000/€5.16 a pop. You enter on the lowest level of seating (the arena floor is off-limits) and take stairs to the upper level.

The term "Colosseum" is actually a nickname for the *Amphitheatrum Flavium*, which Vespatian began building in AD 72 to block out the private lake that Nero had installed for his own seedy purposes. The nickname derives from the colossal bronze statue of Nero as sun-god that used to grace the area next to the amphitheater (see the **Domus Aurea,** p. 80). The Colosseum was completed in 80 by Titus, with spoils from the emperors' campaigns in Judaea. Titus allegedly threw a monster bash for its inauguration: a 100-day fête that saw 5000 wild beasts perish in the bloody arena (from the Latin for sand, *harena*, which was put on the floor to absorb blood). Though the maximum capacity is still debatable, feuding archaeologists have placed the number at at least 50,000. Because the Colosseum events took place for the "public good," tickets to see the slaughter were always free.

Roman Fourum

Chances are that the house was packed for Trajan's celebration of his Dacian victories, when 10,000 gladiators and 11,000 beasts duked it out for a month. Over the centuries, it wasn't only gladiator fights that filled the arena: in the mornings, as a warm-up for the evening's battles, exotic animal hunts were a huge draw—the idea of two Romans stalking a hippopotamus was enough to get bloodthirsty teens out of bed and over to the Colosseum. It's also said that the elliptical interior was flooded for sea battles, although some archaeologists and native Romans insist that it wouldn't have been possible, citing the Circus Maximus as the more probable locale. Sadly, gladiatorial games were suspended in 438 by a Christian-dominated empry and Senate, and animal hunts soon bit the dust as well. The Colosseum was used briefly as a fortress in the Middle Ages and as a quarry in the Renaissance, when popes, beginning with Urban VIII, pillaged marble for use in their own grandiose enterprises, including St. Peter's Basilica (see p. 110) and Palazzo Barberini (see p. 105). The former pagan symbol became the site of Christian liturgical rites in the 17th and 18th centuries, and a chapel and rows of crosses were eventually built on the north end of the hollowed-out amphitheater. The crosses were removed in the 19th century when excavations started on the Colosseum, leaving the structure, with the exception of the ongoing exterior renovations, as it is today.

Church of Santa Maria in Cosmedin

The outside of the arena, with the layers of Doric, Ionic, and Corinthian columns, was considered the ideal orchestration of the classical architectural orders, from the most staid to the most ornamental. On the outer side opposite the entrance, look for five marble posts on the edge of the pavement. These posts are remnants of anchors for a giant *velarium*, the retractable shade that once covered the amphitheater.

Arch of Janus

NERO SUM

Nero, son of Claudius's fourth wife, began a sadistic reign of terror, torture, and debauchery at the tender age of 16, after his mother fed her ex-husband poisonous mushrooms. Nero started out mildly, guided by his overbearing but well-meaning mother; he was too timid even to sign the standard death warrants. Soon, though, he proved to be one of the most ill-adjusted teens in history. He transmogrified into a megalomaniacal monster and ordered the cruel murders of his mother, Agrippina, and his 19-year-old wife, who was found tied up in a hot bath with her veins slashed. He made his best friend and advisor, famed philosopher and tragedian Seneca, cut his own wrists. Nero was haunted by paranoid visions—he often woke up screaming from nightmares of his mother—so he initiated a one-man witch-hunt, condemning senators, army officers, aristocrats, and others to be beheaded as traitors. Many blame Nero for the fire of 64 BC—guilty or not, he certainly took advantage of its destruction, commandeering acres of burnt-out land to construct the Domus Aurea. Ultimately, Nero pushed the patience and the coffers of his empire too far; the Senate sentenced him to death by flogging. Nero, in disguise, escaped on horseback to have a servant slit his throat, as he didn't have the guts to do so himself. The notoriously bad musician and actor did, however, have enough panache to utter in his last moments, "What an artist dies with me." That's style. Style for miles.

During each game, 1000 naval troops operated the *velarium*. Inside, the tremendous wooden floor is gone, revealing brick cells, corridors, ramps, and elevators that were used to transport wild animals from their cages up to the arena level.

Note the large cross across from the side entrance. It symbolizes the Colosseum's escape from total destruction at the hands of pillagers by a lucky mistake. The Pope, in order to commemorate the martyrdom of the thousands of Christians supposedly killed in the amphitheater, declared the monument a sacred place and forbade any more demolition. It was discovered that no Christians had been ever killed in the Colosseum. These days, in fact, the Pope holds occasional masses there. Additionally, in the summer of 2000, the Colosseum was used as a stage for several Italian TV variety show extravaganzas as well as Greek drama and classical music performances. Organizers bragged that it was the first time in 15 centuries that it had been used as an entertainment venue, though the maximum audience of 700 for these events paled by comparison to the arena's former glory.

ARCH OF CONSTANTINE

Between the Colosseum and the Palatine Hill, marking the tail end of the V. Sacra, is the Arch of Constantine, one of the latest and best-preserved imperial monuments gracing the area. The Senate dedicated the arch in 315 to commemorate Constantine's victory over his rival Maxentius at the Battle of the Milvian Bridge in 312 (see **History,** p. 40). The arch's friezes show how heartfelt that dedication actually was: one side's images depict life in Constantine's camps and images of war; on the other side, the images depict life after Constantine's victory and the virtues of peace and humanity. There are a few rough 4th-century friezes that demonstrate just how much Roman sculptural art declined from the onset of the millenium, but otherwise the triple arch is cobbled together almost entirely from sculptural fragments pilfered from earlier Roman monuments. The four sad-looking men near the top, for example, are Dacian prisoners taken from one of Trajan's monuments; the medallions once belonged to a monument for Hadrian and include depictions of his lover, Antinous; and the rest of the scatterings celebrate the military prowess of Marcus Aurelius.

PALATINE HILL

The Palatine rises to the south of the Forum. ***Open*** *daily 9am-6:30pm; in winter M-Sa 9:30am-1hr. before sunset, Su 9am-1pm; sometimes closes M-F 3pm, Su and holidays noon. Last entrance 45min. before closing. L12,000/€6.20; EU citizens between 18 and 24 L6000/€3.20; EU citizens under 18 and over 60 free.*

Palatine Hill (L30,000/€15.50). May be purchased at the booth beyond the Arch of Titus and on the left in the Forum, 100 yards down V.d. S. Gregorio from the Colosseum, or at the Forum's main entrance. ***Visit the Palatine after the Forum;*** *you will better appreciate the views of the Forum after having walked through. The "Orti Farnesini," the hills best for viewing were closed for renovation work in summer 2001. Completion date unknown.*

The Palatine boasts not only vast temples and imperial palaces, but also some of the best views of ancient Rome imaginable—these alone are worth the price of admission. Striking views aside, the hill, a square plateau rising between the Tiber and the Forum, contains a some of the oldest and "newest" Roman ruins.

The first and final chapters of the ancient Empire unfolded atop the Palatine's heights. The she-wolf that suckled Romulus and Remus had her den here, and it was here that Romulus built the first walls and houses of the city, a legend corroborated by the discovery of 9th-century BC huts on the southeastern side of the hill. During the Republic, the Palatine was the city's most fashionable residential quarter, where aristocrats and statesmen, including Cicero and Marc Antony, built their homes. Augustus lived on the hill in a relatively modest house, but later emperors capitalized on the hill's prestige by building progressively more gargantuan quarters for themselves and their courts. By the end of the first century AD, the imperial residence had swallowed up the entire hill, whose Latin name, Palatium, became synonymous with the palace that dominated it. After the fall of Rome, the hill suffered the same fate as the Forum, although Byzantine ambassadors and even popes sometimes set up house in the crumbling palace.

ORTI FARNESIANI

Assuming reconstruction work has been completed, approach this section of the hill by taking your first right as you start up the hill from the Arch of Titus, past the 16th-century Uccelliere, commissioned by Cardinal Alessandro Farnese, to the Orti Farnesiani, which opened in 1625 as the first botanical gardens in the world. For incredible Forum views, follow the signs for the *"Affacciata sul Foro."* At the end opposite from the Forum, terraces look down on several structures that are currently being excavated (and will likely be off-limits until 2002). On the far right are the foundations of the Temple of Cybele, constructed in 204 BC on the orders of a prophecy from a Sibylline book. Immediately to its left are the remains of a 9th-century BC village, the **Casa di Romulo** (House of Romulus). The Iron Age inhabitants (who may well have included the legendary twin) built their oval huts out of wood; all that remains are the holes they sunk into the tufa bedrock for their roofposts.

Left of the temple is the **House of Livia.** Livia was Augustus's wife, the first Roman empress, and according to Robert Graves' *I, Claudius*, an "abominable grandmother." She had the house, with its vestibule, courtyard, and three vaulted living rooms, connected to the House of Augustus next door. Along the pathways between the House of Livia and the House of Augustus, excavation and restoration continues on rooms once lined with marble and gold. Frescoes, hidden from view, decorate the interior walls.

IMPERIAL COMPLEX

Descending the stairs from the terrace to the Domitian's (AD 81-96) imperial complex, you cross the long, spooky **Cryptoporticus,** a tunnel that connected Tiberius's palace with the buildings nearby. Used by slaves and imperial couriers as a secret passage, it was probably built by Nero in one of his more paranoid moments.

DOMUS FLAVIA

First is the sprawling Domus Flavia, site of a gigantic octagonal fountain that occupied almost the entire courtyard. The building was divided into three halls, and was used by the emperor for all sorts of social, political, and religious functions. It was also the site of a huge throne room where Domitian could preside over public audiences. He clearly had a thing for fountains, because the ruins of a smaller, elliptical one remain intact next to the sunken **Triclinium,** where imperial banquets were held between a set of twin oval fishponds. On the other side of the Triclinium, a walkway offers sweeping views of the grassy **Circus Maximus** (see p. 82) and, farther to the left, the **Baths of Caracalla** (see p. 84).

DOMUS AUGUSTANA

Next door, the solemn Domus Augustana was the emperors' private residence. The exterior walls that remain are so high that archaeologists are still unsure how they were roofed over. The palace was built on the side of the hill, and three floors descend below the level of the main hall, including a sunken courtyard with yet another fishpond. The emperor's quarters were in the maze of staircases and corridors behind the courtyard leading toward the side of the hill. Farther down the hill were the **Paedagogium,** the servants' quarters, and the **Domus Praeconum,** which served as the palace's physical plant.

HIPPODROME

The most visible ruins on the Palatine are in the east wing of the palace, where the **Stadium Palatinum,** or Hippodrome, stands. Set below the level of the Domus Augustana, this curious stadium has at its southern end a sunken oval space, once surrounded by a colonnade, now decorated by the Archaeological Superintendency with fragments of porticoes, statues, and fountains. Although it is fairly certain that this was not a racetrack for hippopotamus, its exact nature remains uncertain. There are two prominent theories: first, that it was a private arena, where the imperial family would get their kicks watching the lesser classes fight for their lives; and second, that it was a private garden, where the imperial family would get their kicks watching plants photosynthesize. From the northern end of the stadium, a winding path leads around to the **Domus Severiana,** a later addition to the imperial complex that boasted its own central heating system.

PALATINE ANTIQUARIUM

Between the Domus Augustana and the Domus Flavia. 30 people admitted every 20min. 9:10am-6:20pm. Free with entrance to Palatine.

Built on the ruins of Domitian's imperial palace, this history museum's nine rooms are built around parts of the palace's foundations, and contain 9th-century pottery as well as 5th-century frescoes and sculptures.

DOMUS AUREA

On the Oppian Hill, below Trajan's baths. From the Colosseum, walk through the gates up V.d. Domus Aurea and make 1st right. ☎06 39967700. ***Open*** *Tu -Su 9am-6:45pm. Groups of 30 admitted every 20min. L10,000/€5.16. Visits supervised by guards who give you rather spartan tours in Italian. A better bet is the* ***audioguide*** *(L3000/€1.55). Italian* ***tour*** *with archaeologist L6000/€3.20. Reservations recommended for all visits: additional L2000/€1.03 (L3000/€1.55 for guided tour).*

The recently reopened Domus Aurea was only a small part of Emperor Nero's residence, which once took up one-third of Rome. "Golden House" is something of a misnomer, as this edifice was a series of banquet halls and galleries; Nero's private rooms were likely on the Palatine.

Having decided that he was a god, Nero had the architects Severus and Celer design a palace to suit divinity. "Using art and squandering the wealth of the Emperor," writes Tacitus, they created "eccentricities which went against the laws of nature." Between the Oppian and Palatine palaces was an enclosed lake, where the Colosseum now stands, and the Caelian Hill became private gardens. The Forum was reduced to a vestibule of the palace; Nero crowned it with a colossal statue of himself as the sun. Standing 35m tall, it was the largest bronze statue ever made and was justly called the Colossus.

The party didn't last long, however. Nero was forced to commit suicide only five years after building his gargantuan pleasure garden, and his memory was condemned by the Senate. Following suit, the Flavian emperors who succeeded Nero replaced all traces of the palace with monuments built for the public good. The Flavian Baths were built on top of the Caelian Hill, the lake was drained, and the Colosseum was erected. Trajan filled the Domus Aurea with dirt (so that it would make a stronger foundation) and built his baths on top of it in AD 115, and Hadrian covered the western end with his Temple of Venus and Rome in 135. The Domus Aurea itself was rediscovered in the 14th century.

The Domus Aurea was originally built around a large central courtyard, and designed so that the whole building was perpetually illuminated by sunlight that streamed through skylights and aligned corridors (after all, Nero did fancy himself the sun god). Thanks to Trajan, it's all pitch-black now, though artificial light streams in through aligned floodlights. The best-preserved frescoes are on the ceiling, and that is also where a number of signatures, made with candle-smoke or incised, can be seen. Trajan did not completely fill in the Domus Aurea, and many artists, including Raphael, lowered themselves down into the building with ropes in order to study its artwork. Early archaeologists removed many of the treasures Nero had accumulated during his year of "study" in Greece. Among others, the Laocoön sculpture group and *The Dying Gaul* (now in the **Capitoline Museums,** see p. 152) once graced the Domus Aurea.

The visit begins in a corridor of Trajan's baths, but quickly progresses into the palace itself, meandering through several small rooms before reaching the **Corridor of the Eagles,** notable for the splendid ceiling it once had. While time has taken its toll on the ceiling, fragments of friezes of eagles and vegetation can be made out, as can a central scene thought to be Ariadne after she was abandoned by Theseus.

The tour passes through the **Nymphaeum of Ulysses and Polyphemus,** which was supposed to resemble a natural grotto: fake stalactites and an artificial waterfall were installed. A statue of the Muse Terpsichore was found here, and there is still a pentagonal mosaic of Ulysses and Polyphemus on the ceiling. The next notable sight is the **Golden Vault,** once a sumptuous banquet hall covered in gold leaf. Traces of the precious metal are still visible, but this is also where you can see just how high dirt was piled in the Domus Aurea before its excavation, as there is a huge heap of it in an adjoining room.

Shortly after the Golden Vault is the **Room of Achilles at Scyros.** On the ceiling is an image of cross-dressing Achilles (his father, who had received a prophecy that he would die in the Trojan War, ordered him into drag to avoid it). Farther down the corridor is the most hyped room in the Domus Aurea, the **Octagonal Room.** Ancient authors had written that Nero's palace was so extravagant that he had a rotating banquet hall that turned throughout the day, and this might have been it. Unfortunately, there is no evidence of the equipment needed to achieve this effect, so a few modern scholars have posited that it was all an optical illusion: the room is, in fact, designed so that sunlight circles its walls throughout the day (sunlight still streams into the room, making it by far the brightest), and this may have made the room appear to spin (especially at the end of a drunken banquet). Just off the Octagonal Room is the last stop on the tour, the **Room of Hector and Andromache,** notable for its elaborate friezes and vault.

Arch of Constantine

Palatine Hill

Baths of Caracalla

CIRCUS MAXIMUS

Walk down V.d. San Gregorio from the Colosseum. Open 24hr.

Cradled in the valley between the Palatine and Aventine hills, the Circus Maximus is today only a grassy shadow of its former glory. This rather plain, grassy hollow of a park was the sight of all the uproar depicted by Charlton Heston in *Ben Hur*. After its construction around 600 BC, more than 300,000 Romans often gathered here to watch the careening of chariots around the quarter-mile track. Obelisks in the arena's center served as distance markers, and the turning points of the track were perilously sharp to ensure enough thrills 'n' spills to keep the crowds happy. The excitement of the chariot races was interspersed with a variety of other competitions ranging from bareback horse-racing to more esoteric events like tent-pegging. Emperor Augustus watched from special terraces built onto the Palatine palaces. The Circus may also have been the site of the mythical sea battles that some have attributed to the Colosseum. Circus Maximus refills on happy occasions such as the celebration of AS Roma's smashing soccer successes.

FORI IMPERIALI

The sprawling Fori Imperiali lie on either side of V.d. Fori Imperiali, stretching from the Forum to P. Venezia. **Excavations that will proceed through summer 2002** mean that the area is closed off, but you can still get free views peering over the railing from V.d. Fori Imperiali or V. Alessandrina, which runs diagonally off of V.d. Fori Imperiali. The large conglomeration of temples, basilicas, and public squares was constructed by emperors from the first century BC to the 2nd century AD, in response to increasing congestion in the old Forum. The area was excavated in the early 1930s.

FORUM OF CAESAR

On the left-hand side of V.d. Fori Imperiali, just past the Forum as you walk toward P. Venezia. Julius Caesar was the first Roman leader to expand the city center outside the Forum proper, constructing the Forum of Caesar in 46 BC. Caesar's motivations were political: the new forum and temple he built in honor of Venus, his supposed ancestress, seriously undercut the prestige of the Senate and its older precinct around the Curia. The remains of the **Temple of Venus Genetrix** are marked by three columns. Additions from the reign of Trajan include the brick **Basilica Argentaria,** an ancient bank, and the heated public bathroom—the semi-circular room with holes along the walls. Nearby, a replica of a bronze statue of Caesar from his forum has been placed on the sidewalk of V.d. Fori Imperiali for foreign tourists to have their pictures taken with and Italian teenagers to deface.

FORUM OF AUGUSTUS

The first ruins on the right as you walk up V.d. Fori Imperiali toward P. Venezia (although they are better seen from V. Alessandrina, if it is open) are those of the Forum of Augustus, completed in 2 BC. Dedicated by Augustus to *Mars Ultor* (Mars the Avenger), the huge complex commemorated Augustus's vengeful victory over his adoptive father Julius Caesar's murderers, Brutus and Cassius, at the Battle of Philippi in 42 BC. Three columns remain of the **Temple of Mars Ultor,** which centered upon a statue of Mars (oddly enough, it bore a striking resemblance to a certain avenging Emperor) and lined with statues of Roman history's most important figures. A copy of the Mars statue can be seen at the Capitoline Museums (see p. 152).

The hefty wall behind the temple, built to protect the precious new monument from the seamy Subura slums that spread up the hill behind it, doesn't run exactly straight. Legend says that when the land was being prepared for construction, even Augustus couldn't convince one stubborn homeowner to give up his domicile, so the great wall was built at an angle around it.

The aptly named **Forum Transitorium** (also called the **Forum of Nerva**) was a narrow, rectangular space connecting Augustus's forum with the old Roman Forum and the forum of Vespatian (near present-day V. Cavour). Most of it now lies under the street, but new excavations have begun to uncover more. Although Domitian began it, Emperor Nerva inaugurated the forum in 97, displaying the wit that Roman emperors were known for: he dedicated the temple to "Minerva," the deity whose name was closest to his own.

The nerva of some rulers. All that remains to view is a colossal doorway that once led into Vespatian's Forum; between two Corinthian columns is a relief of Minerva and a decorative frieze.

CHURCH OF SANTI COSMA E DAMIANO

Near the entrance to the Roman Forum on V. Cavour. Open daily 9am-1pm and 3-7pm.

The only remnant of **Vespatian's Forum** was built in 527 out of a library in Vespatian's complex. The interior displays a set of 6th-century mosaics including a multi-color Christ with his robes blowing in the wind. A newly installed viewing window allows for a look into the adjacent Temple of Romulus the Divine.

MARKETS OF TRAJAN

Enter at V. IV Novembre, 94, up the steps in V. Magnanapoli, to the right of the 2 churches behind Trajan's column. ☎06 6790048. Open Tu-Su 9am-6:30pm. L12,000/€6.20. Better yet, save yourself the money and view the markets from the Trajan Forum.

Across V.d. Fori Imperiali from the Vittorio Emanuele II monument stand the brick **Markets of Trajan.** The three-floor, semicircular complex, built during the early 2nd century BC, provides a glimpse of the early Roman shopping malls. Built into the Quirinal Hill, the market had space for 150 shops, selling everything from imported fabrics to Eastern spices. Part of the vast structure housed public administration offices and a stock exchange. The ground- and first-floor rooms of the markets are home to an impressive, if crumbling display of sculpture from the imperial forum, including two colossal torsos of Nerva and Agrippa and part of a frieze of a griffin.

FORUM OF TRAJAN

Marked by an imposing column, the Forum of Trajan, the largest, newest, and most impressive of the imperial *fora*, is hard to miss. Built between 107 and 113, the forum was a celebration of Trajan's campaigns in modern-day Romania. The complex included a colossal equestrian statue of Trajan and a triumphal arch. In the back of the forum, the enormous **Basilica Ulpia** once stood in judicial might. The largest basilica ever built in Rome (17m by 60m), the Ulpia is today just two rows of truncated columns and fragments of the friezes.

TRAJAN'S COLUMN

At one end of the decimated forum stands the almost perfectly preserved spiral of Trajan's Column, one of the greatest specimens of Roman relief sculpture ever found. At 40m, it is exactly the same height as the hill leveled in order to build Trajan's Forum. The continuous frieze that wraps around the column narrates the Emperor's campaigns. From the bottom, you can survey Roman legionnaires preparing supplies, building a stockaded camp, and loading boats to cross the Danube. Twenty-five hundred figures in all have been making their way up the column since 113. The statue of their Emperor that crowned the structure in ancient days was destroyed in the Middle Ages and replaced by the figure of St. Peter in 1588. The column survived the 6th and 7th centuries only because Pope Gregory I was so moved by some of the reliefs that he prayed for Trajan's acceptance into heaven. The Pope then claimed that God had come to him in a vision, ensuring Trajan's safe passage but refusing to admit any other pagans. The small holes in the column are actually windows that illuminate an internal staircase. In the column's base is a door that leads to the tomb of Trajan and his wife, where Trajan's ashes rested in a golden urn only to be stolen in the Middle Ages.

CAPITOLINE HILL

PIAZZA DEL CAMPIDOGLIO

The Capitoline was the smallest of ancient Rome's seven hills, but also the most important and sacred. The highlight of the modern hill is the spectacular P. del Campidoglio, designed by Michelangelo in 1536 in honor of the visit of Emperor Charles V and in celebration of the hill's ancient glory. In ancient times, the hill was the site of a gilded temple to Jupiter (dedicated in 509 BC); also on the hill were the state mint, senatorial archives, and the Department of Throwing People off the Capitoline Hill.

The northern peak of the hill was home to Juno's sacred geese, which saved the city from ambush by the Gauls in 390 BC by honking so loudly that they woke the populace. To get to the *piazza* from P. Venezia, take **La Cordonata,** the second staircase down V.d. Teatro di Marcello. In keeping with the hill's ancient significance, Michelangelo set up the statues of the twin warriors **Castor and Pollux** that flank the wide and gently sloping staircase, as well as the two reclining river gods and the statue of the goddess Roma. To the right and left of P. del Campidoglio stand **Palazzo dei Conservatori** and **Palazzo Nuovo,** home to the **Capitoline Museums** (p. 152). At the far end, opposite the stairs, is the turreted **Palazzo dei Senatori** (Rome's city hall).

In the center of the *piazza* stands the famous equestrian statue of **Marcus Aurelius,** brought here from the Lateran Palace. The gilded bronze was one of a handful of ancient bronzes to escape medieval meltdown, and then only because it was thought to be a portrait of Constantine, the first Christian emperor. Unfortunately, both man and steed succumbed to the assault of modern pollution and were removed for restoration in 1981, leaving behind only their pedestal. The Emperor now resides in climate-controlled comfort in the courtyard of the Palazzo Nuovo, and the statue you see now is a weatherproof copy. Across the way, in the courtyard of the Palazzo dei Conservatori, lie the gargantuan foot, head, arm, and kneecap of the statue of Constantine that once graced the Basilica of Maxentius.

On the open side of the *piazza*, rejoin *La Cordonata* to make the descent to P. Venezia. The staircase was designed so that Charles V, apparently penitent over his sack of the city a decade before, could ride his horse up the hill to meet Paul III during his triumphal visit. On the right-hand side of *La Cordonata* stands a dark statue of a hooded man, **Cola di Rienzo,** the leader of a popular revolt in 1347 that attempted to reestablish a Roman Republic. The statue marks the spot where the disgruntled populace tore him limb from limb shortly after electing him first consul.

SANTA MARIA IN ARACOELI

Climb 124 pilgrims' steps up from the left side of La Cordonata. Open daily 7:30am-6:30pm.

The 7th-century Church of Santa Maria in Aracoeli lies on the site of the Temple to Juno Moneta. "Aracoeli" comes from a medieval legend that Augustus once had a vision of the Virgin Mary, causing him to raise an altar to Heaven *(Ara Coeli)* on the spot she indicated; this explains the rather unusual fresco of Augustus and the Tiburtine Sibyl, in the company of saints and angels. The stunning **Bufalini Chapel** (on the right as you face the altar) is home to Pinturicchio's Renaissance frescoes of St. Bernardino of Siena. Across the aisle is a boarded-up chapel, once the home of the now-purloined **Santo Bambino.** The third chapel on the left houses a beautiful fresco of St. Antonio of Padova, the only one left of a late 15th-century series by Benozzo Gozzoli.

MAMERTINE PRISON

Downhill from Santa Maria in Aracoeli, to the left with your back to the stairs, to V.S. Pietro in Carcere. ☎06 6792902. Open daily 9am-noon and 2:30-6pm. Donation requested. Audioguide L5000/€2.58.

The gloomy Mamertine Prison, consecrated as the **Church of San Pietro in Carcere,** once held St. Peter, who supposedly caused water to flood into his cell and used it to baptize his captors. Although a stairway now leads down to the dank lower chamber, a small hole used to be the only access to the dungeon. The Romans used the light-less lower chamber as a holding cell for prisoners awaiting execution. Inmates were tortured and occasionally strangled to death in the dark by order of the government. Among the more unfortunate residents were Jugurtha, King of Numidia; Vercingetorix, chieftain of the Gauls; and the accomplices of the dictator Catiline.

BATHS OF CARACALLA

From the eastern end of Circus Maximus walk up V.d. Terme di Caracalla. Open daily 9am-6pm; in winter 9am-1hr. before sunset. L8000/€4.13.

The Baths of Caracalla were used continuously from their construction in AD 212 until the Goths cut off the aqueducts that supplied them in the 6th century. They are the largest and best preserved baths in Rome. You might remember their builder, Caracalla, from such sagas as "I killed my brother Geta, took the throne from my father Severus,

and scratched Geta's likeness off the arches of Janus and Septimius Severus."

Although Caracalla wasn't known for his kindly nature, his construction of this monumental complex did do the city some good—some 1500 muddy Romans could sponge themselves off here at the same time (men in the mornings, women in the afternoons, and slaves in the evenings). While the mosaic floors are beautiful, particularly in the *apodyteria* (dressing rooms), it's the sheer magnitude of this proto-health club that boggles the mind. The complex had a central hall opening onto a round, warm swimming pool on one side and a cold pool on the other. Romans would follow a particular regimen for cleaning, beginning with the warm bath, moving from hot *(caldarium)* to cold rooms (the lukewarm *tepidarium* and the cold *frigidarium*), finishing with a dip in the *natatio*, the cold, open-air pool. The original colorful tile floors are reason enough for the walk around the gigantic *thermae*. Remains of a rectangular brick wall mark the boundary of the ancient gym where Romans played sports, sipped juices, and had their body-hair plucked by special servants. Rome's opera company used to stage Verdi's *Aïda* here, complete with horses and elephants, until it was discovered that, due either to the weight of the animals or the sopranos' voices (perhaps it was the other way around), the performances caused structural damage.

Pantheon

VELABRUM

The Velabrum is a low plain west of the Forum and south of the Jewish Ghetto in the shadow of the Capitoline and Palatine hills. The best way to access its sights is to walk down V. Teatro di Marcello (right of the Vittorio Emanuele II monument) from P. Venezia. This flat floodplain of the Tiber was a sacred area for the ancient Romans, and for that reason there are a number of ancient ruins there. It was believed that the mighty Hercules kept his cattle here, and it is also where Aeneas probably first set foot on what was to become Rome. It was also here where baby Romulus and Remus were found by a she-wolf with a ticking biological clock. During the days of the Republic, the area's proximity to a port on the Tiber made it an ideal spot for the city's cattle and vegetable markets. Civic-minded merchants spotted the riverbanks with temples, arches, and a grandiose theater, all dedicated to the gods of trade and commerce. Even after the empire's fall, the area remained a busy market center.

Piazza Colonna

BOCCA DELLA VERITÀ

Two blocks south of the Theater of Marcellus along V. Luigi Petroselli. Portico and church open daily 9am-7pm. Byzantine mass Su 10:30am.

Piazza Farnese

The **Church of Santa Maria in Cosmedin,** one of Rome's eternal tourist attractions, was built in the 6th century to serve the local Greek colony. The interior brims with intricate stonework, from the choir enclosure and pulpits to the geometric, marble-inlaid floor. In the walls, you can see embedded Roman columns, which were once part of the *Statio Annonae,* classical Rome's main food distribution center.

The church is interesting, but most people visit for the famous Bocca della Verità in the portico. Originally a drain cover carved as a river god's face, the circular relief was credited with supernatural powers in the Middle Ages, when it was claimed that the hoary face liked to chomp off the fingers of anyone who dared the gods by speaking an untruth while his hand was in its mouth. To keep the superstition alive, the caretaker-priest used to stick a scorpion in the back of the mouth to sting the fingers of suspected fibbers. The Bocca made a cameo in *Roman Holiday;* during the filming, Gregory Peck stuck his hand in the mouth and jokingly hid his hand in his sleeve when he yanked it out, causing Audrey Hepburn to yelp in shock. The scene wasn't scripted, but it worked so well that it was kept in the movie. For more wacky medieval fun, test the honesty of your friends at home with clay replicas of the Bocca that sell for L4000-150,000/€2.06-77.50 in the church gift shop, which also has a 9th-century mosaic of the epiphany on display inside.

FORO BOARIO

P. della Bocca della Verità is also the site of the ancient Foro Boario, or cattle market. Its two ancient **temples** are among the best-preserved in Rome. The rectangular **Temple of Portunus,** once known as the Temple of Fortuna Virilis, reveals both Greek and Etruscan influences. The present construction dates from the late 2nd century BC, although there was likely a temple on the site for years before. The **circular temple** next door, thought to be the Temple of Hercules Victor, was believed to be dedicated to Vesta because of its similarities to the Temple of Vesta in the Forum (p. 74).

CHURCH OF SAN GIORGIO IN VELABRO

Open daily 10am-12:30pm and 4-6:30pm.

A block from Foro Boario, V.d. Velabro climbs a short way toward the Capitoline Hill. Behind the hulking **Arch of Janus** (built in the 4th century as a covered market for cattle traders) once stood the little Church of San Giorgio in Velabro. A marvelous edifice, it boasted a 9th-century porch and pillars, a simple early Romanesque interior, and a brick and stone arch *campanile* (bell tower). A terrorist car bombing in 1993 reduced the church's famed portico to a single arch and part of a stone beam. Both the church and the arch have been rather summarily rebuilt. To the left of the church, the eroded **Arch of the Argentarii** was erected in the 3rd century AD by the *argentarii* (money changers) and cattle merchants who used the *piazza* as a market in honor of Emperor Septimius Severus. Caracalla, Severus' son and successor, rubbed out both his brother Geta's name from this arch (just like the arch next to the Curia in the Forum) and Geta himself.

CHURCH OF CONSOLATION

From P.d. Bocca della Verità, take V. G. Decollato one block uphill. Open M-Sa 6am-noon and 3:30-6pm.

Here in P. della Consolazione, prisoners in ancient times were given a prayer, a pat on the back, and a "good luck out there," before they were put to death. The Church itself was once home to an order of monks (equipped humanely with smelling salts and liquor flasks) who were dedicated to giving succor to the condemned and accompanying them on their last mortal journey.

THEATER OF MARCELLUS

The Teatro di Marcello was begun by Caesar and finished by Augustus in 13 BC. It is the short, stocky gray structure facing the Tiber, on the right where V. Teatro di Marcello bends to the left. You cannot enter the theater, but excellent views are available from the outside. The theater bears the name of Augustus's nephew, a potential successor whom he was particularly fond of, and whose early and sudden death remains a mystery.

He may have been poisoned by Augustus's wife, Livia, who intended her own son from a previous marriage, Tiberius, to be the next emperor.

The arches and pilasters on the exterior of the theater served as a model for the Colosseum. It represents the classic arrangement of architectural orders, which grow more complex from the ground up: stocky Doric pilasters support the bottom floor, Ionic capitals hold up the middle, and elaborate Corinthian columns once crowned the top tier. Vitruvius and other ancient architects called this arrangement the most perfect possible for exterior decoration, inspiring Michelangelo, Bramante, and other Renaissance architects to copy the pattern. The perfect exterior is all that remains of the theater, as a succession of medieval families used its seats and stage as the foundation for fortified castles. The park around the theater is open for classical concerts on summer nights. See **Entertainment**, p. 198, for more information.

SAN NICOLA IN CARCERE

Across V. Olitorio from the Teatro di Marcello. ☎06 6869972. Open M-Sa 7:30am-noon and 2-5pm, Su 9:30am-1pm and 4-8pm. Closed Aug.

The 12th-century church rests on the foundations of three Republican temples, which were built and dedicated to the gods Juno, Janus, and Spes (Hope) during the hairy times of the First Punic War. The ancient buildings were converted into a prison during the Middle Ages—hence the name *carcere*, meaning "prison." The only captives in the deserted interior today are well-labeled paintings and restored engravings, including part of the church's original dedication from May 12, 1128. On the right side of the church lies the most well-preserved temple, its Ionic columns scattered on the grass and embedded in the church's wall. The left wall preserves the Doric columns of another temple. The third temple is buried beneath the church.

PORTICO D'OTTAVIA

At the bend of V.d. Portico d'Ottavia in the Jewish Ghetto, a shattered pediment and five ivy-covered columns in the shadow of the Theater of Marcellus are all that remain of the once magnificent Portico d'Ottavia, one of Augustus's grandest contributions to Rome's architecture. Built by Quintus Metellus in 149 BC, it was revamped and imperially restyled by Augustus, who dedicated it to his sister Octavia in 23 BC. The portico was a rectangular enclosure sheltering temples to Jupiter and Juno, some libraries, and public rooms adjunct to the Theater of Marcellus next door. The Romans stuck many of their imported Greek masterpieces here, including the famous Mèdici Venus, now in Florence's Uffizi. She was rediscovered under the crumbling detritus and refuse that had accumulated on the site thanks to the ravages of a nearby fish market. In fact, a church was built into its wall in 755 (see p. 101).

TEMPLE OF APOLLO SOSIANUS

Through the fence to the right of the Portico are the polished white columns of the Temple of Apollo Sosianus. The area around the temple, behind the Theater of Marcellus, has been closed in recent years. The temple dates back to 433 BC and needed a little nip and tuck after centuries of neglect, as was also the case when Gaius Sosius rebuilt the temple and attached his own name to it. The three Corinthian columns support a well-preserved frieze of bulls' skulls and floral garlands. The temple's ornate original 5th-century Greek pediment is visible in the **Museo Centrale Termoelettrica Montemartini** (see p. 159).

CENTRO STORICO

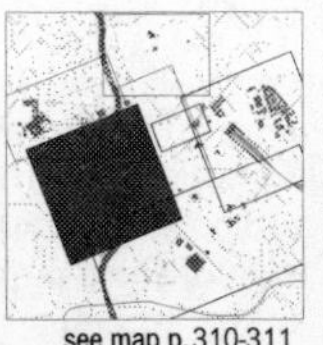
see map p.310-311

This sprawling maze of ancient streets and alleys—the historic center of Rome—brims with dim Baroque churches, cramped picture galleries, ancient ruins, and vast *piazze*. V.d. Corso, runs from P. Venezia nearly a mile north to P. del Popolo, forming a rough eastern boundary of the area; the Tiber is its boundary to the West.

PIAZZA VENEZIA & VIA DEL CORSO

VITTORIO EMANUELE II MONUMENT

Stairs open daily 9am-6pm.

Also known as the *Vittoriano* or "Mussolini's typewriter," this colossal confection of gleaming white marble looms over P. Venezia like a glacier, and many views of the city. It is a memorial to king Vittorio Emanuele II of the House of Savoia (under whom Italy was first united) begun in 1885, the day after his death. Often dubbed "the wedding cake," this awesome monolith stands at the north face of the Capitoline Hill. At the top of the staircase on the exterior is the *Altare della Patria* (Altar of the Fatherland), which has an eternal flame guarded night and day by two members of the armed forces. Behind it is the **Tomb of the Unknown Soldier,** and above is an impressive equestrian bronze of the man of honor. Brave the many stairs for an excellent view of the city, and a close look at all sorts of 19th-century allegorial reliefs. Around the left side toward the forum are the **Sacrario delle Bandiere, Museo del Risorgimento, and the Complesso del Vittoriano.**

PALAZZO DI VENEZIA

This building, on the left as you stand with your back to the *Vittoriano*, is the oldest extant example (begun in 1455) of a Renaissance Roman *palazzo* with its beautiful garden *loggia*, while its formidable tower and fortresslike facade keep one foot in the Middle Ages. It housed the embassy of the Venetian Republic from 1564 to 1797 and later the French and Austrian embassies. Mussolini made the building his personal residence and seat of the Fascist Grand Council, and delivered some of his most famous speeches from its balcony. It is now home to the **Museo Nazionale del Palazzo Venezia,** which has temporary exhibits and a small permanent collection (see p. 162). Walk inside (around the corner, on V.d. Plebiscito) to look at the garden.

BASILICA OF SAN MARCO

In the same building as Palazzo Venezia, in the end toward the Vittorio Emanuele II monument. Enter from P. di San Marco, toward the Vittorio Emanuele monument. Open daily 8:30am-noon and 4-7pm. Dress code enforced.

This church, whose *loggie* date from the Renaissance, is dedicated to the patron saint of Venice, and served as Palazzo Venezia's chapel. Parts of the foundation, however, can be traced to 336, when the church was founded by a Pope Mark quite fond of his namesake saint. Every few centuries parts of the church were redecorated, making it a kaleidoscope of different artistic styles. Inside the church, Melazzo da Forli's *San Marco Evangelista* hangs in the chapel, right of the altar. The 9th-century mosaic in the apse depicts Christ and Pope Gregory IV holding a model of the recently restored church. On the right wall of the Renaissance portico, you'll find the funerary inscription of Vannozza Cattanei, mistress of Borgia Pope Alexander VI and mother of his well-known and well-behaved children Cesare and Lucrezia.

BASILICA DEI SANTI APOSTOLI

One block up V.C. Battisti toward Termini from P. Venezia in P.S. Apostoli. Open daily 7am-noon and 4-7pm..

Tucked in the corner of the *piazza*, this church was built in the 15th century for Pope Martin V. It has an arcaded portico with sculptures above and below. If you're brave enough to get past the lions guarding the entrance, you'll marvel at the imperial eagle, a scary 2nd-century Roman relief, and the largest altarpiece in Rome.

IL GESÙ

Two blocks down from P. Venezia on the left. Open daily 6am-12:30pm and 4-7:15pm. Private apartments: P. del Gesù, 45. Open M-Sa 4-6pm and Su 10am-noon.

The impressive and sumptuous Il Gesù is the principal Jesuit church in Rome, and one of the richest in the city. Its construction was decreed in 1540 by St. Ignatius Loyola, founder of the Jesuit order. The Jesuits were dedicated to advancing Catholicism through the superior education, organization, and dedication of their members, and organized a wide variety of missionary efforts, the founding of colleges, and building their political influence. The church was begun in 1568 by Jacopo Barozzi and completed in 1577 by Giacomo della Porta (who drew from some of Michelangelo's designs for St. Peter's, including the paired pilasters).

Architecturally, Il Gesù became the standard for Baroque churches, and was planned according to the principles of the Counter Reformation. It was designed with a wide single nave in a Latin rather than a Greek cross, so that people attending the church would focus their attention directed to the priest at the main altar.

The interior is lavishly ornate; the Jesuit's motto was "*Ad maiorem dei gloriam*" ("to add to the glory of God") and they believed that impressive churches would glorify God and inspire faith and respect. On the ceiling of the nave, Il Baciccia's celebrated fresco, *Triumph in the Name of Jesus*, uses spectacular perspective, painted panels, and stucco figures to draw the figures in the painting into the same space as the viewers. Baciccia also decorated the brilliant dome. The large monogram "IHS" in the apse is the Jesuits' device and represents the first three letters of Jesus' name in Greek. Check out Bernini's statue of St. Robert Bellarmine to the left of the main altar.

Look left of the dome for the enormous **Cappella di Sant'Ignazio di Loyola,** dedicated to the founder of the order lying under the altar of bronze, marble, and lapis lazuli. Across the apse is another altar with the hand of St. Francis Xavier, Ignatius's friend who led missions to India and Japan. Next to the church, St. Ignatius's **apartments** contain artifacts and paintings.

PIAZZE DEL COLLEGIO ROMANO & SANT'IGNAZIO

V. Lata, two blocks up V.d. Corso from P. Venezia on the left, leads into P. del Collegio Romano. P. di Sant'Ignazio is one block off V.d. Corso on V.d. Caravita (four blocks up from P. Venezia).

PALAZZO DORIA PAMPHILJ

P. del Collegio Romano's stalwart *palazzo* harbors the extensive art collection of the Galleria Doria Pamphilj (see p. 159). It was built in the late-15th century by the Doria-Pamphilj family, who inhabit it to this day. Although their part of the building is off-limits, you can look at one of the *palazzo*'s lavish apartments in the gallery.

CHURCH OF SAN MARCELLO AL CORSO

Across V.d. Corso from Palazzo Doria Pamphilj, opposite V. Lata. Open M-Sa 7:15am-12:30pm and 4:30-7pm, Su 8:30am-noon and 4-7pm; Sept.-June closed Su.

The highlight of the church is a stark and moving *Crucifixion* by Van Dyke in the sacristy. The fourth chapel on the right has three excellent busts by Algardi.

Piazza Mattei

Campo dei Fiori

Teatro de Marcellus

CHURCH OF SANT'IGNAZIO DI LOYOLA

In P. Sant'Ignazio. Open daily 7:30am-12:30pm and 4-7:15pm.

This Jesuit church (begun in 1582 and completed in 1685) is modeled on the Gesu and is equally stunning. The ceiling is decorated with Andrea Pozzo's *trompe l'oeil fresco, The Triumph of St. Ignatius.* Pozzo designed the ceiling so its figures exist in the same space as the church's architecture, and used foreshortening to make it appear as through several more stories continued above before breaking into Heaven. The fresco shows St. Ignatius being received into heaven, while figures from all the continents embrace Christianity, an allegory of the Jesuits' missionary efforts. Be sure to see Legros's reliefs at the altar to St. Louis Gonzaga, a Roman noble who gave up his wealth to join the Jesuits (the right chapel at the crossing). Pozzo painted the false dome after a group of neighboring nuns stopped the construction of the real one, fearing that it would cut off the light to their garden.

PIAZZA COLONNA

COLUMN OF MARCUS AURELIUS

Another seven blocks up the Corso is P. Colonna, named for the massive column that dominates it. The monument was erected after Marcus Aurelius' death in AD 180. Modeled on that of his great grandfather Trajan, the column depicts the Stoic philosopher/emperor's wars against German and Sarmatian barbarians. Trajan's wars had extended the empire so far that Aurelius was forced to spend much of his reign fighting off invasions. Compared to Trajan's, the column's reliefs are rough and unrefined. Unless you're 90 ft. tall or can fly, the best way to look at the column reliefs is to go see the plaster casts of them at the **Museo della Civiltà Romana,** in EUR (p. 158). The statue on top of the column is not Marcus Aurelius, but rather St. Paul, and it was placed there by Pope Sixtus V in the 16th century.

PALAZZI

On the western side of the *piazza* (away from the Corso), **Palazzo Wedekind** (home to the newspaper *Il Tempo*) was built in 1838 with Roman columns from the Etruscan city of Veio. Check out the magnificent clock supported by four strange human figures. **Palazzo Chigi,** built in the 16th and 17th centuries and now the official residence of the Prime Minister, forms the north side of the *piazza*. Guards with really big guns prevent public entrance, but you can look through into the courtyard.

OTHER SIGHTS

Colonna's northwest corner flows into P. di Montecitorio, dominated by Bernini's **Palazzo Montecitorio,** seat of the Chamber of Deputies. The 6th-century BC obelisk in front of the *palazzo* was brought from Egypt to serve as a sundial in Augustus's *Ara Pacis* complex (see p. 82). Running off P. Colonna to the south, V. Bergamaschi leads to **Piazza di Pietra,** where the well-preserved colonnaded portico of the **Temple of Hadrian** (dedicated to the emperor in 145 by his son, Antonius Pius) forms the facade of the **Palazzo della Borsa** (the now-defunct stock exchange). Ah, progress...

PIAZZA DELLA ROTONDA

In the middle of P. della Rotunda, among the hordes of tourists and McDonald's patrons gawking at the Pantheon, Giacomo della Porta's late-Renaissance fountain supports an **Egyptian obelisk.** The phallic monolith was added in the 18th century when obelisks—popular among ancient Romans—had come into fashion. Sometimes an obelisk is just an obelisk.

PANTHEON

In P. della Rotonda. Open June M-Sa 9am-7pm, Su 9am-1pm; July-Aug. M-Sa 9am-7:30pm, Su 9am-1pm; Oct.-May M-Sa 9am-4pm, Su 9am-1pm. Free.

Originally dedicated to all the gods (the name derives from the Greek *pan*—"*all*"—and *theos*—"god"), the Pantheon has stood for nearly 2000 years, with its granite columns, pediment, and soaring domed interior remarkably the same as the day it was erected save superficial decorative alterations. The Pantheon emerged unscathed from centuries of active Christian neglect toward other pagan monuments in Rome because the Byzantine Emperor Phocas gave it to Pope Boniface IV in 606 and it was consecrated as the **Church of Santa Maria ad Martyres,** its official name to this day. Masses are held every Sunday. The Pantheon contains several important tombs: Raphael's final resting place, the third chapel on the right, is decorated by Raphael's beautiful *Madonna del Sasso*, which was commissioned by Lorenzetto. Three members of the Italian royal family are also buried here: King Vittorio Emanuele II (second chapel on the right) and King Umberto I and his wife Margherita (second on the left). The real attraction, though, is the building itself.

Hadrian had the building constructed between AD 118 and 125 (on the site of a 26 BC temple that had served the same purpose); he may have also contributed to its design as well, since he is credited with the revolutionary design of the Temple of Venus and Rome in the Forum (see p. 76), the sprawling Villa Adriana at Tivoli, and his own mausoleum (Castel Sant'Angelo; p. 115).

Following its transformation from pagan temple to Christian church in 606, the Pantheon weathered the Middle Ages with few losses, although it sometimes moonlighted as a fortress and even a fish market (the spotty low holes on the interior walls are marks from the wooden stands vendors built right into the structure). The building has served as the inspiration for countless Renaissance and Neoclassical edifices, including the Jefferson Memorial in Washington, DC. Michelangelo, who used the Pantheon as a model for St. Peter's Basilica, is said to have designed his own dome 2m shorter in diameter, knowing that a dome that wide would not collapse. The 17th century wasn't quite so deferential: when Barberini Pope Urban VIII melted down the bronze door (which has since been replaced), the bronze eagle that adorned the tympanum, and other elements to make cannons for Castel Sant'Angelo (as well as the *Baldacchino* of St. Peter's), horrified Romans remonstrated: "What the barbarians didn't do, the Barberini did."

EXTERIOR

The traditional triangular pediment, inscribed dedication, and Corinthian columns of the exterior are all designed to deceive the first-time visitor into expecting an equally traditional interior: in fact, the only purpose of the large rectangular brick element that rises behind the pediment is to hide the dome from the view of those approaching (this effect worked better in the days of the Roman Empire, when the level of the surrounding *piazza* was some seven meters lower and the temple had to be approached by a staircase). The inscription across the frieze on the facade is

Piazza del'Orlogio

Bar da Benito

Marcus Aurelius

deceptive too: "Marcus Agrippa Lu[c]i fi[l]ius co[n]s[ul] tertium fecit," meaning "Marcus Agrippa, son of Lucius, made this in his third consulship." This refers to the earlier temple, which Hadrian tore down after a fire in AD 117. He presumably had the old inscription copied here to avoid accusations of overweaning pride.

DOME

All modesty was left at the door. Even if you have spotted the dome from outside, the central *oculus* (the big hole in the ceiling), comes as a shock. The dome itself has a radius and a height of 21.3m, making it a perfect half-sphere, and its base is as far from the floor as from the top of the dome, so that if a sphere were placed inside the buiding, it would touch both the top and bottom of the room. The dome was constructed entirely out of poured concrete in a series of rings decreasing in thickness and weight, without supporting vaults, arches, or ribs. The dome is the largest ever covered in masonry, a fact that has perplexed centuries of archaeologists and architects. The 9m *oculus* provides the only source of light. The sunlight that enters via the *oculus* was originally used to mark time on a sundial. The interior is stunning during a rainstorm, when a column of water comes straight down through the *oculus* in a perfect circle.

PIAZZA DELLA MINERVA

ELEFANTINO

A cute little monument marks the center of this tiny *piazza:* a statue of a baby elephant known as the Elefantino, or **Pulcin della Minerva.** Crafted by Bernini, it supports a 6th-century BC Egyptian obelisk. The monument was set up in 1667, in honor of Pope Alexander VI. The gist of the inscription is that it takes a strong mind (the elephant is symbolic of Alexander's mind) to support wisdom (the obelisk).

CHURCH OF SANTA MARIA SOPRA MINERVA

Open M-Sa 7am-7pm, Su 7am-1pm and 3:30-7pm.

The gleaming white Church of Santa Maria Sopra Minerva was built on top of a temple incorrectly attributed to Minerva, Goddess of Wisdom. Begun by the Dominicans in 1280, this is the only Gothic church in all of Rome, although the simple exterior, which was redone in the 19th century, does not belie it. To the right of the entrance, six plaques mark the high-water levels of Tiber floods over the centuries. The interior is pure Gothic, and spangled with colored shadows from the beautiful stained glass windows. The highlight of the church is Fra Filippo Lippi's magnificent fresco cycle showing the life of St. Thomas Aquinas, in the **Carafa Chapel,** the last chapel in the left transept.To the left of the high altar is Michelangelo's 1520 sculpture, **Christ the Redeemer.** The chapels on the right house a number of treasures as well, including (in the fifth) a panel of the *Annunciation* by Antoniazzo Romano, a pupil of Pinturicchio. The altar of many a church in Rome houses a holy relic, and Santa Maria Sopra Minerva has a great one—the body of St. Catherine of Siena, the famous 14th-century ascetic and church reformer who died in a house nearby. To the left of the altar, another medieval great, the painter-saint Fra Angelico, lies under a tomb surrounded by a bronze-leaved fence.

PIAZZA SAN LUIGI DEI FRANCESI

CHURCH OF SAN LUIGI DEI FRANCESI

One block down V.d. Salvatore from C. Rinascimento as it passes P. Navona. Open F-W 7:30am-12:30pm and 3:30-7pm, Th 7:30am-12:30pm.

The simple and sooty Church of San Luigi dei Francesi serves as the French National Church in Rome (Bastille Day is celebrated in the *piazza*) and is home to three of **Caravaggio**'s most famous ecclesiastical masterpieces. The flamboyant artist decorated the last chapel on the left, dedicated to the evangelist St. Matthew, between 1597 and 1602. The *Calling of St. Matthew,* to the left of the chapel's altar, is the most famous piece, but *St. Matthew and the Angel,* in the center, and the *Crucifixion of St. Matthew,* to the right, are also breathtaking. You must pay L200 to shed light on the works, or it'll be impossible to see anything. All of the paintings are characterized by Caravaggio's dramatic use of light to highlight the theological and emotional point of the paintings and to accentuate his careful compositions. His works are also very immediate because of their careful attention to natural and even grimy details, so much so that the picture of *St. Matthew and the Angel* is a toned down version after the patrons of the chapel found the first one inappropriate.

CHURCH OF SANT'IVO

One block down V. Dogana Vecchia from S. Luigi dei Francesi; turn right as you exit the church. Open daily 10am-4pm.

Borromini's stunning and mathematical Church of Sant'Ivo exhibits its famous corkscrew cupola over the Palazzo della Sapienza, the original home of the University of Rome. The entrance to the **cloister** (around the corner at C. del Rinascimento, 40) provides the best view of the recently restored Borromini facade and cupola, designed in 1660. The interior of the church is amazing—completely white, and designed in the form of a star, in a complex geometric pattern. The view of the facade from the courtyard is stunningly lit during the late afternoon.

PIAZZA NAVONA AND ENVIRONS

Navona is the archetypical Roman piazza. Built over ancient ruins, made lavish by Baroque popes, and always the scene of lively street life, almost every visitor to Rome passes through here. The street vendors have shifted from tomatoes and sausages to caricatures and fake soccer jerseys, but the piazza is lively from the morning until well after midnight. Meanwhile, pickpockets ply their trade in the shadow of Navona's three fountains, while customers of the expensive *enoteche* and restaurants nearby do their best to look like jaded sophisticates, even while shooing away rose-selling *vu cumpràs*. It's hustle. It's bustle. For better or worse, it's Rome.

Navona's oblong shape is due to its past as a stadium built by Domitian in AD 86. You can still see some of the stadium's foundations in P. Tor Sanguigna, immediately outside the northern end of Piazza Navona. Contrary to popular belief, Domitian never used this 30,000-person venue to shred Christians; it was a racetrack. From its opening day, the stadium witnessed daily contests of strength and agility: wrestling matches, javelin and discus tosses, foot and chariot races, and even mock naval battles. For the sea-faring fracas, the stadium was flooded and filled with fleets of ships skippered by convicts. If ruins give you a craving for ancient sculpture, continue north to **Museo Nazionale Romano Palazzo Altemps** (p. 155).

As the Empire fell, real-life battles with marauding Goths replaced staged contests, the stadium fell into disuse, and Romans used its crumbling outer walls as foundations for new houses. Crowds returned to the *piazza* when the space hosted the city's general market from 1477 to 1869. Festivals and jousts were commonplace, as was the contest of the *Cuccagna*, in which contestants shimmied up a greased pole to win fabulous prizes. These days, the market, selling beautifully crafted porcelain *presepi* (nativity scenes), marzipan fruit, and *Befane* of every size, comes to the *piazza* only from Christmas until Epiphany (Jan. 6). Legitimate portrait artists and less legitimate caricaturists, roost here year-round, as do multilingual fortune tellers.

Navona owes much of its existence to a case of pure oneupsmanship. Innocent X, the Pamphilj Pope who came to the papal throne in 1644, was eager to distract the Roman people from the achievements of his predecessor, the ubiquitous Barberini Urban VIII. Innocent cleared out the old stadium (where his family had had a palace for centuries) and set about constructing a new *piazza* and palace to rival those of the Barberini family across town (see **Piazza Barberini,** p. 105). If Innocent were alive today, you can be sure that not only would Piazza Navona have a Planet Hollywood like P. Barberini, but it would be bigger and better.

FOUNTAIN OF THE FOUR RIVERS

The towering, rippling bodies in Bernini's famous Fountain of the Four Rivers *(Fontana dei Quattro Fiumi)* command the center of the *piazza* with the grandeur that Innocent intended. In an effort to sabotage his nemesis, the Pope managed to divert the flow of a repaired channel, which had been supplying the Fontana del Tritone in Piazza Barberini. Having stolen old Urban's thunder, Innocent commissioned Bernini to make something impressive out of it, and the artist responded with this work.

Each of the river gods represents one of the four continents of the globe (as they were thought of then): the Ganges for Asia, the Danube for Europe, the Nile for Africa (veiled, since the source of the river was unknown), and the Rio de la Plata for the Americas. Beneath the figure of the Plata is a strange looking armadillo, representing American wildlife, and a bag of coins suggesting the wealth of New Spain.

According to legend, Bernini designed the Nile and Plata statues to shield their eyes from his arch-rival Borromini's Church of San Agnese in Agone. The rivalry continued when Borromini made his statue of St. Agnes perched on top of the church to look out beyond the *piazza*, not deigning to drop her gaze onto Bernini's work. At least half of the story seems to be a sham, however, since the fountain was finished in 1651, before Borromini had even started work on the church.

OTHER FOUNTAINS

At the southern end of the *piazza*, the **Fontana del Moro** attracts pigeons and small children alike. Originally designed by Giacomo della Porta in the 16th century—Bernini renovated it in 1653 and added Il Moro—the central figure perches precariously on a mollusk while struggling with a fish, supposedly modeled on a king of the Congo who died in Rome while on a mission to the Pope. The tritons around the edge of the fountain were moved to the Giardino del Lago in the Villa Borghese in 1874 and replaced by copies. Balancing the whole scene is the **Fountain of Neptune,** flowing in the north end of the *piazza*. It too was designed by della Porta and spruced up by Bernini, but was without a central figure until 1878, when Antonio della Bitta added the Neptune.

CHURCH OF SANT'AGNESE IN AGONE

Western side of P. Navona, opposite Fontana d. Quattro Fiumi. Open Tu-Sa 4:30-7pm, Su 10am-1pm.

According to legend, in ancient times St. Agnes rebuffed the advances of the lascivious son of a magistrate and was stripped naked in Domitian's stadium as punishment. Miraculously, her hair instantly grew to cover her shameful nudity. Unhappy with this miracle, her persecutors tried to burn her at the stake. When the flames didn't singe her, efficient Diocletian decided to cut her head off. It worked. The church marks the spot where she was nearly exposed and houses her severed skull (referred to as the *Sacra Testa*, or Holy Head) in its sacristy. The chapels above the altars are decorated with reliefs and statues instead of paintings, largely by Bernini's pupil Ferrata. Borromini designed the dome and facade with twin bell towers.

PIAZZA SANT'AGOSTINO

CHURCH OF SANT'AGOSTINO

From P. Navona, take V. Agonale north; bear right into P.d. S. Apollinare, then immediately left into P.S. Agostino. Open daily 7:45am-noon and 4:30-7:30pm.

The simple Renaissance facade of the **Church of Sant'Agostino** is a sharp contrast to its ornate interior; its 15th-century design was augmented by layers of Baroque and Rococo stucco and frippery. Keep an eye out for Raphael's shiny *Prophet Isaiah*, on the third pillar of the left aisle. For L200/€0.10, turn on the lights to see the detail of Caravaggio's shadowy *Madonna of the Pilgrims*, in the chapel on the left.

SANTA MARIA DELLA PACE

CHURCH OF SANTA MARIA DELLA PACE

From P. Navona, take V. Agonale north; bear right into P. di S. Apollinare, then immediately left into P.S. Agostino. Open daily 7:45am-noon and 4:30-7:30pm.

To enter the church, pass through **Bramante's cloisters.** Originally built in 1480, the church's facade received a facelift from the imaginative Baroque architect da Cortona in 1656, giving it a charming semicircular porch and making it so popular among Rome's upper crust that the *piazza* became jammed with the carriages of devout patricians. It was only in the 19th century that the *piazza* was expanded, a development so popular that a Latin inscription was put up declaring that no stone in the *piazza* could ever be moved. The **Chigi chapel** (first on the right) is decorated with *The Sybils* by **Raphael.**

The painting of the Virgin over the altar supposedly bled when hit by a stone in the 15th century; the church was built in commemoration.

CHURCH OF SANTA MARIA DELL'ANIMA

V.d. Pace, 20. Across from S. Maria della Pace. Open M-F 8am-7pm, Sa 8am-6pm, Su 8am-1pm and 3-7pm. Ring the bell to enter.

The unassuming German National Church in Rome hides a fragrant courtyard and a spookily deserted, dark interior. Keep an eye out for the bizarre skull-cherub reliefs everywhere and the smooth imitation of Michelangelo's *Pietà*, along with Peruzzi's excellent tomb of the German Pope Adrian IV. Be sure to look for Duqesnoy's beautiful putti on the tomb of van der Eynden.

Piazza del Poppolo

VIA DEL GOVERNO VECCHIO

V.d. Governo Vecchio runs west from the southern end of P. Navona, and is best known for its art and antique galleries and restaurants. The street, which heads west to the Vatican, used to be a papal thoroughfare, lined with the townhouses of prosperous bankers and merchants.

PIAZZA PASQUINO

Here, at the beginning of the road, a misshapen figure is all that remains of poor Pasquino, an ancient Roman bust that has been used as a a *statua parlante* or "talking statue" (basically a communal bitchboard) ever since Cardinal Caraffa put him here in 1501. Bringing together Rome's classical past, popular life, and repressive governments, irate citizens are free to cover Pasquino with their complaints about government, the church, or just about anything else. Though in earlier times people wrote directly onto the statue, nowadays signs and posters are taped to it.

Mausoleum of Augustus

PIAZZA DELL'OROLOGIO

Farther down the street, Borromini's Baroque clock tower stands guard—when it's not shrouded in scaffolding. Don't miss the beautiful Virgin supported by cherubs carved into the rear corner of the oratory below the clock tower. Beyond P. dell'Orologio, V.d. Governo Vecchio becomes V.d. Banchi Nuovi, and ends in P. Banco di Santo Spirito. In the 15th century, the *via* and *piazza* made up a banking district that attracted moguls from all over Italy. Not only did they change and hoard money here, but they also acted as bookies, taking bets on anything from sporting events to papal behavior. (The "pope eating a baby" 300 to 1 longshot was never cashed in.) The **Palazzo di Banco di Santo Spirito** was founded by Pope Paul V to provide credit to poor Romans, and the building is modeled on a Roman triumphal arch. The dank little **Arco dei Banchi,** on the left down V.d. S. Spirito toward the Tiber,

Villa Médici

houses a Virgin and lamp to which Catholic passersby say a quick Hail Mary. Just inside the entrance and to the left, the arch shows the height of the 1277 flood.

CHIESA NUOVA

Bus #64 or 40. Seven blocks down C.V. Emanuele II from P. Sant'Andrea della Valle. Church open daily 8am-noon and 4:30-7pm.

Originally founded in the 12th century as Santa Maria in Vallicella, Chiesa Nuova became the home base for Philip Neri's congregation of Counter-Reformation Oratorians. He remodeled the church in 1605, calling it the "new church" (it was further restored in the 19th century). The compassionate Neri was one of the great church reformers in the Counter Reformation, and organized pious associations that cut across social lines to unite people. He often tested the piety of his aristocratic followers by making them do ridiculous things as a test of faith, such as wearing foxtails through the streets or working as manual laborers on his church. During construction, the future St. Philip had a vision of the Virgin rescuing churchgoers by supporting a collapsing section of the old church; inspection of the beams proved that they were indeed about to fall apart. **Pietro da Cortona** represented this mini-miracle in a 1644 ceiling painting; he also painted the decorations of the dome and the apse over the altar. The altar is decorated with three excellent early paintings by **Peter Paul Rubens** paintings (1606-1608). The chapel on the left holds the remains of St. Philip Neri and is decorated with a mosaic version of Guido Reni's painting of the saint. Head through the door to the left of the altar to enter the sacristy designed by Borromini, and decorated with an excellent statue of St. Phillip Neri by Algardi. Ask if the **rooms of the saint** are open—they contain more paintings by Reni, Cortona, and Guercino. Next door is the 17th-century **Palazzo dei Filippini,** designed by Borromini, featuring the complex concave and convex surfaces that are his trademark.

CAMPO DEI FIORI

Two blocks south of C. V. Emanuele II (on P. della Cancelleria or V.d. Paradiso) stands Rome's most schizophrenic *piazza*, **Campo dei Fiori,** a bustling marketplace during the day that turns into a bustling meatmarket of drunken young foreigners when the sun goes down (see p. 186). Until papal rule ended in 1869, the area was the site of countless executions. In the middle of the Campo, a statue commemorates the death of its most famous victim: **Giordano Bruno** (1548-1600), who rises above the bustle with his arms folded over a book. Scientifically and philosophically out of sync with his time, Bruno sizzled at the stake in 1600 for taking Copernicus one step farther: he argued that the universe had no center at all, and also tried to legitimize magic. Now the only carcasses that litter the *piazza* are those of the fish in the colorful **market** (open M-Sa 6am-2pm).

NEAR CAMPO DEI FIORI

PALAZZO DELLA CANCELLERIA

Just down P. Cancelleria from the Campo and around the corner, left on C. Vittorio Emanuele II. Open daily 7am-noon and 5-8:30pm; in winter 7am-noon and 4:30-8pm. No admission beyond courtyard.

A stone coat of arms marks this early Renaissance *palazzo*. Designed in 1485, it impressed an array of popes and cardinals who affixed their insignia to it. The building's designer remains unknown, but its unprecedented size and style have led the optimistic to suspect Bramante. While Bramante may not have had anything to do with the building itself, his fingerprints are all over the **courtyard,** which is ringed by three stories of *loggie* supported by Doric columns and resembles his restoration of the adjoining **Basilica of San Lorenzo in Damaso.** Today, the Cancelleria is the seat of the three Tribunals of the Vatican and is considered part of the Vatican City.

THEATER OF POMPEY

Walk out of Campo dei Fiori on Passetto del Biscione; go right at V.d. Grotta Pinta.

The V. Grotta Pinta is a canyon of curved palazzi built over the remains of the semi-circular Theater of Pompey. Pompey the Great, one of the power-hungry generals of the first century BC, competed with his rival Julius Caesar in both war and peace.

When Caesar's popular victories in Gaul became too galling, the pompous Pompey built a grandiose theater, the first of its kind in the city. Unfortunately, the prudish Senate had outlawed permanent theaters because they feared they would corrupt public morals. To outwit the censors, Pompey built a small shrine at the top of the stands and called the whole complex a temple. Though Caesar bested Pompey politically, the old general still got the last laugh: it was in Pompey's portico, built to surround his sumptuous theater, that Caesar was assassinated on the Ides of March, 44 BC. A note to archaeology nuts: on the back side of the theater on V.d. Biscione, two restaurants, **Ristorante San Pancrazio** and **Ristorante da Costanza,** have basement dining rooms built out of the theater's substructure.

CHURCH OF SAN CARLO AI CATINARI

Turn right from V.d. Grotta Pinta onto V.d. Chiavar and then left on V.d. Giubbonari. Open daily 6:30am-noon and 4:30-7pm.

Built from 1612 to 1620 by Rosato Rosati, the highlights of the church are decorations by top Baroque artists. Da Cortona painted the altarpiece, showing St. Charles helping plague victims; the apse is decorated with St. Charles's apotheosis by Lanfranco, and Domenico painted the pendentives.

PALAZZO MASSIMO "ALLE COLONNE"

Open for mass M-Sa 7:30am and 7:15pm, Su 7:30 and 11:30am and 7:15pm.

Just across C. Vittorio Emanuele II from P. della Cancelleria in P.S. Pantaleo, this *palazzo* was built by Baldassar Peruzzi in 1527 and is home to a family that traces its origins all the way back to the Roman general Fabius Maximus (hence "Massimo") Cunctator, who kept Hannibal from capturing Rome in the late third century BC. When Napoleon questioned one of the family about their claims of Roman lineage, he replied that he could not say if they were true or not, only that was his family had believed for the last 15 centuries. The *palazzo* has a curved exterior because it rests on the foundations of Domitian's ancient Odeon theater. Behind the *palazzo*, a solitary column remains from the ancient edifice. The back wall of the palace preserves a cycle of 16th-century monochrome paintings; most houses in Rome once boasted such intricate decoration, but few have resisted the assaults of wind and rain as well as this one. Also in P.S. Pantaleo, is the 1216 **Church of San Pantaleo.** Giuseppe Valadier added the strange facade in 1806.

PALAZZO DELLA FARNESINA AI BAULLARI

Just across C. Vittorio Emanuele II from Palazzo Massimo, this little *palazzo*, also known as the **Piccola Farnesina,** holds its own against the Campo's other stunning *palazzi*. Built in 1523 by Antonio da Sangallo the Younger for Thomas Leroy, an English diplomat, it got its name from a case of mistaken identity. Leroy's brilliant career in Rome was rewarded when he was made a nobleman and given special permission to add the lily of France to his coat of arms. The lilies were mistaken for the flowers that represent the Farnese family. The 19th-century interior houses the **Museo Barracco**'s Greek, Roman, Egyptian, and Assyrian art (see p. 160).

PIAZZA FARNESE

PALAZZO FARNESE

The Palazzo is 1 block southwest of Campo dei Fiori on V.d. Baullari. The palazzo is closed to the general public: in order to see the interior, permission from the French embassy is required.

This stately *palazzo* was begun in 1514, and is today considered the greatest of Rome's Renaissance *palazzi*. The Farnese, a noble family from the backwoods of Lazio, parlayed Pope Alexander VI's affair with Giulia Farnese into popehood for her brother Alessandro. He became **Pope Paul III,** set up the Council of Trent, refounded the Inquisition, and commissioned the best architects of his day—da Sangallo, Michelangelo, and della Porta—to design his dream abode. He also continued the trend of papal hijinks, having four illegitimate children, granting legitimacy to three.

Although the facade and entrance passage are remarkable, the most impressive part of the building is **Michelangelo**'s cornice. Note the band of *fleurs de lis* encircling the building. Since 1635, the French Embassy has rented the *palazzo* for L1 per year in exchange for the Hôtel Galiffet in Paris, home of the Italian Embassy. The Farnese family had two huge tubs (the present-day fountains) dug up from the Baths of Caracalla (see p. 84) to serve as "royal boxes" from which members of the patrician family could view the parties and shows they hosted in the square during the 16th and early 17th centuries. The interior is decorated with Annibale Carraci's ceiling relief, showing the loves of the gods, decorated with *tromp l'oeil* architecture. On the northwest side of the *piazza* stands the **Church of Santa Brigida,** whose portal upstages its *palazzo*. The Swedish St. Bridget lived here until her death in 1373.

PALAZZO SPADA

To the east of Palazzo Farnese, off P. Capo di Ferro, the Baroque **Palazzo Spada** houses the picture collection of the **Galleria Spada** (see p. 158) and also all sorts of carabinieri and dignitaries visting the Council of Ministers elsewhere in the building. The *palazzo* is a treasure in itself, recently restored to its original creamy whiteness. Outside, eight ancient Roman kings, generals, and emperors stand proudly under Latin inscriptions describing their achievements. Inside, 18 even less modest Roman gods stand, buck naked, around the court—even the prudish Vesta. Bernardino commissioned the elaborate decorations to compensate for the relatively puny size of his palace, but to make the palace seem bigger he went beyond naked gods and had Borromini design an illusionistic colonnade beyond the library on the right side of the courtyard. The colonnade seems to stretch back through a spacious garden, framing a life-size Classical statue. In reality, Borromini manipulated perspective by shrinking the columns and pavement dramatically. The colonnade is only a few meters long, the statue stands a meter tall, and the garden is no more than a narrow alley.

VIA GIULIA

As part of his campaign in the early 1500s to clean up Rome after the Babylonian Captivity (when the popes moved to Avignon and the city fell into serious disrepair; see p. 42), Pope Julius II commissioned Bramante to construct a straight road leading to the Vatican, and modestly named it after himself. V. Giulia runs parallel to the Tiber northwest from Ponte Sisto to P. d'Oro. Don't be confused by the fact that the odd building numbers begin near Ponte Sisto, while the evens begin at P. d'Oro. This relatively wide road was a contrast to the narrow and winding medieval streets of the day. Throughout the 16th century, the charming road was a fashionable neighborhood, and later architects built its expensive residences in accordance with Bramante's restrained, Classical vision. In the 17th century, Innocent X built a prison here to slum down the area and make his own P. Navona more important. It didn't work: the tiny neighborhood still attracted popes, nobility, and artists, including Raphael, who lived at #85, while P. Navona attracted second-rate caricaturists and pickpockets. The prison provided some prestige—until it fell out of use in the 18th century, experts called it the "most solid and salubrious" in Europe. The V. Giulia remains one of Rome's most exclusive streets, with well-maintained *palazzi*, antique stores, and art galleries.

MICHELANGELO'S FOOTBRIDGE

Perhaps the most striking of the area's sights is the ivy-draped bridge that spans V. Giulia from the back of the **Palazzo Farnese** (p. 97) to the Tiber embankment. Michelangelo designed the bridge, which was originally intended to be the first leg of a much longer bridge that would cross the Tiber. Michelangelo wanted to connect the *palazzo* with the Villa Farnesina on the other side (see **Museums,** p. 156), but funds dried up before its completion. Off the southeast corner of the *palazzo* lurks the **Fontana del Mascherone.** Erected by the Farnesi, its immense marble mask and granite basin are ancient Roman.

CHURCH OF SAN GIOVANNI DEI FIORENTINI

In P. d'Oro, northern end of V. Giulia. Open M-Sa 7am-noon and 4:30-7:30pm, Su and holidays 7:30am-1pm and 4:30-8pm.

Seated at the center of Rome's Renaissance Florentine community, this church was built by Pope Leo X, a Mèdici from Florence, in hopes of illustrating the glories of his hometown. All the famous artists competed for the privilege of building it; Jacopo Sansovino didn't live long enough to finish it, though, so the work was farmed out to da Sangallo and della Porta, and finally wrapped up by Carlo Moderno in 1614. Ask the sacristan to show you the *crypta Falconieri*, an impressive undergroup family tomb designed by Borromini and located behind the altar—Borromini is also buried in the church—look for his garvestone on the pillars on the left. Salvator Rosa painted the dramatic altarpiece on the right transept altar. Notice the church's two busts: Bernini's on the right and a work by his lesser-known father, Pietro, on the left.

PALAZZO SACCHETTI

This *palazzo*, down from S. Giovanni dei Fiorentini on the right, at #66, was designed in 1543 by Sangallo the Younger, who built Palazzo Farnese. The courtyard features a relief of a Madonna and Child illuminated by a candle. In the two blocks between V.d. Gonfalone and V.d. Cefalo, giant stones known as the **Via Giulia sofas** protrude from the buildings on the left. Meant to be the foundation for the never-completed courts of Julius II, they eventually served as bases for Innocent X's prisons. To see the big house, head to **Museo Criminologico** (p. 160). The prison also houses the Ministry of Mercy and Justice. A block north on V.d. Banchi Vecchi is Alexander VI's **Palazzo Sforza Cesarini.**

PALAZZO FALCONIERI

At the southern end of V. Giulia on the river side is the sumptuous Palazzo Falconieri, which was expanded by Borromini and has housed the Hungarian Academy since 1928. The *palazzo* looks out over the river, and easily recognizable by the giant falcons with breasts that roost on each corner. Hot stuff.

SANTA MARIA DELL'ORAZIONE E MORTE

Next to Palazzo Falconieri. Open Su and holidays for 6pm mass.

This Corinthian column-studded church was revamped by Ferdinando Fuga from 1733 to 1737. Its decorated with a *vanitas* skull motif and belongs to a confraternity founded in 1551 to collect unidentified corpses and give them Christian burials.

LARGO ARGENTINA

Toward the beginning of C. Vittorio Emanuele II lies Largo di Torre Argentina (referred to as Largo Argentina), a busy cross-street that sees an unhealthy portion of Rome's bus and taxi traffic. The largo, named for the square *Torre Argentina* (silver tower) that dominates its southeastern corner, is filled with medieval towers and narrow old houses.

Piazza di Siena

Galleria Borghese

Muro Torto

AREA SACRA DI LARGO ARGENTINA

This sunken area in the center of the largo is a complex of four Republican temples unearthed during Mussolini's project of demolishing the medieval city. Their excavation is as much testament to *il Duce*'s disregard for Rome's medieval heritage as it is a tribute to his reverence for its antiquities. Archaeologists don't know to whom the temples were dedicated, but it is believed that they were connected with the larger complex built around the **Theater of Pompey** (see p. 96). The site is now a **cat shelter,** and dozens of cats patrol its grounds, providing the photos of cats sitting on broken columns that postcard and calendar makers love so much. The shelter appreciates small donations to help feed the cats.

CHURCH OF SANT'ANDREA DELLA VALLE

One block down C. Vittorio Emanuele II from Largo Argentina. Open M-Sa 7:30am-noon and 4:30-7:30pm, Su 7:30am-12:45pm and 4:30-7:45pm.

Begun in 1591 by Grimaldi and completed by Baroque bigwig Carlo Maderno, this church sports a 1665 facade by Rainaldi, who challenged the contemporary style by displaying rows of columns and pediments in place of swirls and curls. The conventional interior, where Puccini's opera *Tosca* begins, is modeled on **Il Gesù** (p. 88). The massive interior of the church is dominated by an array of excellent Baroque paintings. Lanfranco frescoed the dome with its depiction of layers of angels, while Domenicino painted the pendetives and the scenes of the life of the saint in the curved area above the altar, with their beautiful landscapes. The most striking paintings are Mattia Preti's scenes of the martyrdom of St. Andrew behind the altar.

JEWISH GHETTO

South of Largo Argentina. Bordered by V. Arenula (tram #8) on the west and by V.d. Teatro di Marcello (bus #44, 63, or 170) on the east. The Service International de Documentation Judeo-Chrétienne, V. Plebiscito, 112, an information center for Jewish-Christian relations, has ½-day walking tours of the Ghetto during the school year (☎06 6795307; L5000/€2.58 donation). Enjoy Rome (p. 23) offers an informative tour of the Ghetto and Trastevere.

Although Dickens declared the area "a miserable place, densely populated, and reeking with bad odours," today's Jewish Ghetto is one of Rome's most charming and eclectic neighborhoods, with family businesses dating back centuries and restaurants serving up some of the tastiest food in the city (see p. 171).

The Jewish community in Rome is the oldest in Europe, and began in the late Roman Republic when migrants arrived to be near the political and economic hub of the Mediterranean. Romans were initially tolerant, but in the 6th century, Pope Paul IV decided that the Jewish population of Rome should be confined to its own neighborhood, and erected the walled ghetto in a neighborhood prone to flooding. He restricted its inhabitants to careers in money-lending and used clothes peddling, and required them to swear oaths of submission to the pope in annual ceremonies by the **Arch of Titus** (p. 76), a monument celebrating the Roman conquest of Jerusalem. The ghetto was torn down after the unification of Italy, but many of Rome's Jews were deported to concentration camps during the Nazi occupation.

CHURCH OF SANTA MARIA IN CAMPITELLI

Off of V.d. Teatro di Marcello in P. di Campitelli. Open M-Sa 7am-noon and 4-7pm, Su and holidays for mass 7:30, 10am, noon, and 6:30pm.

A surprisingly successful project during the Counter-Reformation effort to beautify Rome was relocating an earlier church here to this swanky *piazza*. Carlo Rainaldi designed the church, which exemplifies the theatrics of Baroque architecture. Built in 1662 to give thanks to Mary for delivering the city from plague in 1656, it still houses the statuette believed to have miraculously ended the plague.

PALAZZO CENCI

Technically outside the Ghetto, Palazzo Cenci is at the end of V. Catalana, which runs parallel to V.d. Portico d'Ottavia. This palazzo was home to Beatrice Cenci, made famous by Dickens's and Shelley's accounts of her execution after she, along with her brother and stepmother, murdered her cruel and incestous father at the end of the 16th century in a crime that shocked Rome.

SANT'ANGELO IN PESCHERIA

Toward the eastern end of V.d. Portico d'Ottavia. Prayer meetings W 5:30pm and Sa 5pm.

This church was built right into the Portico d'Ottavia (see p. 87) in 755 and named after the fish market that once flourished here. You can still see an official plaque requiring that the head and body up to the first fin of any fish longer than the length of the plaque be given to the Conservators of Rome. It was here that the Jews of the Ghetto were forced to attend mass every Sunday from 1584 until the 18th century—they quietly resisted the forced evangelism by stuffing their ears with wax.

SINAGOGA ASKENAZITA

At the corner of Lungotevere dei Cenci and V. Catalan, opposite the Theater of Marcellus. ☎06 6875051. Temple open for services only.

The heavily guarded synagogue symbolizes the unity of the Jewish people in Rome and proclaims its unique heritage in a city of Catholic iconography. Built between 1874 and 1904, it incorporates Persian and Babylonian architectural devices, attempting to create a different architecural style from Christian churches. A gray metal dome tops the temple, and, inside, the front is graced with seven massive gold menorahs below the rainbow-colored dome. Orthodox services, to which anyone is welcome, are given entirely in Hebrew. The temple is heavily guarded after a 1982 terrorist attack by a PLO splinter group.To protect worshipers, the doors are bolted from the inside during services. The synagogue houses the **Jewish Community Museum** (see p. 161), a visit to which gets you a brief tour of the temple itself.

PIAZZA MATTEI

The center of the Ghetto, accessible by walking down toward the river on V. Paganica from V.d.Botteghe Oscure (which runs between V. Arenula and P. Venezia).

TORTOISE FOUNTAIN

The 16th-century Fontana delle Tartarughe, in which four little boys are portrayed standing on the backs of small dolphins while pushing tortoises into the water, is the center of this hidden *piazza*. Designed by Florentine Giacomo della Porta, the fountain wasn't graced with turtles until Bernini restored it in 1658. According to local legend, Duke Mattei, a notorious gambler, lost everything in one night, and his father-in-law-to-be was so disgusted that he rescinded his approval of the marriage. The Duke, in a bid to wrest his name from the mud of scandal, had the fountain built in one night to prove that a Mattei could accomplish anything, even when completely destitute. Apparently, speed-fountain-building was a desirable skill for a suitor; he got the girl, although she did block up her window so she would never have to see the fountain that got her married.

RED BRIGADE MURDER

The infamous Red Brigade kidnappers and murderers of former Prime Minister Aldo Moro dumped his body here in P. Mattei in 1978 (see **The 20th Century,** p. 44)—there are occasionally flowers and candles to commemorate the bloody events of that year. They chose the location since it was between the headquaters of the Christian Democrats and the Communists, between whom Moro brokered a reconciliation. Moro's likeness is at V. Caetani, 9, the street to the right of Palazzo Mattei.

PIAZZA DI SPAGNA AND THE CORSO

see map p. 315

M: A-Spagna. Touring the area should take about a half-day.

If you need directions to the Piazza di Spagna, you're lost. The most self-consciously glamorous spot in Rome, the azalea-decked Spanish Steps rise from a crowded *piazza* to a rosy church flanked by palm trees—it's no wonder postcard photographers abound. For years this area was the artistic and literary center of Rome, but today artists of *haute couture* have

TOO MUCH CAPPUCCINO WILL DO THE SAME TO YOU

The bones of 4000 Capuchin friars (for whom cappuccino is named) decorate the four rooms of the Church of L'Immacolata Concezione's Cappuchin Crypt, one of the most bizarre and elaborately macabre settings in Rome. A French monk inaugurated the crypt in 1528, but never saw his brilliant concept brought to its completion because the crypt was not finished until 1870. Angels deck the halls, with hip bones serving as wings. The bodies of more recently dead friars stand, robed and hooded, beneath bone arches. Even the hanging lights are made of bones. Dirt was shipped in especially from Jerusalem to line the floors. The last chapel displays two severed arms with mummy-like skin hanging on the back wall. Also featured in this chapel is a child's skeleton plastered to the ceiling, holding a scale and a reaper, and accompanied by the uplifting inscription: "What you are now we used to be, what we are now you will be."

replaced scribbling poets and portrait painters. Lament the loss over an espresso at **L'Antica Caffe Greco,** indulge in some high-end retail-therapy, or simply sit on the steps with a gelato and enjoy your Roman Holiday—just like Audrey Hepburn.

The Spanish Steps and P. di Spagna were once literally Spanish; the area around the Spanish ambassador's residence, located in the western end of the hourglass-shaped *piazza* since 1622, once held the privilege of extra-territoriality. Wandering foreigners who fell asleep there were liable to wake up the next morning as grunts in the Spanish army. Nowadays, they're more likely to wake up with no wallet.

SPANISH STEPS

Designed by an Italian, paid for by the French, named for the Spaniards, occupied by the British, and currently under the sway of American ambassador-at-large Ronald McDonald, the Spanish Steps *(Scalinata di Spagna)* often appear as if they could be an alternate location for the United Nations. The 137 steps (count 'em) were constructed from 1723 to 1725 to link the *piazza* with important locales above it, including the Pincio and the Villa Mèdici. The beginning of May heralds the world-famous flower show, when the steps are covered with azaleas and photographers, and each July an evening fashion show is held on the steps. When the steps first opened, Romans hoping to earn extra *scudi* as artists' models flocked to the steps dressed as the Madonna and Julius Caesar. Posers of a different sort abound today, and dressing like a virgin does not seem to be the main objective. Each night, hordes of testosterone-injected adolescent males, along with tipsy foreigners imitating their Italian counterparts, descend on the *piazza* in search of women.

FONTANA DELLA BARACCIA

Barges are not known for their inspirational qualities, but when one such vessel washed up in the piazza after the Tiber flooded on Christmas Day, 1598, Gian Lorenzo Bernini's less famous father Pietro decided to immortalize it in stone. The fountain, currently undergoing restorations, has anchored the steps ever since. To compensate for meager water pressure, the fountain was built below ground level.

CHURCH OF SANT'ANDREA DELLE FRATTE

V.S. Andrea, 1. Facing the Spanish Steps, walk to your right and take V.d. Propaganda until it intersects V. Mercede. Open daily 6:30am-12:30pm and 4-7pm.

Capped by a Borromini bell tower (on which 8 delicate angels fold their wings while small faces peek out of the Corinthian columns on the lower ring), this church's strong point is definitely its exterior. If you have time, though, head inside to see the two angels near the altar, Bernini works that originally decorated the Ponte Sant'Angelo. Their companions can still be seen along the bridge in front of Castel Sant'Angelo (see p. 115). Also make sure to stop at the second chapel on the left, dedicated to the miraculous appearance of the Madonna to Jewish banker Alphonse Ratisbonne on January 20, 1842. Alphonse immediately converted to Christianity, became a man of the cloth, and later worked as a missionary in Palestine. Hundreds of lace hearts now hang on the altar and its surrounding columns to commemorate the event.

OTHER SIGHTS

At the southern end of the *piazza* rises the Column of the Immaculata, an 1857 celebration of Pope Pius IX's acceptance of the Immaculate Conception. On December 8, the Pope kneels at the base, while Roman firemen climb their ladders to place a wreath atop the column. Just behind the column stands the Collegio di Propaganda Fide, or, as the Latin inscription above the entrance reads, the *Collegivm Vrbanvm de Propaganda Fide.* Though it sounds like a leftover from the Fascist era, the college was actually founded to train missionaries in the 16th century. The undulating facade along V.d. Propaganda was designed by Borromini. Just across from Sant'Andrea delle Fratte, at V.d. Mercede, 12, a plaque commemorates the building, now full of offices, where Bernini died.

NEAR THE STEPS

CHURCH OF SANTA TRINITA' DEI MONTI

At the top of the Steps. Open daily 9:30am-12:30pm and 4-7pm; upper half open Tu and Th 4-6pm.

After indulging in the 5th sin (gluttony) at your choice of establishments on V. Condotti, climb the stairs of heaven to the **Church of Santa Trinita dei Monti.** (Confessionals on the right.) The Neoclassical church was designed by Carlo Maderno and provides a worthy incentive to climb the steps, not to mention a sweeping view of the city. Known as the Church of the Kings of France, Santa Trinita was Built in 1502 under the auspices of French King Charles VIII. Shortly thereafter the church was unceremoniously pillaged in the infamous 1527 sack of the city by Spanish King Charles V. Maderno. Work was completed on the new building in 1570, and it was consecrated in 1595. This time, the church lasted over 200 years until it was visited and sacked anew in 1798 by armies of Revolutionary France. The church was restored after the fall of Napoleon, and today the only original part of the church is the transept, above the largest altar.

Castel Sant'Angelo

Pietà

St. Peter's Basilica

The third chapel on the right and the second chapel on the left contain works by Michelangelo's star pupil, Daniele da Volterra. The last figure on the right of his *Assumption* depicts his cantankerous teacher, but is currently undergoing restoration. Poussin rated Volterra's other painting, *Deposition from the Cross*, as one of the three greatest paintings ever. Having been restored twice and traveled to the Mèdici Villa and back, the painting is a bit worse for the wear. The fourth chapel on the left in the north transept was frescoed in the 16th century by the Zuccari brothers. The obelisk in the center of the church's *piazza* was brought to Rome in the 2nd century; its hieroglyphics were plagiarized from the obelisk in P. del Popolo.

VILLA MÈDICI

Villa Mèdici, Via Trinita dei Monti, 1. ☎066761320. Open W-M 10:30am-7:30pm. Closed Tuesdays. Exhibits usually L15,000/€7.75.

To the left of Santa Trinità, the Villa Mèdici houses the **Accademia di Francia.** Founded in 1666 to give young French artists an opportunity to live in Rome (Berlioz and Debussy were among the scheme's beneficiaries),the Academy continues to house creative Francophiles and arranges excellent exhibits, primarily of French art. Behind the severe facade lies a beautiful garden (with sweeping views of the city) and elaborate rear facade. The **Pincio,** a park with formal gardens, extends up the hill beyond the villa.

PIAZZA DI TREVI

M: A-Barberini or A-Spagna. Or, take a bus to P.S. Silvestro or Largo del Tritone.

TREVI FOUNTAIN

Nicolo Salvi's (1697-1751) extravagant and now sparkling clean Fontana di Trevi emerges from the back wall of **Palazzo Poli.** The fountain was completed in 1762 by Giuseppe Pannini, who may have altered the original design, but did not make sandwiches. The fountain may also have been based on designs by Bernini which elaborated on a simpler one by Leon Battista Alberti; the idea for combining the fountain and *palazzo* was based on a project by da Cortona. Regardless of its architectural heritage, Fontana di Trevi has become a Roman staple, delighting tourists for centuries.

RELIEFS AND SCULPTURES

Not surprisingly, the guy in the middle of the fountain is Neptune, the god of the sea. Neptune's snazzy chariot is drawn by two winged horses, with two Tritons—representing calm and stormy seas, respectively—guiding his progress. Allegories of Abundance and Health can be found in the two niches on either side of the burly mermen, while the Four Seasons calmly survey the madness from on high, just under the Corsini family arms. In good old Roman style, The fountain's source is an aqueduct—specifically the **Acqua Vergine** aqueduct, which also supplies the spouts in P. Navona and P. di Spagna. The relief at the top of the fountain on the left shows the fountain's namesake, Trivia, the maiden who allegedly pointed out the spring for the aqueduct to thirsty Roman soldiers. The opposite relief shows Augustus's right-hand man, Agrippa, giving the go-ahead for the aqueduct in 19 BC.

The fountain cleverly incorporates the facade of the *palazzo* into its design, effectively becoming a part of the *piazza*'s architecture. Not everyone in the neighborhood was happy about this project however; it's said that the proprietor of 85 Via del Stamperia complained so loudly and for so long that a wave was built in front of his store—business has been bad ever since. Just above the wave, notice that the **window** on the upper right is not a window at all, but a painting of one. A young Corsini took his own life one day by taking a dive out of that window, and his family bricked it up.

TOSSING A COIN

Legend has it that the traveler who throws a coin into the fountain will have a speedy return to Rome. Proper form is to put one's back to the fountain and toss over the left shoulder with the right hand. As the funds increase, so do the rewards—the traveler who tosses two coins will fall in love in Rome, and after three coins the wedding bells begin to toll. Years of romantic hopes have taken their toll; the metal eats away at the travertine and stains the pool. Since the restoration, travelers have been advised not to follow the custom—this hasn't stopped many.

TAKING A DIP

In Fellini's *La Dolce Vita*, the uninhibited Anita Ekberg takes a midnight wade in the fountain. Squads of roving policemen and policewomen armed with whistles and attitude keep others from re-enacting the famous scene. Though we won't say how we came to know this, illicit bathing will cost you upwards of L1,000,000 and a stern talking-to in Italian. Impossibly buxom "model" Anna Nicole Smith tried to do her own Ekberg impression in 1997 and had to cough up the dough.

OTHER SIGHTS

SAN CRISPINO

V.d. Panetteria, 42. Facing the fountain, turn right onto V. Lavatore, and take your 2nd left. ☎06 6793924. Open M and W-Th noon-12:30am, F-Sa noon-1:30am, Su noon-midnight. Cups L3-10,000/€1.55-5.16.

San Crispino won't improve your knowledge of Rome, your aesthetic taste, or your waistline. But it will make you very, very happy. **Gelateria di San Crispino** serves heaven in a cup, and is the best *gelato* in Rome. Suggested combinations appear on a board by the door, and the Armangnac and Zabiglione are particularly fine.

CHURCH OF SANTI VINCENZO AND ANASTASIO

Opposite the Trevi Fountain. Open daily 8am-7:30pm.

The Baroque Church of Santi Vincenzo and Anastasio, rebuilt in 1630, was the parish Church of the Popes for many years. Coincidentally, S.S. Vincenao and Anastasio houses a crypt that preserves the **hearts and lungs of popes** from 1590 to 1903 in marble urns, which, unfortunately for you anatomy fans, is closed to the public.

PIAZZA BARBERINI

Rising from the hum of a busy traffic circle at the end of V.d. Tritone, Bernini's **Triton Fountain** spouts a stream of water high into the air over P. Barberini. Traffic, banks, hotels, a cinema, and Planet Hollywood give the *piazza* a distinctly modern feel. On the corner of V. V. Veneto, Bernini's **Fontana delle Api** (Bee Fountain), buzzes with the same motif that graces the Barberini coat of arms.

CHURCH OF L'IMMACOLATA CONCEZIONE

V. V. Veneto, 27a. Walk up V. V. Veneto away from P. Barberini. Open F-W 9am-noon and 3-6pm. Donation requested.

This severe 1626 Counter-Reformation church holds the tomb of Cardinal Antonio Barberini, the church founder. Seemingly the only modest member of the family, his tomb's inscription reads "Here lies dust, ashes, nothing." Head downstairs for the main attraction: the bones of 4000 dead friars in the **Capuchin Crypt** (see **Too Much Cappuccino**, p. 102). Five rooms of methodically arranged bones show off the creative, if morbid, sides of the 18th-century Capuchin friars. The church upstairs has impressive and less morbid altarpieces by major Baroque painters like Guido Reni.

PALAZZO BARBERINI

Walk on the southern side of P. Barberini, up V.d. Quattro Fontane to the Palazzo.

Carlo Maderno began this *palazzo* in 1624 on commission from Pope Urban VIII, he took on Bernini and Borromini to form a Baroque architecture tag-team and each contributed their unique style to the building. Maderno and Bernini designed the perspective effect that makes the third floor windows look the same size as those on the first floor, while Borromini designed a spiral staircase to the right behind the main facade. Inside, da Cortona decorated the main hall's ceiling with an exaltation of the various virtues of the Barberini, so they could be reminded of just how cool they really were. The *palazzo* houses the **Galleria Nazionale d'Arte Antica** (p. 157).

VIA VITTORIO VENETO

The road curves north toward the Villa Borghese.

This street that once symbolized the glamor of Rome in the 50s and 60s now houses slightly less chic airline offices and embassies. At the turn of the 19th century, pushy real-estate developers demolished many of the villas and gardens, including the wooded preserve of the **Villa Ludovisi.** The speculator who bought the Ludovisi built a colossal palace in its place, but soon even he couldn't afford those crazy 19th-century Italian taxes, and the government repossessed the palace. The US embassy now inhabits the immense palazzo (currently called the Villa Margherita), which it received in return for tons of war surplus goods in 1945. The rise of the movie industry and tourism in the 1950s marked V.V. Veneto's most glamorous days. The grand cafes and hotels attracted bigwigs like Roberto Rossellini and Ingrid Bergman, eager paparazzi, and wide-eyed Americans. V.V. Veneto's prominence has faded, though pricey cafes and restaurants still prey upon tourists.

PIAZZA DEL POPOLO

M: A-Flaminio. Exit the station and pass under the city walls to the northern entrance to the piazza. A visit to the sights below should take about an hour.

The southern end of the square marks the start of three major streets: V.d. Corso, which runs to P. Venezia (you can see the gleaming *Vittoriano* at the end); V.d. Ripetta on the right, built by Leo X for service to the Vatican; and V.d. Babuino on the left. Outside the Porta del Popolo (Bernini designed its southern facade) is an entrance to the **Villa Borghese** (see p. 109).

At Napoleon's request, architect Giuseppe Valadier spruced up the once-scruffy *piazza* in 1814, adding the travertine fountains on the western and eastern sides. To the west, a beefy Neptune splashes in his element with two Tritons. The eastern figures represent Rome flanked by the Aniene and the Tiber. Also present is the she-wolf suckling Romulus and Remus. Walls extending from either side of the fountains form two semicircles that enclose the square. Each end of the walls displays one of the Four Seasons. Once upon a time in a grislier era, P. del Popolo was a favorite venue for popes to perform public executions. Today the "people's square" has become a lively place, though executions are infrequent at best, and the Pope just isn't as lively as he used to be. Masked revelers once filled the square for the torch-lit festivities of the Roman carnival, and the *piazza* remains a favorite arena for communal antics. After a soccer victory or government collapse, the *piazza* resounds with music and celebration.

CHURCH OF SANTA MARIA DEL POPOLO

On the north side of P. del Popolo. ☎06 3610487. Open M-Sa 7am-noon and 4-7pm, Su and holidays 8am-1:30pm and 4:30-7:30pm.

Don't let the unassuming facade of the church deceive you into passing it by—within its early Renaissance walls are many Renaissance and Baroque masterpieces. The gilded relief above the altar depicts the exorcism that led to the church's foundation. Pope Pascal II chopped down a walnut tree marking the legendary spot of Nero's grave, clearing ground for the church and allowing the terrified neighbors to live free of his ghost. The apse behind the altar (sporadically accessible) was designed by **Bramante**—look for his signature shell pattern on the walls. In the vault of the apse, **Pinturicchio** painted a cycle of the *Coronation of the Virgin*. It is illuminated by 16th-century stained glass windows by Frenchman Guillaume de Marcillat, which are the first stained glass windows in Rome.

DELLA ROVERE CHAPEL

Immediately to the right after the main entrance, this chapel harbors an *Adoration* by Bernardino Betti, better known as Pinturicchio (1454-1513). The fresco and its lunettes depict the life of St. Jerome (turn on the light for a better view). More frescoes by Pinturicchio's pupils are found in the third chapel on the right; note its interesting *trompe l'oeil* benches.

CERASI CHAPEL

The Cerasi Chapel, immediately to the left of the altar, houses two spectacular **Caravaggios.** On the right, the *Conversion of St. Paul.* Unlike previous painters, Caravaggio uses contrasts of light and shadow instead of images of angels or God to show the apostle's conversion to Christianity as an internal spiritual experience. On the left, *The Crucifixion of St. Peter* shows the first Pope as a very human and rather confused old man being dragged off by his anonymous executioners. Over the altar, Annibale Caracci's *Assumption of the Virgin* demonstrates his mastery of color, and like Caravaggio, the mass of his figures dominates the painting.

Piazza Sonino

CHIGI CHAPEL

Open daily 7am-noon and 4-7pm.

The Chigi Chapel, second on the left, was designed by **Raphael** for the wealthy Sienese banker Agostino Chigi, reputedly the world's richest man (see **The Era Before Dishwashers,** p. 154). Raphael proved especially ingenious in his designs for the mosaic of the dome. Instead of representing the angels as flat figures, he used clever tricks of perspective and foreshortening to make them seem to stand on top of the chapel, peering down from their gilded empyrean. A century later, Bernini completed the chapel for Cardinal Fabio Chigi, the future Pope Alexander VII. Bernini added two medallions of faces to the pyramids and the marble figure of Death in the floor. Bernini also designed the statues of Habbakuk and Daniel (with the lion at his feet)—note how his statue of Habbakuk is not confined to its niche, but projects into the chapel in many different planes, while the angel moves from the chapel into the niche, breaking down the boundry between the sculpture and the space around it.

Church of Santa Maria

OTHER SIGHTS

OBELISK OF PHARAOH RAMSES II

Restored in 1984, the obelisk commands the center of the *piazza.* Some 3200 years old, it was already an antique when Augustus brought it back as a souvenir from Egypt in the first century BC. Flanked on four sides by floppy-eared lions spouting water, its foundation provides a fantastic perspective of the city.

SALA DEL BRAMANTE

This little art museum is tucked under the stairs to the right of the Church of S. Maria del Popolo, and hosts frequent temporary exhibitions (see p. 162).

G.G. Belli

CHURCH CHAT

St. Peter's interior measures 186m (610.08 ft.) along the nave and 137m (449.36 ft.) along the arms. If you include the walls, the nave is actually 192.76m (632.32 ft.) long and 58m (190.24 ft.) wide. To simplify this, if for some reason the Pope wanted to replace the entire interior with two football fields, he'd have to exclude the end zones, but he could do it. Additionally, if he got a chocolate craving like nobody's business, and wanted to line the Basilica's floor with candy bars, he could pile in roughly 3.96 million Snickers bars. Should parking cars in church become all the rage, 2750 moderately-sized Fiats could be parked within St. Peter's. All of these things the Pope could do but doesn't. Such resolve.

CHURCHES OF SANTA MARIA DI MONTESANTO AND SANTA MARIA DEI MIRACOLI

At the southern end of P. del Popolo. S. Maria di Montesanto open Apr.-June M-F 5-8pm; Nov.-Mar. M-F 4-7pm. S. Maria dei Miracoli open M-Sa 6am-1pm and 5-7:30pm, Su and holidays 8am-1pm and 5-7:30pm.

If you look closely, you'll see that the Baroque "twins" aren't quite identical. S. Maria di Montesano, on the left, with a facade by Bernini, is the older sibling (1662). Santa Maria dei Miracoli was completed by Fontana in 1681. Carlo Rainaldi planned the site to integrate the three streets, the churches, and the *piazza* into a whole.

PIAZZA AUGUSTO IMPERATORE

M: A-Flaminio. Walk down V.d. Ripetta from the south side of P. del Popolo. After years of being closed, the mausoleum has opened for tours: Tu and F at 9pm in German and 10pm in English. L10,000/€5.16; students L8000/€4.13; over 60 and under 18 L6000/€3.20; under 12 free. Ara Pacis is closed for renovation until an undisclosed time; it is typically open Tu-Sa 9am-7pm, Su 9am-1pm. L3750/€1.94, students L2500/€1.29.

The mausoleum, the Ara Pacis, and an obelisk that now stands in P. Montecitorio were once part of an intricate plan to use sculpture, architecture, and even the movements of the sun to legitimize and exalt the Emperor Augustus. His mausoleum and the Ara Pacis were designed to show the legitimacy of his rule and its connection to Roman traditions. On the day and hour of the anniversary of Augustus's birth, the shadow of the obelisk would point directly at the center of the Ara Pacis. In the 2000 years that have passed since the construction of the complex, however, only the mausoleum has remained in its original position.

MAUSOLEUM OF AUGUSTUS

The circular brick mound of the Mausoleum of Augustus once housed the funerary urns of the Imperial family. The oversized tomb was originally crowned by a tumulus of dirt and planted with cypress trees in imitation of archaic Etruscan mound-tombs, and possibly topped by a colossal statue of the emperor. Two obelisks, now relocated to other *piazze*, once guarded the entrance. Later centuries saw the mausoleum converted to a Colonna family fortress, a wooden amphitheater where Goethe watched some bear-baiting in 1787, and even a concert hall, until Mussolini restored it in 1936, and surrounded it with Fascist buildings, trying as always to associate himself with his hero, Augustus.

ARA PACIS

To the right of the mausoleum (coming from P. del Popolo), lies the glass-encased Ara Pacis.

The Ara Pacis stands as a monument to both the grandiosity of Augustan propaganda and the ingenuity of modern-day archaeology. The marble altar, completed in 9 BC, was designed to celebrate Augustus's success in achieving peace after years of civil unrest and war in Gaul and Spain. The reliefs on its front and back include depictions of allegorical figures from Rome's most sacred national myths: a Roman Lupercalia, Aeneas (founder of Rome and Augustus's legendary ancestor) sacrificing a white sow, Tellus the earth goddess, and the goddess Roma. The side panels show the procession in which the altar was consecrated, with realistic portraits of Augustus and his family and various statesmen and priests, all striding off to sacrifice cattle on the new altar to peace.

ARCHAEOLOGY

The altar, which stood alongside the ancient **Via Lata** (now the Corso), was discovered in fragments over the course of several centuries and only pieced together within the last century by Mussolini's archaeologists. The final stages of excavation were almost never completed, as it was discovered that the altar, buried some 10m underground, was supporting one of Rome's larger *palazzi.* To make matters worse, the water table of the city, having risen with the ground level over the past two millennia, had submerged the monument in over 3m of water. Archaeologists and engineers devised a complicated system of underground supports for the palace and, after freezing the water with carbon dioxide charges, painstakingly removed the precious fragments. Mussolini provided the colossal, aquarium-like display case.

VILLA BORGHESE

see map p. 317

M: A-Spagna and follow the signs. Alternatively, from the Flaminio (A) stop, take V. Washington under the archway into the Pincio. From P. del Popolo, climb the stairs to the right of Santa Maria del Popolo, cross the street, and climb the small path. ***BioParco,*** *V.d. Giardino Zoologico, 3 ☎06 3216564. Open daily 9:30am-6pm; in winter 9:30am-5pm. L14,000/€7.23; ages 4-12 L10,000/€5.16, under 4 and over 60 free.* ***Santa Priscilla catacombs,*** *V. Salaria, 430, just before V. Antica crosses V. Ardeatina. The catacombs, along with the gardens of* ***Villa Ada,*** *are best reached by bus #57 or #219 from Termini or bus #56 from V.d. Tritone. Get off at P. Vescovio and walk down V.d. Tor Fiorenza to P. di Priscilla to the entrance to the park and the catacombs. ☎06 86206272. Open Tu-Su 8:30am-noon and 2:30-5pm. L10,000/€5.16.*

The park of the **Villa Borghese** covers 6km^2 north of the Spanish Steps and V.V. Veneto. Its shaded paths, overgrown gardens, scenic terraces, and countless fountains and statues are a refreshing break from the fumes and chaos of the city as well as a great place to spend time when everything else is closed for the afternoon. Many workers eat lunch or enjoy siestas on park benches, ignoring both tourists who tool around in silly bicycle-car contraptions and couples making out on park benches.

In celebration of becoming a cardinal, Scipione Borghese hired architect Flaminio Ponzio and landscaper Domenico Savino da Montepulciano to build a little palace on the hills. They did him proud: the Borghese became the most vast and variegated garden estate in the city and one of the first to follow the Baroque craze of edging ornamental gardens with contrived "wildernesses." Completed by Dutch architect Jan van Santen in 1613, the building remained in the hands of the Borghese until 1902, when it and all the works of art inside were purchased by the Italian state.

Abutting the gardens of the Villa Borghese to the southwest is the **Pincio,** first known as the *Collis Hortulorum* (Hill of Gardens) for the monumental gardens the Roman Republican aristocracy built there. The hill is graced with the **Moses Fountain,** which depicts the future spiritual leader as a wee babe in a basket. During the Middle Ages, it served as a *necropolis* for bodies denied a Christian burial. Claudius's third wife, Messalina, created quite a stir in the nearby **Villa of L. Licinius Lucullus** by murdering the owner. When she later ran off with her lover, her infuriated husband sent his troops to track down and kill her. The Pincio family took possession of the villa in the 4th century. Fleets of Vespas, skippered by surly teenagers,

have replaced the Victorian carriages, but the view is still one of the best in Rome. A bike or a tandem bike or bike-car hybrid is an easy way to see large areas of the park quickly (available for rent for L6-20,000 per hr.).

The elegant terrace of restaurants and cafes in **Casa Valadier,** rising above P. del Popolo, offers an even better view. This locale has fed an unusual clientele of politicians and celebrities, from Gandhi to Chiang Kai-shek. The north and east boundaries of the Pincio are formed by the **Muro Torto,** or "crooked wall," so named for its irregular lines and centuries-old dilapidation. Parts of the wall have seemed ready to collapse since Aurelian built it in the third century. When the Goths failed to break through this precarious pile of rocks in the 6th century, the Romans decided St. Peter must be protecting it and refused to strengthen or fortify it, giving St. Pete a chance to do his job.

Northwest of the Pincio is the rose-planted **Villa Giulia,** home of the resplendent Museo Nazionale Etrusco (see p. 153). Villa Giulia also hosts outdoor classical concerts during the month of July (see **Entertainment,** p. 198). The park's other major museums are the **Galleria Borghese** (see p. 150), which houses one of Rome's finest sculpture collections as well as a gallery of Renaissance paintings, and the **Galleria Nazionale d'Arte Moderna** (see p. 154).

The villa's art is not limited to its museums; in the **Giardino del Lago** (Garden of the Lake), Jacopo della Porta's Tritons look suspiciously like those in Piazza Navona. These are the real thing, moved here in 1984—the ones in Piazza Navona are copies. In the lake itself is the **Temple of Aesculapius.** Get a picturesque close-up from a rowboat. (L5000 for 20min.) Finally, there's an imitation medieval fortress, now the **Museo Canonica** (see p. 161). The **BioParco** is no world-class zoo, but it has plenty of animals, mostly sluggish in the Roman heat. North of Villa Borghese are the **Santa Priscilla catacombs** and the gardens of **Villa Ada.**

VATICAN CITY

see map p.316

M: A-Ottaviano, A-Cipro/Musei Vaticani, bus #64 (beware of pickpockets), #492 from Termini or Largo Argentina, #62 from P. Barberini, or #23 from Testaccio. Central Vatican ☎06 6982.

Perched on the western bank of the Tiber and occupying 108½ independent acres within Rome, Vatican City is the last foothold of the Catholic Church, once the mightiest power in Europe. Since the Lateran Treaty of 1929 (see **History,** p. 44), the Pope has reigned with full sovereignty over this tiny theocracy, but he must remain neutral in Roman and Italian politics. As the spiritual leader of millions of Catholics around the world, however, the Pope's influence extends far beyond the walls of his tiny domain. The nation preserves its independence by minting coins (Italian *lire* with the Pope's face), running a separate postal system, and having its own mayor. The Vatican is protected by the Swiss Guards, the world's most photographed military men. The guards wear flamboyant uniforms designed, *not* by Michelangelo, as tour guides insist, but by some nameless seamstress in 1914, perhaps inspired by a Raphael fresco in the Raphael Rooms of the Vatican Musuem (see below). Although priests, nuns, and other official visitors are allowed in all areas, tourists are only admitted to the Basilica and the stellar **Vatican Museums** (see p. 140).

What's it like to live in the Vatican? It's no party. More than 95% male, the population must conform to a set of rules even the meanest hostel owner would never dare to enforce. The curfew is 10pm, as the last city gates lock up then for the night, and no commercial entertainment is permitted. The 800 inhabitants are nonetheless very well connected: the Vatican's phone per capita ratio is the highest in the world.

ST. PETER'S BASILICA

For information, write to Information Center, Piazza San Pietro, Citta del Vaticano or call 06 82019 or 06 82350. Dress appropriately when visiting or you'll be refused entrance—no shorts, miniskirts (i.e. anything above the knee), sleeveless shirts, or sundresses allowed, though jeans and a t-shirt are fine. Men requested to remove hats upon entering. Multilingual confession available; languages spoken (about 20) are printed outside the confessionals by the main altar. ***The Pilgrim Tourist Information Center*** *is located on the left between the rounded colonnade and the basilica, and offers a multilingual staff, free brochures, and currency exchange.*

*Next to the Information Center is a **first aid** station and free bathrooms. Open daily 7am-7pm, Oct.-Mar. 7am-6pm. Mass M-Sa 9, 10, 11am, noon, and 5pm; Su 9, 10:30, and 11:30am, 12:10, 1, 4, and 5:45pm. Plan on spending at least 2hr. in St. Peter's.*

For the Jubilee year of 2000, the Vatican washed its face and put on a clean shirt, and the results are still visible. The pilgrims have all gone home, but St. Peter's still gleams proudly at the center of Rome. The basilica, perhaps the most famous in Europe, is approached by V.d. Conciliazione, a column-lined avenue built by Mussolini in the 1930s. The road provided Benito with a prime parade route, and offers a grand, if austere, entrance to Bernini's elliptical Piazza San Pietro. It seems that Bernini wanted the marble *piazza* to greet pilgrims as a surprise after their wanderings through the medieval Borgo district. Bernini still has the last word, though, as his *piazza*—with 140 statues overlooking two fountains and an obelisk originally erected in Alexandria—continues to wow the masses daily.

The crown jewel in the papal hat, however, remains the basilica itself. Designed in turn by Bramante, Raphael, and Michelangelo, the basilica marks the resting spot of the bones of St. Peter, the church's founder. (For more on church history, see p. 47.) A Christian structure of some kind has stood on this spot since Emperor Constantine made Christianity the state religion in the middle of the fourth century. In 1506, during the age of exploration, with Constantine's original brick basilica aging, Pope Julius II called upon Donato Bramante to carry out his monumental vision of a new church for what he saw as a new world. Bramante designed the new church with a centralized Greek-cross plan—a decision which proved contentious for the next 100 years. Bramante's work was so expensive that he continually asked the cardinals for money. The cardinals, in turn, sold indulgences, which eventually led to the Protestant Reformation, and a boatload of religious dissidents who settled America.

ESSENTIAL INFORMATION

VATICAN INFO

Vatican Online (www.vatican.va) The official site of the Vatican has information on sights, events, the Vatican museums, and history and news. Yes, you can click on the Pope's head, but nothing will happen.

Pilgrim Tourist Information Office, P.S. Pietro (☎06 69881662). To the left as you face the basilica,after the colonnade. The Vatican's tourist office and official souvenir shop in one. The office conducts free English tours of the Basilica daily usually between 2-3pm. Office open M-Sa 8:30am-6:30pm.

Papal Audiences Every W, John Paul II himself addresses audiences of 2000-3000 rapt pilgrims, usually at 10am in the Piazza San Pietro in front of the basilica. For free tickets, stop by the Prefettura della Casa Pontifica (☎06 69883273) between 3-8pm on Tu before the audience you wish to attend. The office is up a flight of stairs between the right-hand colonnade and the basilica. To secure your tickets in advance, write to the *Prefettura della Casa Pontifica,* 00120 Città del Vaticano, specifying the number of people and the desired and alternate date. Seating is limited, so arrive early. As always, wear appropriate clothing.

When Bramante died before completing his project, **Raphael** took over, followed by **Antonio da Sangallo** the younger, who spent seven years building a 25 ft. model of his design that cost as much as a small church to build. These presumptuous artists usurped Bramante's design and changed St. Peter's to a Latin cross (in which one arm of the church is longer than the others). In 1546, Paul III handed 72-year-old **Michelangelo** the job of completing the basilica, with three times the budget. Even though he and Bramante reportedly hated each other, Michelangelo reverted to the Greek-cross plan because of his love for symmetry. But Michelangelo, too, was finished before his project. **Carlo Moderno** put the finishing touches on the basilica, lengthening St. Peter's nave and adding three chapels, finishing the basilica in the shape of a Latin-cross.The basilica's famous double-shelled dome was designed by Michelangelo, and its central apex lies directly over St. Peter's bones. The dome has a diameter of 42.3m meters, intentionally one meter short of the diameter of the Pantheon—a building Michelangelo greatly admired. Giacamo della Porta altered the ribs and lantern after Michelangelo's death. Make sure to look at the golden ball just below the cross on the top of the dome—16 people can comfortably fit inside.

AROUND THE BASILICA

After walking through Bernini's colonnade, you'll be in the rectangular part of the *piazza* just before the basilica. In the warmer months, a stage and a mind-boggling number of chairs are set up in this area for the Pope's weekly audiences. To the left, before the basilica, are the bathrooms, information center, and first aid station. Just before the steps on the left of the basilica is a courtyard vigilantly protected by Swiss Guards. If you want to see the Tomb of St. Peter and the Pre-Constantine Necropolis (see below) ask the Swiss Guards to let you go to the Ufficio di Scavi, through this courtyard. To the right of the basilica, just at the end of the colonnade, is the entrance to the Prefettura della Casa Pontifica, where you may get tickets to a Papal audience. This entrance is not marked; you must inquire with the Swiss Guards at the top of the stairs to gain admission to this office as well.

PORTICO AND ENTRANCE

Before entering St. Peter's, glance up at the central balcony. Flanked by pink marble, this is where the new pope is announced and subsequently gives his first blessing. Inside the portico, five doors with scriptural themes mark the entrance into the basilica proper. Unless the Pope is celebrating in the basilica, the central bronze door—taken from the Old St. Peter's—is closed. The small door to the right is the *Porta Sancta* (Holy Door) and can only be opened by the Pope, who knocks in its bricked-up center with a silver hammer every 25 years to initiate Jubilee years of holy celebration. (And you thought the the Papal Seal just had the key to heaven.)

PIETÀ

Chances are you'll be blinded by flashbulbs immediately as you enter the basilica. No, it's not the Italian paparazzi, but something more sublime: Michaelangelo's *Pietà*. The marble *Pietà* (1497-1500) lies in the first chapel in the right aisle behind a wall of glass. Created when he was 25, the sculpture established Michelangelo as the preeminent contemporary sculptor in Rome. Michelangelo crowned his achievement by signing his name on the band directly across the Madonna's robe, making the *Pietà* the only sculpture Michelangelo deemed worthy of his signature.

The sculpture was originally created for the chapel of the French Kings (Santa Petronilla) in the Old St. Peter's, where the sculpture would have been viewed from the right. The current frontal display is thus incorrect (Christ should face the viewer, not the Virgin), and it is best to view the *Pietà* from the right. From this angle, the Virgin's piteous gesture is emphasized (she extends her hand toward the viewer) and Christ's elongated limbs and torso are appropriately foreshortened.

Michelangelo's *Pietà* made the artist and the genre famous, but alas, Michelangelo cannot be credited with inventing the genre of the Madonna cradling the dead Christ. The type originated in 14th-century Germany and was popularized in France; Michelangelo was simply the first to portray the unwieldy pose with such elegance. The finish on this statue, most visible on Christ's body, is extraordinary—Michelangelo never again finished a sculpture to this level of refinement. His Madonna is unusually youthful—too young to be the mother of a 32-year-old man. For this, Michelangelo was accused of heresy; he claimed that Mary's virginity preserved her youth. This youthful interpretation of the Madonna could also be based on Michaelangelo's readings of Dante and Petrarch, who thought of the Madonna as both the mother and daughter of God.

In 1962, the work was sent to the World's Fair in New York, but it no longer travels. In 1972, a hammer-wielding maniac attacked the famous sculpture, smashing the nose and breaking the hand off the Madonna. Since then, the *Pietà* has been restored by meticulous sculptors who examined the 1934 copy which stands in the Treasury of St. Peter's (see p. 115). If you cannot stand the crowd and the distance from the sculpture, you can take a closer look at the replicas in the Treasury and just outside the Vatican Museum's Pinoteca—but only as a last resort. Farther down the right aisle is the **Chapel of the Sacrament.** This chapel is solely reserved for prayer, and no photographs are allowed. However, there are thin windows on either side of the entrance through which one can peer into the sanctuary—Bernini's bronze ciborium, a model of Bramante's Tempietto at Rome's other St. Peter's (San Pietro in Montorio, see p.123), and bronze angels definitely merit the snoop.

ST. PETER

Moving from the chapel of the Sacrament into the central nave of the basilica, a **bronze of St. Peter** presides over the crossing from a marble throne on the right-hand pier, his feet worn smooth by those who stop to kiss or rub them. While this statue has been thought to date from the Middle Ages, new research in the 1990s suggests that it may be the work of **Arnolfo di Cambio,** c.1300. St. Peter is outfitted in full religious regalia on holidays and joined in the crossing by statues of St. Helena, St. Veronica, St. Andrew, and St. Longinus holding sacred relics. These saints no longer march, but they stare imposingly. Next to St. Andrew (on the left-hand pier closest to the entrance to the basilica) is the staircase leading down to the **Vatican Grottoes** (p.118).

Isola Tiberina

ST. PETER'S DOME

High above the *baldacchino* (see below) and the altar rises the dome designed by Michelangelo, built with the same double shell as Brunelleschi's earlier one in Florence, but designed more spherically, like the Pantheon (see p. 90). Out of reverence for that ancient architectural wonder, Michelangelo is said to have made this cupola a meter shorter in diameter than the Pantheon's, but the measurements of the dome are still eye-popping. The highest point towers 120m above the floor and the diameter of the dome measures in at 42.3m. At the time of Michelangelo's death in 1564, only the drum of the dome had been completed. Work remained at a standstill until 1588, when 800 laborers were hired to complete it. Toiling round the clock, they finished the dome on May 21, 1590.

Around the bottom of the drum, the key biblical passage of the basilica is inscribed: "You are Peter, and upon this rock I will build my church; I will give you the keys to heaven." As the scriptural justification for the opulence that is St. Peter's, references to these lines abound throughout the rest of the Vatican, especially in the Sistine Chapel. Mosaic representations of Matthew, Mark, Luke, and John adorn one level of the dome; choirs of angels fill up four more levels, and God presides on high.

Casa di Dante

BALDACCHINO

In the center of the crossing, the *baldacchino*, another work by Bernini, rises on spiraling dark columns over the marble altar, reserved for the Pope's use. The Baroque structure, cast in bronze pillaged from the Pantheon, was unveiled on June 28, 1633 by Pope Urban VIII, a member of the wealthy Barberini family. Bees, the symbol of the Barberinis, buzz here and there (as well as on buildings and statues all over Rome), while vines climb up toward Michelangelo's cavernous cupola. The striking spiral-formation of the columns was inspired by columns from the Basilica

Basilica of Santa Cecilia

of Constantine, upon which Jesus used to lean while preaching to his disciples at the even earlier Temple of Solomon. While one of these columns used to reside next to the *Pietà*, it can now be seen in the Treasury of St. Peter's (see p. 119) There's no chance of leaning against these columns now, though, as the marble plinths upon which the *baldacchino* stands would dwarf Hercules himself. The best way to appreciate the scale of the *baldacchino* (and indeed the basilica itself) is to visit the top of the dome on your way to the cupola. In front of the *baldacchino*, 70 gilded oil lamps burn, illuminating Maderno's sunken Confession. Two semi-circular marble staircases lead to St. Peter's tomb, directly beneath the papal altar. As these staircases are closed to the pubic, a better view of the tomb is possible from the grottoes.

TRIBUNE

The Tribune is Bernini's masterpiece dating from 1666. Peter's original wood and ivory chair supposedly lies inside the massive bronze throne, but the wood in the chair was carbon-14 dated in 1968 (at the request of Pope Paul VI) to an embarrassingly recent AD 300; the Vatican has issued no comment. The fact that the throne remains somewhat inexplicably suspended, however, may strengthen the Vatican's position. Above the throne is a stained glass window illuminating the symbol of a dove, and to the throne's right the Bernini tomb of Pope Urban VIII waves to the sarcophagus of Pope Paul III, on the left side of the throne.

To the left of the Cathedral Petri, in the left aisle and behind the statue of St. Veronica in the crossing, is Bernini's last work in St. Peter's, the Baroque **monument to Alexander VII.** A melodramatic example of a rather melodramatic style, a bronze skeleton symbolizing death emerges from a doorway with an empty hourglass in his bony fingers, telling the Pope in no uncertain terms that his time is up. Apparently unconcerned, Alexander placidly prays above miles of fluid drapery, surrounded by the four Christian Virtues. The hourglass had run out for Bernini as well, who died two years after he finished this statue.

Nearby, in the **Cappella della Colonna** (diagonally across from Alexander VII, moving toward the Tribune), is the monument to St. Leo the Great, surrounded by the tombs of smaller St. Leo II and St. Leo III, and Algardi's famous relief of (the great) Pope Leo meeting Attila the Hun. Walking down the left aisle to the doors of the basilica, you'll find **Cappella Clementina,** where a monument to Pius VII (sculpted by Thorvaldsen in 1823) is the only piece of St. Peter's made by non-Catholic hands.

TREASURY OF SAINT PETER'S

To the left of the large Confession Chapel in the left hand aisle of the basilica (just to the left of the tomb of Alexander VII), a door leads into the Treasury. Open M-Su 9am-6:30pm. Closed when the Pope is celebrating in the basilica and on Christmas and Easter. L8000/€4.13, children 12 and under L5000/€2.58. Photographs allowed. Wheelchair accessible. Plan to spend 30min.

The Treasury of St. Peter's contains gifts donated to his tomb in past centuries. The marble plaque to the right on the entrance hall lists all the Popes in order, starting with Peter in AD 64. Among the highlights of the nine-room museum are: the Solomonic column from the Basilica of Constantine; the "dalmatic of Charlemagne," an intricately designed robe that the illiterate Holy Roman Emperor donned for sacred ceremonies; the copy of *Pietà* made in 1934; a clay statue of one of Bernini's angels (for a closer look than on the Ponte S. Angelo); the magnificent bronze tomb of Sixtus IV; and the stone sarcophagus of Junnius Bassius (4th century), which is decorated with 10 biblical episodes from Adam and Eve to the capture of St. Peter.

VATICAN GROTTOES

Near the statue of St. Andrew under the dome (the statue on the left, closest to the doors of the basilica), steps lead down to the Grottoes. Open daily 7am-6pm; Oct.-Mar. 7am-5pm. Wheelchair accessible by entering through the exit, near the entrance to the cupola. Photographs allowed. Plan to spend about 15min.

The Vatican Grottoes are the final resting place of many Catholic VIPs, including emperors and Queen Christina of Sweden. The passages are lined with tombs both ancient and modern, but bright lights, a fresh coat of paint and reassuring guards make this grotto anything but creepy.

CUPOLA

Cupola's ticket office (located directly at the exit of the grottoes; from inside the basilica, exit the building, and reenter the door to the far left with your back to the basilica, marked "cupola." On foot L7000/€3.62, by elevator L8000/€4.13—though there's still a climb to the very top. Rooftop terrace wheelchair accessible, but cupola is not. Lines can be long, especially in the afternoon; you may want to consider visiting the cupola before the basilica, depending on the length of the line. Open daily 7am-5:45pm; Oct.-Mar. 7am-4:45pm. Closed when the Pope's inside.

For not-to-miss views of the interior of St. Peter's and the skyline of Rome, head to the interior observation level in the cupola's dome, which can be reached by elevator, but a macho climb up a winding path of 330 stairs (complete with the sloping roof of the dome) is required to reach the top. No elevator can save you from this climb, which will leave even the fittest *Let's Go* reader bordering on cardiac arrest. But it's well worth it. Standing 370 ft. above the ground, the outdoor ledge around the cupola offers unprecedented views of the Roman skyline, as well as the chance to check out the Pope's backyard, complete with hedges in the shape of the Papal seal, a fleet of shiny automobiles, and 10 satellite dishes. On the way down, drop a postcard in the Vatican mailbox on the terrace—everyone sends a postcard from the Vatican, but how many send a postcard from the top?

TOMB OF ST. PETER AND PRE-CONSTANTINE NECROPOLIS

On the left side of the Piazza San Pietro is the entrance to the necropolis, *just beyond the information office. ☎06 69885318; fax 06 69885518; scavi@fasp.va. Open M-Sa 9am-5pm. Only small, pre-arranged tours may enter. To request a tour, write: The Delegate of the Fabbrica di San Pietro, Excavations Office, 00120 Vatican City. Phone calls only accepted for reconfirmations. As tours fill up (especially in the summer), it is best to book as far ahead as possible, and certainly as soon as you get to Rome. L15,000/€7.75.*

Here, protected by Swiss Guards, you'll find a double row of mausoleums dating from the first century. Multilingual guides remind you that the center of the Catholic Church used to be a pagan burial ground and tell of the discovery of St. Peter's tomb. In 1939, workers came across ancient ruins beneath the Vatican, and, unsure of finding anything, the Church set about looking for St. Peter's tomb secretly. Twenty-one years later, the saint's bones were discovered in a small *aedicula* (temple) directly beneath the altars of both the Constantinian and modern basilicas.

CASTEL SANT'ANGELO

Down V.d. Conciliazione from St. Peter's. To enter the castle, walk along the river with St. Peter's behind you, and the towering castle to your left. Signs will point you to the entrance. Alternately, cross the Tiber on Bernini's Ponte S. Angelo, which leads directly to the entrance of the Castel. ☎06 6875036 or 06 6979111. Open Tu-Su 9am-7pm; in winter daily 9am-7pm. L10,000, EU citizens under 18 and over 65 free. Guided tour with archaeologist summer Tu-F 10:30am and 4:30pm, Sa-Su 4:30pm. L8000/€4.13. Bookstore offers information and reservations; audio guide (in English, French, German, Italian, Japanese, and Spanish) L7000/€3.62.

St. Peter's may have popes, the Colosseum gore galore, and the Forum rocks older than your great-great-great-grandmother, but only Castel Sant'Angelo boasts a three-for-one special, all under one roof. Rising from the banks of the Tiber, the massive Castel Sant'Angelo began as a mausoleum, and was subsequently recycled as a fortress, prison, and palace, and it's easy to see why. The round building lies on prime Roman real-estate (within shouting distance of St. Peter's and a bridge away from the Pantheon), and remained an important political landmark until it was turned into a museum in the 1930s. The metamorphoses of this ancient structure provides a quick-and-dirty general history of Rome after Augustus, as well as the once-in-a-lifetime chance to see a papal bathroom.

Castel Sant'Angelo was originally constructed as a mausoleum by Hadrian (AD 117-138), an emperor who dabbled in architecture. Hadrian's mausoleum didn't last long as such, and was incorporated into the walls of Rome by Aurelian in 271. After the castel was sacked by Alaric in 410 and the besieging Goths in 537, Pope Gregory the Great saw a vision of Archangel Michael atop the fortress, which he interpreted as a sign of the end of the plague. As luck would have it, the plague did end shortly thereafter, and the fortress was renamed Castel Sant'Angelo.

The castle was frequented thereafter by various popes, and during the Sack of Rome in 1527, Pope Clement VII ran for his life along the Leonine wall between the Vatican and the fortress, while the imperial invaders took potshots at his streaming white papal robes. Pope Paul III enjoyed a more leisurely existence in the castle, building a sumptuous suite of apartments atop the ancient foundations. Pesky heretics and troublemakers, including the revolutionary astronomer Giordano Bruno and thieving artist Benvenuto Cellini (who was once stored for a day in one of the structure's larger vertical ventilation ducts), were relegated to the depths of the former mausoleum. If you'd like more information, the **audio guide** is probably your best bet, as the archeology tours tend toward too much minutiae for most peoples' tastes, and actually bypass several of the most beautiful rooms.

RAMPARTS AND MAIN CASTLE ROOMS

Directly opposite the ticket booth, iron stairs lead down to a spiral ramp that may be mistaken as part of Hadrian's private parking garage at first glance. Although the ramp used to be a straight shot to the big guy's tomb, it now serves as a remarkably well-preserved reminder of Imperial Rome. Note the low lighting, damp air, and the occasional floor mosaic. At the top of the ramp, you can turn right and climb to the fortress's ramparts and four circular bastions, named for the four evangelists. From the ramparts you can see the massive cement remains of Hadrian's mausoleum and bits of the travertine and marble that once encased it completely.

Turning back toward the ramp's exit, a bridge leads into the mausoleum. Inside, a wooden ramp (built by Alexander VII) rises steeply over the emperor's tomb while creepy incendiary urns, typical of those that held the ashes of many a Roman emperor, sit in niches in the walls. Go easy with the urns—all of Hadrian's descendants, ending with Caracalla, were cremated in the mausoleum.

The ramp leads outside into **The Court of the Angel,** where Raphael di Montelupo's (not *the* Raphael) original statute of *Archangelo Michael* (sculpted in 1544) stands tall. To the right of the statue is Michelangelo's **Facade of The Medici Chapel,** built for Pope Leo X, a Medici Pope, in 1514. The facade beautifully demonstrates the Renaissance admiration for balanced Classical forms, while the two lions' heads (in reference to the leonine Pope) add a touch of whimsy.

This courtyard leads into the **Sala di Apollo,** whose *grotteschi* frescoes were painted in imitation of ancient Roman designs. Two rooms adjoining the Sala di Apollo display 15th- and 16th-century paintings. From the adjacent **Courtyard of Alexander VI,** you can descend into a dank labyrinth of prison cells and storerooms (including endless rows of vats where oil was kept boiling to douse besiegers) or stop to study the enormous crossbows and cannonballs that once served as the castle's defense. Another stairway, straight ahead when you enter the courtyard, climbs to the **bathroom of Pope Clement VII** nearby. Formerly heated by hot furnace air pumped behind the walls, it is still heavily frescoed with flighty grotesques painted for Clement's personal contemplation.

The stairway to the left of Clement's toilette leads to a gallery that circles the citadel, decorated at intervals with *grotteschi*, stuccos, and *loggie* built by Popes Julius II and Paul III, a bar, and a souvenir stand. The bar offers shady tables in vine-covered niches overlooking St. Peter's, and provides a delightful spot for a pick-me-up. But beauty has a price—a soda is 3000L to take away, and 6000L at a table.

PAPAL APARTMENTS

The extravagant Papal Apartments include the lush **Sala Paolina,** where a fresco of Hadrian stares at a fresco of—who else?—Archangel Michael. Don't miss the out-of-place black-coated man peeking out from a faux doorway on the right as you enter the room—it's speculated to be a caricature of Raphael di Montelupo, the sculptor of the first Michael statue. Also check out the papal bedroom nearby, where a sumptuous double bed consistently raises the eyebrows of pious tourists.

OTHER ROOMS

The rest of the castle is relatively unexciting; high points include the **Camera del Perseo, Camera di Amore e Psyche** (frescoed and filled with furniture), and the **Hall of the Library** (awash with scenes of cavorting sea gods and lined with stucco reliefs).

Political prisoners of the popes were kept in the stone cells along the rim of the fortifications as late as the 19th century.

Keep climbing through temporary exhibition rooms, which usually show the work of recent Italian painters or photographers, to reach a broad, circular terrace with excellent views of the city. A large map outlines principal sites in easily decipherable Italian, and the view of St. Peter's is well worth the 66 stairs. Peter Verschaffelt's version of Michael stands proudly atop a slightly higher terrace sheathing his sword, signaling not impotence but rather the end of the plague, as the Black Death ended shortly after Pope Gregory saw this vision of Michael on top of the castle.

Palazzo del Quirinale

TRASTEVERE

see map p.310-311

Trastevere—a name that refers either to its *trans Tevere* (across the Tiber) location or its settlement during the reign of Tiberius—asserts a vibrance that gives it a character and atmosphere unlike that of the city center. The *Trasteverini* claim to be descendants of the purest Roman stock—*Romani dei Roma* (Romans from Rome). Some residents even claim never to have crossed the river.

The legendary founder of Ostia, King Ancus Martius, first settled Trastevere not as a residential spot but as a commercial and military outpost to protect the valuable salt-beds at the base of the Tiber. The hills beyond Trastevere became important outposts for defending the city from Etruscan invasions. During the Empire, sailors in the imperial fleet inhabited the area, building mud and clay huts along the river's banks. The success of a commercial port started by Hadrian lured Syrian and Jewish merchants to the neighborhood, and the maritime business flourished alongside such cottage industries as tanning, carpentry, milling, and prostitution.

By the Middle Ages, Trastevere's commercial activity began to wane and many residents retreated to the other side of the river. In his 1617 guidebook, editor Fynes Moryson warned readers, "because the aire is unwholesome, as the winde that blows here from the South, Trastevere is onely inhabited by Artisans and poore people." The popes took little interest in the neighborhood and rarely extended their wealth to build churches or monuments here; the community remained self-sufficient. In keeping with its independent spirit, Trastevere backed two revolutions: Mazzini's quest for a Republic in 1849 and Garibaldi's resurgence in 1867.

Fontana del Acqua Felice

Church of Santa Susana

Since World War II, Trastevere has been the victim of aggressive externally-funded gentrification. Today, Trastevere attracts hordes of bitter expatriates, bohemians, and taciturn artists, but thanks to rent control and centuries of fiery patriotism, the area retains its gusto. However, an influx of yoga stores, souvenir vendors, and middle-aged tourists has begun to bring the threat of banality to this famously "authentic" Roman neighborhood. To keep the spirit of independence alive, **Noantri** ("We others," in dialect) is celebrated during the last two weeks of July. Though a bit tacky, the festival features grand religious processions, some kiddie rides, and a *porchetta* (roast pig) on every corner.

ISOLA TIBERINA

According to legend, Tiber Island shares its birthday with the Roman Republic—after the Etruscan tyrant Tarquin raped the virtuous Lucretia, her outraged husband killed him and threw his corpse in the river, where muck and silt collected around it, forming a small land mass. These felonious origins may have deterred Republican Romans from settling the island; its first living inhabitants were slaves abandoned after they'd become too weak to work. On the island, the pitiful slaves prayed to Aesclepius, the Greek god of healing. Rumor has it that when the Romans took his statue from the sanctuary at Kos and dragged it up the Tiber in 293 BC, the god appeared to them as a snake and slithered onto the island. The Romans took this event as a sign that this was where he wanted his temple and, with their typical architectural aplomb, encased the island in marble, building its walls in the shape of a boat to commemorate the god's arrival. Traces of the original travertine decoration on the southeast side of the island are still visible—look for the serpent carved in relief near the "prow." The Romans built a large Aesclepius temple with porticos where the sick could wait for the god to visit them in their dreams and prescribe a cure. Nearby, archaeologists have found pits full of *ex voto* statuettes of arms, legs, and other body parts offered as thanks.

FATEBENEFRATELLI HOSPITAL

The site at Isola Tiberina has long been linked to healing; thus, it comes as a small surprise that the Fatebenefratelli monks established a hospital on the island in 154, which still occupies the northern half. Here, English King Henry I's courtier, Rahere, reputedly fought off malaria, a fatal disease in those pre-quinine days. He was so thankful that he promised to build a church and hospital in gratitude back in England (apparently he thought that Aesclepius already had Rome covered). True to his word, he built the structures that still stand in London's Smithfield district. Expectant Roman mothers consider the hospital the most fashionable place in the city to give birth. That's not surprising since it looks like a tropical villa on the outside and like a church, replete with open-air *piazze* on the inside.

BRIDGES

The footbridge leading from the east bank of the river (on the Centro Storico side) is the **Ponte Fabricio** (commonly known as the **Bridge of Four Heads** for its two busts of Janus, the two-headed god of beginnings and endings). It's the oldest in the city, built by Lucius Fabricius in 62 BC. From the *lungotevere*, you can see the inscription Lucius carved into the bridge to record his public service. From the bridge, the beleaguered **Ponte Rotto,** one of Rome's less fortunate ancient constructions, is also visible to the south. Built in the 2nd century BC, the poor bridge underwent medieval repair after medieval repair, each time succumbing to the Tiber's relentless floods. Since its last collapse in 1598, it's been slowly disintegrating, suffering its final defeat when it was accidentally blown up during the construction of the current metal bridge just downstream, the Ponte Palatino. Now all that remains is a single marble arch planted squatly, but proudly, midstream. The **Ponte Cestio** (originally built by Lucius Cestius in 46 BC and rebuilt in 1892) links the island to Trastevere. The little bridge offers a stellar view of the Gianicolo and the Church of Santa Maria in Cosmedin. Stairs lead to the bank, where lovers, graffiti artists, and other social derelicts enjoy the many charms of secluded anonymity.

CHURCH OF SAN BARTOLOMEO

In P.S. Bartolomeo. Open daily 9am-1pm and 4-6:30pm.

This 10th-century church has been flooded and rebuilt many times, and is now something of an architectural chimera, with a Baroque facade, a Romanesque bell tower, 16 ancient columns, and avant-garde 20th-century stained glass windows.

CENTRAL TRASTEVERE

From the Ponte Garibaldi, V.d. Trastevere opens onto P. G. G. Belli (centered on a statue of the famous dialect poet) and then P. Sonnino, Trastevere's transportation hub (centered on the ever-charming McDonald's Golden Arches). A right onto V.d. Lungharetta takes you to P. di Santa Maria in Trastevere; the fountain that serves as the *piazza*'s centerpiece dates to the first century BC.

PIAZZA SIDNEY SONNINO

The ***Torre degli Anguillara*** *is to the left. The* ***Church of San Crisogno*** *is across the street from the Casa di Dante, off P.S. Sonnino. Open daily 7-11:30am and 4-7:30pm. L3000/€1.55 donation to enter subterranean ruins. To reach the* ***Church of San Francesco a Ripa*** *from P.S. Sonnino, go down V.d. Trastevere, then turn left on V.d. S. Francesco a Ripa. Open M-Sa 7am-noon and 4-7pm, Su 7am-1pm and 4-7:30pm. Free.*

The 13th-century **Torre degli Anguillara** stands over a *palazzo* of the same name. The various members of the Anguillara family were notoriously active as priests, magistrates, warlords, criminals, and swindlers. The building now stands in honor of Dante Alighieri as the **Casa di Dante.** A well-known Roman name is perpetuated in an etching on the facade of the **Church of San Crisogno;** that of Cardinal Borghese. Although founded in the 5th century, the church has been rebuilt many times. Twenty feet beneath the most recent structure lie the remains of the original. To visit the ruins, walk into the room left of the altar; an attendant will lead you down the wrought-iron staircase. Traces of original wall paintings and some well-preserved sarcophagi and inscriptions are visible. On the left side of the church you can view a memorial and listen to an explanation of the life and times of Beata Anna Maria Taigi, housewife and saint who did good works while tending seven sons and her husband, "a difficult, rough character." Wives may wish to use this moment to chastise their husbands for being lazy pigs. One of the first Franciscan churches in Rome, the **Church of San Francesco a Ripa** showcases Bernini's *Beata Lodovica Albertoni* in a chapel on its left side. Shown at her death, she lies in a state of euphoria.

BASILICA OF SANTA CECILIA IN TRASTEVERE

From P.S. Sonnino, walk from the river and go left on V. G. C. Santini, which runs into V.d. Genovesi. From V. Genovesi, go right on V.S. Cecilia. Open daily 8am-12:30pm and 2:30-7pm. Cloister open Tu and Th 10-11:30am, Su 11:30am-noon. Donation requested. Crypt L4000/€2.06.

During the 3rd century, Cecilia converted to Christianity and also managed to convert her husband Valerian and her brother-in-law; the boys were later beheaded for their refusal to worship Roman gods. Cecilia inherited a considerable fortune from them both, becoming one of the richest women in Rome and inciting such resentment that the prefect of Rome ordered her death in 230. She was locked in her own steamroom to die, but miraculously survived. Her relations tried to behead her, but despite three tries, the executioners botched the job and she survived for three more days, slowly bleeding to death. Meanwhile, the hemorrhaging evangelist converted over 400 people. She bequeathed her palace to build this beautiful church. Cecilia is known as the patron saint of music because she was found singing after her three-day stint in the steamroom. A ring of singing nuns often graces the altar in Cecilia's honor. On November 22, St. Cecilia's day of martyrdom, churches hold a musical service. The National Academy of Music in Rome is also named after her.

Pope Urban I consecrated the church in her palace, but Pascal I rebuilt it in 821 when, according to one Vatican account, he dreamed that St. Cecilia revealed her true burial grounds in the catacombs of St. Callisto. He had her body exhumed and moved to the new church. Stefano Maderno's famous **statue of Santa Cecilia** lies under the high altar, showing what she looked like when exhumed from her tomb in 1599 in Maderno's presence—pretty good for a 1200-year-old corpse.

Rococo restorers wreaked untold havoc on the medieval frescoes by **Pietro Cavallini** that once covered the church. However, fragments of his magnificent 1293 *Last Judgment* remain in the gated **cloister** on the right. Beneath the church lie the ruins of Roman buildings and an ancient church. The entrance is on the left as you enter the church and is marked *"cripta e scavi."* Cardinal Rampolla, the man responsible for the excavations, is memorialized in a tomb in the last chapel outside.

SANTA MARIA IN TRASTEVERE

From P.S. Sonnino, take V.d. Lungaretta. Open daily 7:30am-8:30pm.

The church has the distinction of being the first in Rome dedicated to the Virgin Mary. Though this structure dates from the 12th century, an earlier basilica existed on the site under Calixtus in the 3rd century. The mosaics of the Virgin and the 10 saintly women lining the exterior only belie the masculine decor that awaits visitors inside. The 12th-century mosaics in the apse and the chancel arch are in full splendor, depicting Jesus, Mary, and a bevy of saints and popes in rich Byzantine detail.

GIANICOLO

PIAZZA SAN PIETRO IN MONTRORIO

Take Via della Scala from P.S. Encidio to Vico della Scala (1st left). Take a left on V. de Panieri (the 3rd intersection on Vico della Scala). Take a right to climb the stairs to the Piazza. Church and Tempietto open daily 9:30am-12:30pm and 4-6:30pm.

Built on the spot once believed to be the site of St. Peter's upside-down crucifixion, the biggest draw of the **Church of S. Pietro in Montorio** is a masterly *Flagellazione di Gesu*, painted on slate by Sebastiano del Piombo from designs by Michelangelo. The church also contains the tombs of Irish noblemen, exiles persecuted by English Protestants. Next door in the center of a small courtyard is the stunning **Templete of Bramante** (1499-1502). A combination of Renaissance and Classical architecture, it provided the inspiration for the larger dome of St. Peter's.

A decent hike up the hill from P.S. Pietro in Montrorio (take V. Garibaldi past the fountain and then veer right onto Passeggiata del Giancolo, continuing up past the kiddy carousel) is **P. Giuseppe Garibaldi,** the site of a patriotically over-blown statue-complex crowned by an equestrian likeness of the revolutionary leader himself. Blood, sweat, and tears from a statue of embattled soldiers mix with the milk of a she-wolf, as a carved Remus and Romulus are shown suckling from their adopted mother, an appropriate mingling of unlikely strength and sorrow given that the *piazza* marks one of the last places that Garibaldi's ragtag Italian troops tried to hold off Napoleon. Even if you fail to experience a surge of Italian nationalism, you're likely to appreciate the sweeping panoramic view of the city.

BOTANICAL GARDENS

At the end of V. Corsini, off V.d. Scala, at Largo Cristina di Svezia, 23. Grounds open Tu-Sa 9am-6:30pm; Oct.-Mar. M-Sa 9am-5:30pm. Greenhouses open at gardeners' discretion. Closed Aug. and during bad weather. L4000/€2.06; ages 6-11 and over 60 L2000/€1.03, under 6 free.

Filled with well-labeled specimens of trees and flowers, the gardens remain green and luxuriant even when the rest of Rome is brown; there is something in bloom year-round. The impressive assemblage of flora stretches from valleys of ferns through groves of bamboo to a hilltop Japanese garden. Of interest are the garden of roses cultivated during the Baroque period in Rome, containing the two founding bushes from which all domesticated Italian roses supposedly have sprung, and the Garden for the Blind, a star-shaped garden of various plants labeled in Braille.

TERMINI & SAN LORENZO

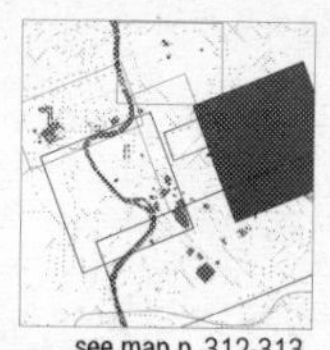

see map p. 312-313

NORTH OF TERMINI

PIAZZA DEL QUIRINALE AND VIA XX SETTEMBRE

Several blocks south of P. Barberini and northeast of P. Venezia.

PIAZZA DEL QUIRINALE

This *piazza*, at the southwest end of V.d. Quirinale, occupies the summit of the tallest of Rome's original seven hills. From the belvedere, the view takes in a sea of Roman domes, with St. Peter's in the distance. In the middle of the *piazza*, the heroic statues of **Castor and Pollux** (mythical warrior twins whom ancient Romans embraced as their protectors) flank yet another of Rome's many obelisks. The fountain over which they preside was once a cattle trough in the Roman Forum.

PALAZZO DEL QUIRINALE

The palazzo is not open to the public.

The President of the Republic officially resides in this imposing *palazzo*, a Baroque collaboration by Bernini, Carlo Maderno, and Domenico Fontana. Maderno designed the front, while Bernini set himself to the *manica lunga* (long sleeve) on V.d. Quirinale. Look through the portals on the *piazza* for a glimpse of the white-uniformed, silver-helmeted Republican Guards (each of whom must be at least 2m tall to get his job) and the *palazzo*'s lush gardens. The *palazzo* was once the papal summer palace and then a royal residence; since 1947, it has hosted the president. The neighboring white stone **Palazzo della Consulta** houses the constitutional court.

CHURCH OF SANT'ANDREA AL QUIRINALE

From P. Quirinale, go east on V. Quirinale. Open W-M 8am-noon and 4-7pm; Aug. W-M 8am-noon.

Another stunning church courtesty of Bernini, Sant'Andrea is built on a small scale in an oval. It highlights both Bernini's ability to combine sculpture with architecture to create a dynamic and lively space, and his use of light and different colored stone in a coherent project. Statues of angels and cherubs clamber over the dome of the church and play with architecural garlands, while Sant'Andrea looks upward to the symbol of the Holy Spirit. Look for the statues of men with nets, representing Saint Andrea's fellow fishermen. This was Bernini's favorite church, and its small scale gives an intimacy lost in larger churches. Right of the altar are the rooms of St. Stanislas and an amazing sculpture of that Jesuit saint. Le Gros used several different colors of marble to create a realistic sculpture of the saint on his deathbed.

CHURCH OF SAN CARLINO

Near the corner of V. Quirinale (V. XX Settembre) and V. Quattro Fontane. Open M-F 9:30am-12:30pm and 4-6pm, Sa 9am-12:30pm; if the interior is closed, ring at the convent next door.

This marvelous Borromini church, officially **San Carlo alle Quattro Fontane,** provides a sharp contrast to neighboring Sant'Andrea al Quirinale and highlights the architect's unique vision. Borromini avoided the kind of mixed-media and multi-colored extravaganzas that Bernini perfected. The interior of the church is undecorated, but is organized in a complex mathematical system incorporating the churches undulating curves and pairs of columns. The dome further illustrates his mathematical approach to architecture, with interlocking geometric forms receeding to give an illusion of depth. The church also has the distinction of being both Borromini's first and last work: though he designed the simple interior early on in his career, he finished the more ornate facade just before his suicide. The complex facade illustrates how he tried to fuse architecture with sculpture, combining the elements of traditional architecture in bold new ways. He also designed the **cloister** next door, which holds the **crypt** where he hoped in vain to be buried.

VIA XX SETTEMBRE

The beginning of V. XX Settembre showcases one of Pope Sixtus V's more gracious additions to the city. In an effort to ease traffic and better define the city's regions, the 16th-century pontiff straightened many of Rome's major streets and erected obelisks at important junctions. From the crossroads here, you can survey the obelisks at P. Quirinale, at the top of the Spanish Steps, and at Santa Maria Maggiore, as well as (in the distance) Michelangelo's famous *Porta Pia.* Two of the four reclining figures in the fountains represent the two virtues, Strength and Fidelity, and the others represent Lazio's two rivers, the Tiber and the Aniene. V. Quirinale becomes V. XX Settembre at V. Quattro Fontane, heading east, and after a few more blocks opens into the Baroque **Piazza San Bernardo,** site of Domenico Fontana's colossal **Fontana dell'Acqua Felice,** built in 1587 where Pope Sixtus V's aqueduct enters the city. Prospero Antichi's beefy and illproportioned statue of Moses was inspired by Michelangelo's, but is supposedly glowering at having been carved by so inept a sculptor.

CHURCH OF SANTA MARIA DELLA VITTORIA

On the south side of P.S. Bernardo, heading from P. Repubblica. Open daily 7:30am-12:30pm and 4-6:30pm.

This church has one of Bernini's most stunning ensembles, dedicated to Spanish mystic St. Teresa of Avila. In the **Cornaro Chapel** (the last one on the left) Bernini shows the saint in ecstasy as an angel pierces her with a golden arrow. He builds the scene like a theater, with members of the Cornaro family looking on. Note how Bernini combined light from a hidden window and golden rays to show divine splendor.

CHURCH OF SANTA SUSANNA

The Church is located on the north side of P.S. Bernardo.

The Church of Santa Susanna, the American National Church in Rome, has a distinctive Counter-Reformation facade by Carlo Maderno. Inside, Baldassarre Croce's Mannerist frescoes of the life of the biblical Susanna cover the walls, and Giovanni Antonio Paracea's four large statues of the prophets stand on pillars dating from the 9th century. St. Susanna, niece of Pope Caius, converted to Christianity as a youth and "sacrificed herself to God, making an offering to him of her virginity." When she refused Emperor Diocletian's orders to marry his son and worship an idol of Jupiter, he had her beheaded in his home.

BATHS OF DIOCLETIAN

P. Repubblica, at the end of V. Nazionale, just north of Termini. Baths and rotunda on right after exiting S. Maria degli Angeli, in the building on V. Romita between V. Parigi and V. Cernaia. Open M-F 9am-2pm, Sa-Su 9am-1pm. Free. Church open daily M-Sa 7am-6:30pm, Su 8am-7:30pm.

The Baths of Diocletian tower over the scattered news kiosks and vendors around Termini. The baths were a colossal construction project, employing 40,000 Christian slaves from AD 298 to 306, and their huge scale provides a sense of the grandeur of ancient Rome absent in the scattered columns of the Forum. The baths, which could serve 3000 people at once, contained gymnasiums, art galleries, gardens, libraries, and concert halls. Going to the heated public toilet was a social event in itself, as it could accommodate 20 people at a time. The cold pool *(frigidarium)* alone measured 2500m^2, the size of a small lake. The baths were modeled on Trajan's thermal baths, the first to abandon a strict north-south axis to make better use of solar energy; the *calidarium*, or hot bath, faced southwest, thus facing the sun during the warmest parts of the day, and the *frigidarium* faced northeast. The complex fell into ruin in 538 when the aqueducts supplying water for the baths were destroyed, perhaps out of jealousy, by Witigis and his dirty Ostrogoths. Damn barbarians.

ROTONDA AND BATHS EXHIBIT

This section of the baths is a dramatic home to two of the most important **Hellenistic sculptures** in existence. One is an aging boxer, looking up tiredly, complete with cauliflower ear, while the other is a general, nude to show his semi-divine prowess. Indeed. Glass sections of the floor provide a peek at the foundations of the baths.

CHURCH OF SANTA MARIA DEGLI ANGELI

Centuries later, a Sicilian priest had a vision of a swarm of angels rising from the baths and pestered Pius IV to build a church on the dilapidated site. So, in 1561 Pope Pius IV ordered Michelangelo, then 86, to undertake what would be his last architectural work and convert the ruins into a church. Imitating the architecture of the baths, his original design used the remains of the *calidarium* as the church facade. This is how it appears today, although much of his interior plan was changed after he and the Pope died three years later. Despite the departure from Michelangelo's plan and the many years of design revisions, the interior gives a sense of the ancient baths. The church was constructed in the ancient *tepidarium* (lukewarm baths); Michelangelo scavenged material from the baths to construct the red porphyry columns that line the church interior. In the floor leading from the east transept to the altar is a sundial, which provided the standard time for Roman clocks for hundreds of years. The sacristy leads to ruins of the *frigidarium* as well as a small exhibit on the construction of the church.

Palazzo del Quirnale

VIA NOMENTANA

Beginning at the Porta Pia (designed by Michelangelo), this breezy road is lined with pleasant villas, embassies, and parks. Hop on bus #36 in front of Termini or head to V. XX Settembre and catch the #60; both traverse the boulevard.

Piazza San Bernardo

VILLA TORLONIA

About a kilometer from the Porta Pia is Mussolini's former estate. The house is now abandoned and somewhat dilapidated, but the grounds have become a public park with scattered fake ruins rapidly turning into the real thing. Walk in through the foreboding gates to see over 50 species of birds and 100 types of trees and shrubs. Don't miss the **Museo della Casina delle Civette** (see p. 162).

CHURCH OF SANT'AGNESE FUORI LE MURA

V. Nomentana, 349. ☎06 86205456. Open daily 9am-noon and 4-6pm; closed M afternoons. Catacombs L8000/€4.12. English guidebook available.

Under this basilica winds a network of Rome's best-preserved and least-crowded **catacombs** containing the remains of **Saint Agnes,** a 12-year-old martyred by Diocletian for refusing to marry. The church's 7th-century apse shows off the extraordinary Byzantine-style mosaic of the young saint with a pair of popes.

Baths of Diocletian

CHURCH OF SANTA COSTANZA

This early round church is decorated with stunning 4th-century mosaics, showing animals, and winemaking, predating most Christian imagery. It was built by Constantine's daughter Constantinia as a mausoleum for herself. She was cured of leprosy while sleeping on St. Agnes's tomb, leading her to convert to Christianity. Her tomb was transformed into a baptistry, then a church.

ESQUILINE HILL

The Esquiline and Caelian (see p. 127) hills, the biggest of Rome's seven original hills, also happen to be home to some of the city's greatest chaos. In ancient times, Nero built his decadent Domus Aurea (see p. 80) between these hills. In the wake of its destruction, many of Rome's early Christian churches were constructed here.

BASILICA OF SANTA MARIA MAGGIORE

From Termini, exit south onto V. Giolitti, and walk down V. Cavour. Walk around to southeastern side to enter. Open daily 7am-7pm. Loggia open daily 9:30am-noon and 2-5:30pm. Tickets in souvenir shop; L5000/€2.58. Dress code enforced.

The Basilica of Santa Maria Maggiore crowns the summit of the Esquiline. One of the city's best-preserved early Christian basilicas, it combines glittering ancient mosaics with the splendor and bravura of Renaissance and Baroque additions. Fourth among the seven major basilicas traditionally visited on the pilgrimage to Rome, it is also one of the five churches in Rome granted extraterritoriality, making it officially part of Vatican City.

According to legend, the Virgin Mary appeared before Pope Liberius in August 352 and requested that he build a church in her honor. The locale was to be the spot on the Esquiline that would be covered in snow the next morning. On the morrow, the Pope discovered that snow had indeed fallen on the hill's crest. Liberius promptly set out to design and build the church, first named Santa Maria della Neve (St. Mary of the Snow). The miracle is recreated by Romans today, who rain white rose petals on the inside of the church to recreate the heavenly snowfall.

It appears that the basilica was actually built 80 years later by Pope Sixtus III, who noticed that Roman women were still visiting a temple to mother goddess Juno Lucina, built on the hill next to Liberius's small, older church. Sixtus enthusiastically tore both down to build his new basilica, not only substituting a Christian cult for a pagan one, but also celebrating the recent Council of Ephesus, which declared Mary to be imbued with a divinity that raised her above general humankind. Most of the mosaics inside are designed to commemorate her new status.

Maria Maggiore has a deceptive exterior: while the shell Ferdinando Fuga built for it in 1750 is 18th-century Baroque, inside it is one of the best-preserved Classical basilicas. Ancient columns divide the rectangular church into a central nave with two side aisles surmounted by clerestory windows. The triumphal arch over the high altar swims in mosaics honoring the Holy Virgin Mary, most excitingly in the 13th-century depiction of her coronation. The rest of the mosaics date from the 5th century, including one on the left which shows details from a story in an apocryphal gospel, in which Mary is featured as a devotee in service of the Jewish temple, spinning a basket of purple wool to make a veil. The coffered ceiling above it all is believed to have been gilded with the first gold sent from America by Columbus.

In the subterranean *confessio* before the altar, a charming marble Pope Pius IX kneels in front of a relic of the baby **Jesus' crib.** Though now sheathed in globs of silver, the crib is revealed each Christmas morning. A dazzling *baldacchino* looms over the altar, which enshrines the famous *acheiropoieton* picture of the Madonna. To the right of the altar, a simple marble slab marks the **tomb of Gian Lorenzo Bernini.** Outside in the P.S. Maria Maggiore, pigeons flock around a statue of the Virgin perched atop a 15m column left over from Constantine's 3rd-century basilica.The **loggia**'s 14th-century mosaics tell the story of Liberius's snowy dream. A visit to the *loggia* grants access to the one-time private chambers of Pope Paul V and Bernini's spiral staircase.

CHURCH OF SANTA CROCE IN GERUSALEMME

M: A-San Giovanni. From P.S. Giovanni north of the Metro stop, go east on V. C. Felice; church on right. From P. V. Emanuele II, take V. Conte Verde (V.s. Croce in Gerusalemme). Open M-Sa 9:30am-noon and 3-6pm, Su and holidays 9:30am-noon and 2:30-5:30pm.

This unique church is home to a motherlode of major relics, housed in the appropriately named and Fascist-designed "Chapel of the Relics," which contains fragments of the "true cross" found by St. Helena. It also houses a chunk of the cross of Dismas (the Good Thief), thorns from Christ's crown, and a nail used in the crucifixion. Perhaps the eeriest of the chapel's relics is the dismembered finger used by doubting Thomas to probe Christ's wounds. The church is believed to have been built around 326, but was rebuilt twice: in 1144, when the *campanile* was added, and in 1744, when the facade got a facelift. At the end of the right aisle in the church's interior, the **Chapel of St. Helena** contains 15th-century mosaics depicting Christ, Peter, Paul, and Helena. On the left side of the church, next to the main entrance, lies the **Chapel of the Crucifixion,** with a 14th-century Giottist fresco of the scene on Golgotha.

CHURCH OF SANTA PRASSEDE

From the front of Santa Maria Maggiore, walk up V. Merulana, taking the first right onto tiny V. San Giovanni Gualberto. The church at dead-end. Open daily 7am-noon and 4-6:30pm. Chapel of Saint Zeno L6000/€3.62.

Built in 822, the Church of Santa Prassede houses what may be the most beautiful set of Christian **mosaics** in Rome. Prassede and Pudenziana, the daughters of the powerful Senator Pudente, reputedly buried the corpses of 3000 persecuted Christians and were converted themselves by St. Peter around AD 50. The Vatican doubted this story enough to remove the girls from the register of saints in 1969. In the apse is the New Jerusalem, a triumphal lamb, and the two sister saints being presented to Christ, with Peter and Paul encouraging them. From the right aisle step into the **Chapel of St. Zeno,** a small glittering room of mosaics (lit by a machine outside the door). The chapel is populated by various saints, while four angels hold up a Byzantine Christ floating in a sea of gold. Note the Empress Theodora, far above your head, who has a square halo, indicating that she was still alive when the mosaics were made. Other scholars think this represents a female bishop. The chapel holds part of a column of rare oriental jasper retrieved from Jerusalem in 1228 during the 6th Crusade, reputedly the column to which Christ was strapped and flogged.

Triton Fountain

Ecstacy of St. Theresa

Church of l'Immacolata Concezione

CHURCH OF SANTA PUDENZIANA

From the back of Santa Maria Maggiore, walk down V. A. Depretis, taking a left onto V. Urbana. The church is on the right. Open Tu-F 7am-7pm, M and Sa 7:30am-5pm.

Legend has it that this small church was built by Pope Pius I in 145 on the property of the late Senator Pudente, in gratitude to his daughters. The original buildings of the church do in fact date to 145, and they were used as places of meeting and worship for Christians in Rome. The church still has substantial traces of its 2nd-century origins. The original windows, though walled up, are still visible, as are remnants of the original buildings in an area behind the altar. The mosaic of Christ teaching the Apostles in the apsidal vault is the oldest known mosaic in a place of worship in Rome. Check out the 12th-century campanile.

PIAZZA VITTORIO EMANUELE II

The Piazza is down V. Carlo Alberto from the front steps of Santa Maria Maggiore.

This large *piazza* contains an outdoor market, with piles of fresh fish, fresh fruit, clothes, shoes, and luggage. Its small park houses the curious remains of a 4th-century fountain. The **Porta Magica,** a few steps away, reveals an alchemist's ancient instructions for turning lead into gold. Nearby, contemporary alchemists are hard at work producing fake Prada bags.

SANTA BIBIANA

Follow V. Giolitti which runs alongside Stazione Termini to the intersection with V. Cairoli, near the end of the station. Church is alongside station wall. Open daily 8am-noon, 4-6:00pm.

Tucked away next to Termini, a water tower and the grime of Esquilino, Santa Bibiana is Bernini's first church and its interior hides several impressive works of art that make it worth a visit. Bernini carved a statue of the saint for the altarpiece, while the great Baroque painter **Pietro da Cortona** painted a series of frescoes showing her life and martyrdom for refusing to sacrifice to pagan gods.

THE AUDOTORIUM OF MAECENAS

In Largo Leopardi, down V. Marulana from S.M. Maggiore, or V. Leopardi from P.V. Emmanuele II. Open Tu-Sa 9am-5pm, Su 9am-1pm. L3000/€1.55.

This underground Roman ruin is a small private theater which was once part of the villa of Maecenas, Augustus's personal advisor and the cultivated patron who encouraged the work of Horace and Virgil, who may have read their works here for their sponsor. The remains of frescoes are still visible behind the seats, including one showing Bacchus characteristically tipsy.

CAMPO VERANO & THE JEWISH CEMETERY

Bus #492 from Termini to P. Verano. To the right of Basilica S. Lorenzo Fuori le Mura, down V. Tiburtina, in San Lorenzo. Bus runs through the cemetery Sa and holidays. Campo Verano open daily 8am-6pm. Jewish cemetery open daily 7:30am-6pm; Oct.-Mar. 7:30am-5pm.

More beautiful than bone-chilling, Campo Verano, Rome's largest public cemetery, features a maze of underground tombs lined with fresh-cut flowers, statuary, and a fetishistic number of photographs of the dead incorporated into tombstones. On November 1 and 2, All Saints' and All Souls' Days, Romans make pilgrimages to the tombs of their relatives, placing chrysanthemums on the stones. The Jewish Cemetery is next door on the far side of the cemetery at Campo Verano.

OPPIAN HILL

CHURCH OF SAN PIETRO IN VINCOLI

M: B-Cavour. Or bus #75 to Largo V. Venosta. Walk southwest on V. Cavour, down toward the Forum. Take stairs on left up to P.S. Pietro in Vincoli. Open daily 7am-12:30pm and 3:30-7pm.

Dating from the 4th century, San Pietro in Vincoli is named for the sacred chains by which St. Peter was supposedly bound after having been imprisoned on the Capitoline.

The two chains were separated for more than a century in Rome and Constantinople, brought back together in the 5th century, and now lie below the altar.

Most tourists don't come for the chains. They head straight for Michelangelo's looming **statue of Moses** in the right aisle of the church. The statue is an unfinished fragment of Michelangelo's *Tomb of Julius II*, Julius wanted the grandest funeral monument ever built, but a series of delays, frustrations, and funding cuts that would have made the Italian bureaucracy proud resulted in a much more limited tomb. Michaelangelo originally designed an enormous rectangular structure decorated with over 40 statues (among them the unfinished *Captives*, now in Florence's Accademia). Pope Julius II quibbled over the cost, his successor popes stalled out of jealousy, and Michelangelo never found the time or money to finish what he had hoped would be his greatest work. Nevertheless, his central figure, the imposing statue of Moses, presides regally over the church. The anomalous goat horns protruding from his head come from a medieval misinterpretation of the Hebrew Bible. According to Exodus, when Moses descended from Sinai with the Ten Commandments, "rays" (similar to "horns" in Hebrew) shone from his brow. Flanking the statue are Leah and Rachel, who represent contemplative and active lives, respectively. For a little extra insight, pick up Freud's fast-paced essay on the statue, *Moses and Michelangelo*.

Aventine Hill

Basilica of Santa Maria Maggiore

SOUTHERN ROME

see map p. 318

CAELIAN HILL

Just east of the Colosseum, the Caelian, along with the Esquiline (see p. 124), is the biggest of Rome's seven original hills.

CHURCH OF SAN CLEMENTE

M: B-Colosseo. Turn left out of the station, walk east on V. Fori Imperiali (V. Labicana) away from the Forum, and turn onto P.S. Clemente. From the Manzoni (A) stop, walk west on V. A. Manzoni (V. Labicana), and turn onto P.S. Clemente. ☎06 70451018. Open M-Sa 9am-12:30pm and 3-6pm, Su and holidays 10am-12:30pm and 3-6pm. Lower basilica and mithraeum L5000/ €2.58.

Split into three levels, each from a different era, the Church of San Clemente is one of Rome's most intriguing churches. The complex incorporates centuries of handiwork into three layers: a 12th-century church on top of a 4th-century church, with an ancient mithraeum and sewers at the bottom.

Church of San Sietro in Vincoli

The upper church holds medieval mosaics of the Crucifixion, saints, and apostles. A fresco cycle by Masolino (possibly executed with help from his pupil Masaccio) dating from the 1420s graces the **Chapel of Santa Caterina.** A fresco of St. Christopher, upon which 15th-century hooligan pilgrims scrawled their names, decorates the left wall that supports the arch of the chapel. The marble choir enclosure, dating from the 6th century, shows off a Romanesque paschal candlestick that belonged to the lower church. The 12th-century courtyard to the upper church is the only extant medieval atrium in Rome; in summer, it is a venue for opera or live music.

The early plan of the sprawling 4th-century lower church has been obscured by piers and walls built to support the upper church. With a little imagination, one can trace the lines of the original nave, aisles, and apse, which retain rare 11th-century frescoes. On this level are a few curiosities, including the tomb of St. Cyril (responsible for the Cyrillic alphabet) and a series of frescoes depicting scenes from the life of St. Clement, the 4th Pope. In one, a Roman general, angry at Clement for converting his wife, sends his men to arrest him. Through divine intervention, they are led to believe that some marble columns are the wily Pope; their swearing when they cannot drag Clement away is rendered in Italian, the first written use of the language.

Another staircase descends to a twisting warren of Roman ruins, including a large shrine to Mithras with a ritual room, dining room, and Mithraic school. More passages lead through Roman basements, while an underground river flows through Republican sewers beneath.

CHURCH OF SANTO STEFANO ROTONDO

V.S. Stefano Rotondo, 7. From P.S. Giovanni, take V.S. Giovanni. The road forks twice; stay to the left. Open M 3:30-6:30pm, Tu-Sa 9am-1pm and 3:30-6pm; July 1-Sept. 3 Tu-Sa morning only. Restoration makes much of the church inaccessible.

Built in the late 5th century, the Church of Santo Stefano Rotondo is one of the oldest circular churches in existence. Long-needed restoration continues on the church; it takes some imagination to picture what the first church must have looked like. It was once structured in three concentric rings, but centuries of decay and remodeling reduced it to the two inner rings by 1450. Partial conclusion of renovations have made the impressive round structure of the church itself and the 17th-century mosaics in the first chapel on the left accessible to visitors.

CHURCH OF SANTI QUATTRO CORONATI

V.d. S.S. Quattro Coronati, 20. From P. di S. Giovanni, take V.d. S. Giovanni, bear left at the 1st fork, right at the 2nd. Open M-Sa 9:30am-noon and 4:30-6pm, Su 6:45am-12:30pm and 3-5:30pm. Chapel L1000/€0.52.

Named for four sculptors of Diocletian who were martyred for refusing to carve statues of pagan gods, this church, though small and inconspicuous, has played a prominent role in Roman ecclesiastical history. Due to its proximity to the Lateran Palace (the early seat of the papacy), the church housed a high-ranking Catholic official *in loco* for many years.

The position of the church on the Caelian Hill made it a perfect location for a fortified defense for the Lateran area, and during the 13th century the massive western walls were raised. As such, the church became a refuge for Popes under siege, as well as visiting royalty like Charles of Anjou, earning it the moniker, "The Royal Hospice of Rome." The little **chapel** to the right off the entrance courtyard contains an extraordinary fresco cycle of the life of Constantine painted in 1248 (ring the bell of the convent; the cloistered nuns will send you a key on a lazy susan). Take a break from your climb to the church to sit on the benches that line the walls of the chapel and gaze on a series of frescoes from the life of Sylvester, including Constantine presenting him with the papal crown.

The 13th-century **cloister** (ring the bell from inside and a sister will let you in) ranks as one of the most beautiful in the city, along with that of the Basilica San Paolo fuori le Mura. While San Paolo's cloister owes its magnificence to size and splendor, the cloister here strikes the senses with its elegant simplicity and utter peacefulness. The marble arches and columns of artisan Pietro dè Maria surround a 12th-century Romanesque cantarus. The result is beautiful.

SAN GIOVANNI

CHURCH OF SAN GIOVANNI IN LATERANO

M: A-San Giovanni or bus #16 from Termini. Open daily 7am-7:30pm. Cloister open daily 9am-6pm; L4000/€2.06. Dress code enforced. Just west of the church on the south end of P. di S. Giovanni in Laterano lies the baptistery. Open only for masses and baptisms, usually on Su.

To the west of the *motorino*-filled P.S. Giovanni stands the immense Church of San Giovanni in Laterano, the oldest Christian basilica in the city, as well as the cathedral of the diocese of Rome, and the end of the traditional pilgrimage route from St. Peter's. The church and its adjoining Lateran Palace, which possess the same rights of extraterritoriality as Vatican City, was the seat of the popes until their flight to Avignon in the 14th century. On Corpus Christi, the ninth Sunday after Easter, a triumphal procession including the College of Cardinals, the Swiss Guard, and hundreds of Italian girl scouts, leads the pontiff back to the Vatican after mass. The doors of the main entrance, facing the P.S. Giovanni, were pillaged from the Curia, the Roman senate house in the Forum. Inside, Borromini's remodeling in the 17th century obscured the original plan of the basilica, creating a dramatic series of niches for statues.

The stately Gothic *baldacchino* over the altar houses two golden reliquaries containing **the heads of Saints Peter and Paul,** and an altar from which only the Pope can celebrate Mass. A door to the left of the altar leads to the 13th-century **cloister,** home to the church's collection of sacred relics and regalia. The twisted double columns and inlaid pavement are typical of the Cosmati family, who designed much of the stone inlaid with marble chips that decorates medieval Roman churches. A terrorist bomb heavily damaged the basilica in 1993 (a simultaneous blast devastated the Church of San Giorgio in Velabro). The facade received the most damage and some frescoes nearly collapsed, but the damage has been contained.

Built by Constantine, the **baptistery of Saint John** is part of the original Lateran Palace, now closed to the public. During that era, all Christians were baptized here, and the octagonal building served as the model for its famous cousin in Florence.

SCALA SANTA

M: A-San Giovanni or bus #16 from Termini. Across from the church. Open M-Sa 6:15am-noon, and 3-6:15pm, Su 6:15am-noon and 3:30-6:45pm.

The Scala Santa houses what are believed to be the 28 marble steps used by Jesus outside Pontius Pilate's house in Jerusalem. Pilgrims win indulgence for their sins if they ascend the steps on their knees, while pausing to recite prayers on each step. Martin Luther experienced one of his key early breaks with Catholicism while on pilgrimage here—in the middle of his way up, he realized the futility and false piety of what he was doing, stood up, and left. If you too have difficulties with the idea of kneeling your way up to the Sancta Sanctorum, use the secular stairs on either side. In the sanctuary you'll find, among other relics, the so-called *acheropite* image, a depiction of Christ supposedly painted by St. Luke with the assistance of an angel, which was carried in processions to stop the plague (though some research claims it to be of 5th- or 6th-century Roman origin).

AVENTINE HILL

Rising outside the city walls, Aventine Hill has been an idyllic haven for Rome's aristocracy since the Imperial era. Along with the Parioli district north of the city, the Aventine continues in its preeminence as one of the city's wealthiest *zone.* In high contrast to less-affluent southern neighborhoods, here luxury sedans careen through lush, tree-lined streets, flanked by villas and pricey apartments.

Alongside the Mercedes Benz zooms a bike maneuvered by a priest—while mainly residential, the Aventine is also home to several churches as well as the famous keyhole view of St. Peter's. A quiet orange grove and a breathtaking rose garden serve as green spaces offering a welcome respite from the intense heat and pollution that blanket Rome in the summer. The best place to start your tour of the Aventine Hill is the **Giardini degli Aranci,** off the P. d'Illiria, where business couples on lunch breaks breathe in the scent of oranges and exude the aroma of *amore;*

a terrace here provides an orienting and generally spectacular view of the city. You can see most of the sights in a few hours, especially if you're near the Palatine or Circus Maximus. Reach the Aventine from the north (via the Circus Maximus Metro (B) stop); a walk down V. Circo Masimo will take you to P. Ugo La Malta. On the right side begins V.S. Sabina, by which many of Aventine's sights may be reached.

PIAZZA DEI CAVALIERI DI MALTA

At the end of V.S. Sabina, past the Church of Santi Bonifacio e Alessio. Entrance to grounds, P. Cavalierie, 4. ☎06 67581234 for information). Open Sat at 10 and 11am; closed July and Aug. L10,000/€5.16 donation requested.

This postcard-perfect *piazza* is home to the Knights of Malta, a charitable organization officially known as the Order of the Knights of St. John of Jerusalem and dating from the 12th century. More easily accessible is the **keyhole view** of St. Peter's Basilica. Peek through the keyhole in the large green gate at #3 for a view of the dome of St. Peter's, framed by perfectly manicured foliage.

CHURCH OF SANTA SABINA

At the southern (uphill) end of Parco Savello, in P. d'Illiria. Open daily 7am-12:30pm and 3:30-7pm.

Built upon Clivos Pubblici, Rome's first paved road, during the 5th century reign of Celestine I, the church has seen its share of remodeling over the years. Despite the unimpressive 20th-century altar, the few original remains, including the mosaic floors, are rather stunning. The carved wooden doors inside the basilica (to the left) served as the original entrance and depict several notable Biblical scenes, including one of the earliest known representations of the Crucifixion.

ROSETO COMUNALE

The garden lies on both sides of V.d. Valle Murcia, up from P. Ugo la Malfa, across the Circus Maximus from the Palatine Hill. Open daily 8am-7pm.

A gardener's dream, the Roseto offers a 10,000m² respite from *motorino*-choked Rome. Take a stroll through over 200 varieties of rose plants and sit at one of the tables under the umbrellas in the lower section to enjoy the view of the Palatine. Each May, the horticultural world descends upon the Roseto to compete for the *Premio Roma*, given to the best new variety of rose. Roses are sent from 21 countries up to two years in advance for evaluation. Winners are featured in the lower section. Built in 1954 after the old Roseto was destroyed in World War II, the new version sits atop the site of the old Jewish Cemetery, which was moved to Campo Verano (see p. 136). When asked for the land by the city, the Jewish community leader agreed, but requested that the old site be memorialized. As a result, steles of the Ten Commandments flank the entrances, and the upper section is shaped like a menorah.

CHURCH OF SANT'ANSELMO

P. Cavalieri di Malta, 5. Open daily 8:30am-1pm and 3-7:15pm; chant mass Su 8:30am.

Constructed between 1893 and 1900, the church has a peaceful garden courtyard with fountain and a weekly Gregorian chant mass. The gift shop hawks *limoncino* and other Benedictine liquors.

APPIAN WAY

Parco dell'Appia Antica info: V. Appia Antica, 42. ☎06 5126314. Bus #218 from San Giovanni; get off before Domine Quo Vadis. Open daily 9am-5:30pm; hours may vary. Or forgo the info office and begin on the other end of the Way by taking the slightly faster and simpler route of bus #660 from Metro Colli Albani; get off the bus at V. Appia Antica and V. Cecilia Metella.

The Appian Way was built by Appius Claudius in 312 BC and has been called the "queen of roads" ever since. It once traversed the whole peninsula, providing a straight path for legions heading to conquests in the East. It also witnessed the grisly crucifixion of Spartacus's rebellious slave army in 71 BC—bodies lined the road from Rome to Capua. 37 BC saw Virgil's 375km pilgrimage to Brindisi; St. Peter followed suit in AD 42 when he traversed the Appian Way on his first trip to Rome in the company of his disciples.

Since burial inside the city walls was forbidden during ancient times, fashionable Romans made their final resting place along the Appian Way, while early Christians secretly dug labyrinthine catacombs under the ashes of their persecutors.

Some of Italy's modern *autostrade* still follow the ancient path, but a sizeable portion of the road remains in its antique state. If you make it far enough south, past the tomb of Cecilia Metella, you will get to a stretch of the road paved with enormous original paving stones, lined with fragments of white tomb statues and cornices, and bordered by horse pastures and views of the valley below. It will also take you past a minor Italian military base. Be careful!

Exercise **caution** when walking on V. Appia Antica, particularly from Porta San Sebastiano toward the Catacombs. As in antiquity, the Appia Antica is a very busy thoroughfare, and the modern day drivers zooming down it during rush hour are hardly saintly (or metaphysical—their cars will feel very substantial when they hit you). Shoulders are virtually non-existent, and you will be walking alongside speeding cars. The road is technically **closed to traffic** on Sundays and holidays from 9:30am to 7pm, making it a safer time to walk or bike along the ancient road. Beyond Cecilia's tomb (see below), the Appian Way continues 7km through rural countryside before it meets the GRA. The remains of circular and turreted tombs, commemorative reliefs, and steles line the road between the country villas of Rome's glitterati. Don't miss the ruins of the large Villa dei Quintilli and the Casal Rotondo.

CATACOMBS

M: A-San Giovanni. Take bus #218 from P.S. Giovanni to intersection of V. Ardeatina and V.d. Sette Chiese. At least 2 catacombs open every day (see individual listings). Each L8000/€4.13. In all 3, visitors follow a free guided tour in the language of their choice (every 20min.).

Outside the city proper lie the catacombs, multi-story cellars for the dead that stretch through tunnel after tunnel for up to 25km on as many as five levels. Of the 60 catacombs near Rome, five are open to the public; the most notable are those of San Callisto, Santa Domitilla, and San Sebastiano, which cater to the catacomb fanatic in their close proximity to one another on V. Appia Antica.

Roman pagans would have found the modern notion of cemeteries repugnant, preferring instead to cremate their dead. Christians were thus driven outside the city walls during the 2nd through the 5th centuries to hack through miles of pliant *tufa* (a type of volcanic rock) beneath the property of wealthy Romans. Bodies were typically swathed in linen before being placed in simple slots in the tunnels, to be sealed with slabs of marble upon which the deceased was identified and eulogized. The graves were mass-produced and thus affordable; even the tufa removed for the sake of burials was used to make saleable bricks. Joining the ranks of impoverished Christian peons were a number of martyrs, whose notoriety transformed the catacombs from mere burial grounds to holy pilgrimage sites.

After a series of lootings, the long-lost mazes fell into utter disuse in the 9th century, to be rediscovered in the 16th century, but excavation didn't begin until the 19th century. Early pilgrims filched bones to sell as relics; consequently, the bones remaining in the parts of the catacombs open to the public have long since been interred in Roman churches. Along with bones, marauding sightseers nabbed marble slabs and mementos buried with the dead, with the result that for the most part all that remains of the burial sites are vacant slots where the bodies were placed and wall paintings with which grave robbers couldn't run off. **Tours through the catacombs are not recommended for people who are claustrophobic or have difficulty walking.** Although the oil lamps of Roman Christians and the candelabras of Victorian tourists have been replaced by a multiplicity of electric lamps, the tunnels are not recommended to those who never travel without their nightlight.

SAN SEBASTIANO

V. Appia Antica, 136. From the #218 bus stop near S. Callisto and S. Domitilla, walk down V. Sette Chiese to V. Appia Antica and turn right. Or walk past the Mausoleum of Cecilia Metella and the Circus of Maxentius from the 660 stop at V. Metella. ☎06 7881035. Open M-Sa 8:30am-noon and 2:30-5:30pm; closed Nov. Adjacent church open daily 8am-6pm.

Arguably the most historically significant of the Appian Way catacombs, San Sebastiano was the most reverenced of the catacombs during the first millenium, having offered safe haven to the bodies of Peter and Paul during a particularly severe period of Christian persecution in the 3rd century BC (or so ancient graffiti on its walls suggests). Despite its former popularity, San Sebastiano tunnels are today among the most under-touristed—their comparative emptiness lends them a unique eeriness (and tour guide audibility). In addition to being comprehensible, guides here tend to be remarkably well informed, expertly leading groups through a sizeable chunk of the 10km of tunnels, whose three levels accommodate 160,000 tombs and are dotted with animal mosaics, disintegrating skulls, and fantastic early Christian iconography. Bernini's bust of St. Peter resides in the chapel on the first level. In addition to the Christian tombs, three elaborate pagan tombs were unearthed comparatively recently and are in marvelous shape.

Your tour will end in the **Basilica di San Sebastiano,** originally constructed by Constantine in AD 340 and the current home to the **arrow** that reputedly **shot Saint Sebastian.** Stubborn Sebastian was met with a clubbing by his persecutors after having survived the onslaught of arrows, later plucked from his body by St. Agnes. His miraculous endurance has induced many painted depictions of the archery death scene. An even more significant relic is the hunk of stone bearing **Christ's footprints,** controversial in that *Domine Quo Vadis* claims to possess a similar remembrance of Jesus' meeting with St. Peter along the Appian Way. In August 1999, the church was burgularized, with the thiefs snatching busts of the apostles but eventually tossing the footprints on the side of the road as they left the church. Criminals with a conscience.

SAN CALLISTO

V. Appia Antica, 110. Take the private road that runs northeast to the catacombs's entrance. ☎06 51301580. Open M-Tu and Th-Su 8:30am-5:30pm, in winter Th-Su 8:30am-noon and 2:30-5pm; closed Feb.

The first public Christian cemetery, the catacombs of San Callisto are Rome's largest, with almost 22km of subterranean paths. They are also the most developed and the most crowded. The four serpentine levels once held 16 popes (nine were buried in what's now called "The Crypt of the Popes" or, more jovially, "The Little Vatican"), seven bishops, St. Cecilia (the patron saint of music—her remains can now be found in the Church of S. Cecilia in Trastevere, see p. 119), and some 500,000 other early Christians. Now they just hold an alarming number of tourist groups—and you can bet you'll be able to hear the guide of the neighboring group better than your own (too bad he's speaking German).

SANTA DOMITILLA

V.d. Sette Chiese, 282. Facing V. Ardeatina from the exit of San Callisto, cross the street and walk right up V. Sette Chiese; catacombs on the left. ☎06 5110342. Open W-M 8:30am-5:30pm, in winter W-M 8:30am-5pm; closed Jan.

Santa Domitilla is acclaimed for its paintings—a 3rd-century portrait of Christ and the Apostles remains intact—and its collection of inscriptions from tombstones and sarcophagi. The tour includes a visit to an ancient frescoed pagan tomb adjoining the catacombs. This is the least crowded of the catacombs on the V. Appia Antica.

OTHER SIGHTS

PORTA SAN SEBASTIANO

V.d. Porta S. Sebastiano, 18. Take bus #218 to the intersection of V. Mura Latine and V. Appia Antica. ☎06 70475284. Museum open Tu-Su 9am-7pm, L5000; EU residents 18-24 L3000/ €1.55; under 18 and over 65 free.

Marking the beginning of the Appian Way, this is one of the nine surviving gates of the ancient Aurelian walls and a fine example of an ingenious Roman defense: the killing gate. The gate was left deceptively weak, but when invaders stormed through, they were trapped in an inner court, where archers picked them off like sitting ducks. Inside, the **Museo delle Mura** tells the walls' history.

DOMINE QUO VADIS? (CHURCH OF SANTA MARIA IN PALMIS)

At the intersection of V. Appia Antica and V. Ardeatina. Bus #218 from P.S. Giovanni. Open daily 9am-noon and 4-7pm.

St. Peter is said to have had a vision of Christ at this spot as he was fleeing Rome. Upon being asked *"Domine quo vadis?"* ("Lord, where are you going?"), Christ replied that he was going to Rome to be crucified again because St. Peter had abandoned him. Peter instead returned to Rome and suffered his own martyrdom. In the middle of the aisle lie the alleged **footprints of Christ** in a piece of stone set into the floor of the church.

MAUSOLEO DELLE FOSSE ARDEATINE

Bus #218 to the intersection of V. Ardeatina and V.d. Sette Chiese. Walk down V. Ardeatina; it's to your right. ☎06 5136742. Open M-F 8:15am-6:45pm, Sa-Su and holidays 8:15am-3:30pm.

One of the only modern monuments on the Appian Way is at the Fosse Ardeatine, site of a WWII atrocity. In these caves, Nazis slaughtered 335 prisoners (75 Jews) as a reprisal for an attack by Roman partisans that killed 32 German military police. To hide the corpses and cover their tracks, the Nazis demolished those sections of the cave with explosives. The bodies were recovered and placed in a mass grave that is marked by a monument and a sculpture.

VILLA MASSENZIO

V. Appia Antica, near the tomb of Cecilia Metella. Open Tu-Su 9am-7pm; in winter Tu-Su 9am-5pm. L5000/€2.58; reduced price L3000/€1.55.

The **Villa of Maxentius** lies half-buried in cricket-filled greenery. Emperor Maxentius built the villa in the first decade of the 4th century, but he never got to enjoy it, having been ejected by the newly Christian Constantine at the Battle of Ponte Milvio. The **Tomb of Romulus,** inside a giant brick portico, housed the remains of the emperor's son, named for the city's founder. The circus is the main attraction (and the only part of the villa that you can really visit). At over half a kilometer in length, it was intended for chariot races and the like, but was left unfinished and unused upon the death of Maxentius.

MAUSOLEUM OF CECILIA METELLA

Intersection of V.d. Cecilia Metella and V. Appia Antica. Open Tu-Su 9am-6:30pm. L4000/€2.06.

This towering turret-like structure was built in the 3rd decade BC for the patrician Cecilia, wife of a powerful Roman nobleman. It was preserved by its conversion into a fortress in the Middle Ages, when its famous crenelations were added. Used as a medieval roadblock of sorts, it stopped travelers to "request" a payment for the Caetni family coffers. The medieval complex includes the ruins of a Gothic church (rare in Rome), the Chiesa San Nicola a Capo di Bove.

TESTACCI

PYRAMID OF GAIUS CESTIUS

M: B-Piramide, bus #175 from Termini, or bus #23 from P. Risorgimento.

Catacombs

Testaccio

Mausoleum of Cecilia Matella

The off-white *Il Piramide di Caio Cestio* towers over Testaccio at the foot of the Aventine. Gaius, tribune of the plebes under Augustus, got caught up in the craze for things Egyptian following the defeat of Cleopatra in the late first century BC and had his slaves build this 27m high marble pyramid to serve as his tomb. It was thrown together in less than 330 days, and the close fit of its marble blocks ensured that it would never be pillaged. For extra protection from the marauding Goths in the 3rd century, Aurelian had the pyramid built into his city walls. Medieval tradition asserts that it stands over Remus's grave. Nowadays, it's a favorite hangout for Rome's feline population.

CIMITERO ACATTOLICO PER GLI STRANIERI

V. Caio Cestio, 6. From the Piramide station, follow V. R. Persichetti onto V. Marmorata, immediately turning left onto V. Caio Cestio. Ring bell for admission. Donation requested. Open Apr.-Sept. Tu-Su 9am-5:30pm; Oct.-Mar. 9am-4:30pm.

The Protestant Cemetery, or, more literally, the Non-Catholic Cemetery for Foreigners, is the only non-ancient burial space in Rome for those who don't belong to the Catholic Church. Crowded tombstones fight for attention with stray teams of meowing cats (take caution, they're known to bite) in the shade of overgrown tamarind trees. In the far left corner of the "Old Cemetery," **John Keats** lies beside his friend, Joseph Severn. At his request, the tombstone itself doesn't mention Keats by name (although placards all over the cemetery do in its stead). It soberly states to contain "all that was mortal of a Young English Poet," and (after a quick disclaimer written by friends) records the words Keats wished to be inscribed on his grave: "Here lies one whose name was writ in water." On the other side of the small "New Cemetery," **Percy Bysshe Shelley** rests in peace beside his friend Trelawny, under a simple plaque hailing him as *Cor Cordium*, "Heart of Hearts." Lying behind the grave sof Keats and Severn is that of Severn's son Arthur, at whose baptism "The Poet Wadsworth was present." The poetic trinity is thus completed. Sort of. Also buried here are Goethe's son Julius, Italian thinker Antoni Gramsci, and Richard Henry Dana, author of *Two Years Before the Mast.* This is also where the heroine of Henry James' novella *Daisy Miller* was buried.

PORTA SAN PAOLO

M: B-Piramide: next to the Pyramid of Gaius Cestius.

Called *Porta Ostiense* in antiquity, this gate began the famous *Via del Mare*, which linked Rome to its major port at Ostia, one of sixteen gates of the 3rd-century Aurelian Walls. Today, this colossal fragment of the city wall keeps watch over the gnarls of traffic converging at Piramide. Inside lies **Museo Della Via Ostiense,** an excellent little history museum with impressive models of life on V. Mare.

MONTE TESTACCIO

Follow V. Caio Cestio from V. Marmorata until it ends at V. Nicola Zabaglia. Continue straight onto V. Monte Testaccio. The hill is ahead and to the right.

One of the most famous and historically significant landfills around, Monte Testaccio once served as a transfer area for grain, oil, wine, and marble unloaded from river barges. After goods were stored, ancient Roman merchants tossed leftover terra cotta urns into a vacant lot. The pile grew and grew, and today the ancient garbage dump (whose name is derived from *testae*, or pot shards) rises in lush, dark green splendor over the drab surrounding streets. While the park is now closed to the public as a *zona archelogica*, and pilfering pot shards is illegal, V. Monte Testaccio, home to most of the Roman nightclubs, surrounds the base of the hill, with many of the clubs built into the side of the hill itself.

OSTIENSE

South of Testaccio lies Ostiense, a neighborhood largely born of turn-of-the-centrury urban migrations. The city's only power plant was once in Ostiense, and though the generator houses are now used for less industrial purposes (such as storing artwork during the Capitoline Museums renovation), the area retains its industrial character. Ostiense and neighboring Garbatella are poor, and their development according to government housing schemes precluded the appearance of many cultural attractions. In keeping with the commerical aspect of the neighborhood, a huge wholesale market *(Mercati Generali)* on V. Ostiense overflows with boxes of fruits and vegetables on weekday mornings.

BASILICA SAN PAOLO FUORI LE MURA

M: B-Basilica San Paolo. Alternatively, take bus #23 or 769 from Testaccio at the corner of V. Ostiense and P. Ostiense. Open daily 7am-6:30pm; in winter 7am-6pm. Cloister open 9am-1pm and 3-6:30pm; in winter 9am-1pm and 3-6pm. Dress code enforced.

This renowned and hulking church holds extraterritorial status (along with San Giovanni in Laterano, Santa Maria Maggiore, and St. Peter's). Until the construction of the new St. Peter's, the church was the largest and (by many accounts) the most beautiful in Rome. St. Paul is believed to be buried under the altar, demarcated by a red light (his body, that is; the head is in San Giovanni). The original church was built in 324 by Constantine; the current incarnation was constructed after a huge fire in 1823 (which Stendhal called "sad as the music of Mozart"). Yet another cataclysm beset the church five years ago when delinquent vandals painted the courtyard's statue of St. Paul fire-engine red.

Warmly lit through high alabaster windows, the church is deserving of its renown. The mammoth layout is in the Latin cross style (in the shape of a "T"), with two aisles flanking the nave on each side. The triumphal arch before the altar is set with 5th-century mosaics, reassembled after the fire, depicting Christ giving benediction in the company of the apostles. Along the basilica's periphery, 264 mosaic medallion portraits of the popes from St. Peter to John Paul II solemnly greet a deluge of tour groups. There is only space for eight more portraits, and legend says that when the wall fills up, the world will end. The popish presence is accentuated by its status as a basilica, which dictates that only the Pope can give mass from the high altar.

Don't miss the **cloister;** its gorgeous twisting columns and mosaics make it one of the most beautiful in the city. Be sure to buy a bottle of monk-made **benedictine liquor** in the gift shop (L16,000).

EUR

South of Ostiense lies what is perhaps the most striking neighborhood in Rome—EUR (AY-oor), an acronym for Universal Exposition of Rome. EUR is designed for function rather than aesthetics. Instead of ancient *piazze*, Roman ruins, and meandering, narrow streets, EUR is composed of wide, straight boulevards in a strangely perfect street grid, brimming with apartment highrises that house many of Rome's white-collar doctors and lawyers. Built in good Fascist style, EUR was to be the site of the 1942 World's Fair that Mussolini intended as a showcase of Fascist and imperial Roman achievements. Apparently, the new, modern Rome was to shock and impress the rest of the world with its futuristic ability to build dozens of rectangular buildings that all look the same. World

Pyramid of Giaus Cestius

Porta San Sebastiano

Appian Way

War II meant cancellation of the fair and demands on manpower and material, ensuring that EUR would never complete Mussolini's dream of extending Rome to the sea.

German and Allied occupation during the war left EUR in such mangled shape that it was labeled a "modern Pompeii." Although the EUR was technically completed thereafter in preparation for the 1960 Rome Olympics, the under-touristed *zona* maintains an interrupted air. Unkempt greenery adorns streets with grandiose yet utilitarian names such as "Piazzale dell'Industria" and "Via dell'Arte."

EUR lies near the end of Metro Linea B (EUR-Palasport or EUR-Fermi stops). You can also take bus #170 from Termini or Piazza Venezia. Arrival via the EUR-Fermi stop delivers you to the foot of the **laghetto** (the little artificial lake). Walking away from the metro stop toward the intersection of V. America and Largo G. Pella, you will see the massive dome of the **Palazzo dello Sport** rising to your left (behind the lake), which is used today as a major concert and sporting event venue. Also rising alongside the lake is Rome's lone **skyscraper.** A turn right, down V. C. Colombo, will take you to **Piazza Marconi,** laden with museums and Mussolini's 1939 **obelisk** (which embodies the Fascist mantra that citizens exist to serve the state, with a ladder of mutually supported human bodies). North (continuing away from the laghetto) on V. Cristoforo Colombo stands the **Palace of the Civilization of Labor,** EUR's definitive symbol. Designed by Marcello Piacentini in 1938, the big white rectangle foreshadows the stylings of post-modern architecture. By wrapping arched windows around the building, Piacentini attempted to evoke Roman ruins and create a "square Colosseum." Slightly farther north, **Piazzale delle Nazioni Unite** embodies EUR's spirit: imposing modern buildings decorated with spare columns meld the ancient empire with Mussolini's.

ABBAZIA DELLE TRE FONTANE

M: B-Laurentina. Exit the metro station and walk straight ahead to V. Laurentina; take a right and proceed about ¾ mi. north on V. Laurentina and turn right onto V.d. Acque Salve. The abbey is at the bottom of the hill. Alternatively, take bus #761 north (catch it on the same side of the street as the metro stop) from the Laurentina stop; ask when to get off for the intersection of V. Laurentina and V. Acque Salve. Open daily 9am-noon and 3-6pm.

St. Paul is said to have been beheaded at the site of this Trappist abbey. According to legend, his head bounced on the ground three times, creating a fountain with each bounce. The now defunct fountains are contained within the Chiesa del Martirio di San Paolo, the last of three churches lying along the path through the compound's gates. Viewing the fountains, one can only imagine the velocity at which his skull hit the ground and the elasticity it possessed to travel so far on each bounce. A millennium later, St. Bernard stayed here during his 12th-century visit to Rome. Pick up some potent eucalyptus liquor (L15-23,000/€7.75-11.83) and divine chocolate (L4-7000/€2.06-3.62 for monstrous bars of the wonderful stuff), as well as marmalade, body cream, and shampoo, all made on the premises by Trappist monks.

LUNEUR PARK

V. Tre Fontane. ☎06 5925933. From P. G. Marconi, walk north on V. C. Colombo, turning right onto P. dell'Industria. The piazzale dead-ends into V.d. Industria; turn left and follow it to V. Tre Fontane. Turn right; the park will be on your right. Open M-F 4pm-midnight, Sa 3pm-2am, Su 11am-midnight; in winter Sa-Su. Pay by the ride, usually L4-5000/€2.06-2.58.

Tired of museums, ruins, and churches? Itching to see some real live Italian carnies? Head to LunEUR park, an old-fashioned amusement park with no high-culture strings attached. Eschewing the grandiose megalomania of, say, Disney, LunEUR park has small-scale rides and games, as well as four not particularly intimidating haunted houses. Enjoy cheap thrills like the "Himalaya Railroad," "Musik Express," and "Gravitron," or acknowledge your incipient old-age and merely take in the sights atop the slow-moving ferris wheel.

LAGHETTO ARTIFICIALE

Just south of Metro (B) stops EUR-Palasport and EUR-Fermi, at Largo G. Pella.

Remember the episodes of *Star Trek: The Next Generation* where Captain Picard and crew landed on some Utopian garden planet with peace-loving natives? They must have filmed those scenes here. The man-made lake and small adjoining park are a spitting image of them, although you'll find nary a klingon kayaking across the lakes and exercising in the greenery along its shores.

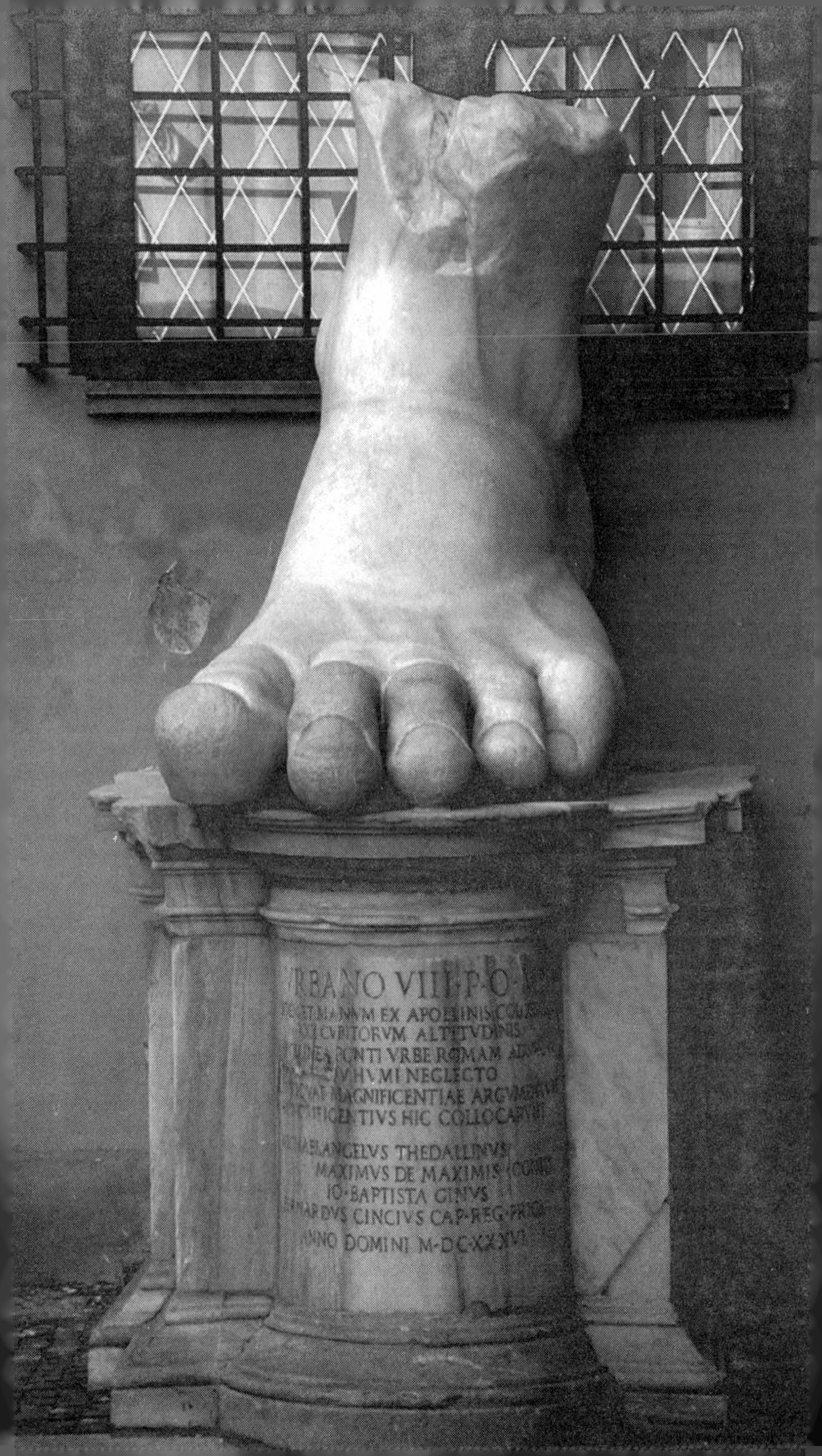

RBANO VIII·P·O·
MANVM EX APO
CVBITORVM ALTITVDINIS
ONTI VRBE ROMAM
VMI NEGLECTO
MAGNIFICENTIAE ARG
TIVS HIC COLLOCA
ANGELVS THEDALLINVS
MAXIMVS DE MAXIMIS
IO·BAPTISTA GINVS
ARDVS CINCIVS CAP·REG·
NNO DOMINI M·DC·XXX

INSIDE

Museums

Museums, you say? Yes siree. Rome offers an astounding array of museums, showing everything from Classical busts of Cicero (Capitoline Museums) and Renaissance goddesses surfing on a half-shell (Galatea at the Villa Farnesina) to Baroque light bulbs (Doria Pamphilj) and Christo drawings of Castel Sant'Angelo wrapped in a giant bedsheet (Galleria Nazionale d'Arte Moderna). Rome's collections are predictably strong in Classical sculpture, Renaissance painting, and the Baroque. The city also holds Italy's best collection of Etruscan art, and has a particular affection for all things Egyptian, perhaps as a result of Antony's yen for Cleopatra. Recent inroads have been made to include work by modern and contemporary Italian artists in the city's repertoire, but progress is slow.

While the quality of art in Rome consistently surpasses expectations, the museums that house this art are often less impressive. Roman museums may have inconvenient hours, galleries that close inexplicably, while some are not handicapped accessible. Many museums retain the 18th-century presentation of their collections (thirty paintings to a wall is not uncommon), and labels range from highly-informative placards translated into multiple languages to nonexistent.

Helpful Hints: For some museums, reservations are a must; for others, they simply alleviate tiresome lines. Rome's museums are generally closed on Sunday afternoons and all day Monday, as well as major holidays (both religious and secular). Be sure to call ahead to make sure all the galleries of the museum you wish to see are open, as renovations and labor shortages cause many unannounced closings. For up-to-the-minute information on many of Rome's museums, visit www.museionline.it.

EU citizens, people under 18 or over 65, and students should never pay full price for admission. Be sure to ask about discounts, and always carry your ISIC card. Students of art and architecture may be eligible for a special pass, or *tessera*, which allows them to visit certain national museums and monuments for free or at a discount.

The bureaucratic bonanza begins at the **Ufficio Centrale Beni Culturali,** Divisione VI, V.S. Michele, 22, 00153 Roma. Applications should include a letter from your school as well as two passport photos. They will be processed more quickly if written in Italian.

PRINCIPAL COLLECTIONS

The museums and galleries described below are the largest and most famous in Rome, and constitute the heart of the city's collections. Most of these museums are wheelchair accessible, but call ahead to request assistance.

VATICAN MUSEUMS

Walk north from the right-hand side of P.S. Pietro along the wall of the Vatican City about 10 blocks. From M: Ottaviano, take a left on V. Ottaviano and continue walking until you reach the Vatican City Wall, turn right and follow the wall to the museum's entrance. ☎06 69883333 or 06 69884341. Information and gift shop (with the very useful official guidebook, L12,000/€6.20) on the ground level past the entrance of the building. ***Currency exchange*** *and* ***first aid*** *stations near ticket booths. Valuable* ***audio guide*** *with information and amusing anecdotes, L8000/€4.13. Guides are available in major languages, and most of the museums' staff are fluent in Italian, with varying levels of English. All major galleries* ***open*** *M-Sa 8:45am-1:45pm. Extended hours Mar. 16-Oct. 30: M-F 8:45am-4:45pm, Sa 8:45am-1:45pm. Last entrance 1hr. before closing. Closed on major religious holidays. L18,000/€9.30, with ISIC card L12,000/€6.20, children under 1m tall free. Free last Su of the month 8:45am-1:45pm. Most of the museum is wheelchair accessible, though less visited parts, such as the upper level of the Etruscan Museum, are not. Various galleries close without explanation; call ahead. Snack bar, between the collection of modern religious art and the Sistine Chapel, is open during the summer. Plan to spend at least 4-5hr.*

Going to the Vatican Museums is a bit like psychotherapy: too much at once is a bad, bad thing. Taken in small doses, the Vatican Museums' world-renowned collections of sculpture, paintings, frescoes and manuscripts can be both delightful and rewarding. With 8 minor museums and millions of visitors a year, the Vatican Museums are not particularly hospitable to aimless wanderers. Plan to arrive 45 minutes prior to the stated opening times to avoid the legendary lines, or enter during lunch-hour. Avoid visiting on Saturdays, which are notoriously crowded, and Mondays, as the museum is closed Sundays and thus gets double the traffic on Monday.

In an attempt at traffic-control, the Vatican has four color-coded routes that guide you through the collections, organized by the amount of time visitors can spend. However, the routes tend to be hard-to-follow and mobbed, as organized tour-groups are required to follow them. The Vatican Museums are best seen over an extended period of time. If you are lucky enough to have the time, follow Routes A and B, but if you have Herculean fortitude and stamina (or you're just strapped for time) Route C will show you the Vatican's best:

Route A: Quattro Cancelli, Egyptian Museum (45min.), Belvedere Courtyard (15min.) Chiaramoni Museum (½hr.), Pio-Clementine Museum (1hr.), Etruscan Museum (1hr.).

Route B:) Gallery of the Candelabra, Gallery of Tapestries, Gallery of Maps (45min. for all three), Raphael Rooms (45min.), Sistine Chapel (45min.), Galleria Urbano VIII, Library of Sixtus V, Galleria Clementina (30min.), Pinoteca (1hr.).

Route C: Quattro Cancelli, Gallery of the Candelabra, Gallery of Tapestries, Gallery of Maps (45min. for all four), Raphael Rooms (45min.), Sistine Chapel (45min.), Egyptian Museum (45min.), Belvedere Courtyard (15min.), Chiaramoni Museum (30min.), Pio-Clementine Museum (1hr.), Etruscan Museum (1hr.), Pinoteca (1hr.).

THE VATICAN MUSEUM, IN 30 SECONDS:

Good, Better, Best...Bestest? Somehow, even superlatives pale before the task of describing a museum that contains half the contents of your art-history book. Nonetheless, some of the Vatican Museum's treasures truly stand above the rest—a few Julia Roberts to a plethora of Sandra Bullocks, if you will. So, take a walk down Vatican Blvd., and take care not to step on the stars.

We begin at the very beginning (a very good place to start), with the creation of light, earth, man and woman in Michelangelo's incomparable **Sistine Ceiling.**

After enjoying the spectacle of creation, hit fast-forward and view your eminent demise in the world's favorite depiction of hell, Michelangelo's **Last Judgment,** also in the Sistine Chapel. Brush up on your Diogenese in the Raphael Rooms with the **School of Athens,** but do behave! Otherwise you'll land in prison, like St. Peter in the nearby Raphael fresco **St. Peter in the Tullarium Prision.** Not content with hell and brimstones? Make your way to the Egyptian Museum, where a **mummy** will lend an ear for as long as you'd like. Giving a nod to the giant **Pine Cone** as you pass through the Belvedere Courtyard, you'll find more learned council in the Chiaramonti Museum, where there are plenty of talking heads. **Augustus of Prima Porta** also hangs out here, and for a small fee will advise on all matters Imperial.

The Vatican's resident hunk, **Apollo Belvedere,** strikes a pose in the Octagonal Court of the Pio-Clementine Museum. If you don't get spit on by a **camel** in the Animal Room, you can drool on the most lusted-after sculptural fragment South of the North Pole, the **Belvedere Torso** in the Hall of the Muses. Afterwards, size up the bronzed **Hercules** in the Circular Hall, or paddle with pterodactyls in the 13m **Monolithic Fountain.** Prance on over to the Pinoteca to see the many faces of St. Peter, as shown by **Giotto** and **Carravaggio.** While you're there, glance at the **Transfiguration Altarpiece** and **Tapestries** in the *other* **Raphael** Room.

EGYPTIAN MUSEUM

Past the information booth in the Quattro Cancelli, to your left, at the top of the first flight, turn right and enter. The Vatican's collection shows a small, high-quality sampling of Egyptian and pseudo-Egyptian (read: Roman-made) statuary, paintings, coffins, and mummies, snatched from Roman excavations or purchased by popes. Among the most remarkable of the Egyptian antiquities can be found in Room 2: brilliantly painted polychrome mummy sarcophagi, a mummy (with traces of hair dye), 3rd-century Coptic (early Egyptian Christian) painted death masks on linen and wood, and a 2010 BC pharaoh bust. The third and fourth rooms are filled with colossal fakes: the enormous, mostly black marble first-century Roman emulations of Egyptian antiquities. Many of these statues were excavated from the site of Hadrian's Tivoli villa. Also tucked into the last rooms are Mesopotamian seals and ceramics and a large variety of Sumerian and Assyrian bas-reliefs, featuring mythological animal-gods and some of the earliest samples of writing.

BELVEDERE COURTYARD

Exiting the Egyptian Museum, you'll find yourself in the **Cortile della Pigna** (Courtyard of the Pinecone), the uppermost end of Bramante's Belvedere Courtyard. It's not hard to see where the courtyard's name came from; a gigantic bronze pinecone stands flanked by two bronze peacocks on the stone railing of the balcony. The first-century pinecone, formerly the center of a fountain, is one of the only works that remains of the original Vatican Museums collection begun by Pope Julius II in 1506. The center of the courtyard features a modern bronze spherical sculpture by Gio Pomodoro. At the end of the courtyard on the right is the **Tower of the Winds,** where Queen Christina of Sweden lived briefly after abdicating her throne, before insisting on more comfortable apartments. The sundial inside was used in the 16th century to cast doubt on the Julian calendar.

CHIARAMONTI MUSEUM

When facing the giant pinecone, a door to your right leads to the **Chiaramonti Museum,** a 300m long vaulted corridor designed by Bramante. The corridor holds over 1000 Classical busts, statues, and reliefs, arranged by Canova in the early 19th century, without any apparent organization. The Chiaramonti Museum is often one of the first to close; ask the guards when it will open as the sculptures are better appreciated up close. The **Braccio Nuovo** (New Wing), another gallery of Roman marble copies of Classical Greek originals, is currently undergoing renovations. Connecting to the midpoint of the corridor of the Chiaramonti, this collection of life-size (and larger) statues includes the famous **Augustus of Prima Porta,** a portrait of the emperor at the height of power, and the reclining **Colossus of the Nile,** surrounded by crocodiles, sphinxes, and 16 small boys—representing the 16 cubits of the river's annual flood, of course.

PIO-CLEMENTINE MUSEUM

Up the stairs at the end of the Chiaramonti corridor, a domed vestibule leads to the stellar Pio-Clementine Museum, thought to be the Western world's finest collection of antique sculpture. The vestibule contains a *basso* (large bowl) and a first-century copy of the athlete Apoxyomenos scraping the oil off his body.

OCTAGONAL COURT

To the left of the vestibule is the outdoor octagonal court, the birthplace of the Vatican Museums. Julius II filled the court with Classical sculpture, thus beginning a rich tradition of papal art collecting. To the left of the entrance stands the sublime **Apollo Belvedere,** the only male nude around that can make Michelangelo's David look shabby. The god's placid features and posture (the sculpture captures the moment just after Apollo has shot an arrow, holding a bow in his left hand) inspired innumerable Renaissance copies in stone and on canvas. During the 18th century, Apollo became the holy grail for aesthetes on their Grand Tours.

Turning clockwise, you encounter the tortured **Laocoön** group, a sculpture that was famous even in ancient times for its vivid grotesqueness. Virgil's *Aeneid* tells the story of Laocoön, a Trojan priest who was punished by Athena, protectress of the Greeks, for advising his people against drawing the Trojan Horse into their city. Athena sent two sea serpents to devour Laocoön and his sons; the Trojans misinterpreted the omen, and happily dragged the "gift" into Troy. Make sure to look at the realistic detail on this sculpture; the veins and muscles are clearly visible. Laocoön's raised arm was discovered and reattached in this century, but many art historians now debate the authenticity of this appendage. Directly across the court stands the **Cabinet of Canova,** which exhibits *Perseus with the Head of Medusa*, flanked by the boxers Kreugas and Damoxenos. These Classical marbles follow violent mythological themes, Perseus turns his enemies to stone, while the surly Damoxenos (on the right), not satisfied with a tie, stabbed his opponent in the stomach and gutted him alive. After a brief Parisian escapade thanks to the plundering Napoleon, Pius IX bought these works back to the Vatican in the early 19th century (see **History,** p. 43).

OTHER ROOMS

Two slobbering Molossian hounds guard the entrance to the Room of the Animals, a marble menagerie that reveals a lot about the importance of brutality in Roman pasttimes. Through the zoo is the Gallery of Statues—home to Apollo, Hermes, Ariadne, and others—at the end of which are stony faces in the Room of the Busts (which showcases a thoroughly engaging 1m foot and calf muscle). The Cabinet of the Masks, also adjacent to the Room of the Animals, houses the Venus of Cnidos. When staff is short, these rooms are often closed.

The **Room of the Muses** opens off the animal room and centers around the inscrutable **Belvedere Torso.** The torso has long been thought to represent Hercules sitting on the skin of the Nemean lion, but recent scholarship has suggested that it could also depict a suicidal Ajax. During the Renaissance, the torso sat in the center of the Octagonal Court (where the fish pond currently serves as a poor substitute) and was drawn by Raphael and Michelangelo. The unusually muscled Christ in the Sistine Chapel's *Last Judgment* (see p. 148) shows that Michelangelo paid close attention. Through the arch, the **Round Room** houses colossal Roman statues (including two of Antinous Hadrian's ill-fated boy-toys,) one of the Emperor Claudius in a general's uniform (his reputed obesity and propensity to drool tactfully forgotten), and a breathtakingly gaudy gilded Hercules. In the middle of the Round Room stands a mammoth fountain (measuring 13m in circumference), once thought to be a pterodactyl bath. The **Greek Cross Room,** the last in the museum, contains the enormous **sarcophagi of St. Helen** on the left, and Constance on the right; mother and daughter, respectively, of Constantine. On either side of the exit, enormous second-century red-granite sphinxes pose riddles before permitting you to leave. No joke.

ETRUSCAN MUSEUM

The next flight of the Simonetti Stairway climbs to the **Etruscan Museum,** which is filled with artifacts from the necropolis of Tuscany and northern Lazio. This newly-renovated museum provides a welcome, peaceful change from the rest of the Vatican, but its galleries are often closed; in particular, rooms 5-8 and 14-end. The splendid contents of the **Regolini-Galassi Tomb,** a *tumulus* (burial mound) found intact and treasure-filled outside the necropolis at Cerveteri (see **Daytripping,** p. 234), are always open, however. In **Room II,** the case on the right holds an extraordinary bronze chariot and bed with which a deceased 7th-century BC couple were supplied for their journey to the other side. **Room III** contains the rare 5th-century BC bronze **Mars of Todi** and Room IX has an excellent display of red- and black-figure amphora (imported from Greece by wealthy Etruscan traders). More far-flung rooms keep smaller bronzes, terra cotta figures, and jewelry. At the end of the Etruscan Rooms, visit the excellent **Rooms of the Greek Originals,** the **Stairway of the Assyrian Reliefs,** and the **Vase Collection.**

OTHER GALLERIES

GALLERY OF THE CANDELABRA

Back on the landing of the Simonetti Staircase is the usually closed **Room of the Biga** to the right. "Biga" means chariot in Greek, and the room appropriately holds a first-century marble chariot outfitted with newly sculpted wheels and horses. The chariot served as an elaborate throne for the bishops of the Church of San Marco. Past the door of the Biga is the Gallery of the Candelabra, named for the marble candlesticks standing under each of six archways. More Roman sculptures reside here, including an Apollo with the lovely huntress of mythology. According to legend, Atalanta (perhaps at the prodding of her incestuously interested father) refused to marry any of her many suitors, but promised to wed any man who could best her in a footrace. Finally, the crafty young Hippomenes distracted her by tossing golden apples in her path, winning the contest and the lady.

GALLERY OF THE TAPESTRIES

The Gallery of the Tapestries is next as you exit the Gallery of the Candelabra. Not surprisingly, its walls are hung with massive tapestries, executed by Raphael's workshop from original cartoons after the artist's death. (Examples of old school Raphael tapestries can be seen in the Vatican's Pinacoteca, p. XX) On the left hang Flemish depictions of the life of Christ, including three gory panels on the slaughter of the innocents. On the right, Roman tapestries illustrate stories of obscure Popes.

GALLERY OF THE MAPS

The Gallery of the Maps is a gilded walkway of cartography designed by Egnazio Danti, the Vatican's true Renaissance man: Danti was a Dominican cosmographer, mathematician, architect, and painter. The 40 frescoes depict maps of Italy, the Apennine Mountains and Avignon, in gorgeous greens, blues and golds. The map of the Adriatic, with winged lions and whiskered fish, is a must see, as is the impressive fresco, stucco, and gold-leaf work on the ceiling.

APARTMENT OF PIUS V

The Apartment of Pius V comes next along the thoroughfare to the Sistine Chapel, holding yet more tapestries. To the right of the "apartment" there is a shortcut staircase down to the Sistine Chapel. To the left, the longer journey through the museum continues with the **Sobieski Room** and the **Room of the Immaculate Conception.**

SOBIESKI ROOM

The Sobieski Room is named for the Polish work that takes up the north wall, "Sobieski Liberates Vienna," in which Sobieski, the king of Poland, defeats the Turks in battle and saves Christendom from takeover by Islamic warriors. What this painting lacks in quality, it more than makes up for in size.

ROOM OF THE IMMACULATE CONCEPTION

The Room of the Immaculate Conception holds 52 rare books in dozens of languages, all delivering a single statement: Pius IX's 1854 decree announcing the doctrine of Mary's permanent and unsullied virginity. The main fresco portrays Pope Pius IX proclaiming the controversial dogma, in case anyone missed it the first time.

RAPHAEL ROOMS

While the Sistine Chapel awes viewers with its vast frescoes and heroic scale, the smaller—but no less exquisite—Raphael Rooms provide an up-close-and-personal look at some of the world's best wall paintings. Known primarily by the self-explanatory adjective *terribilita*, it appears that Pope Julius II had a bit of the suburban housewife in him as well. Upon becoming Pope in 1503, Julius announced his need to redecorate: he simply could not exist in the downstairs apartments, looking at portraits of his predecessor, the nefarious Spanish Pope Alexander VI Borgia. So he promptly hired the best painters of his day (including Perugino, Peruzzi, and Il Sodoma) to decorate a new suite of rooms and a cozy little *cubiculum* (bedroom) for himself. Work was progressing nicely, until a certain Raphael Sanzio coasted into town and painted a trial piece for Pope Julius, a little work called, **The School of Athens.** The Pope was so impressed with Raphael's precocious talent that he immediately fired his other painters, had their frescoes destroyed, and handed the entire suite of rooms over to Raphael. The commission marked the beginning of Raphael's brilliant career in Rome.

CONSTANTINE'S ROOM

A detour down an outdoor walkway over the Belvedere Courtyard takes you to Constantine's Room, where the not-so-subtle theme is Christianity's victory over paganism. The tip-off might be the ceiling where a statue of a pagan god lies broken on the ground in front of a gleaming gold crucifix on a pedestal. On the wall to the left of the entrance, Constantine addresses his soldiers and sees the vision of the cross; on the opposite wall is the baptism of Constantine; on the window wall, Constantine donates the city of Rome to Pope Sylvester; on the wall facing the window, Constantine defeats Maxentius at the Battle of the Milvian Bridge. Despite the tour guides who proclaim otherwise, none of these frescoes were painted by Raphael's hand.

ROOM OF THE CHIAROSCURI AND THE CHAPEL OF NICHOLAS V

The Room of the Chiaroscuri holds coffered wooden ceilings and frescoes of the apostles. The small Chapel of Nicholas V forms the oldest section of the palace, and special permission (obtained at the **Special Tours desk** at the ticket counter) is required to enter. The chapel was decorated by Fra Angelico between 1447-51 with frescoes depicting events from the lives of St. Stephen and St. Lawrence.

HELIODORUS ROOM

Exit Constantine's Room into the Heliodorus Room (1511-14), the secret antechamber of the apartments. The room's obscure subjects were chosen by Julius to illustrate the miraculous protection that God afforded the Church at various times. Directly opposite the door is Raphael's depiction of the miraculous deliverance of St. Peter from the Tullianum Prison on the Capitoline Hill. Raphael's unique composition and his exquisite use of light (daylight, moonlight, angelic light and real light from the window below) make this fresco one of the Vatican's most moving.

The right wall tells the Biblical story of Heliodorus, who had come to loot the Temple of Jerusalem, but was chucked out by a couple of angels and a horseman. On the entrance wall is the miracle of Bolsena: a priest, who had trouble believing in transubstantiation, came to Mass in Bolsena and saw the wine and bread become blood and flesh. Raphael painted Julius himself in the guise of Pope Urban IV, who, after the miraculous appearance of blood on the altar linen at Bolsena, instituted the feast of Corpus Christi. Note the Swiss Guards, dressed just as festively as they are today, kneeling on the right. On the long wall is Leo I expelling Attila from Rome.

STANZA DELLA SEGNATURA

Once a library, the Stanza della Segnatura now holds one of the universal symbols of learning: Raphael's **School of Athens.** The Stanza della Segnatura (1508-1511), once a library, is considered by some to be Raphael's Vatican masterpiece. The walls represent four branches of learning—theology, law, philosophy, and poetry. On the wall of the entrance is the splendid *School of Athens*, in which ancient philosophers and scientists (many of whom Raphael painted with the features of his friends and fellow artists) stroll through an airy architectural fantasy. In the center,

Plato, with the features of Leonardo da Vinci, argues with Aristotle; Euclid, explaining geometry on the ground, has Bramante's face; to the far right of the composition stands Raphael, in three-quarter profile, and his friend and fellow artist, Il Sodoma. In the center, the isolated, brooding figure of Heraclitus is thought to be a portrait of Michelangelo, added as an afterthought when Raphael was given a sneak preview of the Sistine Chapel. Part of what is so remarkable about this fresco is the speed with which it was executed. Raphael supposedly drew up the elaborate cartoons for the frescoes in a matter of days. Furthermore, it appears that Raphael spent as much time working on the face of Heraclitus as the entire left half of the fresco.

Opposite the entrance is the **Disputation of the Holy Sacrament,** in which theologians and church doctors crowd around a monstrance holding the communion host. The remaining scenes depict Mount Parnassus peopled by Italian poets; across are the cardinal and theological virtues, represented by *Gregory IX Approving the Decretals* and *Justinian Publishing the Pandects.*

STANZA DELL'INCENDIO

The final room is the Stanza dell'Incendio (the corner of which you passed through before), containing works by Raphael's pupils, including Giulio Romano. By the time of their painting (1514-17), Pope Leo X Medici had taken up residence in the *stanze,* and portraits of earlier Leos dominate the room. The riotous *Fire in the Borgo* depicts the 847 blaze that was miraculously extinguished when Leo IV made the sign of the cross from the *loggia* of St. Peter's. The painting depicts the facade of the old Constantinian basilica that was pulled down to make way for the new St. Peter's. Other scenes show the coronation of Charlemagne in 800, the victory of Leo IV over the Saracens at Ostia, and, on the window wall, the oath of Leo III. From here you pass through the **Chapel of Urban VIII,** decorated by Pietro da Cortona.

BORGIA APARTMENTS & MUSEUM OF MODERN RELIGIOUS ART

The Vatican is known for old, old things, but the museum has made an effort to spice things up with some modern art, albeit of religious theme. Buttressed with a few big-name works, this collection is not among the Vatican's strongest.

The **Borgia Apartments,** named after the infamous Alexander VI Borgia, father of the even more infamous Lucrezia and Cesare, comprise six rooms decorated from 1492-95 by Pinturicchio. Today, the only visible decorations are the lunettes and ceiling vaults; walls have been covered by the Vatican's collection of modern religious art. Matisse's glorious, colored clerical capes (designed for a chapel despite his atheism), and a cast of Rodin's famous *Thinker* are the stars of the apartments. In the **Room of the Sibyls,** legend has it that the ambitious Cesare Borgia had his brother-in-law Alfonso d'Aragone murdered in order to free his sister Lucrezia to marry to Alfonso d'Este, the guy from Browning's *My Last Duchess.*

Outside the Borgia apartments, the **collection of modern religious art** (largely assembled by Pope Paul VI) continues for many more rooms. The collection is not organized according to any apparent theme and the labels are small and hard to read, but works by Beckmann, Chagall, Dalì, Gauguin, Kandinsky, Klee, Modigliani, Morandi, Munch, Picasso, Rivera, and Shahn can be found by the intrepid wanderer.

SISTINE CHAPEL

With its frescoes plastered on everything from mouse pads and calendars to sweatshirts and coffee mugs, it's easy to forget that the Sistine Chapel is just that—a chapel. Technically part of St. Peter's Basilica, the Sistine Chapel originated as a private chapel for the Popes, and is still the chamber in which the College of Cardinals elects popes, a tradition that dates from the 16th century. While Michelangelo's frescoes receive the most attention, the frescoes along the side wall were painted first, by a host of artists for Sixtus IV in 1481-3. Michelangelo then painted the ceiling from 1508-12, and Raphael's tapestries (now in the Vatican Museum's Pinoteca) were hung below the frescoes on the side walls for Pope Leo X in 1519. Finally, Michelangelo's *Last Judgment* was painted between 1535-41, replacing earlier frescoes by Perugino. In 1980-94 the ceiling frescoes and *Last Judgment* were cleaned, amid much heated debate; the side-wall frescoes were restored in 1999.

While in the chapel, speak quietly and **refrain from taking flash photos,** even if you see others around you doing it. The light of the flash damages the frescoes, and you can buy much better shots (actually cheaper than using your own film) on postcards in the ubiquitous gift shops.

WALL FRESCOES

Before craning your neck, prepare yourself by taking in the older, all too often ignored frescoes on the side walls. Facing the *Last Judgment*, the left wall contains six scenes from the life of Moses, while six scenes from the life of Christ appear on the right wall. The cycle, frescoed in 1481-83, was completed by a team of artists working under Perugino that included Botticelli, Ghirlandaio, Roselli, Pinturicchio, Signorelli, and della Gatta.

LIFE OF MOSES

Starting at the altar, the first fresco in this cycle is Pinturicchio's *Moses and Zepporah*, which shows Moses circumcising his son, and returning to Egypt to free the Israelites from slavery. Botticelli's impressive *Burning Bush* comes next, where Moses hears God speaking out of the burning bush, instructing him to free the Israelites from slavery. A busy man, Moses also defends Jethro's daughters from Midianites at the well, and kills an Egyptian who had beaten an Israelite slave. The third fresco, by Biagio di Antonio, depicts the crossing of the Red Sea. The newly freed Israelite people (left), have passed safely across the sea, which was conveniently lifted to the side, while the pursuing Egyptians, at right, drown with all their troops.

The next fresco, by Cosimo Roselli, shows Moses receiving the Ten Commandments from God. The Israelites, at right, immediately break the new laws by worshipping the golden calf they constructed. Moses breaks the tablets in anger, symbolizing the people's breaking of the laws. Botticelli's *Punishment of Korah, Dathan, and Abiram* follows, in which the said persons are punished for trying to stone Moses. Behind Moses, on the far right, the figure in black is a portrait of Botticelli, the fresco's painter. The last fresco in this cycle ties up loose ends: Moses hands his staff to his successor, Joshua, an angel shows Moses the promised land, and Moses dies.

LIFE OF CHRIST

The first fresco, beginning at the altar, was painted by Perugino and Pinturicchio and shows the baptism of Christ by John the Baptist. In the background, Christ preaches (left) while John steps back in time, predicting Christ's coming (right). In the second fresco, by Botticelli, Christ is tempted by the devil, who suggests that he test God by throwing himself from various high places to see if angels save him. Next, Christ calls the first apostles, fishermen named Peter and Andrew, in a fresco by Ghirlandaio. In the fourth fresco, Cosimo Rosselli shows Christ giving the Sermon on the Mount. In the right foreground, Christ heals a leper. The next fresco (by Perugino and Signorelli) is the most famous in the cycle, showing Christ handing the keys to the kingdom (symbolically the power to decide who enters heaven) to Peter, the first Pope. The final fresco shows the Last Supper, painted by Roselli and Antonio. Judas, the disciple who betrayed Christ, is easy to find: he's sitting across from Christ on the wrong side of the table and is the only one without a halo.

The far inferior frescoes on the wall opposite *The Last Judgment* (*A Resurrection* on the left, and *St. Michael Defending the Body of Moses* on the right) are not original, but were added in the 1570s in the place where Michelangelo was supposed to have painted another full wall masterpiece. Botticelli, Ghirlandaio, and Fra Diamante painted the series of 26 popes who stand in the niches between the high windows.

SISTINE CEILING

Although the Sistine Ceiling is often trumpeted as the pinnacle of Michelangelo's career, the project was given to Michelangelo as a consolation prize by Pope Julius II. Michelangelo's plans to create a massive tomb for Julius II were thwarted by the Pope's sudden edifice fetish, which took the form of improvements to St. Peter's. To keep the hot-tempered artist from fleeing to the hills (as he was wont to do), Julius let Michelangelo repaint the star-studded ceiling of the Sistine Chapel.

Sulking, Michelangelo set about learning how to fresco, firing assistants with remarkable rapidity, and developing a permanent crick in his neck (he did not paint flat on his back, but standing up and craning his head backwards). The complex design primarily depicts the Biblical story of Genesis in the central panels, flanked by Apostles, Sibyls and nudes reclining on thrones along the side of the vault.

Michelangelo began work at the far end of the ceiling, painting the Creation narrative backwards as he moved toward the altar (contrary to Church tradition, in which paintings surrounding the altar always came first). Suffering from a lack of funds, Michelangelo took a six-month hiatus after completing half the ceiling in 1510-11. The division between his earlier, crowded panels and the later, more streamlined panels can be clearly seen. The scale of Michelangelo's figures increased dramatically as he painted as well—check out the size of Zachariah's feet (above the exit) compared to those of Jonah (above the *Last Judgment*).

While focusing on the central panels, don't overlook the expressive Apostles and Sibyls (whose brawny arms are said to be the result of Michelangelo's exclusive use of male models) and the often amusing *ignudi*. Representing some of Michelangelo's best painting, these nudes support green sacks full of acorns (the symbol of the della Rovere family, of which Pope Julius II was a member). In the four corner spandrels are depictions of *David and Goliath*, *Judith and Holofernes*, *The Bronze Serpent*, and *The Punishment of Haman.*

THE CREATION OF EARTH

Looking from *The Last Judgment* toward the chapel's rear, the panels show the first five days of Creation, beginning with *Separation of Light from Darkness.* Both the *Creation of the Sun, Moon, and Planets* and *Separation of Land from Water* focus primarily on the figure of God, surrounded by nebulous clouds.

ADAM AND EVE

In the next panel, *Creation of Adam*, Michelangelo revolutionizes conceptions of the birth of man; by depicting both God and man in human form, Michelangelo places mortals on nearly equal footing with God. Chalk one up for large-scale representations of hubris. Much scholarly attention has been devoted to the "tension" in the gap between the two fingers. In the central panel, *Creation of Eve*, Eve rests next to the stump of a tree, an allusion to the cross. In *Temptation and Expulsion from Paradise*, Adam and Eve reluctantly retire from the garden, while the serpent slithers past.

LIFE OF NOAH

The last three panels take on the life of Noah, with a noticeable absence of the figure of God. These frescoes depict the **Sacrifice of Noah** (where Noah thanks God for saving him and his family from the flood), **The Flood,** and the **Drunkenness of Noah**

Museo Nazionale d'Arte Antica

Arte Antica

Vatican Museums

(in which Noah forgets himself after the flood in a bout of shameful and ungodly revelry, thus proving the sinful nature of all mankind, even God's favorites). Though Michelangelo could have just ended with the *Flood*, it was theologically important to include the *Drunkenness of Noah* as a reminder that the world began anew under a bad light, underlining mankind's need for a savior, thus reinforcing the role of Christ and the Church. A close look at *The Flood* reveals slight damage to a corner, which occurred as a result of an explosion in the nearby Castel Sant'Angelo in 1508.

THE LAST JUDGMENT

Leaving behind frolicking *ignudi* for the flames of hell, Michelangelo turned his brush to the story of *The Last Judgment* (1535-41) for Pope Paul III. In the 23 years between the completion of the ceiling frescoes and the start of the *Last Judgment*, the character of Rome changed dramatically, as the Sack of Rome and the Protestant Reformation wreaked havoc on the city and her beliefs. A known Dante scholar, Michelangelo's interpretation also has some Infernal references, notably in the depiction of Charon whacking the damned in the lower right hand corner of the fresco. The location of *The Last Judgment* above the altar symbolically places the most sacred part of the church in the mouth of hell. Paul III was satisfied with the results of his commission: upon the unveiling of the altarpiece, he fell to his knees on the cold marble floor, crying, "Lord, charge me not with my sins when Thou shalt come on the day of judgment!" Apparently, he didn't know of the later-declared doctrine of Papal infallibility.

In order to paint *The Last Judgment* above the altar, three previous frescoes were destroyed and two windows were filled in. The resulting fresco shows Christ (whose body is supposedly modeled after the Belvedere Torso) in the center, with Mary (averting her eyes from the grotesque spectacle), on the left, and St. Peter, holding his trademark key, on the right. Amid the saintly entourage, is St. Bartholomew holding his own skin, a rather morbid self-portrait of the 65-year-old artist.

On the left of the fresco, angels pull the lucky souls into heaven, while on the right, demons cast the damned into an abyss. The ferryman Charon carts the unfortunate cast of evildoers across the river. On the bottom left corner of the work, where a grim skeleton looks directly at the rest of the chapel, while the famous *Disperato* looks into hell. Also in the lower right corner, Minos, Master of the Underworld, sports a coiling tail and ass-ears. His face is a portrait of Biagio da Cesena, who, speaking for Pope Paul III, objected to Michelangelo's use of "shameless nudity in a holy space." In fact, after Michelangelo's death, during the conservative Counter Reformation, strategically draped, inelegant loin-cloths were painted onto many of the nudes. These additions were largely removed by the recent restoration, but a few loincloths remain.

OTHER MUSEUMS

Plan to spend a total of 20 minutes in these galleries.

CHAPEL OF ST. PIUS V

From the exit along the left-hand wall of the Chapel, several corridors return to the Galleries of the Library and back to the Belvedere Courtyard. The corridors pass numerous rooms containing artifacts collected during the reigns of various popes. In the second room, the Chapel of St. Pius V, a reliquary case contains fragments of saints retrieved from the treasury of *Sancta Sanctorum*, including the Reliquary of the Head of St. Praxedes. The blue and gold starred ceiling above the exit is similar to the ceiling of the Sistine Chapel before Michelangelo's frescoes.

ROOM OF THE ALDOBRANDINI MARRIAGE

A short way up on the left, the Room of the Aldobrandini Marriage hides a series of rare ancient Roman frescoes, including the celebrated wedding scene, set in a flowering park filled with animals.

ROOMS OF THE PAPYRUS

The Rooms of the Papyrus contain 29 facsimiles of medieval papyrus sheets with Latin writings dating back to the 16th century. The corridor continues past cases of uninspiring modern religious art (skip the *Mute Swans of Peace*) as well as antique globes, bells, and maps. The papal geocentric "universe" globes, midway down on the left side, are worth a glimpse.

THE SISTINE HALL

The Sistine Hall, leading off the main corridor to the right, is used for exhibitions from the Vatican Library's superb collection of books and manuscripts. At the end of the corridor, you'll find the Vestibule of the Four Gates, from which the stairs on the opposite side lead up to the Sistine Chapel. On the left is the **Atrium of the Four Gates** and the **Court of the Pinacoteca,** with an excellent view of St. Peter's.

PINACOTECA

The Pinacoteca, the Vatican's eclectic painting collection that spans the 12th to 18th centuries, was started by Pope Pius VI in 1790, and now boasts more than 460 works, including masterpieces by Giotto, Poussin, da Vinci, Titian, Veronese, and Caravaggio. Make sure to look at the gorgeous view of St. Peter's Dome before entering.

ROOMS 1-3

These galleries hold mostly Florentine and Sienese Gothic altarpieces and triptychs from the 12th to 14th centuries, thinly painted in brilliant colors with extraordinary detail and gobs of gold leaf. Particularly impressive is Giotto's two-sided altarpiece in **Room 2.** In **Room 3,** don't miss Fra Angelico's wonderful *Madonna and Child*, and Fra Filippo Lippi's *Coronation of the Virgin.*

ROOM 8

Breeze through Rooms 3-7 to reach the most important room of the Pinoteca, **Room 8.** In the center of the room are three works by Raphael, from left to right: the *Madonna of Foligno*, the sublime *Transfiguration*, and the *Coronation of the Virgin.* Hanging on the walls are the tapestries designed by Raphael, which once hung on the lower walls of the Sistine Chapel until they were plundered during the sack of Rome (only to be returned later). The tapestries were recently restored, and *La Pesca Miracolosa* is among the best.

ROOMS 9-10

These rooms house Giovanni Bellini's *Il Seppellimento di Cristo* and a mutilated Leonardo da Vinci panel of St. Jerome. Prior to its discovery, the panel had been cut in two; the bottom half had served as a coffer lid in an antique store, the top part as a stool seat in a shoemaker's shop. Room 10 holds Titian's *Madonna of San Nicoletta dei Frari* (look for Titian's mark on the wall of the painting).

ROOMS 12-15

Room 12 brings you into the devilishly cruel world of Baroque devotional art.Don't miss Caravaggio's sensual *Deposition from the Cross* and Nicholas Poussin's grisly *Martyrdom of St. Erasmus* (who had his intestines rolled out on a winch). The remaining rooms tend toward the obscure, and can be skipped.

MINOR MUSEUMS

The Gregorian Profane Museum, on the left as one heads toward the museum entrance, makes a quiet change from the bustle and bombast of the other museums. Look for the statues of Marsyas, the satyr who dared to play Athena's pipes (and was skinned alive for doing so), and the fragmentary *Chiaramonti Niobid.* Niobe, a mother of 14 children, had taunted Leto for having given birth to only two. Unfortunately for Niobe, the two were Apollo and Diana, and the irritated gods avenged their insulted mother by shooting down all 14 of Niobe's kiddies. The gallery also contains reliefs from imperial monuments, many depicting buildings of ancient Rome. Next door, the **Pio-Christian Museum** holds artifacts of a fascinating historical synthesis—the marriage of the Greco-Roman sculptural tradition to the newer iconography of the Christian Church. The sarcophagi and statuary here date from the earliest centuries AD, when the Roman Empire and its artistic vocabulary were still alive and well. Many a small statue of the Good Shepherd stand among the many intricately carved sarcophagi. Nearby, the **Ethnological-Missionary Museum** displays non-Christian religious articles alongside missionary-inspired works from Third-World cultures. The **Carriage Museum** contains comparatively recent papal goodies, including armor, guard uniforms, and carriages.

GALLERIA BORGHESE

Piazzale Scipione Borghese, 5. M: A-Spagna; take the exit labeled "Villa Borghese," walk to your right past the metro stop to V. Muro Torto to P. Porta Pinciana, Viale del Museo Borghese will be in front of you. This road will lead you directly to the museum. Alternatively, take **bus** *#910 from Termini to Via Pinciana or follow Villa Borghese exit signs and head left up the road to reach V. del Museo Borghese. Helpful brown signs in the park point the way. ☎06 8548577.* **Open** *Tu-F 9am-7:15pm; entrance only on the hr., visits limited to 2hr.; last entrance 30min. before closing. A limited number of people are admitted every two hours; the gallery does sell out, so book ahead. Admission L14,000/€7.23, EU nationals ages 18-25 L8000/€4.13, EU nationals under 18 and over 65 L2000. Tickets include ground floor galleries and Pinacoteca. The basement of the palace contains: the ticket office, a bookshop selling an informative guidebook for your tour (L20,000), a computer info kiosk, an inexpensive snack bar, restrooms and a cloakroom—all bags must be checked before entering the museum. Tickets may be reserved in advance by phone or in person for an extra L2000/€1.03. Expect to spend 2hr.*

The Galleria Borghese is quite simply one of the most important and enjoyable art collections in Rome. Housed in the former residence of the opulent Cardinal Scipione Borghese (Pope Paul V's brother), the collection attests to the buying power of those close to the Pope. The works include Classical sculptures, important Renaissance and Mannerist paintings, and more Bernini that you thought possible. For more on the Villa Borghese's history and sights, see p. 109.

After getting a ticket in the basement of the villa, you can either go back outside and head up the grand staircase to join the rest of the group in the sculpture-filled **main galleries,** or you can start in the Pinacoteca and enjoy the paintings in relative peace. Judge according to the crowds.

GROUND FLOOR

On your way into the sculpture galleries, don't ignore the spectacular Greek and Roman statuary that litters the porch, including some colossal feet and several figures of Hercules, recognizable by his lion skin cloak and signature club. The grand entrance hall sports a splendid ceiling fresco, *trompe l'oeil* medallions, and a fragment that is said to be a discarded version of the head of Christ from Michelangelo's *Rondanini Pieta*, his last work. Make sure you look at the 4th-century gladiator mosaics on the floor, and Bernini's *Truth*—sculpted for his own front porch.

ROOM 1

To the right of the entrance, this room features 19th-century neoclassicist Antonio Canova's seductive statue of Pauline Bonaparte Borghese as Venus. Supposedly, Pauline's husband thought the figure so luscious that he forbade anybody else to see it. Asked by a 19th-century tabloid writer if she felt uncomfortable posing disrobed Pauline replied, "No, the room was quite warm." The marble figure holds an apple, a reference to the beauty contest that launched the Trojan War, depicted in the ceiling fresco. According to mythology, a beautiful golden apple appeared one day amid the gods of Olympus, inscribed "For the Fairest." Hera, Athena, and Aphrodite claimed the title. Zeus wisely brought in a second opinion, that of Paris, the most beautiful man. Each goddess offered Paris gifts to name her most beautiful: Hera offered unlimited power, Athena unsurpassed knowledge and wisdom, and Aphrodite the love of the most beautiful mortal woman. A typical man, Paris chose the last, and happily made off with a certain Helen. And we all know how well that worked out.

ROOM 2

This is the Borghese's Hero room, where Bernini's **David** crouches in controlled aggression with his slingshot while Perseus and Hercules duke it out with various wild beasts on nearby sarcophagi. David's grimacing face is supposedly Bernini's own—check out Bernini's self-portrait on the second floor and decide for yourself. As will become evident, Cardinal Borghese was a big fan of this emerging star, commissioning several of Bernini's greatest sculptures, most of which remain in the Galleria Borghese.

ROOM 3

Apollo and Daphne shows Bernini at it again: two figures, the hunter-god and a wood nymph, are portrayed in an extraordinarily dynamic pose. Apollo, enamored of the lovely sprite, is depicted in mid-chase, his limbs and draped garment flying; meanwhile, the maiden metamorphoses into a laurel tree, her curls sprouting foliage, her toes twisting into gnarled roots. According to Ovid, the chaste nymph was unable to outrun her insistent suitor, and so called on her father, the river god, for aid. He transformed her into a tree to protect her virginity. As Apollo clasped Daphne in his arms, he could still feel her heart beating beneath the spreading bark. Bernini originally advised Cardinal Borghese to position the sculpture in the far right hand corner as you enter, so that the figure of Daphne was only gradually revealed.

ROOM 4

Follow the religiously themed hallway to Room 4, where pagan myth once more takes over in the form Bernini's **Rape of Proserpina** (1622-5). According to myth, Pluto carried off the young daughter of Ceres (variously Gaia or Demeter), the goddess of harvest, as she picked flowers in a springtime field. This little abduction didn't go over well with Ceres (who withheld the earth's harvest in a brilliant act of collective bargaining) or Zeus, who demanded that Pluto return the girl to her frantic mother. Unfortunately, a hungry Prosperina had already eaten three pomegranate seeds, the *specialita del giorno* of Hades, and was thus eternally bound to her new husband. The Olympic divorce court eventually decided on joint custody; Prosperina would spend six months a year with her mother on earth (summer), and the rest in Hades as queen of the underworld (winter). In Bernini's interpretation, the menacing Pluto is flanked by his three-headed guard dog, Cerberus, while Prosperina's tears are clearly visible on her cheeks. Elsewhere in the room, a dignified marble Artemis, a 2nd-century copy of a 4th-century BC Greek bronze, reaches into her quiver. Meticulously wrought mosaics cover the walls between elegant Renaissance columns.

ROOMS 5-7

In Room 5, a first-century Roman sculpture with a modern head depicts the enigmatic Hermaphrodite. Perhaps the original Lady in Red, Hermaphrodite can also be found in each panel of the ceiling, consistently wearing red draperies. In Room 6, a weary-looking Aeneas, followed by his son Ascanius, carries his elderly father away from the burning city of Troy in *Aeneas and Anchises*, one of the Bernini's first commissions (executed when he was just 21, possibly with help from his sculptor father). While Bernini's characteristic sense of movement is somewhat limited in this early sculpture, he seems to have hit a groove early on with the all-important consideration of hairstyles—they rarely change in any of his later works. Room 7, the Egyptian Room, lives up to its name, showcasing a Roman portrait of the goddess Isis in black marble, six sphinxes, and an marble border featuring pyramids, owls, cranes and hieroglyphics.

ROOM 8

A 2nd-century Roman satyr pirouettes in the center of Room 8, clanging his marble cymbals, but don't let him distract you from the room's real attractions—no fewer than six **Caravaggio** paintings grace the walls. Two early paintings (*Boy with Fruit* and *Self-Portrait as Bacchus*, c.1590) show Caravaggio's exploration with color and light, more fully realized in his famous *St. Jerome* (1605). *David with the Head of Goliath* (1609-10) is considered to be one of Caravaggio's finest works, full of brooding psychological intensity. Carravaggio's concern for the beheaded Goliath is deeply personal—after killing Ranuccio Tommassoni in a 1605 duel, Carravaggio is said to have sent the painting to the Pope with a plea against capital punishment.

PINACOTECA

The Pinacoteca (painting gallery) is accessible from the gardens in back of the gallery by a winding staircase. Go outside by the door you came in and walk around the building to find the door on the opposite face of the building.

ROOMS 10-13

Room 10 showcases Italian mannerism and the dangers of too much lust—the cupid in Cranach's lovely *Venus* eats honeycomb (a symbol of pleasure) while simultaneously getting stung by nasty-looking bees. Inexplicably, Venus remains unscathed. The room also houses Correggio's painting briefly owned by Queen Christina of

Sweden, of Zeus appearing to a reclining Danae as a thunder cloud raining brig golden sparks toward her pelvis. Zeus's infidelity (he was married to Hera) gave ri to an important demigod: Danae gave premature birth to Bacchus, the god of wi several months later when the vengeful Hera struck the unlucky mistress down w lightning. Rooms 11 to 13 hold a variety of smaller, more minor works.

ROOMS 14-16

Room 14, the large hall to the left (as one faces the stairway) provides beauti views of the curlicue French gardens below. Note the macho-macho men holding the ceiling—*trompe l'oeil*, we're afraid. Notable as well are the three small self-p traits by Bernini. The red walls of Room 15 are home to Bassano's sweet *Sheep a Lamb*, juxtaposed (a dark joke by the curators?) with a *Circe* by Dosso Dos Directly across in Room 16 is Zucchi's fabulous *Allegory of the Discovery of New World* and his amusing take on the founding of America.

FINAL ROOMS

The doorway under Cleopatra leads to Room 17 and its excellent 17th-century Dut and Italian interior paintings, notably Frans Francken's whimsical *Antique Deale Gallery* and two views of Rome by Canaletto. A notably pudgy Christ can be fou in a Rubens *Pieta* in Room 18. Titian's *Sacred and Profane Love*, the best Titian Rome, can be seen in Room 20.

CAPITOLINE MUSEUMS

On top of the Capitoline Hill (behind the Vittorio Emanuele II monument). ☎ 06 397462. Open Tu-Su 10am-8pm, holidays 9am-2pm. Ticket office closes 1hr. before closing. L15,0C €7.75, with ISIC L11,000/€5.68, Italian and EU citizens under 18 and over 65 free. Guidebc L30,000/€15.49, audioguide L7000/€3.62, daily tours in English L6000/€3.10. Parts of mu ums wheelchair accessible. Plan to spend 2-3hr.

The Capitoline Museums, founded in 1471 by Pope Sixtus IV, comprise the worl oldest public museum, one of Rome's most important repositories of Greek a Roman sculpture. The beautiful *piazza* and the facades of both *palazzi* we designed by Michelangelo. Entering the museum lands you in a curatorial time-wa as the impressive collection is arranged with a 19th-century view toward 'archit tural symmetry' and 'overall ornamental effect' rather than historical, archaeolo cal, or artistic quality. So bring your sketchbook and revel in the disarray.

The Palazzo Nuovo (to the left as you enter) contains hundreds of unlabeled stat from the 4th century BC through the 3rd century AD, while the Palazzo dei Conservat (on the right), houses some famous Hellenistic Roman bronzes and Renaissance art.

PALAZZO NUOVO

Inside the Palazzo Nuovo's courtyard, the original 2nd-century gilded bronze sta of philosopher-king **Marcus Aurelius** sits astride his horse behind protective glass. copy is in the middle of the P. Campidoglio, where Michelangelo intended the ori nal to stand.) The statue is the only equestrian bronze to survive from ancient Ro most bronzes were melted down during the Middle Ages. Lucky Marcus survived mistake, as he was thought to be Constantine, the first Christian emperor.

On the second floor, notice the delicate *Capitoline Venus* in a polygonal room the right as you walk down the central corridor. The Hall of Emperors, to the left at end of the hallway, showcases a stunning bust of a Roman woman, **Dama Flavia** c. 98-117, with curls that would put Little Orphan Annie to shame. The next room, con niently named the Hall of Philosophers, holds 73 busts, 23 reliefs and one statue of, w philosophers. Homer, Pythagoras, Socrates, Eurpides and Cicero are in attendance, which is which is anyone's guess, as the thinkers are woefully unlabeled. Oh, if the busts could talk. The rest of the rooms are also themed and contain the **Dying Gaul** an **Satyr Resting**, the "Marble Faun" that inspired Hawthorne's book of the same title.

PALAZZO DEI CONSERVATORI

In the underground passageway from Palazzo Nuovo to Palazzo dei Conservatc follow the signs for a quick detour to the Tabularium. The balcony underne ancient arches provides a glorious, elevated view of **The Roman Forum**—withc the crowds or heat. In Palazzo dei Conservatori's courtyard reside sundry limbs long separated from their owner, the 12m 4th-century **Colossus of Constantine;** don't miss your chance to get a picture of yourself beside his big toe. This Colossus stood in the basilica in the Forum, a dedication to Constantine's victory over Maxentius and subsequent conversion to Christianity. On a landing before the first floor, four reliefs from a monument to Marcus Aurelius show scenes (right to left) of the Emperor offering a sacrifice, driving a triumphal chariot, bestowing clemency on captives (with the same gesture as in his equestrian statue), and receiving the ominous "orb of power."

At the second landing, a door leads to the **Sale dei Conservatori.** Cavaliere d'Arpino frescoed the giant main room with episodes from the reigns of the early kings—a little love, a little religion, and a whole lot of carnage. The **Spinario,** an evocative Hellenistic bronze of a boy quietly picking a splinter out of his foot, is in the next room, while the famous **Capitoline She-Wolf,** a 6th- or 5th-century BC Etruscan bronze, stands in the center of the next room. The She-Wolf is perhaps the work of the renowned Vulca of Veii, and Antonio Pollaiuolo added Romulus and Remus to the sculpture in the 15th century. On the walls are the *Fasti*, the archival records of the ancient Pontifex Maximus, excavated from the Regia in the forum. Among the masterpieces not purloined by the popes are (in **Room 2**) Bellini's *Portrait of a Young Man* and Titian's *Baptism of Christ*. Speed through the **Cini Gallery** to see **Caravaggio's** rendition of St. John the Baptist and the recently restored *Gypsy Fortune-Teller* in the Sala di Santa Petronilla, named for the 12m high Il Guernico altarpiece of the burial of said saint.

MUSEO NAZIONALE ETRUSCO DI VILLA GIULIA

In Villa Borghese at P. Villa Giulia, 9. M: A-Flaminio or ***bus*** *#19 from Piazza Risorgimento or #52 from P.S. Silvestro. From Galleria Borghese, follow V. Dell'Uccelliera to the Zoo, and then take V.d. Giardino to V. d. Bell Arte. The museum will be on your left, after the Galleria Arte Moderna. ☎ 06 3201951. L8000/€4.13, EU citizens and Southern and Central Australians under 18 and over 65 free, Canadians under 15 free.* ***Audioguide*** *L8000/€4.13,* ***guidebook*** *L20,000/€10.33, available at the bookstore outside the museum entrance.* ***Open*** *Tu-F, Su, and holidays 8:30am-7:30pm, Sa 9am-8pm. Extended hours June-Sept. Sa 9am-11pm. Plan to spend 1½-2hr.*

The national Etruscan museum is housed in the Villa Giulia, built in 1552 by Pope Julius III, who was criticized by contemporaries for leading a frivolous life while the Council of Trent erupted around him. Designed by Vignola, with some input from Michelangelo, the villa's decorative sculpture was partially scraped away by more conservatives popes. Luckily, Vignola's nymphaeum, a sunken gold-fish pond with prolific ferns and mermaid columns, was preserved.

Though every town in the region seems to host an Etruscan museum, Rome's collection is by far the strongest. The 35 rooms of this museum are well labeled in English and Italian, with instructive maps and historical and archeological details. Don't miss the ceramic uteruses used as fertility charms **(Room 5)** or the statues from the portico of the Temple of Apollo in **Room 7** who brazenly stick their tongues out at passing visitors. Other highlights include a graceful 6th-century BC terra cotta sarcophagus of a husband with his arm around his wife **(Room 9)** and an impressive collection of red and black figure amphoras **(Room 19).**

Room 20 houses a sparkling collection of hundreds of necklaces, bracelets, rings, pins dating from Pre-Colombian times (1500 BC) to the 16th century, including an intriguing Bacchanalian necklace with bunches of amethyst grapes set against gold leaves (Case 6). Catch a glimpse of the Etruscan idea of a good time in **Room 27:** a large jar depicts two men feasting with a nubile female flute player; another shows Eros seated with a naked lass on a panther skin. In **Rooms 30 and 31,** archaeologists have reconstructed fragments of the entire facade of an Etruscan temple, complete with terra cotta gargoyles, chips of original paint, and a fresco of the Greek warrior Tydaeus biting into the brain of a still-living adversary while Athena, who was about to give him the gift of immortal life, turns away in disgust. Before you leave, make sure to see an unusually large skeleton (6 ft. long) lying in a petrified tree trunk in **Room 32.**

THE ERA BEFORE DISHWASHERS

The Villa Farnesina used to be one of *the* spots where that legendary Roman excess took place. Artists, ambassadors, courtesans, cardinals, and even Pope Leo X were known to enjoy Agostino Chigi's extravagantly lavish parties.

Stories of his largesse are legendary. He once invited the Pope and the entire College of Cardinals to dinner in a gold-brocaded dining hall so imposing that the Pope reproached him for not treating him with greater familiarity. Chigi, an honorable man, ordered the hangings removed and revealed to his astonished guests that they'd actually only been eating in his stables.

At another infamous banquet in his *loggia* overlooking the Tiber, Chigi had his guests pay their tab by tossing his gold and silver dishes into the river after every course. Slyly, the shrewd businessman had already hidden nets under the water to recover his original treasures.

GALLERIA NAZIONALE D'ARTE MODERNA

In Villa Borghese, V. delle Belle Arti, 131. M: A-Flaminio; enter park, walk up V. George Washington. ☎06 322981. Open Tu-Su 8:30am-7:30pm. L12,000/€6.20; L6000/€3.10 for art and architecture students. Wheelchair accessible. ***Cafe delle Arte*** *open 7:30am-1am Tu-Sa. Plan to spend 1-1½hrs.*

They say that books should not be judged by their covers, and the Galleria Nazionale D'Arte Moderna proves that art museums should not be either. Despite its overwhelming Neo-classical facade, designed by Cesare Bazzani in 1911 and enlarged in 1933, the museum holds a large collection of mostly Italian 19th- and 20th-century art in a remarkably modern interior. The central salon features well-chosen temporary exhibitions by contemporary Italian artists in a range of media, and deserves careful scrutiny. The 19th-century galleries, to your left as you enter, are mainly arranged by artist and do not present any notable works, with the exception of Canova's depiction of Hercules holding Lica upside down by his ankle.

Time is better spent in 20th-century galleries, in the back of the museum, which feature far more significant works. The collection is large and contains the works of many superstars; however, those works tend to be portraits of the artists' mother, as with de Chirico. Work from 1900 to 1950 is shown in the gallery on the right, containing many paintings from the Italian futurists, including Balla, Carra, Severini and Boccioni. Tucked between the futurists are Klimt's *The Three Ages of Man*, an uninspired Mondrian, Modigliani's *Portrait of a Lady with a Collar* and **Duchamp's "Fountain,"** the famous urinal marked with the words "R. Mutt 1917."

A sculpture-filled hallway, including a Henry Moore and Alberto Viani's voluptous white *Nude*, leads to galleries of art from 1950 to the present. Two skinny Giacomettis stand near one of Arnaldo Popmadoro's broken bronze spheres, "Stera n. 2" Nearby is an undulating bronze wall by another Pomodoro—Gio, to be exact. A smattering of internationals (so-so Pollocks, a Calder and a Kandinsky) also hang in these galleries, but are outdone by the Italian works, such as Lucio Fontana's slashed canvases and Alberto Burri's sexy charred cellophane creations. Upstairs is a jewel case of drawings by Moore, Morandi, and Tw, and a vision of Castel Sant'Angelo wrapped by Christo.

MUSEI NAZIONALI ROMANI

A six-day ticket book is good for all three museums and the Terme di Diocletian for L15,000/€7.75; admission to the Colosseum, the Palatine Hill and the Terme Caracalla bumps the price up to L30,000/€15.49.

MUSEO NAZIONALE ROMANO PALAZZO MASSIMO

Largo di Via Peretti, 1. In the left-hand corner of P. dei Cinquecento as you stand with your back to Termini. ☎06 4815576; group reservations ☎06 39967700. Open Tu-Su 9am-7:45pm; ticket office closes 7pm. L12,000/€6.20, EU citizens ages 18-24 L6000/€3.10, EU citizens under 18 and over 60 free.) Audio guide in Italian and English L7000. For information on archaeological day trips (about L25,000/€12.91), ☎06 4815576 or write: Centro Servizi Per l'Archeologia, Via Giovanne a Mendola 2, Roma. No photographs, video cameras, or cell phones allowed in galleries. Handicapped accessible.

One of the unsung-heroes of the Roman museum circuit, Palazzo Massimo houses many heroes of its own, namely, magnificent Greek and Roman marble statues of Apollo, Dionysus, and Aphrodite, among others. The spacious, well-lit palazzo is designed around an apricot-colored inner courtyard boasting a gold-fish pond. The basement floor holds an impressive catalog of Roman coins, starting in the 4th century BC and ending with Vittorio Emanuele II. Vault doors worthy of Lloyds of London guard the approximately 3600 different coins on display. On the ground floor, Roman sculpture and portraiture from 11 BC to AD 1 is on display, as well as original Greek sculptures and later Roman copies. A Greek sculpture of the *Maiden of Anzio*, taken from Nero's beach bungalow in Anzio, can be found on the first floor. Particularly amusing are the series of gymnast sculptures in the gallery on the right, where the *Discobulo* looks primed for the next Olympics. Look for door knockers in the form of various violent beasts.

A peek at Imperial jewelry in the adjoining rooms is cheaper than a visit to Bulgari and just as gratifying; but beware of the mummy in the corner. The superb mosaics and wall paintings of the top floor are only accessible with a guide, and you must arrive at the time stated on your ticket. The guide leads you though Livia's dining room (painted to resemble a Mediterranean garden), the erotic bedrooms of villa Farnesina, and Nero's fountain in Anzio, built with live coral and seashells.

MUSEO NAZIONALE ROMANO TERME DI DIOCLEZIANO

Museum: P. dei Cinquecento, 78. Opposite Termini. ☎06 39967700. Open Tu-Su 9am-7pm. L8000, EU citizens 18-24 L4000, EU citizens under 18 and over 60 free. Audioguide L7000; guided tour with archaeologist L10,000. Aula Ottagonale: V. Romita, 8. ☎06 39967700. Open Tu-Sa 9am-2pm. Entrance is free.

While the Baths of Diocletian can no longer claim to be the biggest bubble bath in the Western Hemisphere, they left considerably more than rubber duckies in their wake. The newly-renovated museum is partly housed in the huge Baths of Diocletian (see p. 122), and holds permanent exhibitions devoted to ancient epigraphy (writing) and Latin history through the 6th century BC. 100 ancient columns make up the arcade of the *Chiostro Michelangiolesco*, a peaceful cloister littered with fragments of ancient sculpture, including a host of fanciful beasts that jealously guard the central fountain. The bath's vaulted halls provide the most impressive display space, the Aula Grande, where temporary exhibitions about Roman history are often housed (L10,000). If the space is closed, look through the large glass doors—it's well worth the peek. The Aula Ottagonale holds 19 Classical sculptures in a gorgeous octagonal space, including two bronzes found in the baths. To reach the baths, exit the Diocletian Baths and pass S. Maria degli Angeli on your right. The Aula Ottagonale is on the next block on your right.

MUSEO NAZIONALE ROMANO PALAZZO ALTEMPS

P. Sant'Apollinare, 44. Just north of P. Navona. ☎06 7833566. Open Tu-Su, 9am-7pm. L10,000/€5.06, EU citizens 18-24 L5000/€2.58, EU citizens under 18 and over 65 free.

A few steps from the hustling, bustling tourist frenzy that is Piazza Navonna lies Palazzo Altemps, a 16th-century palazzo that houses a collection of ancient Roman sculpture. Arranged around a central courtyard, the galleries show Classical works with a modern twist (most of the sculptures were "restored" in the 19th century). The condition of the sculptures upon excavation is noted in English and Italian on wall placards; by the end of the visit you'll be able to spot a fake a mile away.

On the ground floor, note the Hermae—statues that portray realistic torsos, but turn into columns below the waist. The genitals of these statues were left visible, legend has it, so that travellers could rub them for good luck. Also on the ground floor is a rather more modest *Aphrodite Bathing*, and the *Parthenon Athena*, a first-century BC copy of a 5th-century original by Phidias that stood 12m high and sported a body of gold leaf, a head of ivory, and eyes of precious stones. Upstairs you can find the *Ludovisi Throne*, featuring a relief of Aphrodite being born from the waves. Sculpted in the 5th century BC for the Temple of Epizephiris, the throne was later used by the cult of Aphrodite for annual re-enactments of the goddess's birth. The *Ludovisi Ares* (believed to be derived from the work of Alexander the Great's personal sculptor, Lysippus) and the *Suicidal Gaul* also deserve attention.

VILLA FARNESINA

V. della Lungara, 230. Just across from Palazzo Corsini on Lungotevere Farnesina. Bus #23; get off between Ponte Mazinni and Ponte Sisto. ☎06 68027268. Open M-Sa 9am-1pm. L8000/€4.13, under 18 L6000/€3.10, EU citizens over 65 free. Plan to spend 1hr.

Thought to be the wealthiest man in Europe in his day, Agostino "il Magnifico" Chigi entertained the stars of the Renaissance papal court in his sumptuously decorated villa and its extensive palm gardens. The interior decoration boasts frescoes by Raphael, Peruzzi, Il Sodoma, and Giulio Romano. After the banker's death in 1520, however, the villa fell into disrepair and was bought by the Farnese family.

FIRST FLOOR

To the right upon enetering the villa lies the fantastical Sala of Galatea. The villa's architect, Baldassare Peruzzi, bears most of the responsibility for the frescoes in here. The ceiling frescoes bear symbols of astrological signs, which, taken with the two central panels of Perseus decapitating Medusa and Callisto (in a chariot drawn by oxen), add up to a symbolic plan of the stars in the night sky at 9:30pm, November 29, 1466—the moment of Chigi's birth. But the masterpiece of the room, on the long wall opposite the windows, is Raphael's vibrant fresco, The Triumph of Galatea, in which Galatea appears surfing the seas on a conch-shell chariot drawn by two rather nasty-looking dolphins. Galatea was the lover of Polyphemus, the Cyclops whom Odysseus kills in the *Odyssey*. Prior to his Homeric debut, Polyphemus had his mistress stolen by Venus, who took pity on the nymph's love for another man.

One room over is the lovely **Loggia di Psiche,** which was an entrance hall before the Farnese family glassed it in to protect the frescoes. The 1520 ceiling fresco recreates the adventures of Psyche on Earth, including her love affair with Cupid and the ensuing jealousy of Venus. It's speculated that this love affair is supposed to mirror that of Chigi and his wife, Francesa Ordeaschi, who can be seen to the far left of the second ceiling fresco, offering a bowl to Mercury. **Raphael** was commissioned to paint these, and even drew up designs for them, but rumor has it that he was too obsessed with his new mistress, la Fornarina, to do any work. The frescoes are attributed to Penni, Giovanni da Udine, and Giulio Romano.

SECOND FLOOR

Upstairs you'll find perhaps the most impressive paintings in the palace: two rooms decorated with frescoes to celebrate Chigi's wedding to a young Venetian noblewoman, whom he had abducted and kept cloistered in a convent for several years. The first, the **Sala delle Perspettive,** is embellished on two ends by Baldassare Peruzzi with views of 16th-century Trastevere (right) and the Borgo (left), framed between *trompe l'oeil* columns. The geometry's not all there, but it's worth a look. Vulcan sits above the fireplace, and 11 Olympian gods relax atop vine-covered arches. The adjacent bedroom, the **Stanza delle Nozze** (Marriage Room), is the real reason for coming. This room is undergoing extensive restorations; but should have re-opened to the public by December, 2001. The Stanza delle Nozze was frescoed by Il Sodoma, who had been busy painting the papal apartments in the Vatican until Raphael showed up and stole the commission. Il Sodoma rebounded well, making this masterful fresco of Alexander the Great's marriage to the beautiful Roxanne in 1509. The side walls show the family of Darius the Persian surrendering to Alexander, and a rather awful depiction of Bellerophon the Pegasus-tamer that was painted by another (unknown) hand.

MUSEO NAZIONALE D'ARTE ANTICA

This national collection of 12th- through 18th-century art is split between Palazzo Barberini and Galleria Corsini. The former houses more masterworks, but the latter collection is nothing to sniff at; both galleries deserve a visit.

PALAZZO BARBERINI

V. delle Quattro Fontane, 13. M: A-Barberini. ☎06 4814591. Open Tu-Sa 9am-7pm, Su 9am-8pm. L12,000/€6.20, EU citizens 18-25 L7000/€3.62, EU citizens under 18 and over 65 and students of art and architecture L2000/€1.03. Temporary exhibitions on the second floor, extra L8-10,000/€4.13-5.16. Plan to spend 1-1½hr.

The Barberini contains paintings from the medieval through Baroque periods and an impressive central stairway, full of Barberini bees, designed by Bernini. The Barberini family lived here from 1625, when Pope Urban VIII built it to commemorate his accession, through 1960, despite the sale of the palazzo to the state in 1949. Twice an hour, guards open the upper floor and allow you to wander through the Rococo apartments once belonging to Cornelia Costanza Barberini. The museum holds a healthy number of masterpieces by del Sarto, Il Sodoma, Bernini, Holbein, Lippi, Raphael, Caravaggio, and Poussin. Of particular note on the first floor is Raphael's *La Fornarina*, a portrait of a baker's daughter who also happened to be his mistress, Piero di Cosimo's beautifully restrained *Mary Magdalene*, and a vibrant *Annuciation and Two Donors* by Fillipo Lippi. Upstairs in the first hallway is Guido Reni's *Portrait of a Lady*, depicting the legendary Beatrice Cenci. After a *cause celeb* involving incest, patricide and execution, Beatrice was also immortalized by Shelley, Dickens and Hawthorne.

GALLERIA CORSINI

V. della Lungara, 10. Opposite Villa Farnesina in Trastevere. Take the #23 bus and get off between Ponte Mazinni and Ponte Sisto. ☎06 68802323 Open Tu-Su 8:30am-1pm. L8000/€4.13, EU students L4000/€2.06, Italian art students and EU citizens over 65 free. Guidebooks, in Italian, L20,000/€10.32. Wheelchair accessible. Plan to spend 1hr.

The Corsini houses a crowded collection of mostly 17th- and 18th-century paintings by the Dutch masters Van Dyck and Rubens, Italian virtuosi Fra Angelico, Titian, and Caravaggio, and many others. In **Room II,** note in particular Fra Angelico's ecstatic triptych of the Last Judgment, the Ascension of Christ, and Pentecost to the left of the door, Titian's *Portrait of Philip II of Spain* and Rubens's *St. Sebastian.* Nicolas Poussin's *Triumph of Ovid* in **Room VI** is remarkable. Try not to miss the bedroom where

Laocoön

Vatican Museums

Museo Nazionale d'Arte Antica

Queen Christina of Sweden died—it's marked by a plaque of her dying words in It ian and Swedish ("I was born free, I lived free, and I will die free"), as well a rather unflattering portrait of her, painted as the goddess Diana.

GALLERIA SPADA

P. Capo di Ferro, 13, in the elaborate Palazzo Spada. From Campo dei Fiori, take any of small streets leading to P. Farnese. With your back to Campo dei Fiori, take a left onto Capo Ferro. Bus #64. ☎06 328101. Open Tu-Sa 8:30am-1:30pm, Su 8:30am-12:30pm. Last tick sold 30min. before closing. L10,000/€5.16, EU students L5000/€2.58, EU citizens under 18 . over 60 free. Reservations L2000/€1.03 extra. Plan to spend 1hr.

Yet another Cardinal with money to burn and friends to impress, 17th-century Car nal Bernardino Spada filled his grand palazzo with gorgeous visual goodies. Vario well-connected descendants, added to the stash, which was acquired by the state 1926. Time and luck have left the palatial apartments nearly intact, and a visit to t gallery offers a glimpse of the luxurious Baroque court life. The gallery occup only four rooms of the Palazzo Spada; the rest is the Supreme Court, so mind yo P's and Q's. Before entering the gallery, ask at the ticket counter to see *Perspect*, by **Borromini.** Using a clever combination of light and angles, Borromini's optical il sion makes a 12m hallway look like a fabulous colonnade.

ROOMS 1-2

In **Room 1,** Spada hung three portraits of himself, by Il Guernico, Guido Reni, a Cerini. In **Room 2,** look for the **Tintoretto** work *Portrait of Archbishop of Lu Stella*, Reni's portrait of St. Jerome, and Prospero Fontana's *Astrologer*, compl with astrological globe. **Lavinia Fontana,** one of the few female painters whose wo survived from the 16th century, painted the rather silly-looking *Cleopatra*. Abo the windows is a frieze by del Vaga, originally intended to be placed beneath Micl langelo's far less cherubic *The Last Judgment* in the Sistine Chapel.

ROOMS 3-4

Room 3 houses 17th-century portraits and grandiose mythological scenes along capacious walls. The award for best melodrama goes to *Death of Dido*, by **Il Gu cino,** which shows the scorned Carthaginian queen throwing herself onto both h sword and her funeral pyre simultaneously. In the distance, Aeneas's ships set s for Italy, while an unconcerned Cupid loads another arrow. In Trevisani's *Banqu of Mark Antony and Cleopatra*, a midget holds a dalmation in check, while monkey on a leash skulks in the foreground of *The Rape of Helen* by Campana. **Room 4,** you'll see the **Gentilleschi** paintings which a certain Alessandro Bitti gave the family in return for erasing his (presumably large) debt.

EUR MUSEUMS

M: B-EUR-Palasport or B-EUR-Fermi. Walk north up V. Cristoforo Colombo, or take bus #7 from Termini. Make your final destination P. Giuglielmo Marconi; the museums are splayed ab Mussolini's decidedly phallic obelisk. One morning should be enough to see all the museums.

MUSEO DELLA CIVILTÀ ROMANA

P. Agnelli, 10. Down V. Civiltà Romana. ☎06 5926041. Open Tu-Sa 9am-7pm, Su and holid 9am-1:30pm. L8000/€4.13, reduced price L5000/€2.58, under 18 and over 60 free.

If ever there was an intimidating museum facade, this is it. This museum was co structed with the small task of explaining the history of Rome, and accomplish this through an absurd number of scale models. Elsewhere, a life-size model o Roman library and a cast of Trajan's Column are laid out. Before you leave, ma sure you see the vast scale models of Republican and Imperial Rome. Helpful lab are translated into English.

MUSEO DELL'ALTO MEDIOEVO

V. Lincoln, 3. ☎06 54228199. Open M-Su 9am-8pm; L4000/€2.07, reduced price L200 €1.03, under 18 and over 65 free. Wheelchair accessible.

Come see how the Longobords overran the remains of the Roman Empire in the smallest of the EUR museums. Among the collection of weapons, jewelry and household items are stone fragments with intricate arabesque designs and a collection of finely woven tunics. A morning with the Longobords and their knives can cure cases of Roman museum malaise if you've had it up to here with decadent Renaissance art.

MUSEO NAZIONALE DELLE ARTI E TRADIZIONI POPOLARI

P. G. Marconi, 8. ☎06 5910709; www.ips.it/musis/museo_arti. Open Tu-Su 9am-8pm. Closed New Year's, May Day, and Christmas. Call for tours in Italian or Braille. L8000/€4.13, reduced price L4000/€2.06, under 18 and over 65 free.

This museum is a veritable treasure trove of recent Italian culture. Roman marionettes sway beside wine presses, Carnevale costumes dance next to toy sailboats, and Queen Margherita's sumptuous gondola is beached on the second floor. Be sure to check out the *Bread: Holiday and Everyday* exhibit, which includes roosters, palm trees and a priest made out of bread. Temporary exhibitions are often shown.

MUSEO PREISTORICO ED ETNOGRAFICO LUIGI PIGORINI

P. G. Marconi, 14. ☎06 549521; reservations 06 8412312; guided tours in Italian, call 06 8412312. Open daily 9am-8pm. L8000/€4.13, EU citizens ages 18-25 L4000/€2.07, under 18 and over 65 free.

The collection is strong in ethnographic artifacts from Italy and contains the skull of the famous Neanderthal Guattari Man, discovered near Circeo. The museum holds more than 61 skulls (all in a row) and countless skeletons, in addition to an exhibition that traces the evolution of man from apes to Marilyn Monroe.

RECOMMENDED COLLECTIONS

MUSEO CENTRALE TERMOELETTRICA MONTEMARTINI

V. Ostiense, 106. M:B-Piramide. From P. Ostiense, walk to the right of the train station to V. Ostiense. Then, walk or take bus #702 or #23 three stops. ☎06 5748030. Open Tu-Su 10am-6pm. L8000/€4.13, EU citizens ages 18-24 L5000/€2.58, EU citizens under 18 and over 65 free.

Electric generators and Classical sculptures aren't typical bedfellows, but Athena never looked so good. **Montemartini,** an electrical plant, was converted to hold overflow sculpture from the Capitoline Museums in the 1990s. The fluid lines and pale colors of the sculptures create a striking contrast with the harsh shapes of the cast-iron machinery. Highlights include the *Hercules' Presentation at Mount Olympus* group (a huge, well-preserved floor-mosaic of a hunting scene, best viewed from the staircase to the right), a 5th-century BC statue of *Aphrodite* by Kallimachos found on the Esquilline Hill, and the 1½m head of *Fourtuna.*

GALLERIA COLONNA

V. della Pilotta, 17. Just north of P. Venezia in the Centro Storico. ☎06 0666784330. Open Sa 9am-1pm. L10,000/€5.16, students L8000/€4.13, children under 10, adults over 65, military and disabled persons are free. Closed Aug. Tours of Princess Isabella's apartments available by appointment; groups of 10 needed; L25,000/€13.75 per person. Free tours in English 11:45am.

If you've ever wanted to step into a Merchant-Ivory film, here's your chance. For a mere L8000, you can spend a morning sitting on a plush velvet couch contemplating priceless works of art under a frescoed ceiling. Sort of. This 18th-century palazzo holds the Colonna family's collection, which includes Tintoretto's *Narcissus*, and Bronzino's *Venus, Cupid, and Satyr.* The ebony desk in the next room is adorned with an ivory relief of Michelangelo's *The Last Judgment.*

GALLERIA DORIA PAMPHILJ

P. del Collegio Romano, 2. From P. Venezia, walk up V. del Corso and take your 2nd left. ☎06 6797323. Open F-W 10am-5pm, last tickets 4:15pm. Closed Jan. 1, Easter, May 1, Aug. 15, and Christmas. L14,000/€7.23, students and seniors L11,000/€5.68. Audioguide included. Useful catalogue with L10,000/€5.16 deposit. Private apartments (10:30am-12:30pm) L6000/€3.10.

The Doria Pamphilj family, whose relations with Pope Innocent X coined the term nepotism, still own this stunning private collection, on display in their palatial home.

It is arranged in stackable 18th-century fashion, and includes Titian's *Salome*, Raphael's *Double Portrait*, and only one Bernini, as the sculptor was out of favor with Innocent. Make sure to look closely at Caravaggio's *Rest during the Flight in Egypt*—the sheet music in the painting can be played—and Velasquez's portrait of *Innocent X*, by far the jewel of the collection and the best papal portrait in Rome.

MUSEO BARRACCO

C. Vittorio Emanuele II, 166. At the intersection of C. Vittorio Emanuele II and V. Baullari, across from Piazza Navona. ☎06 68806848. Open Tu-Sa 9am-7pm, Su 9am-1pm. L5000/€2.58, students L3000/€1.55.

Tucked in a *palazzo un poco* near Piazza Navona, the Museo holds a small but choice collection of Greco-Roman, Egyptian and Assyrian art. Particularly impressive are the head of Ramses II and the 3 statues of the God Bes on the 2nd floor. Before you leave, check out the 16th-century BC *Sphynx of Queen Hatshepsut*.

MUSEO NAZIONALE D'ARTE ORIENTALE

V. Merulana, 248. In Palazzo Brancaccio on the Esquiline Hill. ☎06 4874415. Open M, W, and F 9am-2pm, Tu and Th 9am-7pm, Su 9am-1pm. Closed 1st and 3rd M of the month. L8000/€4.13, Italian citizens under 18 and over 60 and humanities students free.

This museum sports an array of artifacts dating from prehistory up to the 19th century, divided into six main sections: evolution of art in the Near East; Islamic art; Nepalese and Tibetan art; Buddhist art from India; and Southeast Asian art. Highlights include Stone Age fertility dolls and psychedelic paintings of the Buddha.

OTHER INTERESTING COLLECTIONS

LARGER COLLECTION

MUSEO CRIMINOLOGICO

V. del Gonfalone, 29. Near Ponte Mazzini. ☎06 68300234. Open Tu 9am-1pm and 2:30-6:30pm, W 9am-1pm, Th 2:30-6:30pm, F-Sa 9am-1pm. May be closed Aug. L4000, under 18 and over 60 L2000

After overdosing on "artwork" and "culture," get your aesthetic stomach pumped at this museum dedicated to crime and punishment (the only museum in Rome run by the Dipartimento dell'Amministrazione Penitenziaria). Torture devices comprise the majority of the first floor, as well as some olde English etchings, among them *Smith Has His Brains Beaten Out With a Hammer*. On the 2nd floor, learn all about the phrenology of criminals and the secret language of tattoos. The 3rd floor contains terrorist, spy, and druggie paraphernalia. Children will learn a great deal.

MUSEO DELLE CERE

P. Santi Apostoli, 67. Two blocks to your left as you stand at the end of V. del Corso facing the Vittorio Emanuele II monument. ☎06 6796482. Open Daily 9am-8pm L8000. Call to arrange discounts for groups over 15.

Billing itself as an "emulation" of London's Madame Tussaud's—it's more like a photocopy of a photocopy—this **wax museum** presents distinctly Italian (and distinctly bizarre) scenes. Lowlights include the *Last Meeting of the Fascist Grand Council in Piazza Venezia*, featuring a very sickly-looking Mussolini, heroes of the Risorgimento, Italian pop stars of the 1960's, and soccer heroes.

MUSEO NAPOLEONICO

V. Zanardelli, 1, first Fl. East of Ponte Umberto. ☎06 68806286. Open Tu-Sa 9am-7pm, Su 9am-1:30pm. L7000.

The Primoli family, to whom this palazzo belonged, married into the Bonapartes in the 19th century and decided this was as good as reason as any to amass a collection of portraits and letters of sundy members of Napoleon's family. Live out your dream of seeing lithographs of every one of Napoleon's nieces.

MUSEO MARIO PRAZ

V. Zanardelli, 1, top fl., east of Ponte Umberto. ☎06 6861089. Hourly visits in small groups Tu-Su 9am-1pm and 2:30pm-6:30pm. L4000; under 18 and over 60 free.

This eccentric, smallish museum is housed in seven rooms in the last home of Mario Praz (1896-1982), an equally eccentric and smallish professor of English literature and 18th- and 19th-century art collector. Neighbors believed that Praz had supernatural powers; when they saw him, they spat or flipped coins.

KEATS-SHELLEY MEMORIAL HOUSE

P. di Spagna, 26. M:A-Spagna. Right of the Steps as you face them. ☎06 6784235. Open May-Sept. M-F 9am-1pm and 3-6pm; Oct.-Apr. M-F 9am-1pm and 2:30-5:30pm. Closed mid-July to mid-Aug. L5000.

The house where Keats lived until his death in 1821 houses both interesting artifacts and morbid curiosities. On the morbid side are plaster casts of Keats's face before and after he succumbed to tuberculosis, a lock of his hair, and his deathbed correspondence with his sister. More scholarly exhibits include the impressive library.

JEWISH COMMUNITY MUSEUM

Lungotevere Cenci, 15. Take bus #23, which runs along the Tiber. ☎06 6840061. To see the synagogue interior, you must take a tour. Open M-Th 9am-7:30pm, F and Su 9am-1:30pm. Oct-Jun M-Th 9am-4:40pm F and Su 9am-1:30pm. No cameras. L10,000.

Sinagoga Askenazita's museum houses a small collection of objects that were hidden during the nine-month Nazi occupation of Rome: magnificently decorated torahs, altar cloths, and various ceremonial objects, as well the original plan of the ghetto (see **Jewish Ghetto,** p. 100). The synagogue itself is lavishly decorated in bright and very beautiful Art Deco designs. Like all Jewish temples in Italy, this is an Orthodox synagogue; services are segregated by gender.

GALLERIA COMUNALE D'ARTE MODERNA E CONTEMPORANEA DI ROMA

V.F. Crispi, 24. M: A-Barberini. Northwest of P. Barberini. ☎06 4742848. Open Tu-Sa 9am-6:30pm, Su 9am-1:30pm. L10,000, students L5000, under 18 and over 60 free. Last Su of the month free. Wheelchair accessible.

If you come mid-week, there's a good chance you'll find yourself pacing the gallery's seven rooms alone. On display: a couple of Rodins and a lot of works by late 19th- and early 20th-century Italian painters and sculptors you've never heard of.

MUSEO CANONICA

V. Pietro Canonica, 2. ☎06 8842279. In Villa Borghese. Open Tu-Sa 9am-7pm, Su 9am-1:30pm. L4000, with student ID L2500, over 60 and under 18 free.

The home and studio of Pietro Canonica, who created the reliefs and statues that decorate many Italian squares, the museum houses a collection of his sculptures.

MUSEUM OF ZOOLOGY

V. d. Giardino Zoologico, 20. ☎06 3216586. Inside zoo in Villa Borghese. Open Tu-Su 9am-5pm. Admission L5000, in addition to 14,000 zoo admission.

While the Italian take on animal reproduction at the entrance is spanking new, the rest of the museum has a distinctly Victorian feeling, betraying a certain lack of funding. Glass cases display birds and mammals stuffed or skeletonized in the 19th and early 20th centuries, with a few reptiles, amphibians, and fish thrown in for variety.

SMALLER MUSEUMS

ARTS AND LETTERS

Museo Comunale Birreria Peroni: *V. Cagliari, 29, ☎06 8844930. Open M-Sa 10am-8pm. L6000.* ***Museo della Casina delle Civette:*** *in the Villa Torlonia, easily reached by bus #36 bus from Termini. ☎06 44250072. Open Tu-Su 9am-7pm; Oct.-Mar. Tu-Su 9am-5pm. L5000.* ***Goethe Museum:*** *V. del Corso, 18,☎06 32650412. Open W-Su 10am-6pm. L6000. Booking required for the* ***Museo Internazionale del Cinema e dello Spettacolo:*** *V. Bettoni, 1. ☎06 3700266.* ***Museo e Biblioteca Teatrale del Burcardo:*** *V. del Sudario, 44. ☎06 6819471. Open M, W, and F 9am-1:30pm, Tu, Th 9am-4pm.*

If you come to the **Museo Comunale Birreria Peroni,** just off V. Nomentana, looking for beer, you'll be disappointed, but if you seek contemporary Italian painting and sculpture in an ex-brewery, look no further. The **Museo della Casina delle Civette,** is full of art nouveau stained glass. The **Goethe Museum,** near P. del Popolo, is in the writer's former house, and celebrates his life. The **Museo Internazionale del Cinema e dello Spettacolo,** lies across the river from Testaccio. The **Museo e Biblioteca Teatrale del Burcardo** contains costumes, scripts, and other artifacts of the stage.

MARTIAL ARTS

Museo delle Mura Porta San Sebastiano: V. di Porta San Sebastiano, 18. Take bus #760 from the Circus Maximus or 218 from San Giovanni, or walk from the baths of Caracalla. Walk around the Aurelian ramparts! ☎06 70475284. Open Tu-Su 9am-7pm. L5000. ***Sacrario delle Bandiere:*** *☎06 647355002. Theoretically open Tu-Su 9am-1pm. L3000.* ***Museo Storico dell'Arma dei Carabinieri:*** *P. del Risorgimento. ☎06 6896691. Open Tu-Su 9am-12:30pm. Free.*

The ancient defense of Rome are chronicled in the **Museo delle Mura Porta San Sebastiano.** The **Sacrario delle Bandiere,** ison the left side of the Vittorio Emanuele II monument as you face it, and salutes 20th-century Italian war efforts, displaying battle-weary flags and hulking World War I submarines. The **Museo Storico dell'Arma dei Carabinieri,** near the Vatican, is dedicated to the glorious history of the machine-gun-toting Italian military police. It's a glorious tribute to the extraordinary heroism of the Carabinieri. Please, don't laugh at the tiny toy Fiats.

OH, THOSE MAD SCIENTISTS

The ***Museo Astronomico Copernicano:*** *V. del Parco Mellini, 84. From the Vatican, take bus #907. ☎06 35347056. Open W and Sa 9am-1pm. L6000.* ***Museo della Matematica:*** *P. Aldo Moro, 5. Take bus #492. ☎06 5833102.)* ***Museo Storico Nazionale dell'Arte Sanitaria:*** *Lungotevere Sassia, 3. ☎06 68351. Open M, W, and F 9:30am-1:30pm. L3000.*

Rome plays host to a number of intriguing museums focusing on mathematic and scientific collections. The **Museo Astronomico Copernicano,** is dedicated to Copernicus and the history of astronomy. The **Museo della Matematica,** which is located in the math department of La Sapienza. All manner of medical instruments from the 16th century to the present are contained in the **Museo Storico Nazionale dell'Arte Sanitaria,** across Ponte Vittorio Emanuele II on the Vatican bank.

PASTA, PRESEPIO, AND PURGATORY

Museo Nazionale delle Paste Alimentari: *P. Scanderbeg, 117. ☎06 6991119. Open daily 9:30am-5:30pm. L15000.* ***Museo Tipologio Nazionale del Presepio:*** *V. Tor dei Conti, 31a, near the intersection of V. dei Fori Imperiali and V. Cavour. ☎ 06 6796146 to arrange a visit.* ***Piccolo Museo delle Anime del Purgatorio:*** *Lungotevere Prati, 12. Open daily 7-11am and 4:30-7:30pm. ☎ 06 68806517.*

The **Museo Nazionale delle Paste Alimentari,** P. Scanderberg, 117, is easy to reach (follow the signs) from P. di Trevi. Its greater purpose is ending world hunger with pasta. While they're working on that, though, the museum will be happy to tell you everything you've ever wanted to know about Italy's favorite first course. Crêches 3000 of 'em, are the focus at the **Museo Tipologio Nazionale del Presepio.** The **Piccolo Museo delle Anime del Purgatorio,** near Ponte Cavour inside the Chiesa del Sacro Cuore del Suffragio, displays communications from souls trapped in Purgatory.

REVOLVING EXHIBITIONS

Rome's museum collections are supplemented by all manner of temporary exhibits. A number of museums listed above host temporary shows. The galleries below are mainly known for their temporary exhibitions. Major exhibitions are usually listed in the English section of *Roma C'è* or in *L'Evento*.

MUSEO NAZIONALE DEL PALAZZO VENEZIA

V. del Plebiscito, 118. On the left-hand side of P. Venezia as you stand with your back to the Vittorio Emanuele II monument. ☎06 67994319. Exhibits usually open Tu-Th, Su 10am-7pm; F and Sa 10am-10pm. Admission varies. Guided tours available. Permanent collection open Tu-Su 9am-2pm. L8000, under 18 and over 60 free.

The museum (an impressive 1455 palazzo that once belonged to the embassy of the Venetian Republic) hosts Rome's most prominent exhibitions. These are held in three large rooms, including the **Sala del Mappamondo,** the office where Mussolini used to deviously leave his light on all night, (earning the title "Sleepless One"). To find out what's showing, to watch the gigantic ads the museum routinely projects onto the facade of the building opposite. Don't miss the inner garden, a remarkable oasis of peace next to one of Rome's busiest intersections.

PALAZZO DELLE ESPOSIZIONI

V. Nazionale, 194. Six blocks in search of an author down V. Nazionale from P. della Repubblica. Open W-M 10am-9pm. ☎06 4885465. L12,000, students L6000, four student tickets L20,000.

This behemoth has no permanent collection, but hosts a varied and ever-changing array of exhibits and film festivals. Film festival movies are included in museum admission. Recent successes have been an Andy Warhol film festival, an El Greco show, and an exhibit on Pirandello.

SALA DEL BRAMANTE

P. del Popolo. M: A-Flaminio. In the small courtyard to the rear of the Church of Santa Maria del Popolo. ☎06 32600569. Open Tu-Su 10am-7pm. L5000.

A small gallery that unveils temporary exhibitions, the most recent being a wildly popular Goya show. Past favorites have included Mark Chagall, Picasso, and Dali.

PALAZZO RUSPOLI

V. d. Corso, 418. ☎06 6874704. Open Su-Th 9:30am-8pm, Sa 9:30am-9pm. L15,000, reduced L11,000.

This palace on the Corso between P. Colonna and V. Condotti hosts major exhibitions, such as an excellent recent show of Velazquez.

MUSEO DEL RISORGIMENTO

Open Tu-Sa 9am-6pm. Free.

Inside the bowels of the Vittoriano, this museum documents the reunification of Italy. More importantly, it's home to Garibaldi's pants, jacket, and his sword.

Caffè Greco

INSIDE

Food & Wine

In ancient Rome, dinners were lavish, festive affairs lasting as long as ten hours, with entertainment considered as vital as the food. Roman writers such as Petronius and Juvenal reported the erotica, exotica, and excess found upon the Imperial dinner table—peacocks, flamingos, and herons were served with their full plumage meticulously replaced after cooking. Acrobats and fire-eaters distracted guests between courses of dormice and camels' feet. Food orgies went on *ad nauseam*, literally—after gorging themselves, guests would retreat to a special room called the *vomitorium*, throw it all up, and return to the party to eat still more.

These days, however, Roman food rituals are considerably tamer. Breakfast, if you're lucky enough to get it, is usually just a gulp of cappuccino and a pastry. Lunch is traditionally the day's main meal, though some Romans now eat lunch on the go during the week, *all'americana*. Keep in mind that restaurants tend to close from 3pm to 7:30pm.

THE ITALIAN MEAL

A full meal begins with **antipasti,** or appetizers. It is acceptable to order *antipasti* alone for lunch, but it is considered gauche at dinner. Next, the **primo piatto** (first course, a.k.a. *primi*) arrives: usually some sort of pasta, risotto, or soup. Especially on Thursdays, many restaurants serve up homemade *gnocchi*, dense dumplings of potato or semolina flour, frequently in a gorgonzola or four-cheese sauce. While *lasagna al forno* (baked lasagna) may be tempting, know that it's often prepared well in advance and will probably not be particularly fresh.

The **secondo piatto** (second course, a.k.a. *secondi*) usually consists of meat or fish. Innards and other odd parts of the cow or pig are often a particularly important part of Roman cuisine. Seafood is common: *calamari* is very good here, especially when grilled.

USE YOUR NOODLE

Selecting the correct pasta for the dish and cooking it right (*al dente*—literally "to the teeth" and slightly chewy) is as close to Italian hearts as the Madonna herself. *Lasagne* come in at least two forms: flat or *ricce* (one edge crimped). The familiar *spaghetti* has larger, hollow cousins, such as *bucatini* and *maccheroni*, as well as smaller, more delicate relatives like *capellini*. Flat pastas include the familiar *linguine* and *fettuccine*, with *taglierini* and *tagliatelle* filling in the size gaps. Short, roughly two-inch pasta tubes include *ziti*, *penne* (cut diagonally and occasionally *rigate*, or ribbed), *sedani* (curved), *rigatoni* (bigger), and *canneloni* (biggest and usually stuffed). More excitingly shaped pastas include *fusilli* (corkscrews), *farfalle* (butterflies or bow-ties), and *ruote* (wheels). Don't be alarmed if you see pastry displays with the label *pasta;* the Italian word refers to anything made of dough and vaguely edible.

There are numerous **contorni** or side dishes, mostly vegetable specialties, which are generally served with the main course. Even the most single-minded carnivores will enjoy dishes like *fagiolini* (early-picked, tender string beans) or *pomodori* (fresh tomatoes in olive oil with salt and fresh basil). Roman mixed salads *(insalata mista)* are usually full of veggies, and, interestingly enough, anise.

Dolce, desserts, are typically accompanied by the essential espresso. Freshly made *tiramisù* (sponge cake soaked in espresso and rum, layered with sweet mascarpone cheese, and dusted with cocoa powder) can be wonderful. *Profiteroles,* delicate rolled pastries with chocolate and cream filling, are also exquisite. *Panna cotta* is a delicious cream custard, covered in chocolate sauce or *frutti di bosco* (blackberries and raspberries). And if *gelato* isn't rich enough for you, try *tartufo,* truffly ice cream usually served in the *bianco* (vanilla) and *nero* (chocolate) versions, sometimes served in *espresso.*

For an after-dinner drink **(digestivo),** try *grappa,* potent, doubly distilled clear liqueur made from old grape pressings or *sambuca con le mosche* (anise liquor "with flies"—that is, flaming with coffee beans floating on top).

The billing at Roman restaurants can be a bit confusing. Bottled water is usually automatically served and charged to your bill: ask for *frizzante* (fizzy) or *naturale* (still), but don't even think of asking for tap water—it's just not done. Many restaurants add a cover or bread charge of L1500 per person. Service charges *(servizio)*, if not included in food prices, may be added to the bill, to the tune of 10-15%.

RESTAURANT TYPES

Ristorantes are the most elegant eateries, with dolled-up waiters, linen tablecloths, and expensive (though not necessarily better) cuisine. A **trattoria** has a more casual atmosphere and lower prices. If you find an original **osteria** or **hostaria,** you'll see old locals sitting around a table, chewing the fat, playing cards, and downing bottles of wine. Another cheap option is the **tavola calda** or **rosticceria,** where you buy platefuls of pastas, cooked vegetables, and well-seasoned meats to eat on the spot or wrap up for a picnic elsewhere.

There are two kinds of **pizzerias.** At a *pizzeria forno a legno*, you sit down to your own plate-sized pizza. A well-prepared Roman-style crust is light, crispy, and blackened a little around the edges, unlike the famous Neapolitan pizzas, which are thicker and made from tastier dough. In a *pizzeria rustica* or *a taglio*, order a slice or particular weight of any of the pizzas displayed at the counter.

MENU READER

ANTIPASTI	
antipasto rusto	assortment of cold appetizers
bruschetta	crisp baked slices of bread with tomatoes or other toppings
prosciutto e melone	cured ham and honeydew melon
PRIMI	
pasta aglio e olio	garlic and olive oil
pasta all'amatriciana	in a tangy tomato sauce with onions and bacon
pasta all'arabbiata	in a spicy tomato sauce
pasta alla bolognese	in a meat sauce
pasta alla boscaiola	in a sauce of cream, peas, and bacon
pasta cacio e pepe	with pepper and pecorino cheese
pasta ai funghi porcini	with a sauce of large wood mushrooms
pasta al pomodoro	in tomato sauce
pasta alla carbonara	in a creamy sauce with egg, cured bacon, and cheese
pasta alle cozze	in a tomato sauce with mussels
pasta alla pizzaiola	tomato based sauce with olive oil and red peppers
pasta alla pescatore	with several kinds of clams and mussels, and sometimes with squid
pasta alla puttanesca	in a tomato sauce with olives and capers
pasta al tartufo	with a truffle sauce
pasta alle vongole	in a clam sauce; *bianco* for white, *rosso* for red
gnocchi	dumpling-like pasta made from potatoes
polenta	deep fried cornmeal
risotto	rice dish (comes with nearly as many sauces as pasta)
PIZZA	
ai carciofi	with artichokes
ai fiori di zucca	with zucchini blossoms
ai funghi	with mushrooms
alla capriciosa	with ham, egg, artichoke, and olives
con alici	with anchovies
con bresaola	with cured beef
con melanzana	with eggplant
con prosciutto	with ham
con prosciutto crudo	with cured ham (also called simply *crudo*)
con rucola (rughetta)	with arugala (rocket for the Brits)
margherita	plain ol' tomato, mozzarella, and basil
napoletana	with anchovies, tomato, and cheese
peperoncini	chillies
polpette	meatballs
quattro formaggi	with four cheeses
quattro stagioni	four seasons; a different topping for each quarter of the pizza, usually mushrooms, *crudo*, artichoke, and tomato
SECONDI	
animelle alla griglia	grilled sweetbreads
calamari alla grigliata	grilled squid
carciofi alla giudia	fried artichokes
coda alla vaccinara	stewed oxtail with herbs and tomatoes
filetto di baccalà	fried cod
fiori di zucca	zucchini flowers; filled with cheese, battered, and lightly fried
involtini al sugo	veal cutlets filled with ham, celery, and cheese, topped with tomato sauce
melanzane parmigiana	eggplant parmesan
osso buco	braised veal shank
pasta e ceci	pasta with chick peas
saltimbocca	slices of veal and ham cooked together and topped with cheese
scamorza grigliata	a type of grilled cheese
suppli	fried rice ball filled with tomato, meat, and cheese
trippa	tripe; chopped, sautéed cow intestines, usually in a tomato sauce

CONTORNI	
broccoletti	broccoli florets
cicoria	chicory
fagioli	beans (usually white)
fagiolini	green beans
funghi	mushrooms
insalata caprese	tomatoes with mozzarella cheese and basil, drizzled with olive oil
insalata mista	mixed green salad
melanzana	eggplant
piselli	peas
spinaci	spinach

PREPARATION	
cruda/o	raw
al sangue	rare
non troppo cotta/o	medium-rare
ben cotta	well-done
al dente	firm to the bite
fresca/o	fresh
frittura	fried
griglia	grilled
marinata/o	marinated
stracotta	overcooked
poco cotta	undercooked
raffermo	stale
ripieno	stuffed
condita/o	seasoned
scottata	scorched
secca	dry
aromatica/o, piccante	spicy
stracetti	strips (of beef, usually)
surgelato	frozen
al vino	in wine sauce
resentin	coffee in a grappa-rinsed mug

RESTAURANTS BY LOCATION

ANCIENT CITY

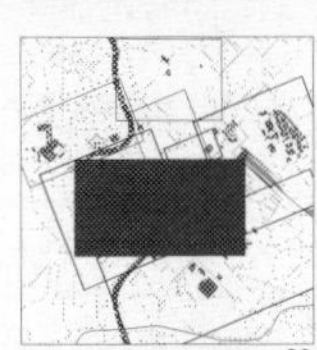
see map p. 69

The area around the Forum and the Colosseum is home to some of Italy's finest tourist-traps, replete with L25,000 *menù turistici*. The snack carts lining the streets will serve you no better; expect to pay L4000 for water and L7000 for a questionably appetizing sandwich. If you forgot to pack a lunch and the stroll down V.d. Fori Imperiali seems too long in the blazing heat, there are a few places that offer tasty meals at fair prices.

Taverna dei Quaranta, V. Claudia, 24 (☎06 7000550), off P. del Colosseo. Shaded by the trees of the Celian Park, outdoor dining at this corner *taverna* is a must. Not at all touristy. The menu changes weekly, and in summer often features delights such as the sinfully good *oliva ascolane* (olives stuffed with meat and fried; L7500/€3.87) and *ravioli all'Amalfitana* (L11,000/€5.68). 0.5L of house wine L5000/€2.58. Cover L2500/€1.29. Reservations suggested, especially for a table outside. Open daily noon-3:30pm and 7:45pm-midnight. AmEx/D/MC/V.

I Buoni Amici, V. Aleardo Aleardi, 4 (☎06 70491993). From the Colosseum, take V. Labicana to V. Merulana. Turn right, then left on V. A. Aleardi. A long walk, but the cheap and excellent food is worth it. Choices include the *linguine all'astice* (linguini with lobster sauce; L12,000/€6.20), *risotto con i funghi* (L10,000/€5.16), and *penne alla vodka* (L10,000/€5.16). Cover L2500/€1.29. Open M-Sa noon-3pm and 7-11:30pm. AmEx/D/MC/V.

Hostaria da Nerone, V.d. Terme di Tito, 96 (☎06 4745207). M: B-Colosseo. Take the stairs to the right (with your back to the Colosseum) and walk up to V.d. Terme di Tito. Outdoor dining near the Colosseum with views of the Baths of Titus through the trees. Traditional specialties like tegamino di cervello burro e funghi (brains with butter and mushrooms; L15,000/€7.75). Pasta L10-12,000/€5.16-6.20. Cover L2500/€1.29. 10% service. Open M-Sa noon-3pm and 7-11pm. MC/V.

CENTRO STORICO

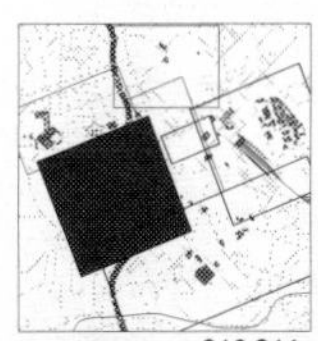
see map p.310-311

PIAZZA NAVONA

There are plenty of delicious, inexpensive *trattorie* and *pizzerias* near P. Navona, but it often takes a short stroll to reach them. A walk down V.d. Governo Vecchio reveals some of the best restaurants in the city, often charging less than their more convenient neighbors in the *piazza*. If you're really lucky, you'll happen upon one of the smaller *enoteche* and *trattorie*, some of which advertise themselves with no more than a beaded curtain guarding an open doorway—Romans who know will tell you that these places offer a constantly changing menu at unbeatable prices. No matter where you eat, you can expect to be subjected to numerous performances by street performers.

Pizzeria Baffetto, V.d. Governo Vecchio, 114 (☎06 6861617). At V. Sora. Once a meeting place for 60s radicals, Baffetto now overflows with hungry Romans. It's gotten famous–be prepared to wait a long while for a table outdoors (as well as for your delicious *pizza* once you've sat down). Always crowded. *Pizze* L8-14,000/€4.13-7.23. Open M-F noon-3pm and 7:30pm-1am, Sa-Su noon-3pm and 7:30pm-2am. Cash only.

Pizzeria Corallo, V.d. Corallo, 10-11 (☎06 68307703). Off V.d. Governo Vecchio near P. del Fico. This pizzeria is a great place to grab a cheap, late dinner before losing your life's savings at the chichi bars nearby. Pizzas L7-14,000/€3.62-7.23. Excellent *primi* options like *Tagliolini ai fiori di zucca* (with zucchini blossoms; L12,000/€6.20). Reservations accepted. Open daily noon-3pm and 7pm-1am. MC/V.

Trattoria dal Cav. Gino, V. Rosini, 4 ☎06 6873434). Off V.d. Campo Marzio across from P. del Parlamente. The very affable Gino greets you at the door at this trattoria, and points a lit-up sign above the door, which announces that *tonnarelli alla ciociala* (L10,000/€5.16) is the house specialty. Want a drink? Another signs proclaims Gino's philosophy: *In Vino Veritas*. Agreed.

Primi L8-10,000/€4.13-5.16; *secondi* L15-17,000/€7.75-8.78. Reservations accepted. Open M-Sa 1-3:45pm and 8-10:30pm. Cash only.

Trattoria Gino e Pietro, V.d. Governo Vecchio, 106 (☎06 6861576). At V. Savelli. Basic Roman food without any frills, like *gnocchi verdi al gorgonzola* (L12,000/€6.20) and *saltimbocca alla romana* (veal with *prosciutto* and sage; L16,000/€8.26). Reservations accepted. Open F-W 12:30-3pm and 6:30-11pm. Closed late July to mid-Aug.

L'Oasi della Pizza, Via della Corda, 3-5. (☎06 6872876; www.info.pizzeriaoasi.tiscalinet.it). While an oasis within shouting distance of Campo dei Fiori is certainly an oxymoron, to say that L'Oasi serves pizza worthy of paradise is not. The *capricciosa* (L14,000/€7.23) is great; you'll get your vegetables with the leafy *margherita* (L10,000/€5.16). A logical first stop before a beer in the Campo. Open Th-Tu, noon-3pm, 7-11:30pm. Closed W.

CAMPO DEI FIORI

If you're not in a rush, take the time to navigate the labyrinth of crooked streets and alleyways that surround Campo dei Fiori. While you might get yourself horribly lost, you will certainly find several exceptional *ristoranti* that can provide sustenance until the search party arrives. If your friends can't find you after dinner, screw 'em: just go pubbing in the Campo and make some new ones (see p. 186).

Trattoria da Sergio, V.d. Grotte, 27 (☎06 6546669). Take V.d. Giubbonari and take your 1st right. Just far enough away from the Campo to keep away the tourists, Sergio offers honest-to-God Roman ambience (the waiters don't bother with menus) and hearty portions of great food. Try the *spaghetti all'Amatriciana* (with bacon and spicy tomato sauce; L10,000/€5.16)—a front runner for the city's best plate of pasta—and the *Straccetti* (shredded beef with tomatoes; L13,000/€6.71). Reservations suggested. Open M-Sa 12:30-3pm and 7pm-12:30am. MC/V.

Hostaria Grappolo d'Oro, P. della Cancelleria, 80-81 (☎06 6897080), between C. V. Emanuele II and the Campo. This increasingly upscale *hostaria* is running out of space in their front window to plaster all the awards they've won over the years. The small menu, which changes daily, offers homestyle dishes like *fregnacce al Casaro* (home-made pasta with ricotta and tomato; L19,000/€9.81) and innovative creations such as *controfiletto di manzo* (steak with herbs and goat-cheese; L24,000/€12.40). Top it all off with a creative dessert like a pistaccio semi-fredo. Cover L2000/€1.03. Open M-Sa noon-2:30pm and 7:30-11pm. Closed Monday lunch. AmEx/MC/V.

Trattoria Da Luigi, P.S. Cesarini, 24 (☎06 6865946), near Chiesa Nuova, four blocks down C. V. Emanuele II from Campo dei Fiore. Enjoy inventive cuisine such as *tagliolini* with shrimp, asparagus, and tomato (L13,000/€6.71), as well as simple dishes like *vitello con funghi* (veal with mushrooms; L15,000/€7.75). Great *antipasti* buffet. Bread L2000/€1.03. Open Tu-Su 7pm-midnight.

La Pollarola, P. Pollarola, 24-25 (☎06 68801654), Off V.d. Biscione on the way into Campo dei Fiori. As the Romans say, *"si mangia bene e si spende giusto"* ("one eats well and pays a fair price"). Enjoy typical Roman dishes like *spaghetti alla carbonara* (with egg and *pancetta*; L10,000/€5.16). Open M-Sa noon-3:30pm and 7:30pm-midnight. No service charge. AmEx/MC/V.

L'Insalata Ricca, Largo di Chiavari, 85-6 (☎06 68803656), off C. Vittorio Emanuele II near P.S. Andrea della Valle. You like salads, damn it, so come here. What kind of salad would you like? They have *all of them* (L10-16,000/€5.16-8.26). If you don't like this location, there are six others around town: P. Pasquino, 72; V.d. Gazometro, 62; P. Albania, 3; V. Polesine, 16; P. Risorgimento, 5; and V. F. Grinaldi, 52. Reservations suggested for dinner. Open daily 12:30-3:30pm and 6:45-11:30pm. AmEx/D/V.

Giardino del Melograno, V.d. Chiodaroli, 16-18 (☎06 68803423). From Campo dei Fiori, take V. Giubbonari, then a left on V. Chiavari. V.d. Chiodaroli is your first right. A highly renowned Chinese restaurant. The vast menu includes a fine dumpling appetizer (L5000/€2.58) and a tempting *gamberi con zenzero* (shrimp with ginger; L12,000/€6.20). Tourist *menù* (antipasti, primi, secondi and drink) is one of the best values in town (lunch L11,000/€5.68; dinner L15,000/€7.75.) Reservations suggested weekends. Open Th-Tu noon-3pm and 7-11:30pm. AmEx/MC/V.

Trattoria Arnaldo ai Satiri, V.d. Grotta Pinta, 8 (☎06 6861915). Take Largo dei Chiavari off C. Vittorio Emanuele II and turn right on V.d. Grotta Pinta. Unusual dishes include spicy

Fusili con melanzane (pasta with eggplant; L11,000/€5.68) and the house specialty, *Rigatoni alla crema di cavoli* (pasta with cream of cabbage sauce; L11,000/€5.68). Glowing with red light bulbs and candles, the interior seems the child of a bordello and a darkroom. Outdoor dining in summer. Open W-M 12:30-3pm and 7:30pm-1am. AmEx/MC/V.

JEWISH GHETTO

On the other side of V. Arenula from Campo dei Fiori, the former Jewish Ghetto has patiently endured centuries of modernization, anti-Semitism, and tourism to remain a proud community. Quiet, cozy *trattorie* line the streets of this neighborhood, each serving traditional Roman-Jewish dishes, like *carciofi alla giudia* (fried artichokes) and *fiori di zucca* (zucchini blossoms filled with cheese and anchovies, battered, and lightly fried).

Ristorante da Giggetto, V.d. Portico d'Ottavio, 21-22 (☎06 6861105). Rightfully famous but increasingly pricey, Giggetto serves up some of the finest Roman cooking known to man in outdoor tables overlooking the ruins of the Teatro Marcello. Their *carciofi alla Giudia* (L8000/€4.13) are legendary, but be daring and go for the fried brains with mushrooms and zucchini (L22,000/€11.36). Cover L3000/€1.55. Reservations needed for dinner. Open Tu-Su 12:30-3pm and 7:30-11pm. AmEx/MC/V.

Al 16, V.d. Portico d'Ottavio, 16 (☎06 6874722), around the corner from the Teatro di Marcello. A neighborhood favorite run by very friendly neighborhood guys, Al 16 offers traditional dishes alongside delicious house specialties like *Pennette al 16* (with eggplant, sausage, and tomato; L14,000/€7.23), all at reasonable prices. Be fearless and try the *Coda alla Vaccinara* (oxtail stew; L14,000/€7.23). Cover L2500/€1.29. Reservations recommended for dinner. Open W-M 12:30-3pm and 7:30-11pm. AmEx/MC/V.

Il Portico, V.d. Portico D'Ottavia (☎06 6874722). Il Portico is a low-key, family restaurant in the middle of the Jewish Ghetto. Tourists go for the tasty pizzas (proscuitto and funghi; L10,000/€5.16), while locals gravitate toward the wide variety of salads (L12-13,000/€6.20-6.71). Open daily 12:30-3pm, 7:30-midnight. MC/V.

PIAZZA DI SPAGNA

see map p. 315

Though the Spanish Steps area may seem very different from the less affluent environs of Termini, there is one big similarity—lots and lots of bad, bad food. The irony of it all is that while a crappy restaurant at Termini might set you back L15,000, the same awful food here will be twice as much. The best food in the area tends to be toward the Ara Pacis, across the V.d. Corso, and away from the crush and press of tourists.

Trattoria da Settimio all'Arancio, V.d. Arancio, 50-52 (☎06 6876119). Take V.d. Condotti from P. di Spagna; take the 1st right after V.d. Corso, then the 1st left. Arrive early to avoid the throngs of natives who come for the great service and tasty seafood on this quiet side street. Excellent grilled *calamari* (L18,000/€9.30). *Primi* L12-15,000/€6.20-7.75; *secondi* L16-26,000/€8.26-13.43. Cover L2000/€1.03. Reservations suggested. Open M-Sa 12:30-3pm and 7:30-11:30pm. AmEx/D/MC/V.

Pizza Re, V.d. Ripetta, 14 (☎06 3211468). A block from P. del Popolo on the left. Even though it's a chain, Pizza Re serves some of the best Neapolitan pizza (L12-18,000/€6.20-9.30) in town. Especially tasty is the (go figure) *Pizza Re* (L17,500/€9.04), with *mozzarella di bufala* and fresh cherry tomatoes. Service is fast and courteous, and the A/C feels sooooo good. Save around L3000 if you order in person and take it out. Open M-Sa 12:45-3:30pm and 7:30pm-12:30am, Su 7:30pm-12:30am. Closed 2 weeks in mid-Aug. AmEx/D/MC/V.

Vini e Buffet, P. Torretta, 60. (☎06 6871445). From V.d. Corso, turn into P.S. Lorenzo in Lucina. Take a left on V. Campo Marzio, a quick right onto V. Toretta. Vini e Buffet is a favorite spot for chic Romans who want to escape the crowds and mediocre food of P. di Spagna. Their popular salads are creative and fresh–the *insalata con salmone,* with salmon and shrimp (L14,000/€7.23), is delightful. Also available are pates, *crostini,* and *scarmorze,* (mozzarella baked with a variety of ingredients), for L12-14000/€6.20-7.23. Don't leave without getting one of their signature yogurt and fruit bowls for dessert; the yogurt, almond, and cassis combination is out of this world. Reservations are recommended but not necessary. M-Sa 12:30-3pm, 7:30-11pm. Cash only.

Il Brillo Parlante, V. Fontanella, 12 (☎06 3243334 or 06 3235017; www.ilbrillopa lante.com), near P. del Popolo. The wood-burning pizza oven, fresh ingredients, and excelle wine attract many lunching Italians. Sophisticated food and shady outdoor tables availabl *Pizze* L10-15,000/€5.16-7.75. Restaurant open Tu-Su noon-3pm and 7:30pm-1am; *en teca* (wine bar) open Tu-Su 11am-2am. MC/V.

Al Piccolo Arancio, V. Scanderbeg, 112 (☎06 6786139). Facing the Trevi Fountain, go rig on V.d. Lavatore; V. Scanderbeg is on the right. This friendly trattoria is a stone's throw fro the Trevi Fountain, but its sidestreet location insulates diners from street vendors. *Ravic all'arancia* (ravioli of ricotta and oranges; L10,000/€5.16) is a specialty, and the *abbacch al forno* (roasted lamb; L18,000/€9.30) is popular. Bread L2000/€1.03. Open Tu-Su noo 3pm and 7-midnight. Closed two weeks in mid-Aug. AmEx/D/MC/V.

Sogo Asahi, V.d. Propaganda, 22 (☎06 6786093). Locals and tourists alike come to e excellent sushi, noodles, and more in this stylish Japanese restaurant. The *miso* sou (L7000/€3.62) is particularly good, as are the *iniri* (sweet tofu), *unaga* (eel), and *sak* (salmon) sushi. *Nigiri* sushi L49,000/€25.31; 13-piece plate L30,000/€15.50; 6-piec *maki* plates L8-15,000/€4.13-7.75. Entrees L15-35,000/€7.75-18.08. Open M-Sa noo 2:30pm and 7-10:30pm. Reservations accepted. AmEx/MC/V.

Margutta Vegetariano RistorArte, V. Margutta 118 (☎06 32650577), off V.d. Babuin near P. del Popolo. This upscale location on artsy V. Margutta is all vegetarian, all the tim The food is green, and the service is excellent. A mushroom and soy burger is L16,00 €8.26; lunch buffet L20,000/€10.33; all-you-can-eat brunch Su L45,000/€23.24. Reserva tions suggested at night. Open Daily 12:30-3:30pm and 7:40-11:40pm. AmEx/MC/V.

Centro Macrobiotico Italiano-Naturist Club, V.d. Vite, 14, 4th fl. (☎06 6792509), just o V.d. Corso. The Naturist Club offers up extremely fresh, well-seasoned macrobiotic fare in a attic restaurant with 70s decor. Probably the only restaurant in Rome where they offer yo ground sesame seeds with your salad. Buffet only in the afternoon (a small bowl of the sala of your choice is L7600/€3.93), but evening brings a full restaurant, where you can eat tas vegetarian entrees and fresh fish to the sound of the Sugar Plum Fairy Waltz. Also includes small health food store. *Primi* L12-15,000/€6.20-7.75; *secondi* L13-20,000/€6.71-10.3 No Smoking. Open M-F 12:30-4pm and 7:30pm-1am. MC/V.

BORGO & PRATI (NEAR VATICAN CITY)

see map p. 316

The streets near the Vatican are paved with bars and *pizzeri* that serve mediocre sandwiches at hiked-up prices. For far be ter and much cheaper food, head to the residential district few blocks north and east of the Vatican Museums, home t specialty shops with fresh bread and pastries and small famil run *osterie*. For picnic supplies, try the immense indoor mark on V. Cola di Rienzo.

Franchi, V. Cola di Rienzo, 200-204 (☎06 6874651; fra chi@franchi.it; www.franchi.it). Benedeto Franchi ("Frankie") has been serving the happy ci zens of Prati superb *tavola calda,* prepared sandwiches, and other luxurious picnic supplie for nearly 50 years, and not an unsatisfied customer yet. Delicacies include *suppli* (fried bal of veggies, mozzarella, and rice or potato, L1800 each), marinated munchies (anchovie peppers, olives, and salmon, all sold by the kilo), and pastas like vegetarian lasagna an *cannellini* stuffed with ricotta and beef (L8800 per generous portion). More expensive tha buying bread and cheese for a midday snack, but certainly cheaper and better than most Va ican area restaurants and snack bars. Open M-Sa 8:15am-9pm. AmEx/MC/V.

Pizza Re, V. Oslavia, 39 (☎06 3721173). Called by many the best pizza in Rome, th chain serves Neopolitan (thick crust) pizzas with every topping imaginable in cheerful yello surroundings. Try it with *alicis* (marinated uncooked anchovies; L14,000). Wonderful de serts, from mousse to tiramisu. Lunch specials (pizza and drink) L13,000. Dinner L7-18,00 Pizzas L3-5500 less if you take them out. Long lines at dinnertime, so get there early. Ope M-Sa noon-3:30pm, daily 7:30pm-12:30am. AmEx/MC/V.

Guido, V. Borgo Pio, 13 (☎06 6875491). Near Basilica San Pietro. Don't let the checkere tablecloths and bow-tie adorned waiters at other establishments nearby distract you from th authentically Roman spot at the foot of Borgo Pio. There's no sign, but you can recognize it by th men sitting outside, playing cards in the sun. Guido himself holds court behind a counter fille with all the makings of a beautiful *tavola calda.* Prices vary, but a *piatti caldi* (plate of marinated vegetables) runs around L6000, while main dishes are L7000. Open daily 9am-9pm. Cash only.

Risky Point Restaurant, P. dell'Unita, 26-27(☎06 32231113). East of P. Risorgimento at V.d. Gracchi and V.C. Mario. This newly refurbished restaurant/bar offers basic pizzas and pastas at reasonable prices (pizzas L8-15,000; delicious *bruschetta con tapenade* L2500.)

Vino!

TRASTEVERE

You can't say you've been to Rome without having savored a pizza and swilled some tasty Peroni in one of the rowdy outdoor *pizzerias* in Trastevere. Trastevere is home to raucous pubs, hopping pizza joints, and a loud bohemian population. By day, the cobblestone streets rumble with the sounds of children and Vespas, but when night falls, hippy expats add their voices to that of the madding throng in P. di Santa Maria di Trastevere.

Formaggio!

Pizzeria San Calisto, P.S. Calisto, 9a (☎06 5818256). Right off P.S. Maria in Trastevere. Quite simply the best damn pizza in Rome. Gorgeous thin crust pizzas so large they hang off the plates. The *bruschetta* (L3-4000) alone is worth a postcard home. Management shoos the rose-sellers away for a peaceful meal. Open Tu-Su 7pm-midnight. MC/V.

Ouseri, V.d. Salumi, 2 (☎06 5818256). Either go left off V.d. Trastevere or take V. Vascellari from Lungotevere Ripa and then go right onto V.d. Salumi. Ouzeri may advertise itself as a "Taberna Greca," but the waiters will tell you its actually a Greek Cultural Association, complete with Greek dancing lessons. Live music and dancing (except when it gets too hot in July and Aug.). Food is out of this world–share the *piatto misto* with a friend (L15-30,000). To get inside, ring the doorbell. L3000 membership required. Reservations suggested. Cash only.

Augusto, P. de' Rienzi, 15 (☎06 5803798). North of P.S. Maria in Trastevere. Enjoy the daily pasta specials at lunch (around L8500), and the *pollo arrosto con patate* (L10,500). The homemade desserts are out of this world. Dinner is chaotic and crowded; lunch tends to feature laid-back discussions between waiters and clientele. Either way, you have to be pushy to get service. No reservation. Open M-F 12:30-3pm and 8-11pm, Sa 12:30-3pm. Closed Aug.

Pizzeria Ivo, V.d. S. Francesco a Ripa, 158 (☎06 5817082). Take a right on V.d. Fratte di Trastevere off V. Trastevere and another right on V.S. Francesco a Ripa. A long-standing favorite in Trastevere, Ivo rests on its laurels a bit, but still serves up a good pizza. Long waits, high prices (pizzas L8-16,000). Open W-M 5pm-2am. Closed Aug. MC/V.

Gelato!

Il Tulipano Nero, V. Roma Libera, 15 (☎06 5818309). Take V.d. Trastevere; turn right on V. E. Morosini. Some of the more innovative pizzas (L8-15,000) in Rome. Almost removed from the nighttime chaos of P.S. Maria in Trastevere, this pizzeria is smack in the middle of the nighttime chaos of P. Cosimato. Iron palates can attempt the *pennette all'elettroshock* (L12,000). Portion size ranges from large to gigantic. Open Tu-Su 6pm-2am.

Osteria der Belli, P. Sant'Apollonia, 11 (☎06 5803782). Off V.d. Lungaretta near P.S. Maria in Trastevere. A bustling *trattoria* specializing in Sardinian cooking, especially seafood. Nice outdoor seating area, if rather full of tourists. *Ravioli sardi* (in tomato cream sauce) L12,000. Excellent grilled *calimari* L20,000. Cover L2000. Reservations suggested. Open Tu-Su 11:30am-2:30pm and 7:30-10:30pm. AmEx/MC/V.

Ristorante al Fontanone, P. Trilussa, 46 (☎06 5817312). North of P.S. Maria in Trastevere. Small restaurant serving traditional Roman cuisine, including *rigatoni cacio de pepe,* with peccorino cheese and pepper (L11,000). Close to the river, it can be a bit touristy, but the porcini mushrooms are fabulous. Open W-Su noon-2pm and 7-11pm. Closed mid-Aug.-early Sept. MC/V.

TERMINI & SAN LORENZO

NORTH OF TERMINI

see map p. 312-313

You're near the train station, hungry, and in a hurry. This is no reason to subject yourself to the gastronomic nightmare of a shady tourist establishment offering a L10,000 "quick lunch." The following provide good service and food for a largely local clientele.

Africa, V. Gaeta, 26-28 (☎06 4941077), near P. Independenza. Decked out in yellow and black, Africa continues its 20-year tradition of serving excellent Eritrean/Ethiopian food. The meat-filled *sambusas* (L5000/€2.58) are a flavorful starter; both the *zighini beghi* (roasted lamb in a spicy sauce; L12,000/€6.20) and the *misto vegetariano* (mixed veggie dishes; L11,000) make fantastic entrees, while the thick yogurt (L3000/€1.55) goes well with spicy dishes. Act out those childhood fantasies of eating with your hands with their spongy Ethiopian flatbread, known as *injera.* Cover L1500/ €0.77. Open M-Sa 8pm-midnight. MC/V.

Trattoria da Bruno, V. Varese, 29 (☎06 490403), from V. Marsala, next to the train station, walk three blocks down V. Milazzo and turn right onto V. Varese. A neighborhood favorite with daily specials. Start with the *tortellini con panna e funghi* (with cream and mushrooms; L10,000/€5.16) or the tasty homemade *gnocchi* (L10,000/€5.16) and continue with the delicious *ossobuco* (L13,000/€6.71). Bruno, the owner, makes créches, and he's very good at what he does: note the picture of him shaking hands with the Pope, upon presentation of one of his little masterworks. Open daily noon-3:30pm and 7-10:15pm. Closed Aug. AmEx/V.

SOUTH OF TERMINI (ESQUILINO)

Eateries closest to Termini aren't exactly known for their high quality and low prices, but a five- to 10-minute walk from the station will reward you with some (almost) hidden gems.

Ristorante Due Colonne, V.d. Serpenti, 91 (☎06 4880852). A right turn off V. Nazionale before the Palazzo delle Esposizioni. By day, Romans on lunch break fill the tables. By night, tourists struggle with the surprisingly broad menu. Excellent pizzas (L8-14,000/€4.13-7.23). *Pasta e fagioli* L9000/€4.65; *linguine alla pescatora* L13,000/€6.71. Tourist *menù* L18-26,000/€9.30-13.43. Open M-Sa 9am-3:30pm and 6:30pm-12:30am. AmEx/D/MC/V.

SAN LORENZO

Though *Let's Go* doesn't recommend communist watching, this would be the place to do it if we did (wink wink). San Lorenzo is Rome's university district, and thank god; a discriminating student palate, combined with student financial resources, have ensured that just about every restaurant here is good and cheap. Definitely a place that travelers should dine if they're spending more than a few days in Rome, although women may find the areas nearest the train station a little uncomfortable if they're alone at night. From Termini, walk south on V. Pretoriano to P. Tiburtino, or take bus #492 to P. Verano (at the other end of V. Tiburtina from P. Tiburtino).

Il Pulcino Ballerino, V.d. Equi, 66-68 (☎06 4941255). Off V. Tiburtina. An artsy atmosphere with cuisine to match. The cook stirs up imaginative dishes like *conchiglione al "Moby Dick"* (shells with tuna, cream, and greens) and *risotto* (various types; L10-12,000/€5.16-6.20). Excellent vegetarian dishes like *scamorrza* and potato casserole (L12,000/€6.20). You can also skip the chef altogether and prepare your own meal on a warm stone at the table. Cover L1000/€0.52. Open M-Sa 1-3:30pm and 8pm-midnight. Closed second and third weeks of Aug. AmEx/MC/V.

Arancia Blu, V.d. Latini, 65 (☎06 4454105), off V. Tiburtina. This elegant and popular little vegetarian restaurant serves up an inventive and excellent take on food. Enjoy elaborate dishes like *tonnarelli con pecorino romano e tartufo* (pasta with sheep cheese and truffles; L12,000/€6.20) or fried ravioli stuffed with eggplant and smoked *caciocavallo* with pesto sauce (L16,000/€8.26). Extensive wine list. Open daily 8:30pm-midnight.

Il Capellaio Matto, V.d. Marsi, 25. From V. Tiburtina, take the 4th right off V.d. Equi. Vegetarians, rejoice! This offbeat place (named for the Mad Hatter) offers pasta and rice dishes like *risotto al pepe verde* (with green peppercorn; L9000/€4.65), imaginative salads like *insalata di rughetta, pere, e parmigiano* (arugula, pears, and parmesan; L7000/€3.62), and a variety of crepes (L7-9000/€3.62-4.65). Plenty of meat dishes, too. Cover L1500/€0.77. Open W-M 8pm-midnight.

La Pantera Rosa, P. Verano, 84-85 (☎06 4456391). At the eastern end of V. Tiburtina. The house specialty is the delicious pink salmon and caviar pizza (L11,000). There's also a variety of excellent *primi* like *bucatini all'Amatriciana* (thick spaghetti with spicy tomato sauce; L9000/€4.65). Open Th-Tu noon-3pm and 6:30pm-12:30am. MC/V.

TESTACCIO

see map p. 318

In the shadow of affluent Aventine lies working-class Testaccio. Once home to a giant slaughterhouse *(il Mattatoio)*, the neighborhood is the seat of many excellent restaurants serving traditional Roman fare and is the center of Roman nightlife. True to their roots, Testaccio eateries offer food made of just about every animal part imaginable. The gastronomically adventurous can sample local delicacies such as *pagliate* (calf intestines with milk), *animelle alla griglia* (grilled sweetbreads), and *fegato* (liver).

Caffe Greco

Filetti di Baccala

Tazza d'Oro

Trattoria da Bucatino, V. Luca della Robbia, 84-86 (☎06 5746886). Take V. Luigi Vanvitel off V. Marmorata, then the first left. A friendly neighborhood *trattoria* bringing you the anima entrails you know and love, and plenty of gut-less dishes as well. Heaping, delicious mound of *tripe all romana* (L12,000/€6.20) stay true to the traditions of Testaccio. More conver tional (but equally good dishes) include *cosse alla marinara* (L10,000/€5.16), more mus sels than anyone in their right mind could hope to eat. Cover L2000/€1.03. Open Tu-S 12:30-3:30pm and 6:30-11:30pm. Closed Aug. D/MC/V.

DESSERT

Though translated as "ice cream," *gelato* is in a league of its own. Unfortunately, shop catering to stupid tourists may sell you commercially made, disgusting imitations c true *gelato:* to avoid this sad fate, try our recommended *gelaterie*, or at least look fo shops advertising *gelato artigianale* or *propria produzione*, which means the make it themselves. If the *gelato* flavors are grayish and barely distinguishable, instea of an artificially colored rainbow, it's a good sign that you're getting the good stuf Saying *"con panna"* when you order will add a mound of fresh whipped cream to you serving for free. Most *gelaterie* require you to pay before you eat, so first head for th *cassa* (cash register) and then present your receipt to the scooper when you order.

Some flavorful vocabulary: *mela* (apple), *ananas* (pineapple), *mirtillo* (blue berry), *stracciatella* (chocolate chip), *cannella* (cinnamon), *cocco* (coconut), *noc ciola* (hazelnut), *miele* (honey), *pompelmo* (grapefruit), *menta/*after eight (min often with chocolate chips), *latte/panna/crema* (cream), *cocomero* (watermelon *nutella* (streaks of hazelnut chocolate spread in vanilla), *meringa* (meringue, ofte with hazelnuts or chocolate chips added), *limone* (lemon), *amareno* (sour cherry *liquirizia* (black licorice), *frutti di bosco* (mixed berries), *arancia* (orange *pesca* (peach), *lampone* (raspberry), *fragola* (strawberry), *baci* (chocolate an hazelnut), *amaretto* (sweet and nutty like the alcohol, and yourself), *cassata* (fruit ice cream with nuts and candied fruits), *riso* (rice pudding), and *tiramisù*.

Another option is a slushy flavored ice treat called **granita.** Three common flavor are *limone* (lemon), *amareno* (sour cherry), and *caffè* (slushy frozen espresso) Alternately, try visiting a **grattachecce** stand. At these little booths (usually aroun parks and busier streets), muscled vendors will scrape shavings off a block of ice fo you on the spot with a metal shovel, then spike your drink with any of the flavoure syrups they have on hand. The Roman specialty in *grattachecce* is a combo flavo called **lemoncocco,** a yummy mix of lemon and coconut flavors with bits of fres coconut fruit mixed in.

San Crispino, V.d. Panetteria, 42 (☎06 6793924). Very near the Trevi Fountain. Facin the fountain, turn right onto V. Lavatore and take your 2nd left; the *gelato* temple is on th right. Positively the best *gelato* in the world. Don't miss their exquisite meringue, armagna (similar to cognac), and grapefruit flavors. No cones; the proprietors claim that they "interfer with the purity of the product." Cups L3-10,000. Also at V. Acaia, 56 (☎06 70450412) south of the center in Appio. Both locations open M and W-Th noon-12:30am, F-Sa noor 1:30am, Su noon-midnight. (see p. 105).

Tre Scalini, P. Navona, 30 (☎06 6880 1996). This chic, old-fashioned spot is famous fo its *tartufo,* a hunk of truffled chocolate ice cream rolled in chocolate shavings (L5000 at th bar, L11,000 sitting). A touristed location has brought high prices, but *tartufo* is not to b missed. Bar open Th-Tu 9am-1:30am; pricey restaurant open Th-Tu 12:30-3:30pm and 7:3C 9pm.

Giolitti, V.d. Uffici del Vicario, 40 (☎06 6991243). From the Pantheon, follow V.d. Par theon (at the northern end of the *piazza*) to its end and then take V.d. Maddelena to its end V.d. Uffici del Vicario is on the right. An old-fashioned ice cream shoppe, Giolitti makes wor derful *gelato* in dozens of flavors, both to take-out or eat-in. Fashionably aloof service peopl don't have much patience with *turisti,* so be sure to pay and get a receipt first, and choos your flavors before you step up to the bar. Very festive and crowded at night. Cones L3-500C Open daily 9am-1am. Nov.-Apr. closed M. AmEx/D/MC/V.

Da Quinto, V.d. Tor Millina, 15 (☎06 686 56 57). West of P. Navona. Eccentric interior dec oration, huge queues, and icy, lighter gelato. The fruit flavors are especially good, as are th house specialty banana splits (L8000). Enormous *macedonia* of fruit (with yogurt, *gelato,* o whipped cream topping; L12,000). Open daily noon-2am. Winter closed W.

Palazzo del Freddo Giovanni Fassi, V. Principe Eugenio, 65-67 (☎06 4464740). Off P. V. Emanuele II, southeast of Termini. This century-old *gelato* factory is famous throughout Rome for its superb, creamy ice cream. Try *riso* (rice), try *coco* (coconut), try them all. Its most famous flavor is *la caterinetta,* a delicate honey and vanilla concoction. Cones L3-7000. *Frulatti* L3-5000. Also at V. Vespasiano, 57, near the Vatican. Open Tu-F noon-midnight, Sa noon-1am, Su 10am-midnight. In summer, also open M noon-midnight.

Il Fornaio, V.d. Baullari, 5-7 (☎06 6880 3947). Across from P.S. Pantaleo, south of P. Navona. Wonderful, fresh-baked cakes, pies, and cookies. *Torta di mele* (L3000 per big slice), delicious *biscotti* (L1800 per *etto*), melting *cornetti* (L1500). Open daily 7am-8:30pm.

Yogufruit, P. G. Tavani Arquati, 118 (☎06 587972). Off V.d. Lungaretta near P.S. Sonnino. No tradition here; it's filled with the young and the fruitful. Tart frozen yogurt blended with just about anything: fruit, M&Ms, even cornflakes. Cups or cones L3-5000. Open M-Sa noon-2am.

CAFFÈ

Italian coffee is the world's best, and coffee itself is the perfect solution to early hostel lockouts, hangovers, and hordes of belligerent tourists. It's also incredibly cheap and readily available. What to order? **Caffè** or **espresso** is a small cup of very strong coffee. A **cappuccino** is *espresso* with steamed milk and foam, often with a sprinkle of *cacao* on top; Italians only drink it for breakfast, but you can get it anytime you like, if you don't mind the bartender's snickering. A **caffè latte** is a shot of *espresso* with an entire glass of hot milk. If you want skim milk, request a **latte scremato. Caffè macchiato** is *espresso* with a spot of milk. **Latte macchiato** is a steamed milk with a spot of espresso. **Caffè ristretto** (or **alto**) is *espresso* with less water than usual. A **caffè lungo** has more water than normal, for non-Italian nervous systems. **Caffè corretto** is a black *espresso* "corrected" with a spot of liqueur. **Caffè americano** may be either filtered coffee or a *caffè lungo.* **Decaffeinato** coffee is available and may be made into any of the above delicacies. Better than decaf, though, is **caffè orzo,** a coffee-like drink made from barley—it tastes better than decaf and contains no trace caffeine.

Note that in most *caffès* and bars, you pay one price to stand at the bar, and a higher price (as much as double) to sit down. There is usually a menu on the wall of the bar listing the prices *al bar* or *al banco* (standing up) and *a tavola* (at a table). The streets around Campo dei Fiori and Trastevere hide some of the best *caffès.* The bars around the Spanish Steps cater to rich tourists and are often packed and over-priced. Also avoid the numerous bars near the Vatican; the prices are some of the highest in Rome, and the quality tends to be poor. Wander a few blocks north to V. Cola di Rienzo to find more authentic *caffès. Pasticcerie* (pastry shops) are scattered around Centro Storico and distinguish themselves from the typical bar with a glorious selection of sweets to wash down with your *caffè.*

Portico d'Ottavia, 1 (☎06 6878637). Not really a cafe, this is a tiny, take-out only pastry bakery deep in the Jewish Ghetto. Little fanfare, just long queues of locals who line up for fabulous blueberry pies, buttery cookies, and chocolate and pudding concoctions, all sold by weight at excellent prices (L2000/€1.03 for a sizeable wedge of pie). Open Su-Th 8am-8pm, F 8am-5:30pm. Closed Jewish holidays.

Tazza d'Oro, V.d. Orfani, 84-86 (☎06 6792768). Standing with your back to the Pantheon's portico, you'll see the yellow-lettered sign on your right. No seating, but the best coffee in Rome (as well as *el mejor del mundo* as well) at great prices (*caffè* L1100/€0.57; *cappuccino* L1400/€0.72). Extensive tea and coffee selection. Superlative *granita di caffè* with mounds of fresh whipped cream (L2500/€1.29). Open M-Sa 7am-8:00pm.

Dagnino, Galleria Esedra, V. V. E. Orlando, 75 (☎06 4818660). Conveniently snuggled between Termini and P. Repubblica, this *pasticceria* extraordinaire serves fabulous Sicilian pastries, *gelato* in special sweet pastry cups, marzipan wonders, almond drinks, and exquisite, never-soggy ricotta *cannoli siciliani* (L2-4000/€1.03-2.06). Don't miss the splendid, sticky *cassatina,* a heavy mix of candied orange and lemon peel, green icing, almond paste, and sweet, moist ricotta. Understandably busy at lunch time, given *primi* that start at L7000/€3.62. Open daily 7am-10pm. MC/V.

Bar San Calisto, P.S. Calisto, 4 (☎06 5835869). Join Trasteverean youth and Roman elders as they engage in conversation over excellent, inexpensive *cappuccino* (L1300/€0.67 sitting or standing), iced tea (L1500/€0.77), or Peroni (L3000/€1.55). Low prices keep the hordes coming. Open M-Sa 6am-1:30am, Su 4pm-1:30am. In winter closed Su.

Antico Caffè Greco, V. Condotti, 86 (☎06 6791700), off P. di Spagna. One of the oldest and most famous *caffès* in the world, this posh house, founded in 1760, has entertained the likes of European kings, Goethe, Wagner, Baudelaire, Byron, Shelley, John F. Kennedy, and others who could afford to spend too much on their caffeine habits. Waiters in ducktails, marble tables, and rows of velvet booths demand that you do the same, if only for one afternoon. *Cappuccino* L2400/€1.24. Pot of tea L3100/€1.60. Hot chocolate with cream L4600/€2.37. Open M-Sa 8am-8:30pm.

Antica Pasticceria Bella Napoli, C. V. Emanuele II, 246 (☎06 6877048). Good coffee and fantastic Neapolitan pastries. Try the *sfogliatelle ricce,* orgasmic ricotta-stuffed pastry flavored with orange peel and cinnamon, or rum soaked *baba* cakes. Available for take-out or eat-in. Pastries L1500-9500/€0.77-4.90 for larger cakes. Open Su-F 7:30am-9pm.

Sant'Eustachio, Il Caffè, P.S. Eustachio, 82 (☎06 6861309). Take a right on via Palombella behind the Pantheon on the right as you face it. Rome's "coffee empire." This cafe was once a favorite haunt of Stendhal; the modern-day struggling artist would do best to find his inspiration elsewhere. Excellent coffee at rather inflated prices. Try a *granita di caffè* with all the works (L10,000/€5.16; L7000/€3.62 at the bar), or their very own *gran caffè speciale* (L5000/€2.58; L3500/€1.81 at the bar). If you don't want your espresso heavily sugared, specify "*caffe amaro.*" Open Su-F 8:30am-1am, Sa 8:30am-2am.

Caffè della Pace, V.d. Pace, 3-7 (☎06 6861216). Off P. Navona. Great people-watching, although you'll see nearly as many Americans sedately writing postcards as Italians wildly gesticulating on their cell phones. Still, a reasonably hip bar for a highly over-touristed area. Cappuccino from L5000/€2.58; beer/wine L6000/€3.10; cocktails L14,000/€7.23, although prices go up after dark. Open daily 9am-3am.

WINE

Renaissance bankroller Lorenzo, perhaps having consumed one too many glasses of Zagarola (a Lazio white, popular in his time), paid poetic tribute to the grapevine-entangled god credited with fetching wine, glorious wine to the Aegean from India. Lorenzo may have been a better politician than a poet, but he certainly conveyed an appreciation for wine that Italian culture continues to embrace. Italians have been winemakers since Ancient Rome, when wine was so widely produced that vineyards were occasionally demolished in order to check the problem of overproduction. The choicest brands may be out of the budget traveler's range, but fortunately there are numerous inexpensive good local wines that will have you feeling the heat of Bacchus in no time. Lazio is best known for its white wine. **Frascati,** the most famous local white, is fruity and dry. Est! Est!! Est!!! is the famous white wine of Montefiascone. **Colli Albani** wines, from the nearby foothills, are pale gold and delicate. **Cerveteri** wines include full-bodied reds and a slightly bitter white. Useful wine terminology: **vecchio** means "old" and **stravecchio** means "very old." **Secco** means "dry," and **abboccato** or **dolce** means "sweet." While house wine varies in quality, it costs only slightly more than bottled water, and one need not be a wine connoisseur to order *un litro* of *vino della casa.*

WINE BARS & ENOTECHE (WINE SHOPS)

Enoteche (or *bottiglierie*), traditional wine and olive oil shops, have become an economical and more authentic lunchtime alternative to pricey *trattorie.* The evolution of wine shops into makeshift restaurants began when shop proprietors had the common decency to feed the men who delivered barrels of the local harvest. Eventually word got out, and the wine shops had to install card tables, put up signs "*vino e cucina,*" and turn family members into waiters. In the 60s and 70s, students, hippies, and political activists gathered in such places to discuss Marx and Marcuse. Anyone looking for tasty, inexpensive food in an informal, personable setting will enjoy the cuisine and company in these neighborhood establishments. Most are open only on weekdays during lunchtime (approximately noon-3pm). *Enoteche* converge into wine bars, which offer more upscale, elegant foods and settings. Here you'll often find smoked fish, imported cheese, delicate desserts in multicolored exotic syrups, in addition to the typical pizza and salad dishes.

Bar Da Benito, V.d. Falegnami, 14 (☎06 6861508), off P.Cairoli in the Jewish Ghetto. A tiny *tavola calda* lined with bottles and hordes of hungry workmen. Glasses of wine from L2000/€1.03; bottle from L15,000/€7.75 One hot pasta prepared daily (L8000/€4.13), along with delicious *secondi* like *prosciutto* with vegetables (L9000/€4.65). Always packed, noisy, and incredibly hectic, with excellent staff. Open M-Sa 6:30am-7pm; lunch noon-3:30pm. Closed Aug.

Trimani Wine Bar, V. Cernaia, 37b (☎06 4469630). Near Termini, perpendicular to V. Volturno (V. Marsala). Their shop is around the corner at V. Goito, 20. Excellent food at reasonable prices. Simple, wonderful salads (like the avocado and feta; L14,000/€7.23), filling quiches (try the spiny lobster and leek quiche; L9000/€4.65), smoked fish (L16,000/€8.26), impressive cheese and sausage plates (L14-20,000/€7.23-10.33), and desserts worth writing home about, such as the heavenly ricotta, amaretto, and raspberry tart (L9000/€4.65). Wines from L3500/€1.81 a glass; L18,000/€9.30 a bottle. Reservations recommended for dinner. Open M-Sa 11am-3:30pm and 6pm-12:30am. AmEx/MC/V.

Cul de Sac, P. Pasquino, 73 (☎06 6880 1094). Off P. Navona. Rome's first wine bar, Cul de Sac has kept the customers coming with a huge selection of great, decently priced wines, outdoor tables, and excellent food. House specialty pate (such as pheasant and mushroom; L9500/€4.90) is exquisite, as are the scrumptious *escargot alla bourguigonne* (L8500/€4.39). Open M 7pm-12:30am, Tu-Sa 12:30-4pm and 6pm-12:30am. MC/V.

La Bottega del Vino da Anacleto Bleve, V.S. Maria del Pianto, 9a-11 (☎06 6865970), off P. Cairoli in the Jewish Ghetto. Wide range of cheese, smoked fish, and cured meats. *Il piatto misto della casa* (L40,000/€20.66) feeds two. Superlative wine list. Wine by the glass from L6000/€3.10. Open M-Sa 9:30am-1:30pm and 5-8pm. AmEx/D/MC/V.

Il Piccolo, V.d. Governo Vecchio, 75 (☎06 68801746), off the southwest corner of P. Navona. Sophisticated but simple food and gentle 20s and 30s jazz floating out to street-side tables make this an indulgent and sunny haven. Glasses of wine from L2000/€1.03. Salads and pasta for lunch (L6-15,000/€3.10-7.75) and assorted *antipasti* at night (L5-10,000/€2.58-5.16). Open daily noon-3:30pm and 4:30pm-2:30am. AmEx/D/MC/V.

Enotecantica, V.d. Croce, 76b (☎06 6790896), off P. di Spagna. Relax at the elegant, semi-circular bar after a draining day at Cartier, or sit outside and gaze in awe at the shoppers who can actually afford to buy something there. Sip wine (L6-13,000 per glass) in a often frenetically over-touristed atmosphere. *Melanzane alla parmigiana* (eggplant parmesan; L14,000/€7.23). Salads L8-18,000/€4.13-9.30; pizza from L12,000/€6.20. Open daily 11am-1am. AmEx/D/MC/V.

Enoteca Buccone, V. Ripetta, 19 (☎06 3612154). Two blocks south of P. del Popolo on the left. Choose from hundreds of wines by the bottle, dozens by the glass, or head into the back room for elegant light fare. Eloquent quiches (L4500/€2.32), tiny *tartini* (L1500/€0.77), and good cold pasta salads (L8500/€4.33). *Secondi* L12-26,000/€6.20-13.43. Wines by the glass (L4500-16,000/€2.32-8.26). Try the marvelous Sardinian dry white (L4500/€2.32). Lunch served noon-3:30pm; dinner Th-Sa evenings. Open M-W 9am-8:30pm, Th-Sa 9am-midnight, Su 10am-5pm. AmEx/D/MC/V.

Curia di Bacco, V.d. Biscione, 79 (☎06 6893893). Off Campo dei Fiori. If you took every bottle of wine in this *enoteche* and lined them up end to end, it would probably make the owners very unhappy. Choose from over 200 choices (L10-130,000/€5.16-67.14). Also offers an extensive imported beer list, and over 20 different salads. If that's not enough, rumor has it that Julius Caesar was slain on the site. Open daily 4pm-2am. AmEx/MC/V.

La Vineria (a.k.a. Da Giorgio), Campo dei Fiori, 15 (☎06 68803268). One of the more lively wine bars, caught between the orbits of the Drunken Ship and Sloppy Sam's. Full of expats during the day; at night, throngs of young Italians and tourists mingle over surprisingly cheap wines and harder drinks. White table wine L2000/€1.03 per plastic cup; gin and tonic L10,000/€5.16. *Tartine* (L2000/€1.03) make a tasty addition to the wine. Open M-Sa 9am-2am. AmEx/D/MC/V.

WINE SHOPS

Some shops still sell just wine (but damn good wine at damn good prices).

Trimani, V. Goito, 20 (☎06 4469661). Near Termini. Founded in 1821, Trimani is indisputably Rome's best wine shop. Vast selection of wines, which range from the very affordable to way-beyond-your-credit-card-limit. Expert staff will be happy to advise you in selecting a bottle to fit your palate and wallet. Don't forget to have a snack at the decadent Trimani Wine Bar, around the corner on V. Cernaia. Open M-Sa 8:30am-1:30pm and 3:30-8pm. AmEx/D/MC/V.

EST! EST!! EST!!! (IN PEACE)

One of the finest golden wines of the region, grown on the slopes of Montefiascone, near Viterbo (p. 224), owes its name, *Est! Est!! Est!!!*, to a German cardinal, Johan Defuk, who was traveling through the district. He sent his valet ahead of him to sample the local wines and chalk "Est" (short for "*est bonum vinum*," or "it's good wine) on the doors of inns with satisfactory offerings, and "Est Est" if it was particularly good. When the valet reached Montefiascone, he was so enraptured with the harvest that he wrote "Est Est Est," a great piece of publicity for the wine which has since assumed the name. The cardinal himself unintentionally spent the last, very happy days of his life in Montefascione. He stayed at the inn for several days and drank such vast quantities of the wine that he died a sudden, if giddy, death. His grave, 20km north of Viterbo in Montefiascone, bears the inscription, "Est Est Est."

SHOPPING FOR FOOD

Food stores tend to be open Monday to Wednesday and Friday 8am to 1pm and 4 to 8pm, Thursday and Saturday 8am to 1pm. For those with rarefied tastes, **alimentari** carry a selection of Italian specialty foods and liquors far superior to that which you might find at your typical Standa. These small stores, sprinkled about the city, carry standard groceries, dry goods, and deli items, but are furthermore superb for food souvenir stock-up. For specialty cheeses, fresh bread, and meats, head to a **panificio** (bakery) or a **salumeria** (delicatessen). A little *pane* (bread) and an **etto** (100g) of meat or cheese will make a cheap but satisfying sandwich. For produce, open-air markets are the best for freshness and price. Seek out small **frutta e verdure** shops and stands. Besides markets, **supermarkets** are generally the cheapest source of everything. They are also quieter, air-conditioned, and open longer. Produce, however, is much less fresh, and there is often a poor selection. Furthermore, Rome's supermarkets tend to be inconveniently far away from the areas tourists frequent. See the Service Directory, p. 293, for listings of major supermarkets in Rome.

ALIMENTARI

Franchi Pietro, V. Cola di Rienzo, 204 (06 874651). Hanging ham hocks, huge wheels of cheese, and a terrific selection of wine and olives are among the more mundane buys to be had at Franchi. Seekers of the exotic, particularly in the area of prepared seafood, will swoon for lobster tails (L180,000/€93.00 per kg) and salmon tart (L85,000/€43.90 per kg) artfully displayed in the well-stocked deli counter. Open Tu-Sa 8:15am-9pm.

Castroni, V. Cola di Rienzo, 196 (06 874383). Craving ramen noodles (L2000/€1.03)? Baked beans (L3500/€1.81)? Hershey's Chocolate Syrup (L10,500/€5.42)? Castroni offers all sorts of American specialty foods, as well as Japanese, Mexican, Greek, German, and Argentinian rarities. An essential store for anyone who's spent a little too much time in Europe and misses...California prunes (L5000/€2.58)? Open Tu-Su 8am-8pm. MC/V.

Fratelli Fabbi, V.d. Croce, 27-28 (☎06 6790612). Well, yes, an astoundingly expensive Gucci bag may be the ultimate Spanish Steps shopping souvenir, but perhaps one could learn to be happy with 1kg bag of meter-long spaghetti (L10,500/€5.42) instead. This well-stocked delicatessen offers all sorts of Italian culinary goodies, including mozzarella wrapped in aromatic grass (L10,000/€5.16) and buns filled with olives (L2000/€1.03). Open Tu-Sa 8am-1:30pm and 4:45-7:45pm. AmEx/D/MC/V.

Albero del Pane, V.S. Maria del Pianto. Ginseng, herb, and aloe are in abundance. Oriented toward vegetarians and sensitive eaters, with a small baked goods section featuring bread made without yeast or milk, and a similarly prepared but wonderful rice pudding and raisin tart (L3000/€1.55 per slice). Open M-F 9am-7:30pm and Sa 9am-1:30pm; Aug. Tu-Su 9am-1:30pm and 5-7:30pm.

Cooperative Latte Cisternino, V.d. Gallo, 20 (☎06 872875), off Camp dei Fiori. Fresh *latte* (milk; 1L from L1800) and *formaggio* (cheese) galore. Open M-F 8am-1:30pm and 5:30-7:30pm, Sa 8am-1:30pm.

OUTDOOR PRODUCE MARKETS

Mercato Rionfale, V. Cola di Rienzo at V. Properzio. Moderate sized, but with a good selection. Open M-Sa 7am-7pm; July and Aug. 6am-4pm.

Mercato Trionfale, Near the Ottaviano Metro Stop at V.S. Maura and V. Andrea Doria. Huge selection of fruit, vegetables, dairy, and meat products, as well as some baked goods.

Mercato Testaccio, P. Testaccio, M: B-Piramide. Come here for juicy fodder. Excellent selection and prices on fish.

Mercato di Piazza San Cosimato, in Trastevere. A raging produce market. Walk up V. Trastevere away from river, turn right on V. Fratte di Trastevere, and left on V.S. Cosimato.

Mercato di Campo dei Fiori. Fruits, veggies, cheese, fish, and a pittance of flowers.

Mercato di Piazza Vittorio Emanuele II, slightly south and west of Termini. The usual produce and mayhem, this time with clothes.

Mercato di Via Milazzo, north of Termini, between V. Varese and V. Palestro.

Mercato Via della Pace, off V.d. Tor Millener. A small-scale produce market.

Mercato di Via del Lavatore, near the Trevi Fountain. Only produce.

Mercato di Via Tomacelli, by Spanish Steps, at Lgo. degli Schiavoni. Produce and flowers.

INSIDE

Nightlife

When you're most frustrated about the random afternoon closing times of restaurants, museums, and just about everything else in the Eternal City, remember this simple fact of Roman life: everyone is sleeping now, so they don't have to after dark. The following lists the best places in Rome to drink, grind, and go bump in the night.

AFTER-DINNER WALKING TOUR

From grub to pub: Spanish Steps to Campo dei Fiori. Begin at P. di Spagna (M:A-Spagna). 1½-2½hr.

As you've no doubt noticed by now, meals in Rome are a serious affair. You'll want to digest, cool off, then gear up before you hit the nightlife—and this after-dinner tour is the perfect way to do such. After a meal at one of Rome's countless *trattorie* (see **Food,** p. 166, for suggestions), take in the vibrant atmosphere of the Spanish Steps (p. 101), where tourists go to sit and watch Bernini's **Barcaccia** fountain and Italians go to *rimorchiarli* (hit on them). Either sit around and ponder the fact that the Spanish Steps were actually paid for by French King Louis XV, or head to **Via Condotti** and **Via Borgognona,** Rome's most exclusive retail space. Either while away the time window-shopping or pick out what you're going to come and buy tomorrow (yeah, right).

In P. di Spagna, head past the column in adjoining P. Mignanelli and bear right along V. di Propaganda (V. San Andrea delle Fratte). Bear left onto V. Nazarena, taking time to notice the **ruins of the Vergine Aqueduct** on the right, which once fed Bernini's fountain. Cross V.d. Tritone onto V.d. Panetteria.

About three-quarters of the way down on the left, you'll find the best *gelato* in Rome at **Gelateria San Crispino** (p. 176), with more than 20 delicious flavors (cups L3-6000). *Gelato* in hand, turn right onto V.d. Lavatore (before the ramp up to the Quirinale) and you'll hit the **Trevi Fountain** (p. 104). Feel free to ensure your own return to Rome.

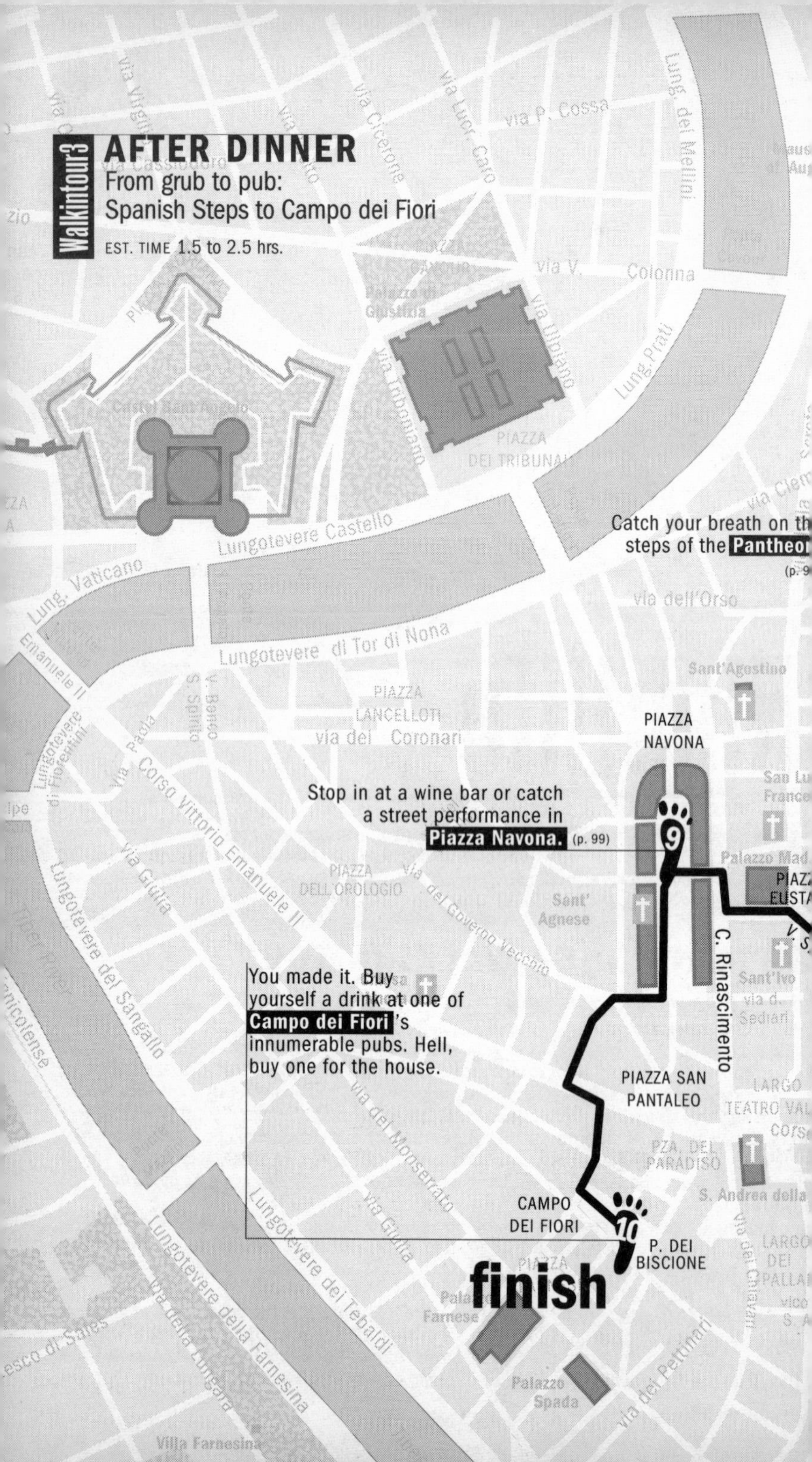

Walkintour3
AFTER DINNER
From grub to pub:
Spanish Steps to Campo dei Fiori
EST. TIME 1.5 to 2.5 hrs.
Catch your breath on th
steps of the Pantheo
(p. 9
Stop in at a wine bar or catch
a street performance in
Piazza Navona. (p. 99)
You made it. Buy
yourself a drink at one of
Campo dei Fiori's
innumerable pubs. Hell,
buy one for the house.
finish
9
10
via P. Cossa
via Cicerone
via Lucr. Caro
Lung. dei Mellini
via V. Colonna
via Ulpiano
via Triboniano
Lung. Prati
PIAZZA
DEI TRIBUNALI
Lungotevere Castello
Lung. Vaticano
via dell'Orso
Lungotevere di Tor di Nona
Sant'Agostino
PIAZZA
LANCELLOTI
via dei Coronari
PIAZZA
NAVONA
Corso Vittorio Emanuele II
via Giulia
PIAZZA
DELL'OROLOGIO
via del Governo Vecchio
Sant'
Agnese
C. Rinascimento
Sant'Ivo
Lungotevere dei Sangallo
PIAZZA SAN
PANTALEO
PZA. DEL
PARADISO
S. Andrea della
CAMPO
DEI FIORI
P. DEI
BISCIONE
via dei Monserrato
Lungotevere dei Tebaldi
Lungotevere della Farnesina
via della Lungara
Palazzo
Farnese
Palazzo
Spada
via dei Pettinari
Villa Farnesina
Tiber River

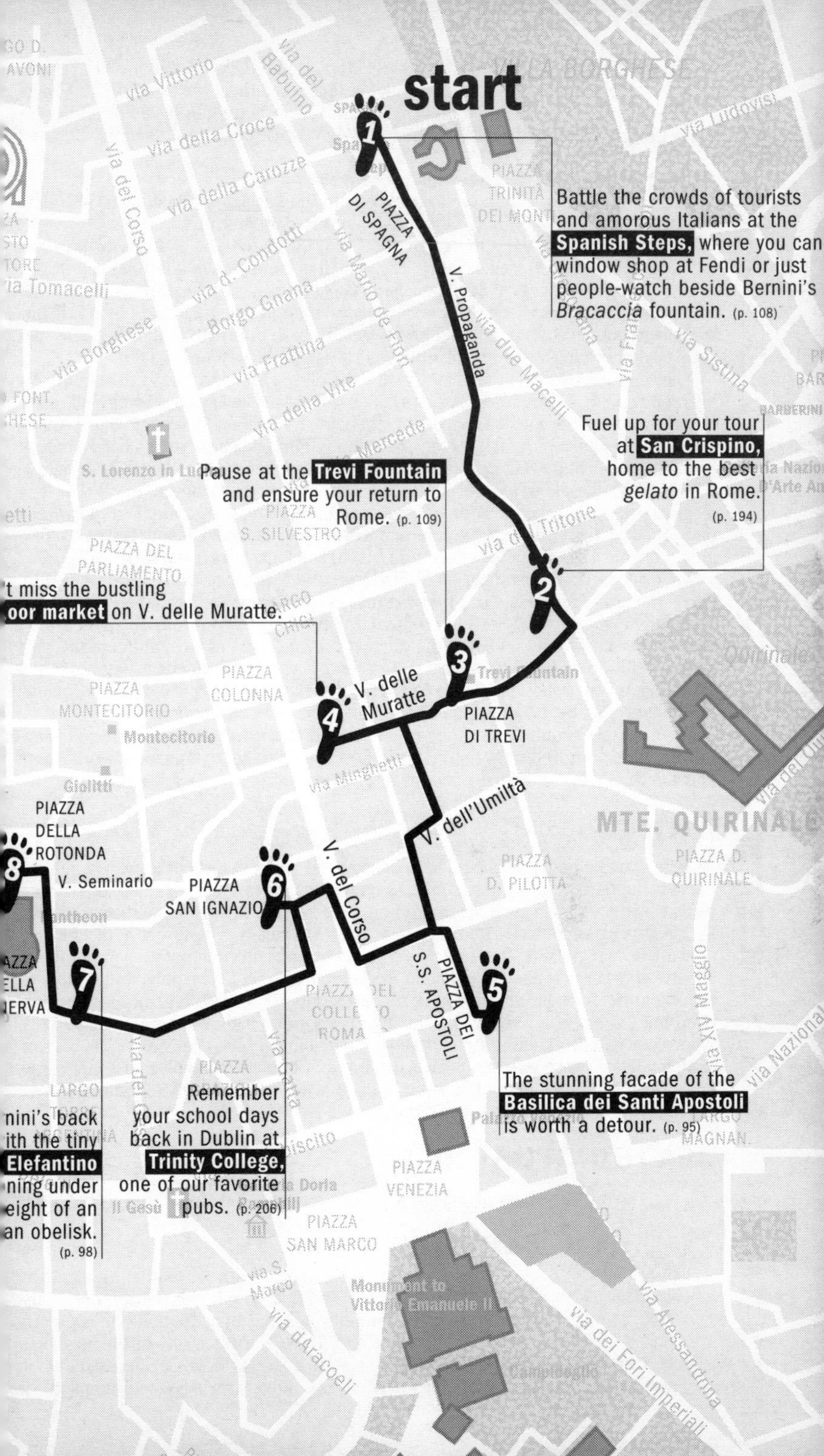

start
Battle the crowds of tourists and amorous Italians at the Spanish Steps, where you can window shop at Fendi or just people-watch beside Bernini's Bracaccia fountain. (p. 108)
Fuel up for your tour at San Crispino, home to the best gelato in Rome. (p. 194)
Pause at the Trevi Fountain and ensure your return to Rome. (p. 109)
't miss the bustling oor market on V. delle Muratte.
The stunning facade of the Basilica dei Santi Apostoli is worth a detour. (p. 95)
Remember your school days back in Dublin at Trinity College, one of our favorite pubs. (p. 206)
nini's back ith the tiny Elefantino ning under eight of an an obelisk. (p. 98)
PIAZZA DI SPAGNA
V. Propaganda
V. delle Muratte
PIAZZA DI TREVI
V. dell'Umiltà
V. del Corso
PIAZZA DEI S.S. APOSTOLI
PIAZZA SAN IGNAZIO
PIAZZA DELLA ROTONDA
V. Seminario
MTE. QUIRINALE
via del Corso
via della Croce
via della Carozze
via d. Condotti
via Frattina
via della Vite
via del Tritone
via due Macelli
via Sistina
via Nazionale
via dei Fori Imperiali
via Alessandrina
PIAZZA VENEZIA
PIAZZA SAN MARCO

Leaving the fountain, walk out onto V.d. Muratte and make a left onto V.d. Vergini. (A little farther down V.d. Muratte, skilled artisans sell their wares outdoors.) Make a right onto V.d. Umiltà and a quick left onto V. San Marcello. If you're thirsty for some Italian beer, try **Birreria Peroni,** on the right, a neighborhood favorite affiliated with the Peroni brewery (L3500-12,000).

Continue down V.S. Marcello and take a quick right onto V. Santi Apostoli. (Continuing straight on Via S. Marcello leads you to the **Basilica dei Santi Apostoli** (see p. 88). It has a beautifully ornate facade and a portico full of sculptures.)

When you arrive at V.d. Corso, turn right, and take a look back down the street at the **Vittorio Emanuele II monument** (p. 88), which is majestically illuminated at night. After passing the **Church of San Marcello al Corso** on your right, cross V.d. Corso and make your first left down V. A. Specchi. On the right at the end of the block is **Trinity College** pub (p. 188), a quintessential Roman Irish pub with much Guinness and Harp paraphernalia and many distinctly non-Irish Italians (pint L6-9000).

Stumbling out of the pub, turn left down V.d. Collegio Romano (V. Pie' di Marmo) and bear right on V.S. Caterina da Siena into P. della Minerva. The **Church of Santa Maria sopra Minerva** was built on top of an ancient temple, but the real eye-catcher is the so-called "Pulcin della Minerva" (p. 92), a cute 18th-century Bernini sculpture of a baby elephant beneath a 6th-century B.C. Egyptian obelisk. With your back to the church, bear right to P. della Rotonda, site of the ancient Roman masterpiece, the **Pantheon** (p. 90). The temple is closed at night, but there are crowds, musicians, and pricey cafes. Exit the *piazza* on Salita de' Crescenzi, and take your first left to P. S. Eustachio. If your spirits are flagging, stop and get your caffeine fix (*caffè* L1600) at **Il Caffè Sant'Eustachio** (p. 178).

Walk out of P. S. Eustachio on V. Staderari and turn right onto C. Rinascimento. Cross the street and take your first left into **Piazza Navona** (p. 93), where street performers, musicians, and portrait painters do their best to entertain. Keep an eye on your wallet and remember that the biggest crowds don't always indicate the best shows.Walk down to the southern end of the *piazza* and turn right to get to P. del Pasquino, where you'll find **Cul de Sac** (p. 179), a classy little wine bar where you can drink tasty *vini* by the glass (L5000 and up) and enjoy fancy appetizers.

From P. del Pasquino, head down V.d. Leutari and turn left on C. Vittorio Emanuele II. Take your first right onto P. della Cancelleria to get to **Campo de' Fiori,** where you can finally become serious about getting your drink on (see **Pubs,** below).

PUBS

Exactly why the Irish pub should have become the *de facto* form of Roman nightlife is unclear, but that's the way it is. Rome has more pubs than Dublin, and more on the way. Not all of Rome's pubs are Irish: some claim to be English, Scottish, American, or Brazilian, and many are distinctly Roman concoctions. Nationality is in the eye of the drinker.

Many Roman pubs feature live music, dancing, and entertainment. The tradition of staying *all'aperto* is alive and well in Rome's pubs—most have substantial outdoor seating areas for your enjoyment in the hot summer months. The more traditional drinking experience lives on in the slightly more upscale **wine bars** (see p. 178), where you can drink without the darkness, smoke, and pick-up scene of the bars.

Listed below are some of our favorites for your pub-crawling pleasure. Of course, *Let's Go* researchers are not allowed to drink while on duty, which, ramble they be gin to ?drinking much merry, vodka be good.

CENTRO STORICO

The area is well served at night by Bus #45N on C. Vittorio Emanuele II.

see map p.310-311

CAMPO DEI FIORI

The statue of Giordano Bruno looks down on the nightly insanity taking place in the Campo with an expression of dismay. During the summer, all hell breaks loose on a nightly basis at Campo dei Fiori. Have a drink at one of the hordes of pubs and bars, grab a slice of watermelon from a street vendor, and go find another lonely backpacker. You diligently threw your coins in the Trevi Fountain; here's your chance to cash in.

The Drunken Ship, Campo dei Fiori, 20-21 (☎06 68300535). Because you're tired of meeting Italians. Because you have a burning desire to commune with the hosteling set. Because you feel the need to have an emotion-free fling with a kindred spirit. Because you're proud to be an American, dammit. A brew will set you back L8000/€4.13. Happy hour daily 5-9pm. Su is Ladies' night, Tu brings half price Tequila, and 9-10pm W power hour—all the beer you can drink (L10,000/€5.16). Ask about the student discount on Heineken. A takeout window completes the American aesthetic. Open 5pm-2am. AmEx/MC/V.

Sloppy Sam's, Campo dei Fiori, 9-10 (☎06 68802637). The poor cousin of the Drunken Ship. Note that once home, wistful stories about that "special someone" you "befriended" at Sloppy Sam's will probably be regarded somewhat cynically. Happy Hour 4-9pm, 2 for 1 special Tu. Beer L8000/€4.13; shots L5000/€2.58. Open Su-Th 4-12:30, F-S 4-1:30am. AmEx/MC/V.

Caipirinha Pub-Café, V.d. Gallo, 10 (☎06 6892561). This fun Brazilian bar serves up tropical drinks and plays Brazilian music for your dancing enjoyment. Cocktails around L10,000. Bud L4000, Guinness L6000. Panini L4000. Open daily 7pm-2am.

Taverna del Campo, Campo dei Fiori, 16 (☎06 6874402). Is it a pub? Is it a wine bar? Gracious me, it's both. And it has damn tasty food and free peanuts to boot. Pannini L7000/€3.62. Wine by the glass L6000/€3.20; beer L7000/€3.62. Less touristy than the rest of the Campo, but of course, everything's relative. Open Tu-Su 8pm-2am. Cash only.

Campo degli Elfi, P. della Cancelleria, 87 (☎06 68308888). More a place for intimate conversation than hard drinkin', this Campo is full of Italian 20-somethings and elves. Very popular among both demographics. Open daily 10pm-2am.

La Taverna di Orusdir, V.d. Cappellari, 130 (☎06 68804654). Celtic environment with a heavy metal crowd. Do be careful. 1.5L beer L7000/€3.62. Cocktails L8000/€4.13. Open daily 8pm-2am. Closed Su.

PIAZZA NAVONA

Also a nightly three-ring circus is elegant P. Navona, which transforms within hours from tourist-packed destination by day to tourist-packed destination by night. Fend off the rose vendors, who become more aggressive as the night (and their bouquets) fades. V.d. Governo Vecchio is home to some fantastic cocktail bars, though these tend toward the wine-bar feel.

Jonathan's Angels, V.d. Fossa, 14-16 (☎06 6893426). West of P. Navona. Take V.d. Governo Vecchio from Campo dei Fiori, turn left at the Abbey Theatre onto V. Parione, and then a left toward the lights. Not since Pope Julius II has there been a case of Roman megalomania as severe as that of Jonathan. Michelangelo's accomplishments pale before the bathroom at Jonathan's Angels, the finest bathroom in Rome, nay, Italy. Jonathan himself holds court in the right bar,

Artu

Jonathan's Angels

Drunken Ship

the BIG $plurge

Bar del Fico, P. del Fico, 26-28 (☎06 6865205). Off V.d. Governo Vecchio. A place to see and be seen with Romans, Fico is almost always mobbed with locals at night. Lounge under the heated, ivy-covered awning or have your drink inside in one of the three oh-so-chic sitting rooms. Wide range of drinks, but pricey: 0.5L beer L12,000/€6.20. Open daily 8am-2am.

Bar della Pace, V.d. Pace, 4-5-7 (☎06 6861216). Off V.d. Governo Vecchio. Its proper name is Antico Caffe della Pace, but you won't hear it called that very often. One of *the* places to be for celebrity-watching in the Eternal City by night, this locale is upscale and it knows it. Sit outside or in one of the two gorgeous rooms, which are tastefully appointed with wood furniture and cushy armchairs. The waitresses seem to have been picked out of a beauty contest, and you know why. Prices are out of sight, but that's why you're here. Open daily 9am-2am.

his son, Jonathan II, spins underground techno on the left. Medium beer on tap L10,000/€5.16; delicious cocktails/long drinks L15,000/€7.75. Mercifully free of pub-crawlers. Open daily 4pm-2am.

Abbey Theatre, V.d. Governo Vecchio, 51-53 (☎06 6861341). One of the only establishments in Rome where you can drop in for a 10am Guinness (L10,000/€5.16). Stay for lunch (a lot of vaguely Irish dishes), watch MTV, and admire the rather touching painting of a drugged-out-looking Yeats. Before you know it, it'll be time for happy hour (daily 11am-9pm). Should you have the staying power, dinner's also available. Open M-Th 10am-2am, F-Sa 10am-3am, Su 1pm-2am. MC/V.

The John Bull Pub, C. V. Emanuele II, 107a (☎06 6871537). A study in contrasts that doesn't quite add up, John Bull's is a dark, cavernous English pub with music just a bit too loud and beer just a bit warm. Often full of pub-crawling kiddies. Food available. Open daily 9pm-2am. Cash only.

ELSEWHERE IN CENTRO STORICO

Trinity College, V.d. Collegio Romano, 6 (☎06 6786472). Off V.d. Corso near P. Venezia. Offers degrees in such diverse curricula as Guinness, Harp, and Heineken. Tuition L6-9000/€3.20-4.50. Fellow students are also foreign. Pub food served for lunch and dinner (Hamburgers L14,000/€7.20). Happy Hour noon-8pm. Classes held every day noon-3am.

The Nag's Head, V. IV Novembre, 138b (☎06 6794620). Off P. Venezia. Pier the bartender, who is straight out of *Cocktail* (and advertises himself as a master of *"flair estremo"*), makes this place worth a visit. After the bottle-twirling and other excesses, you almost don't mind the L1000/€0.52 he tacks on to your bill as a "tip." Dance floor inside; live music twice a week. Guinness L10,000/€5.16; cocktails L14,000/€7.20. Cover (imposed by slick bouncers with gratutious ear pieces) L10,000/€5.16; F and Sa men L15,000/€7.75; *gratis* Su. Open daily 4pm-3am, winter noon-3am. MC/V.

Night and Day, V.d. Oca, 50 (☎06 3202300). Off V. di Ripetta near P. del Popolo. Don't even think of coming until the rest of the bars close. At 2am, Italians who don't let dawn stop their fun stream in. Buy a membership card (L10,000) for discounts on drinks. Beer L5000-7000, Guinness L8000. Happy hour until midnight. Open daily 7pm-6am. Closed part of Aug.

Bartaruga, P. Mattei, 9 (☎06 6892299), in the Jewish Ghetto. Named after the tortoise-shaped fountain in this secluded *piazza,* Bartaruga provides a surreal drinking experience in a myriad of Murano glass, light blue and pink sofas, and tasseled drapery. On weekends it overflows with Italians in tight clothes. Wide variety of cocktails available; beer L8000. Open Tu-Su 10pm-2am.

Rock Castle Café, V. B. Cenci, 8 (☎06 68807999). In the old days, people would wish that there was a discopub with a frat-house atmosphere in the Jewish Ghetto. And they would wish that they could find Red Dog somewhere in the Eternal City. With the advent of the Rock Castle Café there's nothing left to wish for. Resist the urge to drink Budweiser; the Beamish (L7000/€3.62) is much better for you. Popular in winter with study-abroad students. Cover L2000/€1.03. Open 9pm-3am.

Victoria House, V. di Gesù e Maria, 18 (☎06 3201698), near P. del Popolo and marked by a large Union Jack. If this place were any more British, all the Irish pubs would be pissed. Pretty much everything inside was shipped from Sheffield. Shepherd and steak pies, fish and chips (L14,000/€7.20), served with several kinds of beer. Happy hour Tu-F 6-9pm. Pints L8000/€4.13. Open Tu-Th 6pm-12:30am, F-Sa 5:30pm-1am, Su 5pm-12:30am.

BORGO, PRATI, & VATICAN CITY

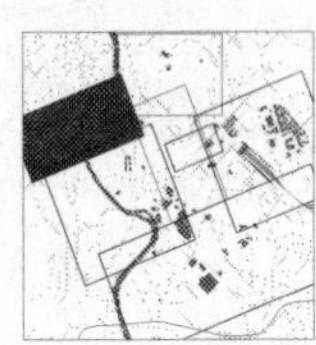
see map p.316

The area around the Vatican is largely residential and full of clergy, making for quiet nights, but a couple of establishments keep the liquor flowing and the music pumping. Pray for us sinners now and in the hour of our death, Amen.

The Proud Lion Pub, Borgo Pio, 36 (☎06 6832841). Located on a relatively highly touristed strip in the shadows of S. Pietro. The outside of the pub says "Rome, Borgo Pio," but the inside says "hey, I don't forget my Highland roots." Affiliated with the Italian Dart Club; call and ask about upcoming tournaments. The Lion's right on target with drink prices: beer L7-8000/€3.62-4.13; cocktails L8000/€4.13. Open Su-Th 8:30pm-1am, F-Sa 8:30pm-2am.

Morrison's, V. E. Q. Visconti, 88 (☎06 3222265). Two blocks north of P. Cavour. Quite an elegant place. Harp, Kilkenny, and Guinness on tap, an excellent selection of Irish and Scotch whiskey and bourbon, and pseudo-Gaelic slogans on the wall. For those in the literary know, the James Joyce (L8000/€4.13, blue caracao and Harp) is a must. Beer L9000/€4.50; cocktails L12,000/€6.20. Open Tu-Su 7pm-2am. AmEx/MC/V.

TRASTEVERE

see map p.310-311

Follow the crowds wandering the narrow streets: you're bound to find something. Still, since wandering time is just wasted drinking time, make a beeline for one of the following:

Artu Cafe, Largo Fumasoni Biondi, 5 (☎06 5880398). In P. San Egidio, directly behind Santa Maria in Trastevere. Artu offers a random melange of people fresh from partying in Trastevere. Good selection of drinks (beer L8000/€4.13; cocktails L12,000/€6.20); beautiful location. Making fun of pub crawl participants will probably not go over very well here. Open Tu-Su 6pm-2am. MC/V.

Sette Mari, V. G. Mameli, 5 (☎06 5882060). A veritable hodgepodge of Danish beer (L8000), English pub, pizza (from L5000/€2.58), and burgers (L12,000/€6.20), and boisterous Italian youth after 11. Open Tu-Su 6:30pm-2am. AmEx/MC/V.

La Scala, P. della Scala, 60 (☎06 5803763). On the left on V.d. Scala behind Santa Maria in Trastevere. Manages to be fun, despite feeling like a cheesy American franchise. Live music (i.e. an electric keyboardist and singer) on Tuesday nights at 9:30 pm. Burgundy lounges and barstools are put to shame by the best seat in the house–the infamous *mezza maquina* (half car) booth. Teeming masses fight to sit in the car, even on weeknights. Also a restaurant with appetizers from L9000/€4.50 (serves dinner until 1am). Cocktails from L10,000/€5.16. Open Th-Tu 7:30pm-2am. AmEx/DC/MC/V.

TERMINI & SAN LORENZO

NORTH OF TERMINI

see map p. 312-313

Termini might have been the convenient *zona* to find a place t sleep, but it's not the best area to take in a lively night-cap. you're in the mood for several night-caps, however, these pub make for a reasonably short stumble home.

Julius Caesar, V. Castelfidardo, 49 (☎06 4461565). Just north Termini near P. dell'Indipendenza, on the corner of V. Solferin Always packed with backpackers and locals, here for live musi cheap drinks, and good times. Upstairs features beer on tap (L10,000/€5.16), cheek Roman busts, and even cheekier Roman babes, while the downstairs is filled with blaring liv music most nights 10:30-11:30pm. Happy Hour half-price in the early evening. Cocktai L10,000/€5.16; wine L30,000/€15.50 per bottle. Inquire about the *Let's Go* discoun Open daily 4pm-2am.

Bandana Republic, V. Alessandria, 44-46 (☎06 44249751). A safari here requires a wa down V. Settembre to P.le Porta Pia, through P. Alessandria, with a right onto V. Alessandri Dumb name, good pub. Despite being English, it has the sense to serve Guinness, Har and Kilkenny (pints L9000, ha'-pints L5000/€2.58). Classy crowd enjoys reasonably price food (appetizers from L6000/€3.20) and laid-back ambience. Open Su-Th 12-2:30 an 7pm1-:30am. AmEx/MC/V.

SOUTH OF TERMINI (ESQUILINO)

Druid's Rock, P. dell'Esquilino, 1 (☎06 4741326). Near S. Maria Maggiore. A pool tab and ample televisions for sports event-viewing draw in Italians and tourists alike. Happy Ho (3pm-9pm) features discounts on drinks, which typically hover around L10,000/€5.16 f cocktails. Open M-F 10am-2am, Sa and Su 3pm-2am.

SAN LORENZO

The university district, San Lorenzo is home to one of the best pub scenes in Rom Tourists rarely venture into San Lorenzo, making it all the more tempting as a slic of genuine Roman youth nightlife. San Lorenzo is a 10min. walk from Termini an from P. Repubblica, through which night buses run every 30min. for your ride home

Il Simposio, V.d. Latini, 11 (☎0328 90778551). Ah, the sweet smell of turpentine. Th symposium's walls are cluttered with the Jackson Pollock-esque works of local artists, an chances are good that on any given night a splattered painter will be hard at work beautifyir a discarded refrigerator. With cocktails from L6000/€3.20 and a glass of *fragolino* f L5000/€2.58, even we starving artists can afford the place. Open daily 9pm-2am.

Pub Hallo'Ween, P. Tiburtino, 31 (☎06 4440705), at the corner of V. Tiburtina and Marsala. Abandon all hope of not having fun, ye who enter here. The plastic skulls and fak spiders and spiderwebs confirm your suspicions that this is indeed a gateway to the darke pits of Hell. Draft beer L6-8000, bottles L7-10,000/€3.62-5.16. Cocktails L10,000/€5.1 Enjoy delicious L10,000/€5.16 sandwiches such as the Freddy (salami and mozzarella), th Candyman (nutella), or the Frankenstein (double cheeseburger). Open daily 8:30pr 2:30am. Closed in Aug.

Legend American Pub, V.d. Latini (☎06 4463881). The stuffed football player on the b does not look particularly happy, but one taste of your *sgroppino* (gin or vodka blended wi strawberry or lemon gelato; L6000/€3.20), and you sure will be. Gleefully rowdy crowds soccer fans gather here to enjoy cheap beer (from L8000/€4.13) and appetizers (fro L5000/€2.58), and the occasional bucket of water thrown by upper-story neighbors unhapp with the loud masses gathered under their windows. Open Tu-Su 7pm-3am. AmEx/MC/V.

Zazerkalje, V.d. Equi, 57. (☎06 5902237). Live music, every night, is this place's big drav Shows start after 11pm, L5000/€2.58 *tessera* required. In the morning, music and painting le sons are given to the disabled, in the afternoon a music school hosts jam sessions. Weekenc offer the most credible music sessions, although the school's experimental performances durir the week attract decent crowds of music lovers. Beer L4-6000/€2.06-3.20, cocktails L8-10,000/€4.13-5.16. Bar open 9pm-5am.

Rivegauche2, V.d. Sabelli, 43 (☎06 4456722). Another addition to the ever-popular Irish pub scene, Rivegauche2 maintains a degree of chumminess despite being arena-like in comparison to other tiny San Lorenzo bars. No gladiators, however, just jovial groups of drinking buddies. Happy hour until 9 (cocktails L9000/€4.50; beers L5000/€2.58). Open daily 7pm-2am. MC/V.

Drome, V.d. Latini, 49-51 (☎06 4461492). A small cocktail bar/lounge with orange chairs straight off the set of The Jetsons and live jazz during non-summer months. An assortment of Middle Eastern foods nicely compliment all sorts of Italian liquors. Internet L6000/€3.20 per hr. Open M-Sa 8pm-3am.

Pigmalione, V. di Porta Labicana, 29 (☎06 4457740). Mellow rock and blues and the occasional Digable Planets tune play under the watchful gaze of a massive Aztec calendar painted on the wall. An eclectic mix of Indian, Egyptian, and astrological decor. It's a bit cheaper than its Irish counterparts, in addition to being better lit and less smoky. Medium beer L7000/€3.62; cocktails L8000/€4.13. Salads and panini L6-7000/€3.20-3.62. Open daily 7pm-2am.

Lancelot, V.d. Volsci, 77a (☎06 4454675). A smoky underground labyrinth of drinkers and lecherous knights. During the winter there can be a wait to get in. Open 8:30pm-2am.

Dalhu' Pub, V.d. Equi, 38-40 (☎06 4457369). Quiet, small Irish pub attracts a somewhat older crowd. Beers from L6000; cocktails from L10,000/€5.16. Open 8:30pm-2am.

TESTACCIO & OSTIENSE

see map p. 318

Testaccio and Ostiense are nightlife-central. Their clubs truly shine, and the pubs aren't too shabby. Bus #20N heads up V. Ostiense, stopping by the pyramid every half-hour.

Il Barone Rosso, V. Libetta, 13 (☎06 5783562). M:B-Garbatella. Left on V. Ostiense, then left at V. Libetta. The closest thing to a German beer garden in Rome. Plenty of room on the two floors and outdoor patio, plenty of snacks, and plenty of beer. Attracts a *telefonini*-toting crowd of young Romans. Beamish and König Pilsener on tap (L7000). Open Tu-Su 7pm-3am.

Mount Gay Music Bar, V. Galvani, 54 (☎06 5746013). Forget the name, just soak in the too-cool ambience as you sit on a pillow on the floor and sip your too-expensive cocktail (L15,000/€7.75). Two cave-like rooms filled with attractive Italians and the sounds of two turntables and a microphone. Open daily 9pm-4am. MC/V.

Four XXXX Pub, V. Galvani, 29 (☎06 5757296). From Piramide, turn left at the pyramid on to V. Marmorata, then left on V. Galvani. Four XXXX serves up its namesake beer (L8000/€4.13) every night and live jazzzz, bluessss, and soullll in its lower level Th-Sa 10pm. Local and Latin American food consumed in crowded tiki huts on the first floor. Open daily 7:30pm-2am. AmEx/D/MC/V.

CLUBS

ANCIENT CITY

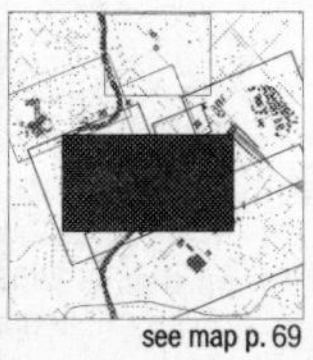
see map p. 69

Ciak Dance, V.S. Saba, 11a (☎06 5782022). Head for the Aventine Hill, but don't go all the way to up to Santa Prisca. Blown-up stills from films such as *Superman, Basic Instinct,* and *The Blues Brothers* line the walls and shake to hip-hop, house, disco, and, yes, sweet electro. Drinks L10,000/€5.16. Cover L30,000/€15.50; Th L15,000/€7.75 (includes a drink). Open Tu-Su 11:30pm-4am. In summer, moves to Ciak Estate, V.d. Artigianato, 34 (☎06 5740093), near LunEUR (p. 136). AmEx.

CENTRO STORICO

see map p.310-311

Dub Club, V.d. Funari, 21a (☎06 68805024), in the Jewish Ghet Bask in the blue light of its subterranean, circular dance floor. Sp techno, funk, acid jazz, and exotica. Cover L10-20,000/€5.16. Op Tu-F 11pm-4am, Sa-Su 11pm-6am. Things get rolling at 2am. Clos most of summer.

Groove, V. Savelli, 10 (☎06 6872427). Head down V.d. Gover Vecchio from P. Pasquino and take the 2nd left. Look for the bla door and unlit neon sign. Lose it to acid jazz, funk, soul, and disco and Sa 1-drink minimum (L10,000/€5.16). Open Tu-Su 10pm-2am. Closed most of Aug.

TERMINI AND SAN LORENZO

see map p.312-313

NORTH OF TERMINI

Alien, V. Velletri, 13-19 (☎06 8412212). One of the biggest discos Rome attracts a well-dressed crowd and plays the house you know a love. As of this writing, the comfy chill-out room had not yet reach 1987. Cover L10-30,000 (includes a drink). Occasional theme nigh Open Tu-Sa 11pm-4am. Moves to Fregene during the summer.

Piper, V. Tagliamento, 9 (☎06 8414459). From V. XX Settemb take V. Piave (V. Salaria). Take a right on V. Po (V. Tagliamento). Alt natively, take bus #319 from Termini to Tagliamento. A popular club that occasionally ho gay nights. 70s, rock, disco, as well as the standard house and underground. Very g friendly all the time. Cover L15-35,000/€7.75-17.60 (includes a drink). Open Sa-Su 11p 3am; in summer Su 11pm-3am.

Club 52, V. Montebello, 102b (☎06 4441331). Take V. Volturno away from Termini; tu right on V. Montebello. Club 52 is the closest disco to Termini and has style to burn. Not y popular with the backpacker crowd; you can make it happen. One drink minimum. Open da 10pm-3:30am.

SOUTH OF TERMINI (ESQUILINO)

Qube, V. Portonaccio, 212 (☎06 4381005). From P. di Porta Maggiore, take V. Prenesti east; turn left on V. Portonaccio. Seedy neighborhood; plan to take a cab home. A warehou style disco, and one of Rome's biggest. Three packed dance floors. "Transmania," on Su, is o of Rome's most popular gay nights. Open Th-Su 11pm-4am. Cover L10-20,000/€5.16-10.3

Black Out, V. Saturnia, 18 (☎06 70496791). From the Colosseum, take V. Claudia (V Navicella/V. Gallia) southeast; turn right on V. Saturnia. Punk and Britpop. Occasional ban Cover L10-15,000/€5.16-7.75. Open Th-Sa 10:30pm-4am. Closed mid-June to August.

SAN LORENZO

Il Giardini di Adone, V.d. Reti, 38a (☎06 4454382). Though it fancies itself a "spaghe pub," the happy students who frequent this little place would remind you that tables are pro erly used for dancing, not for eating linguini. Cover L10,000/€5.16 (includes a drink). Op Tu-Sun 8pm-3am.

TESTACCIO

see map p.318

Welcome to the Carnival. A weekend night of drinking at ba in Trastevere is logically followed up with a trip south acro the river to the area surrounding V. Monte di Testaccio, t club kid's playground. Clubs here cater to goths, gays, plain' party-goers, and lots of scantily clad girls. Most *locali* Testaccio are open air or housed in subterranean tunnels bu into the side of an ancient Roman trashdump (note the potte shads lining some interiors) and so can withstand the heat th closes down many of Rome's nightspots. In June clubs spro up in the parking lot as part of **Testaccio Village**, an outdoor music and dancing extravaganza. The clubs on V. di Monte Testaccio (the road that circles the hill) have only meat-packers and car repair shops as neighbors, so let's get loud. We won't be waking anyone up.

Charro Cafe, V. di Monte Testaccio, 73 (☎06 5783064). So you wanted to go to Tijuana, but got stuck in Rome. Weep no more, *mis amigos:* make a run for Charro, home of the L5000/€2.58 tequila *bum bum*. Italians guzzling a good selection of beer (L10,000) and strong Mexican-themed mixed drinks (L10,000/€5.16) dance themselves silly to pop and house. Cover L10,000/€5.16 (includes a drink). Restaurant M-Sa 8:30-11:30pm, club 11:30pm-3:30am.

Aquarela, V. di Monte Testaccio, 64 ~~3~~ (☎06 5759058). Next door to Radio Londra. You want pottery shards? You got pottery shards. A fine example of urban renewal, Roman-style. Built out of ancient trash, then used for years as a vegetable market, the club consists in part of two underground tunnels that remain cool even when the party's heatin' up. Entrance L20,000/€10.30, which includes a drink. Arrive early to lounge in swank booths eating very expensive Brasilian food. Open Tu-Su 8:30pm-3am.

Caruso, V. di Monte Testaccio, 36 (☎06 5745019). No opera here: Caruso is a reliable venue for live salsa, DJed hip hop, and "music black" (rap and R&B). Five rooms of tropical decor, packed with writhing Latino wannabes on Saturday nights. Live music Fridays. Monthly *tessera* L15-20,000/€7.75-10.30. Open Tu and Th-Su 11:30pm-3am.

Radio Londra Caffè, V. di Monte Testaccio, 65b (☎06 5750044). Admit it: you've always fantasized about watching Italian bands cover rock classics badly. Packed with an energetic, good-looking, young crowd. Pint of Carlsberg L7000/€3.62. Pizza, *panini*, and hamburgers (L8-12,000/€4.13-6.20). Monthly *tessera* L10,000/€5.16. Open Su-F 9pm-3am, Sa 9pm-4am.

C.S.I.O.A. Villaggio Globale, Lungotevere Testaccio (☎06 57300329). Take bus #27 from Termini, get off before it crosses the river, and head left down the river. Women probably don't want to travel alone on the Lungotevere at night. One of the best-known *centri sociali* in Rome—your one-stop shop for all things countercultural. Housed in a huge Testaccio slaughterhouse, it hosts live music, films, art exhibits, poetry readings, African cuisine tastings, and more. Hours and cover vary, Friday nights are usually hopping.

Jungle, V. di Monte Testaccio, 95 (☎06 5746625). A small, smoky disco bar full of black leather-wearing Italian Goths variously dancing to the Cure and Italian pop. Extravagant, if somewhat disorienting, light effects. Cover L10-15,000/€5.16-7.75. Get in free before 11 on Saturday. Beer L10,000/€5.16; cocktails L15,000/€7.75. Open F-Sa 11pm-5am.

Aldebaron

Abbey Theater

Jonathan's Angels

INSIDE

Entertainment

Roman entertainment just isn't what it used to be. Back in the day, you could swing by the Colosseum to watch a man viciously clawed to death by a bear. Now, Romans seeking diversion are far more likely to go to the opera, a soccer game, or the latest Hollywood flick. Is this progress? Perhaps. But this is no reason for you, bloodthirsty traveler, to content your restless heart with eating *gelato* next to a monument or people-watching in a *piazza*. Rome is full of more entertaining entertainment options.

Roma C'è, Time Out, and **TrovaRoma** contain comprehensive lists of events and venues (see p. 24), and *Roma C'è* includes a section in English detailing goings-on of special interest to English speakers. Tourist offices (p. 23) also have lots of information on cultural activities—ask for *Un'Ospite a Roma* and a list of upcoming concerts. Of course, the city's walls are plastered with advertisements for upcoming concerts, plays, operas, parties, and circuses.

THEATER & CINEMA

A FUNNY THING HAPPENED ON THE WAY TO THE THEATER

Contrary to popular belief, there has been Roman theater since Anthony Lane donned a toga in *A Funny Thing Happened on the Way to the Forum.* Current shows are mostly toga-less, thankfully, and Rome is host to a number of quality productions. Shows range from mainstream musicals to black box experimental theater, and are mostly in Italian. For theater listings, check with a tourist office or the major venues listed below.

SPAGHETTI WESTERN

In attempting to jump-start the export of Italian film to America, Italian movie-makers decided to use Rome's Cinecittà studios to make American Westerns. Producers carefully sprinkled token, tow-headed Americans among the extras, and encouraged actors and directors to think up pseudonyms for their spaghetti Western output. Sergio Leone (whose emotion-driven camera work gave the world *The Good, the Bad, and the Ugly* (1966) and *A Fistful of Dollars* (1964)) went as "Bob Robertson."

The spaghetti Western flourished between 1961 and 1973, providing revenue to fund the art-house dreams of directors like Fellini. By the end of the 60s, many other Italian filmmakers had eagerly jumped into the odd but lucrative crossbreed genre. Some of these young talents, inspired by the flavor of the times, began making explicitly Marxist films that built on the Mexican setting of the Western to become what some called "the Zapata-Spaghetti plot." Unfortunately, few of these more revolutionary bandit and cow-herd-gringo flicks ever made it across the ocean to that mother lode of capitalism, distribution, and profits, the United States.

In summer, many plays spring up in open-air theaters, some of them free to the public. The city's two major festivals improve the pickings considerably with international productions: **Festival Roma-Europa** in summer and early fall; and **Festival d'Autunno** in fall. Check newspapers for listings. For information on plays and musicals in English, check tourist offices or the English section of *Roma C'è*. Useful websites include www.romece.it, www.musical.it, and www.comune.rome.it.

Teatro Argentina, Largo di Torre Argentina, 52 (☎06 68804601 or 06 6875445). Bus #64 from Termini. Considered to be the most important theater in Rome, Argentina hosts plays (in Italian), concerts, and ballets. Teatro Argentina is also the head of many drama/music festivals taking place throughout the year around Rome. Call for specific information. Box office open M-F 10am-3pm and 3-7pm, Sa 10am-2pm. Tickets around L40,000/€20.60; students L30,000/€15.50. AmEx/D/MC/V.

Teatro Colosseo, V. Capo d'Africa, 5a (☎06 7004932). M: B-Colosseo. Walk away from the station with the Colosseum to your right for 1 block. Offers a selection of new alternative plays (Italian or translated into Italian), but also has an English-speaking theater night (M in summer), featuring new works from American and British playwrights. Box office open Tu-Sa 8-10pm. Tickets L10-30,000/€5.16-15.50. Student discount L15,000/€7.75.

Teatro Ghione, V.d. Fornaci, 37 (☎/fax 06 6372294). Teatro Ghione puts up 10 plays a year, in addition to their musical program. For further information, see p. 198.

Teatro Nazionale, V.d. Viminale, 51 (☎06 47825140, 06 485498, or 06 4870614). M: A-Repubblica. From P. della Repubblica, walk 1 block toward Termini. Mostly original Italian plays; some translations of international works. Box office open daily 9-5pm. Tickets L35-50,000/€16.75-25.80; L30,000/€15.50 reduced. AmEx/D/MC/V.

Teatro Sistina, V. Sistina, 129 (☎06 4200711). M: A-Barberini. One of the biggies in mainstream musical theater. Recent productions: *Can-Can, Rugantino, L'Anatra all'Arancia,* exclusive engagement of *Sister Act* (in English), and The Who's *Tommy* (in Italian). Box office open daily 10am-1pm and 3:30-7pm. Tickets L35-200,000/€16.75-103.30. AmEx/D/MC/V.

Teatro Valle, V.d. Teatro Valle, 23a (☎06 68803794), near C. V. Emanuele II. A pretty little theater with an excellent repertoire. Box office open Tu-Sa 10am-7pm, Su 10am-1pm. Tickets L40,000. Closed from June-August.

CINEMA

Italy, much to the horror of cineastes foreign and native, insists on dubbing all the film and video it imports. Unless you know Italian well

and get a kick out of hearing Woody Allen speak it, this idiosyncrasy poses a definite obstacle to your Roman cinematic enjoyment. Undubbed English-language films are hard to find, especially more recent releases. Luckily, a few valorous Cineclubs show foreign films, old goodies, and an assortment of favorites in the original language. Check newspapers or *Roma C'è* for listings. A **v.o.** or **l.o.** in any listing means versione originale or *lingua originale* (i.e., not dubbed, usually with Italian subtitles). All first-run theaters offer lower priced tickets for the first two screenings of the day from Monday to Friday (around 4:30 pm and 6:30pm), as well as all day Wednesday.

Though popular Italian film of late has tended toward the banal, it's definitely worth checking out, particularly Nanni Moretti's (p. 59) thoughtful and humorous work. The antics of Roberto Benigni are amusing even without understanding dialogue. In summer, especially July, huge screens come up in *piazze* around the city for **outdoor film festivals.** These night shows can be a lot of fun, especially if you remember to bring insect repellent. One of the most popular is the **San Lorenzo sotto le Stelle** film festival at Villa Mercede, V. Tiburtina, 113, with shows at 9 and 11pm (tickets L10-15,000/€5.16-7.75). In addition, films are usually shown outdoors on the southern tip of Tiber Island. Visit the **I Love Rome** website (www.alfanet.it/welcomeItaly/roma/default.html) for an excellent searchable database of films, theaters, and showtimes. While *Roma C'è* isn't as comprehensive, it does a fairly good job of indexing films, even indexing by director.

Il Pasquino, P.S. Egidio, 10 (☎06 5833310 or 06 5803622), off P.S. Maria in Trastevere. Rome's biggest English-language movie theater. Program changes daily, so call for the schedule or stop by and pick one up. L12,000/€6.20; reduced L8000/€4.13. Theaters 2 and 3 are a film club, pay L2000/€1.03 for a 2-month membership and L10,000/€5.16 for the ticket. Look for the Roma International Film Festival during the summer.

Nuovo Sacher, Largo Ascianghi, 1 (☎06 5818116). This is the famed Italian director Nanni Moretti's theater, and shows a host of Indy films. M films in the original. L13,000/€6.70, matinee and W L8000/€4.13.

Giulio Cesare, V. G. Cesare, 229 (☎06 39720795). M: A-Ottaviano. M films in the original. Tickets L13,000/€6.70; matinee and W L8000/€4.13.

Greenwich, V. Bodoni, 59 (☎06 5745825). In Testaccio, near bus lines #75, 673, and 719. Films frequently in the original with Italian subtitles. Tickets L13,000/€6.70; matinee and W L8000/€4.13.

Stardust

Roman Forum

Festa de l'Unite

LIVE MUSIC & DANCE

CLASSICAL MUSIC & OPERA

The spectacular stage of the Baths of Caracalla (see p. 84) used to host summertime opera performances, but this lively tradition was halted once it was discovered that performers' voices—or "screeching," as the brochure kindly puts it—were bringing the ancient house down—literally. The live elephants that were brought on stage for productions of *Aïda* also did little to fortify the structure. There are still smaller classical music concerts that sporadically pop up in the crazy emperor's baths; or at least there will be until Renzo Piano's immense new auditorium, which has been in the works for several years now, is built.

There are many opportunities to see solid musical performances in Rome. *Telecom Italia* hosts a classical music series at the Teatro dell'Opera (see p. 198). At 9am on concert days, unsold tickets are given out for free at the box office. Be prepared to get in line early; tickets go on a first come, first served basis. Local churches often host free choral concerts—check newspapers tourist offices and church bulletin boards for details. Finally, and perhaps most interestingly, the *carabinieri* frequently give rousing concerts of various Italian composers in P. di San Ignazio and other outdoor forums free of charge. Other venues occasionally offer special discounts, so keep your eyes peeled.

PRINCIPAL VENUES

Accademia Nazionale di Santa Cecilia (main ☎06 3611064, info ☎06 6780742). This conservatory, named for the martyred patron saint of music (see p. 119 for the full story), was founded by Palestrina in the 16th century, and is home to Rome's official symphony orchestra. Orchestra and chamber concerts are held at the **Auditorio Pio,** V. di Conciliazione, 4 (☎06 68801044), near the Vatican, while the Academy's grand new concert hall is being built. Regular season runs Oct.-June, covering the classics, occasional special presentations, such as piano-playing jazz god Keith Jarrett, Jimi Hendrix played by a string quartet. From late June-late July, the company moves outdoors to the *nymphaeum* in Villa Giulia or to the Baths of Caracalla; see **Summer Events,** below. Auditorio Pio box office open Th-Tu 10:20am-1:30pm and 3-6pm, and until showtime on concert days. Tickets L20-50,000/€10.30-25.80. Auditorio Pio's acoustics are notoriously bad, so you might want to splurge on expensive seats to hear more.

Auditorium del Foro Italico, P. Lauro de Bosis (☎06 36865625), near P. Mancini. Home of Rome's RAI Orchestra, this auditorium hosts various classical music concerts. Season runs Oct.-June. Tickets L20-50,000/€10.30-25.80.

Teatro Ghione, V.d. Fornaci, 37 (☎06 6372294), near the Vatican. This red velvet theater hosts Euromusica's classical concerts and other musical guests throughout its season. Season Oct.-Apr. Box office open daily 10:30am-1pm and 4-8pm, with an English-speaking staff. Tickets from L15,000/€7.75. Call for info on morning concerts, with discounts.

Teatro Olimpico, P. Gentile da Fabriano, 17 (☎06 3265991). This newer auditorium with good acoustics is home to many different classical music, theater, and dance events. Season runs Oct.-May. Box office open daily 11am-7pm.

Teatro dell'Opera di Roma, V. Firenze, 72 (main ☎06 481601, info ☎800 016665; www.themix.it). The theater also runs seasonal concerts at Stadio di Olimpico and the Baths of Caracalla (primarily in the summer). Look out for occasional performances during the year at the Teatro Valle, the Teatro Manzoni, and the Loggia della Villa Medici. Box office open M 9-1:30pm, Tu-Sa 9-4pm.Tickets run L50-100,000/€25.80-51.60; students L25,000.

SUMMER EVENTS

The classical scene in Rome goes wild in summer. The smaller festivals that run from mid-May to August are just parts of the larger Roma Estate festival, a city-wide cultural binge featuring work in various genres. (For full information about the festival, consult www.romaestate.com.) Also popular is the Opera-festival di Roma (☎06 5691493), held in the Teatro dell'Opera di Roma. It all starts with the Festa Europea della Musica, a weekend of non-stop music at the end of June—most concerts are free and in fabulous locations (imagine Michalenagelo's Campidoglio in orange and purple strobe lights...) A hop, skip, and jump from Rome is the **Spoleto Festival** in Umbria (☎06 3210288). This world-renowned music and art fest takes place during the last week of June and first week of July. Visit the festival's Rome office at V. Beccaria, 18, for more information. For tickets to summer events, try one of the following venues:

Villa Giulia/Santa Cecilia ticket office, P. della Villa Giulia, 9 (☎06 3611064 or 063611833, credit card reservations ☎06 68801044), in Villa Borghese. The summer home of the Accademia Nazionale di Santa Cecilia. Open Tu-Sa 10am-2pm, Su 10am-1pm. Also buy tickets at Villa Giulia's Etruscan Museum (see p. 153).

Theater of Marcellus, V.d. Teatro di Marcello, 44, hosts evening concerts organized by the Associazione Il Tempietto (see below). Tickets L30,000/€15.50.

MUSIC ASSOCIATIONS

The following associations organize and host concerts and recitals—contact them directly for a full schedule of events, or check newspapers for weekly listings.

Amici di Castel Sant'Angelo, (☎06 8456192). Livens up Hadrian's Mausoleum with free concerts Sa 9pm. Casual concerts are aimed at those simply strolling by the Castel. Look for occasional concerts by the Accademia Filarmonica Romana and the Coro Polifonico Romano.

Associazione Il Tempietto, V. in Selci, 47 (☎06 4814800). Organizes frequent small concerts in churches and, in summer, at the **Theater of Marcellus.** Tickets L30,000/€15.50, though some concerts held in church venues are free.

JAZZ

Rome is no New Orleans. It's no Chicago. It's not even Paris. Rome is Rome (*Roma C'è*, as newsstands will tell you). Even so, jazz swings on within the confines of the eternally hip city. Listings are in *Roma C'è* and *Time Out;* the latter does a slightly better job with jazz, though *Roma C'è* tends to translate most of their jazz listings into English. During the summer, Alexanderplatz (see below) organizes the popular **Jazz & Image** festival, in the **Villa Celimontana,** the ruin-filled park that stretches from the Colosseum to the Baths of Caracalla. For tickets, call **ORBIS** (☎06 5897807). From mid-June to mid-August, films about jazz show on a huge outdoor screen at 9pm. Entrance is usually around L15,000/€7.75, though the price may be hiked up significantly (L40,000/€20.60) for bigger names. In past years, the festival has hosted the Manhattan Transfer, Branford Marsalis, Herbie Hancock, Ray Brown, and Cedar Walton. The world-renowned **Umbria Jazz Festival** in July takes place in Perugia, only a few hours away by train. Past performers include Joao Gilberto, B. B. King, Joe Henderson, and Sonny Rollins (call ☎075 5733363 for information).

PRINCIPAL VENUES

The streets of Trastevere are the best romping grounds for those in search of a good jazz joint. Wander the winding streets, listening for sax riffs and vocalists doing a damn good job with mostly English lyrics, or try some of our favorites:

Alexanderplatz Jazz Club, V. Ostia, 9 (☎06 39742171). M: A-Ottaviano. Near Vatican City. From the station, head west on V. G. Cesare, take 2nd right onto V. Leone IV and 1st left onto V. Ostia. Night buses to P. Venezia and Termini leave from P. Clodio. Known as one of Europe's best jazz clubs, stuffy, smoky atmosphere conveys the mythical feeling of a 40s jazz joint, while sparkling walls and a funky bar suggest a modern side. Read messages left on the walls by the greats who played here, from old pros like Art Farmer and Cedar Walton to young stars like Steve Coleman and Josh Redman. Cocktails L12,000/€6.20. Required *tessera* (L12,000/€6.20), good for 2mos. Open Sept.-June daily 9pm-2am. Shows start 10:30pm.

Big Mama, V.S. Francesco a Ripa, 18 (☎06 5812551), off V. di Trastevere on the left as you face the river. Blues, blues, and more blues. A *tessera* (L20,000/€10.30) is valid for a year and allows you into the club's many free concerts. Occasional L10,000/€5.16 cover for big-name groups. Open Oct.-June daily 9pm-1:30am (sometimes closed Su and M).

Stardust, V. dei Rienzi, 4 (☎06 58320875). Take a right off V. Lungaretta onto V.d. Moro right before P.S. Maria in Trastevere; V. dei Renzi is the 2nd street on the left. Classy cocktail bar; great to chill and listen to live jazz. When's the next time you'll to get to do it while eating crepes? Open daily 7pm-4am; in winter M-F 1:30pm-3am, Sa-Su 11am-2am.

Selarum, V. dei Fienaroli, 12 (☎06 5819130). Off V. di Fratte di Trastevere. More jazz-while-you-eat, as well as South American and blues acts. Treat yourself to some dessert wines (L8-13,000/€4.13-6.70). A gourmet dessert mecca; try the scrumptious *mandorlita* (chocolate, amaretto, and whipped cream; L15,000/€7.75). Open May-Oct. daily 9pm-2am. Music usually starts around 10:30pm.

Berimbau, V. dei Fienaroli, 30b (☎06 5813249). Rome's premier location for Brazilian music. Live music followed by raging disco of salsa, merengue, and a variety of other Latin music. Cover L10-25,000/€5.16-12.90, includes 1 drink. Open W-Su 10:30pm-3:30am.

ROCK & POP

Big-name shows (which usually play at the **Palazzo dello Sport** in EUR or at the **Foro Italico** north of Flaminio) will also invariably have massive poster campaigns. If you still feel inadequately in touch with what the cool kids are up to, ticket agencies and tourist offices have information on big upcoming shows. In summer, the city's pop and rock music scene explodes with outdoor concerts and festivals lasting late into the night. **Ticket agencies** (see p. 294 for a list of them) can arrange reservations and provide more information about major rock concerts. Tickets and info for many concerts are also available at the RicordiMedia (see p. 210) shops scattered throughout the city. The more popular festivals and performances include:

Roma Live, at the Stadio Olimpico. Concerts by the likes of Deep Purple, the Backstreet Boys, Ziggy Marley, Lou Reed, and Joan Baez, among others.

Testaccio Village, V. di Monte Testaccio, 16 (☎06 57287661). Live, mostly local music of all kinds from mid-June to mid-Sept. every night around 9pm.

Roma Incontra il Mondo (☎06 4180369 or 06 58201564), a festival of world music and *"musica etnica,"* livens up the lake in Villa Ada at V. di Ponte Salario. Performers have included the late Nusrat Fateh Ali Khan, Ruben Gonzales, and Blonde Redhead. Late June-early Sept. 6pm-whenever.

Fiesta, Ippodrome di Capannelle, V. Appia, 1243 (☎06 71299855; www.fiesta.it), an extremely popular festival running all summer, featuring all things Latin American. Performers have included Cesaria Evora, Jose Feliciano, and Burning Spear. Don't know how to salsa? Don't worry, you too will be assimilated. Attendance can swell to over 30,000 on weekends.

DANCE

The **Rome Opera Ballet,** affiliated with the **Teatro dell'Opera,** shares its ticket office, information line, and, sometimes, its stage. The ballet company stages joint performances with the opera company in the summer at P. di Siena in Villa Borghese. During the rest of the year, the company performs at the ex-Aquarium, in P. Fanti, south of Termini. (☎06 481601, toll-free info ☎800 016665.) Another tiny venue, a bit farther out, is **Argilia Teatri,** at V.d. Argilia, 18 (☎06 6381058). It can help when you've got to have ethnic dancing, and you've got to have it now. In summer, there is also a festival of dance, art, and culture called **RomaEuropa,** with venues throughout the city. Call ☎06 4742319 or 06 4742286 for information or pick up a program at the **Museo degli Strumenti Musicali** in P.S. Croce in Gerusalemme, one of the performance locations. The theaters listed above may also host dance performances.

SPECTATOR SPORTS

While other spectator sports may exist in Rome (and the key word is "may"), the only one that matters is **calcio** (soccer). Rome has two teams in Italy's Serie A, the most prestigious league in the world: **A.S. Roma** and **S.S. Lazio.** Traditionally, Lazio's fans come from the suburbs and countryside around Rome, while Roma fans are from the city itself, especially the Centro Storico, Trastevere, Testaccio, and the Jewish Ghetto. Lazio, which is literally owned by the man from Del Monte, has lately spent close to a hundred billion *lire* on a revolving cast of expensive players, while Roma relies on the genius of superstar Italian playmaker Francesco Totti, protagonist of the 2000 European national championship, and legendary Argentine striker Gabriel Batistuta.

Games at the **Stadio Olimpico,** in the Foro Italico, are as close to the spectacles that used to happen in the Colosseum as you're going to find these days: *tifosi*, as the hardcore fans are called, show up hours before the games to drink, sing team songs, and taunt rivals. During the thrilling games, fans chant, stomp, and sing their teams on to victory, or at least an honorable defeat. Unfortunately, the cheering sometimes turns ugly, as evidenced by several incidences of Lazio fans displaying racist banners and booing minority players during the last season. For the most part, though, the celebrations are cheerful and melodious: flags are waved madly to the strains of the "Macarena," while Queen's "We Are the Champions" blends imperceptibly into the inspiring sound of fight songs being sung to the tune of the "Battle Hymn of the Republic" by tens of thousands of fans in unison. League matches are held almost every Sunday (sometimes Saturdays) from September to June, with European cup matches often played mid-week. The can't-miss appointments of the season are the two Roma-Lazio *derby* matches, which often prove decisive in the race for the championship. While each team has close to 50,000 season ticket holders, they also sell single-game tickets, which typically start at L30,000/€15.50. Tickets can be bought at the stadium box office before games (although the lines are long and tickets often run out), and also at the team's stores: **A.S. Roma Store,** P. Colonna, 360 (☎ 06 6786514), just off V.d. Corso; and **Lazio Point,** V. Farini, 24 (☎ 06 4826688).

The ultra-trendy, world class **Concorso Ippico Internazionale** (International Horse Show) is held at P. di Siena in the Villa Borghese in May. For information, check *Roma C'è* or call CSIO. (☎ 06 3279939.) The beginning of May also sees the holding of the **Italian Open Tennis Championship,** a warm-up event for the French Open which draws many of the world's top players. For more information, call the Italian Tennis Federation (☎ 06 3233807). Tickets for many sporting events can be bought at the **Orbis Agency,** P. dell'Esquilino, 37 (☎ 06 4827403).

Fiesta de l'Unite

Baths of Caracalla

Stardust

GE

INSIDE

Shopping

You can buy damn near anything in Rome. Here we list only frivolities, so, if you're looking for sustenance, see **Food and Wine,** p. 180. Go now, indulge, you filthy capitalist pig.

CLOTHING & SHOES

Everything you need to know about Italian fashion is summed up in one simple phrase: *la bella figura.* This term describes a beautiful, well-dressed, put together woman, and it is taken very, very seriously in Rome—think Sophia Loren on a good day. But since many of us don't have Sophia's wardrobe, budget, or physical assets (let alone all three), here's a down-and-dirty guide to *la bella figura.* Begin with a pair of big, dark sunglasses with a (preferably gold) logo prominently displayed. If you're under forty, consider tinted sunglasses—but please, no blue or purple. Then you'll need a bag; **Prada** and **Gucci** will immediately increase your social status by a factor of ten, while **Louis Vuitton** and **Fendi** are also acceptable. Logos, of course, should continue to be prominent, and it's also wise to tuck in a pack of cigarettes and an especially expensive telefonino with a signature ring. As for shoes the rules are simple: wear heels. High heels. Very high heels. All the time. Ignore cobblestones, steep stairs, and the high cost of cabs—the Romans all do. With your key accessories in place, wear black. All black, all the time. For men, the best thing to do is to buy one glorious Italian suit—**Armani** or **Dolce & Gabanna**—and then spend the rest of your life praying you don't spill.

Some advice before setting out with credit card in hand: sales in Italy happen twice a year, in mid-January and mid-July. Don't be surprised if you can't try on everything in all stores. Finally, be clear about exchanges and returns *before* giving a store your money; Europe is not exactly known for its customer service. These listings are a teaser; *Roma C'è* publishes a comprehensive shopping guide (in bookstores, about L10,000/€5.16). For those über-shoppers among you, check out our power-hour of a shopping tour, below.

THOU SHALT NOT WANT

Conventional wisdom says that the V. Condotti is *the* shopping street in Rome. While some may argue in favor of V.d. Babuino, those who are *really* in the know head to Via de'Cestari. On this sidestreet next door to the Pantheon,servants of the Christian god meet up with the omnipresent gods and goddesses of fashion. Style-savvy popes, cardinals, priests, and nuns head to **Ghezzi,** at V. de'Cestari 32-3, where mitres (gold and black bishop's hats) retail for L870,000. Nun-pajamas at **De Ritis,** V. Cestari 45-51, sell for L65,000, if you like your nightwear conservative. However, beware, and never try to haggle with those selling clothes on behalf of the almighty. As sales assistants are quick to note—God has yet to go out of style.

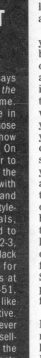

VENI, VIDI, VERSACE

For this shopping tour, you'll need comfy shoes, sharp elbows and a healthy sense of irony. Wallets, be they empty or full, are not necessary, but a bottle of water is a sage idea.

Begin, as one must, at the Spanish Steps. With your back to the steps and facing Via Condotti, bow three times with arms outstretched. On the corner of the piazza and V.d. Carozze are **Kriza** and **Sergio Rossi's** shoes; sigh and continue walking left to reach **Dolce & Gabbana,** where the only thing to distract you from the eye-candy in the window is the piece of man-candy selling it to you. Now take a deep breath, put your hands on your hips (the better to fend off over-sized designer shopping bags) and head down the holy strip of shopping, **V. Condotti.** Immediately to your right lies **Prada,** establishing its supremacy at the top of the street. Careful mannequin-scrutiny is required at this stop, as Prada's windows often set the standard for the season's fashions, but this paragon also merits a trip inside. Take the glass elevator to the second floor. On your left, a round room shows shoes (including children's sizes, for those toddlers with an affinity for lizard skin) and a **spectacular view** of the Spanish Steps. Rest your envious feet while sipping over-priced cappucino in a gilt chair at the famous **Antico Caffe Greco** next door.

As you descend from the lofty heights of Prada, cross the street to **Gucci.** Once inside, do remember that it's much cooler to ask about their line of **motorino helmets** than their handbags. Next-door is **Bulgari,** the undisputed King of Italian jewelry—not to mention the best window displays in all of Rome. A few years back, one display had passersby searching a triangular pile of birch-logs for tiny diamond studs, rings, and bracelets in Bulgari's take on finding "diamonds in the rough." Across the street, **Salvatore Ferragamo's** women's boutique shows classically conservative clothing and beautifully crafted shoes. Inside, hang life-size photographs of Audrey Hepburn, with Salvatore himself at her Ferragamo-shorn feet. **Hermes** displays their trade-mark scarves nearby (guessing what exotic animal will next grace their silk creations has become a neighborhood ritual). **Valentino's Women's Boutique** lies across the street, and serves as the patron saint of *haute-couture* in Rome. Look for one of Valentino's glorious gowns in his signature color, fire-engine red. The ubiquitous logos in the **Louis Vuitton** store next door shouldn't be missed, but try to avoid visiting right after lunch—the lines often stretch all the way to Valentino.

At this point veer off the sacred Condotti, for the shops on **V. Bocca di Leone** cannot be missed without seriously pissing off the style gods. These stores are either discretely elegant, or so well established that they don't need the added status of a V. Condotti address. **Versace Jeans** strikes a youthful note with its fluorescent color scheme, while **Valentino's Men's Boutique** lends an air of paternal distinction, catering to Rome's most distinguished gentlemen. Now cross V.d. Corso, heading to the left of the fork and onto **V. Fontanella Borghese.** Often overlooked by power-shoppers, this street is one of Rome's best. On the left, known for their high-end, avant-guard fashion and lush furs, **Fendi** (and younger sibling **Fendissime**) push the envelope further than any of their contemporaries. If you're hungry, lunch on air kisses and prosecco in leather banquets with well-dressed Italians at **Resturante Ciampini,** on the corner. At 68a Via Fontanella Borghese is the alitier of **Sorelle Fontana,** a spot many feel should be included on the registry of Roman monuments. The Fontana sisters have been quietly creating astounding gowns for queens, duchesses, Jackie O. and the occasional lucky Roman since the 1930s. To the left, continue on V.d. Lupa among intriguing boutiques, framers and upholsterers to V. Preffetti. Go left onto this street, then another left onto V. Campo Marzio. From there, your first right will lead you into Piazza San Lorenzo in Lucia, and to the best profumeria in Rome, **Materozzoli,** which leads you to **V.d. Corso** where you can shop till your heart's content—if it isn't already.

Piazza di Spagna

BOUTIQUES

No matter what anti-capitalist mantra you may espouse, you know you've secretly lusted after that Versace jacket or MaxMara skirt, no matter how ideologically impure it seems. So indulge. Particularly for those coming to Italy from overseas, Rome is one of the best places in the world to sate these forbidden desires, since prices in the boutiques here are well below those in the US and Australia. A stop at Prada is a must; if not to admire the bags, then for the unparalleled view of the Spanish steps from the second floor.

Centro Storico

Bruno Magli, V.d. Gambaro, 1 (☎06 6793802).

Dolce & Gabbana, P. di Spagna, 82-83 (☎06 6792294). Who wouldn't kill for their suits?

Emporio Armani, V.d. Baubino, 140(☎06 36002197). Houses the less expensive end of the Armani line.

Fendi, V. Borgogna, 36-40 (☎06 6794824).

Genny, P. di Spagna, 27 (☎06 6796074).

Gianni Versace, Men: V. Borgogna, 24-25 (☎06 6795037). Women: V. Bocca di Leone, 26 (☎06 6780521).

Giorgio Armani, V.d. Condotti, 75 (☎06 6991460).

Gucci, V.d. Condotti, 8 (☎06 6789340).

Krizia, P. di Spagna, 87 (☎06 6793772).

Laura Biagiotti, V. Borgogna, 43-44(☎06 6795040).

Lacoste, V. Giulia, 18 (☎06 6869590).

Louis Vuitton, V.d. Condotti, 15 (☎06 69940000).

Window Shopping

Max Mara, V.d. Condotti, 17-19. (☎06 6781144).

Moschino, V. Borgognona, 32a (☎06 69922104).

Missoni, P. di Spagna, 78 (☎06 6792555).

Prada, V.d. Condotti, 92-95 (☎06 6790897).

RoccoBarocco, P. di Spagna, 93 (☎06 6797914).

Salvatore Ferragamo, Men: V.d. Condotti, 66 (☎06 6791017). Women: V.d. Condotti, 72-74 (☎06 6792297).

Valentino, V.d. Condotti, 13 (☎06 6790479).

CHEAP AND CHIC

Designer emporiums such as **Cenci,** V. Campo Marzio 1-7 (☎06 6990681), and **David's of Rome** stock many lines of designer clothes at lower prices. Workers won't be as ready to prostrate themselves before you for the contents of your wallet, and you have to buy directly off the rack. These are an especially good deal during the sale months of January and July; look for the *Saldi* sign in the window.

Diesel, V.d. Corso, 186 (☎06 6783933). Off V.d. Condotti. *The* label in retro fashion is surprisingly high-octane. No one said that being a fashion plate was easy. Prices are cheaper than in the US, so it's worth the visit.

Mariotti Boutique, V.d. Frezza 20 (☎06 3227126). This elegant boutique sells modern, sophisticated clothes in gorgeous materials. Prices are steep; watch for the significant sales. Open M 4-8pm, Tu-Sa 10am-1:30pm and 4-8pm; winter M 3:30-7:30pm, Tu-Sa 10am-1:30pm and 3:30-7:30pm. AmEx/MC/V.

Ethic, V.d. Corso, 94 (☎06 3600211091) and V.d. Carozze, 20. The hip yet less adventurous can find a balance between the avant garde and tasteful. Prices won't break the bank.

David Mayer, V.d. Corso, 168 (☎06 69202097), V. Cola di Rienzo (☎06 3243303). www.davidmayer.com. For the inner *fasionista* in all men, David Mayer offers good-loooking attire that doesn't require a trust fund. A short-sleeved button-down shirt is L85,000/€43.90, a sweater L173,000/€89.35, and their popular shoes run L235,000/€121.37.

Invicta, V.d. Baubino, 28 (☎06 36001737) or V.d. Corso, 82-3. (☎06 3613742). When the time has come for a garishly colored backpack (as it surely will), run, don't walk, to Invicta. Chartreuse never looked so good on a backpack. Neither did hot pink or neon blue. Though the senses rebel, social conformity says yes.

Light, V. Nazionale, 197 (☎06 4741612). If leather jackets and leopard print fail to satisfy your disco cravings, then head here, where you'll find *silver* leather jackets and *fuchsia* leopard printed dresses. A great spot to get disco duds, Light carries many youthful brands–Roberto Cavalli, RoccoBarocco, Moschino, etc.

Max&Co, V.d. Condotti, 46-46a (☎06 6787946; also at V. Nazionale, 56). The less expensive line of Max Mara, Max&Co. carries more youthful, colorful clothes.

Simona, V.d. Corso, 82-3 (☎06 3613742 or 06 36001836). This lingerie store has an amusing array of name-brand lingerie, as well as colorful bathing suits during the summer. Prices aren't cheap, but it's full of Italians.

Stefanel, V.d. Corso, 295 (☎06 6789854; www.stefanel.it.). The upscale version of Benetton, with higher prices to match. Skirts L89,000/€45.96; basic dresses L179,000/€92.45; for men: jeans L129,000/€66.62 and button-down shirts L129,000/€66.62.

Xandrine, V.d. Croce, 88 (☎06 6786201). Indulge your inner Princess in this temple to sequins and chiffon. A couture shop that specializes in evening wear. Many ready-to-wear dresses hang along the walls, but if you'd rather have your ball gown in chartreuse taffeta, get your measurements taken and come back in 3 days.

DEPARTMENT STORES

While the Romans lap up American entertainment and munch on fries from McDonalds, one American idea can't seem to get off the ground—the department store. Unlike New York or Paris, Rome's department stores tend to cater to the dowdy and conservative, rather than the young and beautiful. However, the prices are right, and these stores are excellent places to buy necessities like socks and underwear, should the need ever arise.

La Rinascente, Largo Chigi, 20-21 (☎06 6797691; www.rinascenteshopping.com), just off V.d. Corso. The classiest of the bunch, La Rinascente carries sensible, conservative clothing for men, women and children. Caters toward middle-aged crowd; larger sizes available; wide selection of lingerie in basement. Men's khaki shorts L65,000/€33.57; linen dress L200,000/€103.29. Open M-Sa 9:30am-8pm, Su 10:30am-6pm.

COIN, V. Cola di Rienzo, 173 (☎06 3380750). Also P. Appio, 7 (☎06 7080020) and V. Mantova, 1 (☎06 8415884), near Porta Pia. By far the most useful of Rome's department stores, Coin carries attractive, functional merchandise at reasonable prices. Some good deals, especially on cosmetics. All open M-Sa 10am-8pm.

UPIM, V. Nazionale, 215 (☎800 824040). Upim is the bargain basement of department stores in Rome, and their goods tend to be the uninspiring. But if you need a pair of socks, Upim's a cheap, solid option.

Leather Goods

SHOES

It's said that a building's only as good as its foundation. And in Italy, you're only as good as your shoes. In a city where Birkenstocks are only sold at Religious outfitters (Jesus wore sandals, remember), being well shod is not a luxury, but a way of life. Rome may have more shoe stores per square kilometer than any other city in the world, and offers everything from L25,000 lire sandals at outdoor markets to jewel-encrusted silk numbers whose prices are "available upon request." Luckily, there are many stylish, moderately priced stores—so trade your flip-flops for leather sandals, and step out in style. If you feel the perverse desire to tease yourself, drool in front of the picture-perfect windows of Salvatore Ferragamo, Bruno Magli, Sergio Rossi and Raphael Salato—all have stores within walking distance of the Spanish Steps, naturally. For those that judge status in terms of small red stripes or interlocking G's, Prada and Gucci, on V. Condotti, will disdainfully help you enhance Italy's economy. If your paycheck remains within the world of the mortal, the shops listed below will leave you footloose and less lire-free.

Shoes

Trancanelli, P. Cola di Rienzo, 84 (☎06 3234503), V.d. Croce 68-9 (☎06 6791503). This is where the young and the restless of Rome buy their shoes. A must for anyone looking to return home well-shod, with their bank account in tact.

Bata, V. Nazionale, 88a (☎06 6791570), V.d. Due Macelli, 45 (☎06 4824529). With 250 shops in Italy and 6,000 shops world-wide stocked floor to ceiling with functional, affordable shoes that look great, Bata deserves an entire row of gold stars. Bata also has a knack for turning out shoes that look remarkably like Prada's, but at a fraction of the price.

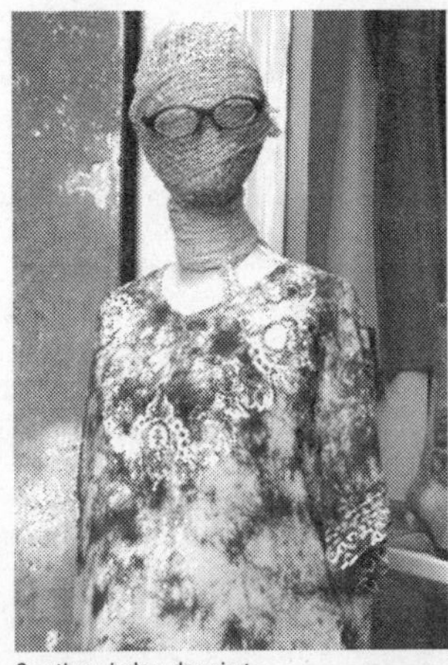
Creative window dressing

Mada, V.d. Croce, 57 (☎06 6798660). A very popular women's shoe store, Mada has been called a "must" for Roman women. Open Tu-Sa 9:30am-1pm and 3:30-7:30pm, M 9:30am-1pm.

Brugnoli Calzature, V. Ripetta, 26 (☎06 3600 1889). Also at V.S. Giacomo, 25 (☎06 3612325). A shoe store selling classic footwear for men and women, along with belts and purses to complete the leather selection. Open Tu-Sa 9:30am-1pm and 3:30-7:30pm, M 9:30am-1pm.

Elisheva, V.d. Baullari, 19 (☎06 6871747) near Campo dei Fiori; P. Irnerio, 41, (☎06 66016077). You want to go out. You can't go out in Italy without high, high heels. You go to Elisheva, and problem solved. A boutique with sexy sandals, as well as a range of daytime flats. Open daily 9:30am-8pm. MC/V.

Loco, V.d. Baullari, 22, near Campo di Fiori. (☎06 68808216; loco@mclink.it, www.loco.com), Loco sells fun, affordable shoes for a younger crowd. Perhaps the only place in Rome that sells flip-flops in candy colors (L30-45,000/€15-23.24).

NON-PRODUCE MARKETS

Rome's markets lay the best and the worst of Rome bare. Markets often have the best deals in town on produce, clothing, and household items, but times and prices vary, pickpockets abound, and successful bargaining is hard work. Arrive at markets early for the best selection, and buy late for the best deals. Expect to bargain, especially on clothing. Often, prices aren't marked in order to allow the vendor to size you up. (As such, don't come to Porta Portese looking as though you just left the Four Seasons.) The best strategy is to check the prices of other vendors to get a base line cost, and then to bargain in the best Italian you can muster. Be prepared to counter the seller's first offer and don't be surprised if a vendor feigns offense—it's all part of the game. Be prepared for a hard sell, and know when to bust out the *"No, grazie"* and walk away. Also, always, *always* check your labels carefully before you buy anything—especially leather jackets. For markets that sell primarily food, see p. 180. Hours are never set in stone—markets begin when everyone gets there and end when they get bored.

Porta Portese, in Trastevere at Porta Portese. Tram #8. A fever dream of a market, where booths selling clothing, shoes, jewelry, bags, toilets, and anything else that you can imagine, extend beyond the horizon. The biggest in Rome–arrive early for the best selection, late for the best bargains. Keep your money close to your person, as this is a notorious spot for pick-pockets. Open Su 5am-2pm.

Borghetto Flaminio–Rigattieri per Hobby, P. della Marina, 32, Borghetto Flaminio. Near the Olympic Stadium. A market primarily dedicated to hobbies of all sorts; if you want it, chances are you can probably find it. L3000. Open Su 5pm-midnight.

Via Sannio, near M: San Giovanni. Clothing and shoe stalls line up to peddle inexpensive new and used wares. Very cheap shoes. Open M-Sa 8:30am-1:30pm.

MISCELLANEOUS

JEWELRY

Rome boasts a large array of jewelers, and many carry work that is quite original and creative. **Bulgari's** windows (V. Condotti 11) are the best in Rome, and celebrities are often spotted at **Massoni,** at the corner of V. Condotti and Largo Goldoni.

Alcozer, V.d. Carozze, 48 (☎06 6791388). Near P. di Spagna. Gorgeous old-world jewelry at remarkably decent prices. Earrings are a bargain at L42,000/€21.69; get a jeweled crucifix Lucrezia Borgia would've been proud of for L250,000/€129.11. Open M 10-2pm, Tu-Sa 10am-1:30pm and 3:30-7:30pm. AmEx/MC/V.

Furla, V.d. Corso, 481 (☎06 36003619). For those who can't afford Bulgari but still like to sparkle, Furla's your best bet. An Italian staple, Furla sells silver jewelry (necklaces L150,000/€77.47) as well as leather handbags (L300,000/€154.94), wallets (L95,000/€49.06), and belts.

Pianegonda, V.d. Croce, 42 (☎06 6786402; ros.v@iol.itwww.pianegondaitalia.com.) Selling provocative jewelry to the upscale client, Pianegonda has comered the market on industrial chic.

Luisella Mariotti, V. di Gesu e Maria, 20a (☎06 3201320; luisella_mariotti@yahoo.it). Between the Spanish Steps and P. del Popolo. This tiny boutique carries funky, original costume jewelry. The style matches the chic-chic location, but prices are reasonable; L70,000/€36.15 will get you a sizeable bracelet.

Siragusa, V.d. Carrozze, 64 (☎06 6797085). Only in Rome could you find an archaeological jewller, but Siragusa is just that, and a darn good one. Ancient coins are set into new gold settings for rings, cuff links, etc. Prices match high quality.

PROFUMERIAS

Perhaps it's the lack of deoderant, perhaps it's the secret to Roman lovers, but in Rome, there's a profumeria on every block.

Materozzoli, P.S. Lorenzo in Lucina, 5, off V.d. Corso (☎06 68892686). This old-world Profumeria carries everything from the exclusive Aqua di Parma line to shaving brushes. Hard to find perfumes and colognes. M 3:30-7:30pm, Tu-Sa 10-1:30, 3:30-7:30pm. Closed two weeks in Aug.

Estivi, V.V.E. Orlando 92-3, near Repubblica (☎06 4881731), V. Condotti 23 (☎06 066792370), P. Barberini, 13 (☎06 4881110). This all-purpose profumeria carries everything from designer sunglasses to floral-printed bathing caps, with 2 floors of perfumes in between. As if all that weren't enough, the V.E. Orlando branch also boasts an indoor waterfall. Open M-Sa 9am-8pm. AmEx/MC/V.

Lekythos, V. Ripetta 16. (☎06 3202012), other locations around the city, including V.d. Quatro Fonata, near V. Nazionale. A Greek store that carries a wide variety of international scents and make-up. Unfortunately, the sea sponges are not for sale. Open M-Sa 10am-1pm and 4-7pm. AmEx/MC/V.

STATIONARY STORES

Campo Marzio Penne, V. Campo Marzio, 41 (☎06 68807877). Gorgeous fountain pens (L50,000/€25.82 and up) and leather goods–the brightly colored diaries and photo albums (L40,000/€20.66) are a welcome respite from typical Italian leathergoods. The small address books (L12,000/€6.20) make great presents.

Vertecchi, V. Croce, 70 (☎06 6790155), by the Spanish Steps. This should be your first stop for all stationary needs. A wide supply of paper and pens, with party supplies and interesting wrapping paper.

TOYS

Don Chisciotte, V. A. Brunetti, 21a (☎06 3224515; www.gallerisdonchisciotte.com.) A bit like walking into Alice's Wonderland, Giuliano de Marsanich's store sells marionettes, puppet theaters, and a wide selection of lead soldiers. For that special child, or the one that's never grown up. Marionettes and soldiers start at L30,000/€15.49. Open M-Sa 10:00am-1:30pm and 4-7:30pm. Closed Aug.

HOME FURNISHINGS

B.B.K., V.d. Frezza, 60. Although B.B. king is not known to frequent this venue, B.B.K. is still attractive for its chic household necessities (wicker tables) and accents (assorted pots, jars, and vases). Not dirt cheap, but helpful in making your hovel home

C.U.C.I.N.A., V. Mario de Fiorio, 65 (☎06 6791275); V. Flamminia Vecchia, 679 (☎06 3332202); P. Euclide, 40 (☎06 6785653). Lots of spiffy kitchen gadgets, particularly of the ultra-shiny chrome variety. AmEx/MC/V.

Modigliani, V.d. Condotti, 24 (☎06 6785653). A large selection of smaller (and quite elegant) housewares. Some of the glassware and ceramic pieces are just gorgeous; and usually priced accordingly.

Linn sui, V.d. Boschetto, 79 (☎06 4820761). If a bed isn't your thing, you can still find a place to lay your head on an average-priced futon (L600,000/€309.87). Open M-Sa 10am-1pm and 4-7:30pm. MC/V.

Archidomus, V. Leonardo da Vinci, 256 (☎06 547945), in Ostiense. Beds, couches, tables, and other such large objects at discounted prices. Open M 4-8pm, Tu-Sa 10am-1pm and 4-8pm. AmEx/MC/V.

UPIM, V. Nazionale 215 (☎800 824040; www.upim.it). Come here for sheets and other household goods at reasonable prices. The branch at S. Maria Maggiore is the cheapest, but the V. Arenula branch tends to have better goods.

MUSIC

Over-stuffed lovers and undying affection parade through the weird wide world of Italian pop. (If you're ready to face this dark side of humanity, see p. 61.) Those looking for cheap music and willing to take a walk on the wild side may look for pirated CDs and PlayStation games. You can find vendors on the street in well-trafficked areas or in outdoor markets. CDs sell for around L10,000, but you can often bargain. A word of warning before you drool over low-cost rip-offs—there is no guarantee of quality or the content matching what is advertised. Many vendors have CD players with them; listen first, then buy. It's usually a good idea to listen to the entire CD—many suddenly end after the fifth track. For a more savory and legal shopping experience, try the following stores.

Disfunzioni Musicali, V. degli Etruschi, 4 (☎06 4461984; fax 06 4451704; mail order 06 4441461). In San Lorenzo. CDs, cassettes, and LPs available, including excellent selections of rock, avant-garde classical, jazz, and ethnic. Helpful staff. Bulletin board, with ads for musicians and roommates/apartments. Open M 3:30-7:30pm, Tu-Sa 10:30am-7:30pm; July and Aug. M-F 10:30am-7:30pm, Sa 10-2pm. Closed major holidays and Ferragosto. MC/V.

Messaggerie Musicali, V.d. Corso, 122 (☎06 6798197). This 3-story music store specializes in CDs and electronics; their music collection is strongest on the pop front and often reasonably priced. A standard, dependable option for most music-lovers. Portable stereos and electronics on 2nd floor. Open daily 10am-8pm. AmEx/MC/V.

RicordiMedia. Several locations: V.d. Corso, 506 (☎06 3612370); V. G. Cesare, 88 (☎06 37351589), in Prati; Termini Galleria (☎06 87406113); V. V. E. Orlando, 73 (☎06 4746254), near Repubblica, and V. C. Battisti, 120 (☎06 6798022), just off P. Venezia. A chain with an average selection of music, average prices. Look for *Prezzi Pazzi* signs for deals on indie music. Open daily 9:30am-8pm. AmEx/MC/V.

BOOKSTORES

Although you already own the only book you'll need during your trip to Rome, sometimes it's nice to read something that's not *so* damn witty and irreverent. **V. di Terme di Diocleziano,** connecting Termini with P. della Repubblica, is lined with booksellers full of dirt-cheap used English paperbacks. **V. di Conciliazione,** the broad avenue leading to St. Peter's, has several bookstores selling English-language histories and guidebooks, as well as devotional materials, but beware of high prices. If you're in Rome for a while (lucky dog, you), introducing yourself to the staff at these bookstores is a good way to get involved in the ex-pat community.

Libreria Feltrinelli International, V. V. E. Orlando, 84-86 (☎06 4827878). Near P. della Repubblica. A Roman fixture, Feltrinelli has an excellent selection of books in several languages, dictionaries, and a wide range of travel guides. Cheaper than most English-language bookstores, this should be your first stop for basics. Open daily 9am-7:30pm. AmEx/MC/V.

Anglo-American Bookshop, V.d. Vite, 102 (☎06 6795222; www.aab.it). To the right of the Spanish Steps. In case the name didn't give it away, this place specializes in English language books. Fiction, history, and poetry abound in this well-stocked bookshop–*The Joy of Cooking* cohabitates with Henry Kissinger's latest. The bilingual staff really knows its stuff and is always willing to help. The bulletin board in back lists apartments for rent. *Wanted in Rome* sold here. In summer open M-F 9am-1pm and 4-8pm, Sa 9am-1pm.

The Lion Bookshop, V.d. Greci, 33-36 (☎06 32654007). Off V.d. Corso, Between P. di Popolo and P. di Spagna. For the Anglophile literature lover, this shop boasts the largest selection of British fiction in Rome. Well-stocked bookstore with poetry, fiction, new releases, and children's books. Coffee/Tea Bar, reading room, and a local bulletin board. Open M-Sa 10am-7:30pm; in winter M 3:30-7:30pm, Tu-Sa 10am-7:30pm. AmEx/MC/V.

ENGLISH LIBRARIES

Centro Studi Americani, V. M. Caetani, 32, 2nd fl. (☎06 68806624). Off P. Mattei in a pretty *palazzo.* Every section of the Dewey Decimal System represented. Check out books with a membership (one-year L30-70,000/€15.49-36.15). Open M-F 9am-7:30pm, Sa 9am-1:30pm. Closed part of Aug. Also look at bulltien boards for concerts, cultural events.

Santa Susanna Lending Library, V. XX Settembre, 15, 2nd fl. (☎06 4827510). In the Church of Santa Susanna. About 9000 English volumes, including the British Council's Fiction Collection. 3mo. membership L20,000/€10.33; yearly L50,000/€25.82. 6mon. family membership L35,000/€18.08; L60,000/€36.99 yearly. Open Tu and Th 10am-1pm, W 3-6pm, F 1-4pm, Sa-Su 10am-12:30pm. July open Tu, W, and Su; Aug. open Su.

INSIDE

Daytripping

In Rome you long for the country; in the country—oh inconstant!—you praise the distant city to the stars.
—Horace

When the speeding *motorini* and the tourist-choked morass of Rome are too much, see sanctuary nearby in rural **Lazio.** The cradle of Roman civilization, Lazio was originally known to the Romans as *Latium*, Latin for "wide land." Today, the standard translation of Lazio for most Romans is "Winner of the 2000 Italian soccer cup." Stretching from the Tyrrhenian coastline through volcanic mountains to the foothills of the Abruzzese Apennines, Lazio encompasses ancient metropoloi, imperial Roman villas, exquisite Baroque estates, beautiful, sandy beaches, tranquil lakeside resorts, and cool, shady woodlands.

Known as *Ager Romanus*, Lazio has always been a rich land. Volcanic soil feeds its farms and vineyards, and travertine marble quarried from its hills was used to build the Colosseum, St. Peter's, and many buildings in between. The territory attracted the Etruscan Empire's notice in the 9th century BC, when it colonized Tarquinia and Cerveteri. The less advanced Latin tribes near Lake Albano spread to the south. While Rome was just a few mud huts on the Palatine, Etruscan and Latin towns enjoyed relative sophistication. After a grueling stint in Rome, take a day and run for the hills (or the forest or the sea). The time required is minimal—most trips are no more than 90min. by train or bus.

Fierce Mediterranean sunshine, sparkling clear waters, and a national predilection for dark tans make Italian beaches an understandably high-in-demand summer destination. While most beaches get crowded on weekends, they don't really become unbearably overcrowded until August. The farther from the city you go, the better your prospects for sunning and swimming in relative peace (see Sabaudia, Pontine Islands, and Sperlonga). Many of Rome's most popular discos close during the summer months and reappear at the beaches of **Ostia** and **Fregene** (see **Nightlife,** p. 183), although you may need a car to get back late at night. *Rome C'è* lists what's going on in the beach scene.

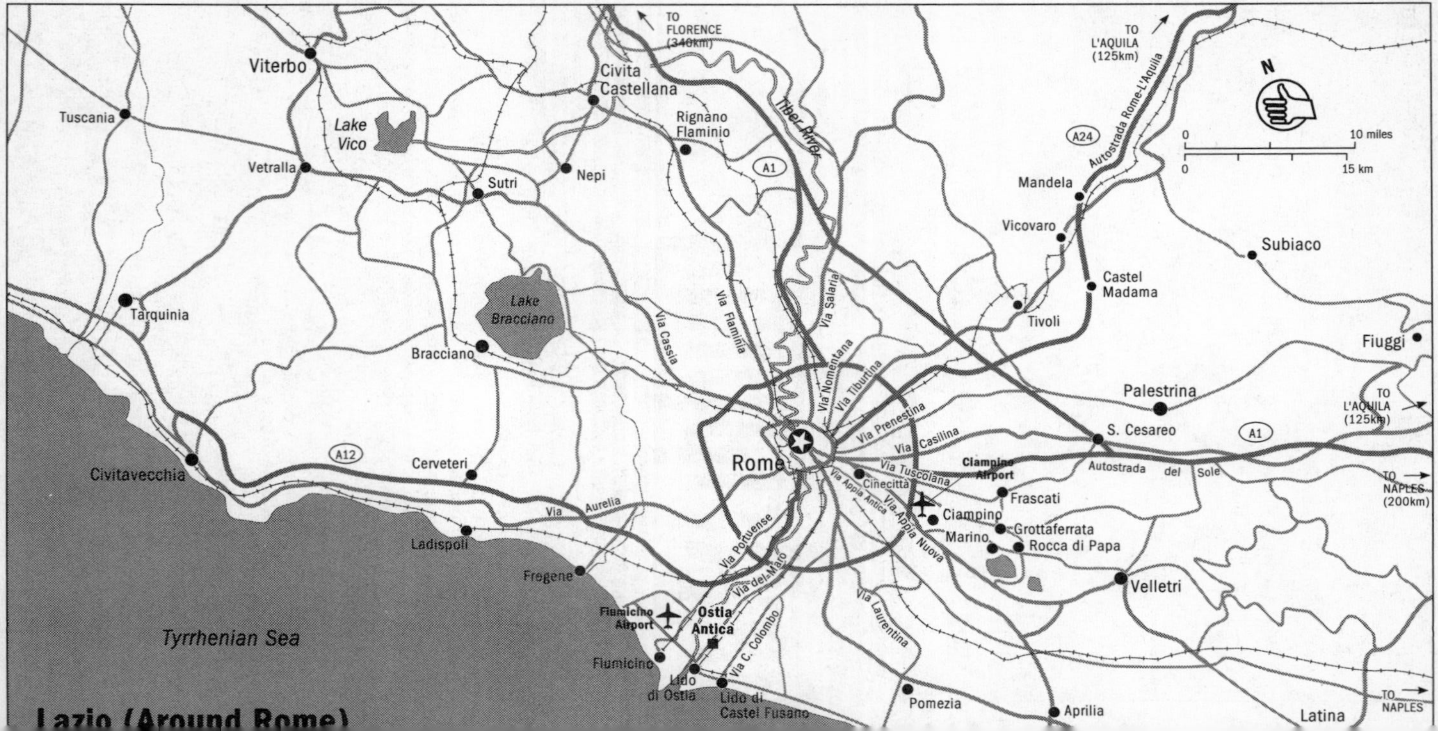

Lazio (Around Rome)

TO FLORENCE (340km)
TO L'AQUILA (125km)
Autostrada Rome-L'Aquila
A24
N
0 10 miles
0 15 km
Viterbo
Civita Castellana
Tuscania
Lake Vico
Rignano Flaminio
Tiber River
A1
Vetralla
Nepi
Sutri
Mandela
Vicovaro
Subiaco
Castel Madama
Tarquinia
Lake Bracciano
Via Salaria
Via Flaminia
Via Cassia
Tivoli
Bracciano
Fiuggi
Via Nomentana
Via Tiburtina
Palestrina
Via Prenestina
TO L'AQUILA (125km)
S. Cesareo
A1
Via Casilina
Civitavecchia
A12
Cerveteri
Rome
Ciampino Airport
Autostrada del Sole
Via Tuscolana
Cinecittà
Via Appia Antica
TO NAPLES (200km)
Frascati
Via Aurelia
Ciampino
Via Appia Nuova
Grottaferrata
Ladispoli
Marino
Rocca di Papa
Via Portuense
Fregene
Via del Mare
Velletri
Fiumicino Airport
Ostia Antica
Via Laurentina
Tyrrhenian Sea
Via C. Colombo
Fiumicino
Lido di Ostia
Lido di Castel Fusano
Pomezia
Aprilia
Latina
TO NAPLES

Great stretches of the Lazio beaches lie under the thumb of nefarious *stabilimenti balneari*—private companies that fence off the choicest bits of beach and charge admission (usually L10-15,000/€5.16-7.75), which includes the use of a changing cabin. Beach chair and umbrella rentals, as well as hot showers, are extra. A little polite inquiry, however, will usually get you to a *spiaggia libera* (public beach).

LAZIO

SABAUDIA

COTRAL buses leave EUR-Fermi for Sabaudia (2hr.; 8:45am-7pm, return 5:35am-6:25pm, or catch the 8:20pm bus to Latina, where a connecting bus to Rome awaits; L6900/€3.50). Orange city buses to the beach leave from P. Oberdan during the week, every 10 min. from P. Savoia on weekends (L2000/€1.03). **Pro Loco tourist office,** *P. del Comune, 18-19 (☎0773 515046; fax 0773 518043; prolocosabaudia@libero.it; www.proloco.sabaudia.net) offers hotel and restuarant listings, as well as maps and info on the National Park and how to hike it. The office also sells train and bus tickets, as do* tabacharie. *Open daily 9am-noon and 5-8pm.*

Constructed as a part of Mussolini's grandiose vision to re-build the Ancient Roman Empire and extend Rome's boundaries to the coastline during the 30s, Sabaudia is an odd mix of breathtaking natural beauty and stupefyingly unappealing Fascist architecture. Located in the Pontine region, Sabaudia is surrounded by Roman ruins, quiet farmland, and the **Circeo National Park** (with its four coastal lakes), all of which more than compensate for the town's rather dour gridded streets and industrial *piazze*. Sabaudia retains its vitality by its proximity to Monte Circeo and serving as a stopover point for caravans of sun-lovers heading over to kayak-filled **Lake Paola** to 23km of dazzling dunes and stretches of breath-taking **beaches** that are comparatively *stabilmenti*-free.

COTRAL buses arrive in P. Oberdan. A right onto C. Vittoria Emmanuele II leads to P. del Comune, where the tourist office is located. Near P. del Comune is V. Principe di Piemonte, which runs to the Giovanni XXIII bridge, V. Lungomare and the beach. *Alimentari*, fruit stores, and *pizzerie* line C. Vittorio Emmanuele II and III. To reach **Hotel Verbania,** V. Verbania, 4 (☎ 0773 517773; fax 0774 517723) from P. del Comune, take a right onto V. Vittorio Emanuele II, and Verbania is to the left, in a quiet residential location, offering clean, simple rooms, many with balconies, and all with telephone, fridge, TV. (Breakfast L10,000/€5.16. Singles L40-90,000/€20.60-45.60, with bath L45-100,00/€23.18-51.60; doubles L60-145,000/€36.20-74.78, with bath L60-195,000/€36.20-99.78, triples L110-160,000/€56.76-87.80. MC/V.)

SPERLONGA

Take the Naples train from Termini to the Formia-Sperlonga stop (1.¼ hr.; every 30min.-1hr.; 6:16am-9:16pm; last return 10:36pm; L10,800/€5.57), where you'll have to catch a bus to Sperlonga (10 min.; every 30 min.; 6:15am-7:45pm, last return 7pm; L2000/€1.03). ***Tourist office*** *on C. San Leone just off the piazza, with maps and hotel listings to share ☎0771 55700; open daily in the summer 9am-12:30pm and 4-8:30pm.*

Sperlonga is a tiny coastal hamlet that was once a favored vacation spot among Roman noblemen. The town's name derives from the Latin word for caves, *speluncae*, one of which was used by Emperor Tiberius as an extension of his waterfront villa in the early decades of the first millennium. Nowadays vacationers forgo the caves for luxury rental condos and vine-covered hotels steps away from lovely stretches of beach. Buses arrive at P. Europa in the *centro storico* upon the hill, where white-washed stairwells give way to stores laden with matronly clothing and artsy-craftsy souvenirs. A left on V.d. III Ripa will take you to staircases cascading past cacti growing between boulders to the beach. The hulking **Toree Truglia** divides the beach into **Spiaggia di Levante** to the left and **Spiaggia di Ponente** to the right. Levante has a tiny, well-maintained marina with sailing and fishing boats, while Ponente offers slightly more public beach space.

On the Ponente side of town you will find the airy beachside **Albergo Amyclae,** V. C. Colombo (☎0771 548051). (Breakfast included in a dining room overlooking the water. During particularly busy periods 1/2 pension is required, which costs L90-120,000 per person, including the price of the room. Singles L100-110,000/€51.60-56.76; doubles L120-150,000/€62.00-77.50. L30-40,000/€15.50-20.30 extra for rooms with A/C, fridge and TV. Private beach and parking.) If you're famished after a long day of sunbathing, try the delicious fried calimari and shrimp (L17,500/€8.78) at **Ristorante La Siesta,** V. Orticello, 15 (☎0771 54617) near P. della Repubblica.

NETTUNO

Take the regionale train from Termini to Nettuno (about 1hr.; every hour; outbound 6:45am-9:25pm, return 6:28am-9:54pm; L5600/€2.88). Nettuno last stop, about 1min. after Anzio. Buses depart for Anzio every 15-30 min. from Piazzale IX Settembre, in front of the train station (10am-9:30pm; L1500/€0.77). ***Pro Loco tourist office*** *in the right corner of marina. ☎06 9803335. www.proloconettuno.it. Open M-F 10am-12:30pm and 5-7:30pm, Sa 10am-12:30pm and 6-8pm.* ***Fortezza Sangallo,*** *and* ***Museo dello Sbarco Alleato*** *open T-Su 9am-1pm and 2-6pm. Free.* ***Cemetary Information Office:*** *open daily 8am-4:30pm; April 16-Sept. 30, M-F 8am-5:30pm, Sa-Su 9am-5pm.*

Following the collapse of the Empire, Roman refugees in flight from marauding Goths installed themselves in the shadows of a coastal temple to Neptune 60km south of Rome. World War II saw the partial destruction of Nettuno and the decimation of nearby Anzio, when amphibious Allied forces emerged from the Tyrrhenian Sea to initiate their advance upon Nazi-occupied Rome.

A walk down V. Colombo from the train station takes you to the perpendicular V. Matteoti. Go left to descend to the marina, teeming with yachts. Continue left past the marina and the church to reach the **public beach** (*spiaggia libera*), a rather sorry stretch of sand that is barely staving off the rapid encroachment of beach-chairs-for-rent. Nettuno fortunately offers more than over-priced skin-scorching. Sites of historical and aesthetic interest include a highly touristed walled, medieval quarter: to the right of the marina, the walls of the **Borgo Medioevale** preserve a congregation of vaulted passageways, narrow *piazze*, and a handful of less archaic nightspots.

A right from V. Colombo onto V. Matteoti will take you to P.S. Francesco, which is dominated by the **Fortezza Sangallo,** a turn-of-the-16th-century fortress that houses the rather musty **Museo dello Sbarco Alleato,** devoted to the Allied landing. A piecemeal collection of photos of Allied soldiers interacting with Italians, random military paraphenalia, and enlarged American newspaper descriptions of the landing, the last of which drip with patriotism and propaganda. An overwhelmingly helpful, Italian-speaking staff awaits to answer questions and point out items of interest.

Another plaintive reminder of Lazio's unfortunate positioning in the path of the World War II juggernaut is the **Sicily-Rome American Cemetery,** stretching over 77 acres of Italian cypress trees, trickling fountains, and muted sadness. To reach the cemetary, turn right coming out of the train station and then right again onto V.S. Maria. The ordered and stately grounds, with row upon row of pristine marble crosses, stand in solemn opposition to the violent and chaotic fashion in which the soldiers interred met their death. A walk among the graves of 7861 Americans (as well as a memorial to the 3095 missing) is both humbling and disquieting. Many of the soldiers died during the 1943-44 Italian campaign, which began with the invasion of Sicily and ended with the liberation of Rome. The memorial at the top of the park contains a chapel, as well as extensive map murals depicting the Allied drive up the peninsula. Americans run the information office to the right of the entrance, and will provide information and help locate graves.

ANZIO

The COTRAL blue bus arrives from and departs for Nettuno in P. Cesare Battisti (6:40am-10pm; L1500/€0.77), or take train from Nettuno to 2nd to last stop. From the train station, walk down V. Palombi to P. C. Battisti; two blocks down and to the left in P. Pia is the ***IAT tourist office,*** *with maps and hotel and ferry information. ☎0669 845147. Open M-Sa 9am-1pm and 4-6pm.*

Majestic palm trees line V. Paolini, the boulevard that runs from the train station to the center of Anzio, past villas that recall Anzio's long-held prominence as the vacation spot of choice for emperors, popes, and pirates. The *vacanza* was interrupted on January 22, 1944 when Allied forces launched an attack from the water upon Anzio and Nettuno, 3km to the south. Within six months, American and British troops would be marching upon the capital. While Rome fared the war reasonably well, Anzio was decimated during the surprise attack. Anzio's beaches have served to recover the town's touristic appeal, but most of the architecture is modern. Anzio is active in the fishing and shipbuilding industries, and the area around the port boasts a shopping center. Anzio is a point of departure for the **Pontine Islands** (see p. 230). Almost all of the prime sand in Anzio is controlled by *stabilimenti*, but if you walk down Riviera Zanardelli you'll find a fairly appealing swath of public coastline.

OSTIA ANTICA

M: B-Piramide. Exit the station and walk left past the bar to the Lido trains. Get off at the Ostia Antica stop. Use same ticket as on Metro. Cross overpass, take road to end, cross street, and walk down parking lot past bar. Go left when the parking lot dead-ends into the lot for the ruins, and follow the signs to the entrance. ☎06 56358099. ***Open*** *Tu-Su 9am-7pm; in winter daily 9am-5pm; last entrance 1hr. before closing. L8000/€4.13. Informative and entertaining* ***audioguide*** *L8000/€4.13. Guided* ***tours*** *Su mornings, except in Aug., L7000/€3.62. For info ☎06 21803030.*

The ruins of the Roman port of Ostia are close and convenient to Rome, and provide the unique experience of exploring a well preserved abandoned Roman city without having to make the long trip to the more famous ruins at Pompeii and Herculaneum. The extensive site also shows the more practical side of ancient Rome absent in the temples and monuments of the Roman Forum—bakeries, bars, and even public toilets. The ruins are also pleasant to visit, dotted with trees and cool sea breezes that keep temperatures tolerable even in summer. The excavations are quite large and require the better part of a day to explore well—bring a picnic if you don't want to eat at the cafeteria.

The city, named for the *ostium* (mouth) of the Tiber, was founded around 335 BC as the first Roman colony. Ostia grew alongside its mother city from a mere fortified camp established to guard the salt fields of the Tiber delta into a port and naval base during the 3rd and 2nd centuries BC. After Rome won control of the seas

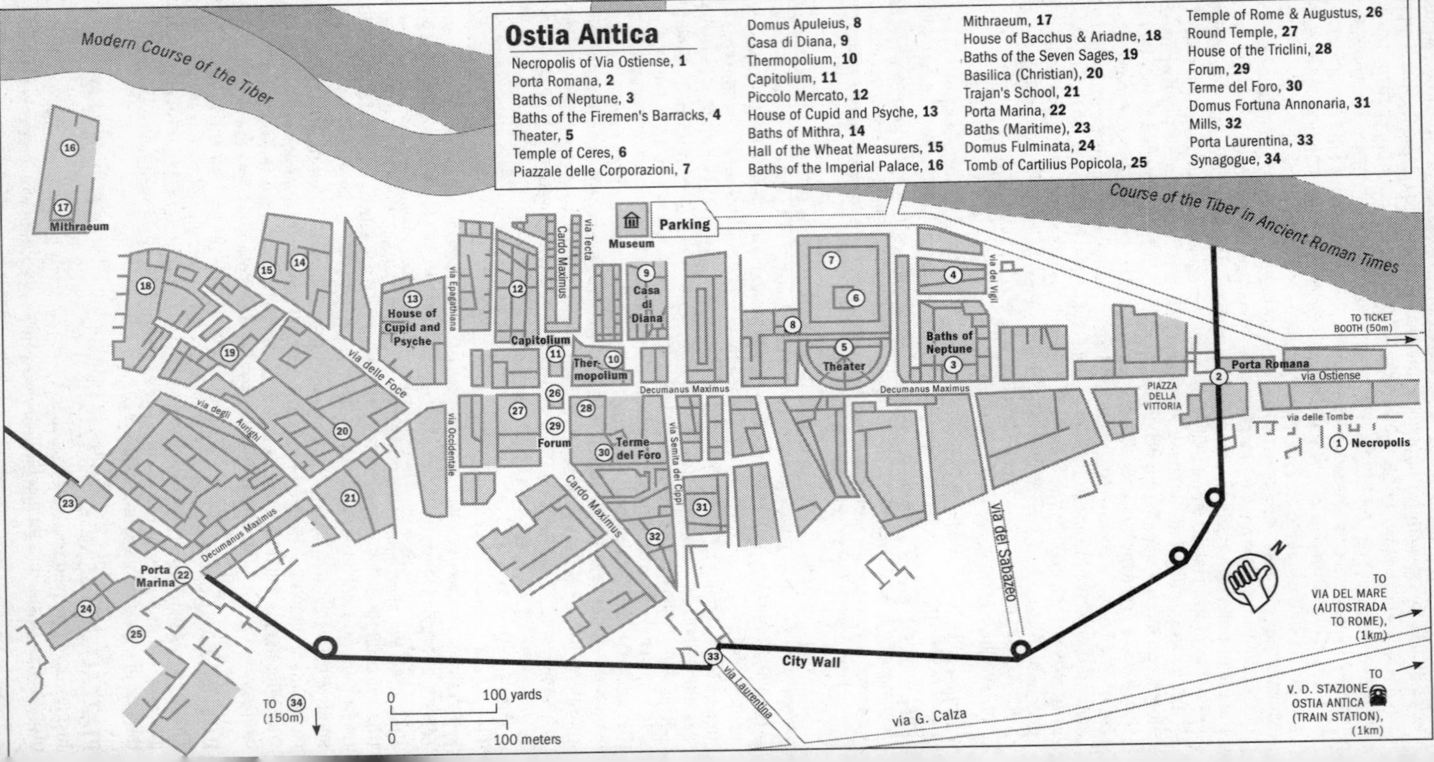

Ostia Antica
Necropolis of Via Ostiense, 1
Porta Romana, 2
Baths of Neptune, 3
Baths of the Firemen's Barracks, 4
Theater, 5
Temple of Ceres, 6
Piazzale delle Corporazioni, 7
Domus Apuleius, 8
Casa di Diana, 9
Thermopolium, 10
Capitolium, 11
Piccolo Mercato, 12
House of Cupid and Psyche, 13
Baths of Mithra, 14
Hall of the Wheat Measurers, 15
Baths of the Imperial Palace, 16
Mithraeum, 17
House of Bacchus & Ariadne, 18
Baths of the Seven Sages, 19
Basilica (Christian), 20
Trajan's School, 21
Porta Marina, 22
Baths (Maritime), 23
Domus Fulminata, 24
Tomb of Cartilius Popicola, 25
Temple of Rome & Augustus, 26
Round Temple, 27
House of the Triclini, 28
Forum, 29
Terme del Foro, 30
Domus Fortuna Annonaria, 31
Mills, 32
Porta Laurentina, 33
Synagogue, 34
Modern Course of the Tiber
Course of the Tiber in Ancient Roman Times
Mithraeum
Museum
Parking
Cardo Maximus
via Tecta
via Epagathiana
House of Cupid and Psyche
Casa di Diana
Capitolium
Thermopolium
Theater
Baths of Neptune
via dei Vigil
TO TICKET BOOTH (50m)
Porta Romana
via Ostiense
PIAZZA DELLA VITTORIA
Decumanus Maximus
via delle Tombe
Necropolis
via delle Foce
via degli Aurighi
via Occidentale
Forum
Terme del Foro
via Semita dei Cippi
Cardo Maximus
via del Sabazeo
Porta Marina
Decumanus Maximus
N
TO VIA DEL MARE (AUTOSTRADA TO ROME), (1km)
City Wall
via Laurentina
TO V. D. STAZIONE OSTIA ANTICA (TRAIN STATION), (1km)
via G. Calza
TO 34 (150m)
0 100 yards
0 100 meters

in the Punic Wars, almost all imports to Rome passed through Ostia. The great bakeries that supplied Rome with much of its bread were here, near the Egyptian grain docks. Rebellious and criminal slaves were often sentenced to labor in these bakeries, pounding grain and shoveling waste into enormous brick ovens. The work was considered second in unpleasantness only to being chained to an oar in a galley.

The late Republican and early Imperial periods saw the construction of the most grandiose (and the most well-preserved) structures in the port. By AD 45, the wharves lining the river had reached their capacity, and the port had begun to be blocked with sand deposits, prompting Claudius to dredge an artificial harbor to the northwest (fragments of which have been found near Fiumicino airport), but Ostia remained important and buildings were built throughout the Imperial period.

The port fell into disuse during the onslaught of the Goths, and the silty Tiber slowly moved the coastline a mile or so west. After the city was sacked by the Goths in the 9th century, Pope Gregory IV built a new fortified town up the road from the present-day entrance gate, and the ancient city receded into malarial swampdom. Fortunately, the mud acted to preserve the ruins. Like the Roman Forum, Ostia was plundered for marble during the Middle Ages—much of it was processed into lime in crude furnaces still present in the city—but many brick buildings survived and much marble was missed.

From the entrance gate, **Via Ostiense** (the same highway that now leads out of Rome), leads to a **necropolis** of brick and marble tombs. The road passes through the low remains of the **Porta Romana**—one of the city's three gates, it's framed by Sulla's 1st-century BC walls—and becomes the city's main street, the **Decumanus Maximus.** To the immediate left are a square and the remains of a fountain where *cisiarii* (cart drivers) who ran between Rome and Ostia parked their vehicles.

SITE MUSEUM

Open Tu-Su 9am-6pm. Free with park ticket.

At the north of Ostia, the park museum displays the more interesting statues recovered at Ostia and a collection of artifacts monumental and mundane. Among the treasures are a colossal statue of Trajan, bas reliefs of various trades and businesses, a statue of Mithras slaying the sacred bull (Room 3), several sarcophagi (Room 9), and a spectacular set of 4th- and 5th-century marble panels of Jesus (Room 11).

BATHS OF THE CISIARII

After entering the gate, turn right at the large plaza to reach the Baths of the Cisiarii, the mule drivers who transported goods between Rome and Ostia (the Roman equivalent of the Teamsters). Loathe to leave their mules even when bathing, they decorated the floor of their baths with mosaics of long-eared mules at work.

THEATER

For events info, check Roma C'è or call the Teatro Roman Scavi Archeologici di Ostia Antica at ☎ 06 5683712 or 06 56352830.

Built in 12 BC, the Ostian theater is almost completely intact thanks to a restoration effort that has left it in usable condition. The large central entrance still has fragments of stucco work added in AD 196. The building once housed several small stores in its bottom levels. A vaulted passage leads to the semicircular *cavea.* The stage itself was backed by a wall several stories high, decorated with columns, arches, niches, and statuary; only the low wall of its foundation survives. Seating around 3500. In summer, the theater hosts plays and concerts.

DOMUS APULEIUS

This house, next to the theatre, is designed like those of Pompeii, with a central graden courtyard. Around the side is a Mithraeum, with a statue of Mithras killing the bull and mosaics representing the planets.

PIAZZALE DELLE CORPORAZIONI

Just north of the theater are the remains of this expansive and beautiful plaza for the offices of shipping companies. Lining the walkway are the mosaics that advertised the different agencies. Many show ships and their cargos, the lighthouse of Ostia, and describe where their goods were shipped from. The mosaics of elephants represent the ivory trade. At the center of the plaza are the remains of a small temple to Ceres, the goddess of the grain that poured into Ostia.

BATHS OF NEPTUNE AND WINE SHOP

The large baths rise on the right a few hundred yards down the road from the entrance gate. Up the stairs from the *decumanus* is a platform to see the large mosaic of Neptune driving his chariot, surrounding by sundry sea creatures and nymphs frolicking. Next to the baths is the *palestra* where bathers would exercise. Go behind the right wall of the palestra to see a break in the wall which shows how the hot baths were set on platforms under which hot air circulated through-*(laconicum)* and a standard *caldarium*. Past the baths is a wine shop, with a mosaic in the floor showing a large cup and an advertisement for the shop—"Fortunatus says: if you're thirsty have a cup of wine." In the road in front of the baths is a medieval well—look in the grating next to it to see the piping that brought water through Ostia. Near the well is a small alley running alongside the baths, with a mosaic representing the four winds (men with wings on their heads) and the Roman provines that traded with Ostia (women wearing agricultural products in the hair, and the three legged wheel of Sicily).

FULLONICA AND MITHRAEUM

Off the Decumanus to the left of the baths, the V.d. Fontana, a well-preserved street lined with stores and apartment houses, leads back to a Fullonica, or ancient cleaning shop. Its deep pits were filled with clothing and fresh urine, which contains bleaching agents; slaves had to jump in and splash around to agitate the wash, a means of washing clothes which backpackers probably shouldn't try in their hostel bathrooms. Past the Fullonia are the remains of a mithraeum, with seven mosaic symbols laid in the ground which represent the seven degrees of initiation members of the religion went through.

FORUM

Occupying a wide rectangular space to the west of the Thermopolium is the Forum of Ostia, anchored by the imposing **Temple to Jupiter, Juno, and Minerva** (called the **Capitolium**) with its imposing staircase. During the 1700s, however, it was used as a sheepfold, dubbed "the red house" by shepherds. At the other end of the forum is a temple to Augustus, with a marble staue representing Rome with her foot on a globe as ruler of the world. Between the two temples is a small well, the shrine to the *lares* (household gods) of the imperial family. The largest baths at Ostia, the **Terme del Foro** complex sits just southeast of the Forum. Note the remains of the complex heating system in the subterranean passage and the exquisite veined marble columns rising in the *frigidarium*. Near the baths is a well preserved 20 seat public toliet, showing where a current of water used to run constantly under the seats. A hole in the stone doorway shows where a revolving door used to turn.

HOUSE OF CUPID AND PSYCHE

At the fork in the Decumanus, V.d. Foce leads right to this elaborate, marble-paneled dwelling, where the statue of the two lovers (now in the museum) was found. Down from the house and to the right on V. di Terme del Mitra, a staircase descends to a shadowy mithraeum (see Mithraism, p. 47) and the beginning of the maze of sewers and cisterns that sprawls beneath the city.

SCHOLA OF TRAJAN

A marbled *exedra* greets the visitor to the Schola of Trajan, believed to be owned by a corporation of shipbuilders. The first-century BC *domus* contains beautiful and rare mosaics; the interior court and fountain are striking.

ANCIENT SYNAGOGUE

South of the city through the **Porta Marina,** through which disembarking sailors entered the city, is a large synagogue. Two architraves with Jewish symbols led to the discovery that these ruins, which include an oven and a podium for religious services, were a Jewish temple. The entrance is marked by two steps that lead into a vestibule. On the right lies the *mikvah*, or ritual bath. The tabernacle contains two columns that once held corbels resembling seven-branched candelabra.

BATHS OF MARCIANA AND TOMB OF L. CARTILIUS POPLICOLA

Between the synagogue and the gate are the remains of still more baths, proving that there was no excuse to be dirty in ancient Ostia. Like any self respecting bath, it's decorated with mosaics, showing athletes, philosophers, and a woman who looks like the Statue of Liberty. Closer to the gate is a marble wall marking the tomb of a prominent citizen, L. Cartilius Popicola, decorated with the *fasces* of authority. Budding Latinists can have a go at the inscription describing his accomplishments.

OIL SHOP+GRAIN MILLS+SYNAGOGUE=PARTY!

Down the stairs from the museum are the remains of an oil shop. The huge amphorae buried in the ground were used to store oil. Next door ar the remains of another synagogue, decorated with menorahs on top of the pillars. One street over toward the theatre is Via Mulini, enter the building with a large dark stone outside to see the remains of a grain mill. The dark stone contraptions were used to grind grain; donkeys walked around them to turn the stones and crush the grain, blindfolded so they wouldnt get dizzy and makes asses of themselves.

CASA DI DIANA

East of the Theater off V. dei Molini lies the Casa di Diana (named for the terra-cotta relief of Diana in the main courtyard), the best preserved Roman house at Ostia and among the most complete in the world. At the time of its construction, the edifice reached a height of almost 18m, encompassing three or four floors. Buildings like this, known as *insulae,* once filled most Imperial Roman cities. Unlike the large, single-family villas at Pompeii (see p. 236), *insulae* were three-story apartments where several dozen people lived together, sharing the courtyard and kitchen facilities. The ground floor housed *tabernae* (shops), which opened onto the street. The grooves in the thresholds show where sliding wooden screens served as doors. At the back of the ground floor, a dark, windowless room holds a **mithraeum.**

THERMOPOLIUM

Ancestor to the modern coffee/snack bars that adorn the streets of modern Italy, this place offered the Ostian a chance to walk in for a drink and a bite to eat, and since many of the smaller apartments lacked kitchens, many Ostians ordered meals from places like this. An elegant marble counter greeted customers from the street; they could drink beverages out of the sunken clay jars or cold wine from the cellars. A still life in the central room depicts what are possibly popular foods of the time.

BATHS OF THE SEVEN SAGES

Consderably less scholarly than the name implies, this bath has a public toliet decorated with famous philosophers giving some tips on using the bathroom. A less scatological highlight of the baths is their huge circular mosaic of a hunt.

PALESTRINA

Cotral buses stop at the foot of the hill that makes up most of Palestrina. From the bus stop take the stairs up through the garden to reach the city center. Seminary open daily 9am-1hr before sunset. Free. Temple and museum open Tu-Su 9am-6pm. A single ticket admits you to both L8000/€4.13.

Climbing up a hillside in the countryside of Lazio, Palestrina's greatest attractions date from when it was known as Praeneste, a cosmopolitan city sitting astride the trade routes between Etruria, Rome, and the Greek world. In the 2nd century BC, the prosperous city built a temple to Fortune on an unprecedented scale. The complex is well preserved today, and a museum highlights finds from the aea, especially a huge and detailed Nile Mosaic.

The city is composed of layers of streets climbing up the hill, though the streets are fairly short in length. The main **church** is located in P. Margherita, just up from the gardens. The church was built over the remains of an ancient temple, and still has its rough early Middle Age facade. The *piazza* is also decorated with a statue of local boy made good, Giovanni Pierluigi di Palestrina, inventor of polyphonic church music. On the right next to the church is the old seminary, with parts of ancient mosaics, including some impressive fragments depicting fish.

The real highlights of Palestrina (the temple and its museum) are further up the hill. The temple dedicated to the goddess Fortune, known by the maxim "Fortune favors the bold," was a turning point in Classical architecture. It marked a departure from traditional temples like the Parthenon toward massive complexes designed with the new concrete. It spread over the hills in a series of ceremonial ramps and plazas, topped by a theatre, extending up the slope almost five stories. Almost the entirety of the ancient temple exists and is open to visit. The ruins also provide a maginifcent panorama of the hills of Lazio. The palace holds a sculpture collection of sculpture from Palestrina, but the showpiece is the massive Nile Mosaic on the top floor, which was built during the time of the Roman Republic, when Palestrina was a trading hub between Italy and the Greek East. This huge mosaic is one of the most impressive in existence, and shows the Nile valley from Nubia to Alexandria, with a wealth of smaller scenes depicting temples, fishermen, hippopotomus hunters, lurking crocodiles, and all other sorts of Egyptiana.

TIVOLI

M: B-Rebibbia (15min. from Termini); exit the station and follow signs for Tivoli through an underpass to reach the other side of V. Tiburtina. Find the marker for the blue **ACOTRAL** *bus to Tivoli (25min.). Get a ticket (L3000/€1.55) in the bar next door or in the subway station. Once the bus climbs up to Tivoli, get off past the green P. Garibaldi at P. delle Nazioni Unite (the bus back to Rome leaves from P. Garibaldi). On the street leading from P. Garibaldi, the* ***tourist office,*** *a round shack with a big "I" in front, is loaded with information, restaurant and hotel maps, and bus schedules. ☎0774 311249. Open M-Sa 9:45am-3pm.*

If the heat of Rome has you longing for a water park but the demons of culture refuse to stop whispering in your ear, Tivoli's the answer to your dilemma. Only an hour and a half from Termini, this cool hilltop town, perched 120m above the Aniene River, has been the suburban retreat for some of Rome's finest—Horace, Catullus and Propertius once vacationed nearby—for years. The main attraction is the abundant water, which flows fancifully in the many fountains of the Villa D'Este. Two other villas, Villa Adriana and Gregoriana, comprise the area's principal sites. Though not expressly permitted, the best lunch option in Tivoli is a picnic in the gardens of the Villa D'Este; pick up some water and a panini from any of the bars in P.za Garibaldi. If you'd rather not chance getting chased out of a garden by well-meaning guards, head to **Er Piu,** directly across from the castle on V. Trieste, which leads off of P. delle Nazioni Unite. Tramezzini and panini (L2500 and L3500, respectively) are made in house, and there are shady tables outside. Tivoli is best visited as a daytrip from Rome, where cheaper accommodations are available.

HADRIAN'S VILLA (VILLA ADRIANA)

Take ***orange bus*** *#4x 5km from P. Garibaldi. L1400/€0.70, tickets at the news kiosk. The bus will let you off right in front of a long path down to the Villa. The return bus stop is halfway down the street to the right, diagonally from the bar with an ice-cream cone outside it. ☎0774 530203.* ***Open*** *daily 9am-1½hr. before sunset. L12,000/€6.20; L6000/€3.20 for EU students.* ***Audioguide*** *L7000/€3.62. Parking L3000/€1.55.*

In the valley below Tivoli, Emperor Hadrian, a fairly sophisticated patron of art and architecture, built this enormous complex according to his own unique design. Perhaps the earliest example of suburban sprawl, Hadrian's pad was the largest and most costly villa ever built in Ancient Rome. The ruins, now scattered in fields of olive trees and purple thistles, are among the best-preserved imperial architecture near Rome. Though his predecessor, Trajan, expanded the borders of the empire to their furthest reaches, Hadrian, who came to power in 117, simply expanded the reaches of his own house. As long as the citizens were happy, this "emperor of the arts" was satisfied with amusing himself through building projects—each section of the estate was built in the style of a monument Hadrian had seen during his travels in Greece and Egypt.

Tickets are available at the ticket counter in the building behind the entrance. Stop in the bookshop to grab a map of the ruins, and if you haven't brought a large bottle of water along, it's essential that you buy one in the bar. (There is no place to buy water once inside the villa, and the sun is scorching.) The ruins are large and have little shade, and so a hat and sunscreen are also a sage idea.

From the entrance, two paved roads in front of you lead to the **Pecile,** a great, once-colonnaded court built to recall the famous Painted Porch *(Poikile)* in Athens where Hadrian's heroes, the Greek Stoic philosophers, met to debate. The large pool of the Pecile is now home to ducks and some very hostile swans. To the left of the Pecile, the Philosopher's Hall (its 7 niches that probably held the seven Greek sages' tomes) leads to the circular **Maritime Theater.** This was the emperor's private study and bedroom, cloistered inside a courtyard and protected by a green moat.

To the right of the Pecile is the **Stadio,** where Hadrian enjoyed athletic amusements. Taking a left after passing the Stadio, you'll approach the Piccole and Grande **thermae** (baths) crumbling beneath the remnants of a large dome, suspiciously like that of the Pantheon. After the baths is the **Canopus,** a green expanse of water surrounded by plasters of original Egyptian sculptures (including some very lifelike crocodiles) and broken columns, replicates a famous canal near Alexandria. At the end of the Canopus is the **Serapeum,** a semicircular dining hall modeled after the Alexandria's Temple of Serapis, anchors the far end of the canal. Here the emperor and his guests dined on a platform completely surrounded by water cascading down from the fountains at rear.

To the left of the Maritime Theater is the so-called **Court of the Libraries,** now believed to have been an assembly hall, a summer triclinium or a belvedere tower. Fragments of mosaics survive here, so keep your eyes open; one archaeologist did and found a complete statue of Dionysus and 2,672 coins in 1881, which are now in the Museo Nazionale Romano. Beneath the **Court of the Libraries** is a shadowy **cryptoporticus,** one of several in the villa which hid the emperor's army of slaves from view as they ran the enormous complex. Other rooms of the palace—the Hospitalia, or guest house, the Tre Esedere and the Peristilio di Palazzo—lie nearby in heavily labeled enclaves.

VILLA D'ESTE

From P. Garibaldi, weave your way through the gauntlet of souvenir stands through P. Trento down the path to the Villa d'Este. ☎*0774 312070. Open daily May-Aug. 8:30-6:30pm; Sept.-April 9am-1hr. before sunset. On Sundays, the villa closes 1½hr. earlier. L8000/€4.13; EU citizens under 18 and over 65 free.*

The Villa d'Este was laid out by Cardinal Ercole d'Este (son of Lucrezia Borgia) and his architect Pirro Ligorio in 1550 to combine the feel of ancient Roman *nymphaea* and pleasure palaces with that modern *je ne sais quoi* of the cutloose 1550s. The palace is decorated with amusing grotesque frescoes, shell-studded grottoes, and large picture windows. The gardens are built along the slope of the hill; cleverly constructed terraces above them offer views of the greenery and the distant countryside. The fountains (which are the real attractions) and the park are an ideal setting for a picnic or some casual frolicking, preferably in the company of small children spitting mouthfuls of water.

The gardens make up Italy's most cultured water park, with fountains of every imaginable shape and size. Unfortunately, splashing and inner-tubes are frowned upon, and the water in the fountains is hardly drinkable, as it comes from the semi-clean Aniene River. Immediately below the villa's main terrace is the **Fontana del Bicchierone,** a shell-shaped goblet of Bernini's design. To the left (with your back toward the villa), a path leads to the **Grotto of Diana,** which contains mythological scenes in its shiny mosaic nooks, but is currently being restored. Another path (on the right) leads to the **Rometta,** or Little Rome, directly below the Grotto of Diana. The stately lady in the center of this fountain is Roma herself, surrounded by emblems of the Eternal City—among them a boat with a spurting obelisk representing the Tiber and miniatures of principal temples, and a suckling Romulus and Remus. From the Rometta, the **Viale delle Cento Fontane** runs the width of the garden, where plumes of water spring from grimacing masks between Este eagles.

At the other end from the Rometta, the **Fontana dell'Ovato or di Tivoli**, designed by Pirro Ligorio, shows a central goddess flanked by nymphs, and Venus trying to emerge from her half-shell in the pool. Down the semi-circular steps from the center of the Viale delle Cento Fontane is the **Fontana dei Draghi,** a round pool where reclining four dragons are having a spitting contest. To the right of the dragons stand the **Fontana di Proserpina** and the **Fontana della Civetta e degli Uccelli,** both currently under going restoration, which is said to emit the chirps of birdsong.

(Not to ruin the magic and mystery, but there are actually unseen pipes inside th fountain creating the peeps.) At the bottom of the park, two large goldfish pon sit among some of Italy's oldest cypress trees. With your back to the villa, th ornate marble and stucco **Fontana dell'Organo Idraulico** is on your right, which onc used water pressure to power a hydraulic organ. This behemoth fountain is act ally two; the bottom half is the **Fountain of Neptune.** To the left of the arbor in th back of the garden is the **Fountain of the Ephesian Goddess,** which spouts curve streams of water from each of her 18 breasts.

VILLA GREGORIANA

Follow the signs to the northern end of the city, along the bend in river, then cross the bridg Open June-Aug. Tu-Su 9:30m-7:30pm; Sept.-May Tu-Su 9:30am-1hr. before sunset. L3500/€1.8 under 12 L1000/€0.52. ***The Villa has been closed indefinitely for restorations. Call the Tivo tourist office (☎0774 311249) for more information.***

The **Villa Gregoriana** is a park designed around a man-made waterfall by Pope Gre gory XVI in 1835. There are waterfalls and grottoes, but the star of the show is th Great Cascade, a thundering 160m waterfall. For the best view, bear right at th entrance. If you want more, follow the signs to **Grotta delle Sirene** and the **Grotta del Sibilla,** two natural grottoes carved by the falls. Enjoy the walk down (through som non-descript ruins) and try not to think about the taxing climb back up. The we exit leads you past the 2nd-century BC **Temple of Vesta** and the **Temple of Tiburnus.**

VITERBO

The easiest way to get to Viterbo from Rome is to take the ***train*** *from S. Pietro station (1¾hr., eve hr. 5am-9pm, L6500/€3.45). Viterbo's 2 stations are* ***Porta Romana*** *(near the historical district) a* ***Porta Fiorentina*** *(to the north).* ***Romana*** *is 2 blocks north of Porta Romana on V. Romiti. The* ***bus sta tion*** *is just outside the northeast corner, on the Tangenziale Ovest near V. A. Volta. (Open daily 7a 7pm.) Bus tickets can be purchased at the biglietteria to the left of the bar in the parking lot of the b station. Buses to: Civitavecchia (1¾hr., L6000/€3.20); Orvieto (1½hr., L6000/€3.20); and Tarquin (1hr., L5000/€2.58). The* ***tourist office*** *is off P. Plebecita on V. Ascenzi. They also make reservations f accommodations. ☎0761 325992; portavt@isa.it. Open M-Sa 10am-noon and 4:30-6:30pm.*

Sick of hearing about Romulus and Remus, Caesar and Augustus? If you've had your fi of Ancient and Imperial Rome, head to Viterbo's narrow streets and quirky *piazze* f some Medieval relief. Visit the Piazza della Morte (square of death), make a pilgrima to the church where St. Thomas Aquinas once spoke, or have lunch under a mediev arch with the local soldiers—and all in weather decidedly cooler than Rome's. Viterb began as an Etruscan center but earned fame as the papal refuge from Frederick Ba barossa's siege of Rome in the 12th century. When Viterbo became a Guelph strongho in the aristocrats' civil war, the (literally) torturous process of papal elections first too shape. The *capitano* (city dictator) locked the cardinals in their palace, threatening t cut off food deliveries and remove the roof from the conference room (so that co could creep in), until they chose a new one. Today Viterbo serves as an induction poi for Italian military draftees; the streets brim with more than their share of boys in un form. There aren't many tourists in Viterbo, but it still draws some curious (and perha ailing) sightseers to its sulphurous **Bulicane hot spring** (3km from the center), famous f its curative powers. During the winter, the soothing waters are used to fill a large publ swimming pool. The city's cathedral and medieval remnants are also prime attraction

The medieval part of Viterbo lies to the south, around P. Fontana Grande, P. del Morte, P. del Gesu and P. del Plebiscito, near the Porta Romana. These piazzas com prise the historical neighborhoods of **San Sisto, San Lorenzo, San Pelligrino, San Pietr** and **Verita,** although the town is so small that they all seem to run into each other. To th north, Trinita houses Chiesa S. Trinita, while Santa Rosa also is home to Chiesa S. Ros P. della Rocca is just by the Porta Fiorentina.

SIGHTS

Church of Santa Rosa: *open Th and Su 8:30am-12:30pm and 4-5:30pm.* ***Museo del Macchina di Santa Rosa,*** *V.S. Pellegrino, 60. Open W-Su 10am-1pm and 4-7pm. L2000/€1.0* ***Palazzo dei Papi*** *open M-Sa 10am-12:30pm.* ***Museo d'Arte Sacra:*** *open daily 9:45am-1pm. Fre* ***Church of Santa Maria Nuova:*** *open M-Sa 10am-1pm and 4-7:30pm.* ***Chiesa della Trinità:*** *ope 8am-2pm. Free. Church of Sant'Angelo: open daily 8am-noon and 4-6:30pm.* ***Museo Archeologi Nazionale:*** *☎0761 325929. Open Tu-Su 9am-7pm. L4000/€2.06.*

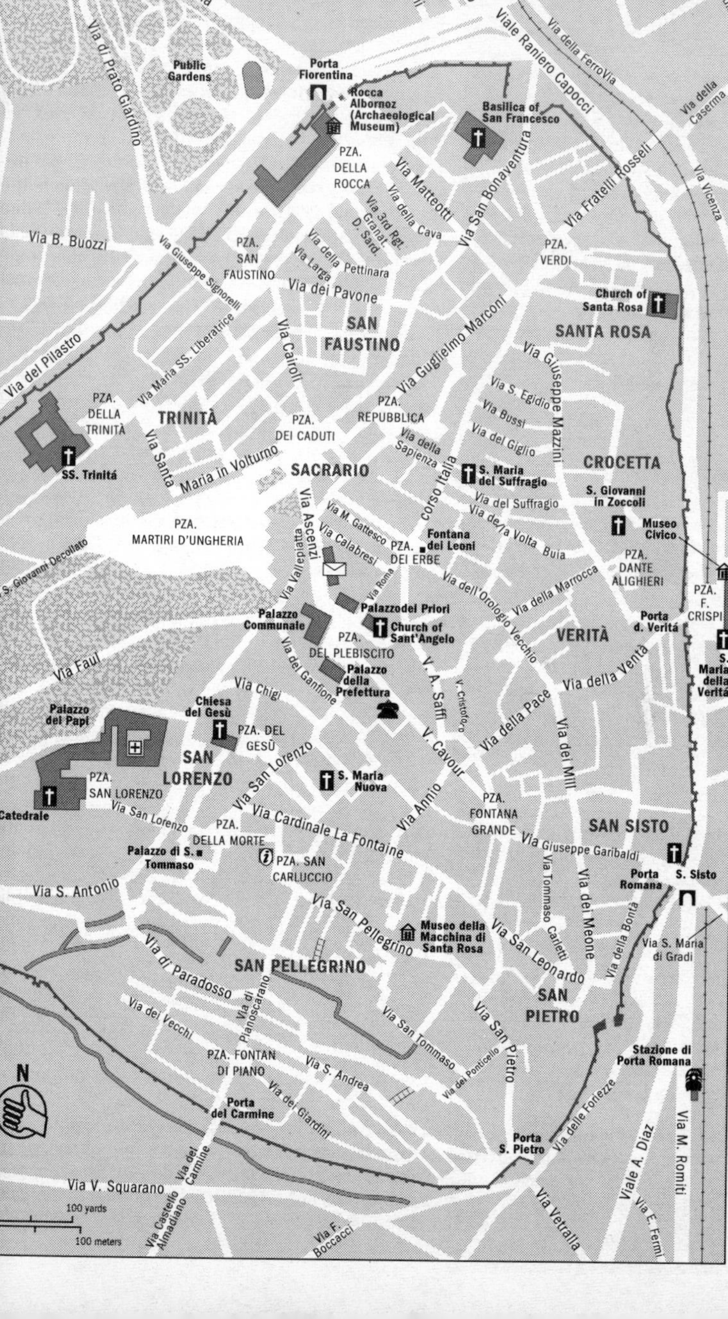
Viterbo
Via L. Rossi Danielli
Via della Palazzina
Via di Prato Giardino
Public Gardens
Stazione di Porta Fiorentina
Via Igino Garbini
Viale Trento
Via F. Baracca
Via Sauro
Viale Trieste
Via Gorizia
Via Pola
TO POLICE (100 m)
Via del Paradiso
Viale Raniero Capocci
Via della FerroVia
Porta Fiorentina
Rocca Albornoz (Archaeological Museum)
Basilica of San Francesco
Via della Caserma
PZA. DELLA ROCCA
Via Matteotti
Via della Cava
Via 3rd Rgt. Granat. D. Sard.
Via San Bonaventura
Via Fratelli Rosselli
Via Vicenza
Via B. Buozzi
Via Giuseppe Signorelli
PZA. SAN FAUSTINO
Via della Pettinara
Via Larga
Via dei Pavone
PZA. VERDI
Church of Santa Rosa
SAN FAUSTINO
SANTA ROSA
Via del Pilastro
Via Maria SS. Liberatrice
Via Cairoli
Via Guglielmo Marconi
Via Giuseppe Mazzini
Via S. Egidio
Via Bussi
Via del Giglio
PZA. DELLA TRINITÀ
TRINITÀ
PZA. DEI CADUTI
PZA. REPUBBLICA
Via della Sapienza
SS. Trinitá
Via Santa Maria in Volturno
SACRARIO
Corso Italia
S. Maria del Suffragio
CROCETTA
Via del Suffragio
S. Giovanni in Zoccoli
PZA. MARTIRI D'UNGHERIA
Via Ascenzi
Via M. Gattesco
Via Calabresi
Fontana dei Leoni
PZA. DEI ERBE
Via della Volta Buia
Museo Civico
Via S. Giovanni Decollato
Via Vallepiatta
Via Roma
Via dell'Orologio Vecchio
Via della Marrocca
PZA. DANTE ALIGHIERI
PZA. F. CRISPI
Palazzo Communale
Palazzodei Priori
Church of Sant'Angelo
PZA. DEL PLEBISCITO
Porta d. Verità
VERITÀ
S. Maria della Verità
Via Faul
Via del Ganfione
Palazzo della Prefettura
V. A. Saffi
V. Cristoforo
Via della Pace
Via della Verità
Via Chigi
Palazzo del Papi
Chiesa del Gesù
PZA. DEL GESÙ
V. Cavour
Via dei Mili
SAN LORENZO
Via San Lorenzo
S. Maria Nuova
PZA. SAN LORENZO
Catedrale
Via Annio
PZA. FONTANA GRANDE
Via Cardinale La Fontaine
PZA. DELLA MORTE
SAN SISTO
Via Giuseppe Garibaldi
Palazzo di S. Tommaso
PZA. SAN CARLUCCIO
Via Tommaso Carletti
Via dei Meone
Porta Romana
S. Sisto
Via S. Antonio
Via San Pellegrino
Museo della Macchina di Santa Rosa
Via San Leonardo
Via della Bontà
Via S. Maria di Gradi
Via di Paradosso
SAN PELLEGRINO
Via di Pianoscarano
Via dei Vecchi
Via San Tommaso
Via San Pietro
SAN PIETRO
PZA. FONTAN DI PIANO
Via S. Andrea
Via del Ponticello
Stazione di Porta Romana
N
Via dei Giardini
Porta del Carmine
Via delle Fortezze
Via A. Diaz
Via M. Romiti
Porta S. Pietro
Via V. Squarano
Via del Carmine
Via Castello Almadiano
100 yards
100 meters
Via F. Boccacci
Via Vetralla
Via E. Fermi

the BIG $plurge

Hotel Chiaia di Luna (☎0771 80113; fax 0771 809821). Above the beach bearing the same name. The views and service here are worth the extra cost; many rooms overlook the awe-inspiring Chiaia di Luna. All quarters with private bath, TV, phone, and elegant hardwood furniture; some have balconies. Also enjoy the large swimming pool and terrace below. Breakfast included; half board available. Van service to and from the port at arrival/departure and every morning. Rooms L90-180,000/€45.50-90.00 per person per night, depending on the season; single rooms pay 50% surcharge.

Ristorante Acqua Pazza, P. Carlo Pisacane, 10 (☎0771 80643). Pass a truly unforgettable evening under the awnings of Acqua Pazza. Savor the excellent seafood on beautiful blue and yellow place settings overlooking the harbor. Quite possibly one of the best restuarants on the island, though the bill reflects this fact. Booked solid almost every night in high season; reserve in advance. *Primi* L15-25,000/€7.75-17.25 (including great *linguini ai scampi e gamberi;* L22,000/€11.60), *secondi* are bought by the *etto:* L7-8000/€3.62-4.13 for most whole fish; L20,000/€10.30 per fillets; expect whole fish to cost L35-L40,000/€17.60-20.60. Pane L3000/€1.55; servizio 10%. Open daily 8pm-"until we finish." AmEx/MC/V.

Entering the city from the Porta Romana, the **Church of San Sisto** is immediately on your right. The church is built right into the medieval wall on the site of a 9th-century pagan cult. Continuing down V. Garibaldi, the **P. Fontana Grande** features (you guessed it) a large fountain dating from the beginning of the 13th century. A short walk down V.d. Fabbriche leads to picturesque **V.S. Pellegrino,** once the principal axis of medieval Viterbo. It's the parade route for the festival of Viterbo's patron saint, Santa Rosa, who is honored every September 3rd at 9pm, when 100 burly citizens carry the **Macchina di Santa Rosa,** a 30m illuminated tower of iron, wood, and paper-mâché, through the streets. The bearers lug it around town, then sprint uphill to the **Church of Santa Rosa,** off P. Verde, where the saint's 700-year-old body is preserved in a glass sarcophagus. (In 1814, the *macchina* fell on its bearers, and in 1967 it had to be abandoned in the street because it was too heavy. The frenzied celebrations accompanying this event are well-documented in the **Museo della Macchina di Santa Rosa.**

Just past the Piazza della Morte, the 1267 **Palazzo dei Papi** was the site of three drawn-out papal conclaves, and remains Viterbo's most important site. On the right side of the edifice is the impressive *loggia*, which has excellent views of the city and the Church of S. Trinita. Inside is the **Museo d'Arte Sacra,** which contains 16th- and 17th-century religious paintings and sculptures. Next door is the 13th-century (the facade is from 1570) **San Lorenzo Cathedral,** its *faux*-Sienese bell tower dominating the *piazza*. Weaving through tiny medieval streets, you'll find the 11th-century **Church of Santa Maria Nuova** off V.S. Lorenzo. Note the pulpit outside: Thomas Aquinas once delivered a sermon here.

The medieval quarter's administrative center, **P. del Plebiscito,** is farther up V.S. Lorenzo. The medallion-bedecked building with the tall clock tower is the **Palazzo del Popolo,** across from the **Palazzo della Prefettura.** Both are guarded by large, decidedly unfierce stone lions, symbols of Viterbo. Between them stands the **Palazzo Comunale.** The odd frescoes in its Sala Regia (painted in 1592) depict the history of Viterbo, mixing in Etruscan, classical, Christian, and medieval legends. Peek into the **Capella dei Priori** (because all they let you do is peek) on the right at the top of the stairs for Sebastiano del Piombo's compelling *Flagellation of Christ* and *Pietà*. Visit the *loggia* for a dazzling view of the community garden and the **Chiesa della Trinità,** and the delightful ground-floor courtyard. Outside, across from the clock tower, the facade of the **Church of Sant'Angelo** incorporates a late Roman sarcophagus containing the body of the beautiful and virtuous Galiana.

At the other end of town near the Porta Fiorentina is the imposing 14th-century **Rocca Albornoz,** home to the **Museo Archeologico Nazionale.** The museum spans the history of the area from Neolithic times to the Middle Ages, with particular emphasis on Etruscan settlements of the 6th and 7th centuries BC. Be sure to visit the second floor galleries, where Roman statues of the Muses grace the rooms.

FOOD

Local specialties include *lombriche* (a type of pasta) and a chestnut soup known as *zuppa di mosciarelle.* While these may sound innocuous, Viterbo's potables have a sinister bent. *Sambuca,* a sweet anise-flavored liqueur, is native to the city. Light it on fire, but blow it out before drinking. Also dangerous is the local wine that goes by the name of *Est! Est!! Est!!!;* one happy German cardinal actually tippled himself to death on it (see p. 180 for the juicy details). Pope Martin IV experienced doom of a different sort—Dante postmarked him for purgatory—for his weakness for another local dish, the tasty roasted eel from Lake Bolsena.

For those with a taste for danger, *alimentari* can be found along V.d. Orologio Vecchio, up one block up from P. del Plebiscito on C. Italia and right, and at the huge **outdoor market** in P. Martiri d'Ungheria, up V. Ascenzi from P. del Plebiscito. (Open Sa 7am-2pm.) Restaurants in the city are cheap and plentiful. **Trattoria L'Archetto,** V.S. Cristoforo, 1, off V. A. Saffi and P. delle Erbe, makes local Italian delights that you can enjoy under a medieval arch. (☎0761 325769. *Primi* L7-10,000/€3.62-5.16. Open M-Sa 10am-4pm and 7-9:30pm.) For a taste of local wine and a more creative lunch, join the locals and head to **Cantina Palazzo dei Mercanti,** V.d. Torre, 1. Be sure to ask about the daily specials. (☎0671 226467. *Primi* L9,000/€4.64; glass of wine L4-6,000/€2.06-3.20. Open M-Sa 12:45-3pm, 7:45pm-12am. AmEx/MC/V.) If you're around for dinner, **Enotecca la Torre,** next door at V.d. Torre, 5, is a particularly tempting splurge. Just inside the walls of the Porta Romana, **Ristorante Porta Romana,** V.d. Bonita, 12, offers typical local cuisine in a friendly (and very convenient) locale. (☎0671 307118. *Primi* L12,500/€6.72. Open M-Sa 12:30-2:30, 7-10:30pm. AmEx/MC/V.)

CASTELLI ROMANI

M:A and take Blue COTRAL buses from Anagnina Station to Frascati (every 30 min. 5:30am-10:30pm, on weekends every 1½hr.; L2400/€1.23) and Albani (every 30min., L2000/€1.03). Trains from Termini connect Rome to Frascati and Albano (departures throughout the day; L3200/€1600), but take longer than the bus. For bus travel between the Castelli Romani, ask at the tourist offices in the region's towns. The COTRAL busses are inexpensive, but not always reliable–the best way to see these towns is to rent a motorino or a car, and travel at your own pace. Otherwise, bring a good book and some sunscreen.

Volcanoes are notoriously unfriendly creatures (remember Pompeii?), but the quiet volcanoes that surround Rome have tried to make up for their more inflammatory southern counterparts by providing lush landscapes, famed wines and succulent strawberries for world-weary Romans. The 16 hill towns that comprise the Castelli Romani, perched on these volcanoes and overlooking Rome, are famed for their Renaissance villas and their white wine. Fortunately, the pace of life has slowed since the good old days, when feuding families built imposing forts and slung insults across the hills.

FRASCATI

Frascati is a 15min. bus ride from Anagnina Station; the bus driver will let you off at the bus depot in P. Marconi, the town center and train station. The tourist office, P. Marconi, 1 (☎06 9420331), is across the street, next to the town hall. Open M 8-2,Tu-Sa 8am-2pm and 4-7pm; winter M-F 8am-2pm and 3:30-6:30pm. ***Gardens*** *open M-F 9am-1pm and 3:30-6pm; winter M-F 9am-1pm. Free pass available at tourist office.* ***Ethiopian Museum,*** *V. Cardinale G. Massia, 26, ☎06 94286601. Open daily 9am-noon and 3-6pm. Free.*

From its lofty position on an ancient volcanic ridge, Frascati has attracted fugitives from the stifling Roman heat for centuries. Frascati's patrician villas and famed fruity, dry white wines remain two of the town's finest attractions. Those lucky enough to be in Frascati in October or November can get caught up in the fevered

CULT OF SAN SILVERIO

Prominently displayed near the cash registers and by the corners and crossroads of much of Ponza is San Silverio, aged graybeard and martyr of choice in the Pontine archipelago. Who is this saintly man, you ask? Ah. Silverio was a minor deacon when a web of intrigue propelled by the Ostrogothic king Theoda had him elected as pope in 536 to keep the Goths in charge. The angry empress Theodora sent her husband Justinian's general to convince him to stand down. When Silverio refused, forged letters of plots between the pope and the Goths were suddenly brought to light. Poor Silverio was summarily degraded to the rank of monk, deposed in a hasty trial, forced to sign an abdication by his successor pope, and sent into exile on the island of Pomarola, just off the coast of Ponza, where he soon died of starvation and the hearty island life. His grave quickly became a center of miracles and cures for the faithful *Pontinesi*, who encouraged the Vatican to have him elevated to sainthood in the 11th century. His image is still enthusiastically plastered about the islands; his somewhat dubious memory is celebrated on June 20th and February 2nd.

dipsomania of the annual **vendemmia,** the celebration of the grape harvest. The 1598 **Villa Aldobrandini** dominates the hill over town. Up V. Catone from P. Marconi, hang a right onto V. G. Massaia, which leads to the Renaissance *villa*. Financed by Clement VIII and designed by Giacomo della Porta, the villa was built as a quiet retreat for Clement's favorite nephew, Pietro Aldobrandini. Visit the sculpture-filled gardens, Bernini fountains and the Ninfeo—a "theater of water" featuring Pan, Atlas and a Satyr—and see what a lucky, lucky boy Pietro was. Before you leave, make sure to see the panoramic views of town from the terrace.

About 1km uphill from the *villa* on G. Massaia is the tiny sixteenth-century **Chiesa dei Cappuccini,** perched at the top of a wooded staircase. A sign on the door announces that you need reservations for marriages, but the unique **Ethiopian Museum,** just next door, is open daily and requires no such forethought. The **Museum,** was built in honor of Cardinal Massaia, who spent 35 years as a missionary in Ethiopia, and houses a collection of weapons, handmade crafts, and the cardinal's personal paraphernalia, including his death mask.

The entrance to **Villa Tuscolana,** the highest of Frascati's villas, is a few meters left of the church's exit. Built on the foundations of the ruins of Cicero's villa, the building has now been turned into an up-scale hotel, but provides views of Monteporzio, a neighboring hill town.

While the foundations of Cicero's house are no longer visable, the ruins of nearby Tusculum—an ancient resort for the who's who of Roman society, including Cato and Cicero—can still be seen. From the entrance of the Villa Aldobrandini, turn right onto V. Tusculo, which climbs 5km over winding country roads to reach the ruins of Tusculum. The town was destroyed in 1191 during a feud between its residents and the Romans, but the small Roman theater, scattered ruins and stunning view of Lazio make the ghost town worth the climb. The citadel of Tusculum, marked by an iron cross at the hill's summit, affords a 360° view of southern Lazio, with Rome to the right, the Tyrrhenian Sea in front, and the extinct volcano Monte Cavo to the left. Check at the tourist office in Frascati to see if tours are being given; if not, ask for a map.

Frascati's 17th-century duomo, reconstructed after damage in WWII, rises above P. Mercato with a Baroque facade that is currently undergoing restorations. Half a block down the street is the **Chiesa del Gesù,** designed by Pietro da Cortona with interior frescoes by Andrea Pozzi.

Death masks and churches not withstanding, the main attraction here is still wine. Pick up a bottle and other picnic supplies at the market at P. del Mercato, off P. del Duomo (open M-Sa 9am-noon), or try **Bar Baioni,** to the right of the duomo at P. del Duomo, 16, where the locals flock for homemade pastries (L.1500/€0.78), pannini (L.3500/€1.75) and capuccino (L1300/€0.65). (Open every day, 6am-midnight.)If you'd rather sit down, **Trattoria Sora Irma,** V.S.S. Filippo e Giacomo, 12, located above the center of Frascati. From P. Marconi, take a left up the steps of V. Pietro Campana; V.S.S. Filippo e Giacomo is on your left. (Open W-Su 11am-3pm and 7-11pm.) The local specialty is *porchetta*, a greasy, sliced, fried pork dish said to complement the fine Frascati vintages perfectly. **Zaraza,** V. R. Margherita, 2, is another *trattoria* with simple, good food at low prices, and a terrace with an unbeatable view. (☎06 9422053. L.15,000/€7.75 for primi and wine. Open Tu-Su noon-2:30pm and 7:30-10:30pm. AmEx/MC/V.) Another place to soak up the local culture—and wine—is at the **Cantina Il Pergolato,** V. del Castello, 20, off P. del Mercato. It serves homemade wine, pizza, and other fare in a cave-like dining room. (☎06 9420464. L20,000/€10.30 for *antipasti* and *primi.* Open daily 12:30-2:30pm and 3:30-10:30pm. MC/V.)

LAKE ALBANO & LAKE NEMI

From Frascati, take a ***bus*** *marked "Albano" from P. Marconi (1 per hr., 6:35am-8:35pm). The bus should let you off in P. Mazzini, the center of Albano. Free map at* ***tourist office,*** *V. Risorgimento, 1 (☎06 9324082 or 06 9324081; fax 06 9320040). From the piazza, take a right onto Corso Matteotti; after about 7 blocks take a left on V.S. Martino and a right onto V. Risorgimento. The tourist office is left after the intersection. Open M-F 9am-1pm and 4-7pm, Sa 9am-12:30.* ***Museo Civico,*** *☎06 9323490. Open daily 8:30am-noon, W-Th 4-7pm, Sa 8-4. L4000/€2.06; under six or over 60 L3000/€1.55.*

A few kilometers across the hills from Frascati, the other Castelli Romani cling to the sides of an extinct volcanic crater, now filled with the shimmering blue waters of **Lago Albano,** one of Lazio's cleanest and chilliest swimming spots. Crisp wines, clear mountain views, and a taste of Italian country life are the main attractions among these *castelli.* **Albano** lies on the Appian Way, and was once home to the villa of Emperor Domiziano and the less palatial camp of Septimus Severus' soldiers. Today, emperors and soldiers are harder to find, but Albano remains the largest and most commercial town of the Castelli Romani.

An outdoor market in P. Luigi Sabatini (down C. Matteoti and up the stairs from P. Mazzini), sells the region's fruits, vegetables, and gigantic fish. (Open M-Sa 7am-2pm.) A bit farther on, artifacts and pictorial reconstructions of the Paleolithic through Renaissance ages, gathered in Albano and surrounding areas, are housed in the **Museo Civico,** V. Risorgimento, 3, next to the tourist office. At the end of June, look for gladiators (in skimpy costumes weilding daggers, tridents and various blunt objects) duking it out in the town's *Spettacolo Gladiatorio.*

CASTEL GANDOLFO

Buses go to the beach from Castel Gandolfo and Albano (every 1-1½hr., L1200/€0.62).

North of Albano, tiny **Castel Gandolfo** owes its fame to the Pope, who occupies its volcanic ridge in the summer. He likes to stop by when the Vatican gets too stifling, to enjoy his famed gardens, which spread down the outer rim of the crater toward the sea. The palace, declared an inalienable dominion of the Holy See in 1608, was enlarged according to a plan by Maderno and is topped by a modern dome, the center of the old Vatican Observatory. (Just in case the Pope wants to check and see if the Big Guy's still up there.) The Pope is in residence in Castel Gandolfo from July to September, and audiences are held Wednesdays at 11am. On Sundays at noon, the Pope says mass.

The town's public street and one tiny *piazza*, dominated by Maderno's early Baroque papal palace, offer glimpses of the lake and mountain scenery which have drawn pontiffs here for centuries. The *piazza* also houses the **Church of San Tommaso di Villanova,** an early work by Bernini, along with a Bernini fountain. A lake road opens out to several belvederes, from which you can catch better views of Lake Albano. A winding road leads down to a public beach (about 2km), where you can rent sailboats.

ARICCIA

South of Albano, the same lake road passes a spacious park (open 8am-7pm; Oct.-May 8am-5pm. Free.) and the curious **Tomb of the Horatii and Curiatii,** a Republican-age funeral monument believed to mark the graves of the famous triplets whose duel secured Rome's supremacy over ancient Alba Longa. **Ariccia**, 1km east of Albano on the same road, isn't noted for much other than the soaring viaduct that brings you into town; unless you have a craving for *porchetta* in one of the piazza's many *porchetterias*, it's best to keep driving. Ariccia's *piazza* is graced by the remains of a Republican temple, the medieval **Palazzo Chigi** (spruced up by Bernini in the 17th century), and—for the obsessive Bernini fan—another minor Bernini original, the round **Santa Maria dell'Assunzione.**

GENZANO

Catch a COTRAL bus to Nemi (L1500/€0.78); they leave on the hour from P.T. Frasconi.

Kings and rock stars get red velvet carpets, Dorothy gets a yellow brick road, and lucky souls who visit Genzano the Sunday after Corpus Christus get an avenue of flowers. Since 1778, the *Infiorata* has covered Via Livia with elaborate floral designs, often representing famous works of art. (The theme for 2001 was Michelangelo's Sistine Ceiling.) Look for posters in Rome, or consult an ecclesiastical calendar for the exact date.

NEMI

Nemi Museum of Ships: open Tu-Su 9am-2pm. L8000/€4.13; EU citizens under 12 free.)

From Ariccia, the road continues south to Lake Nemi, another flooded crater where life is a little more tranquil than in other, more touristed *castelli.*. Ancient Romans, marveling at Nemi's placid blue waters, called the lake "the Mirror of Diana" and graced its sloping shores with a **temple** to the goddess. Surrounded by a sacred grove, the temple was presided over by a eunuch priest who got his job by killing his predecessor and plucking a golden bough off one of the grove's trees. The village boasts more staircases than streets, but miniature strawberries *(fragoline di Nemi)*, grown along the lake's shores, are its real glory. A bowl filled with the tiny fruits, soaked in lemon juice, and topped with a dollop of fresh *panna* (cream) is a specialty at bars lining the belvedere overlooking the lake. **Locanda Specchio di Diana,** Corso V.Emanuele, 13, is a good bet. (☎ 06 9368805; fax 06 9368016. Claims to be *sempre aperto*—always open.) In late June and early July, the town hosts a strawberry festival.

The **Nemi Museum of Ships,** 15 minutes down the road from Nemi, was built to house two of Caligula's Roman barges. Although L. Battista Alberti tried to refloat the Emperor's party boats in 1487, all efforts failed until the ships were dredged from the lake in the late 1920s. During WWII, the ships were torched by the Nazis as they retreated from Italy, so the museum displays two scale models and the few bits of lead and bronze that weren't melted in the blaze.

ROCCA DI PAPA

Marino's a good place to make COTRAL bus connections back to Rome (L2000/€1.03).

The lake road continues north to the summit of Monte Cavo, where **Rocca di Papa,** the highest of the Castelli Romani, glowers over Lake Albano. The town, dating from the 3rd century BC, doesn't offer much in the way of architecture anymore, but the views of the lake are the reason for the hike. On the other side of Monte Cavo, **Marino** closes the circle of *castelli* to the north. If you're in town on the first Sunday in October, you'll see the town's fountains flowing with wine during the annual Sagra dell'Uva.

PONTINE ISLANDS

Several companies run aliscafi *(hydrofoils) and slower, cheaper* traghetti *(larger car ferries).* ***From Rome,*** *take the* ***train*** *from Termini to Anzio (L56,000/€29.00) and then the* ***CAREMAR*** *ferry from Anzio to Ponza (June 16-Sept. 23 M-F 1pm, Sa 8:30am, Su and holidays 8:30am and 3pm; return M-F 5pm, Sa 5:15pm, Su and holidays 11am and 5:15pm; L35,000/€17.60).*

*CAREMAR **ticket office** in Anzio (☎06 98600083; www.caremar.it) is in the white booth on the quay; in Ponza (☎0771 80565). Or, take the faster **Linee Vetor** hydrofoils (3-5 per day; 8:15am-5:15pm; return 9:50am-6pm; L36,000/€18.20, resident L13,000/€6.75). Linee Vetor **ticket office** in Anzio (☎06 9845083; www.vetor.it) is on the quay; in Ponza (☎0771 80549). **From Formia,** CAREMAR runs 2 boats a day (L35,000/€17.60; 9am-5:30pm, return 5:30am and 2:30pm), as does Vetor (8:10am-2:30pm, return 10am-6:30pm; L36,000).*

The sorceress Circe reputedly ensared Odysseus on the Homeric isle of Eea contained in this archipelago off the southern coast of Lazio, the Isle of Sirens (Ventotene) likewise seducing his crew. Nero was expatriated to the *isole;* Mussolini cast enemies to the state upon the 30 million year old volcanic residuum, only to later be imprisoned here himself. For nearly two centuries Anarchists and the like were jailed in a Neapolitan king's prison. The prison's been out of use since the 60s, but Romans continue to surrender themselves as captives to the Pontine's soaring natural beauty and soothing calm, in self-banishment from summertime traffic, smog, and stifling heat.

Not a bad place to get locked up in; the Isole Pontine, including Ponza, Palmarola, Zannone, and Ventotene, are awash with stunning, cliff-sheltered beaches connected by rugged Mediterranean coastline knifing into the clean, turquoise-blue water of the Tyrrhenian. The blues are reflected in painted shutters hung on cloud-white cement houses, the domes overrun with fuschia blossoms. Coves, inlets, and grottoes cut from the volcanic stone lie in all their natural beauty around each turn of the winding roads.

Yet here the cars slow down, and so do the people. Grocery shoppers don bikinis, spoiled twelve-year olds sell seashells by the twinkling seashore, swim fins joust playfully with speedboat blades. A man's wife passes him his cellphone—he takes one look at the display and shakes his head. The cellphone goes back in her purse, and the man returns to his lobster and linguini.

A 60-mile ferry ride is a long way to go, and the 60,000+ lira fare a lot to pay—but entirely worth it for two or three or four days here (you'll inevitably stay chained to the beach longer than you planned). Join the ranks of Greek heroes, suicidal emperors, and violent hippy revolutionaries: become an exile.

PONZA

*To navigate Ponza, **Autolinee Isola di Ponza buses** leave from V. Dante (every 15-20min. until 1am; buy tickets from driver L1750/€0.75). Follow C. Pisacane until it becomes V. Dante (past the tunnel); stop is to your left. Buses stop by request, so flag them down at stops. Look for **private taxis** near the main bus stand or pick up a list of phone numbers at tourist office. **Water taxis** leave near the docks and go to beaches and harbors around the island (from L6000/€3.20 roundtrip; arrange pick-up time with driver unless going to well-frequented spots). **Pro Loco tourist office,** V. Molo Musco, at the far right of the port, next to the lighthouse, in the long red building. Offers "alternative" tours of the island's many Roman and Bourbon-era archaeological sites. ☎0771 80031; prolocoponza@libero.it. Open summer M-Sa 9am-1pm and 4-8:30pm, Su 9am-1pm and 5-8:10pm. **Emergency:** ☎113. **Post Office:** P. Pisacane. ☎0771 80672. Open M-F 8am-2pm, Sa 8am-12:10pm. **Postal code:** 04027.*

The craggy cliffs of this island were created in the late Tertiary, when volcanic activity thrust the precipices up out of the water during a three million-year long growth spurt. Imperial Romans built a port and fortifications on this island, known as Circide or Enotria. The collapse of the Roman empire depopulated the islands, and until the arrival of the Bourbons in 1734, the island was in the hands of pirates, who enslaved the few remaining *ponzese.* Mussolini used Ponza as a depository for dissenters, and in a beautiful piece of historical irony, was imprisoned here himself for two weeks in summer 1943. The island entertains boatloads of tourists every summer, with the occasional Italian celebrity joining in the migration to the beach. Marauding pirates, belligerent dictators, and Gucci-wearing glitterati aside, *dunque, tutti siamo in vacanza*—we're all equal in the eyes of the sun gods.

In Ponza, the laid-back island lifestyle has resulted in a happy disregard for street signs, addresses, or maps. There are only a handful of streets and addresses you'll ever need to know: **V. Banchina Nuova,** which runs along the docks and changes to **V. Dante** on the other side of the **S. Antonio tunnel; Corso Pisacane,** which runs along the port above the docks; **V. Molo Musco,** jutting out along the pier to your right as you face the water; and **P. Carlo Pisacane,** where V. Molo Muscolo meets C. Pisacane. Everything you could want is on the docks or nearby, and the locals are friendly and more than helpful in showing you the way, even if they don't know English (which, be forewarned, most Ponzese do not). *Isole Pontine*, a comprehensive guide to the islands is L12,000/€6.20 at newsstands.

SIGHTS

Excellent beaches are everywhere on Ponza. **Cala dello Schiavone and Cala Cecata** (on the bus line) are excellent spots. Essential points of sun-bathing intrest, however, are **Chiaia di Luna** and **Piscine Naturali.** A 10-minute walk from the port will take you to chiaia, set at the foot of a spectacular 200-meter cliffside. Go down C. Pisacane and turn left before reaching the tunnel. Soon, a path to the left will lead you under the road and through a series of tunnels to the beach. A sheer wall of tufo rises 20 feet from the water's edge. The rocky beach still provides ample room for sunbathing, though it does get crowded. A lovely ride through Ponza's hillside will take you to the even lovelier Piscine Naturali (take the bus to Le Foma and ask to be let off at the Piscine. Cross the street and make go down the long, steep path.) Cliffs crumbling into the ocean create a series of deep, crystal-clear natural pools separated by smooth rocky outcroppings perfect for sunbathing. Rumor has it that there are spots for cliff-diving in the area, though Let's Go does not officially recommend throwing yourself off of a 15m cliff. Locals know the right spots; jump at your own risk. One word of **caution:** spiny sea urchins line the rocks.

Water taxis (from L6000/€3.20) run from the port to the beach of Frontone on the east side of the island north of Ponza, Punta della Madonna (where you can still see rock-carved pools in which the ancient Romans farmed fish) just east of Ponza, as well as such unspoiled beaches farther away from Ponza as Core, Spaccapolpi, Cala Fonte, and Cala Feola. You can rent kayaks, paddle-boats, motorized rafts, and scuba gear along the port. **Settemari,** V. Banchina, 25 (☎0771 80653) rents boats with especially helpful guides who will show you around for L15,000/€7.75 per person per hour. The tourist office also offers tours of the sites on the island. The **Ponza Diving Center,** V. Banchina (☎0771 809788; www.ponzadiving.com) charges L50,000/€25.80 for 2-hr. guided submersions. Open water diver courses start at L500,000/€258.00. (Open daily 10am-1pm and 5-8pm. AmEx/MC/V.)

ACCOMMODATIONS & FOOD

Hotel rooms on Ponza hover in the L200,000/€103.30 zone. Let's Go recommends forgoing hotels entirely and checking out one of many *immobiliare vacanze* (vacation property) offices instead. The tourist office has a list of over 10 helpful agencies that can assist you in finding a room or apartment. The folks at **Isotur,** Corso Piscacane, 18 (☎0771 80339; agenzia.isotur@tin.it; www.isotur.it) are friendly and, more importantly, can set you up with a double room with a bath, kitchen, terrace, and beautiful views in nearby Santa Maria (really an extension of Ponza) for as little as L70,000/€36.20 per night in June; up to L90,000/€45.50 in July and L130,000/€67.10 in August. Apartments for six for a week L800,000-L2,500,000/€406.00-1288.00. They have over 100 apartments under their keep, and the office is conveniently located on the port next door to the very visible Hotel Mari. (Open May M-F 9:30am-12:30pm and 4:30-8pm, Sa 9:15am-1pm and 4-8:30pm; June-August daily 9:15am-8:30pm. MC/V.) If you're not up for a trip from the port, **Hotel Mari,** C. Piscacane, 19 (☎0771 80101; hotel.mari@tin.it) has classy decor and clean, air-conditioned rooms with bathrooms, telephone, and TV. (Breakfast included. Internet L6000/€3.20 per 30 min. Singles L80-120,000/€40.30-61.90; doubles, many with brilliant views of the water, L110-L240,000/€56.76-123.60. AmEx/D/MC/V.)

The islands are known and loved for their lentil soup, fish, and spiny lobster. Restaurants and bars line the port and grocery stores crowd the streets running along the docks. The restaurants are on the expensive side, with plates of pasta costing L20,000, but Ristorante da Antonio, on the water at V. Dante (☎0771 809832), has seafood and a view well worth the splurge. A full meal with wine will cost in the area of L60,000. *Raviolini ai gamberoni* (with shrimp, L10,000/€5.16 per etto; L25,000/€12.88 per serving) and *pesce spada alla griglia* (grilled swordfish, L7000/€3.62 per etto; L20,000/€10.30 per serving) are excellent.

PALMAROLA

Palmarola is only accessible by boat. Either rent one (from L65,000/€34.58 per day) or sign up for a guided boat tour offered by one of the many offices at the port advertising una gita a Palmarola. Cooperativa Barcaioli Ponzesi, *C. Piscacane at the S. Antonio tunnel, provides excursions to Palmarola (☎0771 809929; departure 10:30am, return 6pm; L35,000/€17.60).*

Palmarola is an uninhabited islet perched off the northeast coast of the island. The clear, turquoise water, irregular volcanic rock formations, and steep white cliffs (tinted red by iron deposits and yellow by sulphur) of the island are incredible. As you approach Palmarola, you will see **Dala Brigantina,** a natural lime amphitheater. Also visible are houses built upon prehistoric sites lodged into the mountainside. Most excursions visit the **Pilatus Caves** at Ponza, a breeding ground for fish.

ZANNONE

Zannone is only accessible by boat. Trips offered by Cooperativa Barcaioli Ponzesi, *C. Piscacane at the S. Antonio tunnel (☎0771 809929; departure 10:30am, return 6pm; L35,000/€17.60).*

Zannone is a nature and wildlife preserve whose lands are encompassed by the National Park of Circeo. Zannone offers the nature-lover a refreshing break from the beach and the opportunity to see virgin Mediterranean wildlife at its least tainted. Tours will take you around the coast, allowing time for walks on the *mufloni*-strewn island, through the *lecci* forrests, and to the large medieval monastery of S. Spirito.

VENTOTENE

Motor ***boat rentals*** *from the port L60,000/€32.00; rowboats L20,000/€10.30.* ***Ponza-Ventotene: CAREMAR hydrofoil*** *from Ponza, daily (except Su Oct.-Apr.) 6:10am; from Ventotene, returns 4pm Oct. 16-April14, 5:40pm Sept. 23-Oct. 15, 7:10pm Aug.15-Sept. 22; L20,500/€10.55. ALISCAFI SNAL* ***hydrofoils*** *go from* ***Ponza to*** *the smaller island of* ***Ventotene*** *(50min.; 11:15am-6:15pm, return 10:05am-5pm; L15,000/€7.75). The* ***Tourist office,*** *Centro Servizio Ventotene, Località Porto Romano (☎0771 85273; fax 0771 854107), is at the port (follow the "i" signs), managed by an English-speaking staff. Open daily 9am-1pm and 4:30-7pm, winter 4-7pm.* ***Archaeological Museum:*** *Call the Comune di Ventotene to arrange a visit ☎0771 85193. L4000/€2.06.* ***Tours of: Villa Giulia:*** *L6-8000/€3.20-4.13,* ***Necropoli:*** *L6-8000/€3.20-4.13,* ***Carcere of Santo Stefano:*** *L18,000/€9.20, including roundtrip boat ride.*

Far less accessible than Ponza (and freer of summer vacationing hordes) Ventotene is more striking, too. Here, the island lifestyle is untainted even by the roar of engines—cars and *motorini* are forbidden; the only homage to internal combustion is the outboard motor. Ventotene awaits you with the last vestiges of untouristed peace near Rome. The **Archaeological Museum** of Ventotene covers everything from Roman ruins and underwater archaeology to the prison Mussolini built here for "enemies of the state." The tourist office also arranges Italian-language tours of archaeological sites, including the **Villa Giulia** (a well-preserved villa where Augustus exiled his daughter, Giulia, for crimes of indecency), the prehistoric **Necropoli,** and the **Carcere of Santo Stefano,** the citadel where Mussolini enjoyed locking up anti-Fascists. Splendid beaches flank the port.

Pompeii

Inside Pompeii

Pottery

ETRURIA

The rolling hills north of Rome were once home to the Etruscans, a people who gave Rome much of its early art and culture, and provided its first kings. Their fascinating tombs still dot the landscape and provide a beautiful and fascinating glimpse of the lives and pleasures of their makers. Cerveteri boasts a field of dozens of large tombs, while well preserved tomb paintings lie outside the medieval walls and churches of Tarquinia. Many of the objects and statues originally found in the tombs are now in the **Villa Giulia** and the Vatican Museums.

CERVETERI

M: A-Lepanto or bus #70, then take the blue ***COTRAL*** *bus run to Cerveteri from Lepanto (every 30min.-1hr., L4900/€2.32). Last bus to Rome 8:05pm. Less frequent on Su. From the village, it's 1.5km to the* necropolis *along a country road; follow the signs downhill and then to the right. Whenever you see a fork in the road without a sign to guide you, choose the fork on the right, but don't follow the* "Da Paolo Vino" *sign at the final fork.* ***Tourist office,*** *V.d. Necropoli, 2, will answer queries. ☎06 9952304. Open Tu-Su 9:30am-12:30pm and 6-7:30pm.* ***Tomba dei Rilievi*** *☎06 9940001. Open M Tu-Su 9am-7:30pm; Oct.-Apr. Tu-Sa 9am-4pm. L8000/€4.13.* ***Museo Nazionale di Caerite:*** *☎06 9941354. Open May-Sept. Tu-Su 9am-7pm; Oct.-Apr. Tu-Sa 9am-4pm. Free.*

Cerveteri's lure lies in is its extensive Etruscan *necropolis*, a remnant of Kysry, the Etruscan town once located here, which was a port that conducted a lively trade business throughout the Mediterranean from the 7th to 5th century BC. The town was actually much larger than is visible from the excavated area; archeologists estimate that Kysry was about 20 times larger than modern Cerveteri.

The **Banditaccia Necropolis** is made up of dozens of Etruscan tombs up to 30 ft. high, designed to look like the round roofed houses the Etuscans once lived in, and laid out in orderly streets. The grass growing on top makes them resemble huge haystacks, but while the scene may be styled in the vein of Monet, exploring it is an experience straight out of Indiana Jones. Only a few tombs are lighted, but almost all are accessible, so you can wander around the tombs and underground chambers. Archaeologists have removed the objects of daily life (chariots, weapons, cooking implements) with which the dead were equipped, but the carved *tufa* columns and couches remain. Small rooms off each tomb's antechamber were the resting places of slaves and lesser household members; the central room held the bodies of the rest of the family, and the small chambers off the back were reserved for the most prominent men and women. Triangular headboards on a couch mark a women's graves, while a circular ones indicate that the deceased was male. Only some 50 of an estimated 5000 tombs have been excavated, mostly in a cluster of narrow streets at the heart of this city of the dead. Don't miss the **Tomb of the Shields and the Chairs,** the smaller **Tomb of the Alcove** (with a carved-out matrimonial bed), and the **row houses** where less well-to-do Etruscans rested in peace. Look for the colored stucco reliefs in the **Tomba dei Rilievi.**

Also worthwhile is the **Museo Nazionale di Caerite,** on the P.S. Maria Maggiore, in **Ruspoli Castle,** whose crenellations and ancient walls now protect Etruscan artifacts as painted vases and funerary statues that have been dug from the *necropolis* in the last 10 years (most of the rest having been carted off to the Etruscan museums of the Villa Giulia and the Vatican).

TARQUINIA

Trains *leave from Termini (1hr., 11 per day; last train leaves Tarquinia at 10:12pm, L10,200/ €5.26). Buses run from the train station to the beach (L1100/€0.57) and to the city center (L1500/€0.77) about every 30min. until 9:30pm.* ***Buses*** *link the town with Viterbo (1hr., L6000/ €3.20). For bus schedules and info on Etruria, try the* ***tourist office*** *in P. Cavour, near the medieval walls. ☎0766 856384. Open daily 8am-2pm and 4-7pm.* ***Museo Nazionale:*** *☎0766 856036. Open Tu-Su 9am-7pm. L12000.* ***Necropolis:*** *☎0766 856308. Open 9am-1hr. before sunset.*

When Rome was little more than a mud hut shanty town clinging to the Palatine Hill, Tarquin kings held the fledgling metropolis under their sway. Their vibrantly decorated tombs make their lives and pleasures seem vivid despite the intervening centuries. The city of Tarquinia is an attraction in itself, with a large and excellent Etruscan museum, walls overlooking the countryside, and medieval churches.

Buses stop just outside the medieval ramparts. Just inside P. Cavour is the majestic **Museo Nazionale,** one of the most comprehensive collections of Etruscan art outside of Rome and English explanations. It houses a superb collection of Etruscan sarcophagi (some with bright paintings still visible), several complete Etruscan tombs with beutiful frescoes on the top floor, votive statues, and an enormous range of Etruscan and (occasionally sexy) Greek vases. Look for the famous 4th-century BC terra cotta **Winged Horses** upstairs.

The museum ticket will admit you to the **necropolis.** Walk (15min.) from the museum. Head up C. V. Emanuele from P. Cavour past the main square with its fountain and turn right on V. Porta Tarquinia (V. Tombe Etruschi), and head out through the city gate, then continue left. The tombs are decorated with paintings of their occupants feasting, dancing, and hunting, depicted remarkably realisticly in warm red, yellow, and green paints and surrounded with beautiful abstract patterns. D. H. Lawrence's section on Tarquinia in *Etruscan Places* will give you a picture of the tombs as they were before they museumification.

Tarquinia's medieval churches are also worth exploring. Don't miss **San Pancrazio,** with its spiny-egg tower, or **San Martino,** with its simple interior and Romanesque arches. The most interesting church, the crumbling **Santa Maria del Castello,** must be reached by the old city bastions overgrown with climbing honeysuckle—from P. Cavour follow V. Mazzzini until the medieval gates, then go through them. The asymmetrical facade is due to the fact that the 12th-century church was built over the foundations of an earlier edifice. The white marble flooring, inscribed with cabalistic pictures, can still be seen at the edges of the later multi-colored mosaic. Ask the custodian to unlock the church doors—she lives to the left of the church. The brick towers dotted around the city were once private fortresses during those crazy Middle Ages. If you'd like a meal check out the excellent **Le Due Orfanelle,** V. Breve, 4, near the Church of San Francesco. (☎0766 856307. Open W-M noon-3pm and 7:30-11pm.)

LAKE BRACCIANO

M: A-Lepanto, then take the Cotral buse(L3900). Anguillara and Bracciano are accessible by train on the Rome-Viterbo line (every hr.; from Rome's San Pietro station 5:35am-9:45pm, last train to Rome 10:14pm; L5300/€2.74). ***Orsini-Odescalchi Castle:*** *☎06 99804348; www.odescalchi.it. Open Apr.-Sept. Tu-Su, mandatory tours in English at 10:30, 11:30am, 3:30, 5:30pm. L11,000/€5.67, children under 12 and military L9000/€4.50.*

Scenic Lake Bracciano lies in the hills an hour north of Rome, its clear, fresh water ringed by small beaches with swimming, and set against a charming backdrop of wooded farms on the surrounding slopes. Bracciano's large and impressive medieval castle towers over the quiet town below, and local restaraunts serve up platters of tasty fish or eel from the lake.

To get to Bracciano's main attraction, the **Orsini-Odescalchi Castle,** take V. A. Fausti from P. Roma to V. Umberto and turn right. The castle was built in the late 15th century for the Orsini, an ancient, independent-minded Roman family who managed to provoke (and more impressively, to withstand) the jealous rages of a succession of autocratic Renaissance popes. Even Cesare Borgia, Alexander VI's Machiavellian and rogueish son and commander-in-chief, never breached the castle's towers (the castle only succumbed in the 1670s, when the Odescalchi family tried a weapon more powerful than any pillaging army or battering ram—cold, hard, beautiful...cash. Inside, a series of salons and chambers wraps around two medieval courtyards, their walls and ceilings frescoed with the bears and roses of the Orsini arms, and a few stellar cycles by Antoniazzo Romano (a pupil of Pinturicchio), Taddeo, and Federico Zuccari. The rooms house more arms and armor than you can shake a halberd at and a **furry collection** of stuffed wild boars. In the summer, **classical music concerts** are hosted in the castle. Should you find yourself in the mood to burn large sums of cash , you can rent parts of the castle for receptions. To get to the lake from the castle (about 1km), head down V. Umberto and turn right, following the signs along V.d. Lago. The narrow strip of rough sand stretches in both directions, and stands rent **canoes** (L10-20,000 per hr.) and umbrellas and chairs (L5000 per day), while large amounts swaths of the beach are free. During the week the beaches are amazingly uncrowded, though on weekends many daytrippers pour in from Rome.

When you find yourself hungry, dine with the locals at **Trattoria del Castello,** in Piazza Mazzini, with tables outside in the shadow of the castle for big plates of pasta and grilled lake fish (L14,000; ☎06 998 04339; closed Tu). *Gelaterie* and a video arcade also promise relief from tedium to anyone who finds sunbathing and swimming too hot or insufficiently intellectually stimulating.

CAMPANIA

The fertile crescent of Campania, in the shadow of Mt. Vesuvius, cradles the Bay of Naples and the larger Gulf of Salerno. The fiery fields of Hades to the west and the ruins of Pompeii hiding beneath the crater captivate visitors year after year.

POMPEII (POMPEI)

The easiest way to get to Pompeii is to take one of many Rome-based bus tours. ***Enjoy Rome****'s self-guided tour (p. 23) is a deal at L70,000/€36.20 per person. On your own from Termini, take the train to Naples (every 15min.-1hr., 6:10am-10:30pm, L18,600-39,500/€9.77-20.30). From there, take the Circumvesuviana train (☎081 7722111), getting off at "Pompeii Scavi/Villa dei Misteri" (ignore "Pompeii Santuario"). Eurailpasses are not valid. Stop by the* ***tourist office,*** *V. Sacra, 1, for a free map. (☎081 8507255. Open M-F 8am-3:30pm, Sa 8am-2pm.) Store your pack for free at the entrance to the ruins. There is a* ***police station*** *at the entrance to the ancient site, but the main station is at P. Schettini, 1 (☎081 8506164), in the modern town, on the corner of P. B. Longo, at the end of V. Roma. Food at the ruins cafeteria is horribly expensive, so bring a lunch. Of the few restaurants and fruit stands that cluster outside the excavation entrances, the best is* ***La Vinicola,*** *V. Roma, 29 (☎081 863 12 44; cover L1500/€0.77; open daily 9am-midnight). Site* ***open*** *8:30am-1hr. before sunset: in summer around 6pm; in winter around 3:30pm. L16,000/€8.26.* ***Guidebooks*** *from L8000/€4.13. Useful* ***audioguide*** *recommended. A comprehensive exploration of Pompeii will probably take all day.*

On August 24, AD 79, life in the prosperous Roman city of Pompeii suddenly halted. A fit of towering flames, suffocating black clouds, and seething lava from Mt. Vesuvius buried the city—temples, villas, theaters, and all—under more than 7m of volcanic ash. Except for the few lucky ones who dropped everything and ran at the first tremors of catastrophe, the inhabitants of Pompeii suffered a live burial. Perhaps the most ghastly and evocative relics of the town's untimely death are the "frozen people," ash casts made of the victims' bodies, preserving their last contortions and expressions of horror. These amazing exhibits are visible (in glass cases) all over the ancient site. The excavation of Pompeii is ongoing, so many sights are poorly labeled. (Hey, it could be worse—you could be trapped under molten lava for 2000 years.) Since the first unearthings in 1748, every decade has brought new discoveries to light, slowly creating a vivid picture of life in the ancient Roman era.

PORTA MARINA

The **basilica** (Roman law court) walls are decorated with stucco made to look like marble. Walk farther down V.d. Marina to reach the **Forum,** which is surrounded by a colonnade. Once dotted with statues of emperors and gods, this site was the commercial, civic, and religious center of the city. Cases along the side display some of the gruesome body-casts of Vesuvius's victims. At the upper end rises the **Temple of Jupiter,** mostly destroyed by an earthquake that struck 17 years before the city's bad luck got worse. To the left, the **Temple of Apollo** contains statues of Apollo and Diana (originals in Naples' Museo Archeologico Nazionale,) and a column topped by a sundial. On the opposite side of the forum, the **Temple of Vespasian** houses a delicate frieze depicting preparation for a sacrifice. To the right, the **Building of Eumachia** has a carved door frame.

V. DELLA FORTUNA

Exit the Forum through the upper end, by the cafeteria, and enter the **Forum Baths** on the left. Here, chipping away parts of the bodycasts has revealed teeth and bones beneath. A right on V.d. Fortuna leads to the **House of the Faun,** where a bronze dancing faun and the spectacular Alexander Mosaic (originals in the **Museo Archeologico Nazionale,** p. 224) were found. Before the door, a floor mosaic proclaims *Have* (welcome). The sheer size and opulence of this building lead archaeologists to believe that it was the private dwelling of one of the wealthiest men in town.

Continuing on V.d. Fortuna and turning left on V. dei Vettii will bring you to the **House of the Vettii,** on the left, decorated with the most vivid frescoes in Pompeii. In the vestibule, a depiction of Priapus, the god of fertility, displays his colossal member. And while in ancient times, phalli were believed to scare off evil spirits; these days they seem only to make tourists titter.

VIA DEGLI AUGUSTALI

Back down V.d. Vetti, cross V.d. Fortuna over to V. Storto, and then turn left on V. degli Augustali, which displays the deep ruts of carriages on either side. The Romans who were repaving this worn path when the volcano struck left their task incomplete. A quick right leads to the small **brothel** (the Lupenar) containing several bedstalls. Above each stall, a pornographic painting depicts with unabashed precision the specialty of its occupant. After 2000 years, this remains the most popular place in town; you may have to wait in line. The street continues down to the main avenue, V.d. Abbondanza. To the left lie the **Stabian Baths,** which were privately owned and therefore fancier than the Forum Baths (think ritzy spa vs. YMCA). The separate men's and women's sides each include a dressing room, cold baths *(frigidaria)*, warm baths *(tepidaria)*, and hot steam baths *(caldaria)*.

VIA DEI TEATRI

V.d. Teatri, across the street, leads to a huge complex consisting of the **Great Theater,** constructed in the first half of the 2nd century BC, and the **Little Theater,** built later for music and dance concerts. North of the theaters stands the **Temple of Isis,** Pompeii's monument to the Egyptian fertility goddess. Through the exit on the right, the road passes two fine houses, the **House of Secundus** and the **House of Menander.** At the end of the street, a left turn will return you to the main road. The Romans believed that crossroads were particularly vulnerable to evil spirits, so they built altars (like the one here) designed to ward them off.

DELL'ABBONDANZA

On V.d. Abbondanza, red writing glares from the walls, expressing everything from political slogans to love declarations. Popular favorites include "Albanus is a bugger," "Restitutus has decieved many girls many times," and the lyrical "Lovers, like bees, lead a honey-sweet life"—apparently graffiti hasn't changed much in 2000 years. At the end of the street rest the **House of Tiburtinus** and the **House of Venus,** huge complexes with gardens replanted according to modern knowledge of ancient horticulture. The nearby **amphitheater** (80 BC), the oldest standing in the world, held 12,000 spectators. When battles occurred, crowds decided whether a defeated gladiator would live or die with a casual thumbs up or thumbs down.

To reach the **Villa of the Mysteries,** go to the far west end of V.d. Fortuna, turn right on V. Consolare, and walk all the way up Porta Ercolano. The best preserved of Pompeii's villas, it includes the Dionysiac Frieze, perhaps the largest painting from the ancient world, depicting the initiation of a bride into the cult of Dionysus. Head through the door in the Porta for a great view of the entire city.

HERCULANEUM (ERCOLANO)

Go 500m downhill from the Ercolano stop on the Circumvesuviana train from Naples (dir.: Sorrento, 20min., L3200/€1.65). Archaeological site open daily 8:30am to 1hr. before sunset. L16,000/€8.30. Tourist office ☎081 788 12 43. Open M, W-F 9am-1pm, Tu 4-6:30pm.

TEMPLE OF CERES AND ENVIRONS

There are three entrances to Paestum's ruins. The northernmost entrance leads to the Temple of Ceres. Built around 500 BC, this temple became a church in the early Middle Ages but was abandoned in the 9th century. The ancient Greeks built Paestum on a north-south axis, marked by the paved V. Sacra. Farther south on V. Sacra is the Roman **forum,** which is even larger than the one at Pompeii (p. 236). The Romans leveled most of the older structures in the city's center to build this proto-piazza, the commercial and political arena of Paestum. To the left, a pit marks the pool of an ancient **gymnasium.** East of the gymnasium lies the Roman **amphitheater.**

TEMPLE(S?) OF POSEIDON

Museum open daily 9am-6:30pm. Ticket office open daily 9am-5:30pm; closed 1st and 3rd Monday of each month. L8000, EU citizens over 60 and under 18 free.

South of the forum lies the 5th-century BC Temple of Poseidon (actually dedicated to Hera), which incorporates many of the optical refinements that characterize the Parthenon in Athens. Small lions' heads serve as gargoyles on the temple roof. The southernmost temple, known as the **basilica,** is the oldest, dating to the 6th century BC. Its unusual plan, with a main interior section split by a row of columns down the middle, has inspired the theory that the temple was dedicated to two gods, Zeus and Hera, rather than one. A **museum** on the other side of V. Magna Graecia houses an extraordinary collection of pottery, paintings, and artifacts taken primarily from Paestum's tombs, with outstanding bilingual descriptions and essays on site. It also includes samples of 2500-year-old honey and paintings from the famous **Tomb of the Diver,** dating to 475 BC.

Neatly excavated and impressively intact, the remains of the prosperous Roman town of Herculaneum (modern Ercolano) hardly deserve the term "ruins." Indeed, exploring the 2000-year-old houses, complete with frescoes, furniture, mosaics, small sculptures, and even wooden doors, feels like an invasion of privacy.

Herculaneum does not evoke the tragedy of Pompeii—most of its inhabitants escaped the ravages of Vesuvius. Only a small part of the southeastern quarter of the city has been excavated, and between 15 and 20 houses are open to the public. One of the more alluring is the **House of Deer** (named for the statues of deer in the courtyard), which displays the statue, *Satyr with a Wineskin,* and one of Hercules in a drunken stupor trying to relieve himself. The **baths,** with largely intact warm and hot rooms and a vaulted swimming pool, conjure up images of ancient opulence. The **House of the Mosaic of Neptune and Anfitrite,** which belonged to a rich shop owner, is famous for its namesake mosaic, and the front of the house has a remarkably well-preserved wine shop. A mock colonnade of stucco distinguishes the **Samnise House.** Down the street, the **House of the Wooden Partition** still has a door in its elegant courtyard, and an ancient clothes press around the corner. Cardo IV shows you what a Roman street must have looked like. Outside the site, 250m to the left on the main road, lies the **theater,** perfectly preserved underground. The **Villa dei Papiri,** 500m west of the site, recently caused a stir when it was thought that a trove of ancient scrolls in the library included works by Cicero, Virgil, and Horace. Unfortunately, neither of these sites is generally open.

MT. VESUVIUS

Trasporti Vesuviani buses run from the Ercolano Circumvesuviana station to the crater of Vesuvius. Schedule available at tourist office; buy tickets on the bus (round-trip L6000/€3.10). L9000/€4.65.

Peer into the only active volcano on mainland Europe. It's a 20 to 30min. walk from the bus stop to the top of Mt. Vesuvius, so bring plenty of water and wear sturdy shoes. Scientists say volcanoes should erupt about every 30 years—Vesuvius hasn't erupted since March 31, 1944. Nevertheless, experts say the trip is safe.

PAESTUM

*From Termini, take the **train** to Naples (every 15min.-1hr., 6:10am-10:30pm, L18,600-39,500), then take the train to Paestum (1¼hr., 9 per day 5:30am-10pm, L8200) via Salerno (35min., L4700). **CTSP buses** from Salerno (1hr., every hr. 7am-7pm, L4700) stop at Via Magna Graecia, the main modern road. The tourist office in Salerno provides a helpful list of all return buses from Paestum. The **AAST Information Office,** V. Magna Graecia, 155, is next to the museum. (☎082 811016; fax 082 8722322. Open July-Sept. 15 M-Sa 8am-2pm and 3:30-7:30pm, Su 9am-noon; Sept. 16-June M-Sa 8am-2pm.) The pleasant beachside **Ostello "La Lanterna" (HI),** V. Lanterna, 8, in Agropoli, is the nearest budget accommodation. (☎/fax 0974 838364. 56 beds. Sheets and shower included. Dorms L17,000; quads L68,000.) To get to Agropoli, take the CTSP buses from Paestum (10min., 1 per hr. 7am-7pm, L2000) or from Salerno (1hr., L4700). Agropoli is also connected by train to Paestum (10min., L2200); Salerno (45min., L4700); and Naples (1½hr., L8200). Temples **open** daily 9am-1hr. before sunset; closed 1st and 3rd Monday of each month; last admittance 2hr. before sunset. L8000, EU citizens over 60 and under 18 free.*

Not far from the Roman ruins of Pompeii and Herculaneum, the three Doric Greek temples of Paestum are among the best preserved in the world, even rivaling those of Sicily and Athens. They rank among the best preserved in the world. Originally built without any mortar or cement (they were simply covered by roofs of terra-cotta tiles supported by wooden beams) the temples remained standing even after the great earthquake of AD 69 reduced Pompeii's streets to a pile of rubble. When excavators first uncovered the three temples, they misidentified (and thus misnamed) them, and the names have stuck. Misnomers have been Paestum's M.O. from the beginning. Greek colonists from Sybaris founded Paestum as Poseidonia in the 7th century BC, and it became a flourishing commercial and trade center. After a period of native Italian control in the 5th and 4th centuries BC, Poseidonia fell to the Romans in 273 BC, was renamed Paestum, and remained a Roman town until the deforestation of nearby hills turned the town into a swampy mush. Plagued by malaria and syphilitic pirates, Paestum's ruins lay relatively untouched until they were rediscovered in the 18th century.

INSIDE

Planning Your Trip

DOCUMENTS & FORMALITIES

All applications should be filed several weeks or months before departure. Demand for passports is highest between January and August, so try to apply as early as possible.

PASSPORTS

REQUIREMENTS

Citizens of Australia, Canada, Ireland, New Zealand, South Africa, the UK, and the US need valid passports to enter Italy and to re-enter their home countries.

PHOTOCOPIES

Be sure to photocopy the page of your passport with your photo, passport number, and other identifying information, as well as any visas, travel insurance policies, plane tickets, or traveler's check serial numbers. Carry one set of copies in a safe place, apart from the originals, and leave another set at home. Consulates also recommend that you carry an expired passport or an official copy of your birth certificate in a part of your baggage separate from other documents.

LOST PASSPORTS

If you lose your passport, immediately notify the local police and the nearest embassy or consulate of your home government. To expedite its replacement, you will need to know all information previously recorded and show ID and proof of citizenship. In some cases, a replacement may take weeks to process, and may be valid for a limited time. Any visas stamped in your old passport will be irretrievably lost. In an emergency, ask for immediate temporary traveling papers that will permit you to re-enter your home country. Your passport is a public document belonging to your nation's government. You may have to surrender it to a foreign government official, but if you don't get it back in a reasonable amount of time, inform the nearest mission of your home country.

NEW PASSPORTS

Citizens of Australia, Canada, Ireland, New Zealand, the United Kingdom, and the United States can apply for a passport at the nearest post office, passport office, or court of law. Citizens of South Africa can apply for a passport at the nearest office of Foreign Affairs. Any new passport or renewal applications must be filed well in advance of the departure date, although most passport offices offer rush services for a very steep fee. Citizens living abroad who need a passport or renewal services should contact the nearest consular service of their home country.

VISAS & WORK PERMITS

British, Irish, and **EU** citizens need only carry a valid passport to enter Italy, and they may stay in the country for as long as they like. Citizens of **Australia, Canada, New Zealand,** and the **US** do not need visas for tourism or business stays of up to three months. US citizens can take advantage of the **Center for International Business and Travel (CIBT;** ☎800-925-2428), which, for a service charge, secures visas for travel to almost any country. As of August 2000, citizens of South Africa need a visa—a stamp, sticker, or insert in your passport specifying the purpose of your travel and the permitted duration of your stay—in addition to a valid passport for entrance to Italy. Visas cost US$25 (for business or tourism visas) and US$10 (for transit visas) and US$30 (student visa). Visas can be purchased at your home country's consulate. Any visa granted by Italy will be respected by the following countries: which make up the Schengen area: Austria, Belgium, France, Germany, Greece, Luxembourg, Portugal, Spain, and The Netherlands. The extensive requirements for this visa include: passport (valid for 10 months from departure), recent passport photo, application form, itinerary including border of entry and duration of stay in each country, proof of sufficient funds, proof of insurance, a valid return airline ticket and a photocopy of it, proof of accommodations, or if residing with friends or relatives, a letter of invitation certified by Italian Police Authorities. The duration of one stay or a succession of stays may not exceed 90 days per six months. The cost of a visa varies with duration and number of entries; one entry with the maximum 90-day stay costs 198 ZAR. Double-check on entrance requirements at the nearest embassy or consulate of Italy (listed under **Embassies & Consulates,** on p. 243) for up-to-date info before departure. US citizens can also consult the website at www.pueblo.gsa.gov/cic_text/travel/foreign/foreignentryreqs.html.Within eight days of arrival, all foreign nationals staying with friends or relatives or uptaking private residence must register with the local police office and receive a *permesso di soggiorno* (permit of stay) for L20,000. If you are staying in a hotel or hostel, the officials will fulfill registration requirements for you and the fee is waived. Those wishing to stay in Italy for more than three months for the sole purpose of tourism must apply for an extention at a local *questura* at least one month before the original permit expires. Extensions are granted at the discretion of the local authorities. EU citizens do not need permission to **work** in Italy. Non-EU citizens seeking work must apply for an Italian work permit before entering the country.

IDENTIFICATION

When you travel, always carry two or more forms of identification on your person, including at least one photo ID; a passport combined with a driver's license or birth certificate is usually adequate. Many establishments, especially banks, may require several IDs in order to cash traveler's checks. Never carry all your forms of ID together; split them up in case of theft or loss.

For more information on all the forms of identification listed below, contact the organization that provides the service, the **International Student Travel Confederation (ISTC),** Herengracht 479, 1017 BS Amsterdam, Netherlands (☎+31 20 421 2800; fax 421 2810; istcinfo@istc.org; www.istc.org).

TEACHER & STUDENT IDENTIFICATION

The **International Student Identity Card (ISIC),** the most widely accepted form of student ID, provides discounts on sights such as the Vatican and Capitoline museums, hostel rooms, bike rentals, and admission to nightclubs, among other things. The ISIC is preferable to an institution-specific card (such as a university ID) because it is more likely to be recognized abroad. Cardholders have access to a 24hr. emergency helpline for medical, legal, and financial emergencies (in North America call ☎877-370-ISIC, elsewhere call US collect +1 715-345-0505), and US cardholders are also eligible for insurance benefits (see **Insurance,** p. 250). Many student travel agencies issue ISICs, including STA Travel in Australia and New Zealand; Travel CUTS in Canada; usit in the Republic of Ireland and Northern Ireland; SASTS in South Africa; Campus Travel and STA Travel in the UK; Council Travel (www.counciltravel.com/idcards/default.asp) and STA Travel in the US (see p. 251).

The card is valid from September of one year to December of the following year and costs US$22. Applicants must be degree-seeking students of a secondary or post-secondary school and must be of at least 12 years of age. Some services (particularly airlines) require additional proof of student identity. The **International Teacher Identity Card (ITIC)** offers the same insurance coverage as well as similar but limited discounts. The fee is US$22.

YOUTH IDENTIFICATION

The International Student Travel Confederation also issues a discount card to travelers who are 25 years old or under, but are not students. This one-year **International Youth Travel Card** (**IYTC;** formerly the **GO 25** Card) offers many of the same benefits as the ISIC. Most organizations that sell the ISIC also sell the IYTC (US$22).

EMBASSIES & CONSULATES

For foreign **consular services** in Rome, check the **Service Directory** p. 290.

ITALIAN CONSULAR SERVICES ABROAD

Address questions concerning visas and passports to consulates, not embassies.

Australia: Embassy, 12 Grey St., **Deakin, Canberra** A.C.T. 2600 (☎612 6273 3333; fax 6273 4223; embassy@ambitalia.org.au; www.ambitalia.org.au). Open M-F 9am-12:30pm; M 2:30-4pm. **Consulates:** AMP Place, 10 Eagle St., 14th level, **Brisbane** QLD 4000 (☎00617 3229 8944; fax 3229 8643; italcons.brisbane@bigpond.com). Open M-F 9am-1pm; Th 9am-3pm; 509 St. Kilda Rd., **Melbourne** VIC 3004 (☎613 867 5744; fax 866 3932); Level 45, "The Gateway," 1 Macquarie Pl., **Sydney** NSW 2000 (☎612 9392 7939; fax 9392 7935; office@iisyd.org). All consular information is available through the embassy website.

Canada: Embassy, 275 Slater St., 21st fl., **Ottawa,** ON K1P 5H9 (☎613-232-2401; fax 233-1484; italcomm@trytel.com; www.italyincanada.com). **Consulate,** 496 Huron St., **Toronto,** ON M5R 2R3 (☎416-921-3802; fax 962-2503).

Ireland: Embassy, 63, Northumberland Rd., **Dublin** (☎3531 660 1744; fax 668 2759; italianembassy@tinet.ie; homepage.eircom.net/~italianembassy). Open M-F 10am-12:30pm.

New Zealand: Embassy, 34 Grant Rd., **Wellington** (☎006 4473 5339; fax 472 9302; ambwell@xtra.co.nz).

UK: Embassy, 14, Three Kings Yard, **London** W1Y 2EH (☎020 7312 2200; fax 7499 2283; emblondon@embitaly.org.uk; www.embitaly.org.uk). **Consulates:** 38 Eaton Pl., **London** SW1X 8AN (☎440 20 7235 9371; fax 7823 1609); Rodwell Tower, 111 Piccadilly, **Manchester** M1 2HY (☎440 161 236 9024; fax 236 5574; passaporti@italconsulman.demon.co.uk); 32 Melville St., **Edinburgh** EH3 7HA (☎440 131 226 3631; fax 226 6260; consedimb@consedimb.demon.co.uk).

US: Embassy, 1601 Fuller St, **Washington, D.C.** 20009(☎202-328-5500; stampa@itwash.org; www.italyemb.org). **Consulates:** 100 Boylston St., Suite #900, **Boston,** MA 02116 (☎617-542-0483/4; fax 542-3998; it.conbos@ix.netcom.com; www.reference.it/cgboston); 500 N. Michigan Ave. Suite #1850, **Chicago,** IL 60611 (☎312-467-1550; fax 467-1335; consul@consitchicago.org; 12400 Wilshire Blvd. Suite #300, **Los Angeles,** CA 90025 (☎310-820-0622; fax 820-0727; Cglos@conlang.com; www.conlang.com); 690 Park Ave. (visas 54 E. 69th St.), **New York,** NY 10021 (☎212-737-9100; fax 249-4945; italconsny@aol.com; www.italconsulnyc.org);

1026, Public Ledger Building, 100 South 6th St., **Philadelphia,** PA 19106-3470 (☎215-592-7329 or 592 7370; fax 592 9808; conphila@op.net).

TOURIST OFFICES

The privately owned **Enjoy Rome** (p. 23) and the official **EPT** (p. 24) and **PIT** (p. 23) are the best places to turn when you have questions about Rome.

Italian Government Tourist Board (ENIT), 630 Fifth Ave. Suite #1565, **New York,** NY 10111 (☎ (212) 245-5095; fax (212) 586-9249; www.enit.it). Write or call their travel brochure hotline (☎ (212) 245-4822) to receive a free copy of their guide *Italia: General Information for Travelers to Italy* (containing train and ferry schedules). **Branch offices:** 1 Princess St., **London** WIR 9AY-1 (☎ (0044) 20-73551557; fax (0044) 20-7493 6695); Enitolond@globalnet.co.uk; 12400 Wilshire Blvd. Suite #550, **Los Angeles,** CA 90025 (☎ (310) 820-1898; fax (310) 820-6357);17 Bloor St., M4W3R8 **Toronto** ON (☎(416) 925-4882; fax (416) 925-4799); enit.canada@on.aibn.com.

Italian Cultural Institute, 686 Park Ave., New York, NY 10021 (☎ (212) 879-4242; fax (212) 861-4018). Often more prompt and helpful than ENIT.

CUSTOMS

Upon entering Italy, you must declare certain items from abroad and pay a duty on the value of those articles that exceeds the allowance established by Italy's customs service. Note that goods and gifts purchased at **duty-free** shops abroad are not exempt from duty or sales tax at your point of return and thus must be declared as well; "duty-free" merely means that you need not pay a tax in the country of purchase. Duty-free allowances were abolished for travel between EU member states on July 1, 1999, but exist for those arriving from outside the EU. Upon returning home, you must declare all articles acquired abroad and pay a duty on the value of articles in excess of your home country's allowance. In order to expedite your return, list any valuables brought from home and register them with customs before traveling abroad. Also be sure to keep receipts for all goods acquired abroad.

MONEY

CUSTOMS IN THE EU. As well as freedom of movement of people within the EU, travelers in the countries that are members of the EU (Austria, Belgium, Denmark, Finland, France, Germany, Greece, Ireland, Italy, Luxembourg, the Netherlands, Portugal, Spain, Sweden, and the UK) can also take advantage of the freedom of movement of goods. This means there are no customs controls at internal EU borders (i.e., you can take the blue customs channel at the airport), and travelers are free to transport whatever legal substances they like as long as it is for their own personal (non-commercial) use–up to 800 cigarettes, 10L of spirits, 90L of wine (60L of sparkling wine), and 110L of beer. You should be aware that duty-free was abolished on June 30, 1999 for travel between EU member states; however, travelers between the EU and the rest of the world still get a duty-free allowance when passing through customs.

CURRENCY & EXCHANGE

The currency chart below is based on August 2001 exchange rates between local currency and Australian dollars (AUS$), Canadian dollars (CDN$), Irish pounds (IR£), New Zealand dollars (NZ$), South African Rand (ZAR), British pounds (UK£), US dollars (US$), and European Union euros (€). Check our currency converter at www.letsgo.com/thumb or a newspaper for the latest exchange rates.

As a general rule, it's cheaper to convert money in Rome than at home. However, you should bring enough foreign currency to last for the first 24 to 72 hours of a trip to avoid being penniless should you arrive after bank hours or on a holiday.

EXCHANGE RATES

AUS$ = 1,173L	1L = 0.00085AUS$
CDN$ = 1,469L	1L= 0.00068CDN$
IR£ = 2,459L	1L = 0.0004IR£
NZ$ = 950L	1L = 0.001NZ$
ZAR = 284L	1L = 0.0035ZAR
US$ = 2,258L	1L = 0.0004US$
UK£ = 3,216L	1L = 0.0003UK£
EUR€ = 1,936L	1L = 0.0005EUR€

Travelers from the US can get foreign currency from the comfort of home: **International Currency Express** (☎888-278-6628) deliver foreign currency or traveler' checks 2nd-day (US$12) at competitive exchange rates.

When changing money abroad, go to banks that have at most a 5% margin betwee their buy and sell prices. Since you lose money with every transaction, **convert larg sums** (unless the currency is depreciating rapidly), **but no more than you'll need.**

If you use traveler's checks or bills, carry some in small denominations (the equiv alent of US$50 or less) for times when you are forced to exchange money at disad vantageous rates, but bring a range of denominations since charges may be levie per check cashed. Store your money in a variety of forms; ideally, you will at an given time be carrying some cash, some traveler's checks, and an ATM and/or credi card. All travelers should also consider carrying some US dollars or German mark (about US$50 or DM95 worth) which are often preferred by local tellers. Note, how ever, that throwing dollars around for preferential treatment may be offensive, an can attract thieves. It marks you as a foreigner and invites locals to raise their prices.

GETTING MONEY FROM HOME

AMERICAN EXPRESS

Cardholders can withdraw cash from their checking accounts at any of AmEx' major offices and many representative offices (up to US$1000 every 21 days; no ser vice charge, no interest). AmEx "Express Cash" withdrawals from any AmEx ATM in Italy are automatically debited from the cardholder's checking account or line o credit. Green card holders may withdraw up to US$1000 in any seven-day period (2% transaction fee; minimum US$2.50, maximum US$20). To enroll in Express Cash cardmembers may call 800-227-4669 in the US. The AmEx number in Rome is 06 67641. The AmEx branches in Rome are listed in the **Service Directory** on p. 291.

WESTERN UNION

Travelers from the US, Canada, and the UK can wire money abroad by using Western Union. In the US, ☎800-325-6000; in Canada, ☎800-235-0000; in the UK, ☎0800 83 38 33; in Italy ☎06 6484583. To wire money within the US using a credit card (Visa, Mastercard, Discover) ☎800-225-5227. The rates for sending cash are generally US$10-11 cheaper than with a credit card, and the money is usually available at the place you're sending it to within an hour. To locate the nearest Western Union location, consult www.westernunion.com.

US STATE DEPARTMENT (US CITIZENS ONLY)

In dire emergencies only, the US State Department will forward money within hours to the nearest consular office, which will then disburse it according to instructions for a US$15 fee. You must contact the Overseas Citizens Service division of the US State Department (☎202-647-5225; nights, Sundays, and holidays ☎202-647-4000).

TRAVELER'S CHECKS

Traveler's checks (American Express and Visa are the most recognized) are a safe means of carrying funds. Several agencies and banks sell them for a small commission. Each agency provides refunds if checks are lost or stolen, and many provide additional services, such as toll-free refund hotlines abroad, emergency message services, and stolen credit card assistance.

While traveling, keep check receipts and a record of which checks you've cashed separate from the checks themselves. Also leave a list of check numbers with someone at home. Never countersign checks until you're ready to cash them, and always bring your passport to cash them. If your checks are lost or stolen, contact a refund center (of the company that issued your checks) to be reimbursed; they may require a police report verifying the loss or theft. Less-touristed countries may not have refund centers at all, in which case you might have to wait to be reimbursed. Ask about toll-free refund hotlines and refund centers when purchasing checks, and always carry emergency cash.

American Express: Call ☎800 25 19 02 in Australia; in New Zealand 0800 441 068; in the UK 0800 521 313; in the US and Canada 800-221-7282. Elsewhere call US collect +1 801-964-6665; www.aexp.com. Traveler's checks are available in lira at 1-4% commission at AmEx offices and banks, commission-free at AAA offices. *Cheques for Two* can be signed by either of 2 people traveling together.

Thomas Cook MasterCard: In the US and Canada call 800-223-7373; in the UK call 0800 62 21 01; elsewhere call UK collect +44 1733 31 89 50. Checks available in 13 currencies at 2% commission. Thomas Cook offices cash checks commission-free.

Visa: In the US, ☎800-227-6811; in the UK, ☎0800 89 50 78; elsewhere UK collect +44 020 7937 8091. Call for the location of their nearest office.

ESSENTIAL INFORMATION

THE EURO

On January 1, 1999, 11 countries of the European Union, including Italy, officially adopted the Euro as their common currency. Euro notes and coins will not be issued until January, 1, 2002, and until that time the Euro will exist only in electronic transactions and traveler's checks. On June 1, 2002, the *lira* will be withdrawn from circulation and the Euro will become the only legal currency in Italy. *Let's Go* lists all prices in Italian *lire,* as these will still be most relevant in 2001. However, all Italian businesses must quote prices in both *lire* and Euros.

Travelers who will be passing through more than one nation in the Euro-zone should note that exchange rates between the 11 national currencies were irrevocably fixed on January 1, 1999. Henceforth, *cambiari* will be obliged to change Euro-zone currencies at the official rate with **no commission,** though they may still charge a nominal service fee. Euro-denominated traveler's checks may also be used throughout the Euro-zone, and can be exchanged commission-free in any of the 11 Euro nations.

CREDIT CARDS

Where they are accepted, credit cards often offer superior exchange rates—up to 5% better than the retail rate used by banks and other currency exchange establishments. Credit cards may also offer services such as insurance or emergency help, and are sometimes required to reserve hotel rooms or rental cars. **MasterCard** (a.k.a. EuroCard or Access in Europe) and **Visa** are the most welcomed; **American Express** cards work at some ATMs and at AmEx offices and major airports. However, budget travelers will probably find that few of the establishments they frequent will accept credit cards; aside from the occasional splurge, you will probably reserve use of your credit card for financial emergencies.

Credit cards are also useful for **cash advances,** which allow you to withdraw lire from associated banks and ATMs throughout Rome instantly. However, transaction fees for all credit card advances (up to US$10 per advance, plus 2-3% extra on foreign transactions after conversion) tend to make credit cards a more costly way of withdrawing cash than ATMs or traveler's checks. In an emergency, however, the transaction fee may prove worth the cost. To be eligible for an advance, you'll need to get a **Personal Identification Number (PIN)** from your credit card company (see **Cash Cards (ATM Cards),** below). Check with your credit card company before you leave home, though; some companies have started to charge a foreign transaction fee.

CREDIT CARD COMPANIES

Visa (US ☎800-336-8472) and MasterCard (US ☎800-307-7309) are issued in cooperation with banks and other organizations. American Express (US ☎800-843-2273) has an annual fee of up to US$55. AmEx cardholders may cash personal checks at AmEx offices abroad, access an emergency medical and legal assistance hotline (24hr.; in North America ☎800-554-2639, elsewhere US collect +1 715-343-7977), and enjoy American Express Travel Service benefits (plane, hotel, and car rent reservation changes; baggage loss and flight insurance; mailgram and internation cable services; and held mail). Discover Card (in US ☎800-347-2683, elsewhere U +1 801-902-3100) offers cashback bonuses on purchases, but it may not be accepte in Rome .

CASH CARDS (ATM CARDS)

Cash cards—popularly called ATM cards—are widespread in Rome. Depending o the system that your home bank uses, you can most likely access your personal ban account from abroad. ATMs get the same wholesale exchange rate as credit card but there is often a limit on the amount of money you can withdraw per day (aroun US$500), and unfortunately computer networks sometimes fail. There is typicall also a surcharge of US$1-5 per withdrawal. Memorize your PIN code in numeri form since machines elsewhere often don't have letters on their keys. Also, if you PIN is longer than four digits, ask your bank whether you need a new number.

In Rome, ATMs are *Bancomats*. The banks with the most reliable ATMs, accep ing Visa and Mastercard, are Banca Nazionale del Lavoro and Banca di Roma (se **Service Directory,** p. 289). **Credit card ATMs** abound on V. Arenula, V.d. Tritone, V. Corso, and near the Pantheon. The 5-block radius surrounding Termini is chock fu of banks and machines, as is the 10-block radius surrounding St. Peter's Basilic The ATM at the AmEx office at the Spanish Steps accepts **AmEx** cards, as does th Banca Popolare di Milano. Some machines shut down after midnight. In case of ser ous problems with ATMs, contact Smarrimento Bancom (☎(800) 822056).

The two major international money networks are **Cirrus** (US ☎800-424-7787) an **PLUS** (US ☎800-843-7587). To locate ATMs around the world, call the above num bers, or consult www.visa.com/pd/atm or www.mastercard.com/atm. Most ATM charge a transaction fee that is paid to the bank that owns the ATM.

Visa TravelMoney allows you to access money from any ATM that accepts Vis cards. You deposit an amount before you travel (plus a small administration fee and you can withdraw up to that sum. The cards, which give you the same favorabl exchange rate for withdrawals as a regular Visa, are especially useful if you plan t travel through many countries. Obtain a card by either visiting a nearby Thoma Cook or Citicorp office, by calling toll-free in the US 877-394-2247, or checking wit your local bank or to see if it issues TravelMoney cards. **Road Cash** (US ☎877-762 3227; www.roadcash.com) issues cards in the US with a minimum US$300 deposit.

COSTS

The cost of your trip will vary considerably, depending on where you go, how you trave and where you stay. The single biggest cost of your trip will probably be your round-tri (return) **airfare** to Italy (see **Getting to Rome: By Plane,** p. 251). A **railpass** (or **bus pass)** wi be another major pre-departure expense. Before you go, spend some time calculating reasonable per-day **budget** that will meet your needs.

STAYING ON A BUDGET

To give you a general idea, a bare-bones day in Rome (sleeping in hostels/, buying foo at supermarkets) would cost about US$45 (L100,000); and for a luxurious day, the sky' the limit. Also, don't forget to factor in emergency reserve funds (at least US$200) whe planning how much money you'll need.

TIPS FOR SAVING MONEY

Considering that saving just a few dollars a day over the course of your trip might pa for days or weeks of additional travel, the art of penny-pinching is well worth learning Learn to take advantage of freebies: for example, **museums** in Rome are typically fre once a month, and Rome hosts free open-air **concerts** and/or **cultural events** (especiall in summer). Bring a **sleepsack** to save on sheet charges in Roman hostels, and do you own laundry in the sink (unless you're explicitly prohibited from doing so). You ca split **accommodations** costs (in hotels and some hostels) with trustworthy fellow trav elers; multi-bed rooms almost always work out cheaper per person than singles. Th same principle will also work for cutting down on the cost of restaurant meals.

You can also buy food in **supermarkets** like **STANDA** instead of eating out. With that said, don't go overboard with your budget obsession. Though staying within your budget is important, don't do so at the expense of your sanity or health.

TAXES

Upon entering Italy, you must declare certain items from abroad and pay a duty on the value of those articles that exceeds the allowance established by the Italian customs service. Note that goods and gifts purchased at **duty-free** shops abroad are not exempt from duty or sales tax at your point of return and thus must be declared as well; "duty-free" merely means that you need not pay a tax in the country of purchase. Duty-free allowances were abolished for travel between EU member states on July 1, 1999, but still exist for those arriving from outside the EU.

Italy allows duty-free importation of the following for non-EU citizens: 200 cigarettes or 100 small cigars or 50 cigars or 250g of loose tobacco, 750 ml of spirits over 22% or 2L of wine; 50cc of perfume and 500g of coffee or 100 grams of tea. EU citizens may bring in the above items in larger quantities: 800 cigarettes or 400 small cigars or 200 cigars or 1kg of tobacco, 90L of wine, 10L of spirits over 22%, 110L of beer. Non-EU tourists may also bring in two cameras, film, a video camera, one radio, one television, one tape recorder, one bicycle, one boat (with or without motor), two pairs of skis, two tennis rackets, one canoe, and one surf board.

Upon returning home, you must declare all articles acquired abroad and pay a duty on the value of articles in excess of your home country's allowance. In order to expedite your return, make a list of any valuables brought from home and register them with customs before traveling abroad. Be sure to keep receipts for all goods acquired abroad. Upon departure from the EU, non-EU citizens can claim a refund for the **value added tax** (VAT or IVA) paid on major purchases. The VAT (in Italian, *imposto sul valore aggiunta*, or IVA) is a sales tax levied in the European Union. VAT (generally around 19%) is usually part of the price paid for goods and services. Upon departure from the EU, non-EU citizens can get a refund of the VAT for purchases over L650,000. The receipt, purchases, and purchaser's passport must be presented at the Customs Office as you leave the EU, and the refund will be mailed to you. "Tax-Free Shopping for Tourists" at some stores enables you to get your refund in cash when at the airport or a border crossing.

HEALTH

Common sense is the simplest prescription for good health while you travel. Drink lots of fluids to prevent dehydration and constipation, wear sturdy, broken-in shoes and clean socks, and use talcum powder to keep your feet dry. For a basic **first-aid kit,** pack: bandages, pain reliever, antibiotic cream, a thermometer, a Swiss Army knife, tweezers, moleskin, decongestant, motion-sickness remedy, diarrhea or upset-stomach medication, an antihistamine, sunscreen, insect repellent, burn ointment, and a syringe for emergencies (get an letter from your doctor).

In your **passport,** write the names of any people you wish to be contacted in case of a medical emergency, and also list any allergies or medical conditions of which you would want doctors to be aware. Matching a prescription to a foreign equivalent is not always easy, safe, or possible. Carry up-to-date, legible prescriptions or a statement from your doctor stating the medication's trade name, manufacturer, chemical name, and dosage. Be sure to keep all medication with you in your carry-on luggage.

IMMUNIZATIONS & PRECAUTIONS

Travelers over two years old should be sure that the following vaccines are up to date: MMR (for measles, mumps, and rubella); DTaP or Td (for diptheria, tetanus, and pertussis), OPV (for polio), HbCV (for haemophilus influenza B), and HBV (for hepatitus B). Consult the CDC (see below) in the US or the equivalent in your home country, and check with a doctor for guidance.

USEFUL ORGANIZATIONS & PUBLICATIONS

The US **Centers for Disease Control and Prevention** (**CDC;** ☎877-FYI-TRIP www.cdc.gov/travel) is a source of information for travelers and maintains an inte national fax information service. The CDC's comprehensive booklet *Health Infor mation for International Travel*, an annual rundown of disease, immunizatio and general health advice, is free online or US$25 via the Public Health Foundatio (☎877-252-1200). Consult the appropriate government agency of your home countr for consular information sheets on health, entry requirements, and other issues fc various countries. For quick information on health and other travel warnings, ca the **Overseas Citizens Services** (☎202-647-5225; after-hours 202-647-4000), contact passport agency or an embassy or consulate abroad. US citizens can send a sel addressed, stamped envelope to the Overseas Citizens Services, Bureau of Consula Affairs, #4811, US Department of State, Washington, D.C. 20520. See the US goverr ment's website at http://travel.state.gov/medical.html or the **British Foreign and Com monwealth Office** (www.fco.gov.uk).

For detailed information on travel health, including a country-by-country ove view of diseases, try the **International Travel Health Guide,** Stuart Rose, MD (Trave Medicine, US$24.95; www.travmed.com). For general health info, contact the **Ame can Red Cross** (☎800-564-1234).

MEDICAL ASSISTANCE ON THE ROAD

In general, English-speaking health care services in Rome are reliable and readil available, but if you are concerned about being able to access medical support whil traveling, there are special support services you may employ. The *MedPass* fror **GlobalCare, Inc.,** 2001 Westside Pkwy., #120, Alpharetta, GA 30004, USA (☎800-86C 1111; fax 770-475-0058; www.globalems.com), provides 24hr. international medica assistance, support, and medical evacuation resources. The **International Associatio for Medical Assistance to Travelers** (**IAMAT;** US ☎716-754-4883, Canada ☎416-652-013 New Zealand ☎03 352 20 53; www.sentex.net/~iamat) has free membership, list English-speaking doctors worldwide, and offers detailed info on immunizatio requirements and sanitation. If your regular **insurance** policy does not cover trave abroad, you may wish to purchase additional coverage (see p. 250).

Those with medical conditions (diabetes, allergies to antibiotics, epilepsy, hea conditions) may want to obtain a stainless-steel **Medic Alert** ID tag (first year US$3 annually thereafter US$20), which identifies the condition and gives a 24hr. collec call number. Contact the Medic Alert Foundation, 2323 Colorado Ave, Turlock, C 95382, USA (☎888-633-4298; www.medicalert.org).

INSURANCE

Travel insurance covers four basic areas: medical/health problems, property los trip cancellation/interruption, and emergency evacuation. Although your regula insurance policies may well extend to travel-related accidents, you may conside purchasing travel insurance if the cost of potential trip cancellation/interruption i greater than you can absorb. Prices for travel insurance purchased separately gene ally run about US$50 per week for full coverage, while trip cancellation/interruptio may be purchased separately at a rate of about US$5.50 per US$100 of coverage.

Medical insurance (especially university policies) often covers costs incurre abroad; check with your provider. **US Medicare** does not cover foreign travel. **Canad ans** are protected by their home province's health insurance plan for up to 90 day after leaving the country; check with the provincial Ministry of Health or Health Pla Headquarters. **Australians** traveling in Italy are entitled to many of the services tha they would receive at home as part of the Reciprocal Health Care Agreement. **Home owners' insurance** (or your family's coverage) often covers theft during travel and los of travel documents (passport, plane ticket, railpass, etc.) up to US$500.

ISIC and **ITIC** (see p. 244) provide basic insurance benefits, including US$100 pe day of in-hospital sickness for up to 60 days, US$3000 of accident-related medica reimbursement, and US$25,000 for emergency medical transport. Cardholders hav access to a toll-free 24hr. helpline for medical, legal, and financial emergencies over seas (US and Canada ☎800-626-2427, elsewhere call US collect +1 713-267-2525). **American Express** (US ☎800-528-4800) grants most cardholders automatic car rental insurance (collision and theft, but not liability) and ground travel accident coverage of US$100,000 on flight purchases made with the card.

Council and **STA** (see p. 251) offer a range of plans that can supplement your basic coverage. Other private insurance providers in the US and Canada include: Access America (☎800-284-8300); Berkely Group/Carefree Travel Insurance (☎800-323-3149; www.berkely.com); Globalcare Travel Insurance (☎800-821-2488; www.globalcare-cocco.com); and Travel Assistance International (☎800-821-2828; www.worldwide-assistance.com). Providers in the UK include Campus Travel (☎01865 25 80 00) and Columbus Travel Insurance (☎020 7375 0011). In Australia, try CIC Insurance (☎9202 8000).

ESSENTIAL INFORMATION

ATM ALERT!

All automatic teller machines require a four-digit Personal Identification Number (PIN), which credit cards in the United States do not always carry. You must ask your credit card company to assign you one before you leave. Without this PIN, you will be unable to withdraw cash with your credit card abroad. Also, if your PIN is longer than four digits, ask your bank whether the first four digits will work, or whether you need a new number.

There are no letters on the keypads of most European bank machines, so work out your PIN here: QZ correspond to 1, ABC correspond to 2; DEF to 3; GHI to 4; JKL to 5; MNO to 6; PRS to 7; TUV to 8; and WXY to 9.

If you mistakenly punch the wrong code into a Italian ATM three times it will eat your card. If you lose your card in Rome, call for help at the following numbers, all of which have English-speaking operators: Mastercard (☎ (800) 870 866); Visa (☎ (800) 819 014); American Express (call US collect (301) 214-8228)

GETTING TO ROME

BY PLANE

When it comes to airfare, a little effort can save you a bundle. If your plans are flexible enough to deal with the restrictions, courier fares are the cheapest. Tickets bought from consolidators and standby seating are also good deals, but last-minute specials, airfare wars, and charter flights often beat these fares. The key is to hunt around, to be flexible, and to ask persistently about discounts. Students, seniors, and those under 26 should never pay full price for a ticket.

AIRFARES

Airfares to Rome peak between mid-June and early September; holidays are also expensive. Midweek (M-Th morning) round-trip flights run US$40-50 cheaper than weekend flights, but they are generally more crowded and less likely to permit frequent-flier upgrades. Traveling with an "open return" ticket can be pricier than fixing a return date when buying the ticket. Round-trip flights are by far the cheapest; "open-jaw" (arriving in and departing from different cities) tickets tend to be pricier. Patching one-way flights together is the most expensive way to travel. **Fares** for roundtrip flights to Rome from the US or Canadian east coast cost around US$600 or US$400 off season; from the US or Canadian west coast US$900/US$500; from the US$200/$175; from Australia $1100/$900; from New Zealand $950/$1100.

BUDGET & STUDENT TRAVEL AGENCIES

Travel agents can help you save, but they may not find you the lowest fare. Travelers holding **ISIC and IYTC cards** (p. 244) qualify for discounts from student travel agencies. Most flights from budget agencies are on major airlines, but in peak season some sell seats on less-reliable chartered aircraft.

usit world (www.usitworld.com). Over 50 **usit campus** branches in the UK (www.usitcampus.co.uk), including 52 Grosvenor Gardens, **London** SW1W 0AG (☎0870 240 10 10); **Manchester** (☎0161 273 1880); **Edinburgh** (☎0131 668 3303). Nearly 20 **usit NOW** offices in Ireland, including 19-21 Aston Quay, O'Connell Bridge, **Dublin** 2 (☎01 602 1600;

www.usitnow.ie), and **Belfast** (☎02 890 327 111; www.usitnow.com). Offices in Athe Auckland, Brussels, Frankfurt, Johannesburg, Lisbon, Madrid, Paris, Sofia, and Warsaw.

Council Travel (www.counciltravel.com). Countless US offices, including branches in Atlan Boston, Chicago, L.A., New York, Rome, Seattle, and Washington, D.C. Check the website call 800-2-COUNCIL (226-8624) for the office nearest you. Also an office at 28A Poland (Oxford Circus), **London,** W1V 3DB (☎0207 437 77 67).

CTS Travel, 44 Goodge St., **London** W1T 2AD (☎0207 636 0031; fax 0207 637 532 ctsinfo@ctstravel.co.uk).

STA Travel, 7890 S. Hardy Dr., Ste. 110, Tempe AZ 85284 (24hr. reservations and ir ☎800-777-0112; fax 480-592-0876; www.sta-travel.com). A student and youth travel or nization with over 150 offices worldwide (check their website for a listing of all their office including US offices in Boston, Chicago, L.A., New York, Rome, Seattle, and Washington, D Ticket booking, travel insurance, railpasses, and more. In the UK, walk-in office 11 Good St., **London** W1T 2PF or call 0870-160-6070. In New Zealand, 10 High St., **Auckland** (☎ 309 0458). In Australia, 366 Lygon St., **Melbourne** Vic 3053 (☎03 9349 4344).

Travel CUTS (Canadian Universities Travel Services Limited), 187 College St., **Toronto,** M5T 1P7 (☎416-979-2406; fax 979-8167; www.travelcuts.com). 60 offices across Canac Also in the UK, 295-A Regent St., **London** W1R 7YA (☎0207-255-1944).

Wasteels, Skoubogade 6, 1158 Copenhagen K., (☎3314-4633 fax 7630-086 www.wasteels.dk/uk). A huge chain with 165 locations across Europe. Sells Wasteels tickets discounted 30-45% off regular fare, 2nd-class international point-to-point train tick with unlimited stopovers for those under 26 (sold only in Europe).

COMMERCIAL AIRLINES

The commercial airlines' lowest regular offer is the APEX (Advance Purcha Excursion) fare, which provides confirmed reservations and allows "open-jaw" tic ets. Generally, reservations must be made seven to 21 days ahead of departure, wi seven- to 14-day minimum-stay and up to 90-day maximum-stay restrictions. The fares carry hefty cancellation and change penalties (fees rise in summer). Bo peak-season APEX fares early; by May you will have a hard time getting your desir departure date. Use Microsoft Expedia (msn.expedia.com) or Traveloci (www.travelocity.com) to get an idea of the lowest published fares, then use t resources outlined here to try and beat those fares. Low-season fares should appreciably cheaper than the high-season (mid-June to Aug.) ones listed here. Pop lar carriers to Rome, and the typical fares they offer, include:

TRAVELING FROM NORTH AMERICA

Basic round-trip fares to Western Europe range from roughly US$200-750: to Lo don, US$200-600; Paris, US$250-700. Standard commercial carriers like Americ (☎800-433-7300; www.aa.com) and United (☎800-241-6522; www.ual.com) offer t most convenient flights, but they may not be the cheapest, unless you manage grab a special promotion or airfare war ticket. Flying one of the following airlin may be a better deal, if any of their limited departure points is convenient for you.

TRAVELING FROM THE UK & IRELAND

Because of the myriad carriers flying from the British Isles to the continent, we or include discount airlines or those with cheap specials here. The **Air Travel Advisc Bureau** in London (☎020 7636 5000; www.atab.co.uk) provides referrals to trav agencies and consolidators that offer discounted airfares out of the UK.

Aer Lingus: Ireland ☎01 886 88 88; www.aerlingus.ie. Return tickets from Dublin, Cork, G way, Kerry, and Shannon to Amsterdam, Madrid, Milan, Paris, and Rome (IR£102-244).

buzz: UK ☎0870 240 70 70; www.buzzaway.com. A subsidiary of KLM. From London to B lin, Milan, Paris, and Vienna (UK£50-80). Tickets can not be changed or refunded.

Go-Fly Limited: UK ☎0845 605 43 21, elsewhere call UK +44 1279 66 63 88; www.g fly.com. A subsidiary of British Airways. From London to Barcelona, Madred, Naples, Rom and Venice (return UK£53-180).

KLM: UK ☎0870 507 40 74; www.klmuk.com. Cheap return tickets from London and els where to Amsterdam, Brussels, Frankfurt, Milan, Paris, and Rome.

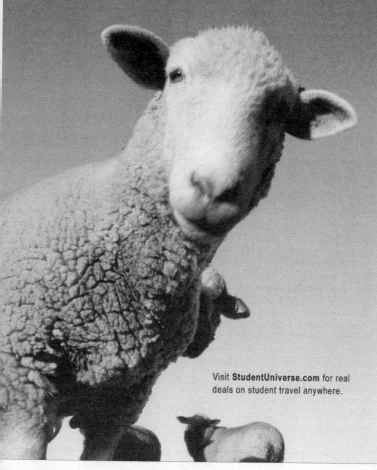

TRAVELING FROM AUSTRALIA & NEW ZEALAND

Singapore Air: Australia ☎13 10 11, New Zealand ☎0800 808 909; www.singaporeair.com. Flies from Auckland, Sydney, Melbourne, and Perth to Western Europe.

TRAVELING FROM SOUTH AFRICA

British Airways: ☎0860 011 747; www.british-airways.com/regional/sa. Cape Town and Johannesburg to the UK and the rest of Europe from ZAR3400.

Virgin Atlantic: ☎011 340 34 00; www.virgin-atlantic.co.za. Flies to London from both Cape Town and Johannesburg.

AIR COURIER FLIGHTS

Those who travel light should consider courier flights. Couriers help transport cargo on international flights by using their checked luggage space for freight. Generally, couriers must travel with carry-ons only and must deal with complex flight restrictions. Most flights are round-trip only, with short fixed-length stays (usually one week) and a limit of a one ticket per issue. Most of these flights also operate only out of major gateway cities, mostly in North America. Round-trip courier fares from the US to Rome run about US$200. Most flights leave from New York, Los Angeles, Rome, or Miami in the US; and from Montreal, Toronto, or Vancouver in Canada. Generally, you must be over 21 (in some cases 18). In summer, the most popular destinations usually require an advance reservation of about two weeks (you can usually book up to two months ahead). Super-discounted fares are common for "last-minute" flights (three to 14 days ahead).

TRAVELING FROM NORTH AMERICA

Round-trip courier fares from the US to Western Europe run about US$200-500. Most flights leave from New York, Los Angeles, Rome, or Miami in the US; and from Montreal, Toronto, or Vancouver in Canada. The first four organizations below provide their members with lists of opportunities and courier brokers worldwide for an annual fee (typically US$50-60). Alternatively, you can contact a courier broker (such as the last three listings) directly; most charge registration fees, but a few don't. Prices quoted below are round-trip.

Air Courier Association, 15000 W. 6th Ave. #203, Golden, CO 80401 (☎800-282-1202; elsewhere call US +1 303-215-9000; www.aircourier.org). Ten departure cities throughout the US and Canada to London, Madrid, Paris, Rome, and throughout Western Europe (high season US$150-360). One-year US$64.

International Association of Air Travel Couriers (IAATC), 220 South Dixie Highway #3, PO Box 1349, Lake Worth, FL 33460 (☎561-582-8320; fax 582-1581; www.courier.org). From 9 North American cities to: London, Mardid, Paris, Rome, and more. One-year US$45-50.

Global Courier Travel, PO Box 3051, Nederland, CO 80466 (www.globalcouriertravel.com). Searchable online database. Six departure points in the US and Canada to Amsterdam, London, Madrid, Milan, Paris, and Rome. One-year US$40, 2 people US$55.

NOW Voyager, 74 Varick St. #307, New York, NY 10013 (☎212-431-1616; fax 219-175[illegible]; www.nowvoyagertravel.com). To Amsterdam, Brussels, Dublin, London, Madrid, Milan, Paris, Rome (US$499-699). 1-week max. stay. 1-yr. US$50. Non-courier discount fares available.

Worldwide Courier Association (☎800-780-4359, ext. 441; www.massiveweb.com). From New York, Rome, Los Angeles, and Chicago to Western Europe, including London, Milan, Paris, and Rome (US$259-299). One-year US$58.

FROM THE UK, IRELAND, AUSTRALIA, & NEW ZEALAND

Although the courier industry is most developed from North America, there are limited courier flights in other areas. The minimum age for couriers from the **UK** is usually 18. **Brave New World Enterprises,** P.O. Box 22212, London SE5 8W[illegible] (guideinfo@nry.co.uk; www.nry.co.uk/bnw) publishes a directory of all the companies offering courier flights in the UK (UK£10, in electronic form UK£8). The **International Association of Air Travel Couriers** (see above) often offers courier flights from London to Rome. **Global Courier Travel** (see above) also offer flights from London and Dublin to continental Europe. **British Airways Travel Shop** (☎0870 606 11 33; www.british-airways.com/travelqa/booking/travshop/travshop.shtml) arranges some flights rom London to destinations in continental Europe (specials may be as low as JK£60; no registration fee). From **Australia** and **New Zealand, Global Courier Travel** see above) often has listings from Sydney and Auckland to London.

STANDBY FLIGHTS

raveling standby requires considerable flexibility in arrival and departure dates nd cities. Companies dealing in standby flights sell vouchers rather than tickets, long with the promise to get to your destination (or near your destination) within certain window of time (typically 1-5 days). You call in before your specific window of time to hear your flight options and the probability that you will be able to oard each flight. You can then decide which flights you want to try to make, show p at the appropriate airport at the appropriate time, present your voucher, and oard if space is available. Vouchers can usually be bought for both one-way and ound-trip travel. You may receive a monetary refund only if every available flight vithin your date range is full; if you opt not to take an available (but perhaps less onvenient) flight, you can only get credit toward future travel. Carefully read greements with any company offering standby flights as tricky fine print can leave ou in a lurch. To check on a company's service record in the US, call the Better Business Bureau (☎212-533-6200). It is difficult to receive refunds, and clients' ouchers will not be honored when an airline fails to receive payment in time. One tandby company within the US is **Whole Earth Travel,** 325 W. 38th St., New York, NY 0018 (☎800-326-2009; fax 212-864-5489; www.4standby.com) and Los Angeles, CA ☎888-247-4482), which offers one-way flights to Europe from the Northeast US$169), West Coast and Northwest (US$249), Midwest (US$219), and Southeast US$219). "Intracontnental" connecting flights within Europe cost US$79-139.

TICKET CONSOLIDATORS

Ticket consolidators, or **"bucket shops,"** buy unsold tickets in bulk from commercial irlines and sell them at discounted rates. Look in the Sunday travel section of any najor newspaper (such as the *New York Times*), where many bucket shops place iny ads. Call quickly, as availability is typically extremely limited. Not all bucket hops are reliable, so insist on a receipt that gives full details of restrictions, refunds, nd tickets, and pay by credit card (2-5% fee) so you can stop payment if you never eceive tickets. For more, see www.travel-library.com/air-travel/consolidators.html.

Travel Avenue (☎800-333-3335; www.travelavenue.com) rebates commercial fares o or from the US (5% for over US$550) and will search for cheap flights from anywhere for a fee. **NOW Voyager,** 74 Varick St., Ste. 307, New York, NY 10013 (☎212-431-.616; fax 219-1793; www.nowvoyagertravel.com) arranges discounted flights, nostly from New York, to Barcelona, London, Madrid, Milan, Paris, and Rome. Other consolidators worth trying are **Airfare Busters** (☎800-232-8783; www.af.busters.com); **Interworld** (☎305-443-4929; fax 443-0351); **Pennsylvania Travel** (☎800-331-947); **Rebel** (☎800-227-3235; travel@rebeltours.com; www.rebeltours.com); **Cheap ickets** (☎800-377-1000; www.cheaptickets.com); and **Travac** (☎800-872-8800; fax 12-714-9063; www.travac.com). Yet more consolidators on the web include the **nternet Travel Network** (www.itn.com); **Travel Information Services** (www.tiss.com); **ravelHUB** (www.travelhub.com); and **The Travel Site** (www.thetravelsite.com). Keep n mind that these are just suggestions to get you started in your research; *Let's Go* loes not endorse any of these agencies. As always, be cautious, and research companies before you hand over your credit card number.

In London, the **Air Travel Advisory Bureau** (☎0207 636 50 00; www.atab.co.uk) can rovide names of reliable consolidators and discount flight specialists. From Australia and New Zealand, look for consolidator ads in the travel section of the *Sydney Morning Herald* and other papers.

CHARTER FLIGHTS

Charters are flights a tour operator contracts with an airline to fly extra loads of passengers during peak season. Charter flights fly less frequently than major airlines, nake refunds particularly difficult, and are usually fully booked. Schedules and itineraries may also change or be cancelled at the last moment (as late as 48 hours efore the trip, and without a full refund), and check-in, boarding, and baggage claim re often much slower. However, they can also be cheaper.

Discount clubs and **fare brokers** offer members savings on last-minute charter an tour deals. Study contracts closely; you don't want to end up with an unwanted ove night layover. **Travelers Advantage,** Trumbull, CT, USA (☎203-365-2000; www.travele sadvantage.com; US$60 annual fee includes discounts and cheap flight directorie specializes in European travel and tour packages.

BY TRAIN

Most major Italian cities and European hubs lie on a direct line to Rome or can reac it with a single change. **Tickets** can be bought and **reservations** made in any train sta tion and at many travel agencies (see **Tourist Offices,**p. 23). Reservations are manda tory for **Eurostar** (☎(440) 20 7298 5163; www.eurostar.com,) trains and some expres trains (usually less than L10,000). Machines opposite the ticket counter at Termi station provide instructions in English and handle most transactions, accepting bil up to L50,000, ATM, Diner's Club, Matercard, and Visa.While economical, efficien and romantic, as well as the first choice of many budget travelers, trains are nc always safe. While passengers sleep, they risk robbery. Sleep wearing your mone belt or neck pouch, and if you are traveling with a companion, try to sleep in shift see **Personal Safety,** p. 257. **Termini,** the transportation hub of Rome, is the focal poi of most train lines and Rome's subway. Services including hotel reservations (acros from track #20), ATMs, luggage storage (at track #1), and police (at track #13, or ca 112) are available in the station. Not to be missed are **Termini's bathrooms,** a black wonderland off track #1 (L1000). Be warned, they become a way of life.

The various other stations on the fringe of town—**Tiburtina, Trastevere, Ostiens San Lorenzo, Roma Nord, Prenestina**—are connected by bus and/or subway to Termin. Trains that arrive in Rome after midnight and before 5am or so usually arrive a Tiburtina or Ostiense, which are connected to Termini during these hours by th 40N and 20N-21N buses respectively. Be particularly wary of pickpockets and co artists in and around the stations.

For information on **train service within Italy,** contact **Ferrovie dello Stato (FS),** th Italian state railway (☎06 4730 6599; www.fs-on-line.com). FS offers **Cartaverde** fc people under 26; the card (L45,000) is valid for one year, and entitles you to a 20 and 30% discount on first- and second-class seats, respectively. If you qualify an plan to travel extensively, it should be your *first* purchase upon arrival. Families c four or more and groups of up to 10 adults traveling together also qualify for di counts on Italian railways. Persons over 60 receive a 20% discount on train ticke with purchase of a **Carta d'argento** (L45,000 per year).

For more information on service from outside Italy, contact Rail Europe (U ☎(877) 456-RAIL; www.raileurope.com); for extended travel, a variety of passes ar available. The following are rates and times for second-class seats, one-way to Rom from: **Florence** (1-2hr., L68,740); **Venice** (5hr., L103,115); **Milan** (4½hr., L107,700 **Naples** (2hr., L55,000); **Vienna** (13hr., US$50); **Paris** (14½hr., US$295).

BY BUS

An often cheaper alternative to rail passes for travelers visiting many cities is a **international bus pass,** which allows unlimited travel between major cities on a ho on, hop-off basis. Buses are most popular among non-American backpackers.

Busabout, 258 Vauxhall Bridge Rd., London SW1V 1BS (☎207 950 1661; fax 950 166 www.busabout.com; info@busabout.co.uk). Offers 5 interconnecting bus circuits covering 7 cities and towns in Europe; rolls into Rome twice daily. Consecutive Day Passes and Fle Passes both available. Connections to Rome available from **Florence** (4hr.); **Sorrento** (5hr. and **Venice** (9hr.). Consecutive Day Standard/student passes allow unlimited travel to a destinations, and are valid 2 weeks (US$249/219), 3 weeks (US$359/329), 1 mon (US$479/429), 2 months (US$739/659), 3 months (US$909/829), or season (US$1089 979). Flexicards also available, which allow travelers to allow themselves more time in loca tions (for example allowing them to spread 10 days of unlimited travel out over 2 months).

Eurolines, 52 Grosvenor Gardens, London SWIW OAG (☎1582 404 511; www.eur lines.com). Unlimited 15-day (UK£109; under 26 and over 60 UK£90), 30-day (UK£22 under 26 and over 60 UK£179) or 60-day (UK£259/195) travel in 30 major European cities.

BY CAR

For specific information on traveling by car in Italy, check out **When in Rome** (p. 17).

INTERNATIONAL DRIVING PERMIT (IDP)

If you plan to drive a car while in Italy, you must have an International Driving Permit (IDP). Your IDP, valid for one year, must be issued in your own country before you depart, and is generally available at the local automobile club, for a fee of US$10. An application for an IDP usually needs to include one or two photos, a current local license, an additional form of identification.

CAR INSURANCE

Most credit cards cover standard insurance. If you rent, lease, or borrow a car, you will need a **green card,** or **International Insurance Certificate,** to certify that you have liability insurance and that it applies abroad. Green cards can be obtained at car rental agencies, car dealers (for those leasing cars), some travel agents, and some border crossings. Rental agencies may require you to purchase theft insurance in countries that they consider to have a high risk of auto theft.

SPECIFIC CONCERNS

WOMEN TRAVELERS

Italy has long been viewed as a particularly difficult area for female travelers, largely due to the amount of unsought attention they routinely, constantly, and universally receive from Italian men. In general, harassment does not go beyond honking, whistling, obnoxious hissing noises, and raucous "compliments." To minimize harassment, adopt the attitude of Roman women: walk like you know where you are going, avoid eye contact—**sunglasses** are indispensable—and meet all advances with dignity, silence, and an impassive gaze. Try not to show too much skin if you aren't comfortable attracting attention, avoiding "touristy" attire (college shirts, sneakers, Tevas, or Birkenstocks) can also prevent unwanted attention.

If you are physically harassed on the bus or in some public place, don't talk to the person directly (this often encourages him). Most Italians are embarrassed by the treatment that foreign women receive in Italy and will be supportive and helpful if they see that you are being bothered. Don't travel alone at night, if

ESSENTIAL INFORMATION

INTERNET FLIGHT PLANNING

The Internet is one of the best places to look for travel bargains—it's fast and convenient, and you can spend hours exploring options without driving your travel agent insane.

Many airline sites offer special last-minute deals on the Web. For fares, see Alitalia (www.alitalia.it), Air-One (www.air-one.it/airone.htm), and Gandalf Air (www.gandalfair.com). For a great set of links to practically every airline in every country, see www.travelpage.com/air/airlines. Other sites do the legwork and compile the deals for you—try www.bestfares.com, www.onetravel.com, www.lowestfare.com, and www.travelzoo.com.

Other sites do the legwork and **compile deals** for you:

www.bestfares.com
www.onetravel.com
www.lowestfare.com
www.travelzoo.com

For **student quotes,** try:

www.sta-travel.com
www.counciltravel.com
www.studentuniverse.com

Full travel services:

Expedia (msn.expedia.com)
Travelocity.Com (www.travelocity.com)

Priceline (www.priceline.com) allows you to specify a price, and obligates you to buy any ticket that meets or beats it; be prepared for antisocial hours and odd routes.

Skyauction (www.skyauction.com) allows you to bid on both last-minute and advance-purchase tickets. Just one last note—to protect yourself, make sure that the site you use has a secure server before handing over any credit card details. Happy hunting!

you can help it. All travelers to Italy should be aware that the Italian conception o **personal space** might be different from that to which they are accustomed. The gu crowded next to you on the bus or the woman gesticulating madly in your face is no necessarily threatening you or being rude; it is fairly normal in Italian culture t stand close to the person you're addressing and to gesture wildly. Beyond this, if yo feel at all uncomfortable, don't hesitate to seek out a police officer or passerby Memorize the **emergency numbers** in Italy (113 and 112). Always carry a phone car and enough extra money for a bus or taxi, and consider carrying a whistle on you keychain. A self-defense course will not only prepare you for a potential attack, bu will also raise your level of awareness of your surroundings as well as your confi dence.

Hitchhiking is never safe for lone women, or even for two women travelin together. When choosing a train compartment, look for other women, couples, o better yet, nuns. Nuns, both on and off trains, rival the police, guard dogs, and th most state-of-the-art personal protection devices in their effectiveness in warding o potential danger. **Never sit in an empty train compartment.** Be especially careful o overnight trains; many women have had the unpleasant surprise of waking up to fin themselves being pawed by a lecherous stranger. A simple but loud *"non mi toc care"* ("don't touch me") will alert the other riders that you're being bothered an may humiliate your harasser enough to make him leave. Some travelers recommen wearing a fake (or real, if you've got one) wedding or engagement ring and even ca rying pictures of their "children," who are back at the "hotel" with their "husband. Blondes and redheads will probably be harassed more than others with calls o *"Psssst, biondina"* and other, less flattering phrases, but even brunettes an native Romans have to deal with harassment fairly regularly.

Women exploring on their own inevitably face some additional safety concerns but it's easy to be adventurous without taking undue risks. If you are concerned consider staying in hostels which offer single rooms that lock from the inside or i religious organizations with rooms for women only. Communal showers in som hostels are safer than others; check them before settling in. Stick to centrally locate accommodations and avoid solitary late-night treks or metro rides.

TRAVELING ALONE

There are many benefits to traveling alone, including independence and greate interaction with locals. Without distraction, you can write a great travelogue (or a least some interesting letters) in the grand tradition of Henry James, Ernest Heming way, or St. Paul. You may also be a more visible target for robbery and harassmen Lone travelers need to be well organized and look confident at all times. Try not t stand out as a tourist. **If questioned, never admit that you are traveling alone.** Maintai regular contact with someone at home who knows your itinerary. For more tips pick up *Traveling Solo* by Eleanor Berman (Globe Pequot Press, US$17) or sub scribe to **Connecting: Solo Travel Network,** 689 Park Road, Unit 6, Gibsons, BC V0N 1V (☎604-886-9099; www.cstn.org; membership US$28). Alternatively, several service link solo travelers who desire companions with travelers that have similar trave habits and interests; contact the **Travel Companion Exchange,** P.O. Box 833, Amityvill NY 11701 (☎631-454-0880; www.whytravelalone.com; US$48)

OLDER TRAVELERS

Older travelers in Italy are generally treated with considerable respect, and senio travelers are often entitled to travel-related discounts. Always ask about them, an be prepared to show proof of age (you probably look younger than you are). Agen cies for senior group travel are growing in enrollment and popularity.

For more info, check out: *No Problem! Worldwise Tips for Mature Adventur ers*, by Janice Kenyon (Orca Book Publishers, US$16); *A Senior's Guide t Healthy Travel*, by Donald L. Sullivan (Career Press, US$15); *Unbelievably Goo Deals and Great Adventures That You Absolutely Can't Get Unless You're Ove 50*, by Joan Rattner Heilman (Contemporary Books, US$13). For more informatio contact one of the following organizations:

Elderhostel, 11 Ave. de Lafayette, Boston, MA 02111 (☎877-426-8056; www.elderhostel.org). Organizes 1- to 4-week "educational adventures" in Rome for those 55+.

The Mature Traveler, P.O. Box 15791, Sacramento, CA 95852 (☎800-460-6676). Deals, discounts, and travel packages for the 50+ traveler. Subscription$30.

BISEXUAL, GAY, & LESBIAN TRAVELERS

While Rome does not have a thriving gay and lesbian community like those to be found in many northern Italian cities, the gay scene is slowly but surely expanding. Italian society is, unfortunately, not the most gay-friendly in the world. Straight Roman men and women are open in showing affection for members of the same sex; embracing, holding hands or walking arm-in-arm is common; sadly, however, this homosocial ease hasn't translated into tolerance for men or women who want to express a *different* kind of affection for one another. However concealed public gay life may be, the scene is on the rise. In 2000, Rome hosted World Pride 2000, drawing thousands of men and women from around the world. Sexual acts between members of the same sex have been legal for those above the age of consent (16) since 1889—more than many Anglo-Saxon countries can say.

The national organization for gay men, **Arci-Gay,** has its headquarters in Bologna, P. di Porta Saragozza, 2, 40123 (☎051 6447054; www.malox.com/arcigay/link.htm). Arci-Gay (www.gay.it/arcigay/roma) and **Arci-Lesbica** (www.women.it/~arciles/roma.) share two offices in Rome: V. Orvinio, 2 (☎06 86385112) and V. Lariana, 8. (☎06 8555522). Both groups hold group discussions, dances, and many special events. It might be a good idea to buy an Arci-Gay membership card (L20,000 annually), which gives admission to many gay clubs all over Italy.

Rome's Arci-Gay office publishes the monthly newsletter *Pegaso*. In addition, the monthly *Babilonia* (published by Babilonia Edizioni, V. Ebro, 11, 20141 Milan; ☎02 5696468) and the annual *Guida Gay Italia* (available at most newsstands) confront gay issues and list events. Finally, the **Italian Gay and Lesbian Yellow Pages** (www.gay.it/guida/italia/info.htm) includes listings of gay bars, hotels, and shops. Other useful websites include www.women.it and www.gay.it.

In Rome, the **Circolo Mario Mieli di Cultura Omosessuale,** V. Corinto, 5, provides loads of info about gay life in Rome. Take M: B-San Paolo, walk one block to largo Beato Placido Riccardi, hang a left, and walk 1½ blocks to V. Corinto to find gay-related brochures, pamphlets, and a bulletin board with announcements and special events. The staff offers group discussions, social events, a welcome group every Friday at 7pm, and info sessions on topics such as gay health concerns. (☎06 5413985; fax 06 5413971; www.mariomieli.org. Open M-F 9am-1pm and 2-6pm; closed Aug.)

Unfortunately, there isn't much organized lesbian activity for the traveler in Rome. The best source of info is the **Coordinamento Lesbico Italiano,** V.S. Francesco di Sales, 1a (☎06 6864201), off V.d. Lungara in Trastevere. Rome's one and only gay bookstore, **Libreria Babele,** V.d. Banchi Vecchi, is across the bridge from Castel Sant'Angelo. (☎06 6876628. Open M.-Sa. 10am-7:30pm.) It is also one of the only places that sells the *Gay and Lesbian Map of Rome* (L12,000).

Gay and lesbian Romans crowd the **gay beach** *Il Buco* at Lido di Ostia. The dunes along the beach hide an amusing pick-up scene, with many middle-aged Italians standing gopher-like atop mounds of sand; the beach itself accommodates a more relaxed, younger crowd. Take the train from Piramide or Magliana (M: A-Lido di Ostia), then bus #7 to the *capolinea;* from there, walk 2km south along the beach.

For **general travel concerns,** check out **Out and About** (www.planetout.com), which offers a biweekly newsletter addressing travel concerns. Contact the **International Gay and Lesbian Travel Association,** 4331 N. Federal Hwy. #304, Fort Lauderdale, FL 33308, an organization of 1350 companies serving gay and lesbian travelers worldwide. (☎954-776-2626; www.iglta.com.) Listed below are contact organizations, mail-order bookstores, and publishers that offer materials addressing some specific concerns. **Out and About** (www.planetout.com) offers a biweekly newsletter addressing travel concerns and a comprehensive site addressing gay travel concerns.

RESOURCES

Gay's the Word, 66 Marchmont St., London WC1N 1AB (☎+44 20 7278 7654; www.gaystheword.co.uk). The largest gay and lesbian bookshop in the UK, with both fiction and non-fiction titles. Mail-order service available.

Giovanni's Room, 1145 Pine St., Philadelphia, PA 19107 (☎215-923-2960; www.queerbooks.com). An international lesbian/feminist and gay bookstore with mail-order service (carries many of the publications listed below).

International Lesbian and Gay Association (ILGA), 81 rue Marché-au-Charbon, B-1000 Brussels, Belgium (☎+32 2 502 2471; www.ilga.org). Provides political information, such as homosexuality laws of individual countries.

FURTHER READING

Spartacus International Gay Guide 2001-2002. Bruno Gmunder Verlag (US$33).

Damron Men's Guide, Damron Road Atlas, Damron's Accommodations, and *The Women's Traveller.* Damron Travel Guides (US$14-19). For more info, call 800-462-6654 or visit www.damron.com.

Ferrari Guides' Gay Travel A to Z, Ferrari Guides' Men's Travel in Your Pocket, and *Ferrari Guides' Inn Places.* Ferrari Publications (US$16-20). Purchase the guides online at www.ferrariguides.com.

TRAVELERS WITH DISABILITIES

Romans are making an increased effort to meet the needs of people with disabilities. Still, many of the sights (like the Ancient City) can be difficult to navigate in a wheelchair, and in general, establishments are not wheelchair accessible unless stated otherwise. The **Italian Government Travel Office (ENIT)** will let you know which hotels and buildings are wheelchair accessible. When making arrangements with airlines or hotels, specify exactly what you need and allow time for preparation and confirmation of arrangements. Many of the larger **Ferrovie dello Stato (FS)** trains are marked wheelchair accessible; they suggest that you call ahead to reserve a space (☎ (800) 888088). For more info, call the **Italian State Railway Representative** in New York (☎ (212) 730-2121). If you plan to bring a **seeing-eye dog** to Italy, contact your vet and the nearest Italian consulate. You'll need import documents and records certifying your dog's health. For additional info, try **Global Access** (www.geocities.com/Paris/1502/disabilitylinks.html), which has several great links for disabled travelers in Italy. Those with disabilities should inform airlines and hotels of their disabilities when making reservations; some time may be needed to prepare special accommodations. Call ahead to restaurants, museums, and other facilities to find out about the existence of ramps, the widths of doors, the dimensions of elevators, etc. **Guide dog owners** should inquire as to the quarantine policies of each destination country. At the very least, they will need to provide a certificate of immunization against rabies. **Rail** is probably the most convenient form of travel for disabled travelers in Europe: many stations have ramps, and some trains have wheelchair lifts, special seating areas, and specially equipped toilets. All Eurostar, some InterCity (IC) and some EuroCity (EC) trains are wheelchair-accessible amd CityNightLine trains and Conrail trains feature special compartments. In general, Italy has one of the most **wheelchair-accessible rail networks** in Europe; all Pendolino and many Ec and IC trains are accessible. For those who wish to rent cars, some major **car rental** agencies (Hertz, Avis, and National) offer hand-controlled vehicles.

USEFUL ORGANIZATIONS

Mobility International USA (MIUSA), P.O. Box 10767, Eugene, OR 97440 (☎541-343-1284; www.miusa.org). Sells *A World of Options: A Guide to International Educational Exchange, Community Service, and Travel for Persons with Disabilities* (US$35).

Society for the Advancement of Travel for the Handicapped (SATH), 347 Fifth Ave., #610, New York, NY 10016 (☎212-447-7284; www.sath.org). An advocacy group that publishes free online travel information and the travel magazine *OPEN WORLD* (US$18, free for members). Annual membership US$45, students and seniors US$30.

TOUR AGENCIES

Directions Unlimited, 123 Green Ln., Bedford Hills, NY 10507 (☎800-533-5343). Books individual and group vacations for the physically disabled; not an info service.

MINORITY TRAVELERS

Until recently, the Roman population was relatively homogeneous. Immigration in the latter half of the 20th century from Eastern Europe, North Africa, the Philippines, and former Italian colonies like Somalia and Ethiopia has changed the make-up of the city. Many Romans have not quite gotten used to these newcomers and blame them for—among other things—the rise in crime and social unrest. Although immigrants of color do experience discrimination, tourists of color from the West, who are easily distinguishable by western clothes and language, are not the usual targets of racism. Women of Asian heritage may be referred to as *giapponese*. Women from India may be called *Indiana*. African-American women may find that Italian men can't get past *bellissima*.

Let's Go does not list known discriminatory establishments. If, in your travels, you encounter discriminatory treatment, let us know so that we can check the establishment and warn travelers. If you have trouble, contact your country's embassy or consulate in Rome (many are listed in the **Service Directory,** p. 290.

TRAVELERS WITH CHILDREN

Long bus rides and longer walks are usually required to see just about anything in Rome, making traveling with children quite challenging. Your children will almost certainly find historical sites far less interesting than you will. On the other hand, they will find all sorts of unexpected things interesting, especially if you take the time to explain things to them. Rome also boasts a bountiful supply of *gelaterias*, candy stores, and free water fountains, which are surprisingly helpful in keeping a kid's morale up. Don't forget to schedule an afternoon nap for *everyone*, which will correspond with the siesta planned right into Roman business hours anyway.

If you're going beyond Rome, note that while car rental is convenient, train travel might be more fun for the kids, and certainly cheaper. **Discount Eurailpasses** are available for groups, families, and children. Make sure that your children have some sort of ID (including your hotel info) on their person in case they get lost.

Caffè della Palma (near the Pantheon) and **Jolly Pop candy stores** (in P. Navona and in the entrance of Termini Station) are always good for a rest stop or a bribe. The **Villa Borghese** park is a cool respite from ancient monuments and churches, and you can rent bicycles or a rowboat to paddle in the small lake. There are **boat rides** down the Tiber and **horse-drawn carriage rides** around the city, originating from P. di Spagna. Children also love the **caricatures** and portraits done in P. Navona—either watching or posing. There are puppet shows in English on Saturday and Sunday at **Teatro dei Satiri,** V.d. Grotta Pinta, 19, off Campo dei Fiori. (☎06 68806244.) Check out the genuine Sicilian puppet shows at the **Teatro Crisogno,** V.S. Gallicano, 8, off viale di Trastevere. **LUNEUR** park (see p. 136) is an old-fashioned amusement park, with a hokey wax museum, roller coaster, and carnival attractions.

Backpacking with Babies and Small Children, Goldie Silverman. Wilderness Press (US$10).

Take Your Kids to Europe, Cynthia W. Harriman. Cardogan Books (US$18).

DIETARY CONCERNS

Vegetarians should have no problems in Italian restaurants, since the majority of first courses (primi, the pasta course) are meatless, and most restaurants will also supply you a mixed plate of their vegetable side dishes upon request—ask for verdure miste (mixed vegetables). *Let's Go: Rome* includes some vegetarian restaurants (see the **Index,** under vegetarian) and you can always ask for a dish *senza carne*. If you aren't sure of the contents of a particular dish, ask *"c'è carne?"* Be wary, since Italians don't believe that fish is meat, and many seemingly veggie treats may hide meat. Soups are never vegetarian: they're made with a meat base, even if no meat is added.

Since many Italian dishes count pork as their principal ingredient, and lots of the rest consist of little other than meat and cheese, those who keep kosher may have to turn vegetarian. Travelers who keep **kosher** should contact the synagogue of Rome in the Jewish Ghetto (☎06 6875051) for information on kosher restaurants (also see the **Index,** under kosher).Your own synagogue or college Hillel should have access to lists of Jewish institutions across the nation. If you are strict in your observance, you may have to prepare your own food on the road. A good resource is the *Jewish Travel Guide*, by Michael Zaidner (Vallentine Mitchell; US$17).

The North American Vegetarian Society, P.O. Box 72, Dolgeville, NY 13329 (☎518-568-7970; www.navs-online.org), publishes information about vegetarian travel, including Transformative Adventures, a Guide to Vacations and Retreats (US$15), and the Vegetarian Journal's Guide to Natural Food Restaurants in the US and Canada (US$12). For more information, visit your local bookstore, health food store, or library, and consult *The Vegetarian Traveler: Where to Stay if You're Vegetarian*, by Jed and Susan Civic (Larson Publications; US$16) and *Europe on 10 Salads a Day*, by Greg and Mary Jane Edwards (Mustang Publishing; US$10).

OTHER RESOURCES

Let's Go tries to cover all aspects of budget travel, but we can't put *everything* in our guides. Listed below are jumping off points for your own research.

TRAVEL PUBLISHERS & BOOKSTORES

Hippocrene Books, Inc., 171 Madison Ave., New York, NY 10016 (☎212-685-4371; orders 718-454-2366; www.netcom.com/~hippocre). Free catalog. Publishes foreign language dictionaries and language learning guides.

Hunter Publishing, 130 Campus Dr., Edison, NJ 08818, USA (☎800-255-0343; www.hunterpublishing.com). Has an extensive catalog of travel guides and diving and adventure travel books.

Rand McNally, 150 S. Wacker Dr., Chicago, IL 60606, USA (☎800-234-0679 or 312-332-2009; www.randmcnally.com), publishes road atlases (each US$10).

WORLD WIDE WEB

Almost every aspect of budget travel is accessible via the web. Within 10min. at the keyboard, you can reserve a room in a hostel, ask other travelers where the hotspots are in Rome, or find out just how much the train from Rome to Milan costs. Listed here are some budget travel sites to start off your surfing; other relevant web sites are listed throughout the book. Because website turnover is high, use search engines (such as www.google.com) to strike out on your own.

THE ART OF BUDGET TRAVEL

How to See the World: www.artoftravel.com. A compendium of great travel tips, from cheap flights to self defense to interacting with local culture.

Rec. Travel Library: www.travel-library.com. A fantastic set of links for general information and personal travelogues.

Lycos: cityguide.lycos.com. General introductions to Rome, accompanied by links to applicable histories, news, and local tourism sites.

Backpacker's Ultimate Guide: www.bugeurope.com. Tips on packing, transportation, and where to go. Also tons of country-specific travel information.

INFORMATION ON ROME

CIA World Factbook: www.odci.gov/cia/publications/factbook/index.html. Tons of vital statistics on Rome's geography, government, economy, and people.

Foreign Language for Travelers: www.travlang.com. Provides free online translating dictionaries and lists of phrases in Italian.

MyTravelGuide: www.mytravelguide.com. Country overviews, with everything from history to transportation to live web cam coverage of Rome.

Geographia: www.geographia.com. Highlights, culture, and people of Italy.

Atevo Travel: www.atevo.com/guides/destinations. Detailed introductions, travel tips, and suggested itineraries.

World Travel Guide: www.travel-guides.com/navigate/world.asp. Helpful practical info.

TravelPage: www.travelpage.com. Links to official tourist office sites in Italy.

PlanetRider: www.planetrider.com. A subjective list of links to the "best" websites covering the culture and tourist attractions of Italy.

A.S. Roma and **S.S. Lazio:** www.asromacalcio.it and www.sslazio.it. Rome's two soccer teams. Deciding which you like better before you go will make your time in Rome far less confusing.

Comune di Roma: www.comune.roma.it. An intimidating Roman site with up-to-the-minute events information and metric tons more.

Romeguide: www.romeguide.it. An amazingly complete site; particularly strong in the area of accommodations, transportation, and cultural events

AND OUR PERSONAL FAVORITE...

Let's Go: www.letsgo.com. Our constantly expanding website features photos and streaming video, online ordering of all our titles, info about our books, a travel forum buzzing with stories and tips, and links that will help you find everything you ever wanted to know about Rome.

INSIDE

Accommodations

Everyone sooner or later comes round by Rome," wrote poet Robert Browning, and chances are they're coming at the same time you are and have the reservations you wanted. Many hotels now let you **book rooms** directly over the Internet, which is significantly cheaper than calling or sending a fax from abroad. English may not be spoken at some smaller places, but this shouldn't dissuade a non-Italian speaker from calling; most Useful phrases for making a room reservation in Italian are on p. 28, but most *pensione* owners are used to calls from travelers. Useful phrases for making a room reservation in Italian are included in **Let's Speak Italian,** p. 28. When you check in, the proprietor will ask for your passport to register you with the police, as required by Italian law. They should only need it to write down the number—be sure to retrieve it. If the hotel asks for a deposit, send a bank draft (unless a credit card is required). Prices vary widely according to season. You'll pay the most during high season, June and July.

If you arrive in Rome **without reservations,** it is usually possible to find a place to stay, although you may not like it very much and may have to pay more than you ought to for it. Termini is full of officials ready to direct you to a hotel. Some of them are the real thing and have photo IDs issued by the tourist office. Some, however, are sneaky impostors who issue themselves fake badges and cards, and they may well direct you to a sketchy location charging a ridiculous rate, particularly if you arrive late at night. Private tourist agencies like Enjoy Rome (see p. 23) are also a good resource.

The APT(Azienda di Promozione Turistica) classifies all Italian hotels on a five-star system. An official rate card is then put on the inside of the door of each room. Prices are set each October, which explains why you may sometimes encounter rates slightly above those listed in *Let's Go: Rome 2002*, which was researched during the summer of 2001. No hotel can legally charge more than the maximum permitted by the inspector, but be warned that some proprietors increase their prices up to double at the sound of a foreign voice. If you find that your hotel is charging more than the maximum posted rate, complain by calling APT at 06 488991 or visiting any tourist office. Illegal *pensioni* and hostels abound in the area around Termini. While some of these establishments are cheap and may suit your needs, be aware that they have no price controls, and often have no insurance. If you have a problem at these establishments, complaints to the officials at APT will get you nowhere. All establishments listed in *Let's Go: Rome 2002* are registered with APT.

Rates tend to be lower per person in a shared room; it will be less expensive for you to share a triple with two friends than to get a single on your own. A single (which will often be quite small) is called a *camera singola*, a double with separate beds is a *camera doppia*, and a double with one big bed is a *camera matrimoniale.* A triple *(camera tripla)* will occasionally be a large double with an extra bed. This is almost always the case with quads *(camera quadrupla)* and larger rooms (with the exception of hostels). Note that **children are not allowed in most dorm rooms.**

By Italian law, you are not allowed to have unregistered visitors in your room, so don't be surprised or upset if the proprietor isn't keen on letting you invite your new Italian friend in for a nightcap (or more). Equally illegal is hanging laundry out the window or on a balcony to dry, so don't try it.

ACCOMMODATIONS BY PRICE

The accommodations listed below are grouped according to prices as they are posted in the high season (June and July in the Eternal City). Low season prices tend to be anywhere from L10,000 cheaper than the high season price to half the high season price. The price listed below is for the cheapest single room, dorm room, or equivalent space available (accurate as of August 2001), without any extra amenities such as A/C or bath (suck it up, budgeteer!). The following key to the neighborhoods of Rome (roughly equivalent to the neighborhood breakdown of the rest of the book) will help you to decipher the neighborhood codes listed directly across from the accommodation name.

NEIGHBORHOOD KEY			
Borgo and Prati (270)	BP	Piazza di Spagna (269)	PS
Centro Storico (266)	CS	Termini and San Lorenzo (270)	TSL
Esquilino–south of Termini (273)	ESQ	Trastevere (268)	TRV
Near Vatican City (270)	VC	West of Termini (274)	WT

ACCOMMODATIONS BY NEIGHBORHOOD

Unless explicitly stated (AmEx, D, MC, V), the following budget accommodations do not accept credit cards. Remember that **price increases,** though regrettable, are inevitable at most establishments. When prices are listed as a range, lower prices are for low season .

CENTRO STORICO

see map p.310-311

The *Centro Storico* is the ideal, if increasingly expensive, base for living as the Romans do. Most sights are within walking distance, and the market at nearby Campo dei Fiori yields cheap, fresh nourishment. You can expect to pay a 10-15% premium for the classical Roman charm lacking in Termini-area accommodations.

Albergo Pomezia, V.d. Chiavari, 12 (☎/fax 06 6861371; hotelpomezia@openaccess.it). Off C. V. Emanuele II behind Sant'Andrea della Valle. The rooms on the first and 2nd floors have been renovated and are nicer than those on the 3rd; all of the redone rooms have baths. Clean, quiet rooms with phones, fans, and heat in the winter. You haven't had too much to drink–the managers really are twins. Breakfast in the pleasant dining room included (8-11am). Singles L90,000/€45.00, L110,000/€56.70

L35,000 AND UNDER	
Associazione Cattolica Int'l (275)	ESQ
Colors (270)	BP
Hotel Il Castello (273)	ESQ
Ostello dei Foro Italico (HI)	BP
Pensione Fawlty Towers (270)	TSL
Pensione Ottaviano (270)	VC
Pensione Sandy (274)	WT
L50,000 AND UNDER	
Hotel Bolognese (271)	TSL
Pensione di Rienzo (273)	ESQ
L75,000 AND UNDER	
Pensione Monaco (272)	TSL
Pensione Panda (269)	PS
Pensione Piave (273)	TSL
Pensione Tizi (272)	TSL
Hotels Castelfidardo & Lazzari (272)	TSL
Hotel Cervia (272)	TSL
Hotel Des Artistes (271)	TSL
Hotel Giu' Giu' (273)	ESQ
Pensione Katty (272)	TSL
Hotel Ventura (272)	TSL
YWCA Foyer di Roma (275)	BP
Hotel Orlanda (273)	ESQ
Hotel San Paolo (274)	WT
L80,000 AND UNDER	
Hotel Boccaccio (269)	PS
Hotel Roxena (272)	TSL
L90,000 AND UNDER	
Albergo della Lunetta (267)	CS
Hotel Baltic (272)	TSL
L90,000 AND UNDER (CONT.)	
Hotel Magic (271)	TSL
Albergo Pomezia (266)	CS
Hotel Pensione Cathrine (271)	TSL
L100,000 AND UNDER	
Hotel Dolomiti (271)	TSL
Hotel Fenicia (272)	TSL
Hotel Carmel (268)	TRV
Hotel Galli (272)	TSL
Hotel Piccolo (267)	CS
Hotel Sweet Home (273)	ESQ
Pensione Cortorillo (273)	ESQ
Pensione Jonella (269)	PS
Hotel Selene (273)	ESQ
Hotel Lachea (271)	
L110,000 AND UNDER	
Albergo Abruzzi (267)	CS
Albergo del Sole (268)	CS
Hotel Kennedy (273)	ESQ
Hotel Mimosa (268)	CS
Hotel Pensione Joli (270)	BP
L140,000 AND UNDER	
Hotel Florida (270)	BP
Hotel Trastevere (268)	TSV
Hotel Navona (267)	CS
Hotel Pensione Suisse S.A.S. (269)	PS
Hotel Teti (274)	ESQ
Hotel Lady (270)	BPV
OVER L140,000	
Hotel Adventure (271)	TSL
Hotel/Pensione Parlamento (268)	PS
Residenza dei Quiriti (268)	VC

with bath; doubles L150,000/€77.50, L200,000/€103.00 with bath; triples L210,000/€108.60, with bath L255,000/€127.50; extra bed 35% surcharge. AmEx/MC/V.

Albergo della Lunetta, P. del Paradiso, 68 (☎06 6861080; fax 06 6892028). The first right off V. Chiavari from C. V. Emanuele II behind Sant'Andrea della Valle. Clean, well-lit rooms with phones; some around a small, fern-filled courtyard, and a roof garden. Fairly good value in a great location (between Campo dei Fiori and P. Navona). Singles L90,000/€45.00, with bath L110,000/€56.70; doubles L150,000/€77.50, with bath L200,000/€103.00; triples L210,000/€108.16 with bath L255,000/€177.50. Reservations with credit card or check. MC/V.

Albergo Abruzzi, P. della Rotonda, 69 (☎06 6792021). Location, location, location! 200 ft. from the Pantheon, these are indeed rooms with a view. The facilities abetting your viewing are old-fashioned but clean. Hall bathrooms are the only option here, but every room comes equipped with a sink. Singles L90-115,000/€45.00-58.60; doubles L140-170,000/€72.00-87.60; triples L220,000/€116.00.

Hotel Piccolo, V.d. Chiavari, 32 (☎06 6892330). Off C. Vittorio Emanuele II behind Sant'Andrea della Valle. Recently renovated, family-run establishment next to a bustling grocery store. All rooms have fans and telephones. No elevator. English spoken. Curfew 1am. Checkout noon. Breakfast L7000/€3.62. Singles L100,000/€51.60, with bath L120,000/€62.00; doubles L120,000/€62.00, with bath L160,000/€82.00; triples with bath L170,000/€87.60; quads with bath L180,000/€90.00. AmEx/ MC/V.

Hotel Navona, V.d. Sediari, 8, first Fl. (☎06 6864203; fax 06 68211392, call before faxing; www.hotelnavona.com; info@hotelnavona.com. Take V.d. Canestrari from P. Navona, cross C. del Rinascimento, and go straight. This 16th-century building has been used as a *pensione* for over 150 years, counting among its guests Keats, Shelley, and the University of Alabama

the BIG $plurge

Hotel/Pensione Parlamento, V.d. Convertite, 5 (☎/fax 06 6792082). **Near the Spanish Steps:** off V.d. Corso. The rooms are very well-apportioned, with comfortable mattresses, each with bath, safe, hair dryer, A/C, telephone, and TV, as well as high ceilings, plush velvet chairs, and static-free CNN. Giorgio, the receptionist, speaks English, French, Spanish, and German. Singles L160-180,000/€82.60-90.00; doubles L180-200,000/€90.00-103.00; triples L235-255,000/€120.00-128.80; quads L300-320,000/€155.00-165.00. Ample breakfast included; in the summer you can eat outside on the glamorous terrace. Reservations recommended. AmEx/MC/V.

Residenza dei Quiriti, V. Germanico, 198, 4th Fl. (☎06 3600 5389; fax 06 3679 0487). **Near the Vatican:** in same building as Hotel Lady. While a bit more expensive than other area lodgings, the brand new Quiriti is a big step up in comfort and style–definitely worth the splurge. Ten snug, beautiful yellow rooms with private baths and elegant furnishings offer all the crucial details: A/C, mini fridges, hair dryers, satellite TV, daily maid service, and several even have bathtubs! The friendly staff speaks good English. Singles L160,000, doubles L240,000, triples L280,000; prices drop to L120,000, L160,000, and L180,000 in late July, Aug. and March. AmEx/MC/V.

chapter of the ΑΠΘ fraternity. Checkout 10am. Breakfast included. Singles with bath 160,000/€82.00; doubles with bath L210,000/€108.60; triples with bath L290,00/€145.00. A/C L30,000/€15.50 Pay in cash only before 1st night.

Albergo del Sole, V.d. Biscione, 76 (☎06 68806873; fax 06 6893787). Off Campo dei Fiori. Allegedly the oldest *pensione* in Rome. 61 comfortable modern rooms with phone, fan, TV, and fantastic antique furniture. Some rooms look out on the rowdy street, while others ring a pleasant courtyard garden. Parking garage (L30-40,000). Singles L120,000/€62.00, with bath 140-170,000/€72.00-86.00; doubles L160-180,000/€82.00-92.00, with bath L200-240,000/€103.00-124.00.

Hotel Mimosa, V.S. Chiara, 61, 2nd Fl. (☎06 68801753; fax 06 6833557). Off P. della Minerva behind the Pantheon. Spacious rooms in a a remarkably quiet and convenient part of the Centro Storico. No elevator or champagne and orange juice cocktails. Drunkenness not tolerated. Curfew 1am, but keys are available. Singles L90-120,000/€45.00-62.00, with bath L120-130,000/€62.00-66.00; doubles L130-160,000/€65.00-82.60, with L150-180,000/€77.50-90.00.

TRASTEVERE

see map p.310-311

Trastevere is a beautiful old Roman neighborhood famous for its separatism, medieval streets, and pretty-far-from-the-tourist-crowd charm. Hotels here are scattered, most of them flung well beyond the budget traveller's budget, but nice to stay in, if you'd like to be near the Vatican as well as great nightlife.

Hotel Carmel, V. G. Mameli, 11 (☎06 5809921; fax 6 5818853, hotelcarmel@hotmail.com). Take a right on V. E. Morosini (V. G. Mameli) off V.d. Trastevere. Though a good walk from the heart of Trastevere, this simple hotel offers nine no-frills, smallish rooms for reasonable prices. A comfortable atrium-like sitting room leads to a beautiful garden terrace with seating for breakfast. All with bath. Breakfast included. Singles L100,000/€51.60; doubles L150,000/€77.50; triples L190,000/€98.13; quads L220,000/€113.62. AmEx/MC/V.

Hotel Trastevere, V. Luciano Manara, 25 (☎06 5814713, fax 06 5881016). Take a right off V.d. Trastevere onto V.d. Fratte di Trastevere. This homey establishment overlooks colorful P.S. Cosimato in the heart of Trastevere. Extravagant neighborhood murals give way to nine simple and airy rooms with bath, TV, and phone. English spoken. Breakfast included. Singles L130,000/€67.14; doubles 160,000/€82.63; triples L170,000/€87.80; quads L240,000/€123.95. Short-term apartments for 2-6 persons with neat little kitchens and loft beds available. AmEx/D/MC/V.

NEAR PIAZZA DI SPAGNA

see map p. 315

Accommodations in this area might run you a few thousand more *lire* per day, but can you really put a price tag on living but a few steps from Prada? John Keats couldn't.

Pensione Panda, V.d. Croce, 35 (☎06 6780179; fax 06 69942151; www.hotelpandaparadise.com). Between P. di Spagna and V.d. Corso. Newly renovated, the Panda sports lovely, immaculate rooms, arched ceilings (some with frescoes), and neo-Roman reliefs in the hallways. 11am checkout. Reservations recommended. Singles L70,000/€36.20, with bath L100-120,000/€51.60-62.00; doubles L120-180,000/€62.00-90.00; triples with bath L210,000/€108.16; quads with bath L320,000/€160.00. Ask about Let's Go discount. AmEx/MC/V.

Pensione Jonella, V.d. Croce, 41 (☎06 6797966). Between P. di Spagna and V.d. Corso. Run by same guys as Hotel des Artistes (see p. 271), this *pensione* offers four beautiful rooms. Quiet, roomy, and cool in summer. No reception: call ahead to arrange for someone to meet you when you arrive. 4th floor location; no elevator. No private bathrooms. Singles L100,000/€51.60; doubles L120,000/€62.00. Cash only.

Hotel Boccaccio, V.d. Boccaccio, 25 (☎/fax 06 4885962; www.hotelboccaccio.com). M: A-Barberini. Off V.d. Tritone. This well-situated hotel offers 8 elegantly furnished rooms near many sights. Singles L80,000/€41.30; doubles L120,000/€62.00, with bath L160,000/€83.60; triples L162-216,000/€85.00-111.00. AmEx/D/MC/V.

Hotel Pensione Suisse S.A.S., V. Gregoriana, 54 (☎06 6783649; fax 06 6781258; suisse.hotel@tiscalinet.it). Turn right at the top of the Spanish Steps, Madame. Renovated winter 2001. Sleek, old-fashioned furniture, comfortable beds, and phone and fan in every room. Close to the wisteria-hung heights of the Steps, but away from the hubbub; at night you'll think you're in another city. Curfew 2am. In-room breakfast included. All rooms with bath. Triples L285,000/€147.19; quads L340,000/€175.60. Half the bill may be paid by credit card. MC/V.

Home away from home

Sweet Dreams!

Hotel des Artistes

BORGO AND PRATI (NEAR VATICAN CITY)

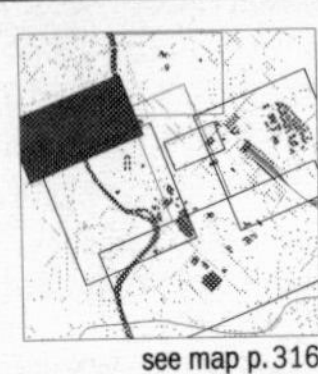

see map p.316

The *pensioni* on the other side of the Tiber aren't the cheapest in Rome, but they tend to be comfortable, spotless, and fairly quiet (which might appeal to families looking to get plenty of rest). It's convenient to the Vatican but a hike from many central sights. Nearby Metro (A) stops are Lepanto and Ottaviano.

Colors, V. Boezio, 31 (☎ 06 6874030, fax 06 6867947). M: A-Ottaviano, or take a bus to P. Risorgimento. Take V. Cola di Rienzo to V. Terenzio. Sporting lots of amenities and a super-cool English-speaking staff, Colors is located in the elegant and quiet Prati area and offers 18 beds in rooms painted with a bravado that would put Caravaggio to shame. Kitchen, hair dryers, internet (L5000/€2.58 per hour), laundry service (L8000/€4.13 per load, the best deal in town). Beautiful terrace open until 11:00pm. Dorm beds L35,000/€17.60; doubles L120-150,000/€61.97-77.50; triples L140-180,000/€72.30-92.96. Credit card needed for reservations; cash only.

Pensione Ottaviano, V. Ottaviano, 6 (☎06 39737253 or 06 39737253; www.pensioneottaviano.com; gi.costantini@agora.stm.it), just north of P. del Risorgimento, a few blocks from the Metro stop of the same name and a few steps away from St. Peter's. This comfortable hostel has been open since 1956, and just keeps getting better. 3 to 6 beds per room. Amenities include satellite TV, individual lockers, fridges, a microwave, hot showers, free linens, and free email access for guests. Friendly Aussie and British staff. Smoking allowed. No curfew. Lock-out 11:30am-2pm. Dorm-style rooms L30,000/€15.50, winter L25,000/€17.00 in the winter. Doubles L90,000/L70,000/€45.50-36.20; one triple L120,000/€61.97. Cash only.

Hotel Pensione Joli, V. Cola di Rienzo, 243, 6th Fl. (☎06 3241854; fax 06 36006637; jolihit@yahoo.it), at V. Tibullo, *scala* A. Winding blue-striped walls and low ceilings make you feel a little like Alice in Wonderland, if Wonderland were a *pensione* with nice beds, ceiling fans, and gorgeous views of the Vatican. Most of the 18 rooms have bath, all have telephone. Breakfast included. Singles L95,000/€49.06, with bathroom L120,000/€61.97; doubles L160-180,000/€82.63-92.96; triples L243,000/€125.50; quads L318,000/€164.23. MC/V.

Hotel Florida, V. Cola di Rienzo, 243 (☎06 3241872 or 06 3241608; fax 06 3241857), on the 2nd and 3rd floors. Floral carpets, floral bedspreads, floral wall decorations. Very comfortable, with kind, English-speaking staff. A/C, TVs, phones, and hair dryers in each of the 16 rooms. Delightfully clean bathrooms. Singles with sink L140,000/€72.30, with bath L160,000/€82.63; doubles with bath L200,000/€103.00; triples with bath L260,000/€134.23; quads with bath L300,000/€154.94. Call ahead to reserve and ask about discounts. 5% discount if you pay in cash. AmEx/MC/V.

Hotel Lady, V. Germanico, 198, 4th Fl. (☎06 3242112; fax 06 3243446), between V. Fabbio Massimo and V. Paolo Emilio. A non-English-speaking Roman couple has been running this small, peaceful *pensione* for 38 years. 8 rooms, some with beautiful loft-style open woodwork ceilings. Spacious common room. Singles without bathroom L130,000/€67.14; doubles L160,000/€82.63, with bath L200,000/€103.00.

TERMINI AND SAN LORENZO

see map p. 312-313

NORTH OF TERMINI

Although the area right next to the train station has its fair share of tourist traps, there are many comfortable, reasonably priced *pensioni* and hotels. This area has recently experienced a revival and consequent influx of reasonably-priced lodgings, making it a haven for budget travelers. It's also cheaper than the historic center and safer than the sometimes seedy Esquilino area. For a quieter stay, ask for rooms on internal courtyards.

Pensione Fawlty Towers, V. Magenta, 39 (☎/fax 06 4450374; www.fawltytowers.org or www.fawltytowersrome.com; info@fawltytowers.org). Exit Termini to the right from the middle concourse, cross V. Marsala onto V. Marghera, and turn right onto V. Magenta.An extremely popular 15-room hotel/hostel,

Fawlty Towers never fails to satisfy its customers. The flower-filled terrace provides a peaceful respite from the panic of Termini. Common room with satellite TV, library, refrigerator, microwave, and cheap Internet access. Check-out 9am for dorms and 10am for private rooms. Frequently full, but the reception will do their utmost to find you a place. Reservations possible a week in advance; confirm all reservations 48 hours before arrival. Native English speaking staff. Dorm-style quads L30-35,000/€15.50-17.60 per person (no children); singles L75,000/€38.73, with shower L90,000/€45.00; doubles L110,000/€56.81, with shower L140,000/€72.30, with bath L150,000/€77.50; triples with bath L165,000/€85.22.

Hotel Des Artistes, V. Villafranca, 20 (☎06 4454365; fax 06 4462368; www.hoteldesartistes.com; info@hoteldesartistes.com). From the middle concourse of Termini, exit right, turn left onto V. Marsala, right onto V. Vicenza, and then left onto the 5th cross-street. 3-star, 40-room hotel with clean, elegant rooms with bathrooms, safes, refrigerators, and TVs. Amenities include a lovely rooftop terrace and lounge with satellite TV. Cheap Internet access. Breakfast (L8000/€4.13). 24hr. reception. Cancel Reservations at least 5 days before. Check-out 11am. Singles L70,000/€36.20; doubles L110-170,000/€56.81-87.80; triples L130-210,000/€67.14-108.46; dorms (rooms with 4-6 beds) L35,000/€17.60. Winter 20-30% less. AmEx/MC/V.

Hotel Papa Germano, V. Calatafimi, 14a (☎06 486919 or 06 47825202; fax 06 47881281; www.hotelpapagermano.com. From the middle concourse of Termini, exit right, and turn left onto V. Marsala, which shortly becomes V. Volturno; V. Calatafimi is the 4th cross-street on your right. Clean, affordable rooms (all with TV and telephone) and outstanding service from friendly owners Gino and Pina. English Spoken. Internet access. 18 rooms. Check-out 11am. Singles L45-70,000/€23.24; doubles L70-130,000/€36.20-67.14, with bath L100-160,00/€51.60-82.63; triples L105-150,000/€54.23-77.47, with bath L135-200,000/€69.72-103.29; dorms L30-40,000/€15.50-20.60. AmEx/MC/V.

Hotel Dolomiti and **Hotel Lachea,** V.S. Martino della Battaglia, 11 (☎06 4957256; fax 06 4454665; www.hotel-dolomiti.it; dolomiti@hotel-dolomiti.it). From the middle concourse of Termini, exit right, turn left onto V. Marsala and right onto V. Solferino (V.S. Martino della Battaglia). Aging 19th-century *palazzo* houses sparkling new hotels, offering a bar, breakfast room, and Internet access (L10,000). Rooms in three-star Dolomiti have satellite TV, telephones, minibars, safes, and A/C. Lachea offers the same excellent service in a simpler hotel (for lower prices). Some rooms with a balcony. Breakfast L12,000/€6.20. A/C L25,000/€12.91 per night. Check-out 11am. Rooms with baths. Singles L100-130,000/€51.60-67.14; doubles L140-200,000/€72.30-103.00; triples L180-240,000/€92.96-123.94; quads L220-260,000/€113.62-134.28; quints available. Rooms without bath and tv available: Singles L75-90,000/€38.73-45.00; doubles L90-120,000/€45.00-61.97; triples L110-130,000/€56.81-67.14.

Hotel Pensione Cathrine, V. Volturno, 27 (☎06 483634). From the middle concourse of Termini, exit right, and turn left onto V. Marsala (V. Volturno). Comfortable *pensione* run by friendly southern Italian man. Two uncommonly clean common bathrooms serve the spacious singles and doubles that only have a sink. More rooms at V. XX Settembre, 58a. Breakfast L13,000/€6.71. *Let's Go* discount L10,000/€5.16. Singles L90,000/€45.00; doubles L130-140,000/€67.13-72.30; triples with bath L170,000/€87.80.

Hotel Adventure, V. Palestro, 88 (☎06 4469026; fax 06 4460084; www.hoteladventure.com; hotel.adventure@flashnet.it). From the middle concourse of Termini, exit right, cross V. Marsala onto V. Marghera, and take the 4th right onto V. Palestro. Newly renovated rooms (all with bath, satellite TV, telephone, and fridge) at excellent rates. Breakfast included. Check-out 11am. Singles 150,000/€77.47 including A/C; doubles L160,000/€82.63; triples L220,000/€113.62. A/C L25,000/€12.91. AmEx/MC/V.

Hotel Bolognese, V. Palestro, 15 (☎/fax 06 490045). In a land of run-of-the-mill *pensioni,* this place is spruced up by the artist-owner who provides scattered extra amenities: some of the 14 bedrooms have attached sitting rooms, some bathtubs, and still others terraces. Probably the only hotel near Termini to have won an award from the Knights of Malta. Check-out 11am. Curfew 2am. Singles L50,000/€25.80, with bath L70-L80,000/€36.20-41.30; doubles L80-120,000/€41.20-62.00; triples L120-150,000/€62.00-77.50.

Hotel Magic, V. Milazzo, 20 (☎/fax 064959880). Alacazam! The owners of Hotel Magic will make a clean, modern room and a beautiful bar appear before your very eyes. Almost all rooms include private baths, TVs, and in-room safes. Singles L100,000/€51.60;

doubles L140,000/€72.30; triples L180,000/€92.96; quads L220,000/€113.62. A/C L20,000/€10.30. MC/V.

Hotel Galli, V. Milazzo, 20 (☎06 4456859; fax 06 4468501; www.albergogalli.com; info@albergogalli.com), off V. Marsala. Clean and modern. Many a green plant in the white hallways invite you to stay a little longer. All 12 rooms have bath, TV, mini-bar, and safe. Breakfast included. Singles L120,000/€62.00; doubles L160,000/€82.63; triples L210,000/€108.46; quads L250,000/€129.11. Winter 10-15% lower . A/C Included. AmEx/MC/V.

Hotel Fenicia, V. Milazzo, 20 (☎/fax 06490342; www.fenicia.it; hotel.fenicia@tiscalinet.it). 11 sparkling, modern rooms close to Termini, all with bath and TV. Singles L90,000/€45.00; doubles L140,000/€72.30. Extra beds L45,000/€23.24. A/C L20,000/€10.30.

Hotel Cervia, V. Palestro, 55 (☎06 491057; fax 06 491056; hotelcervia@wnt.it). The TV room, breakfast room with bar, and clean rooms and bathrooms are nice, but guests stay on for the friendly atmosphere. Rooms with bath include breakfast; otherwise, it's L5000/€2.58. 24hr. reception. Check-out noon. Singles L70,000/€36.20; doubles L90,000/€45.00, with bath L140,000/€72.30; triples L135-210,000/€69.72-108.46. AmEx/MC/V.

Pensione Katty, V. Palestro, 35 (☎06 4441216). The 23 rooms are plain but large, and you can ask for one with an elegant painted ceiling. The nicest rooms are on the second floor, while all rooms have high ceilings and sinks. Lounge with espresso machine. Key deposit L5000/€2.58. Check-out 11am. Singles L75,000/€38.73, with bath L100,000/€51.60; doubles L100-130,000/€51.60-67.14; triples L150-180,000/€77.50-92.96; quads L200-230,000/€103.00-118.79. Big discounts Nov.-Mar. L10,000/€5.16 extra per night for A/C. Traveler's checks accepted. MC/V.

Hotel Ventura, V. Palestro, 88 (☎06 4451951). In a building with many other hotels, Ventura distinguishes itself by rooms with TVs, telephones, and a truly inordinate number of pictures covering their walls. Breakfast L10,000/€5.16. Doubles with bath L100-150,000/€51.60-77.50; triples with bath L50-80,000/€25.80-41.30. AmEx/MC/V. No reservations.

Hotel Roxena, V. Marghera, 13 (☎06 4456823; fax 06 4452629). A little drab, but you could trip on your way out of Termini and be here. Breakfast L10,000/€5.16. Curfew 1am. Singles L60,000/€32.00; doubles L100,000/€51.60, with bath L140,000/€72.30; triples L150-180,000/€77.50-92.96.

VIA XX SEPTEMBRE AND ENVIRONS

Although not far from the train station, this area has a very different character, and is dominated by government ministries and private apartments, so there's less noise and tourists than in the Termini area.

Pensione Tizi, V. Collina, 48 (☎06 4820128; fax 06 4743266). A 10 min. walk from the station. Take V. Goito from P. dell'Indipendenza, cross V. XX Settembre onto V. Piave, then go left on V. Flavia, to V. Collina. Or take bus #319 or 270 from Termini. The nice people at Tizi have served student travelers in this peaceful neighborhood for years. Marble floors and inlaid ceilings adorn spacious and recently renovated rooms. Breakfast L10,000/€5.16. Check-out 11am. Singles L70,000/€36.20; doubles L90,000/€45.00, with bath L110,000/€56.81; triples and quads L40,000/€20.60 per person, L45,000/€23.24 with bath.

Hotel Castelfidardo and **Hotel Lazzari,** V. Castelfidardo, 31 (☎06 4464638; fax 06 4941378; www.castelfidardo.com). Two blocks off V. XX Settmebre. Both run by the same friendly family. Renovated rooms with spanking clean floors and soothing pastel walls. Three floors of modern, shiny comfort and bodacious bathroom space. Hall bathrooms shared by three rooms at most. Check-out 11am. Singles L75,000/€38.73, with bath 100,000/€51.60; doubles L110,00/€56.81, with bath 130,000/€67.14; triples L140,000/€72.30, with bath 165,000/€85.22; quads with bath L200,000/€103.00. AmEx/MC/V.

Hotel Baltic, V. XX Settembre, 89 (☎06 4814775; fax 06 485509). Just past the intersection with V. Palestro. Sleek and well maintained, quiet rooms are more like those in a business hotel than the typical pensione, and all have telephone, televsion, microfridge, and safe. A friendly manager and marble lobby sweeten the deal. 23 rooms Breakfast L8000/€4.13. Check-out 11am. Singles L90,000/€45.00; doubles L120,000/€62.00; triples L150,000/€77.50; quads L195,000/€100.71. Traveler's checks accepted. AmEx/MC/V.

Pensione Monaco, V. Flavia, 84 (☎/fax 06 42014180). From V. XX Settembre, turn left onto V. Quinto Sellia and right onto V. Flavia. Friendly Italian woman and English-speaking children keep these 11 sunlit rooms clean. Comfortable mattresses, bright courtyard. Washing machines available. Check-out 9am. Let's Go discount prices: singles L60,000/€32.00, with bath L75,000/€38.73; doubles L85,000/€43.90, with bath L110,000/€56.81; triples and quads L45,000/€23.24 per person. Winter prices about 10% lower.

Pensione Piave, V. Piave, 14 (☎06 4743447; fax 06 4873360). Off V. XX Settembre to the left. Piave offers plain, well lit and quiet rooms at a moderate price. Check-in 11:30am. Check-out 11am. Reservations recommended. Singles L65,000/€33.57, with bath L95,000/€49.06; doubles with bath L120,000/€62.00; triples with bath L165,000/€85.22; quads with bath L180,000/€92.96. AmEx/MC/V.

SOUTH OF TERMINI (ESQUILINO)

While not the most posh part of town, it has decent rooms at good prices and is still close to many of the major sights.

Pensione di Rienzo, V. Principe Amedeo, 79a (☎06 4467131; fax 06 4466980). A tranquil, family-run retreat with spacious, newly renovated rooms. Large windows overlook a courtyard. Extremely friendly, helpful staff. It's plain and it's cheap. Sixteen rooms, some with balconies, TVs, and baths. Breakfast L20,000/€10.30. Check-out 10am. Singles without bath L40-80,000/€20.60-41.30; doubles L60-120,000/€32.00-62.00. MC/V.

Pensione Cortorillo, V. Principe Amedeo, 79a, 5th Fl. (☎06 4466934; fax 06 4454769). A family runs this small and friendly *pensione.* TV in all fourteen rooms. Cheap lobby phone. English spoken well. Breakfast included. Check-out 10am. Singles L80-120,000/€41.30-62.00; doubles L70-130,000/€36.20-67.14; rooms can be made into triples and quads for an additional L30,000/€15.50 per person. AmEx/D/MC/V.

Hotel Kennedy, V. Filippo Turati, 62-64 (☎06 4465373; fax 06 4465417; www.hotelkennedy.net; hotelkennedy@micanet.it). Ask not what you can do for Hotel Kennedy, ask what Hotel Kennedy can do for you. Classical music in the bar, leather couches, and a large color TV in the lounge. Private bath, satellite TV, phone, and A/C. Some rooms offer a view of Roman ruins. Hearty all-you-can-eat breakfast in three pleasant breakfast rooms included. English, French, and Spanish, and Portugese spoken. Check-out 11am. Reservations by fax/email only. Singles L65-169,000/€33.57-87.28; doubles L100-299,000/€51.60-154.42; triples L149-349,00/€76.95-180.240. 10% *Let's Go* discount. AmEx/D/MC/V.

Hotel Il Castello, V. Vittorio Amedeo II, 9 (☎06 77204036; fax 06 70490068; www.ilcastello.com). M: A-Manzoni. Far beyond Termini, but well within the backpacker's budget. Walk down V. San Quintino and take the first left. Housed in a castle with smallish white rooms and eager serving knaves (mostly native English speakers). Spot damsels in distress from the quaint balcony outside four of the rooms. Continental breakfast L5000. Check-out 10:30am. Dorm room beds L30,000/€15.50; singles without bath L80,000/€41.30; doubles L110,000/€56.81, with bath L130-150,000/€67.14; triples L120,000/€62.00, with bath L140-180,000/€72.30-92.96. MC/V.

Hotel Giu' Giu', V.d. Viminale, 8 (☎06 4827734; fax 06 48912616). Two blocks south of Termini, in an elegant but fading *palazzo.* Pleasant breakfast area, 12 large, quiet rooms, and a friendly family running the place. Breakfast L15,000/€7.75. Check-out 10am. Singles L65,000/€33.57; doubles L105,000/€54.23, with bath L115,000/€59.39; triples with bath L155,000/€80.05; quads with bath L195,000/€100.71.

Hotel Orlanda, V. Principe Amedeo, 76, 3rd Fl. (☎06 4880124; fax 06 4880183). At V. Gioberti. Take the stairs on the right in the vestibule. Frequented by Italian businesspeople. All 23 rooms have sinks, even if they don't have a bathroom; some have hair dryers. English spoken. Breakfast included. 24hr. reception. Can check in at noon, must check-out by 10am. Singles L55-130,000, with bath L60-170,000/€32.00-36.20; doubles L80-160,000/€41.30-82.63, with bath L100-270,000/€51.60-138.44; triples L105-190,000/€54.23-98.13, with bath L125-370,000/€64.56-191.09; quads L140-240,000/€72.30-123.95, with bath L160-460,000/€82.63-237.57. A/C L30,000/€15.50 extra. AmEx/D/MC/V.

Hotel Selene, V.d. Viminale, 8 (☎06 4824460; fax 06 4782 1977; www.hotel_seleneroma.com; hotelseleneroma@mclink.it). Above Hotel Giu' Giu'. 27 clean rooms with bath, TV, and telephone. Breakfast included. Singles L100,000/€51.60; doubles L150,000/€77.50; triples L210,000/€108.46; quads L240,000/€123.95. MC/V.

Hotel Sweet Home, V. Principe Amedeo, 47 (☎/fax 06 4880954). At V.d. Manin. The newly renovated rooms are of above average quality (with candy on the pillows, no less) and the proprietors are very welcoming. Checkout 11am. Singles L80-100,000/€41.30-51.60, with bath L150-180,000/€77.50-92.96; doubles L120-200,000/€62.00-103.00; triples 30% additional. AmEx/D/MC/V.

Hotel Teti, V. Principe Amedeo, 76 (☎/fax 06 48904088; hotelteti@iol.it). Take the stairs at the end of the courtyard. Spacious rooms, but costly for the neighborhood. Satellite TV, bathroom, and telephone in all rooms. A/C L25,000. English spoken. Breakfast L10,000/€5.16. Check-out 11am. Reservation can be made via email. Singles L90-160,000/€45.00-82.63; doubles L130-210,000/€67.14-108.46; triples L160-250,000/€82.63-129.11; quads L190-310,000/€98.13-160.10. 10-15% discount for students. AmEx/ D/MC/V.

WEST OF TERMINI

Just steps west from all the hustle and bustle of beloved Termini, the neighborhood becomes less decrepit and contains more sights and stores. It is also home to the city's two women-only establishments. Streets here are busier than those north of Termini and not nearly as grid-like.

Hotel San Paolo, V. Panisperna, 95 (☎06 4745213; fax 06 4745218; hsanpaolo@tin.it). Exiting from the front of the train station, turn left onto V. Cavour. After you pass Santa Maria Maggiore (on the left), bear right onto V.d. Santa Maria Maggiore (V. Panisperna). 10 min. from Termini, San Paolo's 23 rooms are housed in a bright little *palazzo* with tranquil, whimsically decorated rooms. Hall baths are clean and private. Public stereo in the cafe. Breakfast L10,000/€5.16. Check-out 10:30am. Singles L75,000/€38.73; doubles L110,000/€56.81, with bath L150,000/€77.50; triples L150,000/€77.50. Lovely, large 6-10 person suite L50-65,000/€25.80-33.57 per person. AmEx/MC/V.

Pensione Sandy, V. Cavour, 136 (☎06 4884585; gi.costantini@agora.stm.it; www.sandyhostel.com). Just past the intersection of V.S. Maria Maggiore. No sign; look for the Hotel Valle, Sandy is next door to the right. 4th floor, no elevator (ouch). Under the same ownership as Pensione Ottaviano, but not quite as nice. 25 beds. Free internet access and individual lockers (bring your own lock) in each room. No curfew, no lock-out. Simple, hostel-style rooms, usually for 3-5 people, in a central location. L30,000/€15.50 per person. Cash only.

ALTERNATIVE ACCOMMODATIONS

BED AND BREAKFASTS

While Italians may have appropriated the American terminology, the reality of "Bed and Breakfast" services in Rome differs from the typical American concept of a quaint countryside inn. Guest rooms are arranged in private homes throughout the city, with the owners of the home generally obliged to provide breakfast every morning. Apartments have kitchens where clients are expected to make their own breakfast. The rooms and apartments can vary greatly in quality and size. Be sure to pinpoint just how "centrally located" your appartment is—they can be flung toward the outskirts of the city.

Bed & Breakfast Association of Rome, P. del Teatro Pompeo, 2 (☎/fax 06 6877348; info@b-b.rm.it; www.b-b.rm.it), is a reservation service with a website that gives very explicit information and pictures of the rooms and apartments offered. Prices range from L80,000/€41.30 per night for a single room to L270,000/€139.44 per night for an apartment for six. (Office phone answered M-F 9am-1pm.)

Bed and Go, V.S. Tommaso d'Aquino, 47 (☎06 39750907 or 06 39746484; fax 06 39760553; www.bedandgo.com bedandgo@tin.it), offers rooms and apartments of all types, with prices in the city center ranging from L330,000/€170.43 per night for a six-bedroom apartment to L125,000/€64.56 for a single bedroom. (Open M-F 9:30am-1pm and 2-6pm.)

INSTITUTIONAL ACCOMMODATIONS

Rome's only HI-affiliated hostel is certainly not the cream of the crop; you should only consider this inconveniently located hostel if central Rome's many hostels are completely filled.

Ostello del Foro Italico (HI), V.d. Olimpiadi, 61 (☎06 3236267 or 06 3236279; fax 06 3242613). M: A-Ottaviano. Exit onto V. Barletta and take bus #32 to Cadorna (get off when you see pink Foro Italico buildings and an obelisk). 350 beds, in 6-12 person single-sex rooms. Close to the "Big Gym," Rome's largest public sports complex. No family rooms. Huge, free lockers (bring a lock). Reception 2pm-midnight. Lockout 10am-2pm. Strictly enforced curfew midnight. Check-out 7-10am. Lunch and dinner available (L10,000/€5.16). Small continental breakfast and hot showers included. Bar open 10am-10:30pm, restaurant open noon-2:30pm 6:30pm-9:30. L28,000/€14.46 with HI card (L30,000/€15.50). Cash only. Wheelchair accessible.

RELIGIOUS HOUSING

Certain convents and monasteries host guests (for a fee hovering around L50,000/€25.80 or more per night) who come with letters of introduction from their local diocese. Contact your home parish for details. Most religious accommodations involve single-sex housing, early curfews, services, and light chores.

CAMPING

In August, when most Italians go on vacation, call ahead or arrive early (well before 11am) to secure a spot. Rates average L12,000/€6.20 per person and another L8000/€4.13 per tent. The **Touring Club Italiano** publishes an annual directory of all camping sites in Italy, *Campeggi in Italia*, available in bookstores throughout Italy. Camping on beaches, roads, and inconspicuous plots is illegal and dangerous.

Seven Hills Village, V. Cassia, 1216 (☎06 303310826; fax 06 303310039) is 8km north of Rome. Take bus #907 from the Cipro-Musei Vaticani Metro(A), or bus #201 from P. Mancini. Ask where to get off–it's 3-4km past the GRA (the big highway that circles the city). Daily shuttles to Rome will fetch you back and forth to Ple. Flaminio (L6000/€3.20) or to a train staion near the campgrounds (L2000/€1.03). From the stop, follow the country road about 1km until you see the sign. Spend a lazy poolside afternoon and dance the night away in the disco. It also houses a bar, market, restaurant, and *pizzeria.* No *lire* allowed: buy a Seven Hills card for use all over the campground. Doctor on hand during the day. Check-in anytime, check-out by noon. L14,000/€ per person, L1500/€0.77 per tent, L7000/€3.62 per car; campers L15,000/€7.75. Bungalows sleep up to 4 and start from L85,000/€43.90. Open late Mar. to late Oct. Cash only.

WOMEN'S HOUSING

Beware the strict curfews and guest policies.

YWCA Foyer di Roma, V. C. Balbo, 4 (☎06 4880460; fax 06 4871028). From P. dei Cinquecento (in front of Termini), walk down V.d. Viminale, turn left onto V. Torino and right onto V. C. Balbo. The YWCA (pronounced EEV-kah) is a pretty, clean, and secure hostel. Breakfast included, M-Sa 8am-9am. Tell reception by 10am the same day if you want lunch (1pm-2pm, L20,000/€10.30). Reception open 7am-midnight. Curfew midnight. Check-out 10am. Singles L70,000/€36.20, with bath L90,000/€45.00; doubles L120,000/€62.00, with bath L140,000/€72.30; triples and quads L50,000/€25.80 per person. Cash only.

Associazione Cattolica Internazionale al Servizio della Giovane, V. Urbana, 158 (☎ 06 4880056). From P. Esquilino (in front of Santa Maria Maggiore), walk down V.d. Pretis and turn left. Church-run establishment makes living arrangements for women (27 and younger) of any religion. The garden will make you weep, but so may the 10pm curfew. Doubles and triples L35,000/€17.60 per person; dorms with 5 or 8 beds, L30,000/€15.50 per person. Open M-Sa 6:30am-10pm, Su 7am-10pm. Cash only.

AX·546 PC

INSIDE

Living in Rome

You yearn to tread in the footsteps of Goethe, Keats, Shelley, and Hemingway (not to mentions scads of former *Let's Go* researchers). Before you jump on that plane, however, you might want to think just a bit about what you're going to do about immigration, your living situation, daily necessaries, and that biggest pain in most of our collective asses, making money.

USEFUL RESOURCES

Enjoy Rome, the tourist and travel agency, also offers help in finding short-term apartments, and offers access to many community resources. See p. 23.

Roma Online: www.roma-online.com. Helps the longer-term visitor by including information on moving to Rome, as well as an online map and street database.

Welcome Home Relocation Services, V. Barbarano Romano, 15 (☎06 3036 6936; fax 06 3036 1706; welcome.home@slashnet.it). All kinds of housing plus assistance in documentation (permits, visas, licenses) and orientation. English spoken. Open M-F 9am-6pm.

Transitions Abroad, P.O. Box 1300, 18 Hulst Rd., Amherst, MA 01004-1300 (☎ (800) 293-0373; fax (413) 256-0373; www.transabroad.com). Publishes a bi-monthly magazine listing opportunities and printed resources for those seeking to study, work, or travel abroad. The possibilities are almost endless. They also publish *The Alternative Travel Directory,* an exhaustive listing of information, and *Work Abroad*, a comprehensive guide to finding and preparing for a job overseas. For subscriptions (in US US$28 for 6 issues, in Canada US$32, in other countries US$46), write to them at the address listed above.

VISAS & PERMITS

Italy, in keeping with the predominant European model of large, social welfare government, will throw loads of confusing paperwork at you before you can take part in the utopia that is European living. Not surprisingly—Italy being Italy—the big bureaucracy in Rome is not as well-oiled as its counterparts in Paris, Brussels, or London; be prepared for frustration. Many of the organizations listed throughout this chapter can provide advice on how to cut through the red tape. The City of Rome even realizes the confusion documentation can cause, and publishes *Roma per te*, a guide to obtaining permits and other documents, with the phonebook. Private companies such as the **Center for International Business and Travel,** 25 W. 23rd St. #1420, New York, NY 10036 (☎ (800) 925-2428), can obtain documentation for a fee.

LONG-TERM VISAS

All non-EU citizens are required to obtain a visa for any stay longer than 3 months, even if they are staying only as tourists. For information and applications, contact the Italian Embassy or Consulate in your country (see p. 243).

PERMIT TO STAY

All Non-EU citizens are also required to obtain a *Permesso di Soggiorno* (Permit to Stay) within eight days of arrival in Italy. If you are staying in a hotel or hostel, this requirement is waived, but if you are living on your own, you must apply at a police station or the foreigners office at the main police station *(Quaestra Centrale)*, V. Genoa, 2. (☎06 46861. Open M-F 9am-12:30pm.) EU citizens must apply for a *Permesso di Soggiorno* within three months.

RESIDENCY

Once you find a place to stay, bring your Permit to Stay (it must have at least one year's validity) to a records office *(circoscrizione;* for the nearest location, look up *Come di Roma: Circoscrizione* in the phone book). This certificate, which confirms your registered address, will expedite such procedures as clearing goods from abroad through customs and making large purchases (such as automobiles).

TAX CODE

Anybody who works in Italy must carry a *Codice Fiscale* card, which is often required for procedures such as opening bank accounts and receiving medical coverage. Applications require a passport and Permit to Stay, and should be submitted to the *Ufficio delle Entrate*, V. Ippolito Nuevo, 36, in Trastevere. (☎06 583191. Open M, W, and F 9am-1pm, Tu and Th 9am-1pm and 2:50-4:50pm.)

WORK PERMITS

EU passport holders do not require a visa to work in Italy. Non-EU citizens seeking work in Italy must apply for an Italian work permit *(Autorizzazione al lavoro in Italia)* before entering the country. The employer must receive a work permit from the Provincial Employment Office where the foreigner will be working. The Employment Office, upon determining that there are no Italian workers willing or able to fill the position, may issue a permit. The employer proceeds with the permit to the appropriate *questura* for necessary approval. Next, the employer must send the work permit to the prospective employee in her home country, where she presents the document along with a valid passport in order to obtain a work visa.

STUDY VISAS

EU citizens do not need a visa to study in Italy. Non-EU citizens wishing to study in Italy must obtain a study visa *(permisso di studio)* prior to departure from their nearest embassy or consulate. To obtain a visa, you will need to provide proof of enrollment from your home institution or the school in Italy. US citizens also require a notarized statement that the student has adequate financial means, and that the student will purchase an Italian health insurance policy in Italy as a supplement to

American health insurance. The visa fee for US citizens is $32.43 (payable in money order only) and for Australian citizens is AUS$51. Upon arrival in Italy, students must register with the Foreigners' Bureau *(Ufficio degli Stranieri)* of the local *questura* in order to receive their permit of stay.

WORK & VOLUNTEER

Many years ago, Romulus and Remus, after their long journey up the Tiber, landed on the shores of what we now know to be modern-day Rome. Unfortunately, as unnaturalized immigrants without work permits and the proper tax information, they found themselves ineligible for most employment opportunities and were forced to wait tables at 3rd-rate *trattorie.*

And just as unfortunately for their modern-day progeny, unemployment is high in central and southern Italy, making job searches in Rome difficult and sometimes fruitless. Italian law requires employers to pony up substantial sums of money for pensions and benefits even for short-term employees, making new hires very substantial investments.

In such a situation, firms are inclined to prefer naturalized Italian labor to your foreign sweat and blood. Work with Italian companies is almost impossible to find if you are not an EU citizen; your best bet is either a position in a foreign firm from an English-speaking country (preferably your own), or under-the-table jobs in the tourism sector. However, it's not easy in this sector, either. Openings are coveted by herds of would-be expats, so competition is fierce.

Officially, you must have a **work permit** (p. 278) to work in Italy. Your prospective employer must apply for this document, usually by demonstrating that you have skills that locals lack. You will also need a **working visa,** available from an Italian consulate. EU citizens can work in Italy without working papers. Students can check with their university's foreign language department, which may have access to jobs abroad.

Unofficially, there is the cash-based, untaxable **underground economy** *(economia sommersa* or *economia nera)*. Many permitless agricultural workers go untroubled by local authorities, who recognize the need for seasonal labor. Many foreigners go unnoticed through this route, too, though rarely through the back-breaking and thankless labor of the migrant farm worker. Many expats, for instance, find work (cash-based and official) with well-to-do families as nannies-*cum*-English teachers. Again, your best resource for these jobs is community bulletin boards and magazines such as *Wanted in Rome*, or placement organizations such as those listed below.

Jewish Ghetto

Piazza Farnese

Centro Storico

GENERAL WORK RESOURCES

Wanted in Rome (www.wantedinrome.com). This bi-weekly magazine (L1500) offers cultural information and a wealth of classified advertisements, all delivered in a very British tone. Annual subscription (21 issues) L60,000 overseas, L25,000 within Italy. Available at most newsstands, English-language bookstores, and from their main office, V.d. Delfini, 17 (☎06 6790190; fax 06 6783798).

Vacation Work Publications, 9 Park End St., Oxford OX1 1HJ, UK (☎ (01865) 24 19 78; fax 79 08 85; www.vacationwork.co.uk). Publishes variety of directories with job listings and info for the working traveler. Opportunities for summer or full-time work in numerous countries.

OPTIONS FOR WORK

TOURISM INDUSTRY

The Roman tourism industry is primarily targeted at the English-speaker, and with some persistence, you may be able to find a position there, albeit with little financial security. Many tourist offices look for tour guides over the summer. These jobs are usually not salaried; you work for a commission by convincing people to come to expensive tours given by the agency. Often, this entails giving free "teaser" tours all day in the hot sun at Roman ruins, working for tips, and begging your fellow countrymen to come to paid events and say that you sent them there. It's not for the faint of heart nor quiet of mouth, but it just might be enough to pay the bills. Besides tour guides, English-speaking hotel and hostel personnel are always in high demand, especially during the summer months. Due to the sometimes unofficial nature of the jobs, often the best course of action is to call establishments directly.

TEACHING ENGLISH

Assuming you lack the stamina to till the fields, consider that teaching English, one of the few long-term job possibilities, can be particularly lucrative. No more than minimal Italian is necessary to teach conversation, though many language institutes require a college degree and/or some sort of TEFL or RSA certificate (or completion of a shorter training course on teaching English as foreign language).

There are numerous English-language institutes in Rome that offer jobs through ads in *Wanted in Rome* (available at most newsstands; see p. 280) and in Rome's daily newspaper *Il Messagero*. Some schools simply post signs in stores, hair salons, or cafes. Many people poster their services around universities and on community bulletin boards. A common method is to set up a small class of four to six students for which the going rate, depending on the size of the class, is about L15-35,000 per hour.

Language schools are listed under *Scuole di Lingua* in the Italian yellow pages and are also listed in the English yellow pages. **International House Academia Britannica,** V. Manzoni, 22, one block from the Manzoni (A) Metro stop, which offers TEFLA and EFL courses, has a good bulletin board and advertises teaching jobs throughout Italy. (☎06 70476894; fax 06 70497842. Open M-F 9am-1pm and 3-7:30pm.) Also try:

International Schools Services, Educational Staffing Program, P.O. Box 5910, Princeton, NJ 08543 (☎ (609) 452-0990; fax (609) 452-2690; www.iss.edu). Recruits teachers and administrators for American and English schools in Italy. All instruction in English. Applicants must have a bachelor's degree and two years of relevant experience. Nonrefundable US$100 application fee. Publishes *The ISS Directory of Overseas Schools* (US$35).

PROFESSIONAL TEACHING

You may be able to secure a teaching position with an American school in Italy through the **Office of Overseas Schools,** Room H328, SA-1, Dept. of State, Washington, DC 20522. (☎ (202) 261-8200; fax (202) 261-8224; www.state.gov.) **International Schools Services,** Educational Staffing Program, 15 Roszel Rd., P.O. Box 5910, Princeton, NJ 08543, can also assist in finding a teaching job. (☎ (609) 452-0990; fax 452-2690; www.iss.edu.) Another short-term option, albeit horrifying, is to be a substitute teacher at one of the American or British schools; generally, you need a college degree, nerves of steel, and a *Codice Fiscale* (tax code).

INTERNSHIPS

The best bet for finding an above-board job that will take care of all documentation requirements is to look for internships with large domestic and multinational firms with offices in Rome. It is probably also your best bet to find professional work as a foreigner without substantial experience and complete fluency in Italian. Most companies post job descriptions and human resources contact information on their websites. Some Embassies offer internships throughout the year; contact your government for more information, or contact your embassy in Rome (see **Service Directory,** p. 290).

ARCHAELOGICAL DIGS

The Archaeological Institute of America, 656 Beacon St., Boston, MA 02215-2010 (☎ (617) 353-9361; fax (617) 353-6550; www.archaeological.org), puts out the *Archaeological Fieldwork Opportunities Bulletin* (US$16 for non-members), which lists over 250 field sites throughout the world. The bulletin can also be purchased from Kendall/Hunt Publishing, 4050 Westmark Dr., Dubuque, Iowa 52002 (☎ (800) 228-0810). For info on anthropology, archaeological digs, and art history in Italy, write to the **Centro Comune di Studi Preistorici,** 25044 Capo di Ponte, Brescia (☎0364 42091; fax 0364 42572; globalnet.it/ccsp/ccsp.htm), a research center involved with the management of cultural property and the organization of congresses, research projects, and exhibitions. They publish *BCSP*, the world journal of prehistoric and tribal art, and offer volunteer work, grants, and research assistant positions for prehistoric art.

Local colleges and universities in your home country are another excellent source of information on archaeological digs in Rome and elsewhere. Check with the departments of the classics, archaeology, anthropology, fine arts, and/or other relevant area studies at your local university or college; many excavations send information and applications directly to individual professors or departments rather than to the general public.

AU PAIR

Accord Cultural Exchange, 750 La Playa, Rome, CA 94121 (☎ (415) 386-6203); fax 386-0240; www.cognitext.com/accord), offers *au pair* jobs to people aged 18-29 in Italy. Au pairs work 5-6hr. per day, 30hr. per week, plus 2 evenings of babysitting. Light housekeeping and childcare in exchange for room and board plus US$250-400 per month salary. Program fees US$750 for the summer, US$1200 for the academic year. US$40 Application fee.

Childcare International, Ltd., Trafalgar House, Grenville Place, London NW7 3SA (☎ (020) 8906 3116; fax (020) 8906 3461; www.childint.demon.co.uk) offers *au pair* positions in Italy. The organization prefers long-term placements but does arrange summer work. Member of the International Au Pair Association. UK£80 application fee.

InterExchange, 161 Sixth Ave., New York, NY 10013 (☎ (212) 924-0446; fax 924-0575; www.interexchange.org) provides information on international work, *au pair* programs, and *au pair* positions in Italy and other European countries.

VOLUNTEER

Volunteering is a good way to immerse yourself in a foreign culture without all the bother of being paid for your services. You may receive room and board, and the work can be fascinating. The high application fees charged by the organizations that arrange placement can sometimes be avoided by contacting the individual workcamps directly; check with the organizations. The extensive listings found in Vacation Work Publications' (see **General Work Resources,** p. 280) *International Directory of Voluntary Work* (UK£10; postage UK£2.50, within UK £1.50) can be especially helpful. Also try:

Council's Voluntary Services Dept., 205 E. 42nd St., New York, NY 10017 (☎ (888) 268-6245); fax (212) 822-2699; www.ciee.org), offers 1-2 week construction and environmental projects July-Sept. Minimum US$300 placement fee.

Service Civil International Voluntary Service (SCI-VS), 814 NE 40th St., Seattle, WA 98105 (☎/fax (206) 545-6585; sciivsusa@igc.apc.org). Arranges placement in workcamps in Italy for those age 18 and over. Local organizations sponsor groups for physical or social work. Registration fees US$50-250, depending on the camp location.

STUDY

Full-time university programs will often offer assistance in terms of living and documentation. Language schools, which tend to be less formal, with a smaller time and financial commitment, aim toward providing the foreigner with basic speaking and living skills.

GENERAL STUDY RESOURCES

Institute of International Education (IIE), 809 United Nations Plaza, New York, NY 10017 (☎ (212) 984-5413; fax 984-5358). For book orders: IIE Books, Institute of International Educations, P.O. Box 371, Annapolis Junction, MD 20701 (☎ (800) 445-0443; fax (301) 953-2838; iie-boks@iie.org). A nonprofit, international and cultural exchange agency. Publishes *Academic Year Abroad* (US$43, postage US$4) and *Vacation Study Abroad* (US$37, postage US$5). Write for a complete list of publications.

Peterson's, P.O. Box 2123, Princeton, NJ 08543 (☎ (800) 338-3282; fax (609) 243-9150; www.petersons.com). Their comprehensive, annual study-abroad guide lists programs in countries all over the world and provides essential information on the study abroad experience in general. Find a copy at your local bookstore (US$27), call their toll-free number in the US, or order through their online bookstore.

The College Connection, Inc., 1295 Prospect St., Ste. B, La Jolla, CA 92037 (☎ (619) 551-9770; fax (619) 551-9987; www.eurailpass.com). Publishes *The Passport,* a booklet listing hints about every aspect of traveling and studying abroad. This booklet is free to *Let's Go* readers; send your request by email or fax only. The College Rail Connection, a division of the College Connection, sells railpasses with student discounts.

American Field Service (AFS), 310 SW 4th Avenue, Suite 630, Portland, OR 97204 (☎ (800) AFS-INFO (237-4636); fax (503) 241-1653; afsinfo@afs.org; www.afs.org/usa). AFS offers summer, semester, and year-long homestay exchange programs in Italy for high school students and graduating high school seniors. Financial aid available.

Centro Turistico Studentesco e Giovanile (CTS) provides info on study in Italy (see p. 294).

Council Travel sponsors over 40 study abroad programs worldwide (see p. 282).

Youth For Understanding International Exchange (YFU), 3501 Newark St. NW, Washington, D.C. 20016 (☎ (800) TEENAGE (833-6243); fax 895-1104; www.yfu.org). Places US high school students worldwide for a year, semester, or summer.

UNIVERSITIES

If you're fluent in Italian, consider enrolling directly in an Italian university. Alternatively, there are several American universities in Italy. Universities are crowded, but you'll probably have a blast and get a real feel for the culture. For further advice, contact **Ufficio Centrale Studenti Esteri in Italia (UCSEI),** Lungotevere dei Vallati 14, 00186 Roma (☎06 8804062; fax 06 8804063), a national organization for foreign students who have already started their course of study in Italy. Remember that student visas are required for study abroad (see **Visas,** p. 278).

La Sapienza, one of the main universities in Rome. M:B-Policlinico. From the Metro station, walk up V. Regina Margherita/Elena past the hospital and Blockbuster to V. Università. For application info, write to the nearest Italian consulate (see p. 243). In Rome, contact the **Segretaria Stranieri,** Città Universitaria, P. Aldo Moro 5, 00185 Roma (switchboard ☎06 49911; fax 06 4452824; direct ☎06 49912707; www.uniroma1.it. Open M, W, and F 8:30am-1pm). Though the university does not offer any week- or month-long classes, the range of activities on campus is as good as any major university; theatrical, musical, and dance productions, debates, and sports—all in Italian, of course.

John Cabot University, V.d. Lungara, 233, 00165 Roma (☎06 6819121; fax 06 6832088). US office at 339 South Main St., Sebastopol, CA 95472 (☎ (707) 824-9800; fax (707) 824-0198; www.johncabot.edu; jcu@johncabot.edu.) This American international university in Trastevere offers undergraduate degrees in art history, business, English literature, and international affairs. Foreign students can enroll for summer, semester ($5500), and year-long ($10,600) sessions. Students are aided in finding internships in their fields of study. Like any college named after a confused British navigator who stumbled upon Canada, John Cabot has a number of conferences, lectures, and dramatic productions that are open to the public.

LANGUAGE SCHOOLS

If you are planning to be in Rome for two weeks or more and desire to learn the language that everybody around you seems to speak all the time (or at least learn how to say something else besides "*Buon giorno, principessa!*" and other choice phrases from Italian import movies),

Italidea, P. della Cancelleria, 85, 00186 Roma (☎06 68307620; fax 06 6892997; www.italiaidea.com). Offers every level of Italian study from an intensive short-term course to more advanced, semester-long courses meeting once or twice per week. Intensive groups meet 3hr. per day M-F for 4 weeks, at a total price of L780,000 and a L30,000 registration fee. The less intensive group meets 3hr. per day twice a week for 4 weeks, at the same price. Private lessons are also available at higher prices. Flexible scheduling. College credit courses offered through some US college and university programs in Italy. Homestays with Italian families are also available.

DILIT-ih, V. Marghera, 22, 00185 Roma (☎06 4462592 or 06 4462593; fax 06 4440888; www.dilit.it). Near Termini. Resources include a language lab, video and listening center, a computer, and reading room. Intensive courses of 3, 4, or 6hr. per day (min. 2 weeks). 6hr. per day 2-week program L780,000 (plus L50,000 enrollment fee). Individual courses also available. Students of all levels of Italian are accommodated according to a placement exam. Private and home-stay lodgings available. Open summer daily 8:30am-8pm.

Istituto Italiano Centro di Lingua e Cultura, V. Macchiavelli 33, 00185 Roma (☎06 70452138; fax 06 70085122; istital@uni.net). Near the Manzoni Metro stop on Linea A. Courses offered for students who want a slower pace or for those who seek an intensive setting. Or for people who just want to learn how to say the school's name 3 times quickly. 4-week intensive course (22½hr. per week) L1,020,000. The less intensive 4-week program (15hr. per week) is L760,000. Groups size 3-12. 1 month of accommodations with a family (L760,000) or a student flat with a kitchen (L620,000) are available through the office. Office open M-F 8:30am-7pm. AmEx, MC, V.

Torre di Babele, V. Bixio 74, 00185 Roma (☎06 7008434; fax 06 70497150; www.torredibabele.it). Small groups of students (max. 12) enjoy personal attention from the instructor in non-intensive or intensive courses for an even number of weeks (min. 2 weeks). 2-week intensive program (4hr. per day) L540,000; 4-week intensive program (4hr. per day) L1,000,000. Additional weeks L250,000 apiece. Students can find lodging through the school. MC, V.

Centro Storico

Roman Forum

Trastevere

CIAO MEOW

One of the most important things you should know about living in Rome is that there are cats. Lots of them. Everywhere.

After living in the city for a while, you may come to think that you own the place–think again. That honor has long been conferred upon the eternal feline inhabitants of the Eternal City. In fact, Italian composer Ottorino Respighi was so struck by the presence of cats in the city that he named the third piece in his *Rome* trilogy for orchestra *Cats of Rome* (after *Pines of Rome* and *Hills of Rome*).

The cats in Rome live the good life (unlike dogs, many of whom are abandoned when their owners skip town for *Ferragosto*). Thanks to a bizarre 1988 law, Rome's stray cats are granted the right to live where they are born. This has led to the proliferation of an estimated 10,000 cat colonies throughout the city, many of which are cared for by the city (as well as Italians who feed them leftover pasta). Look for the felines among the ruins, especially near Largo di Torre Argentina.

LONG-TERM ACCOMMODATIONS

Finding a long-term apartment rental in Rome can be downright painful, since many potential landlords are wary of renting out properties because of convoluted Italian laws that can make the process of evicting a tenant take up to 20 years. Not wanting to have a squatter on their hands, many apartment owners prefer to keep their properties empty. Short-term rentals are comparatively easier: the months with the most vacancies are July, August, and December, when vacationing times set in, and homeowners are willing to lease out their places. During the rest of the year, the real estate market is extremely tight. In the last decade, prices for even the most simple pad have skyrocketed; expect to pay no less than L1,300,000 per month for a one-bedroom in the Centro Storico. The longer you stay, the better your chances of finding a cheap rent. In general, the cheaper areas include the Nomentana neighborhood, the area around Piazza Bologna, and San Lorenzo. Utilities are inordinately expensive in Rome; they can augment your rent by up to 25%. Check the English classified ads in *Wanted in Rome* (see p. 280) and Italian ads in *Porta Portese*. Community **bulletin boards** often carry advertisements for roommates—check the English-language ones in bookstores (see p. 210) or the Pasquino movie theater (see p. 197). **Real estate agencies** can help, but many charge fees; definitely avoid agencies that charge a non-refundable fee.

You can also prowl around a particular neighborhood you'd like to live in and look for *"affitasi"* ("for rent") signs. Check with **foreign university programs** as well; they often rent out apartments for their students which are vacant in summer. The best way to find a pad is through connections.

ACCOMMODATIONS AGENCIES

The following real estate agents specialize in finding apartments for foreigners. They may be out of your price range, but they're often willing to give advice. Calling well ahead of time will greatly increase your chances of securing a place on time. Once you've finally found a place and need to furnish it, see **Shopping** (p. 203) for some of our favorite home furnishing stores. When all else fails, head to IKEA.

Romeguide (www.romeguide.it). A great web site to use while searching for an apartment.

Property Center, V.d. Gesù è Maria, 25 (☎06 3212341). Near P. del Popolo. Arranges short- and long-term apartment and villa rentals in various price ranges.

specializes in Centro Storico and Trastevere. English spoken. Open M-F 9:30am-6:30pm, Sa 10am-2pm.

Welcome Home Relocation Services, V. Barbarano Romano, 15 (☎06 3036 6936; fax 06 30361706; welcome.home@slashnet.it). All kinds of housing placement services plus assistance in documentation (permits, visas, licenses) and orientation. English spoken. Open M-F 9am-6pm.

Homes International, V. L. Bissolati, 20 (☎06 4881800; fax 06 4881808; homesen-int@tin.it). Arranges short- and long-term rentals for apartments and villas; can also locate cheaper places in the outskirts of Rome. Open M-F 9am-7pm, Sa 9am-noon.

MONEY MATTERS

Anyone who's ever tried to change a few *lire* will attest to the horrors of the Roman banking administration: employees are snippy, computers crash frequently, and the amount of paperwork required is enough to give any Greenpeace member a coronary. Opening a bank account is no exception. In order to open a bank account in Rome you must present the following: *certificato di residenza* (a certificate of residence, which you receive from the *comune* when you register as a resident) or your *permesso di soggiorno;* a passport or photo ID; and a *Codice Fiscale*, equivalent to an American Social Security number, which you also get from the *commune*. Sound simple? Think again. Getting a *Codice Fiscale* is next to impossible. Check with the institution with which you hope to do business or the international desk of your local bank for requirements and other information. For banks in Rome, see **Service Directory,** p. 289.

COMMUNITY RESOURCES

Even though there are upwards of 200,000 registered foreigners living in Rome (and probably many unofficial residents on top of that), the life of an expat can be daunting and lonely, especially at first. Even the establishments listed throughout this book, which often serve a tourist and backpacker crowd, may not provide you with the social network you need to acclimate yourself to your new home. To fill the gap, **Welcome Neighbor** organizes events and support groups for English-speaking expats in Rome. (☎06 3036 6936.) For gay and lesbian resources, and other special concerns, see p. 257.

HEALTH & FITNESS

For emergency rooms, clinics, hospitals, and dentists, see **Service Directory,** p. 290.

INSURANCE

Non-EU citizens should first contact their home health insurance provider to see what coverage options are available for long-term stays in Italy. Coverage under the Italian state system costs around L1.2 million per year, and involves significant co-payments for prescriptions, laboratory work, specialist visits, and hospital stays. Family planning services are covered, but non-emergency dentistry is not. To register for coverage, bring your visa, passport, and any other documentation to the nearest INPS (Italian state insurance board).

EU citizens, on the other hand, are eligible for state health care in Italy. Before leaving your home country, pick up an E111 form, and bring it to a hospital in Rome. If you don't have the form, bring your passport, permit to stay, and tax forms instead.

HEALTH CLUBS

Though American-style athletic clubs are few and far between, exercise opportunities present themselves in the form of gargantuan fitness complexes. Consult *Roma C'è* for a more extensive listing. Even if you don't have a membership, you can still use the recreational facilities at Rome's **YMCA** (EEM-kah), V.d. Oceano Pacifico, 13 (pool), in EUR, and V. Libomo, 68 (gym). For L40,000 you can use the Y's pool, gym, and tennis courts for an entire day (you must be under 45 years old). Call 06 5225247 for more info.

Big Gym (☎06 3208666; www.biggym.it). In the Stadio dei Marmi at the Foro Italico . Bus #32, 232, or 280. An open air fitness extravaganza that is everything its name suggests. Under the watchful gaze of the numerous uncomfortably naked statues that line the stadium, customers can choose from aerobics, basketball, fun ball (a game that seems to be the result of a tennis hybridization experiment gone horribly awry), *calcetto* (five-on-five small-field soccer), thunderball, free climbing, tennis, swimming and an aggressive in-line course complete with half-pipe. Open Jun. 1-Aug. 11 daily 9am-1am. L15,000.

Roman Sport Center, V.d. Galoppatoio, 33 (☎06 3201667 or 06 3218096). M:A-Spagna. In Villa Borghese. This large gym offers non-members a day of sweating (aerobics, pool, sauna, Turkish baths, weight room) for L50,000. Open M-Sa 9am-10pm.

Associazione Sportiva Augustea (A.S.A.), V. Luciani, 57 (☎06 23235112). M:A-Cinecittà. In Cinecittà. Alternatively, take bus #558 or 54. Indoor pool (L16,000 for a day's swim, L20,000 on the weekends), gym (L20,000), and tennis courts (L15,000/1hr.). Open M-Sa 10am-6pm.

Body Image, V. E. Fermi, 142 (☎06 5573356). For women only, this club boasts a weight room, aerobics, and a sauna. L80,000 per month. Open daily 9:30am-9pm. Closed Aug.

Navona Health Center, V.d. Banchi Nuovi, 39 (☎06 6896104). In the Centro Storico. Small gym with weights, 2 fitness rooms, and a sauna. L20,000 per day, L160,000 per month, but ask about student discounts.Free trainers available M-F 11-3pm and 5-9:30pm. Open M-F 9am-9:30pm, Sa 10:30-8pm. Closed Aug.

PARTICIPANT SPORTS

JOGGING

Rome has some spectacular parks, providing the perfect spot for jogging. A note of **caution:** if the air is particularly polluted, stay indoors. Rome suffers from extremely high levels of smog which can at times be dangerous. On clear days, you can head up to **Villa Borghese** for a run. **Villa Ada** also has places to run, along with an exercise course through the park, as does **Villa Doria Pamphilj,** the largest park in the city. Using real running tracks entails declaring yourself a member of **Fidal,** followed by a long bureaucratic process of submitting money, pictures, and proof of health. Head down to the Stadio delle Terme di Caracalla, V. G. Bacelli, 5 (☎06 5780602), if you're up to the challenge of all those steps.To meet a lively group of ex-pats who run from bar to bar, consult www.hashhouseharriers.com for the time and location of the next outing in Rome.

SWIMMING

For chlorinated relief from the Roman heat, ask at a tourist office for locations of public pools or check out the yellow pages under *piscine.* Entertainment magazines often list pools. Many major hotels in Rome open their pools to the public, but often charge a large fee. (The Hilton is one such hotel; call 06 35092950 for information.) At **Piscina della Rosa,** V. America, 20 in EUR, the pool is a short walk from the Metro (B) EUR-Palasport stop. (☎06 5926717. Open June-Sept. daily 9am-7pm. Full-day swim in the outdoor pool L20,000, half-day L15,000, 1-4pm L8000.) The **Centro Sportivo Italiano,** Lungotevere Flaminio, 59, accessible by bus #926 or tram #19 or #225, is just north of the city along the Tiber. (☎06 3234732. Open June-Sept. daily 10:45am-6:30pm; full day L22,000, half-day L15,000.)

ICE SKATING

If you prefer water in the solid state and have a car, head for the skating rink **Palaghiacco di Marino**, on V. Appia Nuova, km 19, which has 1½hr. skating sessions. (☎06 9309480. Open late Aug.-Apr. Rentals M-F 5, 9, and 11pm; Sa-Su 3, 5, 7, 9, and 11pm; Su also 11am. Rentals of skates and pads L10,000, on weekends L12,000.)

BOWLING

"Do you have 12-pound balls?" If you really miss bowling (pronounced *booling* in Italy, thank you very much), head for **Bowling Roma,** V. R. Margherita, 181, off V. Nomentana past the Porta Pia (accessible by bus #62), an A/C time warp to the 1960s

☎06 8551184. Open M-Sa 10am-1am, Su 5pm-midnight. L3000 per game per person, shoes included, after 9pm L6000.) Or *bool* on over to **Bowling Brunswick,** Lungotevere dell'Acqua Acetosa, 10. Take bus #4 or #230. Three nights a week, this unassuming bowling alley is transformed into the home of "Cosmic Bowling." Lanes and pins glow, accompanied by music and lights of the stroboscopic variety. (☎06 8086147. Open Su-Th 10-2am, F-Sa 10-2am. L5000 per game per person, after 8pm L6800, shoes L2000.)

TENNIS

One club in particular is very friendly to foreigners, open to non-members, and affordable. **Circolo della Stampa** is in P. Mancini and owned by the Italian Journalist's Association. (☎06 3232452. Open M-F 9am-midnight, Sa-Su 8am-8pm. L18,000 for a singles for an hour, L24,000 doubles. Lights L4000.) **Foro Italico** (Viale dei Gladitori 31) also has courts at comprable prices; call 06 36858218.

YOGA

Yoga has not yet become a very widespread practice in Rome, but it is growing, and there are a few places in the city where you can find instruction and community. The **Accademia Yoga,** V. XX Settembre, 58a (☎06 4885967), on the corner of V. Piave near P. della Repubblica, offers courses in mental and physical yoga exercise, concentrating mainly on the raja yoga technique of Patanjali, which is theoretically best-suited to the western mind. It has links with various yoga schools in India and frequently brings over visiting teachers. Courses in Hindi and Sanskrit are also available. a yearly membership costs L80,000/€41.30, and a package of 10 lessons is L120,000/€62.00. (Open M, Tu, F 10-1pm and 3:30-8pm, Th 3:30-8pm, closed W and Sa.) Contact the **Federazione Italiana Yoga,** V. Belisario, 7, off V. Piave near V. XX Settembre, for further assistance finding a teacher suited to your needs. (☎06 4287 0191.) Other listings are available in *Roma C'è's* guide *La Città Invisibile.*

BIKING

Sick of walking, and too cash-strapped to buy a motorino? Spend a day peddling around on a bike. A lovely afternoon can be had on a two-wheeler in the Villa Borghese; **I Bike Rome** (Via Veneto 156, near the V. Borghese car park; 06 3225240) rents bikes for L10,000/€5.16 a day. Open daily, 9am-7pm. **Collalti**, V.d. Pellegrino 82 (06 68801084) also rents bikes: L15,000/€7.75 for 12hrs, L20,000/€10.30 for 24hrs. T-Su 9am-7:30pm. Also consult tourist agencies (p. p. 23), as many offer scenic bike tours of the city.

GOLF

If bread, water and golf are what you need to survive, then Rome will not leave you hungry. You can tee-off at **Country Club Castel Gandolfo**, V.S. Spirito 13, 06 9312301, daily from 8:30am-5pm. Weekday rounds are L90,000 and weekends are L110,000/ €56.60. Driving range fees are L10,000. Carts available; call in advance to reserve a caddy. **Circolo del Golf di Roma**, V. Appia Nuova 716a (☎06 7803407) offers a round for L120,000/€62.00 weekdays, L140,000/€72.63 weekends. The driving range is L17,000/ €8.50 weekdays, L30,000 weekends. Closed Monday.

TAXI

Service Directory

ACCOMMODATIONS

*See also **Tourist Services,** p. 294.*

Welcome Home Relocation Services, V. Barbarano Romano, 15 (☎06 3036 6936; fax 06 30361706; welcome.home@slashnet.it). English spoken. Open M-F 9am-6pm.

Property Center, V.d. Gesù è Maria, 25 (☎06 3212341). English spoken. Open M-F 9:30am-6:30pm, Sa 10am-2pm.

Homes International, V. L. Bissolati, 20 (☎06 4881800; fax 06 4881808; homesen-int@tin.it). Open M-F 9am-7pm, Sa 9am-noon.

Italian Youth Hostels Association (HI-IYHF), V. Cavour, 44 (☎06 4871152; fax 06 4880492). Open M-Th 8am-5pm, F 8am-3pm, Sa 8am-noon.

Associazione Cattolica Internazionale al Servizio della Giovane, V. Urbana, 158 (☎ 06 4880056). Open M-Sa 6:30am-10pm, Su 7am-10pm. Closed part of Aug.

Bed and Go, V. S. Tommaso d'Aquino, 47 (☎06 39750907 or 06 39746484; fax 06 39760553; bedandgo@tin.it). Open M-F 9am-1pm and 2-6pm.

Bed & Breakfast Association of Rome, P. del Teatro Pompeo, 2 (☎/fax 06 6877348; www.b-b.rm.it; info@b-b.rm.it).

AIRPORTS

Ciampino Airport (☎06 794941).

Fiumicino Airport (☎06 65951), also known as Leonardo da Vinci International.

BANKS

Banca Popolare di Milano, P. Flamina.

Banca Nazionale del Lavoro, V. Marsala, 6; V.d. Rosetta, 1; P. Venezia, 6; and V. Veneto, 111. Cirrus/PLUS.

Banco di Roma, V.d. Banco di Santo Spirito, 31 (☎06 68809710; fax 06 68808651). Open M-F 8:30am-1:30pm and 2:30-4pm. Also at V. Tiburtina, P. Barberini, V.d. Monti Tiburtini, V.d. Corso, and others. Cirrus/PLUS.

Istituto Bancario San Paolo di Torino, Termini. Cirrus.

BIKE & MOPED RENTAL

Happy Rent, V. Farini, 3 (☎06 4818185). Take a bus to V. Cavour. Motorbikes L50,000/€25.80 per day; 600cc bikes L120,000/€62.00 per day. Open daily 9am-7pm. AmEx/MC/V.

Romarent, V.d. Bovari, 7a (☎06 6896555). Bikes L15,000/€7.75 per day, L75,000/€38.73 per week; motorbikes L35,000/€17.60 per day. AmEx/D/MC.

Rent-a-Scooter, V. F. Turati, 50 (☎06 4469222). Mopeds from L50,000/€25.80 per day. Lock, helmet, insurance, and free souvenir included. Open daily 9am-7pm.

Scooters for Rent, V.d. Purificazione, 84 (☎06 4885485), off P. Barberini. Bicycles L20,000/€10.30 per day; L100,000/€51.60 per week; mopeds L50,000/€25.80 per day, L250,000/€129.11 per week. Open daily 9am-7pm. AmEx/MC/V.

I Bike Rome, V. Veneto, 156 (☎06 3225240), in the Villa Borghese parking garage. Bikes L5-8000/€2.58-4.13 per hr., L10,000/€5.16 per day, L40,000/€20.30 per week. Mopeds L40,000/€20.30 for 4hr., L60,000/€32.00 per day, L250,000/€129.11 per week. Open daily 8:30am-7pm.

BUSES

See ***Transportation,*** *p. 295.*

CAR RENTAL

Avis: ☎06 41998; www.avis.com.
Maggiore: ☎06 2291530; www.maggiore.it.
Hertz: ☎06 4740389; www.hertz.com.
Europcar: ☎06 4882854; www.europcar.it.

CLINICS

See also ***Hospitals*** *(p. 291) and* ***Emergency Services*** *(p. 291).*

Ospedale San Camillo in Monteverde, Circonvallazione Gianicolense, 87 (☎06 58701), in Gianicolo. Pregnancy tests, STD tests, gynecological exams, and pap smears. Open for info daily 8am-7pm; call for appointment.

Unione Sanitaria Internazionale, V. Machiavelli, 22 (☎06 70453544), M: A-Vittorio Emanuele. Open for info daily 7am-7pm; tests daily 7-11am.

Analisi Cliniche Luisa, V. Padova, 96a (☎06 44291406). M: B-P. Bologna. Pregnancy, STD, HIV tests (L20-90,000/€10.30-46.48). Open M-F 7:30am-8pm, Sa 8am-noon.

Studio Polispecialistico Nomentano, V. Nomentana, 550/552 (☎06 86895611). HIV tests L85,000/€43.90. Open daily 7am-12:30pm and 3-10pm.

Circolo di Cultura Omosessuale Mario Mieli. See p. 290.

COMMUNITY RESOURCES

See also ***Gay & Lesbian Resources*** *(p. 291).*

Welcome Neighbor (☎06 30366936). Events and support groups for English speakers.

CONSULATES & EMBASSIES

Australia, V. Alessandria, 215 (☎06 852721, emergency 800 877790; fax 06 85272300). Consular and passport services around the corner at C. Trieste, 25. Open M-Th 9am-5pm, F 9am-12:30pm.

Canada, Consulate, V. Zara, 30 (☎06 44598421; fax 06 44598912). Consular and passport services open M-F 10am-noon and 2-4pm. **Embassy,** V. G.B. De Rossi, 27 (☎06 445981).

Ireland, Consulate, P. Campitelli, 3 (☎06 6979121). Passport services open M-F 10am-12:30pm and 3-4:30pm.

New Zealand, V. Zara, 28 (☎06 4417171; fax 06 4402984). Consular and passport services open M-F 9:30am-noon. Embassy services M-F 8:30am-12:45pm and 1:45-5pm.

South Africa, V. Tanaro, 14 (☎06 852541; fax 06 85254300). Bus #86 from Termini to P. Buenos Aires. Open M-F 9am-noon.

U.K., V. XX Settembre, 80/A (☎06 4825441; fax 06 42202334; consulate 06 42202600), near the corner of V. Palestro. Consular and passport services open M-F 9:15am-1:30pm.

United States, V. Veneto, 119/A (☎06 46741; fax 06 46742217). Passport and consular services open M-F 8:30-noon and 1:30-3:30pm. Visas M-F 8:30-10:30am; IRS M-F 9am-noon in person, 1:30-3:30pm by phone. Closed US and Italian holidays.

CRISIS LINES

Centro Anti-Violenza, V.d. Torrespaccata, 157 (☎06 23269049 or 06 23269053). For victims of sexual violence. Branch offices for legal and psychological consultation throughout the city. Available 24hr.

Telefono Rosa, V. Tor di Nona, 43 (☎06 6832675; fax 06 6833748). For victims of sexual abuse or harassment. Open M-F 10am-1pm and 4-7pm.

Samaritans, V. San Giovanni in Laterano, 250 (☎06 70454444). Native English speakers. Anonymous or face-to-face counseling available. Open for calls and visits (call ahead) daily 1-10pm.

Alcoholics Anonymous (☎06 6636620).

CURRENCY SERVICES

*See also **Banks** (p. 289).*

American Express, P. di Spagna, 38 (☎06 67641; lost or stolen cards and/or checks ☎06 72281; fax 06 67642499). Open Sept.-July: M-F 9am-7:30pm, Sa 9am-3pm; Aug. M-F 9am-6pm, Sa 9am-12:30pm. Mailing address: P. di Spagna, 38; 00187 Roma.

Thomas Cook, P. Barberini, 21a (☎06 4828082). Open M-Sa 9am-8pm, Su 9:30am-5pm. **Other branches:** V.d. Conciliazione, 23/25 (☎06 68300435; open M-Sa 8:30am-6pm, Su 9am-5pm); V.d. Corso, 23 (☎06 3230067; open M-Sa 9am-8pm, Su 9am-1:30pm); P. della Repubblica, 65 (☎06 486495; open M-F 9am-5pm, Sa 9am-1pm).

Western Union, P. di Spagna, 92 (toll-free ☎06 6484583). Open M-F 9am-7pm.

EMBASSIES

*See **Consulates & Embassies,** p. 289.*

EMERGENCY SERVICES

*See also **Police** (p. 293) and **Hospitals** (p. 291).*

Carabinieri: ☎112.

Police/Fire/Ambulance: ☎113.

Medical Emergencies: ☎118.

Fire Service: ☎115.

Policlinico Umberto I, V.le di Policlinico, 155 (emergency ☎06 49971, non emergency 06 49971). M: B-Policlinico or #9 bus. Free first aid *(pronto soccorso).* Open 24hr.

Nuovo Regina Margherita, V. Trastevere, 72 (☎06 58441). Walk-in first aid. Open 24hr.

Condomeria, V.d. Prefetti, 25. Open M-Sa 10am-1pm and 4-7:30pm.

Accademia Yoga, V. XX Settembre, 58a (☎06 4885967).

Federazione Italiana Yoga, V. Belisario, 7, (☎06 4287 0191).

ENTERTAINMENT

*See **Tickets,** p. 294.*

GAY & LESBIAN RESOURCES

Circolo Mario Mieli di Cultura Omosessuale, V. Corinto, 5 (☎06 5413985; fax 06 5413971; www.mariomieli.it). M: B-San Paolo. Open M-F 9am-1pm and 2-6pm; closed Aug.

Arci-Gay, V. Orvinio, 2 (☎06 86385112; www.gay.it/arcigay/roma). Also at V. Lariana, 8 (☎06 8555522).

Arci-Lesbica (www.women.it/~arciles/roma), in the Same offices as Arci-Gay.

Libreria Babele (☎06 6876628), V.d. Banchi Vecchi, across the bridge from Castel Sant'Angelo. Rome's only gay and lesbian bookstore. *Gay and Lesbian Map of Rome* L12,000/€6.20. Open M-Sa 10am-7:30pm.

Italian Gay and Lesbian Yellow Pages (www.gay.it/guida/italia/info.htm).

Coordinamento Lesbico Italiano, V. S. Francesco di Sales, 1a (☎06 6864201).

GROCERS

*See **Supermarkets,** p. 293*

HEALTH CLUBS

Big Gym, Stadio dei Marmi at the Foro Italico (☎06 3208666; www.biggym.it). L7000/€3.62 before 6pm, L12,000/€6.20 after 6pm. L3000/€1.55 discount with stamped bus ticket. Open Jun. 1-Aug. 5 daily 9am-2am.

Roman Sport Center, V.d. Galoppatoio, 33 (☎06 3201667 or 06 3218096). M: A-Spagna. 1-day membership L50,000/€25.80. Open M-Sa 9am-10pm and Su 9am-3pm.

Associazione Sportiva Augustea (A.S.A.), V. Luciani, 57 (☎06 23235112). M: A-Cinecittà. Open daily 10am-7pm.

Body Image, V. E. Fermi, 142 (☎06 5573356). Women only. L80,000/€41.30 per month. Open daily 9:30am-9pm; closed Aug.

Navona Health Center, V.d. Banchi Nuovi, 39 (☎06 6896104). L15,000/€7.75 per day, L100,000/€51.60 per month. Open M-F 9am-9pm, Sa 11am-8pm; closed Aug.

HOSPITALS

*See also **Emergency Services** (p. 291) and **Clinics** (p. 290).*

International Medical Center, V. G. Amendola, 7 (☎06 4882371; nights and Su 06 4884051). Call first. Prescriptions filled, paramedic crew on call, referral service to English-speaking doctors. General visit L130,000/€67.14. Open M-Sa 8:30am-8pm. On-call 24hr.

Rome-American Hospital, V. E. Longoni, 69 (☎06 22551; fax 06 2285062). Private emergency and laboratory services, HIV tests, and pregnancy tests. No emergency room. On-call 24hr.

HOTLINES

*See **Crisis Lines,** p. 290.*

INTERNET ACCESS

Marco's Bar, V. Varese, 54 (☎06 44703591). L5000/€2.58 per hr. with *Let's Go*. Open daily 5:30am-2am.

Trevi Tourist Service: Trevi Internet, V.d. Lucchesi, 31-32 (☎/fax 06 6920 0799). L5000/€2.58 per 30min., L10,000 per 90min. Open daily 9am-10pm.

Internet Café, V.d. Marrucini, 12 (☎/fax 06 4454953; www.Internetcafe.it; info@Internet-cafe.it.) L5000/€2.58 per 30min., L8000/€4.13 per hr.; after 9pm L6000/€3.20 per 30min., L10,000/€5.16 per hr. Open M-F 9am-2am, Sa-Su 5pm-2am.

Bolle Blu (p. 292). Laundromat with Internet accesss (L7000/€3.62 per hr.).

Freedom Traveller, V. Gaeta, 25 (☎06 4782 3682; www.freedom-traveller.it). L10,000/€5.16 per hr., students L8000/€4.13. Open M-Sa 9am-midnight.

Internet Café, V. Cavour, 213 (☎06 4782 3051). L10,000/€5.16 per hr. Open daily 9am-1am.

The Netgate Internet Point, P. Firenze, 25 (☎06 6893445). W and Sa free 8pm-8:30pm; otherwise L10,000/€5.16 per hr.

X-plore, V.d. Gracchi, 83-85 (☎06 50797474; www.xplore.it). L10,000/€5.16 per hr. Open M-Th 10-1am, F-Sa 10-3am.

LAUNDROMATS

OndaBlu, V. La Mora, 7 (info ☎800 861346). Other locations throughout Rome. Wash L6000 per 6½kg load; dry L6000/€3.20 per 6½kg load; soap L1500/€0.77. Open daily 8am-10pm.

Bolle Blu, V. Palestro, 59/61 (☎06 4465804), and V. Milazzo, 20b. Wash L6000/€3.20 per 6½kg load; dry L6000/€3.20 per 6½kg load; special L10,000/€5.16 per 16kg; soap L1500/€0.77. Open daily 8am-midnight.

Acqua & Sapone Lavanderia, V. Montebello, 66 (☎06 4883209). Wash L6000 per 6-8kg; dry L6000/€3.20 per 6-8kg. Open daily 8am-10pm.

LIBRARIES

Biblioteca Alessandrina, P. Aldo Moro, 5 (☎06 4474021). La Sapienza's inefficient but public library. Open M-F 8:30am-7:45pm, Sa 8:30am-1:30pm.

Biblioteca Nazionale, V. Castro Pretorio, 105 (☎06 49891 or 06 4989249; fax 06 4457635). M-F 8:30am-7pm, Sa 8:30am-1:30pm. Closed mid-Aug.

Centro Studi Americani, V. M. Caetani, 32, 2nd fl. (☎06 68806624). Open M-F 9am-7:30pm, Sa 9am-1:30pm. Closed some Aug.

Santa Susanna Lending Library, V. XX Settembre, 15, 2nd fl. (☎06 4827510). Open Tu and Th 10am-1pm, W 3-6pm, F 1-4pm, Sa-Su 10am-12:30pm; July open Tu, W, and Su; Aug. open Su.

LOST PROPERTY

*See also **Police** (p. 293).*

Oggetti Smarriti, V. Nicolo Bettoni, 1 (☎06 5816040; items lost on trains 06 47306682). Open Tu and F 8:30am-1pm, M, W 8:30am-1pm and 2:30-6pm, Th 8:30am-6pm.

Termini, in the glass booth in the main passageway. Open daily 7am-11pm.

MARKETS

*See also **Supermarkets** (p. 293). For outdoor markets, see p. 208 or p. 181.*

MOPED RENTAL

*See **Bike & Moped Rental** (p. 290).*

POSTAL SERVICES

Main Post Office (Posta Centrale), P. San Silvestro, 19 (☎06 679 8495; fax 06 6786618). Open M-F 9am-6pm, Sa 9am-2pm. Another **branch,** V.d. Terme di Diocleziano, 30 (☎06 4745602; fax 06 4743536), near Termini. Same hours as San Silvestro branch.

Vatican Post Office (☎06 69883406), 2 locations in P. San Pietro. No *Fermo Posta*. Open M-F 8:30am-7pm, Sa 8:30am-6pm. **Branch office** 2nd fl. of Vatican Museum. Open museum hours.

FedEx, V. Barberini, 115-119 (☎800 123800). Open M-F 9am-1pm and 2-6pm. AmEx/MC/V.

UPS, V.d. Traforo, 136. (☎800 877877), just next to the tunnel that connects V.d. Tritone and V. Nazionale. Open M-F 9am-1pm and 3-7pm. AmEx/MC/V.

PHARMACIES

*Most **Hospitals** (p. 291) have pharmacies.*

Farmacia Internazionale, P. Barberini, 49 (☎06 4871195). Open 24hr. MC/V.

Farmacia Piram, V. Nazionale, 228 (☎06 4880754). Open 24hr. MC/V.

Farmacia Arenula, V. Arenula, 73 (☎06 68803278). Call for hours.

Farmacia Grieco, P. della Repubblica, 67 (☎06 4880410). Open 24hr.

Farmacia Di Stazione Notturna, P. del Cinquecento, 51 (☎06 4880019). Call for hours.

PHONE SERVICES

See ***Telehone Services,*** *p. 293.*

POLICE

Police: Foreigner's Office (Ufficio Stranieri), V. Genova, 2 (☎06 46862876). Open 24hr.
Police Headquarters (Questura Centrale), V. San Vitale, 15 (☎06 46861).
Railway Police (☎06 47306959), track #1 and facing track #2 in Termini. Open 24hr.

RADIO TAXIS

See ***Taxis & Radio Taxis,*** *p. 294.*

RELIGIOUS SERVICES

All Saints Church (Anglican), V.d. Babuino, 153 (☎06 36001881). English services, usually Su 8:30 and 10:30am and 6:30pm. Prayers M-Tu and Th-F 8am and noon. Eucharists M-Tu and Th-F 6pm.
Rome Baptist Church, P. di San Lorenzo in Lucrina, 35 (☎06 6876652). Sunday service 10am; Bible study 11am. Confession M-W 10am-1pm, F 6-8pm.
Confessionals (Catholic) are in St. Peter's (p. 110), Santa Maria Maggiore (p. 124), San Giovanni in Laterano (p. 129), San Paolo fuori le Mura (p. 135), Il Gesù (p. 88), Santa Maria sopra Minerva (p. 92), Sant'Anselmo (p. 130), and Santa Sabina (p. 130). Languages spoken by priest noted on door.
San Silvestro (Catholic), P. San Silvestro, 1 (☎06 6797775). Masses in English Su 10am and 5:30pm.
Santa Susanna (Catholic), V. XX Settembre, 15 (☎06 4882748). Mass in English M-Sa 6pm, Su 9 and 10:30am.
San Paolo fuori le Mura (Episcopalian), V. Napoli, 58 (☎06 4883339). English services Su 8:30 and 10:30am.
Comunita Israelitica di Roma (Jewish), Lungotevere Cenci (☎06 6840061). Hebrew services M-F 7:45am and sunset, Sa 8:30am.
Ponte Sant'Angelo Church (Methodist), P. Ponte Sant'Angelo (☎06 6868314). Su service 10:30am. Communion first Su each month.
La Moschea di Roma (Muslim), V.d. Moschea (☎06 8082258). Prayers in Arabic daily 3:22am, noon, 1:15, 5:13, 8:50, and 10:20pm. Services W and Su 9-11:30am.
St. Andrew's Church (Presbyterian), V. XX Settembre, 7 (☎06 4827627). Services in English Su 11am. Another congregation holds Korean services in the same building daily 6am, W 7pm, and Su noon.

SPORTS FACILITIES

See also ***Health Clubs,*** *p. 291.*
Accademia Yoga, V. XX Settembre, 58a (☎06 4885967).
Bowling Brunswick, Lungotevere dell'Acqua Acetosa, 10 (☎06 8086147). Cosmic bowling! L3300/€1.70 per game per person, after 8pm L5300/€2.74, shoes L1000/€0.52. Open Su-Th 10-2am, F-Sa 10-4am.
Bowling Roma, V. R. Margherita, 181 (☎06 8551184). L3000/€1.55 per game per person, shoes included; after 9pm L6000/€3.20. Open M-Sa 10am-11:30pm, Su 5pm-midnight.
Centro Sportivo Italiano, Lungotevere Flaminio, 59 (☎06 3234732). Swimming pool. One-time membership fee L10,000/€5.16; full day L22,000/€11.00; half-day L15,000/€7.75. Open June-Sept. daily 10:45am-10:30pm.
Circolo della Stampa, P. Mancini (☎06 3232452). Tennis. L16,000/€8.26 per court per hr. Lights L6000/€3.20. Open M-F 8am-11pm, Sa-Su 8am-8pm.
Federazione Italiana Yoga, V. Belisario, 7, (☎06 42870191).
Palaghiacco di Marino, V. Appia Nuova, km 19 (☎06 9309480). Ice skating. 1½hr. skating sessions. Rentals of skates and pads L10,000/€5.16, on weekends L11,000/€5.67. Rentals M-F 5, 9, and 11pm; Sa-Su 3, 5, 7, 9, and 11pm; Su also 11am. Open late-Aug. to Apr.
Piscina della Rosa, V. America, 20 (☎06 5926717). Full-day swim in the outdoor pool L20,000/€10.30, half-day L15,000/€7.75, 1-4pm L6000/€3.20. Open June-Sept. daily 9am-7pm.
SC Ostiense, V.d. Mare, 128 (☎06 5915540). Tennis. L16,000/€8.52 per singles match per hr., L24,000/€12.40 per doubles match per hr. Lights L10,000/€5.16. Open daily 9am-6:30pm; closed Aug.

SUPERMARKETS

STANDA (☎800 358758). V. Cola di Rienzo, 173 (in Prati, near the Vatican), V.d. Trastevere, 62, and other locations.
Alimentari Coreani (Korean Grocery Store), V. Cavour, 84. Near P. di Santa Maria Maggiore. Open M-Sa 9am-1pm and 4-8pm.

Billo, V. S. Ambrogio, 7 (☎06 687 79 66), off V. Portico, in the Jewish Ghetto. Kosher.

Castroni, V. Cola di Rienzo, 196-198 (☎06 6874383). Coffee bar and phenomenal foreign foods market. Other locations include V. Ottaviano, 55 (☎06 39723279) and V.d. Quattro Fontane, 38 (☎06 44824 35).

TAXIS & RADIO TAXIS

Radiotaxi: ☎06 3570.
Radiotevere: ☎06 4157.
Prontotaxi: ☎06 6645.
Cosmo la Capitale: ☎06 4994.

TELEPHONE SERVICES

AT&T: ☎1721011.
MCI: ☎1721022.
Sprint: ☎1721877.
Bell Canada Direct: ☎1721001.
British Telecom Direct: ☎1720044.
Telecom Éireann Direct: ☎1720353.
Telstra Australia Direct: ☎1721161.
Telecom New Zealand: ☎1721064.
Telkom South Africa: ☎1721027.

TICKETS

Teatro Argentina Box Office, Largo di Torre Argentina, 52 (☎06 68804601 or 06 6875445). Tickets for any and all goings-on in Rome. Open M-F 10am-2pm and 3-7pm, Sa 10am-2pm.

Interclub, P. Ippolito Nievo, 3 (☎06 5880564), in Trastevere. Covers just about everything going on in the city.

Orbis, P. Esquilino, 37. (☎06 4827403). Rock/pop and sporting events. Open M-Sa 9:30am-1pm and 4-7:30pm.

RicordiMedia, 2 locations: V.d. Corso, 506 (☎06 3612370), and V. G. Cesare, 88 (☎06 37351589). Rock/Pop concerts. Both open daily 9:30am-8pm.

Auditorio Pio Box Office, V.d. Conciliazione, 4 (☎06 68801044). Classical music. Open Th-Tu 10:20am-1:30pm and 3-6pm, and until showtime on concert days.

Villa Giulia/Santa Cecilia ticket office, P. della Villa Giulia, 9 (☎06 3611064 or 06 3611833, credit card reservations ☎06 68801044). Summer classical music. Open Tu-Sa 10am-2pm, Su 10am-1pm, and until showtime on performance days.

TOURIST SERVICES

Enjoy Rome, V. Marghera, 8a (☎06 4451843 or 06 4456890; fax 06 4450734; www.enjoyrome.com). **Branch** office, V. Varese, 39. Open M-F 8:30am-2pm and 3:30-6:30pm, Sa 8:30am-2pm.

PIT (Tourist Information Point) (☎06 48906300), track #4 in Termini. **Kiosks:** Castel Sant'Angelo (P. Pia; ☎06 68809707); Fori Imperiali (V.d. Tempio della Pace; ☎06 69924307); P. di Spagna (Largo Goldoni; ☎06 68136061); P. Navona (P. delle Cinque Lune; ☎06 68809240); Trastevere (P. Sonnino; ☎06 58333457); San Giovanni (P. S. Giovanni in Laterano; ☎06 77203535); Santa Maria Maggiore (V.d. Olmata; ☎06 47880294); V.d. Corso (V. Minghetti; ☎06 6782988); V. Nazionale (Palazzo delle Espozioni; ☎06 47824525); Termini (P. dei Cinquecento; ☎06 47825194); Fiumicino (international arrivals area; ☎06 65956074). All kiosks except Fiumicino open daily 9am-6pm. Fiumicino open daily 8:15am-7:15pm.

Call Center Comune di Roma (☎06 36004399). Open daily 9am-7pm.

Centro Turistico Studentesco (CTS), V. Genova, 16 (☎06 4620431; general info ☎06 441111; fax 06 4679207; www.cts.it). Open M-F 9am-1pm and 2-6pm. Branch offices: V.d. Ausoni, 5 (☎06 4450141); V. Appia Nuova, 434 (☎06 7857906); C. Vittorio Emanuele II, 297 (☎06 6872672); Terminal Ostiense (☎06 5747950); P. Imerio 43 (☎06 6628597).

EPT (Rome Tourist Authority), V. Parigi, 5 (☎06 48899255 or 06 48899253; fax 06 48899228). Open M-F 8:15am-7:15pm, Sa 8:15am-1:45pm. **Termini branch** (☎06 65956074). Open daily 8:15am-7pm.

Italian Youth Hostels Association (HI-IYHF), p. 289.

APT (Azienda di Promozione Turistica), ☎06 488991.

Transalpino, P. dell'Esquilino, 8a (☎06 4870870; fax 06 4883094). Open M-F 9am-6:30pm. **Booth** (☎06 4880536) at track #22 in Termini. Open M-Sa 8am-8:30pm; in summer also Su 8:30am-5:30pm.

TOURS

Enjoy Rome: Walk Through the Centuries, V. Varese, 39 (☎06 4451843; www.enjoyrome.com). Four three-hour English tours (under 26 L25,000/€12.70; ages and over L30,000/€15.50): The Ancient and Old Rome; the Vatican City; Trastevere and the Jewish Ghetto; and night tour of the Ancient City and the Centro Storico **Bike tour** from Villa Borghese to the Circus Maximus (L35,000/€17.60). "Hollywood on the Tiber," a bus tour (with film clips) of Rome's famous cinematic areas (L50,000/€25.80). Day-long Pompeii bus trips L70,000/€36.20. Tickets at the Enjoy

Rome office (p. 294), Pensione Fawlty Towers (p. 270), Hotel Colors (p. 270), Pensione Sandy (p. 274), or Pensione Ottaviano (p. 270).

Appian Line, P. dell'Esquilino, 6 (☎06 4878 6601; fax 06 4742214; www.appianline.it). To the left as you face the Church of Santa Maria Maggiore. 11 different bus tours of the city, including Ancient Rome (L53,000/€27.30), Papal Blessing (L60,000/€32.00), Tivoli, Florence, Pompeii, and others (L130-215,000/€67.14-111.04); tours within Rome (L25-77,000/€12.70-39.77) include all expenses. Free pick-up from hotel. English, French, Spanish, and German spoken. Open daily 6:30am-8pm. AmEx/MC/V.

American Express, P. di Spagna, 38 (☎06 6764 2413; fax 06 6794953). All expenses paid 4hr. bus-and-walking tours of Vatican City (L75,000/€38.00), Ancient City (L70,000/€36.20), and Tivoli (L80,000/€41.30) daily except Su and winter holidays 9:30am and 2:30pm. Daytrips to Florence, Pompeii, Capri, Assisi, and Sorrento (L125-210,000/€64.56-108.46). English spoken. Open M-F 9am-5:30pm, Sa 9am-12:30pm. AmEx.

Associazione Culturale dell'Italia, V. Trionfale, 148 (☎06 3972 8186; fax 06 3972 8187). Guided tours of the city in English, French, Spanish, and German. 12,000/€6.20 per person, 15-20 people L150,000/€77.50 for 2hr. of whatever sights you want to see. Closed Aug.

ATAC 110 City Tour (☎06 4695 2256). City transit authority. 2hr. bus tour along bus #110 line, both leaving from Termini (L15,000/€7.75). Sightseeing Tour (2½hr.; daily departure 10:30am, 2, 3, 5, 6pm) and Basilicas Tour (3hr.; daily departure 10am and 2:30pm). Buy tickets at info booth inside train station. English spoken. Reservations possible.

TRANSPORTATION

See also ***Airports*** *(p. 289),* ***Bike & Moped Rental*** *(p. 290),* ***Car Rental*** *(p. 290),* ***Taxis & Radio Taxis*** *(p. 291).*

Aziende Tramvie Autobus Communali (ATAC): ☎800 555666. Open daily 8am-8pm.

COTRAL: ☎06 5915551.

Ferrovie dello Stato (FS): ☎1478 88088; www.fs-on-line.com.

VESPA RENTAL

See ***Bike & Moped Rental,*** *p. 290.*

Index

A

B

C

D

E

F

G

N

O

P

Q

R

S

T

U

V

W

X

Y

Z

Maps

Maps

INSIDE

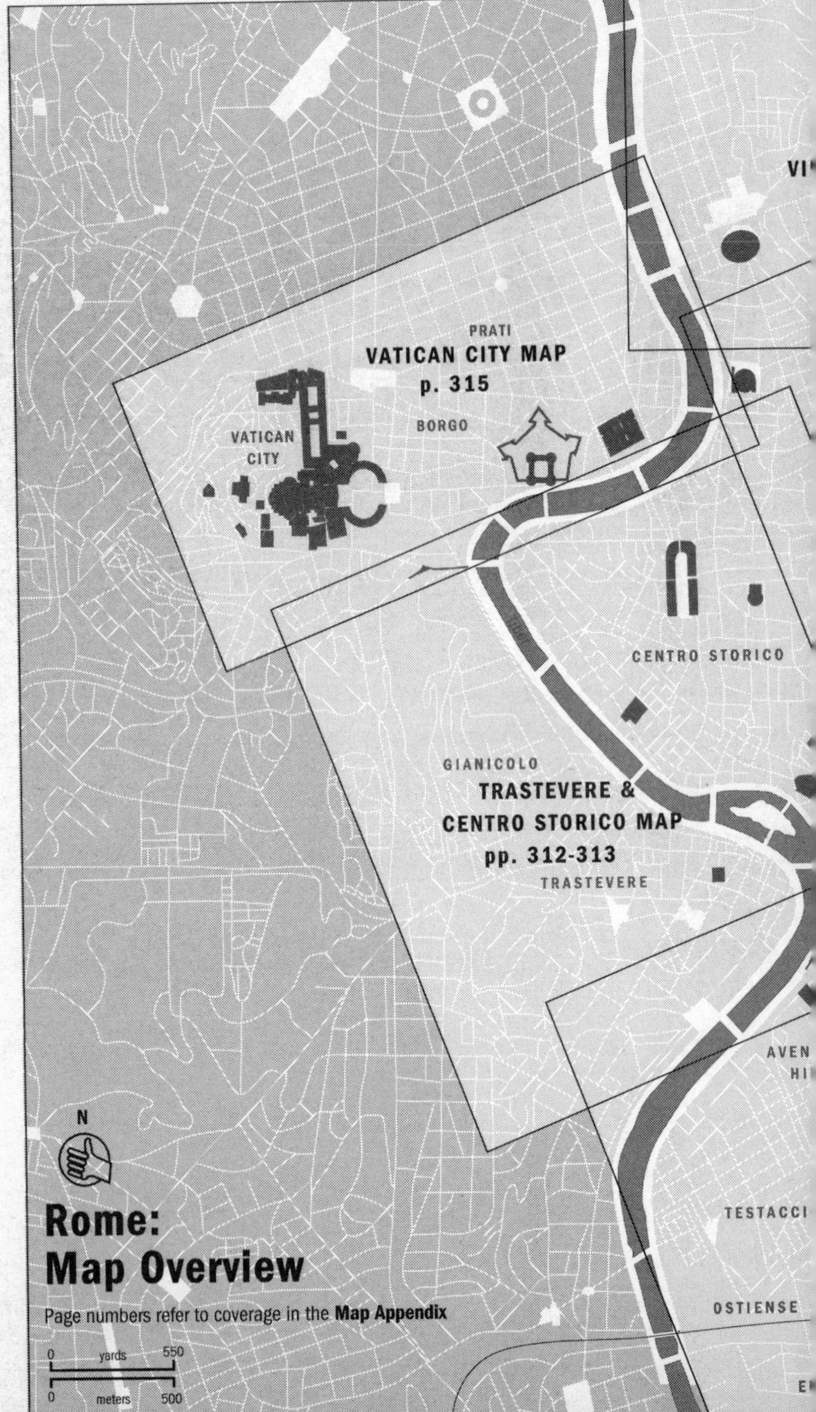
PRATI
VATICAN CITY MAP
p. 315
BORGO
VATICAN
CITY
CENTRO STORICO
GIANICOLO
TRASTEVERE &
CENTRO STORICO MAP
pp. 312-313
TRASTEVERE
TESTACCI
OSTIENSE
N
Rome:
Map Overview
Page numbers refer to coverage in the Map Appendix
0 yards 550
0 meters 500

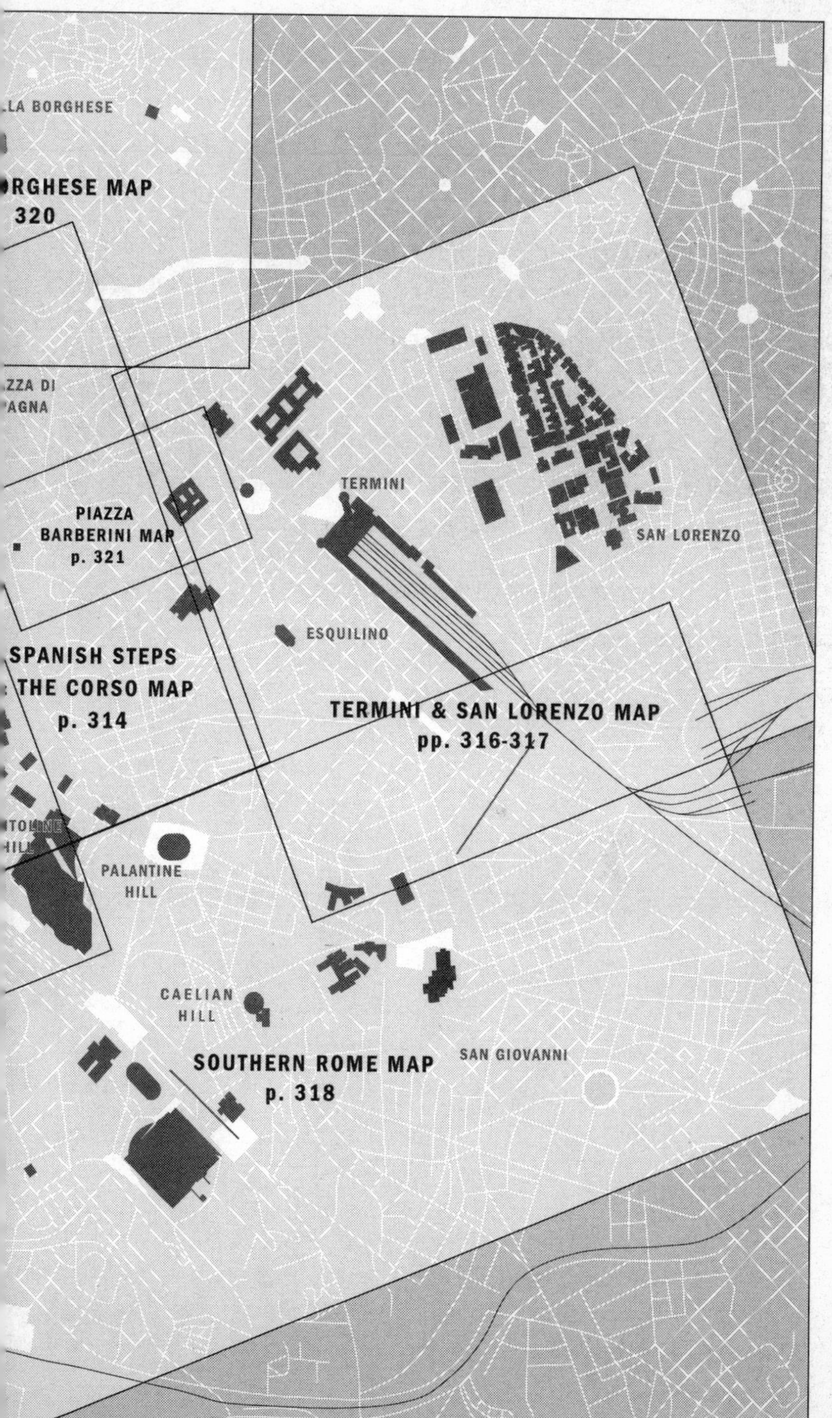
LLA BORGHESE
ORGHESE MAP
320
ZZA DI
AGNA
PIAZZA
BARBERINI MAP
p. 321
TERMINI
SAN LORENZO
ESQUILINO
SPANISH STEPS
THE CORSO MAP
p. 314
TERMINI & SAN LORENZO MAP
pp. 316-317
PALANTINE
HILL
CAELIAN
HILL
SOUTHERN ROME MAP
p. 318
SAN GIOVANNI

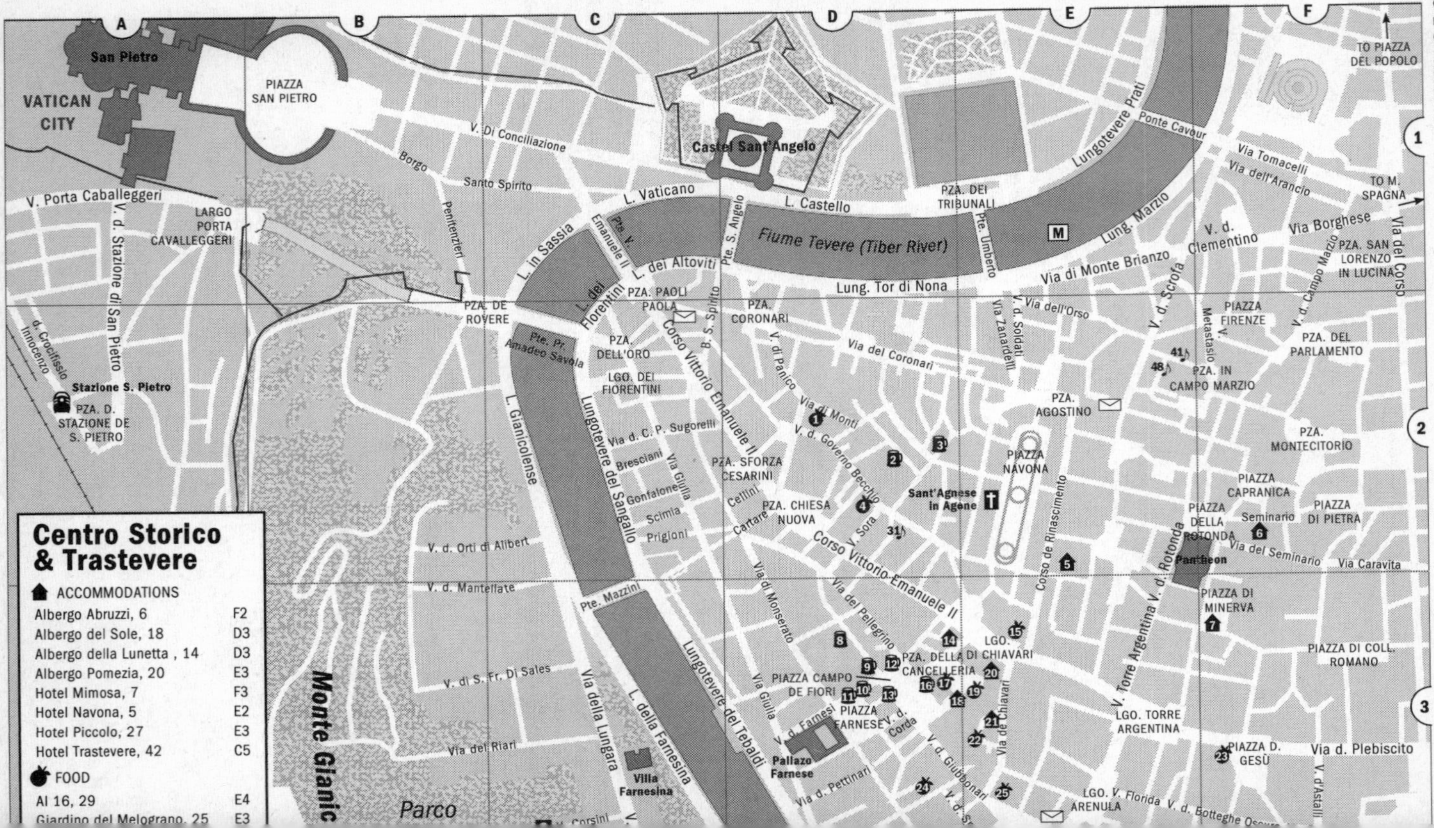

Centro Storico & Trastevere

ACCOMMODATIONS

Albergo Abruzzi, 6	F2
Albergo del Sole, 18	D3
Albergo della Lunetta , 14	D3
Albergo Pomezia, 20	E3
Hotel Mimosa, 7	F3
Hotel Navona, 5	E2
Hotel Piccolo, 27	E3
Hotel Trastevere, 42	C5

FOOD

Al 16, 29	E4
Giardino del Melograno, 25	E3

VATICAN CITY
San Pietro
PIAZZA SAN PIETRO
V. Di Conciliazione
Borgo
Santo Spirito
Penitenzieri
V. Porta Caballeggeri
LARGO PORTA CAVALLEGGERI
V. d. Stazione di San Pietro
d. Crocifissio Innocenzo
Stazione S. Pietro
PZA. D. STAZIONE DE S. PIETRO
Castel Sant'Angelo
L. Vaticano
L. Castello
PZA. DEI TRIBUNALI
Pte. Umberto
Lungotevere Prati
Ponte Cavour
Lung. Marzio
Fiume Tevere (Tiber River)
Pte. S. Angelo
Pte. V. Emanuele II
L. in Sassia
L. dei Altoviti
L. dei Fiorentini
Lung. Tor di Nona
Via di Monte Brianzo
PZA. DE ROVERE
Pte. Pr. Amadeo Savoia
L. Gianicolense
Lungotevere del Sangallo
PZA. PAOLI PAOLA
B. S. Spirito
PZA. CORONARI
Corso Vittorio Emanuele II
PZA. DELL'ORO
LGO. DEI FIORENTINI
Via d. C. P. Sugorelli
Bresciani
Via Giulia
Gonfalone
Scimia
Prigioni
Cellini
Cartare
PZA. SFORZA CESARINI
PZA. CHIESA NUOVA
V. di Panico
Via di Monti
V. d. Governo Becchio
Via del Coronari
V. Sora
V. d. Soldati
Via Zanardelli
Via dell'Orso
PZA. AGOSTINO
PIAZZA NAVONA
Sant'Agnese in Agone
Corso de Rinascimento
V. d. Orti di Alibert
V. d. Mantellate
V. di S. Fr. Di Sales
Via del Riari
Via della Lungara
L. della Farnesina
Villa Farnesina
Pte. Mazzini
Lungotevere del Tebaldi
Monte Gianic
Parco
Via di Monserato
Via del Pellegrino
Via Giulia
V. d. Farnesi
Pallazo Farnese
PIAZZA FARNESE
PIAZZA CAMPO DE FIORI
PZA. DELLA CANCELLERIA
LGO. DI CHIAVARI
V. d. Corda
Via de Chiavari
V. d. Giubbonari
Via d. Pettinari
LGO. V. Florida ARENULA
V. d. Botteghe Oscure
TO PIAZZA DEL POPOLO
TO M. SPAGNA
Via Tomacelli
Via dell'Arancio
Via Borghese
V. d. Clementino
V. d. Campo Marzio
PZA. SAN LORENZO IN LUCINA
Via del Corso
V. d. Scrofa
V. Metastasio
PIAZZA FIRENZE
PZA. DEL PARLAMENTO
PZA. IN CAMPO MARZIO
PZA. MONTECITORIO
PIAZZA CAPRANICA
PIAZZA DI PIETRA
PIAZZA DELLA ROTONDA
Seminario
Via del Seminario
Via Caravita
Pantheon
V. d. Rotonda
PIAZZA DI MINERVA
V. Torre Argentina
PIAZZA DI COLL. ROMANO
LGO. TORRE ARGENTINA
PIAZZA D. GESÙ
Via d. Plebiscito
V. d'Astalli

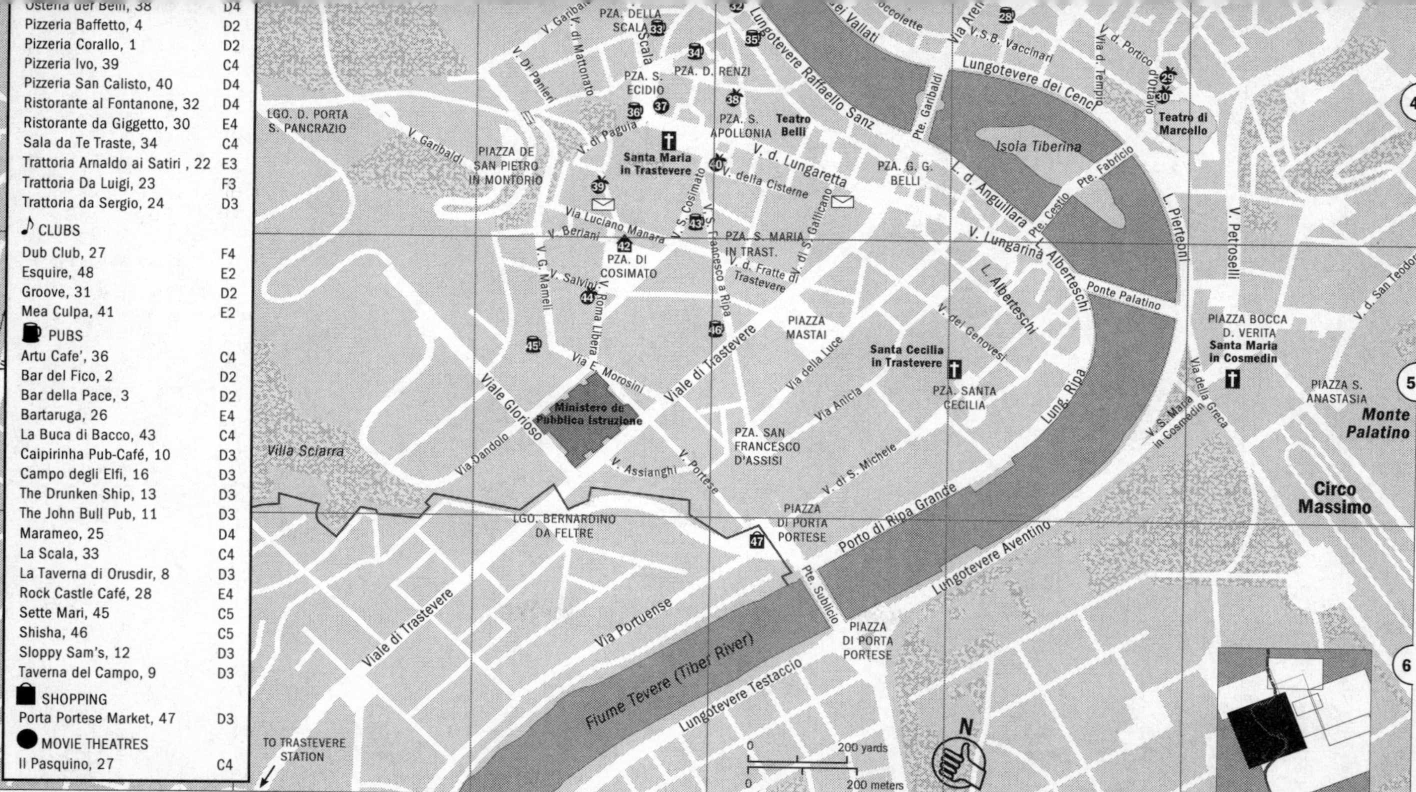
Osteria del Belli, 38 D4
Pizzeria Baffetto, 4 D2
Pizzeria Corallo, 1 D2
Pizzeria Ivo, 39 C4
Pizzeria San Calisto, 40 D4
Ristorante al Fontanone, 32 D4
Ristorante da Giggetto, 30 E4
Sala da Te Traste, 34 C4
Trattoria Arnaldo ai Satiri , 22 E3
Trattoria Da Luigi, 23 F3
Trattoria da Sergio, 24 D3
CLUBS
Dub Club, 27 F4
Esquire, 48 E2
Groove, 31 D2
Mea Culpa, 41 E2
PUBS
Artu Cafe', 36 C4
Bar del Fico, 2 D2
Bar della Pace, 3 D2
Bartaruga, 26 E4
La Buca di Bacco, 43 C4
Caipirinha Pub-Café, 10 D3
Campo degli Elfi, 16 D3
The Drunken Ship, 13 D3
The John Bull Pub, 11 D3
Marameo, 25 D4
La Scala, 33 C4
La Taverna di Orusdir, 8 D3
Rock Castle Café, 28 E4
Sette Mari, 45 C5
Shisha, 46 C5
Sloppy Sam's, 12 D3
Taverna del Campo, 9 D3
SHOPPING
Porta Portese Market, 47 D3
MOVIE THEATRES
Il Pasquino, 27 C4
LGO. D. PORTA S. PANCRAZIO
V. Garibaldi
PIAZZA DE SAN PIETRO IN MONTORIO
V. Di Panieri
V. di Mattonato
PZA. DELLA SCALA
Scala
PZA. S. ECIDIO
V. di Paglia
Santa Maria in Trastevere
PZA. D. RENZI
PZA. S. APOLLONIA
Teatro Belli
Lungotevere Raffaello Sanz
V. d. Lungaretta
V. della Cisterne
V. S. Cosimato
Via Luciano Manara
V. Beriani
PZA. DI COSIMATO
V. G. Mameli
V. Salvini
V. Roma Libera
Via E. Morosini
PZA. S. MARIA IN TRAST.
V. di S. Gallicano
V. d. Fratte di Trastevere
V. S. Francesco a Ripa
Viale di Trastevere
Viale Glorioso
Ministero de Pubblica Istruzione
Via Dandolo
Villa Sciarra
V. Assianghi
V. Portese
PZA. SAN FRANCESCO D'ASSISI
PIAZZA MASTAI
Via della Luce
Via Anicia
V. di S. Michele
Santa Cecilia in Trastevere
PZA. SANTA CECILIA
V. dei Genovesi
L. Alberteschi
V. Lungarina
L. Alberteschi
L. d. Anguillara
PZA. G. G. BELLI
Pte. Garibaldi
Isola Tiberina
Lungotevere dei Cenci
Pte. Cestio
Pte. Fabricio
Ponte Palatino
L. Pierleoni
V. S.B. Vaccinari
Via Arenula
Lungotevere dei Vallati
V. d. Portico d'Ottavio
Via d. Tempio
Teatro di Marcello
V. Petroselli
V. d. San Teodoro
PIAZZA BOCCA D. VERITA
Santa Maria in Cosmedin
Via della Greca
V. S. Maria in Cosmedin
PIAZZA S. ANASTASIA
Monte Palatino
Circo Massimo
Lung. Ripa
Porto di Ripa Grande
PIAZZA DI PORTA PORTESE
LGO. BERNARDINO DA FELTRE
Pte. Sublicio
Lungotevere Aventino
PIAZZA DI PORTA PORTESE
Via Portuense
Viale di Trastevere
Fiume Tevere (Tiber River)
Lungotevere Testaccio
TO TRASTEVERE STATION
0 200 yards
0 200 meters
N
4
5
6

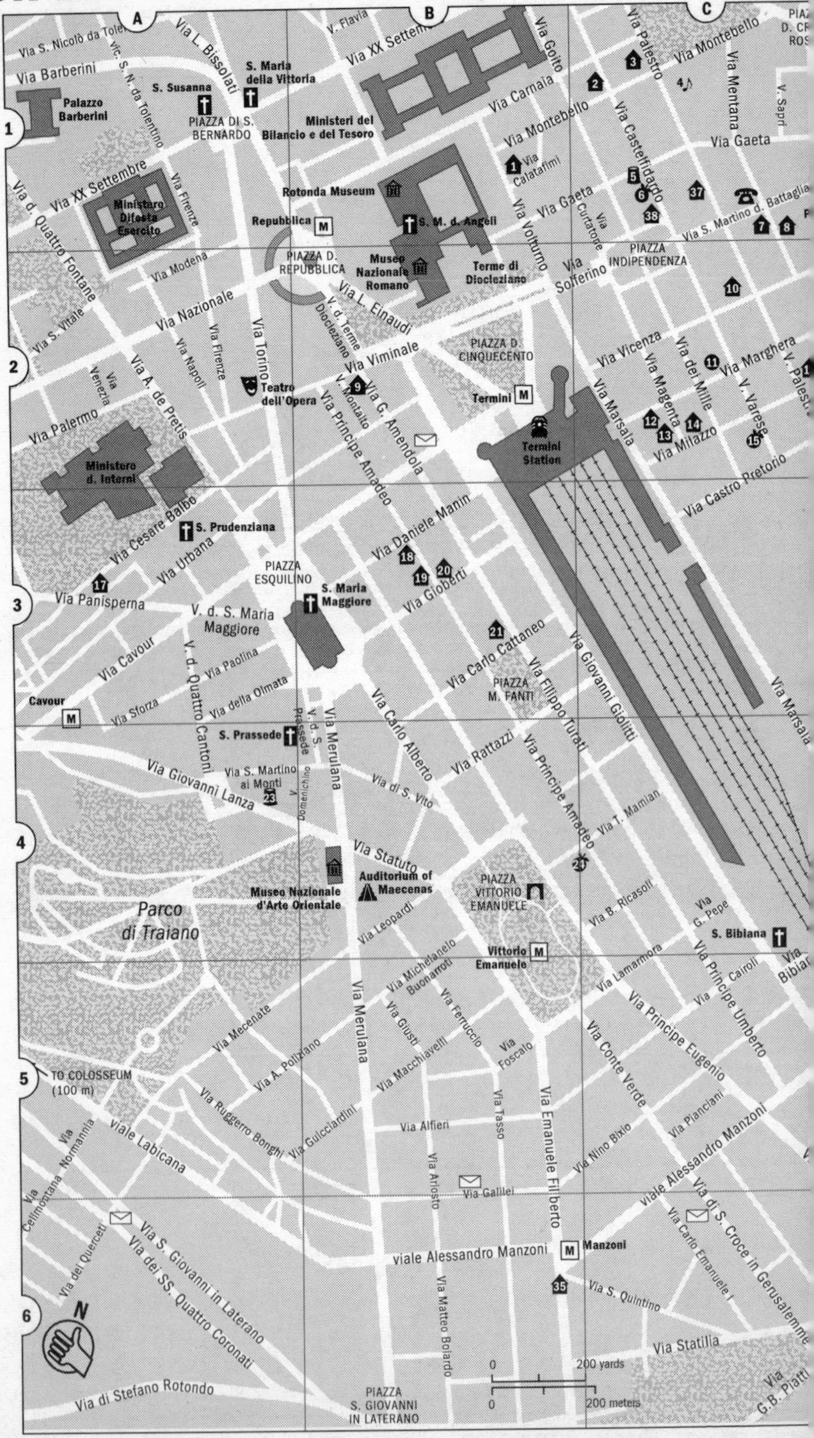

A B C
1 2 3 4 5 6

Palazzo Barberini
S. Susanna
PIAZZA DI S. BERNARDO
S. Maria della Vittoria
Ministeri del Bilancio e del Tesoro
Ministero Difesa Esercito
Rotonda Museum
Repubblica
PIAZZA D. REPUBBLICA
S. M. d. Angeli
Museo Nazionale Romano
Terme di Diocleziano
PIAZZA INDIPENDENZA
PIAZZA D. CINQUECENTO
Termini
Termini Station
Teatro dell'Opera
Ministero d. Interni
S. Prudenziana
PIAZZA ESQUILINO
S. Maria Maggiore
Cavour
S. Prassede
PIAZZA M. FANTI
Auditorium of Maecenas
Museo Nazionale d'Arte Orientale
PIAZZA VITTORIO EMANUELE
Vittorio Emanuele
Parco di Traiano
TO COLOSSEUM (100 m)
S. Bibiana
Manzoni
PIAZZA S. GIOVANNI IN LATERANO
0 200 yards
0 200 meters
N

Via S. Nicolò da Tolentino
Via Barberini
Vic. S. N. da Tolentino
Via L. Bissolati
V. Flavia
Via XX Settembre
Via Goito
Via Palestro
Via Montebello
Via Mentana
V. Sapri
Via Carnaia
Via Castelfidardo
Via Gaeta
Via Calatafimi
Via d. Quattro Fontane
Via Firenze
Via Volturno
Via Curtatone
Via S. Martino d. Battaglia
Via Modena
Via Solferino
Via L. Einaudi
Via Nazionale
Via S. Vitale
Via Torino
V. d. Terme Diocleziano
Via Viminale
Via Napoli
Via A. de Pretis
Via Venezia
V. Montalto
Via G. Amendola
Via Principe Amadeo
Via Vicenza
Via Magenta
Via dei Mille
Via Marghera
V. Palestro
Via Marsala
V. Varese
Via Milazzo
Via Castro Pretorio
Via Palermo
Via Cesare Balbo
Via Urbana
Via Daniele Manin
Via Gioberti
Via Panisperna
V. d. S. Maria Maggiore
Via Cavour
V. d. Quattro Cantoni
Via Paolina
Via della Olmata
Via Sforza
V. d. S. Prassede
Via Merulana
Via Carlo Alberto
Via Carlo Cattaneo
Via Filippo Turati
Via Giovanni Giolitti
Via Giovanni Lanza
Via S. Martino ai Monti
V. Domenichino
Via di S. Vito
Via Rattazzi
Via T. Mamiani
Via Statuto
Via Leopardi
Via B. Ricasoli
Via G. Pepe
Via Michelangelo Buonarroti
Via Lamarmora
Via Cairoli
Via Bibiana
Via Principe Umberto
Via Principe Eugenio
Via Giusti
Via Ferruccio
Via Foscalo
Via Mecenate
Via A. Poliziano
Via Macchiavelli
Via Conte Verde
Via Tasso
Via Emanuele Filiberto
Via Ruggerro Bonghi
Via Guicciardini
Via Alfieri
Via Nino Bixio
Via Pianciani
viale Alessandro Manzoni
Via Normannia
Viale Labicana
Via Celimontana
Via Ariosto
Via Galilei
Via Carlo Emanuele I
Via di S. Croce in Gerusalemme
Via del Querceti
Via S. Giovanni in Laterano
Via dei SS. Quattro Coronati
Via Matteo Bolardo
Via S. Quintino
Via Statilia
Via G.B. Piatti
Via di Stefano Rotondo

D
E
F
Termini & San Lorenzo
Castro Pretorio
Biblioteca Nazionale
Min. Difesa Aeronautica
CITTÀ UNIVERSITARIA
Policlinico
Bologna
PIAZZA SASSARI
PIAZZA SALERNO
PIAZZA LECCE
PIAZZALE DELLE PROVINCE
LARGO MARCHIAFAVA
PIAZZA VALERO MASSIMO
PIAZZALE ALDO MORO
PIAZZALE S. LORENZO
PIAZZALE DEL VERANO
Cimitero del Verano
LARGO D. OSCHI
SAN LORENZO
LARGO E. TALAMO
PIAZZA DI PORTA MAGGIORE
del Policlinico
V. G. B. Morgani
Via Bari
Via Catanzaro
Via Padova
Via Cremona
Via G. M. Lancisi
Vle. Regina Margherita
Via Forlì
Via Como
Via Arezzo
Via Catania
viale delle Province
V. Caserta
Via Treviso
Via Chieta
Via Imperia
Via Brianza
Via Lucca
Via Pavia
viale del Policlinico
Viale Regina Elena
Via Borelli
V. Vigevano
V. P. Zacchia
V. Giano della Bella
viale Ippocrate
Via Antonio Scarpa
Via Castro Laurenzia
dell'Universit'a
viale delle Scienza
Via Tiburtina
e Piero Gobetti
d. Frentani
Via d. Taurini
Via Dauni
V. D. Liburni
Via Cesare de Lollis
Via dei Ramni
Via dei Marrucini
V. dei Dalmati
Via di Tizi
Via dei Luceri
Via dei Corsi
Via dei Volsci
Via dei Reti
V. Ernici
V. Falisci
V. dei Etruschi
V. Latina
V. degli Equi
Via degli Ausoni
Via dei Piceni
Via dei Sardi
via dei Sabelli
via dei Aurunci
Via degli Enotri
Via dei Marsi
Via degli Apuli
Circonvallazione Tiburtina
Via di Campani
Via dei Lucani
Via del Anamari
Via dei Liguri
Viale dello Scalo di S. Lorenzo
Via Prenestina
Via Eleniana
Giolitti
di Porta Labicana
22
25
26
27
28
29
30
31
32
33
34

Termini & San Lorenzo

ACCOMMODATIONS

Hotel Adventure, 16	C2
Hotel Bolognese, 3	C1
Hotel Castelfidardo and Hotel Lazzari, 2	C1
Hotel Cervia, 10	C2
Hotel Des Artistes, 8	C1
Hotel Dolomiti and Hotel Lachea, 7	C1
Hotel Fenicia, 14	C2
Hotel Galli, 14	C2
Hotel Giu' Giu', 9	B2
Hotel Il Castello, 36	B6
Hotel Kennedy, 21	B3
Hotel Magic, 14	C2
Hotel Orlanda, 19	B3
Hotel Roxena, 12	C2
Hotel San Paolo, 17	A3
Hotel Selene, 9	B2
Hotel Sweet Home, 19	B3
Hotel Teti, 19	B3
Hotel Ventura, 16	C2
Pensione Cortorillo, 20	B3
Pensione di Rienzo, 19	B3
Pensione Fawlty Towers, 13	C2
Pensione Katty, 37	C1
Pensione Papa Germano, 1	B1
Pensione Sandy, 38	C1

SHOPPING

Disfunzioni Musicali, 22, 36	D3, D4

SERVICES

Enjoy Rome, 11	C2

FOOD

Africa, 6	C1
Arancia Blu, 34	D5
Il Capellaio Matto, 32	D5
Il Pulcino Ballerino, 33	D5
Indian Fast Food, 24	B4
La Pantera Rosa, 29	E4
Trattoria da Bruno, 15	C2

PUBS

Dalhu' Pub, 31	D5
Drome, 27	D4
Druid's Den, 23	A4
Julius Caesar, 5	C1
Lancelot, 28	E4
Legend Pub, 27	D4
Pub Hallo'Ween, 35	D4

CLUBS

Club 52, 4	C1
Il Giardini di Adone, 30	E4

Piazza di Spagna & the Corso

ACCOMMODATIONS

Hotel Pensione Suisse S.A.S., 11
Pensione Jonella, 1
Pensione Panda, 1

FOOD

Al Piccolo Arancio, 12
Birreria Peroni, 14
Centro Macrobiotico Italiano-Naturist Club, 7
McDonald's, 10
Le Pain Quotidien, 3
Sogo Asahi, 9
Trattoria da Settimio all'Arancio, 4
Vini e Bultet, 5

SHOPPING

Messaggerie Musicali, 6
Anglo-American Bookshop, 8
Mada, 2

PUBS

The Nag's Head, 15
Trinity College, 13

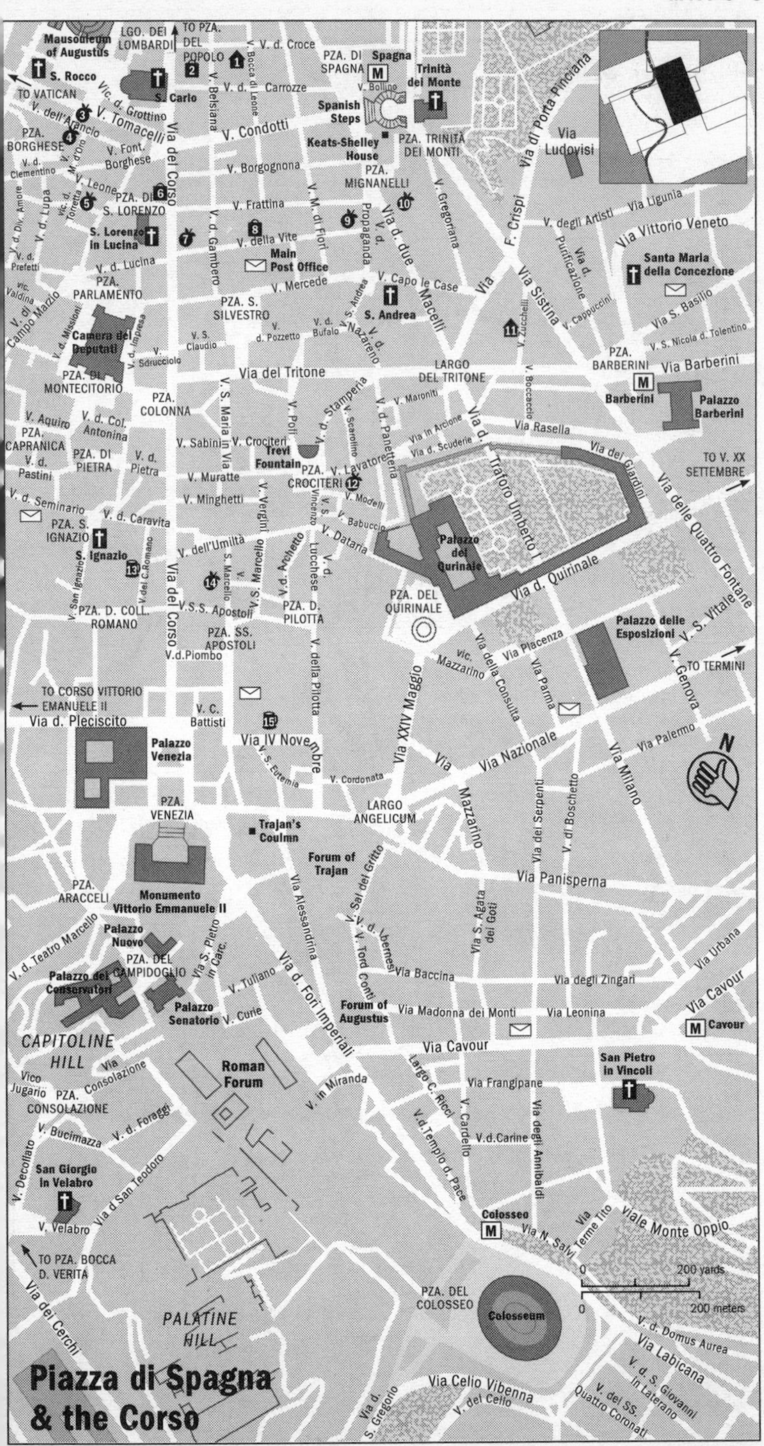
Piazza di Spagna
& the Corso
Mausoleum of Augustus
LGO. DEI LOMBARDI
TO PZA. DEL POPOLO
S. Rocco
TO VATICAN
S. Carlo
V. Tomacelli
PZA. BORGHESE
V. Condotti
Via del Corso
V. Belsiana
V. d. Croce
V. d. Carrozze
V. Bocca di Leone
PZA. DI SPAGNA
Spagna
Trinità dei Monte
Spanish Steps
Keats-Shelley House
PZA. TRINITÀ DEI MONTI
PZA. MIGNANELLI
V. Borgognona
V. Frattina
V. della Vite
V. d. Gambero
Main Post Office
V. M. di Fiori
Propaganda
V. Gregoriana
Via d. due Macelli
Via di Porta Pinciana
Via Ludovisi
F. Crispi
Via Sistina
V. degli Artisti
Via Ligunia
Via Vittorio Veneto
Santa Maria della Concezione
Via S. Basilio
V. S. Nicola d. Tolentino
PZA. BARBERINI
Via Barberini
Barberini
Palazzo Barberini
V. Capo le Case
V. Mercede
S. Andrea
PZA. S. SILVESTRO
PZA. DI S. LORENZO
S. Lorenzo in Lucina
V. d. Lucina
PZA. PARLAMENTO
Camera dei Deputati
PZA. DI MONTECITORIO
PZA. COLONNA
Via del Tritone
LARGO DEL TRITONE
V. Boccaccio
Via Rasella
V. d. Col. Antonina
PZA. CAPRANICA
PZA. DI PIETRA
V. d. Pietra
V. Sabini
V. Crociferi
Trevi Fountain
PZA. CROCITERI
V. Lavatore
V. d. Stamperia
V. d. Panetteria
Via d. Traforo Umberto I
Via dei Giardini
TO V. XX SETTEMBRE
Via delle Quattro Fontane
V. Muratte
V. Minghetti
V. d. Seminario
PZA. S. IGNAZIO
S. Ignazio
V. d. Caravita
V. dell'Umiltà
V. Dataria
Palazzo del Quirinale
Via d. Quirinale
PZA. DEL QUIRINALE
PZA. D. COLL. ROMANO
V.S.S. Apostoli
PZA. SS. APOSTOLI
PZA. D. PILOTTA
V. della Pilotta
Palazzo delle Esposizioni
V. S. Vitale
Via Placenza
Via della Consulta
Via Parma
V. Genova
TO TERMINI
V.d.Piombo
TO CORSO VITTORIO EMANUELE II
Via d. Pleciscito
V. C. Battisti
Via IV Novembre
Via XXIV Maggio
Via Nazionale
Via Milano
Via Palermo
Palazzo Venezia
PZA. VENEZIA
Trajan's Coulmn
LARGO ANGELICUM
Via Mazzarino
V. dei Serpenti
V. di Boschetto
Via Panisperna
Forum of Trajan
PZA. ARACCELI
Monumento Vittorio Emmanuele II
Palazzo Nuovo
PZA. DEL CAMPIDOGLIO
Palazzo dei Conservatori
Palazzo Senatorio
V. d. Teatro Marcello
Via Alessandrina
V. Sal del Gritto
Via S. Agata dei Goti
Via Baccina
Via degli Zingari
Via Urbana
Via Cavour
Forum of Augustus
Via Madonna dei Monti
Via Leonina
Cavour
Via d. Fori Imperiali
CAPITOLINE HILL
Roman Forum
San Pietro in Vincoli
Via Frangipane
V. in Miranda
Largo C. Ricci
V. Cardello
V.d.Carine
Via degli Annibaldi
V.d.Tempio d. Pace
Vico Jugario
PZA. CONSOLAZIONE
Via Consolazione
V. Bucimazza
V. d. Foraggi
V. Decollato
San Giorgio in Velabro
V. Velabro
Via d San Teodoro
TO PZA. BOCCA D. VERITA
Via dei Cerchi
Colosseo
Via N. Salvi
Via Terme Tito
Viale Monte Oppio
0 200 yards
0 200 meters
PZA. DEL COLOSSEO
Colosseum
PALATINE HILL
V. d. Domus Aurea
Via Labicana
V. d. S. Giovanni in Laterano
V. dei SS. Quattro Coronati
Via Celio Vibenna
V. del Celio
Via d. S. Gregorio
N

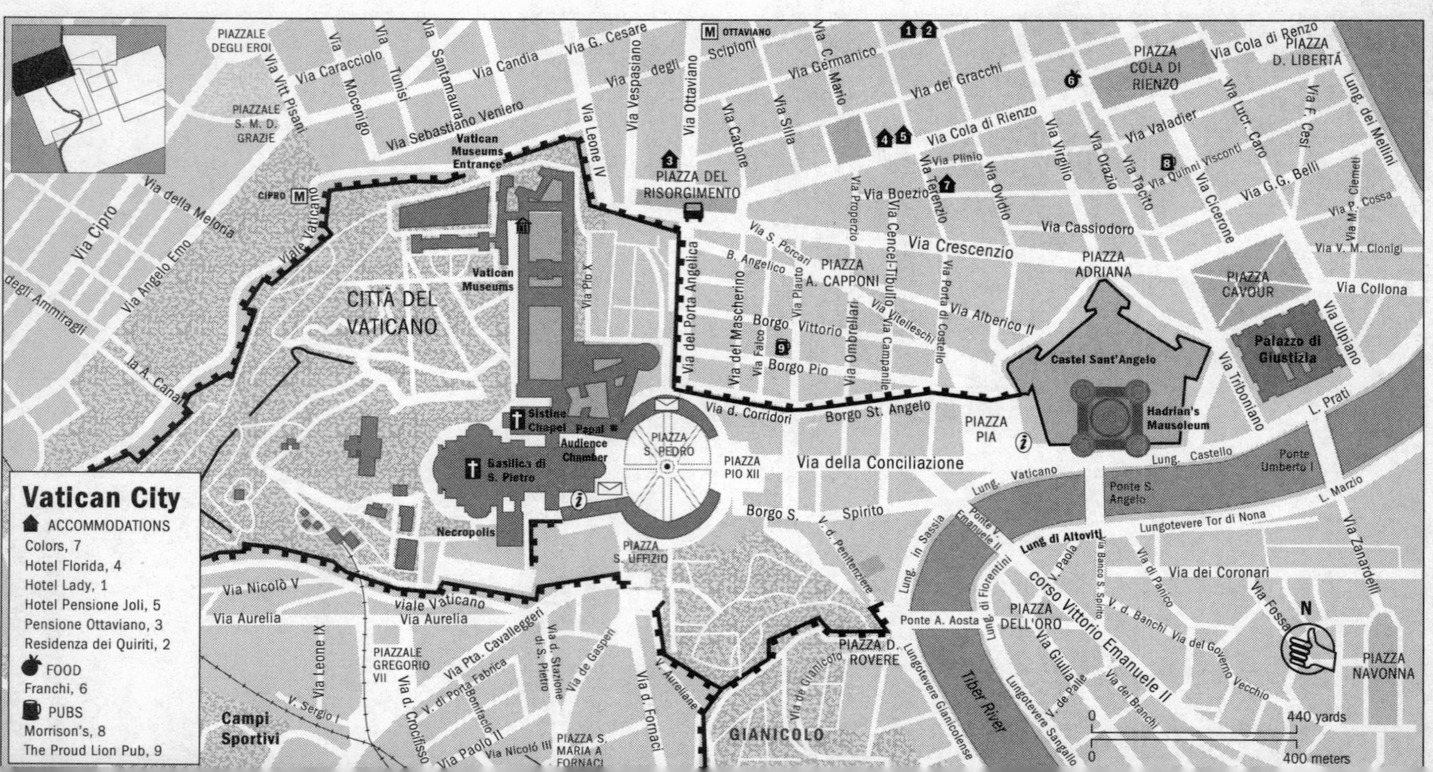

Vatican City
ACCOMMODATIONS
Colors, 7
Hotel Florida, 4
Hotel Lady, 1
Hotel Pensione Joli, 5
Pensione Ottaviano, 3
Residenza dei Quiriti, 2
FOOD
Franchi, 6
PUBS
Morrison's, 8
The Proud Lion Pub, 9
N
440 yards
400 meters
CITTÀ DEL VATICANO
Vatican Museums
Vatican Museums Entrance
Sistine Chapel
Papal Audience Chamber
Basilica di S. Pietro
Necropolis
PIAZZA S. PIETRO
Castel Sant'Angelo
Hadrian's Mausoleum
Palazzo di Giustizia
PIAZZA CAVOUR
PIAZZA ADRIANA
PIAZZA PIA
PIAZZA PIO XII
PIAZZA DEL RISORGIMENTO
PIAZZA COLA DI RIENZO
PIAZZA D. LIBERTÀ
PIAZZA NAVONA
PIAZZA DELL'ORO
PIAZZA D. ROVERE
PIAZZA A. CAPPONI
PIAZZA S. UFFIZIO
PIAZZA S. MARIA A FORNACI
PIAZZALE GREGORIO VII
PIAZZALE DEGLI EROI
PIAZZALE S. M. D. GRAZIE
GIANICOLO
Tiber River
Campi Sportivi
OTTAVIANO
CIPRO
Via della Conciliazione
Via Crescenzio
Via Cola di Rienzo
Via Ottaviano
Via Leone IV
Viale Vaticano
Via Aurelia
Via Nicolò V
Via d. Fornaci
Via Giulia
corso Vittorio Emanuele II
Via dei Coronari
Via Zanardelli
Via Cipro
Via della Meloria
Via Angelo Emo
Via Candia
Via G. Cesare
Via dei Gracchi
Via Germanico
Via Sebastiano Veniero
Via Vespasiano
Via Cassiodoro
Via Alberico II
Via Tribonaniano
Borgo Pio
Borgo Vittorio
Borgo St. Angelo
Borgo S. Spirito
Via d. Corridori
Lungotevere Tor di Nona
Lungotevere Gianicolense
Lungotevere Sangallo
Ponte Umberto I
Ponte S. Angelo
Ponte V. Emanuele II
Ponte A. Aosta

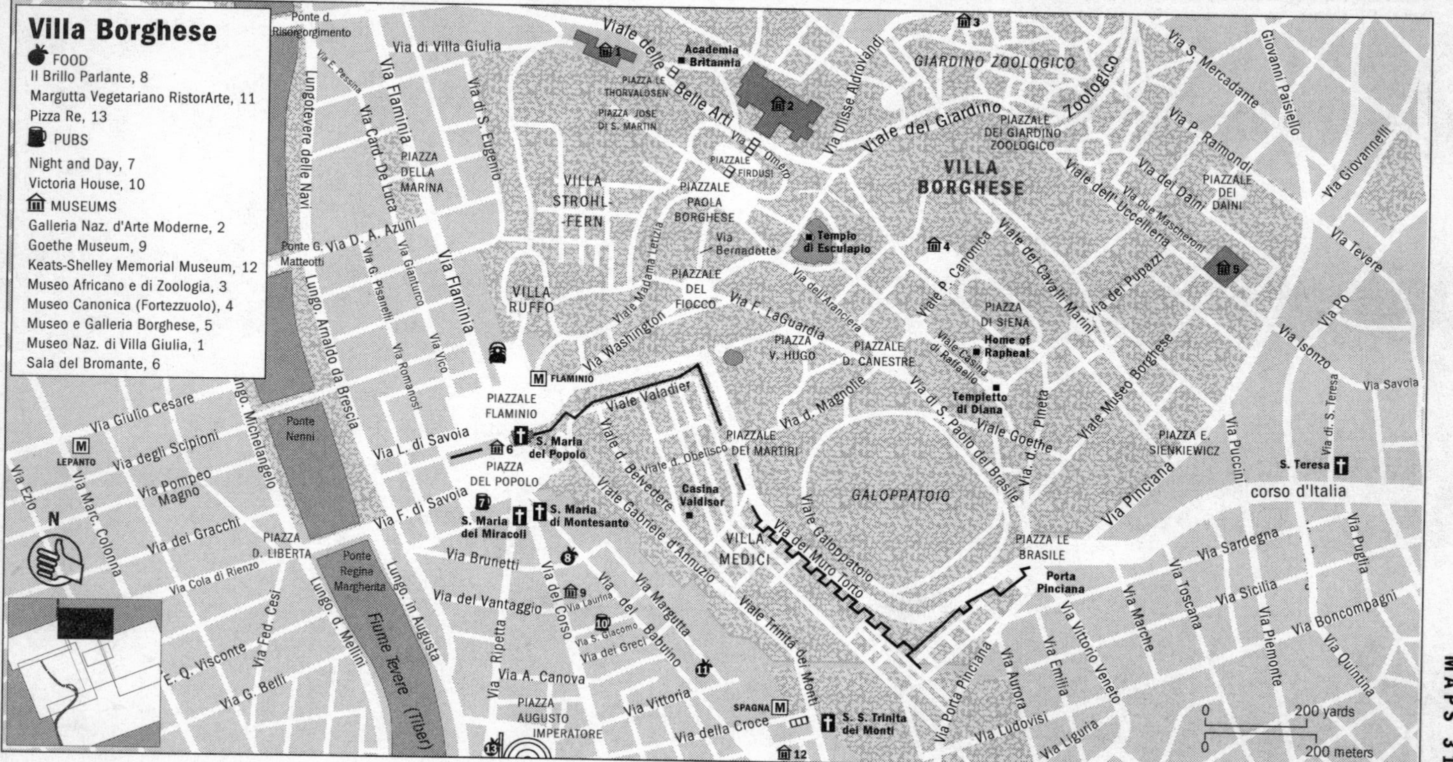
Villa Borghese
FOOD
Il Brillo Parlante, 8
Margutta Vegetariano RistorArte, 11
Pizza Re, 13
PUBS
Night and Day, 7
Victoria House, 10
MUSEUMS
Galleria Naz. d'Arte Moderne, 2
Goethe Museum, 9
Keats-Shelley Memorial Museum, 12
Museo Africano e di Zoologia, 3
Museo Canonica (Fortezzuolo), 4
Museo e Galleria Borghese, 5
Museo Naz. di Villa Giulia, 1
Sala del Bromante, 6
VILLA BORGHESE
GIARDINO ZOOLOGICO
VILLA STROHL-FERN
VILLA RUFFO
VILLA MEDICI
GALOPPATOIO
Academia Britannia
Tempio di Esculapio
Home of Rapheal
Tempietto di Diana
Casina Valdisor
S. Maria del Popolo
S. Maria di Montesanto
S. Maria dei Miracoli
S. S. Trinita dei Monti
S. Teresa
Porta Pinciana
PIAZZALE FLAMINIO
PIAZZA DEL POPOLO
PIAZZALE DEI MARTIRI
PIAZZALE D. CANESTRE
PIAZZA V. HUGO
PIAZZALE DEL FIOCCO
PIAZZALE PAOLA BORGHESE
PIAZZALE FIRDUSI
PIAZZA LE THORVALDSEN
PIAZZA JOSE DI S. MARTIN
PIAZZALE DEI GIARDINO ZOOLOGICO
PIAZZALE DEI DAINI
PIAZZA DI SIENA
PIAZZA E. SIENKIEWICZ
PIAZZA LE BRASILE
PIAZZA DELLA MARINA
PIAZZA D. LIBERTA
PIAZZA AUGUSTO IMPERATORE
Viale delle Belle Arti
Viale del Giardino Zoologico
Via Ulisse Aldrovandi
Via S. Mercadante
Giovanni Paisiello
Via P. Raimondi
Via dei Daini
Via Giovannelli
Viale dell' Uccelliera
Via due Mascheroni
Via Tevere
Via Po
Via Isonzo
Via Savoia
Via di. S. Teresa
Via Puccini
corso d'Italia
Via Puglia
Via Sardegna
Via Sicilia
Via Boncompagni
Via Quintina
Via Piemonte
Via Toscana
Via Marche
Via Vittorio Veneto
Via Emilia
Via Aurora
Via Ludovisi
Via Liguria
Via Porta Pinciana
Via Pinciana
Viale Museo Borghese
Via dei Pupazzi
Viale dei Cavalli Marini
Viale P. Canonica
Via d. Pineta
Viale Goethe
Viale Casina di Raffaello
Via di S. Paolo del Brasile
Via dell'Aranciera
Via F. LaGuardia
Via d. Magnolie
Viale Valadier
Viale d. Obelisco
Viale d. Belvedere
Viale Gabriele d'Annuzio
Viale Galoppatoio
Via del Muro Torto
Viale Trinita dei Monti
Via Omero
Via Bernadotte
Viale Madama Letizia
Via Washington
Via di Villa Giulia
Via di S. Eugenio
Via Flaminia
Via Card. De Luca
Via D. A. Azuni
Via G. Pisanelli
Via Gianturco
Via Romanosi
Via Vico
Via E. Pessina
Ponte d. Risorgorgimento
Lungotevere delle Navi
Ponte G. Matteotti
Lungo. Arnaldo da Brescia
Ponte Nenni
Lungo. Michelangelo
Via L. di Savoia
Via F. di Savoia
Via Giulio Cesare
Via degli Scipioni
Via Pompeo Magno
Via dei Gracchi
Via Ezio
Via Marc. Colonna
Via Cola di Rienzo
Via Fed. Cesi
E. Q. Visconte
Via G. Belli
Ponte Regina Margherita
Lungo. d. Mellini
Lungo. in Augusta
Fiume Tevere (Tiber)
Via Brunetti
Via del Vantaggio
Via Ripetta
Via A. Canova
Via del Corso
Via Laurina
Via del Babuino
Via S. Giacomo
Via dei Greci
Via Margutta
Via Vittoria
Via della Croce
FLAMINIO
LEPANTO
SPAGNA
N
0
200 yards
0
200 meters

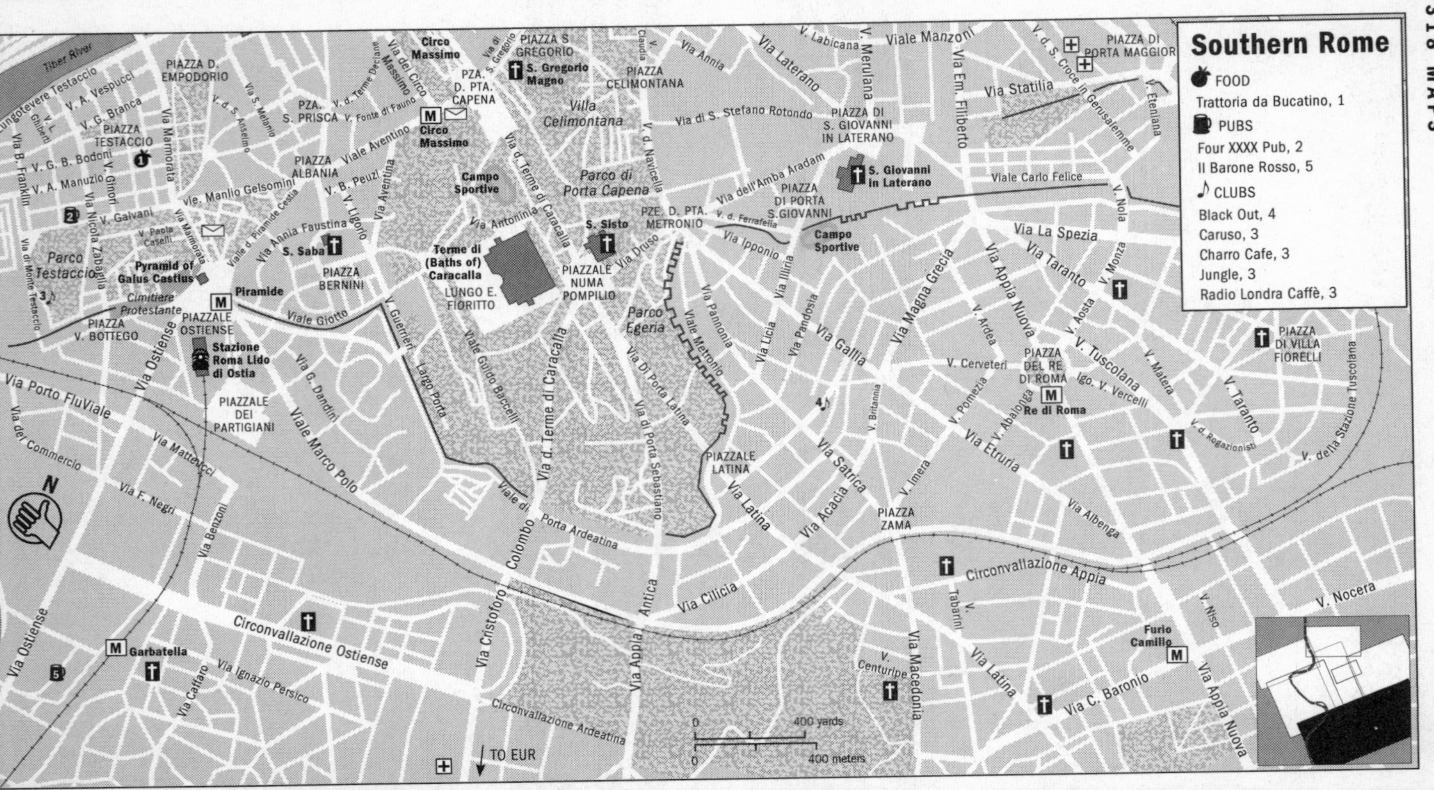
Southern Rome
FOOD
Trattoria da Bucatino, 1
PUBS
Four XXXX Pub, 2
Il Barone Rosso, 5
CLUBS
Black Out, 4
Caruso, 3
Charro Cafe, 3
Jungle, 3
Radio Londra Caffè, 3
Tiber River
Lungotevere Testaccio
PIAZZA D. EMPODORIO
PIAZZA TESTACCIO
Via Marmorata
Parco Testaccio
Pyramid of Galus Castius
Cimitiere Protestante
PIAZZA V. BOTTEGO
PIAZZALE OSTIENSE
Piramide
Stazione Roma Lido di Ostia
PIAZZALE DEI PARTIGIANI
Viale Giotto
Viale Aventino
PIAZZA ALBANIA
S. Saba
PIAZZA BERNINI
Circo Massimo
PZA. D. PTA. CAPENA
PIAZZA S. GREGORIO
S. Gregorio Magno
Campo Sportive
Terme di (Baths of) Caracalla
LUNGO E. FIORITTO
Villa Celimontana
PIAZZA CELIMONTANA
Parco di Porta Capena
S. Sisto
PIAZZALE NUMA POMPILIO
PZE. D. PTA. METRONIO
Parco Egeria
Viale Metronio
PIAZZALE LATINA
PIAZZA DI PORTA S.GIOVANNI
S. Giovanni in Laterano
PIAZZA DI S. GIOVANNI IN LATERANO
Via Laterano
V. Merulana
Viale Manzoni
Via Em. Filiberto
Via Statilia
PIAZZA DI PORTA MAGGIOR
Viale Carlo Felice
Via La Spezia
Via Taranto
Via Appia Nuova
Via Magna Grecia
Via Gallia
Via Satrica
Via Acacia
PIAZZA ZAMA
Via Etruria
PIAZZA DEL RE DI ROMA
Re di Roma
V. Tuscolana
PIAZZA DI VILLA FIORELLI
Via Porto FluViale
Viale Marco Polo
Via Ostiense
Via d. Terme di Caracalla
Viale di Porta Ardeatina
Via Cristoforo Colombo
Via di Porta Sebastiano
Via Appia Antica
Via Cilicia
Via Latina
Circonvallazione Appia
Circonvallazione Ostiense
Circonvallazione Ardeatina
Garbatella
Via Macedonia
Furio Camillo
Via C. Baronio
V. Nocera
0
400 yards
400 meters
TO EUR

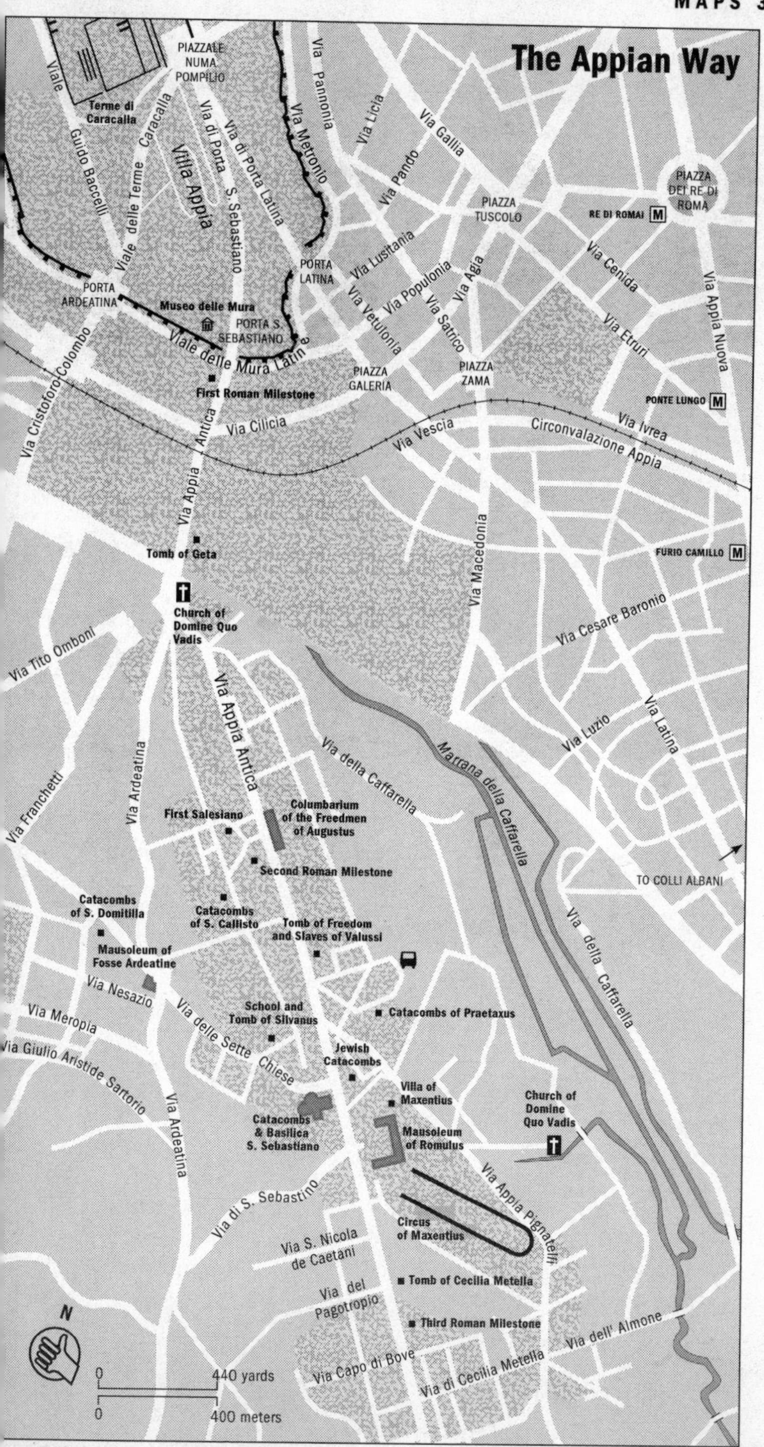
The Appian Way
PIAZZALE NUMA POMPILIO
Terme di Caracalla
Viale Guido Baccelli
Viale delle Terme Caracalla
Villa Appia
Via di Porta S. Sebastiano
Via di Porta Latina
Via Metronio
Via Pannonia
Via Licia
Via Gallia
Via Pando
PIAZZA TUSCOLO
PIAZZA DEI RE DI ROMA
RE DI ROMA
PORTA LATINA
Via Lusitania
Via Populonia
Via Agia
Via Cenida
Via Appia Nuova
PORTA ARDEATINA
Museo delle Mura
PORTA S. SEBASTIANO
Via Vetulonia
Via Satrico
Via Etruri
Viale delle Mura Latina
Via Cristoforo Colombo
First Roman Milestone
PIAZZA GALERIA
PIAZZA ZAMA
PONTE LUNGO
Via Cilicia
Via Vescia
Circonvalazione Appia
Via Ivrea
Via Appia Antica
Tomb of Geta
FURIO CAMILLO
Via Macedonia
Church of Domine Quo Vadis
Via Tito Omboni
Via Cesare Baronio
Via Latina
Via Luzio
Via della Caffarella
Marrana della Caffarella
Via Franchetti
Via Ardeatina
First Salesiano
Columbarium of the Freedmen of Augustus
Second Roman Milestone
TO COLLI ALBANI
Catacombs of S. Domitilla
Catacombs of S. Callisto
Tomb of Freedom and Slaves of Valussi
Mausoleum of Fosse Ardeatine
Via Nesazio
Via Meropia
Via delle Sette Chiese
School and Tomb of Silvanus
Catacombs of Praetaxus
Via Giulio Aristide Sartorio
Jewish Catacombs
Villa of Maxentius
Church of Domine Quo Vadis
Catacombs & Basilica S. Sebastiano
Mausoleum of Romulus
Via Appia Pignatelli
Via di S. Sebastino
Via S. Nicola de Caetani
Circus of Maxentius
Tomb of Cecilia Metella
Via del Pagotropio
Third Roman Milestone
Via dell' Almone
Via Capo di Bove
Via di Cecilia Metella
N
0 440 yards
0 400 meters

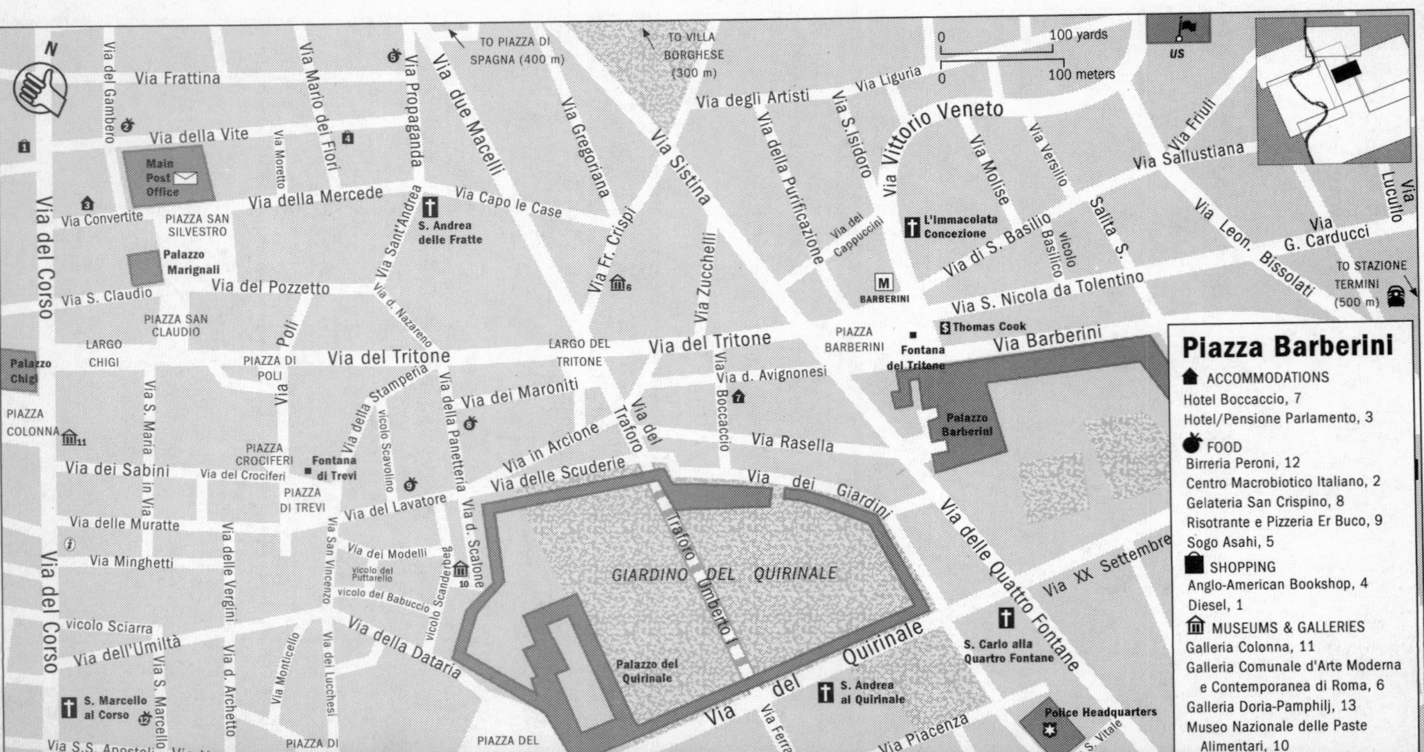
Piazza Barberini
ACCOMMODATIONS
Hotel Boccaccio, 7
Hotel/Pensione Parlamento, 3
FOOD
Birreria Peroni, 12
Centro Macrobiotico Italiano, 2
Gelateria San Crispino, 8
Risotrante e Pizzeria Er Buco, 9
Sogo Asahi, 5
SHOPPING
Anglo-American Bookshop, 4
Diesel, 1
MUSEUMS & GALLERIES
Galleria Colonna, 11
Galleria Comunale d'Arte Moderna e Contemporanea di Roma, 6
Galleria Doria-Pamphilj, 13
Museo Nazionale delle Paste Alimentari, 10
N
TO PIAZZA DI SPAGNA (400 m)
TO VILLA BORGHESE (300 m)
0 100 yards
0 100 meters
US
TO STAZIONE TERMINI (500 m)
Via Frattina
Via del Gambero
Via della Vite
Main Post Office
Via Moretto
Via Mario dei Fiori
Via Propaganda
Via due Macelli
Via Gregoriana
Via Sistina
Via degli Artisti
Via Liguria
Via della Purificazione
Via S.Isidoro
Via Vittorio Veneto
Via Molise
Via Versilio
Via Sallustiana
Via Friuli
Via Lucullo
Via Convertite
PIAZZA SAN SILVESTRO
Via della Mercede
Via Sant'Andrea
S. Andrea delle Fratte
Via Capo le Case
Via Fr. Crispi
Via Zucchelli
Via dei Cappuccini
L'Immacolata Concezione
Via di S. Basilio
vicolo Basilico
Salita S.
Via Leon. Bissolati
Via G. Carducci
Palazzo Marignoli
Via del Pozzetto
Via S. Claudio
Via d. Nazareno
BARBERINI
Via S. Nicola da Tolentino
PIAZZA SAN CLAUDIO
Poli
LARGO CHIGI
PIAZZA DI POLI
Via del Tritone
LARGO DEL TRITONE
PIAZZA BARBERINI
Fontana del Tritone
Thomas Cook
Via Barberini
Palazzo Chigi
Via della Stamperia
Via dei Maroniti
Via d. Avignonesi
Via Boccaccio
Palazzo Barberini
PIAZZA COLONNA
Via S. Maria in Via
Via
vicolo Scavolino
Via della Panetteria
Via del Traforo
Via Rasella
PIAZZA CROCIFERI
Fontana di Trevi
Via in Arcione
Via dei Sabini
Via del Crociferi
Via delle Scuderie
Via dei Giardini
PIAZZA DI TREVI
Via del Lavatore
Via delle Muratte
Via delle Vergini
Via San Vincenzo
Via dei Modelli
vicolo del Puttarello
vicolo Scanderbeg
Via d. Scalone
Traforo Umberto I
GIARDINO DEL QUIRINALE
Via delle Quattro Fontane
Via XX Settembre
Via Minghetti
vicolo del Babuccio
vicolo Sciarra
Via dell'Umiltà
Via Monticello
Via dei Lucchesi
Via della Dataria
Via del Quirinale
S. Carlo alla Quartro Fontane
Palazzo del Quirinale
S. Andrea al Quirinale
S. Marcello al Corso
Via S. Marcello
Via d. Archetto
Via del Corso
Via S.S. Apostoli
PIAZZA DI
PIAZZA DEL
Via Ferra
Via Piacenza
Police Headquarters
Via S. Vitale

NOTES:

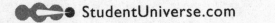